Free Trade and Uneven Development

The North American Apparel Industry after NAFTA

EDITED BY

Gary Gereffi, David Spener, and Jennifer Bair

TEMPLE UNIVERSITY PRESS

PHILADELPHIA

Temple University Press, Philadelphia 19122
Copyright © 2002 by Temple University
All rights reserved
Published 2002
Printed in the United States of America

Library of Congress Cataloging-in-Publication Data

Free trade and uneven development : the North American apparel industry after NAFTA /
edited by Gary Gereffi, David Spener, and Jennifer Bair.
   p. cm.
  Includes bibliographical references and index.
  ISBN 1-56639-967-X (cloth : alk. paper) — ISBN 1-56639-968-8 (pbk. : alk. paper)
    1. Clothing trade—North America. 2. Clothing trade—Government policy—North
America. 3. Textile industry—North America. 4. Textile industry—Government
policy—North America. 5. Free trade—North America. 6. Canada. Treaties, etc. 1992
Oct. 7. I. Gereffi, Gary. II. Spener, David, 1961– III. Bair, Jennifer, 1973–

HD9940.N72 F74   2002
382'.45687'097–dc21   2001050820

Free Trade and Uneven Development

Contents

Part III: The U.S.-Mexico Border Region

Part IV: Interior Mexico

Part V: Central America and the Caribbean

Part VI: Conclusion

List of Tables and Figures

Tables

Figures

Acknowledgments

This book grew out of a conference on "Global Production, Regional Responses, and Local Jobs: Challenges and Opportunities in the North American Apparel Industry" that was held at Duke University in November 1997. Financial support for this meeting came from a variety of sources, including the Howard E. Jensen Fund in the Sociology Department at Duke, the North American Studies Program and the "Globalization and Equity" Common Fund project at Duke, and the Canadian Studies Conference Grant Program in the Office of the Canadian Embassy in Washington, D.C. Gary Gereffi and Jennifer Bair co-organized the Duke conference, with the assistance of a large number of administrative support staff and student volunteers at the university.

David Spener wishes to acknowledge several institutions and individuals for their support in making publication of this book possible. First, the Ford Foundation's Mexico City and New York offices supported the efforts of a research team, in which he was a participant, that examined economic development issues in the U.S.-Mexico border region and in the Mexican interior. This research was supported by a grant to the Population Research Center of the University of Texas at Austin and the Colegio de la Frontera Norte and included collection and analysis of data on the apparel industry in El Paso, Los Angeles, Ciudad Juárez, Monterrey, Mexico City, and Guadalajara. Second, Bryan R. Roberts, who holds the C. B. Smith Centennial Chair in U.S.-Mexico Relations at the University of Texas at Austin, provided generous financial support to Spener and other contributors to this book that permitted their participation in several meetings in diverse locales. Third, the Tom and Mary Turner Faculty Fellowship of Trinity University underwrote Spener's contribution to the writing and editing of several of the chapters herein.

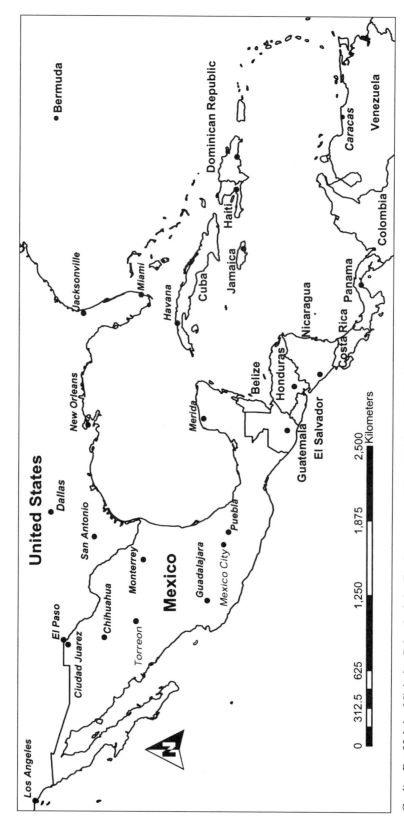

Credit: Pat Halpin, Nicholas School of the Environment and Earth Science, Duke University

Part I

Analytical Overview

David Spener, Gary Gereffi,
and Jennifer Bair

1   Introduction: The Apparel Industry
and North American
Economic Integration

The economic and social consequences of international trade agreements have become a major area of inquiry in development studies in recent years. As evidenced by the energetic protests surrounding the Seattle meeting of the World Trade Organization (WTO) in December 1999 and the controversy about China's admission to the WTO, such agreements have also become a focus of political conflict in both the developed and developing countries. At issue are questions of job gains and job losses in different regions, prices paid by consumers, acceptable standards for wages and working conditions in transnational manufacturing industries, and the quality of the environment. All these concerns have arisen with regard to the North American Free Trade Agreement (NAFTA) and can be addressed through an examination of changes in the dynamics of the apparel industry in the post-NAFTA period.[1] In this book, we examine the evolution of the apparel industry in North America in order to address some of these questions as they pertain to North America, with an eye toward the broader implications of our findings. We also consider the countries of the Caribbean Basin and Central America, whose textile and apparel goods are now allowed to enter the U.S. market on the same basis as those from Canada and Mexico (Odessey 2000).

Globalization and Regionalization of the Apparel Industry

As Michael Mortimore notes in Chapter 14, the apparel industry has served as a crucial stepping-stone in the economic development of all the advanced industrialized nations and it has also been an important engine of growth for the successful newly industrializing economies of East Asia. Apparel manufacturing is traditionally one of the largest sources of industrial employment for most countries. In addition, apparel is a quintessential global industry. It exemplifies, more than any other industry, the process by which firms have relocated their labor-intensive manufacturing operations from high-wage regions in the advanced industrialized countries to low-cost production sites in industrializing nations.

Traditional low-tech forms of production are linked with advanced communications and information technologies in a complex post-modern web of design, manufacturing, marketing, and distribution.

The internationalization of garment manufacturing began earlier and has extended further than that of any other industry. Since the 1960s, the newly industrializing economies, led by East Asia and followed more recently by Latin America, have seen a massive increase in export-oriented production (Appelbaum, Smith, and Christerson 1994; Bonacich et al. 1994; Christerson and Appelbaum 1995; Gereffi 1994, 1999; Mittelhauser 1996, 1997; Murray 1995). World apparel exports grew from a modest $3 billion in 1965, with developing countries accounting for just 14 percent of the total, to $119 billion in 1991, with developing countries supplying 59 percent (Murray 1995). The U.S. market was the recipient of the largest share (around one-third) of apparel exported by the newly industrializing economies (Murray 1995), and U.S. apparel imports grew from just $1 billion in 1970 to nearly $22 billion by 1990 (Bonacich and Waller 1994, 24). By 1998 the world market for apparel exports was valued at $200 billion, and U.S. apparel imports represented more than one-quarter ($54 billion) of the world total (see Tables 2.1 and 2.2 in Chapter 2).

By 1995 imported garments accounted for over half of apparel purchases in the United States (Mittelhauser 1996). More than any other industry, apparel manufacturing has exemplified the emergence of a new international division of labor, as the rise in Third World imports has been accompanied by massive declines in employment in advanced industrial countries such as the United States. Table 1.1 documents the resulting employment shifts in the North American apparel industry. U.S. apparel employment peaked at around 1.4 million workers in 1974. By 1990

around a third of those jobs had either disappeared or been transferred to overseas production sites (Bonacich and Waller 1994; Mittelhauser 1996, 1997; Murray 1995), and this trend of increasing import penetration coupled with massive job loss continued through the end of the twentieth century. By 1998 garment employment in the United States had fallen to just over 750,000 workers (American Apparel Manufacturers Association 1999), while garment imports had risen to nearly $50 billion, more than double their 1990 level (U.S. Department of Commerce 1999).

Canadian apparel employment has been more uneven throughout this period. The Canadian industry suffered its greatest decline in the late 1980s, following the implementation of the Canadian-U.S. Free Trade Agreement. The industry has since rebounded under NAFTA, with apparel employment in Canada increasing from 82,800 in 1994 to 93,700 in 2000 (see Table 1.1).

Whereas the Northeast Asian economies once dominated developing-country apparel exports to the United States, since the mid-1980s the countries of the Caribbean Basin and Mexico have risen to prominence. In 1990 the Northeast Asian economies (China, Hong Kong, Taiwan, South Korea, and Macao) exported a total value of $13.7 billion worth of garments to the United States, accounting for more than half of total U.S. imports. By 2000, however, these economies' share of total U.S. garment imports declined to less than 30 percent. Meanwhile, garment exports from Central America,[2] the Caribbean, and Mexico skyrocketed from $2.7 billion in 1990 to over $18.4 billion in 2000, accounting for nearly 30 percent of U.S. total apparel imports. Particularly dramatic was Mexico's rise to become the top-ranked garment exporter to the United States at the end of the century, as its exports grew from just $709 million in 1990 to over $8.7 billion in 2000 (see Table 2.2 in Chapter 2).

TABLE I.I. Employment in the North American Apparel Industry, 1985–2000 (thousands of workers)

	1985	1988	1991	1994	1995	1996	1997	1998	1999	2000
Canada	89.9	95.8	64.3	82.8	85.5	89.9	87.4	91.9	91.1	93.7
United States	1,120.4	1,085.1	1,106.0	974.0	935.8	867.7	823.6	765.8	690.1	633.2
Mexico[a]	146.8	196.4	221.3	231.3	263.2	395.6	454.9	761.9	607.0	557.0

Sources: Statistics Canada, *Employment, Earnings and Hours;* U.S. Bureau of Labor Statistics; INEGI, *Censos Economicos.*

[a]Mexico's figures in this table include maquiladora and non-maquiladora apparel employment. The 1999 and 2000 employment figures are estimates based on data from the Camara Nacional de la Industria del Vestido and *Apparel Industry Magazine,* respectively.

The movement of garment production to the Caribbean Basin and Mexico has been promoted by U.S. government policies, including:

- provisions of the U.S. tariff code that have encouraged the growth of production in maquiladoras, which are plants that assemble U.S.-made components that are then exported back into the United States, with tariff paid only on the value added in the exporting country;
- the Caribbean Basin Initiative (CBI), which gave preferential access to U.S. markets to the countries of Central America and the Caribbean beginning in the 1980s;
- the progressive lifting, since the late 1980s, of U.S. quotas limiting apparel imports from developing countries; and, most recently,
- the North American Free Trade Agreement, which, together with the 1994–95 peso devaluation, has cemented Mexico's position as "the low-cost manufacturing center of North America" (Martin 1995).

These policy changes have substantially altered the conditions that confront garment manufacturers who wish to produce for the U.S. market. Particularly dramatic has been the effect of NAFTA on Mexico's garment production for export. In 1994, the first year that NAFTA was in effect, 412 maquiladoras employed 82,500 workers sewing garments (Figure I.I). By December 2000 there were more than 286,000 workers sewing garments in 1,119 maquiladoras in Mexico.[3] The number of maquiladora workers fell in 2001 to 276,700, though the number of maquiladora plants dedicated to apparel production increased to 1,125. Despite this dip in employment, the number of workers employed in apparel maquiladoras in 2001 was more than three times greater than in 1994 (INEGI 2001). The expansion of the maquiladora sector is evidence of Mexico's impressive NAFTA-era export dynamism in the apparel industry. Although exports from the Caribbean Basin countries have also been strong in recent years, these economies were disadvantaged by the region's exclusion from NAFTA. The passage of the Trade and Development Act of 2000 by the U.S. Congress extends a weak version of NAFTA parity to the region, but it is too early to tell what impact it will have in increasing the CBI's export dynamism relative to Mexico.

In addition to the quantitative boom in Mexico's apparel exports in the post-NAFTA period, production in this economic sector is undergoing a qualitative transformation. Beside the growth of maquiladora sewing operations Mexico has witnessed the emergence of cutting, laundering, and finishing operations, as these parts of the production process are moved south of the U.S. border to various sites that are undertaking "full-package" production. This upgrading of Mexico's productive capacity has, in turn, attracted a number of

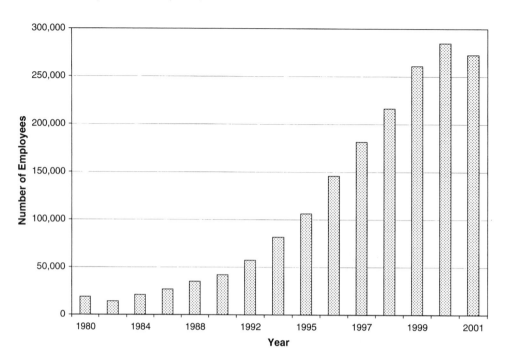

FIGURE 1.1.   Employment in Mexico's Apparel Maquiladoras, 1980–2001
Source: INEGI, "Banco de información económica," data available at <http://www.inegi.
gob.mx>.

large textile producers, including Burlington Industries and Cone Mills, which alone or in concert with Mexican firms have opened plants in Mexico's interior for the production of fabrics.

With regard to product segments, Mexico is not only gaining in standardized apparel but also making inroads in the fashion sector that has traditionally been dominated by Asian firms. The emphasis is, nevertheless, still on men's sport-fashion apparel (e.g., designer jeans) rather than women's apparel (although some women's brands are being produced in Mexico for labels such as Donna Karan, DKNY, and the Limited). As a consequence, Mexico's apparel exports to the United States remain dominated by such mass-produced, standardized garments as men's trousers and shirts, women's trousers, and brassieres (U.S. Department of Commerce 1999; Gereffi 2000).

Most studies indicate that the overall impact of NAFTA on employment and wages in the United States has been quite small; implementation of the agreement, however, has contributed greatly to the elimination of direct production jobs in apparel manufacturing. Although the apparel industry accounted for just 7.3 percent of all manual jobs in U.S. manufacturing in 1998, 30 percent of the NAFTA-induced job losses documented by the U.S. Department of Labor between 1994 and 1999 were accounted for by apparel workers whose plants moved to Mexico or laid off workers in response to surging imports. Overall, apparel employment in the United States declined by 14 percent from 1993 to 1997, with the bulk of this loss occurring in states such as Tennessee and the Carolinas that, like Mexico, specialized in the mass production of standardized garments (Spener and Capps 2001).

As mass-production jobs in the industry were lost, the leading garment districts in New York City and especially Los Angeles retained jobs not only in design but also in direct production by relying on immigrant workers to sew small-batch, high-fashion garments. Indeed, although overall U.S. apparel employment declined precipitously in the 1990s, the net number of immigrant workers engaged in sewing and other direct-production tasks actually grew from 265,000 in 1990 to 296,000 by 1999, an increase of more than 10 percent. As native U.S. employees lost their apparel jobs or found better work in other fields, the immigrants' share of direct-production apparel jobs rose dramatically, from around one-quarter of the total U.S. garment workforce in 1990 to nearly one-half by 1999 (Spener and Capps 2001; see also Chapters 3 and 4 in this volume, by Florence Palpacuer and Judi Kessler, respectively).

The principal reason for the growth of immigrant employment in the U.S. apparel industry during the 1990s was Los Angeles' prominence as the leading garment district in the United States. There employment in the industry grew throughout the decade, while it declined nearly everywhere else. In 1990 more than 90 percent of Los Angeles garment workers were foreign born, the majority being Mexican, even though Mexicans made up just 9 percent of all garment workers nationwide. By the end of the decade, however, 20 percent of all garment workers in the United States were Mexican immigrants, with most of these working in Los Angeles. Thus we see that Mexico has come to play a doubly important role in the production of garments for the U.S. market, with more than 280,000 Mexicans working in apparel maquiladoras south of the border and another 128,000 sewing, cutting, and finishing garments north of it (Spener and Capps 2001).

Apparel Production in the Era of NAFTA: The Dynamics of Interfirm Networks

The purpose of this book is to document the ways in which firms in the textile-apparel complex have responded to the changed trade environment in terms of new production and marketing strategies and, in turn, to consider the implications for job creation and retention, wages, and working conditions in various regions in Mexico, the United States, Central America, and the Caribbean. Given the rapid pace of change in the geography of production in recent years, there is a great deal of room for new documentation and analysis in the academic literature on the organization of the industry. This is in itself an important task, given that the textile-apparel complex has, until recently, been the largest U.S. manufacturing sector in terms of employment and also has come to play a substantial role in the Mexican, Central American, and Caribbean economies. With this collection of essays we are able, at a minimum, to provide a useful service to readers by updating the extant literature on the global apparel industry (e.g., Bonacich et al. 1994; see also chapters on apparel in diverse edited volumes, such as Gereffi and Korzeniewicz 1994; Gereffi and Kaplinsky 2001).

Nevertheless, this book does much more than update earlier works. The emergence of an integrated North American regional economy in the latter half of the 1990s constitutes a qualitative change in the dynamics of the apparel industry that requires new forms of analysis. While a great deal can be gained by simply studying the effects of national trade policies and exchange rates on the geography of production, such an approach fails to explain the important shifts that are occurring within countries as well as the socioeconomic consequences of such subnational or local transformations. Contributors to this book address the new regional dynamics of production in the apparel industry by taking a firm-centered approach that focuses on the ways in which interfirm networks are creating new textile-apparel supply chains in a more interdependent and complex North American production and trade landscape. This firm-centered approach has several advantages.

First, this approach allows us to identify the "lead firms" in the textile and apparel commodity chain and to document the evolution of the strategies and organizational behaviors they adopt in response to changes in the regulatory regime for international trade. Often these lead firms are not themselves garment manufacturers but rather are to be found in the retail, design, or textiles and fiber segments of the supply chain. Thus we are able to demonstrate how apparel producers are dynamically linked to other strategic actors in the textile-apparel complex. In addition, by focusing on the behavior of lead firms in vertically structured interfirm networks, we can trace the actual mechanisms through which the geography of apparel production is changing, accounting for spatial shifts in regional employment, the upgrading or downgrading of productive technologies, job quality, and so forth.

Second, the network approach allows us to examine the extent to which cooperative ties exist among small- to medium-scale firms that participate in cross-border networks in particular locales in the United States and Mexico. This permits us to talk about the emergence or renewal of industrial districts in the United States and Mexico and whether such districts are following the "high road" to development exemplified by the famous "Third Italy" case of Emilia-Romagna.[4] Thus, a network perspective provides a unique opportunity to link multiple levels of analysis: from the strategic decision making of lead firms, to the modes of insertion into the apparel commodity chain of small-scale garment enterprises, to the dynam-

ics of local industrial districts, to an investigation into the wages and working conditions prevalent among peripheral contractors.

Third, an interfirm network perspective allows us to demonstrate how a variety of subnational regions in Mexico and the United States are dynamically linked with one another across the national boundary dividing the two countries (e.g., El Paso, Texas, and Torreón, Coahuila; Los Angeles and Tehuacán, Puebla; San Francisco, California, and Aguascalientes). In this regard, our edited collection complements the publication of new monographs on the industry, such as Edna Bonacich and Richard Appelbaum's *Behind the Label: Inequality in the Los Angeles Apparel Industry* (2000), that center on a single production locale rather than on the web of relations among multiple sites.

Fourth, the network perspective integrates a variety of research methodologies, ranging from strategic interviews with key personnel of lead firms in order to trace transborder production chains, to plant surveys, analysis of official trade and employment data, and the examination of published records and data from the textile-apparel firms themselves.

The Contexts in Which Networks Operate

Focusing our attention on interfirm networks in the garment industry gives us considerable analytical leverage. In concert with one another, firms make a series of decisions that shape the textile-apparel commodity chain: where different aspects of the design–production–marketing–distribution process take place; how each aspect is organized and managed; and what types of workers are hired, under what sorts of conditions, at what pay levels, and with how much opportunity for upward mobility.

Nevertheless, it is important to bear in mind that firms are not the only actors in the apparel commodity chain that determine its evolution. Rather, they contend with other collective or institutional participants that influence not only production decisions but also the relevant economic and social outcomes. These participants include national, state, and local governments, supranational regulatory agencies (e.g., the NAFTA Secretariat and the World Trade Organization), labor unions, nongovernmental advocacy groups, banks, local entrepreneurial elites, advertising and media companies, households, and transnational migrant communities. Thus, although we grant analytical primacy to the role of different types of interfirm networks in determining the evolution of the textile-garment chain and the generation of wealth at different points along it, we recognize that the socioeconomic consequences of this process are embedded in a multilayered institutional setting that incorporates a variety of other factors as well.

In this regard, it is instructive to contemplate the interaction between firm strategies and macroeconomic and macropolitical contexts, that is, the dynamic relation between private firms and nation-states. These contexts play a powerful role in determining what strategies are pursued at a given point in an industry's development and in limiting the benefits and costs to a particular region that result from changes in firm strategies. For example, it is clear that changes in the macro context—in the form of NAFTA and a severely devalued peso—have led brand-name apparel firms vigorously to pursue opportunities to manufacture garments in Mexico, such as mass-produced men's and boys' trousers. The structural advantages of Mexico as a production site include:

- the relatively low cost and high productivity of its labor force;

- the existence of a Mexican entrepreneurial class within the industry that is capable of undertaking assembly and in some cases also full-package production;
- the generally acceptable quality of its transportation, utilities, and communications infrastructure, especially in comparison to other developing nations;
- its physical proximity to the United States (which keeps transportation costs from wiping out other cost savings); and
- its preferential tariff and quota treatment under NAFTA.

At the same time, the varying structural conditions that firms encounter *within* Mexico influence their strategic decisions with regard to production. For example, we see that the possibilities for expansion of garment production on Mexico's northern border are limited by the saturation of the labor and commercial real estate markets with auto-parts and electronics maquiladoras. This has made production at the border relatively more expensive than elsewhere in Mexico, encouraging a shift toward interior production locations. Although the majority of maquiladora employees continue to work in plants located along Mexico's northern border—79 percent in 1998—this proportion has declined from 93 percent in 1988 (Buitelaar and Padilla Pérez 2000). At present, the rate of growth in the maquiladora sector is higher in the interior of Mexico than along the border, and this is particularly true for apparel plants.

As a consequence, in some interior locations of the Mexican garment industry (e.g., Monterrey, Guadalajara, and Torreón) we see established domestic producers shifting to the export market on an original equipment manufacture (OEM) basis, that is, manufacturing ready-made garments for branded U.S. customers, or selling to new foreign retail chains in the Mexican market (see Chapters 9, 10, and 11 in this

book; see also Bair 2001). In other interior locations (e.g., the rural municipalities near Gómez
Palacio, Durango), we see garment production
undertaken on a "green field" basis, tapping
heretofore unutilized labor reserves, especially
those constituted by young women in smaller
towns and rural areas. We also find variation in
the types of garments that dominate production in different regions. In general terms, the
"new" production centers concentrate on
mass-produced men's and boys' garments,
such as blue jeans, while the types of garments
made in regions that are experiencing a shift
from domestic- to export-oriented production
depend more on the preexisting infrastructure
that has served the Mexican market.

Shifts in the geography of apparel production within Mexico, with sites in southern and
central Mexico growing rapidly, are driven by
the combination of push and pull factors
alluded to above. The push factors, as noted,
are high turnover and increasing wages on the
border, which have led many leading U.S.
firms to relocate production and sourcing
operations to the interior. State governments,
seeking to attract foreign investment and create jobs, offer various incentives to these firms
in order to pull them to particular locations
that are often green-field (i.e., new and potentially "fertile") sites with respect to apparel
production. Another pull factor is the existence in several parts of Mexico of national
firms that are looking for maquiladora orders
either to replace or to supplement production
for a stagnant domestic market.

While in the past Mexico's apparel production for export was limited to assembly,
NAFTA has prompted a substantial flow of
additional capabilities to Mexico, including
textile production, cutting, trimming, laundering, and distribution. The growth in nonassembly production activities has been especially pronounced in interior regions. In
addition, the post-NAFTA period has wit-

nessed the emergence of a number of "full-
package" production networks linking the
United States and Mexico. Such full-package
manufacturing in Mexico has a number of
advantages, including local "backward" linkages,[5] technology transfer, and skill upgrading
at the direct-production, technician, and managerial levels, as high-status, brand-name companies contract to local producers that can
meet exacting standards for quality, timely
delivery, and cost. These local producers may
be U.S.-owned, Mexican-owned, or joint ventures. Meeting such standards typically involves the use of state-of-the-art technologies
and forms of work organization that, in turn,
require a trained, disciplined, and stable workforce.

The ability to fill full-package orders for
U.S. buyers gives Mexican firms a competitive
edge vis-à-vis their maquiladora competitors
in Central America and the Caribbean. The
transition to full package may also benefit
Mexican workers in the form of better working conditions and perhaps even higher wages
than those of their peers with jobs in "low-
road" maquiladoras and smaller producers
that are more technologically and organizationally backward.

Nevertheless, the macro context in which
even such "elite," high-productivity garment
networks operate can place strong limits on the
benefits accruing to Mexican workers. Thus,
while the expansion of garment production for
the world market has generated considerable
employment in Mexico in recent years and has
led to productivity growth in some regions of
the country, workers' incomes may not rise
concomitantly if their purchasing power is
reduced by currency devaluations or government attempts to keep exports competitive by
deliberately limiting wage growth. Indeed,
research by Harley Shaiken (1990) into technologically advanced, export-oriented plants in
Mexico in the automobile, consumer electron-

ics, and computer industries demonstrates that such an outcome for the garment industry is not out of the question.[6] In this regard, it is important to bear in mind that firms in the garment industry do not set the average wage levels in most of the local labor markets in which they operate, that is, they are "price takers" with respect to wages. The wages they pay may be relatively high in local labor markets but may still be insufficient to lift workers above the subsistence level. At the same time, macroeconomic factors that depress worker wages give transnational firms an incentive to shift production to low-wage regions.

Evaluation of the impact of NAFTA on Mexican development must also take account of changes that have occurred in the country's political and economic landscape since the mid-1980s. Mexico transformed itself from one of the world's most closed economies to one of the most open in little more than a decade. Its modernizing agenda, dramatically accelerated by President Carlos Salinas de Gortari (1988–94), placed a high priority on increasing labor flexibility and making Mexico an attractive site for foreign direct investment. In effect, this has meant falling real wages for most Mexican workers and a serious decline in the influence of the once-powerful (if never democratic) unions that for decades provided important support to the country's ruling party, the Partido Revolucionario Institucional (PRI). The analytical approach taken in this collection focuses attention precisely on this sort of interplay between the macroeconomic and political landscape, local environments of specific production sites, and interfirm networks connecting national and foreign companies and their workers.

While the firm-focused approach taken here means that this book contains only a few chapters that analyze developments within the North American garment workforce, it suggests a network-oriented path for other ana-lysts who wish to explore these developments. Similar to the way in which networked firms devise production strategies in response to structural factors, workers and their communities participate in networks that help organize their labor market participation. This can be seen most clearly in the existence of transnational migrant networks that link communities of garment workers and their families across national boundaries.

Mexican workers participating in migrant networks that transcend the U.S.-Mexico border face strategic decisions in a way similar to those of networked firms in the garment industry. Both confront a North American landscape altered by increased economic integration between Mexico and the United States and a transformed legal framework that regulates their activities. Mexican workers enmeshed in social networks in certain regions in Mexico may find it attractive to remain in Mexico in order to pursue employment opportunities with the dynamic export-oriented firms that are coming to dominate Mexico's manufacturing sector. Workers in different social settings in other regions may find it attractive to migrate to the United States in order to pursue productive opportunities there. With regard to the North American garment industry, Mexican laborers are crucial to subsidizing its development whether they work in El Paso, Los Angeles, Torreón, or Puebla. The relative benefits they derive from employment as garment workers depend on the types of firms they work for, their productivity, the effort they put forth as individuals, the degree to which they are represented by strong and responsible unions, and the national macroeconomic context, as well as on social and cultural factors inherent to the communities in which they live and work.

Within this "social economy" framework seemingly peculiar outcomes may arise. Workers employed in Mexico as sewing machine operators in progressive, state-of-the-art apparel firms may enjoy wages and benefits that are substantially higher than those offered by other types of firms in their communities. They may gain new skills and find opportunities for occupational advancement. Their incomes, while perhaps not sufficient to support an entire family, may contribute to sustaining low-income multiearner households. Mexicans working for garment producers in Los Angeles might find themselves in similar circumstances. By contrast, especially if they are undocumented, they may work for substandard U.S. wages, receive no benefits, have little chance for occupational advancement, and toil in sweatshop conditions.[7]

In spite of the considerable disadvantages experienced by Mexican workers relative to U.S. natives in Los Angeles, national macroeconomic factors allow Mexicans working there to earn wages up to ten times higher than those earned by compatriots laboring in the garment industry in Mexico. Just as this national income gap influences firm strategies in the North American garment industry, so too it influences Mexican worker strategies. Thus, Mexican women who lose their jobs sewing jeans in El Paso are unlikely to move home to Torreón in order to continue plying their trade. But by the same token, their nieces, who in earlier times might have migrated to the border to work in the industry, may be less likely to move to El Paso to join other kin and friends there. Undocumented Mexicans in Los Angeles may tolerate wages and working and living conditions that are abysmal by U.S. standards but that allow them to remit a substantial portion of their dollar income home to family members in their communities of origin. Some of these family members may labor in the same industry and may even use the remitted dollars to set up their own garment shops as subcontractors.[8]

The Chapters in This Book

Given that this collection directs its attention to the "new geography" of the North American apparel industry, we have chosen a geographic order of presentation of its chapters. But before introducing the individual chapters and highlighting their contributions, we ask readers to bear two points in mind. First, for the purposes of description and analysis we have deliberately chosen a broad definition of North America. Hence we include chapters dealing with apparel production not only in the United States and Mexico but also in Central America and the Caribbean. As noted above, by the early 1990s the Central American countries and certain Caribbean Basin economies such as the Dominican Republic had become major exporters of garments to the U.S. market. After the implementation of NAFTA, the Caribbean Basin region lost market share relative to Mexico, although its exports to the United States continued to grow rapidly. Now that the Trade and Development Act of 2000 grants Caribbean Basin countries U.S. market access on more favorable terms, they are in a better position to compete with Mexico, and the Caribbean Basin economies are even more thoroughly integrated into the development of the North American regional apparel market. For these reasons, we have included two chapters (by Michael Mortimore and Dale Mathews) focusing on apparel production in Central America and the Caribbean Basin.

This book does not, however, contain chapters focused on the textile-apparel complex in Canada, in spite of that country's participation in NAFTA. In terms of North American regional trade, Canada occupies a relatively minor niche in the apparel industry, specializing in a small number of products such as men's and women's wool suits. It is a more important exporter of textile products, but for the most part these are not destined for apparel production, instead being used in household and automotive upholstery. Like the United States, although on a much smaller scale, Canada has seen employment declines in both textiles and apparel owing to competition from Asian and Mexican imports. For these reasons, we have not included individual chapters dedicated to the Canadian experience.

The second point we ask readers to remember is that, although the chapters are organized by the geography of the principal production sites they examine, the fact that contributors have taken a firm-centered, network-oriented analytical approach means that most chapters relate developments in the industry to more than one place in the North American region. For example, Judi Kessler's discussion of the Los Angeles garment district also considers its relationship to emerging Mexican production sites in Puebla and Cuernavaca, while Florence Palpacuer's chapter on New York perforce relates developments there to those in Los Angeles, its principal geographic competitor in the United States. Similarly, David Spener's and Robine van Dooren's chapters on El Paso take into account the emergence of Torreón as a rival to the Texas city's claim to be the "blue jeans capital of the world," while Gary Gereffi, Martha Martínez, and Jennifer Bair discuss Torreón's relationship with textile and garment producers in the U.S. Southeast. Thus the reader of any given chapter in this book will learn not only about apparel production in the principal site described therein but also about how and why production there relates to clothing production and consumption elsewhere in the region.

Part I: Analytical Overview

In addition to this introductory chapter, Part I includes a chapter by Jennifer Bair and Gary Gereffi that describes the emergence of full-

package production networks in Mexico that link new types of U.S. "lead firms" with a range of Mexican partners, including textile, fiber, and apparel companies. Chapter 2 begins with a review of the evolution of the global apparel industry since the 1970s. The authors then discuss the types of data necessary for a firm-level network analysis, including trade and production statistics, strategic interviews with lead companies, and on-site fieldwork. Research conducted by the authors over several years reveals that firms are developing strategies to respond both to the changing institutional environments created by trade regimes such as NAFTA and to their own concerns about profitability and control in increasingly global commodity chains. In addition, the authors discuss how the developmental implications of "full-package" networks differ from those associated with the maquiladora or assembly model of production.

Part II: The Apparel Industry in the United States

The initial two chapters in this part of the book address contemporary developments in New York and Los Angeles, the two largest garment districts in the United States in terms of employment and cities that are also among the world's most important fashion design centers. In Chapter 3, Florence Palpacuer analyzes how the structure of the New York garment industry has evolved under the impact of globalization by focusing on its main industrial niche, the fashion-oriented segment of the women's wear industry, and on the subcontracting networks through which production in this segment is organized. Globalization is here associated with two major trends: (1) the development of international subcontracting networks that link garment firms in New York City to foreign producers in a variety of countries; and (2) the entry of Asian and Hispanic immigrants, which has produced significant diversification in the social and ethnic composition of the New York garment industry.

Palpacuer finds that the majority of New York garment firms are still small, but a few have grown significantly by adopting new competitive strategies in marketing, product design, and production management. Most New York garment firms use local subcontractors for garment manufacturing, but the largest have developed transnational production networks in which local producers account for only a small portion of productive activities. Although ethnic ties remain an important channel for entry into the New York garment industry, Palpacuer finds, subcontracting networks have developed across ethnic communities, creating new patterns of social and industrial segmentation in the local industry.

In Chapter 4, Judi Kessler focuses on the evolution of Los Angeles as a major center for garment production and on the changes that have occurred there since 1994. She presents evidence that although NAFTA has helped promote Southern California as a center for apparel services for North America, it has also pulled segments of the apparel commodity chain from Los Angeles to Mexico. In particular, she highlights a survey of Los Angeles apparel manufacturers that she conducted in 1997 and 1998, in which half the respondents reported that they sourced at least some of their production in Mexico—up from just 15 percent of the same respondents surveyed in 1992. The vast majority of respondents in 1997–98 maintained that NAFTA was a primary reason for shifting production to Mexico, more important than the 1994–95 peso devaluation that lowered Mexican labor costs.

In conducting in-depth interviews with managers of Los Angeles firms that sourced production to Mexico, Kessler found that the interior states of Guanajuato, Puebla, Tlaxcala, and Jalisco, as well as the greater Mexico City region, figured most prominently as new production states. Many of the managers stated that a principal reason for sourcing production to Mexico was to avoid the burden of complying with state and federal labor regulations governing production in Los Angeles. At the same time, Kessler found that many small manufacturers lack the "global reach" to relocate production to Mexico or other offshore sites and continue to exploit a vulnerable immigrant workforce, many of whose members are undocumented Mexicans. Should employment of direct-production workers in Los Angeles remain constant or grow in the future, it will likely be in this small-scale, immigrant-dominated sector.

As both Palpacuer and Kessler note in their chapters, many immigrant workers in the New York and Los Angeles garment districts toil in substandard conditions. In Chapter 5, Robert Ross takes up the issue of sweatshop employment in the U.S. apparel industry. He examines a variety of statistical and historical records to measure the extent of sweatshop exploitation during the evolution of the U.S. apparel industry in the twentieth century. Adopting the U.S. General Accounting Office's definition of a "sweatshop" as "a business that regularly violates both wage or child labor and safety or health laws," Ross estimates that in 1998 around 60 percent of the eight hundred thousand garment workers in the United States labored in sweatshops.

Based on his examination of historical records, including documents and statements from officials of the International Ladies Garment Workers Union (ILGWU); studies conducted by independent scholars; and an examination of the conditions of Puerto Rican workers in New York City's garment industry in the 1950s, Ross concludes that sweatshop employment, which had been endemic early in the century, had declined to a marginal level by the 1960s. He then describes the four significant factors in the resurgence in sweatshop employment in the apparel industry since the late 1960s: the declining capacity of the state to enforce labor law; the increasing market power of retailers through concentration of sales; the competitive pressure brought about by massive imports from low-wage export platforms; and the availability of a large pool of vulnerable immigrant labor.

In Chapter 6, the final chapter in Part II of this book, Edna Bonacich shows how organized labor is confronting global production in the apparel industry. The shift to global outsourcing in the last decades of the twentieth century led to huge losses in membership in the two leading unions in the U.S. apparel sector: the ILGWU and the Amalgamated Clothing and Textile Workers Union (ACTWU). When the ILGWU and ACTWU merged in 1995 to form UNITE (the Union of Needletrades, Industrial, and Textile Employees), a new chapter in the U.S. labor movement was launched. Bonacich describes how each of these three unions (ILGWU, ACTWU, and UNITE) responded to the challenges of globalization, with an emphasis on the key limitation of labor's strategy in the North American apparel industry: its reluctance to try to link domestic organizing of apparel production workers with organizing efforts directed at garment workers in developing countries. The chapter ends with a discussion of new strategies by labor that include linking solidarity initiatives associated with the "anti-sweatshop movement," a strategic ally of the North American labor movement, to real organizing in offshore production locations.

Part III: The U.S.-Mexico Border Region

The apparel industry was an important employer in the border region long before the maquiladora system and NAFTA were implemented. In many ways, the border region was the first place where, prior to Mexico's unilateral trade opening of the 1980s and its subsequent entry into NAFTA, North American economic integration occurred, in the form of export-oriented assembly on the Mexican side coupled with commercial distribution of industrial and consumer goods and large-scale employment of Mexican nationals in agriculture, manufacturing, and services on the U.S. side. Business organizations in the region were strong proponents of NAFTA, and the border was seen as a harbinger of the economic benefits that U.S.-Mexican free trade could bring (see Spener 1995). Ironically, the border region has been hard hit by NAFTA-related dislocations, especially in the apparel industry. Three chapters in this book address themselves to developments in the border region.

In Chapter 7, David Spener describes how bilateral trade regulations negotiated under the auspices of the Multifiber Arrangement (MFA)[9] promoted the development of El Paso as a low-cost producer of denim apparel in the United States and how subsequent liberalization of the regime encouraged firms to relocate cutting, sewing, and finishing operations to sites in Mexico. Spener pays special attention to the case of Levi Strauss, El Paso's largest private employer, which has laid off nearly three thousand employees in El Paso since the implementation of NAFTA began. He argues that while NAFTA was not the proximate cause of the company's plant shutdowns in El Paso, the trade agreement favored its greatly increased reliance on a network of overseas contractors, especially in Mexico. The new

NAFTA trade regime has also negatively affected smaller subcontractor firms in El Paso, whose activities (such as cutting and laundering of denim garments) were formerly protected from Mexican competition. Spener concludes his analysis by highlighting the challenges created for the El Paso community by job loss in its principal industry. The apparel sector had traditionally provided employment for large numbers of Mexican immigrant women, whose lack of education and English-language ability makes them especially difficult to retrain for jobs in other industries.

In Chapter 8, Robine van Dooren also directs attention to the El Paso case, but she focuses on the lack of cross-border linkages between the Texas city's garment district and apparel production in Ciudad Juárez, El Paso's "twin" city across the border and the home to Mexico's largest concentration of maquiladoras. From her examination of a survey of sixty companies in this binational metropolitan area, van Dooren concludes that very little complementarity exists between the two cities' industries, largely because of their differing product specializations—El Paso focuses on blue jeans production, whereas Ciudad Juárez makes a much wider variety of garments, ranging from women's wear to uniforms, with very little emphasis on jeans. In the free-trade environment, low-cost production in Juárez is favored in the short run, while the production of standardized garments in El Paso is seriously threatened by competition not from Juárez but rather from cities in the Mexican interior, such as Torreón/Gómez Palacio, Aguascalientes, and Puebla. In the long run, however, Juárez may experience a decline in garment production due to a tight labor market brought on by large-scale maquiladora production in electronics and auto parts. This tight labor market and high real estate costs make Juárez an increasingly unattractive site for garment production relative to other Mexican locales.

In Chapter 9, Jorge Carrillo, Alfredo Hualde, and Araceli Almaraz compare the different experiences with free trade of the apparel sectors of Monterrey, in the state of Nuevo León, and Ciudad Juárez. Specifically, the authors identify the different types of interfirm networks that have arisen in each city. In Monterrey these include traditional assembly, OEM (or full-package production, as it is better known in the apparel industry), and original brand-name manufacture (OBM) networks, in which local firms have moved beyond OEM production for foreign buyers to establishing their own brand names that they market themselves. Ciudad Juárez has two distinct forms of international subcontracting networks, one that features significant backward linkages to the local market and one with no such linkages. In examining the international competitiveness of firms participating in each type of network, the authors conclude that, contrary to the predictions of development theory, firms participating in networks without local backward linkages tend to be more flexibly competitive in the new free-trade environment, while locally linked firms tend to suffer from a number of disadvantages, including technological and organizational limitations and a lack of forward linkages to the international market.

Part IV: Interior Mexico

Mexico's rise to prominence as an apparel exporter has resulted from the rapid expansion of production in its interior, far from the traditional sites of maquiladora assembly on the border with the United States. Three chapters in this part examine the export-oriented apparel sector in the Mexican interior, while a fourth addresses the evolution of the domestic retail market for apparel. Together, these chapters outline the challenges and opportunities facing the Mexican apparel industry in the free-trade period. Mexican producers have confronted the double challenge of the penetration of Asian imports and the shrinking of the domestic apparel market caused, respectively, by the country's entry into the General Agreement on Tariffs and Trade (GATT) in the 1980s and by the drastic devaluation of the peso in the mid-1990s. As a consequence, many Mexican producers have had to shift to producing for the U.S. market in order to survive. For the most part, this has meant working as subcontractors for U.S.-based manufacturers and retailers or for larger Mexican producers, an opportunity that has been enhanced by both NAFTA and the devalued peso.

Nowhere in Mexico has the rise of apparel production for export been more dramatic than in Torreón, Coahuila, which by the end of the twentieth century had replaced El Paso as the "blue jeans capital of the world." In Chapter 10, Gary Gereffi, Martha Martínez, and Jennifer Bair detail the rapid rise of Torreón as an exporter and discuss its potential as a model for surpassing the traditional maquiladora form of production in the apparel sector. They describe how Torreón's blue jeans firms have transformed themselves in just a few years from producers for the domestic market, to maquiladora exporters, and then to full-package exporters working as partners with U.S. "lead firms," for whom they manufacture on an OEM basis. In this process, apparel employment has mushroomed in the area, from just twelve thousand jobs in 1993 to seventy-five thousand by 2000. In addition, Torreón's rise as a jeans exporter has attracted U.S. textile producers to the region, leading to the opening of new denim mills close to local producers.

Although the authors establish that Torreón has moved well beyond the traditional maquiladora model, with positive consequences that include improved wages and conditions for workers, skill upgrading, and the deepening of

local backward linkages, firms there do not have the institutional support associated with a traditional "industrial district," and no firm has been able to move into the most profitable activities in the apparel chain, namely, design and marketing. The authors also question the extent to which Torreón's experience is replicable in other Mexican locales that do not share some of the city's strategic advantages, including close proximity and easy transport to the U.S. border, the existence of an apparel-manufacturing tradition prior to NAFTA, and a class of local entrepreneurs able to upgrade their factory operations.

In Chapter 11, Enrique Dussel Peters, Clemente Ruiz Durán, and Michael Piore elaborate further on how Mexican apparel producers can upgrade their operations by partnering with foreign firms. They note that trade liberalization in Mexico has created a split between a relatively small set of companies with current technology and manufacturing methods that are able to compete in a global market, on the one hand, and a larger group of firms catering to domestic demand that have been negatively affected by the opening of markets, on the other hand. Firms that have made a successful transition to exporting have relied heavily on their relationships with foreign firms placing orders in Mexico. The authors examine the learning process that accompanied these successful transitions and argue that the type of investment required of both foreign and Mexican manufacturers limits the likelihood that these tutelage relationships will prove common enough to upgrade the Mexican apparel industry on a wide scale. The chapter concludes with a set of policy recommendations for a "bootstrapping strategy" that can extend to a broader range of companies the benefits created by one-on-one relationships between foreign and national firms.

In Chapter 12, Ulrik Vangstrup examines the experiences of domestic knitwear manufacturers in the central and western states of Guanajuato, Hidalgo, México, Michoacán, and Jalisco that have recently begun exporting. He focuses on the potential benefits provided to these primarily small and medium-sized enterprises as a result of their location in industrial clusters. Drawing on industrial-districts and collective-efficiency literature, Vangstrup asks if the *empresas integradoras* ("integrative firms") and credit unions that emerged in the early 1990s, during Mexico's most intense period of economic reform, have encouraged Mexican entrepreneurs to export. Contrary to the emphasis that the industrial-districts literature has placed on the importance of *inner-cluster* dynamics for small and medium-sized enterprises, the rich case studies presented in this chapter reveal that *external links* to global commodity chains have been critical in allowing companies to initiate successful export programs. Specifically, contacts with foreign (and especially U.S.) buyers were found to be more important than the advantages provided by membership in a producer association or location in a cluster. Vangstrup concludes with recommendations for increasing the efficacy of the producer associations, noting the potential competitiveness of Mexican knitwear manufacturers in the global market.

In Chapter 13, Jorge Mendoza, Fernando Pozos Ponce, and David Spener describe the evolving structure of the Mexican retail market for apparel in terms of the growing importance of large-scale discount chains and department stores and the persistence of informal distribution channels. In reviewing trends in Mexican clothing imports and consumption in the 1980s and 1990s, the authors present a typology of enterprises engaged in the retail sale of clothing in Mexico and describe the market segment served by each type, as well as trends in the overall market share of each. In addition, they undertake a case study of informal distribution channels for imported cloth-

ing in Guadalajara that link Mexican entrepreneurs, workers, and consumers of modest means with manufacturers and brokers of U.S.- and Asian-made clothing located in the Los Angeles garment district. In their conclusions, the authors argue that the emergence of Mexico in the early 1990s as a consumer market for U.S.- and Asian-made apparel was theoretically significant, as buyer-driven commodity chains came full circle, with First World firms bringing their Third World–produced goods to an emerging market that was itself located in the Third World.

Part V: Central America and the Caribbean

We have included Central America and the Caribbean in our examination of the "North American" apparel industry because these regions are significant exporters to the United States and have enjoyed preferential access to the U.S. market under the Caribbean Basin Initiative and Item 9802 of the U.S. tariff code. The two chapters in Part V analyze the challenges facing apparel producers and national governments in the Caribbean Basin region as their special advantages for exporting to the United States were being eroded by NAFTA in the latter half of the 1990s. Now that a version of NAFTA parity has finally been granted to the Caribbean Basin countries, it remains to be seen how the region's exporters will fare relative to Mexico and Asia.

Michael Mortimore discusses in Chapter 14 how apparel production served as an engine of growth and development for all the world's advanced national economies in earlier stages of their industrial development. He notes that the apparel industry has been an important stepping-stone for developed countries and several of their Asian challengers to promote industrialization and to generate significant exports to the international market. Nonetheless, he questions whether the apparel industry can serve such a function for the small countries of Central America and the Caribbean today. Reviewing relevant trade statistics and taking Costa Rica as a case study, Mortimore concludes that over the long run apparel production is unlikely to produce positive developmental outcomes for the region. This is so because only low-value-added assembly operations take place in the Caribbean Basin; producers are not competitive with their Asian counterparts without preferential access to the U.S. market; no significant backward linkages into local economies are being developed; and little tax revenue is being generated that could be invested by governments in other important development projects. In addition, because of the small size of their domestic markets and the lack of local textile suppliers, no national firms are capable of moving beyond maquiladora-style subcontracting and into full-package production, as has been occurring in some Mexican locations. Although the Caribbean and Central American countries' disadvantage vis-à-vis Mexico has been reduced by the awarding of "NAFTA parity" for their garment exports, they still face the threat posed by the termination of the MFA in 2005.

Dale Mathews finds that Mortimore's concerns also apply to the Dominican Republic, where the export-oriented apparel industry has been a leading source of employment since the Caribbean Basin Initiative was implemented in the 1980s. In Chapter 15, Mathews describes how the competitiveness of the Dominican Republic's assembly industry is threatened by two recent trends: the liberalization of the global apparel trade regime, as represented by the phaseout of the Multifiber Arrangement and the establishment of the World Trade Organization, and the emergence of Mexico as the Caribbean's main competitor for the U.S. apparel market since the passage of NAFTA. He argues that the costs of trade diversion from the Caribbean to Mexico are particularly high for the Dominican Republic, although it is not yet clear if the U.S. Trade and Development Act of 2000, which helps level the playing field between the Caribbean Basin countries and Mexico, will slow or reverse this trend. Much like the contribution from David Spener in Chapter 7, this chapter underscores how changes in trade regimes can dramatically reshape a country's competitiveness in the global apparel industry. For the relatively homogeneous and less-industrialized economies characteristic of the Caribbean Basin, these changes can mean not only job losses but also the need to rethink a national development strategy dependent on the vitality of export processing zones.

Part VI: Conclusion

The relationship of apparel production and uneven development between and within nations is revisited in Chapter 16. Mexico's meteoric rise to the number-one spot among apparel exporters to the United States is emblematic of the costs and benefits associated with the export-oriented development model that the country has followed since the mid-1980s. The last two decades have witnessed a profound transformation not just of Mexico's economy but also of the political and social relationships underlying its peculiar brand of postrevolutionary, authoritarian corporatism (Middlebrook 1995). This corporatist model has become increasingly less tenable, especially since the abandonment of the import-substitution industrialization strategy in the early 1980s, the subsequent liberalization and industrial restructuring of the economy, and the onset of a new era of electoral democracy in Mexico. What is emerging in its place is still unclear, but the extent to which

Mexico's shift in development strategy will produce positive outcomes for Mexican firms and workers will depend to a significant degree on the organization and performance of inter-firm networks that link capital and labor on both sides of the border.

Notes

1. Throughout the book we use the terms *apparel industry* or *garment industry* to refer to the production of clothing and *textile industry* to refer to the production of fibers and fabric. When we wish to emphasize the links between these two related industries, we speak of the "textile-apparel complex."

2. Guatemala, Honduras, El Salvador, and Costa Rica.

3. This includes only those workers who are directly employed in a plant registered as a maquiladora. Because much maquiladora production is carried out by subcontractors in small and medium-sized firms working for registered maquiladoras, these data underestimate the number of both firms and workers involved in export-oriented apparel production, although it is difficult to know to what extent.

4. Since the 1984 publication of *The Second Industrial Divide* by Michael Piore and Charles Sabel, much has been written about the renewed potential for local "districts" of small- to medium-scale enterprises to lead regional economic development (Saxenian 1994; Sengenberger 1993; Storper and Scott 1990). Inspired by Piore and Sabel's description of the successful example of the Emilia-Romagna region of Italy, where an industrial renaissance occurred as the result of the organization of small-scale metalworking, ceramic, apparel, and furniture firms into flexible production networks, analysts have constructed a variety of industrial-district models that are based on a number of common elements, including (1) highly skilled, well-compensated employees working in a craft tradition; (2) small-batch production facilitated by computer-assisted, multitask tools and cross-trained workers; (3) intense local social networks that link workers

and managers across enterprises in the district; (4) competitive cooperation, such that small firms routinely compete for orders from the same set of clients but then collaborate with one another as partners when a given work order exceeds a single firm's immediate capacity; and (5) local and regional government policies that support districts' institutional infrastructure.

5. Industrial commodities are manufactured, marketed, and distributed by producers and sellers linked to one another in a chainlike fashion. Thus, for any set of companies located at a particular point along a supply chain, *backward linkages* refers to the source of needed inputs for their stage of the production–marketing–distribution process. Locating multiple segments in a supply chain within the same community or geographic region can be especially beneficial to local economic development because these businesses create ancillary employment opportunities for other firms in the community, in addition to diversifying the community's productive infrastructure.

6. To take one example, Shaiken found that a plant run by one of the U.S. Big Three auto manufacturers was as productive as any of the company's plants located in the United States. Labor disputes arose in the plant in the late 1980s when workers claimed that productivity gains associated with specialized training for many of its workers were not accompanied by proportional raises in wages (Shaiken 1990). Indeed, Shaiken (1990, 49–50) reports that in April 1989 workers at the top of the plant's pay scale were earning around $2.20 per hour (entry-level workers earned just $1.00 per hour). At the same time, the average hourly wage for all manual workers in the U.S. automobile industry was $13.58 per hour (calculation made by the authors of this chapter using the 5 Percent Public Use Microdata Sample of the 1990 U.S. Census of Population and Housing).

7. In Los Angeles, 57 percent of garment workers in 1990 were Mexican born and earned an average hourly wage of $5.11, compared to $7.43 per hour for U.S. natives (calculation made by authors using 5 Percent Public Use Microdata Sample of the 1990 U.S. Census of Population and Housing). See Chapter 5 by Robert Ross on the rise of sweatshop conditions in the Los Angeles garment district.

8. Research on Mexican migrant communities shows that this possibility is not at all far-fetched. See Massey et al. (1987), Massey (1998), and Massey and Parrado (1998).

9. From 1974 to 1994, international trade in textiles and apparel was governed by the Multifiber Arrangement, a framework for bilateral agreements or unilateral actions established within the General Agreement on Tariffs and Trade. The MFA established quotas for limiting textile and apparel imports into countries whose domestic industries were threatened by rapidly increasing imports. In 1995 the MFA was superceded by the WTO's Agreement on Textiles and Clothing (ATC). A more detailed explanation of the history of the MFA and its replacement by the ATC can be found on the WTO Web site at <http://www.wto.org>.

References

American Apparel Manufacturers Association. 1999. "1998: The Year in Numbers." In *Apparel Industry Trends* (March). Arlington, Va.: American Apparel Manufacturers Association.

Appelbaum, Richard P., David Smith, and Brad Christerson. 1994. "Commodity Chains and Industrial Restructuring in the Pacific Rim: Garment Trade and Manufacturing." In *Commodity Chains and Global Capitalism,* ed. Gary Gereffi and Miguel Korzeniewicz, pp. 185–204. Westport, Conn.: Greenwood.

Bair, Jennifer. 2001. "Successful Cases of Small and Medium Enterprises in Mexico: Lessons from the Aguascalientes Apparel Industry." In *Condiciones y retos de las pequeñas y medianas empresas en México: Estudios de casos de vinculación de empresas exitosas y propuestas de política,* ed. Enrique Dussel Peters, pp. 63–105. Santiago, Chile: United Nations Economic Commission for Latin America and the Caribbean.

Bonacich, Edna, and Richard P. Appelbaum. 2000. *Behind the Label: Inequality in the Los Angeles Apparel Industry.* Berkeley: University of California Press.

Bonacich, Edna, Luci E. Cheng, Norma Chinchilla, Nora Hamilton, and Paul Ong. 1994. "The Garment Industry in the Restructuring Global Economy." In *Global Production: The Apparel Industry in the Pacific Rim,* ed. Edna Bonacich, Lucie Cheng, Norma Chinchilla, Nora Hamilton, and Paul Ong, pp. 3–20. Philadelphia: Temple University Press.

Bonacich, Edna, and David V. Waller. 1994. "Mapping a Global Industry: Apparel Production in the Pacific Rim Triangle." In *Global Production: The Apparel Industry in the Pacific Rim,* ed. Edna Bonacich, Lucie Cheng, Norma Chinchilla, Nora Hamilton, and Paul Ong, pp. 21–41. Philadelphia: Temple University Press.

Buitelaar, Rudolf, and Ramón Padilla Pérez. 2000. "Maquila, Economic Reform, and Corporate Strategies." *World Development* 28, 9: 1627–42.

Christerson, Brad, and Richard P. Appelbaum. 1995. "Global and Local Subcontracting: Space, Ethnicity, and the Organization of Apparel Production." *World Development* 23, 8: 1363–74.

Gereffi, Gary. 1994. "The Organization of Buyer-Driven Global Commodity Chains: How U.S. Retailers Shape Overseas Production Networks." In *Commodity Chains and Global Capitalism,* ed. Gary Gereffi and Miguel Korzeniewicz, pp. 95–122. Westport, Conn.: Praeger.

———. 1999. "International Trade and Industrial Upgrading in the Apparel Commodity Chain." *Journal of International Economics* 48, 1 (June): 37–70.

———. 2000. "The Transformation of the North American Apparel Industry: Is NAFTA a Curse or a Blessing?" *Integration and Trade* 4, 11 (May–August): 47–95.

Gereffi, Gary, and Raphael Kaplinsky, eds. 2001. "The Value of Value Chains: Spreading the Gains from Globalisation." Special issue of *IDS Bulletin* 32, 3 (July).

Gereffi, Gary, and Miguel Korzeniewicz, eds. 1994. *Commodity Chains and Global Capitalism.* Westport, Conn.: Praeger.

Instituto Nacional de Estadística, Geografía e Información (INEGI). 2001. *Banco de información económica.* Retrieved on October 15, 2001, from <http://dgcnesyp.inegi.gob.mx>.

Martin, Philip. 1995. "Mexican-U.S. Migration: Policies and Economic Impacts." *Challenge* (March–April): 56–62.

Massey, Douglas S. 1998. "March of Folly: U.S. Immigration Policy after NAFTA." *American Prospect* 37 (March–April): 22–33.

Massey, Douglas S., Rafael Alarcón, Jorge Durand, and Humberto González. 1987. *Return to Aztlán: The Social Process of International Migration from Western Mexico.* Berkeley: University of California Press.

Massey, Douglas S., and Emilio A. Parrado. 1998. "International Migration and Business Formation in Mexico." *Social Science Quarterly* 79, 1: 1–20.

Middlebrook, Kevin. 1995. *The Paradox of Revolution: Labor, the State, and Authoritarianism in Mexico.* Baltimore: Johns Hopkins University Press.

Mittelhauser, Mark. 1996. "Job Loss and Survival in the Textile and Apparel Industries." *Occupational Outlook Quarterly* 40, 3 (Fall): 18–27.

———. 1997. "Employment Trends in Textiles and Apparel, 1973–2005." *Monthly Labor Review* 121: 24–35.

Murray, Lauren A. 1995. "Unraveling Employment Trends in Textiles and Apparel." *Monthly Labor Review* 118: 62–72.

Odessey, Bruce. 2000. "Senate Passes Africa-Caribbean Trade Bill by 77–19 Vote." *Trade Compass Daily Brief* 48, 10 (May 12): 1.

Piore, Michael J., and Charles F. Sabel. 1984. *The Second Industrial Divide.* New York: Basic Books.

Saxenian, Annalee. 1994. *Regional Advantage: Culture and Competition in Silicon Valley and Route 128.* Cambridge, Mass.: Harvard University Press.

Sengenberger, Werner. 1993. "Local Development and International Economic Competition." *International Labour Review* 132, 3: 313–29.

Shaiken, Harley. 1990. *Mexico in the Global Economy: High Technology and Work Organization in Export Industries.* La Jolla: Center for U.S.-Mexican Studies, University of California, San Diego.

Spener, David. 1995. "Small Scale Enterprise and Entrepreneurship in the Texas Border Region: A Sociocultural Approach." Ph.D. diss., Department of Sociology, University of Texas at Austin.

Spener, David, and Randy Capps. 2001. "North American Free Trade and Changes in the Nativity of the Garment Industry Workforce in the United States." *International Journal of Urban and Regional Research* 25, 2: 301–26.

Storper, Michael, and Allen J. Scott. 1990. "Work Organisation and Local Labour Markets in an Era of Flexible Production." *International Labour Review* 129, 5: 573–91.

U.S. Department of Commerce. 1999. *National Trade Data Base.* Washington, D.C.: U.S. Department of Commerce.

Jennifer Bair and Gary Gereffi

2   NAFTA and the Apparel Commodity
      Chain: Corporate Strategies,
      Interfirm Networks, and
      Industrial Upgrading

The apparel industry is one of the oldest and largest export industries in the world, with global trade and production networks that connect firms and workers in countries at all levels of economic development. This chapter examines the impact of the North American Free Trade Agreement (NAFTA) as one of the most recent and significant developments to affect patterns of international trade and production in the apparel and textile industries. Trade policies are changing the institutional environment in which firms in this industry operate, and companies are responding to these changes with new strategies designed to increase their profitability and strengthen their control over the apparel commodity chain. Our hypothesis is that lead firms are establishing qualitatively different kinds of regional production networks in North America from those that existed prior to NAFTA, and that these networks have important consequences for industrial upgrading in the Mexican textile and apparel industries. Post-NAFTA cross-border production arrangements include full-package networks that link lead firms in the United States with apparel and textile manufacturers, contractors, and suppliers in Mexico. Full-package production is increasing the local value added provided by the apparel commodity chain in Mexico and creating new opportunities for Mexican firms and workers.

The chapter is divided into four main sections. The first section uses trade and production data to analyze shifts in global apparel flows, highlighting the emergence and consolidation of a regional trade bloc in North America. The second section discusses the process of industrial upgrading in the apparel industry and introduces a distinction between assembly and full-package production networks. The third section includes case studies based on published industry sources and strategic interviews with several lead companies whose strategies are largely responsible for the shifting trade patterns and NAFTA-inspired cross-border production networks discussed in the previous section. The fourth section considers the implications of these changes for employment in the North American apparel industry.

Regionalization in the Global Apparel Industry

The world textile and apparel industry has undergone several migrations of production and trade since the 1950s, and prior to the 1990s all these migrations revolved around Asia. The first was from North America and Western Europe to Japan in the 1950s and early 1960s, when a sharp rise in imports from Japan displaced Western textile and clothing production. The second supply shift was from Japan to the "big three" Asian apparel producers (Hong Kong, Taiwan, and South Korea), which permitted the latter group to dominate global textile and clothing exports in the 1970s and 1980s. The mid-1980s through the 1990s saw a third migration of production, this time from the Asian big three to a number of other developing economies. In the 1980s the principal shift was to mainland China, but it also encompassed Southeast and South Asian nations as well as Turkey. In the 1990s the proliferation of new suppliers included apparel exporters in Eastern Europe, Central America and the Caribbean, and, above all, Mexico (Khanna 1993; Gereffi 1999).

The shifting patterns of international trade in the apparel industry are highlighted in Table 2.1, which lists the twenty-five leading apparel exporters in the world. Each economy in the table (with the exception of Costa Rica) had at least $1 billion of apparel exports to the world market in 1999,[1] which in total were valued at just over $200 billion. Examining the growth in apparel exports of these nations in 1980, 1990, and 1999, one sees a stair-step pattern of entry into the global apparel market. In 1980 only four developing countries had apparel exports of at least $1 billion: the Northeast Asian economies of Hong Kong, South Korea, Taiwan, and China. By 1990 seven more countries had passed this threshold: Indonesia, Thailand, and Malaysia in Southeast Asia; India and Pak-

istan in South Asia; Turkey in Central Europe; and Tunisia in North Africa. Finally, by 1999 the billion-dollar club of apparel exporters had added ten new members: the Philippines and Vietnam in Southeast Asia; Bangladesh and Sri Lanka in South Asia; Poland, Romania, Hungary, and the Czech Republic in Eastern Europe; the Dominican Republic in the Caribbean Basin; and Mexico.[2]

How can we explain these international trade shifts? A simple market explanation is that the most labor-intensive segments of the apparel supply chain will be located in countries with the lowest wages. This account is supported by the sequential relocation of textile and apparel production from the United States and Western Europe to Japan, the Asian big three, and China, since each new tier of entrants to the production hierarchy had significantly lower wage rates than its predecessors. While differences in wage rates help explain the shift of apparel production from more-expensive to less-expensive sites globally, labor costs alone fail to reveal a key structural feature of the apparel industry: It is not just global in scope but also regional in its organization.

Each macro global region (Asia, Europe, and North America) is characterized by a regional division of labor whereby countries at different levels of development carry out complementary activities and play distinct roles in the apparel commodity chain. The ability of the East Asian newly industrializing economies (NIEs) to sustain their export success over several decades and to develop a multilayered sourcing hierarchy in Asia must be examined in the context of an interrelated regional economy (Gereffi 1999). The apparel export boom in the less-developed southern tier of Asia has been driven to a significant extent by industrial restructuring in the northern-tier East Asian NIEs. As Northeast Asian firms began to move their production offshore, they devised ways to coordinate and control their sourcing networks.

Ultimately they focused on the profitable design and marketing segments in the apparel commodity chain to sustain their competitive edge. This transformation can be conceptualized as a process of industrial upgrading, based in large measure on building various kinds of economic and social networks between buyers and sellers. An analogous division of labor exists between high-cost and low-cost countries in each region of the world.

Triangle Manufacturing in Asia

In Asia triangle manufacturing arrangements have shifted the geography of production and allowed the dominant apparel exporters in the region (Hong Kong, South Korea, and Taiwan) to move to higher-value-added activities (Gereffi 1999). "Triangle manufacturing," which the East Asian NIEs initiated in the 1970s and 1980s, describes an international production and trade network in which U.S. or other overseas buyers place their orders with suppliers in the NIEs with whom they have done business in the past. These companies, in turn, shift some or all of the requested production to affiliated offshore factories in low-wage countries, such as China, Indonesia, and Vietnam. The triangle is completed when the finished goods are shipped directly to the foreign buyer. Triangle manufacturing thus changes the status of these NIE companies from established suppliers for U.S. retailers and marketers to "middlemen" in commodity chains that create a regional division of labor in Asia between the higher-wage countries that coordinate these networks and the lower-wage countries that perform the more labor-intensive portion of the production process.

Outward Processing Trade in Europe

Outward processing trade (OPT) in the European clothing sector is the practice by which companies export fabrics or parts of garments to be assembled in another country. These are then reimported as finished garments in a European Union (EU) country. Regulated within the European Union since 1982, OPT is widely recognized as accelerating the shift of apparel manufacturing from high-wage to low-wage countries in Eastern Europe and North Africa (most notably Tunisia and Morocco). Trade policy is, however, designed to retain textile production in the higher-wage countries. Companies exporting fabrics for assembly under OPT that are not manufactured in an EU country are penalized by a tariff of 14 percent levied on their reimports. The level of tariff duties offsets the advantage of lower production costs made possible through the OPT arrangement.

Garments made under the OPT option constitute a significant portion of the EU market in apparel, given the European Union's relatively high labor costs. More than 80 percent of OPT clothing imports are concentrated in only four EU member states: Germany, Italy, France, and the United Kingdom. The ratio of OPT imports to total clothing imports in 1995 was highest in Germany (21 percent of all German clothing imports) and Italy (17 percent) (OETH 1996, 51–52).

OPT trade is particularly significant for Central and Eastern European countries. In the mid-1990s, OPT exports represented 25 percent of total exports from these economies to the European Union, although the relative importance of OPT arrangements varied for different products. Textile products dominate OPT in Europe, but OPT arrangements in electrical machinery are also prevalent. Fully 80 percent of the garments exported to Western Europe from Central and Eastern Europe were assembled under the OPT regime (Henriot and Inotäi 1998). In recent years, OPT trade in textile products between this region and the European Union has weakened somewhat, reflecting the increased competitiveness of some Asian suppliers to the European market.

TABLE 2.1.   World's 25 Leading Apparel Exporters, 1980–99

Region/Country	Population (millions) 1999[a]	GNP (U.S.$ billions) 1999[a]	GNP/capita (U.S.$) 1999[a]	Total national exports (U.S.$ billions)			Apparel exports to the world market (U.S.$ billions)			Apparel as percent of total national exports (%)			Hourly apparel labor costs (wages & fringe benefits, U.S.$) 1998[c]
				1980[b]	1990[b]	1999[b]	1980[b]	1990[b]	1999[b]	1980[b]	1990[b]	1999[b]	
Northeast Asia													
China	1,250	980	780	19	65	210	1.7	10.2	32.4	8.8	15.7	15.4	0.43
Hong Kong	7	162	23,520	21	84	177	5.3	15.7	22.8	25.4	18.7	12.9	5.20
South Korea	47	398	8,490	18	66	150	3.1	8.3	5.1	16.8	12.5	3.4	2.69
Taiwan	22[d]	291[d]	13,235[d]	21	71	139	2.6	4.2	3.4	12.3	5.9	2.4	4.68
Southeast Asia													
Indonesia	207	120	580	24	28	53	0.6	2.9	5.9	2.5	10.3	11.1	0.16
Thailand	62	121	1,960	7	24	61	0.3	2.9	3.7	4.4	12.2	6.1	0.78
Malaysia	23	77	3,400	14	31	89	0.2	1.4	2.4	1.5	4.6	2.7	1.30
Vietnam	78	28	370	0	1	11	0.0	0.1	1.4	5.5	7.2	12.7	0.22
Philippines	77	78	1,020	6	8	37	0.3	0.7	1.3	4.9	8.3	3.5	0.76
South Asia													
India	998	442	450	8	19	39	0.6	2.6	5.4	7.4	14.0	13.8	0.39
Bangladesh	128	47	370	1	1	5	0.0	0.6	4.0	0.0	41.0	80.0	0.30
Sri Lanka	19	16	820	1	2	5	0.1	0.7	2.4	8.9	35.5	48.0	0.44
Pakistan	135	64	470	3	6	9	0.1	1.1	2.0	3.9	19.2	23.0	0.24
Central and Eastern Europe													
Turkey	64	186	2,900	3	13	28	0.1	3.4	6.9	3.5	26.1	24.8	1.84
Poland	39	153	3,960	15	12	29	0.6	0.4	2.3	4.0	3.2	7.9	2.77
Romania	22	34	1,520	12	6	9	0.4	0.4	2.2	3.3	7.1	25.6	1.04
Hungary	10	47	4,650	9	10	26	0.3	0.4	1.4	3.5	4.1	5.4	2.12
Czech Republic	10	52	5,060	12	7	39	0.4	0.3	1.3	3.5	4.1	3.3	1.85

TABLE 2.1. *Continued*

Region/Country	Population (millions) 1999[a]	GNP (U.S.$ billions) 1999[a]	GNP/capita (U.S.$) 1999[a]	Total national exports (U.S.$ billions)			Apparel exports to the world market (U.S.$ billions)			Apparel as percent of total national exports (%)			Hourly apparel labor costs (wages & fringe benefits, U.S.$) 1998[c]
				1980[b]	1990[b]	1999[b]	1980[b]	1990[b]	1999[b]	1980[b]	1990[b]	1999[b]	
Africa													
Morocco	28	34	1,200	2	4	8	0.1	0.7	2.6	4.2	16.4	33.8	1.36
Tunisia	9	20	2,100	2	3	6	0.3	1.1	2.5	14.1	31.8	42.5	0.98[e]
Mauritius	1[f]	4[f]	3,590[f]	0	1	2	0.1	0.6	1.0	21.7	47.7	57.6	1.03
Caribbean Basin													
Dominican Republic	8	16	1,910	1	2	5	0.0	0.8	2.5	0.0	38.0	47.5	1.48
Costa Rica	4	10	2,740	1	2	7	0.0	0.1	0.4	1.8	6.4	5.7	2.52
North America													
United States	273	8,351	30,600	240	418	734	1.3	2.7	8.7	0.5	0.6	1.2	10.12
Mexico	97	429	4,400	16	29	143	0.1	0.1	8.0	0.6	0.3	5.6	1.51
World[g]	5,975	29,232	4,890	2,014	3,471	5,874	39.6	110.6	201.3	2.0	3.2	3.4	—

[a] World Bank, *World Development Report 2000/2001* (New York: Oxford University Press, 2001), 274–75.

[b] World Trade Analyzer, based on United Nations trade data. Apparel is defined as SITC (Standard Industrial Trade Classification) 84.

[c] Werner International, Inc., *Hourly Labor Cost in the Apparel Industry* (Reston, Va.: Werner International, Infotext Division, 1998).

[d] 1999 data from *Taiwan Statistical Data Book 2001*, Council for Economic Planning and Development, Republic of China.

[e] 1996.

[f] World Bank, *World Development Indicators 1999* (New York: Oxford University Press, 1999).

[g] Includes all exporters of apparel.

Production Sharing in North America

Like their European counterparts, U.S. firms are also able to export cut parts of garments to lower-wage countries for assembly and reimport. The United States' analogue to OPT is known as production sharing or "807 production" for the numbered clause in the U.S. trade laws that regulates this type of offshore assembly network. The 807 trade law (now clause 9802) provides preferential access to U.S. firms importing garments that were assembled offshore from fabrics cut in the United States. Under an amended version of the 807/9802 clause, known as 807A, these companies receive further incentives (in the form of even lower tariff rates and essentially limitless quotas, known as Guaranteed Access Levels, or GALs) if they use fabrics that are manufactured as well as cut in the United States.

Each of these arrangements—triangle manufacturing, OPT, and 807 production—is associated with intraregional production networks that create a division of labor between relatively high-wage and low-wage countries. The latter primarily assemble apparel, which remains the most labor-intensive part of the production process, while the higher-wage countries have more developed supporting industries, including textile and fiber manufacturers that supply apparel companies with the materials needed for clothing production. Within each of the regional economies, the lowest-wage countries are attempting to consolidate their importance in existing assembly networks, while relatively developed economies (such as Mexico, Turkey, and China) want to expand or upgrade their apparel industries by moving to a new export role.

Assembly versus Full-Package Production: The Upgrading Challenge

The global apparel industry is characterized by a hierarchy of export roles (Gereffi 1995). Less-developed countries with inexpensive labor are typically linked to the global apparel industry through assembly. This type of production system is the one associated with OPT in Europe and production sharing in North America and generally refers to subcontracting networks between foreign buyers and local producers for the assembly of apparel from imported fabrics, which are often precut. Entry into the apparel commodity chain in the assembly export role requires that an economy have low labor costs, relative political stability, and favorable quotas or other forms of trade access to major export markets. Participation in assembly networks (often associated with export-processing zones) is considered the first step in the upgrading process because it teaches apparel exporters about the price, quality, and delivery standards used in global markets. The assembly role requires that firms learn how to work with organizational buyers (e.g., manufacturers, trading companies, and brokers) that supply the exporting firm with orders, as well as with the fabrics and other inputs needed to assemble garments.

The most typical upgrading trajectory for countries is to shift from the assembly export role to the original equipment manufacturing (OEM) or "full-package" role (as it is more often referred to in the apparel industry). Unlike assembly networks through which exporting firms are provided with inputs, full-package networks require the company receiving the order to perform steps in the production process beyond assembly, such as making samples; purchasing and cutting fabrics; procuring other needed inputs, such as buttons and zippers; and performing whatever finishing processes are required, such as laundering or pressing garments. Generally the shift from the assembly to the OEM role is also facilitated by a local infrastructure of firms capable of supplying a variety of apparel inputs (e.g., textiles, thread, buttons, zippers, labels) at the quality and quantity levels required for export production, as well as a good working relationship between local firms and a new set of foreign buyers (e.g., retailers and marketers) willing to place full-package orders.

At the level of the firm, full-package production changes the relationship between buyer and supplier in a direction that gives more autonomy and learning potential for industrial upgrading to the supplier. It also expands a firm's potential customer base beyond the branded manufacturers that typically place assembly orders (such as Fruit of the Loom or Levi Strauss) to include retailers and marketers (such as Liz Claiborne and the Gap).[3] At the level of the national economy, the development of full-package networks represents a form of upgrading because it stimulates linkages between related segments of the apparel commodity chain. Unlike assembly networks, which usually require the importation of foreign inputs, full-package networks provide opportunities for firms to find local suppliers for materials such as fabric, buttons, and thread.

The competitive edge that the full-package role has historically given the East Asian exporters to the U.S. market is apparent in Table 2.2, which shows trends in U.S. apparel imports by region and country between 1983 and 2001. During the 1980s, Hong Kong, South Korea, and Taiwan dominated the U.S. market for imported apparel. In 1983 these three economies, along with China and Macao, accounted for 68 percent of total apparel imports. Although their share of the U.S. mar-

ket has declined in recent years, the Asian NIEs remain significant exporters to the United States, despite their higher labor costs.

Table 2.2 also reveals the significant growth in North American sources of apparel imports in the 1990s. The countries of Central America and the Caribbean increased their share of U.S. apparel imports from a negligible 4 percent in 1983 to 15 percent in 1998 (a level they maintained through 2001), while Mexico's percentage of the U.S. import market jumped nearly sevenfold, from 2 percent to 13 percent between 1986 and 2001. This growth in imports from the Caribbean Basin and Mexico underscores the increasingly regional nature of trade and production flows in apparel. The production-sharing program that allows U.S. companies to assemble apparel in low-wage sites in North America is largely responsible for this boom in intraregional trade.

Apparel Production in Mexico and the Caribbean Basin

Production activities performed in export-processing plants in the Caribbean's Free Trade Zones or in Mexico (where these factories are called maquiladoras) are generally of a very low value-added nature, which is a direct result of U.S. policy. Under the production-sharing program, export-processing plants have an incentive to minimize locally purchased inputs because only U.S.-made components are exempt from import duties when the finished product is shipped back to the United States. This constitutes a major impediment to increasing the integration between the activities in the zones and the local economy, and it limits the usefulness of export-processing activities as stepping-stones to higher stages of industrialization.

The majority of apparel produced for the U.S. market in Mexico and the Caribbean Basin

TABLE 2.2. U.S. Apparel Imports by Region and Country, 1983–2001

Region/Country	1983 Value U.S.$ millions	1983 Value %	1986 Value U.S.$ millions	1986 Value %	1990 Value U.S.$ millions	1990 Value %	1994 Value U.S.$ millions	1994 Value %	1998 Value U.S.$ millions	1998 Value %	2001 Value U.S.$ millions	2001 Value %	% Change 1990–94	% Change 1994–2001
Northeast Asia														
China	759	8	1,661	10	3,439	13	6,338	17	7,180	13	8,853	14	84.3	39.7
Hong Kong	2,249		3,392		3,977		4,393		4,494		4,282		10.5	−2.5
South Korea	1,685		2,581		3,342		2,245		2,047		2,355		−32.8	4.9
Taiwan	1,800		2,621		2,489		2,269		2,224		1,907		−8.8	−16.0
Macao	132		229		417		605		1,019		1,126		44.9	86.3
Total	6,625	68	10,484	60	13,664	54	15,850	43	16,963	31	18,523	29	16.0	16.9
Southeast Asia														
Indonesia	75		269		645		1,182		1,857		2,344		83.3	98.3
Thailand	125		213		483		1,006		1,733		2,151		108.2	113.8
Philippines	319		473		1,083		1,457		1,797		1,919		34.6	31.7
Malaysia	93		257		604		1,051		1,360		1,256		74.0	19.5
Singapore	193		386		621		472		307		299		−23.9	−36.7
Total	805	8	1,598	9	3,436	13	5,168	14	7,054	13	7,969	12	50.4	54.2
South Asia														
Bangladesh	7		154		422		885		1,628		2,101		109.9	137.5
India	220		344		636		1,309		1,636		1,927		105.9	47.2
Sri Lanka	126		257		426		871		1,342		1,534		104.2	76.2
Pakistan	32		92		232		508		771		1,017		118.9	100.1
Total	385	4	847	5	1,716	7	3,573	10	5,377	10	6,579	10	108.2	84.2

TABLE 2.2. *Continued*

Region/Country	1983 Value U.S.$ millions	%	1986 Value U.S.$ millions	%	1990 Value U.S.$ millions	%	1994 Value U.S.$ millions	%	1998 Value U.S.$ millions	%	2001 Value U.S.$ millions	%	% Change 1990–94	% Change 1994–2001
Central America and the Caribbean														
Honduras	20		32		113		650		1,905		2,438		476.9	275.2
Dominican Republic	139		287		723		1,600		2,358		2,286		121.2	42.9
El Salvador	7		11		54		398		1,170		1,634		635.1	310.9
Guatemala	4		20		192		600		1,150		1,634		212.1	172.2
Costa Rica	64		142		384		686		827		774		78.7	13.0
Jamaica	13		99		235		454		422		188		93.4	−58.6
Other	142		207		284		151		516		648		−46.9	329.0
Total	389	4	798	5	1,985	8	4,539	12	8,349	15	9,602	15	128.6	111.6
Mexico	199	2	331	2	709	3	1,889	5	6,812	13	8,128	13	166.3	330.3
All Other Countries	1,328	14	3,283	19	4,009	16	5,859	16	9,318	17	12,989	20	46.2	121.7
Total Apparel[a]	9,731	100	17,341	100	25,519	100	36,878	100	53,873	100	63,790	100	44.5	73.0

Source: Compiled from official statistics of the U.S. Department of Commerce, International Trade Administration, Office of Textiles and Apparel: U.S. imports for consumption, customs value.

[a]Percentages may not sum to 100 due to rounding.

is imported under the 807 program (see Table 2.3). In the Caribbean the production-sharing program is known as the Caribbean Basin Initiative, which was implemented in the mid-1980s. In Mexico, 807 trade is governed by the Border Industrialization Program, which established the maquiladora or in-bond industry along Mexico's northern border in 1965.

While Mexico and the nations of the Caribbean Basin are similar in that they export large amounts of apparel to the United States under the 807 program, the apparel industries of these countries differ in important respects. Table 2.4 reveals the diversity of the export-oriented apparel industries in Mexico and the Caribbean Basin economies. In 2000, Mexico had the largest apparel sector by far, with nearly thirteen thousand plants and 560,000 garment workers. However, these statistics encompass both the domestic and the export-oriented apparel firms. Many of the companies that supply Mexico's domestic market are undercapitalized, traditional family-owned workshops or microenterprises (94 percent of Mexico's garment plants are considered small), which brings the national average for the sector down to forty-four employees per plant.

The apparel sector in the Central American and Caribbean countries, by contrast, is dominated by large export-oriented firms that supply the U.S. market under the 807/9802 production-sharing program. Among the Caribbean Basin nations, the Dominican Republic has the biggest apparel industry with 145,000 employees, followed by Honduras (111,000 garment workers), Guatemala (77,000 workers), and El Salvador (60,000 workers). Apparel is the main manufacturing industry in each of these economies. Especially striking is the large size of the apparel plants in these four Caribbean Basin economies, where the average factory employs 260 to 555 workers. This suggests that Caribbean Basin apparel exports are channeled through giant

TABLE 2.3. U.S. Apparel Imports: Total and 807/9802 Trade by Mexico and Caribbean Basin Initiative (CBI) Countries, 1994–2000

Year	Total apparel imports (U.S.$ millions)	807/9802 trade (U.S.$ millions)	807/9802 trade as a share of total imports (percent)
World			
1994	36,878	5,707	15
1995	39,438	7,631	19
1996	41,679	8,719	21
1997	48,287	11,322	23
1998	53,874	12,791	24
1999	56,376	13,474	24
2000	64,181	12,953	20
Mexico			
1994	1,889	1,470	78
1995	2,876	2,282	79
1996	3,850	2,967	77
1997	5,349	4,096	77
1998	6,812	5,102	75
1999	7,845	5,417	69
2000	8,730	5,071	58
CBI Countries			
1994	4,539	3,617	80
1995	5,487	4,497	82
1996	6,076	4,999	82
1997	7,664	6,411	84
1998	8,349	6,929	83
1999	8,889	7,301	82
2000	9,702	7,181	74

Source: Compiled from official statistics of the U.S. Department of Commerce, International Trade Administration, Office of Textiles and Apparel: U.S. imports for consumption, customs value.

assembly plants that are capable of filling the big orders that come from U.S. apparel manufacturers, rather than through traditional family firms or more flexible forms of networked production.

Mexico's export-processing plants are known as *maquilas,* and along with electronics and autos, apparel has been one of the most important industries in generating employment in these in-bond factories. In 1993, Mexico's

TABLE 2.4. Apparel Plants in Mexico and the Caribbean Basin, 2000

Country	Population (millions)	No. of apparel plants	Plant breakdown[a] (%)			No. of apparel employees	Average employees/ plant
			Small	Medium	Large		
Mexico	95.5	12,774	94	4	2	557,000	44
Guatemala	11.1	267	28	34	38	77,107	289
Dominican Republic	8	490	35	45	20	145,000	296
Honduras	5.5	200	19	51	30	110,923	555
El Salvador	6.5	230	56	29	15	60,000	261
Nicaragua	4.4	31[b]	15	25	60	19,357	624
Costa Rica	3.5	460	75	11	14	38,494	84
Panama	2.7	117	15	35	50	8,000	68

Source: *Apparel Industry Magazine,* September 2000.

[a]Size distribution of plants in El Salvador and Costa Rica based on 1998 data.

[b]Plants registered in free-trade zones.

maquiladora industry generated $22 billion in exports and employed 540,000 Mexicans in 2,143 plants; by 1996, the industry had grown by 50 percent, with a total of 811,000 workers in 2,553 plants. Exports rose by 54 percent over the same period, to $34 billion (USITC 1997). Expansion of the maquiladora sector continued over the next five years. By April 2001, 3,750 maquiladoras throughout the country were registered with the Mexican government, and these in-bond factories provided employment for 1,264,400 workers (INEGI 2001).

Until the 1990s, Mexico's maquiladora plants typified low-value-added assembly operations, with virtually no backward linkages. (Local materials typically accounted for only 2 percent to 4 percent of total inputs.) In the 1980s a new wave of maquiladora plants began to push beyond this enclave model to a more advanced type of production, making components for complex products such as automobiles and computers (Gereffi 1996; Carrillo 1998). Although debate continues over the extent to which the maquiladora industry contributes to Mexico's overall development, the consensus is that it has been a critical source of employment creation and export dynamism, especially since the implementa-

tion of NAFTA (Buitelaar and Padilla Pérez 2000; Gereffi 2000).

The maquiladora sector benefited dramatically from Mexico's opening to trade in the mid-1980s. Although the maquiladora program began in the mid-1960s, over 80 percent of the jobs that exist in today's maquiladoras date from the later period of economic reform. Four hundred thousand of these jobs were created between 1994 and 1998 alone—the first four years after the implementation of NAFTA (Buitelaar and Padilla Pérez 2000). Post-NAFTA job growth has been particularly impressive in the maquiladoras that assemble apparel. In the year 2000, 286,600 Mexicans worked in 1,120 apparel maquiladoras located throughout Mexico. In 1993, the year prior to NAFTA, there were 400 apparel maquiladoras employing sixty-six thousand workers. The growth in exports of apparel products assembled in maquiladoras also points to NAFTA-era dynamism. Apparel exports to the United States from Mexican maquiladora plants more than tripled between 1994 and 1998, from just under $1.5 billion to $5.1 billion (USITC 2001).

The assembly trade typical of the maquiladora industry still predominates in the North American garment sector, accounting in 2000 for 58 percent of U.S. apparel imports from Mexico (down from 75 percent in 1998) and 74 percent of those from the Caribbean and Central America (down from 83 percent in 1998) (Table 2.3). However, the growth in Mexico's non-807/9802 apparel exports to the United States is impressive, having nearly doubled in percentage terms between 1994 and 2000 from 22 percent to 42 percent.[4] In value terms, these imports have increased nearly tenfold, from $420 million to almost $3.7 billion, in the 1994–2000 period. The surge in Mexico's non-807 exports can be taken as one indicator of a qualitative shift in the Mexican apparel sector beyond apparel assembly to full-package programs that involve more value added through the provision of textiles and other local inputs.[5]

Our analysis of trade and production statistics in the apparel industry reveals two trends related to the consolidation of a regional economy in North America. First, the relative decline in Asian exports to the U.S. market and the increase in 807/9802 exports from Mexico and the Caribbean suggest that the production-sharing program has increased the importance of low-cost apparel producers in North America. Second, the increase in non-807/9802 exports from Mexico underscores the impact of NAFTA in promoting the growth of full-package networks between U.S. buyers and Mexican manufacturers.[6] The next section examines the emergence of full-package networks in Mexico, focusing on how lead firms in the U.S. apparel and textile industries are reshaping their trade and production networks to take advantage of the opportunities NAFTA creates for firms on both sides of the U.S.-Mexico border.

Lead Firms in the North American Apparel Commodity Chain

To understand the nature of full-package networks and their implications for industrial upgrading in Mexico, it is useful to think of the different steps involved in the production of apparel in terms of a commodity chain. The commodity chain for apparel extends from the upstream sectors that supply the garment industry with its raw materials and intermediate products—the fiber and textile industries—to the downstream sectors that manage the distribution of finished apparel, including marketing and retail. Sectors at both ends of the chain tend to be characterized by more advanced technology and greater capital intensity than are associated with the production of garments. For example, the fiber industry invests millions of dollars in research and development of high-performance materials such as Gore-Tex and Lycra. Although for many years textile production was considered a labor-intensive manufacturing process, massive investment in technology and automation since the mid-1980s has made this an increasingly capital-intensive sector, at least in industrialized countries. The retail segment of the apparel commodity chain is also fairly capital intensive, due to computerized point-of-sale technology that is becoming an essential tool for managing inventory.

Several types of lead firms drive the apparel commodity chain in North America: retailers, marketers, branded manufacturers, and textile companies. As apparel production has become globally dispersed and the competition among these lead firms has intensified, each has responded with new strategies designed to strengthen its position in the commodity chain. For example, retailers and marketers have developed extensive global sourcing capabilities; branded manufacturers are shifting out of production and fortifying their activities in the high-value-added design and marketing segments of the apparel chain; and some textile companies are making their own apparel products in an effort to augment the competitiveness of their fabrics vis-à-vis Asian imports. NAFTA is an important factor influencing the development of these strategies, which are blurring the boundaries that traditionally separated these firms and altering their interests within the chain. A quick look at the strategic position of each type of lead firm in the apparel commodity chain is provided below.

Retailers

In the past retailers were apparel manufacturers' main customers, but now they are increasingly their competitors. As consumers demand better value, retailers have turned to imports. In 1975 only 12 percent of the apparel sold by U.S. retailers was imported; by 1984 retail stores had doubled their use of imported garments (AAMA 1984). In 1993 retailers accounted for 48 percent of the total value of imports among the top one hundred U.S. apparel importers (which collectively represented about one-quarter of all apparel imports). U.S. apparel marketers, which perform the design and marketing functions but contract out the actual production of apparel to foreign or domestic sources, represented 22 percent of the value of these imports in 1993, and domestic producers made up an additional 20 percent of the total[7] (Jones 1995, 25–26).

The 1980s witnessed many mergers and acquisitions across the retail landscape, resulting in a far more concentrated industry structure. The strategies that apparel retailers are adopting to confront competitive pressures include: (1) reducing inventory; (2) leveraging their bargaining power over apparel manufacturers to "demand lower prices and to transfer to them part of the risk of sales slumps"; and (3) creating their own private labels or store brands[8] (Secretariat of the Commission for Labor Cooperation 2000, 9).

Marketers

These manufacturers without factories include companies such as Liz Claiborne, Donna Karan, Ralph Lauren, Tommy Hilfiger, Nautica, and Nike that literally were "born global" because most of their sourcing has always been done overseas. To deal with the influx of new competition, marketers have adopted several strategic responses that are altering the content and scope of their global sourcing networks: shrinking their supply chains, using fewer but more capable contractors; instructing contractors where to obtain needed components, thus reducing their own purchase and redistribution activities; discontinuing certain support functions (such as making samples and patterns) and reassigning them to contractors; adopting more stringent vendor certification systems to improve performance; and shifting the geography of their sourcing networks from Asia to the Western Hemisphere.

Branded Manufacturers

The decision facing many large manufacturers in developed countries is no longer *whether* to engage in foreign production but *how* to organize and manage it. These firms often supply intermediate inputs (cut fabric, thread, buttons, and other trim) to extensive networks of offshore suppliers, which are typically located in neighboring countries that have reciprocal trade agreements allowing goods assembled offshore to be reimported with a tariff charged only on the value added by foreign labor. From a global commodity chains perspective, the main significance of branded manufacturers is that they generally coordinate international *industrial* subcontracting networks, while retailers and marketers coordinate *commercial* subcontracting networks.

Textile Manufacturers

As producers of the most important input for clothing, textile companies have traditionally sold fabrics to domestic apparel manufacturers. However, the dramatic growth in the amount of apparel being sourced overseas since 1980 by U.S. retailers, marketers, and branded manufacturers has led textile companies to worry about the continued viability of their customer base. In an effort to stem the tide of Asian textiles entering the U.S. market in the form of imported apparel, several textile companies have begun to offer "full-package service," by which they provide finished garments instead of fabrics to customers such as retailers and marketers. This strategy, which one textile-company executive described as "selling fabrics but delivering garments," is based on the expectation that potential clients will choose competitively priced, high-quality fabrics made in North America if textile manufacturers can offer the same kinds of subcontracting services that are available in Asia. As the next section explains, NAFTA allows textile companies to pursue this strategy by expanding both textile and apparel production in Mexico.

The Evolution of U.S. Corporate Strategies in the NAFTA Era

The production-sharing program has been important in stimulating apparel exports from low-wage countries in North America. While the maquiladora program in Mexico and its counterpart in the Caribbean Basin have created employment and generated needed export earnings for these countries, they have been criticized for trapping low-wage economies in the dead-end role of providing cheap labor for assembly jobs without generating backward and forward linkages to related industrial sectors (see Chapter 14 in this book). As noted

earlier, the enclave nature of these programs is a direct result of U.S. trade policy, which intends to take advantage of low-cost labor in Mexico or the Caribbean Basin for the assembly portion of the production process while providing a degree of protection for other, related manufacturing jobs. For instance, companies that want to assemble garments under the production-sharing or 807/9802 program have to cut in the United States the fabrics they will send offshore for assembly. The 807 law was amended in 1986 to address the fact that some companies were importing Asian fabrics, cutting them in the United States, then sending them to Mexico or the Caribbean for assembly and eventual reimport to the U.S. market under the preferential terms of the production-sharing program. The new provision of the trade law, called 807A, provided additional benefits for companies assembling fabrics offshore that were manufactured as well as cut in the United States.

While these measures provided some protection to the domestic U.S. textile industry and its workers, they also prevented backward linkages between the assembly plants and upstream segments of the commodity chain in Mexico and the Caribbean. NAFTA has changed this scenario for Mexico, however, in ways that are promoting growth in the Mexican textile and fiber industries. NAFTA replaced the terms of the 807 regime, which was designed to protect U.S.-made fabrics, with new rules of origin that allow a garment to be imported into any one of the three NAFTA countries duty-free, as long as it contains yarns manufactured in Mexico, the United States, or Canada.[9] Effectively, this gives companies that assemble garments in Mexico from Mexican-manufactured fabrics the same preferential access to the U.S. market as companies that assemble garments from U.S.-formed and -cut fabrics under the production-sharing program. This eliminates one of the major obstacles to increasing backward linkages between the export-oriented apparel sector and Mexican fiber and textile manufacturers.

In addition to the protectionist nature of the 807 regime, another factor that has limited the development of backward linkages to Mexican suppliers is the shortage of export-quality fabrics manufactured in Mexico. The few apparel exporters in Mexico that attempted to use domestically manufactured fabrics found they were plagued by consistent problems with quality and on-time delivery. However, new investments in textile production, particularly in denim, are increasing both the quality and quantity of fabrics available in Mexico. For example, industry experts estimate that prior to NAFTA, Mexico produced about 200 million square yards of denim annually. This amount increased to about 400 million square yards by 1998, largely as a result of new investments in Mexico on the part of U.S. textile companies. Virtually all this increment is in export-quality denim.

The growth in Mexican denim production underscores the important role that U.S. firms are playing in Mexico's transition from assembly to full-package exports in apparel. Key to this transition are networks organized and coordinated by U.S. firms that want to increase their security and enhance profits by coordinating the activities associated with full-package supply in North America. Large firms in different segments of the apparel supply chain, mainly from the United States, are vying to become coordinating agents in new North American networks that would strengthen Mexico's capabilities to carry out full-package production (Gereffi 1997; Gereffi and Bair 1998):

- *Synthetic fiber companies* in the United States and Mexico have been lobbying with U.S. apparel manufacturers and retailers, trying to get the apparel firms to develop products using their fibers and encouraging retailers to bring their orders to Mexico.

- *Textile mills* have been forging alliances with apparel suppliers that could allow for more integrated textile and apparel production in different regions of Mexico. In addition, some textile firms are exploring the possibility of creating their own product-development teams for select apparel categories, and a few have entered into joint ventures with Mexican textile manufacturers for the production of fabrics in Mexico.

- *U.S. branded apparel manufacturers* are reorganizing their supply base in Mexico, looking for smaller numbers of more capable suppliers, and reducing their domestic and offshore production operations by divesting themselves of manufacturing assets in favor of building up the marketing side of their business, with an emphasis on global brands.

- A handful of *Mexican integrated apparel manufacturers* that own modern plants that go from spinning and weaving through apparel production and finishing are beginning to develop strong reputations with U.S. retailers and marketers that are looking to place full-package orders in Mexico.

- *U.S. and Latin American retailers* are beginning to set up sourcing networks in Mexico, aided by government-supported vendor certification programs.

- *Mexican sourcing agents* are emerging to serve as intermediaries for U.S. buyers and Mexican factories, a pattern already widespread in East Asia.

Below we discuss a number of firms in greater detail in order to show how each type of lead company is responding to the opportunities that NAFTA presents. Our highlights of these firm strategies are based on two types of data: (1) information published in secondary sources, such as apparel and textile industry trade publications, and (2) strategic interviews conducted in the United States and Mexico with firms at each segment of the apparel commodity chain, including fiber and textile manufacturers, apparel companies, retailers, and trading companies.[10]

Synthetic Fiber Companies

DuPont. U.S. chemical and fiber giant DuPont has several initiatives in Mexico that mirror its global efforts to play a role in connecting different parts of the apparel commodity chain. In Mexico, DuPont has a joint venture with Grupo Alfa (one of Mexico's leading fiber manufacturers) for the production of nylon, Lycra (or Likra, as it is called in Spanish), and daycron staple fibers. Besides its importance as a manufacturer of fibers, DuPont is attempting to work closely with its customers at the downstream links of the apparel commodity chain to coordinate full-package apparel production using DuPont materials. The company has a global sourcing division with offices in several countries, including Mexico, Spain, Germany, Hong Kong, Honduras, and Israel, as well as the United States. The goal of DuPont's sourcing program is to create demand for DuPont fibers at the retail and marketing end of the chain and then to develop relationships with textile and apparel manufacturers in order to carry that demand throughout the chain. DuPont's "Lycra Assured" initiative thus attempts to convince retailers and marketers to use DuPont-brand Lycra, as opposed to less-expensive, Asian-made substitutes, in their apparel. DuPont then works with these clients to find manufacturers who can produce garments containing Lycra.

For DuPont, the "Lycra Assured" initiative is analogous to the full-package strategy that is being adopted by the textile companies that are offering garment services to their clients. Worried about the decline of their traditional customer base—domestic apparel manufacturers—these upstream suppliers are trying to ensure the continued use of their inputs by controlling the critical downstream segment of the chain, apparel assembly, which is no longer viable in the United States. Both U.S. fiber and textile companies realize that they need to coordinate Mexican production networks for apparel if they hope to make a North American alternative more attractive to their customers than importing Asian-made garments that use foreign fibers and fabrics.

U.S. Textile Mills

Burlington Industries. Burlington Industries recently celebrated its seventy-fifth anniversary as one of the world's largest textile manufacturers, with sales of $1.6 billion in the year 2000. Burlington employs 13,700 people worldwide, with facilities in several U.S. states as well as in Mexico and India. Production of textiles for apparel accounts for 60 percent of Burlington Industries' revenue. Burlington serves four major product categories in apparel: denim, synthetics, worsted wool, and cotton sportswear. Based in Greensboro, North Carolina, the relevance of Burlington Industries for our analysis of the North American apparel commodity chain is twofold. First, it is a prime example of the textile industry trend toward offshore production. Second, Burlington is diversifying into apparel. From being a manufacturer of textiles only, it has embarked on a risky and ambitious strategy of forward integration by venturing into sewing and garment assembly.

Mexico is a key growth area for Burlington. Although the manufacturer has been involved in Mexico for more than forty years through its subsidiary Textiles Morelos, these interests had previously been limited to supplying home textiles for the domestic market. In 1994, Burlington had only three plants in Mexico, two of which were for the production of cotton and synthetic fabrics. Yet layoffs at U.S.

plants were an early indicator that the company was looking south. Burlington claimed as late as 1996 that it would "keep core production based in the United States" (Krouse 1996), but this strategy soon began to change rapidly. In 1998 the company announced that it would invest $80 million over the next three years in five garment-making facilities coordinated by its Garment Service Center in Mexico. The plants were expected to employ two thousand workers, and the garment business was expected at the time to add $225 million to Burlington's annual sales. Although initial projections about the size and scope of Burlington's Mexican apparel operations proved inaccurate, the company's interest in Mexico as a production site for apparel and textile production is underscored by the approximately $250 million it invested there between 1996 and 2000 (Hill 2000a).

The expansion of apparel production in Mexico is part of Burlington's strategy to provide garment services to its customers. One Burlington executive described this move into apparel production as "one-stop shopping" for the company's clients: "The strategy is to offer fabric in garment form as a service to branded customers, many of whom have to outsource production anyway" (Hill 2000b, 29). Initially, two of Burlington's divisions were offering garment services. In 1999 the Performance Wear division, which manufactures wool and synthetic fabrics for career apparel such as men's and women's suits, initiated cut-and-sew operations for worsted slacks in an industrial park located near Cuernavaca, south of Mexico City. This facility was plagued with problems, however, including difficulties with its inexperienced labor force, and Burlington announced its sale in September 2000, when it decided that the Performance Wear division of the company would abandon the garment-making business (Rudie 2000).

The Casual Wear division of Burlington Industries, in contrast, continues to pursue its strategy of integrated denim apparel production in Mexico. Burlington manufactures denim in Yecapixtla and assembles jeans in its manufacturing plant in the central Mexican state of Aguascalientes (which was acquired from jeans manufacturer Lucky Star in March 1999). These jeans are then sent to a laundry in northern Mexico for finishing. The laundry, located in the state of Chihuahua, is a joint venture between Burlington and a Texas-based company, International Garment Processors.

Cone Mills Corporation. Cone Mills Corporation, another North Carolina–based textile giant, also tried to "virtually" integrate into garment production in order to offer package services to its clients. Cone Mills planned to pursue this strategy through a partnership with a Mexican apparel manufacturer based in Puebla. The company has since abandoned its plans to provide garment services, although one executive notes that it is still committed to building good relationships with sewing contractors in order "to link [Cone's] fabrics into the region's supply chain" (Rudie 2000, 19). Like Burlington, Cone Mills has invested in denim production in Mexico. This investment took the form of a joint-venture operation with Mexican textile manufacturer Parras. Together the two companies built Parras-Cone de México, a state-of-the-art denim mill in northern Mexico, which began operations in 1996.

Guilford Mills. Guilford Mills, under the leadership of chief executive officer (CEO) Chuck Hayes, has been among the most daring of U.S. textile companies in terms of envisioning the possibilities that NAFTA creates for the industry. Hayes believes that NAFTA provides an opportunity to strengthen the fiber-textile-apparel chain in North America, thereby repatriating textile and apparel production that had gone to Asia. In 1995 Hayes talked with Mexican government officials about his plan to create a large modern industrial park dedicated to apparel production in Mexico. The Zedillo government, at the time reeling from the December 1994 peso crisis, was receptive to the idea, and it was agreed that the park would be developed through a tripartite alliance of the Mexican federal government, the state government, and the private sector. Like Guilford, Alpek (the petrochemical division of Mexican conglomerate Grupo Alfa) provided financial support for the project, and eventually DuPont and Burlington Industries came to be involved in the initiative as well.

After the alliance considered several sites for the proposed park, it settled on the state of Morelos. The complex, known as NuStart or "Apparel City" (Ciudad de la Confección), is located in the municipality of Emiliano Zapata, a rural area outside Cuernavaca in central Mexico.[11] It was inaugurated in July 1997 (with President Zedillo in attendance), and as of June 2000, seven companies (mostly maquiladoras) from Canada, the United States, and Mexico were operating in the park. The project's developers encountered a number of unexpected obstacles, including problems selling all the available production facilities. Other difficulties arose in implementing the parkwide recruitment, hiring, and training program, which NuStart's founders had promoted as one of the park's main benefits, believing it would lure companies that had no experience producing in Mexico and that might otherwise be reluctant to move south of the border. During an interview in June 2000, park representatives maintained that employment at NuStart was expected to increase from three thousand to seven thousand workers, but in September of the same year the park received a major setback when Burlington announced it was selling its apparel factory there. This

plant, Confecciones Burlmex, which was producing men's and women's pants for the company's Performance Wear division, was the largest employer in the park.

Despite the problems that have plagued NuStart, Guilford Mills is heading an initiative to create a second industrial park in the Mexican state of Tamaulipas. Located in the city of Altamira, this park will be an integrated apparel complex, and, unlike NuStart, it will include fiber, yarn, and fabric production, as well as cut-and-sew apparel operations.

Branded Apparel Manufacturers

VF Corporation. VF Corporation, based in Greensboro, North Carolina, is an apparel manufacturer whose sales reached $5.7 billion in the year 2000. The top-selling jeans maker in the United States, with 27.5 percent market share, VF owns the number-one brands for men's and women's jeans (Wrangler and Lee, respectively). VF's group of brand names also includes Vanity Fair and Vassarette (intimate apparel), Jansport (the top brand in backpacks), Jantzen (swimwear), and Healthtex (children's apparel). During the 1980s and 1990s, VF made a number of strategic acquisitions to serve its goal of growth in four areas: jeans, intimate apparel, work apparel, and day packs.

VF's production strategy has been to maintain a balance between U.S. production and contracting in East Asia, Mexico, and the Caribbean. The corporation is aiming to update technology and skills in all its plants as part of a global strategy to streamline operations in order to better handle the rapid speed at which apparel producers must run. In 1995, VF underwent a restructuring that resulted in corporate savings of $80 million. It closed fourteen U.S. plants, moving more of its production to Mexico and the Caribbean, and it laid off seventy-eight hundred workers. In 1996 it formed a Global Sourcing Organization to study a variety of global sourcing options.

In 1997, VF launched its new "consumerization" plan. As part of this intense consumer focus, VF's seventeen decentralized divisions were consolidated into five product-based coalitions, and a $1.25 billion brand-investment program was announced. This consumerization initiative marked a major point in VF's plan to move into marketing and away from domestic production (Hill 1999a, 1999b). It has been acquiring companies to boost its brand names (including the Gitano, Chic, and North Face brands, which it added in 2000), but increasingly these acquisitions either outsource production to other countries or own facilities offshore. For example, from 1990 to 1996, Wrangler added three plants in Costa Rica, two in Honduras, and one in Mexico. Whereas offshore production accounted for 30 percent of VF's domestic product sales in 1995, this percentage rose to 57 percent in 1998, and VF plans to increase it to 80 percent in the near future. VF is now augmenting its brand-name appeal through licensing agreements with such big names as Tommy Hilfiger and Nike. These agreements allow VF to reap the profits associated with already established brands while sourcing production offshore.

Sara Lee Corporation. Sara Lee Corporation is a global food, apparel, and consumer-products conglomerate that has operations in more than forty countries, markets its branded products in over 170 nations, and employs 141,500 people. Sara Lee manufactures women's intimates, men's underwear, hosiery, and athletic apparel under the Hanes, Hanes Her Way, Playtex, Bali, and L'eggs labels. In 1998, Sara Lee held a 32 percent share of the U.S. bra market, a 36 percent share of the U.S. women's and girls' panties market, and a 38 percent share of the men's and boys' underwear market. Sara Lee reported $7.6 billion in sales of its intimate and underwear products in 2000.

Throughout the early to mid-1990s, Sara Lee's global strategy lay in acquisitions. In 1992 it announced plans to invest $700 million in acquisitions of hosiery, underwear, and other apparel concerns. Much of this occurred in Mexico. By December 1992, Sara Lee had purchased the six-thousand-employee Rinbros company (annual sales of $25 million), Mexico's leading maker of men's and boys' underwear, as well as Mallorca S.A. de C.V., the second-largest hosiery maker in Mexico. These acquisitions led analysts to conclude that Sara Lee's primary emphasis would be on growth outside the United States. A 1994 restructuring of worldwide operations reinforced this notion.

Sara Lee shifted gears in 1997. During the previous five years, the company had focused on building brand equity and improving returns. With the continuing goal of improving shareholders' equity, Sara Lee announced its plan to "de-verticalize" operations through the divestiture of fixed assets, moving away from involvement in every step of the manufacturing process and concentrating on sales and marketing. Said John H. Bryan, the company's chairman and CEO, "The business of Sara Lee Corp. has been and will continue to be the building of branded leadership positions. This program will significantly reduce the capital demands on our company, enhance our competitiveness and let us focus even more sharply on our mission of building brands" (*Bobbin* 1997). As part of this strategy, in 1998, Sara Lee sold ten of its yarn and textile plants to National Textile, a company formed in January 1998 by former Sara Lee employees, and signed a buying agreement with National Textile. Sara Lee also announced plans to increase outsourcing, which in 1997 accounted for 42 percent of apparel sales. In February 1999 the company announced a projected investment of

$45 million in Puerto Rico, where it already owns twelve plants and is the commonwealth's largest employer.

Levi Strauss and Company. Levi Strauss and Company is one of the world's largest producers of brand-name clothing and the second-largest maker of jeans, behind VF Corporation. Levi Strauss manufactures and markets jeans, dress pants, and casual sportswear under the Levi's, Dockers, and Slates labels. Based in San Francisco, Levi's posted sales of $4.6 billion in 2000, down from a peak of $7.1 billion in 1996. Over the course of the 1990s, its share of the U.S. jeans market plummeted from 31 percent to 14 percent. This drop is attributable to two factors: Levi's failure to pick up on consumer trends and the high prices of Levi's jeans. The latter factor has resulted from Levi's long insistence on keeping production in the United States, while its competitors were moving offshore to take advantage of lower labor costs. Deciding that U.S. production is no longer profitable, Levi's has recently laid off many of its U.S. workers and closed a large number of its domestic manufacturing plants. Most production will be moved to contract operations in Mexico and the Caribbean (Emert 1999). Levi's is now focusing on regaining market share and encouraging its brand-name appeal through a strategy of consumer-focused brand management. It is devoting resources to innovative marketing and product design aimed at the youth market, and it has opened an online store on its Web page to promote Levi's as hip and up-to-date (Hill 1999c).

Mexican Integrated Apparel Manufacturers

Avante Textil. Avante Textil is a vertically integrated apparel manufacturer, located outside Mexico City, that manufactures and sells yarn, knit fabrics, and apparel. Employing a total workforce of five thousand, Avante also owns about one hundred retail outlets that market its apparel products. The company has a monthly apparel production capacity of 3 million pieces, of which 30 percent is dedicated to full-package programs for U.S. clients. Full-package clients include JCPenney's private-label Stafford line. The remaining 70 percent of production consists of T-shirts, intimate wear, and underwear for Avante's own brands and the foreign brands for which it holds licenses. The company is a licensee for Disney and Warner Brothers apparel and the sole North American licensee for the upscale German underwear line Skiny, which is sold in high-end Mexican department stores. Avante also offers two brands of its own: Optima Cotton Wear, and Tops and Bottoms.

Kaltex. While Avante is the largest vertically integrated manufacturer of knit fabrics in Mexico, a company called Kaltex, which is twice the size of Avante, claims this distinction for woven fabrics. Kaltex was founded in 1925, and since that time Grupo Kaltex has grown to be one of the most significant textile companies in the country. As recently as October 1998, it was considered to be the largest user of U.S.-grown cotton in Mexico (*Daily News Record* 1998). The company has expanded beyond its textile roots in yarn and fabric production to include garment making, initiating full-package apparel programs in 1994. In 1996, Kaltex inaugurated its first denim mill, and it is already considered one of the largest denim manufacturers in Mexico as well as a major player in the full-package jeans market. Kaltex's denim arm, Denimex, exports virtually all its denim to the United States in the form of fabric or apparel. Denimex has a close relationship with the Lee jeans company, meaning that much of its production is sold to Lee's parent company, VF Corporation.

U.S. and Latin American Retailers

JCPenney Corporation. The middle-tier U.S. retailer JCPenney opened its first department store in Mexico in May 1995, in Monterrey, Nuevo Leon. It has since opened other retail outlets in Leon, Guanajuato, and Mexico City. JCPenney's Mexican stores are upgraded versions of their U.S. counterparts, focusing on higher-quality, fashion-oriented apparel and including upper-end brands such as Liz Claiborne and Nautica. About 40 percent of the merchandise sold in the Mexican department stores is manufactured domestically, while the remaining 60 percent is imported, much of it from the United States. The ratio of domestic-to-offshore production is about fifty-fifty in JCPenney's U.S. stores.

In 1994, JCPenney established a buying office in Mexico City with the goal of sourcing apparel from Mexican manufacturers for its private label lines. In 1994 it sourced $7 million of apparel in Mexico, an amount that increased to about $98 million by 1999. Currently, JCPenney sources from twenty-two Mexican companies, including the vertically integrated manufacturer Avante. T-shirts, underwear, and jeans are the principal products. JCPenney is interested in building long-term relationships with its contractors and works closely with its Mexican suppliers, providing them with detailed specifications regarding the inputs to be used for their full-package orders (such as specific fabrics and zippers for jeans). If the Mexican contractor wants to use an alternative fabric or trim, the proposed substitute has to be sent to a JCPenney brand manager, who will decide if it is an acceptable equivalent. Each manufacturer also has to undergo a rigorous evaluation process before being accepted as a JCPenney supplier, with inspectors visiting the plant to ensure that it meets stringent requirements. Some of the apparel for JCPenney's most successful private label line, Arizona jeans wear, is manufactured in the northern Mexican town of Gómez Palacio, Durango, by the Original Mexican Jean Company, which is a joint venture between a U.S. manufacturer, Aalfs, and a Mexican partner, Gerardo Martín. (See Chapter 10 in this book.) In addition to its own plants, Aalfs uses contractors in the Laguna area of northern Mexico to fill its orders from JCPenney for Arizona jeans.

JCPenney is only one of several retailers that are increasing their purchases of Mexican-made apparel. Mexican manufacturers are also selling to retailers in South America, particularly from Chile, Colombia, and Venezuela. These sales are facilitated by Mexico's Banco Nacional de Comercio Exterior (Bancomext), which has been playing a "matchmaking" role by bringing foreign buyers into contact with Mexican apparel manufacturers. Bancomext promotes Mexican apparel producers in several ways, including a vendor certification program that carries out plant-level evaluations of Mexican suppliers, especially small and medium-sized firms, and provides them with some of the technical advice needed to become successful exporters; providing modest financial assistance in terms of working capital to credit-worthy Mexican enterprises; and sponsoring annual trade fairs designed to familiarize foreign buyers with the offerings of Mexican manufacturers (Gereffi and Bair 1998).

Mexican Sourcing Agents

Aztex Trading Company. Aztex Trading Company represents a new breed of broker emerging in Mexico in order to link U.S. companies that are looking to source full-package apparel in Mexico with Mexican manufacturers. Aztex works with U.S. clients such as Liz Claiborne and DKNY that want to source apparel in Mexico but do not have their own manufacturing facilities or a developed network of subcontractors. Its owners describe Aztex as "a service company," meaning it provides its customers with whatever services they require to fill their full-package orders in Mexico: finding fabrics or working with textile companies to develop the desired fabrics, working on specifications for the garments, locating an appropriate contractor, overseeing quality, and ensuring on-time production. Based in Mexico City, with a staff of forty people throughout the country, Aztex serves as an intermediary between its clients and the Mexican manufacturer. Historically, many of these branded manufacturers, retailers, and marketers have sourced large amounts of apparel from Asia, but the cost of buying from Asia as opposed to Latin America has increased with NAFTA, leading many of them to reevaluate Mexico. The role Aztex plays in establishing and managing these foreign companies' full-package networks makes it possible for a new set of buyers that do not want to take on this coordinating role to source apparel in Mexico.

These examples of firm strategies show that companies all along the commodity chain are responding to the opportunities NAFTA creates for more integrated regional production networks, and Mexico is figuring prominently in these companies' plans. In the final section of this chapter, we briefly discuss the implications of these changes for firms and workers in the North American apparel industry before offering some concluding thoughts about Mexico's transition from the assembly to the full-package export role.[12]

NAFTA and Jobs

In addition to strategic interviews with firms, our study of NAFTA's impact on the apparel commodity chain in North America included visits to some of the Mexican cities and towns that are export-oriented apparel manufacturing centers. Since Chapter 10 in this book discusses in detail the developmental implications of full-package networks for the most dynamic of these centers, the Torreón/Gómez Palacio cluster in northern Mexico (see Bair and Gereffi 2001; also Bair 2001), this section offers a more general treatment of the issue.

The firm strategies outlined in the preceding section have two clear consequences in terms of employment: a decline in apparel manufacturing jobs in the United States and a corresponding expansion in both the number and types of jobs being created in Mexico's apparel-related industries. In terms of U.S. job losses, the case of Levi Strauss and Company is particularly notable. Levi's announced in February 1999 that it would close eleven U.S. plants and lay off fifty-nine hundred workers[13] (Emert 1999). This move was the culmination of a series of layoffs throughout the 1980s and 1990s and left only eleven plants remaining in the United States. Earlier layoffs reflected weak sales, but the 1999 announcement signaled a new conviction on the part of Levi's that large-scale apparel production in the United States was no longer feasible.

The same trends characterize the U.S. apparel sector as a whole. During 1993–97 alone, restructuring by U.S. apparel companies caused an estimated loss of 176,000 jobs in the domestic industry (Jones 1998, 37). Apparel employment in 2000 stood at a little over 633,000 workers, and U.S. textile employment was at an all-time low of 541,000[14] (U.S. Bureau of Labor Statistics 2001; AAFA 2000). Furthermore, the only types of jobs in the U.S. apparel sector that are expected to grow from 1994 to 2005 are in professional specialty occupations, such as systems analysts, engineers, and programmers. While the quality of these positions in terms of conditions of work and pay may be considered superior to the sewing jobs that have been lost in recent decades, professional specialty occupations represent only 1.4 percent of total employment in the U.S. textile industry (Mittelhauser 1997, 32).

The local impact of these job losses is more marked than the statistics indicate, given the geographic concentration of apparel and textile manufacturing employment. Employment in the U.S. textile complex is geographically concentrated in the Southeast, with 63.7 percent of total employment in the industry located in five states in the region in 1996. These states, in descending order of textile employment, are North Carolina (which alone accounts for 29 percent of total U.S. textile employment), Georgia, Alabama, Virginia, and South Carolina (ATMI 1998). Although apparel production is less geographically concentrated than textile manufacturing, the five states with the largest number of apparel jobs accounted for almost 47 percent of 1996 employment in the industry: California, New York, Texas, North Carolina, and Alabama (in descending order). Textile and apparel employees are similar in that workers in both sectors generally have relatively low levels of education, making their successful transition to alternative employment particularly difficult.

However, job declines in the United States have been accompanied by two related and less well-recognized phenomena: improved productivity and higher U.S. wages. Since 1995 the productivity of the average U.S. apparel worker has increased by about 11 percent because of advances in technology, production practices, and inventory management. The hourly earnings of the average U.S. apparel worker increased from $7.64 in 1995 to $9.09 in 2000, while the hourly wages of U.S. textile workers rose from $9.41 to $10.95 in the same period[15] (AAFA 2000). Thus, contrary to popular opinion, productivity and wage levels in the U.S. textile and apparel industries appear to have improved since NAFTA went into effect, despite an accelerated rate of job loss over this period.[16]

Although manufacturing jobs in high-wage countries such as the United States will most likely continue to decline, the regionalization of commodity chains means that other types of U.S. jobs related to the management and coordination of increasingly complex cross-border production networks are being created. As the corporate strategies of the firms discussed above suggest, most of the future growth in production jobs will occur in the low-wage countries that are today's preferred sites for apparel assembly.

How Has NAFTA Affected Mexico?

Despite impressive export growth since NAFTA, there is considerable debate about how most manufacturers in the Mexican apparel and textile industries are faring. Small and medium-sized enterprises have faced significant difficulties in adjusting to the country's liberalized economic environment. In a short time, Mexico went from being one of the most protected economies in the world to one of the most open, a process initiated by the country's accession to the General Agreement on Tariffs and Trade (GATT) in 1986. The pace of liberalization was accelerated during the administration of President Carlos Salinas de Gortari (1988–94). Economic policy under Salinas, who championed the NAFTA cause in Mexico, marked the consolidation of neoliberal economic reforms begun during the administration of his predecessor, Miguel de la Madrid (1982–88). Mexico's rapid entry into the global economy from the mid-1980s through the mid-1990s signaled a clear break with the country's history of import-substituting industrialization.

The hardships caused by Mexico's economic opening have been borne disproportionately by smaller manufacturing firms. These are often undercapitalized, family-owned enterprises that lack access to current technology and modern manufacturing methods, but they are overwhelmingly the kinds of firms that dominate the apparel and textile industries in Mexico. This is particularly true for the labor-intensive apparel industry, which is made up of more than 22,500 mostly small companies. However, micro- and small enterprises (companies employing up to fifteen and one hundred workers, respectively) also dominate the more capital-intensive textile sector. The number of establishments in the Mexican textile sector fell steadily between 1992 and 1997, but the employment profile in the industry underscores the importance of growth in the sector's largest firms: While employment fell in micro-, small, and medium-sized enterprises between 1992 and 1997, overall employment in the Mexican textile industry increased slightly, from 164,400 in 1992 to 166,500 in 1997. This growth is even more impressive in light of the fact that employment had declined significantly between 1992 and 1995 (when it reached a low of 133,200 workers), before rebounding in 1996 and 1997 (Knight 1999).

The commodity-chains approach can help shed light on these macro trends by revealing the dynamics that account for shifts in employment patterns. NAFTA has positively affected the Mexican apparel industry in terms of stimulating growth in both 807 and non-807 exports. To the extent that the latter exports represent full-package production, NAFTA has also had a positive effect on the Mexican textile industry because full-package networks between U.S. buyers and Mexican manufacturers are increasing the amount of Mexican-made fabric used in this apparel. Chapter 10 in this book discusses in detail how these networks are generating growth in apparel and textile employment, as well as upgrading

working conditions in many of the Torreón area's factories. However, we can make two broad observations about the implications of NAFTA for the North American apparel commodity chain in general and for Mexican firms and workers in particular.

First, instead of having a uniform impact on the Mexican textile and apparel industries, NAFTA-era interfirm networks are changing the geography of production in these sectors. The emergence of clusters, such as the one for jeans production in the Torreón/Gómez Palacio region, is creating growth in apparel and textile employment in particular regions. Companies looking to place full-package orders in Mexico are attracted to Torreón because of the area's large apparel-manufacturing capacity, as well as the availability of locally produced denim and the presence of local trim suppliers. While NAFTA's impact on subnational regions in Mexico is not evident in the aggregate trade data presented in the first section of this chapter, strategic interviews with lead firms allowed us to identify the particular locations favored by U.S. firms. Our findings indicate that in clusters that are connected to the U.S. market by means of networks with U.S. lead firms, jobs are increasing in number (as a result of booming exports), expanding in type (as full-package networks generate growth in textile mills and laundering and finishing plants), and on average improving in quality (as manufacturers need to meet the quality-control standards imposed by U.S. buyers such as JCPenney and the Gap).[17]

Second, companies lacking connections to foreign lead buyers face significant obstacles in Mexico's current economic environment. Although exports have increased since a major devaluation of the peso at the end of 1994, domestic demand has not recovered. Consequently, companies accustomed to serving the Mexican consumer must compete against low-cost imports for a more open but stagnant market. Many of these companies are smaller firms. Furthermore, most of the U.S. companies that are establishing full-package networks in Mexico are doing so through joint ventures with large Mexican counterparts, such as textile mills, and buyers placing full-package orders are also looking to large manufacturers. Although these companies often rely on tiers of smaller subcontractors to assemble garments for the full-package orders they receive from U.S. firms, small and medium-sized enterprises are increasingly marginalized in Mexico's transition to the full-package export role. While smaller companies may benefit from these NAFTA-inspired networks, they are incorporated at the lowest levels of the networks, where the risks are highest, the wages lowest, and the work conditions poorest.

Conclusions

Our study of NAFTA's impact on the North American apparel commodity chain has yielded three main conclusions. First, the trade data reveal that regional production blocs based on divisions of labor between high- and low-wage countries are becoming more significant in the global apparel industry. NAFTA is promoting Mexico as a privileged exporter to the U.S. market, and changes introduced by the NAFTA regime are allowing Mexico to move beyond the limited export role of apparel assembly, associated with the maquiladora industry, to the new export role associated with full-package production.

Second, we have been able to show how this transition is occurring by identifying the types and consequences of interfirm networks that U.S. enterprises establish in Mexico. U.S. companies, in alliance with Mexican partners, are playing a critical role in reconfiguring and more fully developing the North American apparel commodity chain in Mexico.

Third, growth in apparel and textile manufacturing and employment is occurring in clusters where Mexican firms are linked to U.S. buyers. Since these export networks are critical for firm performance and job growth in Mexico, the challenge for policy makers is to promote institutional environments that create opportunities for Mexican enterprises to access networks that offer the greatest possibilities for local development and industrial upgrading.

Appendix: Companies Interviewed

Aalfs, Gómez Palacio, Mexico, July 9, 1998; July 10, 2000.

Avante Textil, Toluca, Mexico, July 18, 1997; July 20, 2001.

Aztex Trading Company, Mexico City, Mexico, January 20, 1999; June 11, 2000; June 30, 2000.

Banco Nacional de Comercio Exterior (Bancomext), Mexico City, Mexico, July 26, 1999.

Burlington Industries, Greensboro, North Carolina, December 15, 1998.

Cone Mills Corporation, Greensboro, North Carolina, September 4, 1998.

DuPont de México, Mexico City, Mexico, July 16, 1997; July 24, 2000; July 31, 2000.

JCPenney Comercializadora, Mexico City, Mexico, July 17, 1997; January 21, 1999.

NuStart, Emiliano Zapata, Mexico, July 20, 2000.

Notes

1. West European apparel exporters are excluded from Table 2.1 because the majority of their exports involve intra-European trade. Several Caribbean Basin nations are missing from this list because of incomplete information regarding their apparel trade.

2. These dollar amounts are not adjusted for constant dollars.

3. Branded manufacturers have experience in producing garments domestically or globally, making

it possible for them to supply assembly contractors directly with the inputs needed to fill their orders. Retailers and marketers, in contrast, often rely entirely on an extensive network of contractors to produce the garments they design and sell.

4. Some caution needs to be exercised in interpreting the 807 trade data since NAFTA. Because NAFTA reduces the incentives for firms to register as maquiladoras, some of the apparent growth in non-807 exports likely represents apparel that is assembled in Mexico from U.S. fabrics but not officially imported under the 807 regime. Despite this statistical effect, our primary data have confirmed that the growth in what we call "full-package" exports has been significant since NAFTA.

5. In the Caribbean Basin countries the non-807/9802 apparel trade is not an indicator of full-package production because their textiles tend to be imported from Asia rather than produced domestically.

6. Although the Trade and Development Act of 2000 is often referred to as a version of "NAFTA parity" for the Caribbean Basin, this characterization is inaccurate because the act does not change the rules of origin, which specify that only apparel exports assembled in the region from U.S.-made inputs are eligible for preferential access to the U.S. market. Consequently, this region is not likely to follow Mexico's example in developing the full-package model of more locally integrated and higher-value-added production. For more on the role of the Caribbean and Central American economies in the North American apparel complex, see Chapters 14 and 15 in this book.

7. These figures do not include the production-sharing activities of U.S. apparel firms in Mexico and the Caribbean Basin, which also have been expanding rapidly (USITC 1997).

8. "Private-label apparel" refers to store-brand merchandise that is made for specific retailers and sold exclusively in their stores. It constituted 25 percent of the total U.S. apparel market in 1993 (Dickerson 1995, 460).

9. There are some exceptions to this so-called yarn-forward rule. For example, sweaters made of man-made fibers are subject to a fiber-forward rule, meaning that the fibers must originate in a NAFTA country in order to receive preferential access to the

NAFTA markets. Furthermore, apparel that is made from fabrics that are not widely produced in any of the NAFTA countries, such as silk, linen, and velveteen, can be imported to any of the NAFTA countries without tariffs as long as they undergo a "single transformation" in North America, meaning they must be assembled in Canada, the United States, or Mexico (Knight 1999).

10. These interviews were conducted between May 1996 and July 2000, with several firms interviewed on more than one occasion. Interviews typically lasted from one to two-and-a-half hours. Interview sites in the United States were concentrated in and around the North Carolina Piedmont region, while Mexican sites included Mexico City, Morelos, Toluca, and Gómez Palacio. Rather than adhering to a standard survey instrument, these strategic interviews took the form of extended conversations with managers and owners of firms and representatives of industry associations. Respondents were asked specific questions about their organization's global and North American operations, and they also were invited to reflect more generally on the direction of the apparel and textile industries in the era of NAFTA. A list of the firms interviewed is provided in an appendix to this chapter.

11. The NuStart project is analyzed in greater detail in Bair (2002).

12. Describing the development of full-package networks in Mexico as a transition from the assembly to the full-package export role is not meant to imply that 807/9802 production in Mexico will disappear. Although aspects of the maquiladora program will officially cease to exist with the full phasing in of NAFTA, the assembly networks between U.S. and Mexican companies under the production-sharing program remain strong. In fact, the maquiladora industry continues to grow, having received a significant boost from a devaluation of the peso in late 1994 and the consequent decrease in the price of Mexican labor. From a developmental perspective, however, the emergence of full-package networks is significant because it signals that Mexico has moved up in the export hierarchy to include the OEM role as its most advanced export capability.

13. CEO Robert Haas says that most production will be moved to contract operations in Mexico and

the Caribbean: "We can't swim against the tide. . . .
We have invested tens of millions of dollars to try
[to] find a way to make our owned-and-operated
factories enough of an asset [to offset wage differ-
ences]. . . . [February's] announcement is just facing
the realities" (Emert 1999).

14. In relative terms, the plunge in U.S. textile
and apparel employment mirrors what happened in
Hong Kong, one of the most successful Asian
exporters to the U.S. market in the 1970s and 1980s.
Employment in the Hong Kong textile industry fell
from 67,000 in 1984 to 36,000 in 1994—a drop of
46 percent. Meanwhile, Hong Kong's clothing jobs
plummeted from 300,000 in 1984 to 137,000 in
1994—a decrease of 54 percent in a single decade
(De Coster 1996, 65).

15. These wages are not adjusted for constant
dollars.

16. Over three times as many apparel jobs were
lost between 1994 and 2000 as during the preceding seven-year period. U.S. apparel employment
declined by 340,000 jobs during the first seven years
of NAFTA, compared to 110,000 lost jobs between
1988 and 1994 (U.S. Bureau of Labor Statistics
2001).

17. Largely due to a number of well-publicized
cases in which U.S. companies were revealed to have
sourced apparel from factories with "sweatshop"
work conditions, an increasing number of U.S. buyers are inspecting their domestic and foreign contracting networks. These inspections are designed
to ensure that suppliers meet a host of standards
that apply not only to the quality of their products
but also the quality of their workplaces. These standards range from environmental regulations to
safety measures designed to reduce the risk of
workplace injury (see Gereffi, Garcia-Johnson, and
Sasser 2001).

References

AAFA (American Apparel and Footwear Association). 2000. *2000 Footwear and Apparel Industry
Data.* Arlington, Va.: AAFA.

AAMA (American Apparel Manufacturers Association). 1984. *Apparel Manufacturing Strategies.*
Arlington, Va.: AAMA.

ATMI (American Textile Manufacturers Institute).
1998. *Textile HiLights.* Arlington, Va.: ATMI.

Bair, Jennifer. 2001. "Successful Cases of Small and
Medium Enterprises in Mexico: Lessons from
the Aguascalientes Apparel Industry." In *Claroscuros: Integración exitosa de las pequeñas y medianas empresas en México,* ed. Enrique Dussel
Peters, pp. 63–105. Mexico City: Editorial Jus.

———. 2002. "Is Mexico Sewing Up Development? NAFTA and Mexico's Changing Role in
the North American Apparel Industry." Ph.D.
diss., Department of Sociology, Duke University.

Bair, Jennifer, and Gary Gereffi. 2001. "Local Clusters in Global Chains: The Causes and Consequences of Export Dynamism in Torreón's Blue
Jeans Industry." *World Development* 29, 11 (November): 1885–1903.

Bobbin. 1997. "Sara Lee Announces $1.6 Billion
Restructuring Program." *Bobbin* 39, 3 (November): 8.

Buitelaar, Rudolf M., and Ramón Padilla Pérez.
2000. "Maquila, Economic Reform, and Corporate Strategies." *World Development* 28, 9
(September): 1627–42.

Carrillo, Jorge. 1998. "Third Generation Maquiladoras? The Delphi–General Motors Case."
Journal of Borderlands Studies 13, 1 (Spring):
79–97.

Daily News Record. 1998. "Hahn to Revamp Kaltex
America." Harrisonburg, Va., October 13.

De Coster, Jozef. 1996. "Hong Kong and China:
The Joining of Two Giants in Textiles and
Clothing." *Textile Outlook International* 68 (No-
vember): 63–79.

Dickerson, Kitty G. 1995. *Textiles and Apparel in the
Global Economy.* 2d ed. Englewood Cliffs, N.J.:
Prentice-Hall.

Emert, Carol. 1999. "Levi's to Slash U.S. Plants:
Competitors' Foreign-Made Jeans Blamed." *San
Francisco Chronicle,* February 23, A1.

Gereffi, Gary. 1995. "Global Production Systems
and Third World Development." In *Global
Change, Regional Response: The New International Context of Development,* ed. Barbara Stallings, pp. 100–142. New York: Cambridge University Press.

———. 1996. "Mexico's 'Old' and 'New' Maquiladora Industries: Contrasting Approaches to

North American Integration." In *Neoliberalism Revisited: Economic Restructuring and Mexico's Political Future*, ed. Gerardo Otero, pp. 85–105. Boulder, Colo.: Westview Press.

———. 1997. "Global Shifts, Regional Response: Can North America Meet the Full-Package Challenge?" *Bobbin* 39, 3 (November): 16–31.

———. 1999. "International Trade and Industrial Upgrading in the Apparel Commodity Chain." *Journal of International Economics* 48, 1 (June): 37–70.

———. 2000. "The Transformation of the North American Apparel Industry: Is NAFTA a Curse or a Blessing?" *Integration and Trade* 4, 11 (May–August): 47–95.

Gereffi, Gary, and Jennifer Bair. 1998. "U.S. Companies Eye NAFTA's Prize." *Bobbin* 39, 7 (March): 26–35.

Gereffi, Gary, Ronie Garcia-Johnson, and Erika Sasser. 2001. "The NGO-Industrial Complex." *Foreign Policy* 125 (July–August): 56–65.

Henriot, Alain, and András Inotaï. 1998. "What Future for the Integration of the European Union and the Central and Eastern European Countries?" Working Paper 127, Berkeley Roundtable on the International Economy, University of California at Berkeley.

Hill, Suzette. 1999a. "Fashion or Five-Pocket, VF Jeanswear Values Basics." *Apparel Industry Magazine* 60, 1: 58–62.

———. 1999b. "Brittania: Going to Extremes." *Apparel Industry Magazine* 60, 1: 63–64.

———. 1999c. "Levi Strauss & Co.: Icon in Revolution." *Apparel Industry Magazine* 60, 1: 66–69.

———. 2000a. "Burlington Down, but Coming Up Swinging." *Apparel Industry Magazine* 61, 6: 66.

———. 2000b. "Burlington Adds Retail-Ready with Garment Services." *Apparel Industry Magazine* 61, 1: 28–34.

INEGI (Instituto Nacional de Estadística, Geografía, e Informática), Banco de Información Económica. 2001. Data available at <http://www.inegi.gob.mx>. Web site consulted in July.

Jones, Jackie. 1995. "Forces behind Restructuring in U.S. Apparel Retailing and Its Effects on the U.S. Apparel Industry." *Industry, Trade, and Technology Review* (March): 23–27.

———. 1998. "Apparel Sourcing Strategies for Competing in the U.S. Market." *Industry, Trade, and Technology Review* (December): 31–40.

Khanna, Sri Ram. 1993. "Structural Changes in Asian Textiles and Clothing Industries: The Second Migration of Production." *Textile Outlook International* (September): 11–32.

Knight, Patrick. 1999. "Profile of Mexico's Textile and Clothing Industry." *Textile Outlook International* (January): 76–103.

Krouse, Peter. 1996. "Caught in the Middle: Apparel Jobs Are on the Move." *Greensboro* (N.C.) *News and Record*, February 4, E1.

Mittelhauser, Mark. 1997. "Employment Trends in Textiles and Apparel, 1973–2005." *Monthly Labor Review* 121 (August): 24–35.

OETH (L'Observatoire Européen du Textile et de l'Habillement). 1996. *The EU Textile and Clothing Industry 1995*. Brussels: OETH.

Rudie, Ray. 2000. "U.S. Mills in Mexico: The Status of Their Strategies." *Bobbin* 42, 3 (November): 18–24.

Secretariat of the Commission for Labor Cooperation in North America. 2000. *"Standard" and "Advanced" Practices in the North American Garment Industry*. Washington, D.C.: Secretariat of the Commission for Labor Cooperation.

Scheffer, Michael. 1994. *The Changing Map of European Textiles: Production and Sourcing Strategies of Textile and Clothing Firms*. Brussels: OETH.

U.S. Bureau of Labor Statistics. 2001. Data available at <http://www.bls.gov>. Web site consulted in September.

USITC (United States International Trade Commission). 1997. *Production Sharing: Use of U.S. Components and Materials in Foreign Assembly Operations, 1992–1995*. USITC Publication 3032. Washington, D.C.: USITC.

———. 2001. Data Web. Data available at <http://www.dataweb.usitc.gov>. Web site consulted in July.

Part II

The Changing Face of the
Apparel Industry in the
United States

Florence Palpacuer

3   Subcontracting Networks in the
     New York City Garment Industry:
     Changing Characteristics in a Global Era

Introduction

This chapter analyses how the structure of the
New York garment industry has evolved under
the impact of globalization. The focus is the
industry's main industrial segment, the highly
fashion-oriented women's wear industry, and
the subcontracting networks through which
production is organized in this segment. Globalization is here associated with two major
trends: (1) the development of international
subcontracting networks that link garment
firms in New York City to foreign producers
located in a variety of countries; and (2) the
entry of Asian and Hispanic immigrants, which
has contributed to a significant diversification
of the social and ethnic composition of the
New York garment industry.

Two analytical perspectives will be combined to study these evolutions: the industrial-
district model, which captures many of the
traditional characteristics of the New York
garment industry, and the global commodity-
chain framework, which better accounts for
the integration of the local industry into transnational production networks. The New York

garment industry traditionally matched the
characteristics of an industrial district, including a geographical and sectoral concentration
of firms, the predominance of small firms,
vertical disintegration, cooperative competition, a common sociocultural identity that facilitated trust, and local support institutions
(Piore and Sabel 1984; Schmitz 1995). However, global dynamics have substantially altered the industrial and social structure of this
district since the 1970s, as local firms became
integrated into global production networks
and new immigrant communities entered the
local industry. To study such transformations,
I highlight the specific organizational and
social processes that underlie globalization in
this industry and assess their impact from the
perspective of economic performance and social cohesion.

New York remains a major pole in the U.S.
apparel industry, despite a continuous erosion
of employment since the 1970s: the state ranks
second in terms of employment behind California, with 73,200 apparel jobs in 2000, of
which 83 percent are located in New York City.[1]
The local concentration of apparel activities is

linked to the dominance of New York City as a trade center, with important retailing and wholesaling activities; as a fashion center, with significant artistic and cultural activities; and as an immigration center, with a constant inflow of newcomers feeding both the labor force and the entrepreneurial base of the local garment industry. Apparel firms located in New York also benefit from a concentration of related activities, including the supply of fabrics, accessories, and specialized services (Waldinger 1986). These characteristics are especially important to the women's wear segment of the apparel industry, which accounted for 44,400 jobs in 2000, or 73 percent of apparel employment in New York City.[2] Women's wear tends to be more fashion sensitive than other apparel segments, such as men's wear or undergarments, and being located in New York allows firms to quickly catch and respond to fashion changes. Because products are varied and constantly changing, production activities do not easily lend themselves to automation and remain highly labor intensive, relying on the local pool of immigrant labor. In response to such constraints, the New York women's wear industry has long been organized on the basis of a subcontracting system in which the so-called jobbers or manufacturers specialize in design and marketing activities and contract out most or all of their production activities to "contractors" specialized in cutting and assembling garments. Such a system allows manufacturers to limit their fixed costs and be more responsive to market changes, while making entry easier in the subcontracting segment. Contractors absorb seasonal and cyclical fluctuations in output demand and rely on ethnic ties in immigrant communities to mobilize labor (Waldinger 1986).

Cooperative competition among local firms was historically promoted through the constitution of the International Ladies' Garment Workers' Union (ILGWU) at the beginning of the twentieth century and the National Industrial Recovery Act (NRA) in 1933. These institutions provided the backbone of an industrial-relations system aimed at preventing excess competition in interfirm and intrafirm relations. Collective agreements stipulate that manufacturers are to select a stable pool of contractors and distribute work equitably among them; that they should pay contract prices allowing for the payment of union wages within contracting firms; and that these firms should, in turn, distribute work equitably among garment workers (Carpenter 1972; Schlesinger 1951). This industrial-relations system extends the role of collective agreements beyond employment to the sphere of interfirm relations and industrial organization. An important precondition to its establishment in the 1930s was the bounded nature of the local immigrant communities, which were both closely knit from a social perspective and restricted in size due to changes in immigration flows. From the mid-1920s up to the mid-1960s, immigration to the United States slowed down considerably, limiting the flow of new firms and workers entering the garment industry. The small New York manufacturers also used local or regional contractors, thus restricting the geographical scope of their production networks. The industrial-relations system thus embodied values rooted in a shared sociocultural background, thereby exerting community pressure on both workers and employers to adhere to labor agreements (Piore 1990).

The share of New York's employment in the national apparel industry steadily declined in the post–World War II period, when the development of a mass market boosted standardized apparel production in southern states (Blumenberg and Ong 1994; Taplin 1997). Although the decline of employment continued in New York City's women's wear industry until the end of the century, its relative position increased from 17 percent of U.S.

women's wear employment in 1975 to about 24 percent in 2000.[3] Over the same period, a new growth pole emerged in California, where employment in the women's wear industry nearly doubled from 52,700 to 106,100 employees between 1975 and 1996, before declining to 93,000 in 2000 under the impact of the North American Free Trade Agreement (NAFTA).[4] The relative stabilization of New York City and the growth of Los Angeles, where 70 percent of California's apparel employment is concentrated, reflect a new dynamic of polarization of the women's wear industry in the country's major urban centers.

What favored such stabilization of the New York garment industry? In the mid-1980s, Roger Waldinger (1986) convincingly argued that the small, specialized firms making up the New York garment industry were better equipped than their large southern counterparts to meet the more diversified and changing needs of consumers. This argument may also apply to the Los Angeles garment industry, which is similarly organized in networks of predominantly small firms (see Chapter 4 in this book). It supports the thesis developed by Michael Piore and Charles Sabel (1984), who contend that greater fragmentation and instability in consumer markets favored a resurgence of industrial districts based on craft production principles. This thesis explains at least part of the relative performance of the garment industry in New York City, as well as the industry's growth in Los Angeles in the late twentieth century. The two cities also benefited from the upsurge in immigration flows that followed the Immigration Act of 1965 and brought a flexible and low-cost labor force to their local garment industries.

Since the 1970s, however, the New York garment industry also has undergone a number of structural transformations that do not easily fit the industrial-district model and that reveal the emergence of a more complex form of orga-

nization in this center of the U.S. women's wear industry. To analyze how this new model has emerged over time, the rest of this chapter focuses on changes in the economic and social characteristics of manufacturers and contractors and on the relationships that developed between these two types of firms. This analysis shows how the New York garment industry evolved from a traditional industrial district to a central location in global production networks, highlighting three major patterns of change: the rise of large firms among the predominantly small concerns that make up the New York garment industry, the development of transnational subcontracting networks that link local manufacturers to contractors in a variety of countries, and the entry of new immigrant communities that are building up new manufacturing capabilities and contracting linkages with New York manufacturers.

The Rise of Large Manufacturers

During the 1950s and 1960s, small firms dominated the fashion-oriented women's wear sector. Associated with the small size of manufacturers in New York City were a number of organizational characteristics, including strong product specialization, high instability of sales, and limited product development and managerial capabilities. High specialization meant that firms designed and marketed one type of product, such as dresses, coats, blouses, or suits, in a particular price category, ranging from "popular," "moderate," and "better" to "design" and "couture" in the industry's terminology.[5] As a result, the task of combining products into broad-ranging lines to meet the diversified clothing needs of consumers was left to retailers, who bought complementary items from a variety of manufacturers. Specialization increased the vulnerability of manufacturers vis-à-vis demand fluctuations. As explained by Roy Helfgott (1959, 42), "Success for the apparel firm depends upon getting a 'hot number' which will result in enough re-orders during the season to create a profit." Luck and intuition, rather than sophisticated product development and marketing techniques, played an important role in that success. Rudimentary management systems, limited capital, and high turnover were the dominant characteristics of manufacturers in the local industry.

Some firms departed from this typical profile and were able to stabilize their sales by becoming "established names" in the trade, particularly in the high-price segment, where some degree of product differentiation could be achieved among garment firms (Helfgott 1959). But it was not until the 1970s that such strategies were developed on a large scale, leading to the emergence of large manufacturers in New York's women's wear industry (Waldinger 1986). Compared to traditional manufacturers, these firms developed broad lines of products designed to meet the range of needs of specific consumer segments, and they applied strong brand-building and marketing strategies aimed at strengthening their market position. Liz Claiborne was the champion user of this growth strategy from the 1970s to the end of the century: From a standing start in 1976, the company became the largest American firm specializing in women's wear products, with sales growing to $2.8 billion in the late 1990s.[6] Although its products are marketed as "designer" items, most are priced in the "better" category and targeted toward young to middle-aged working women.

In higher-price segments, a group of firms created in the late 1960s successfully grew to annual sales over $100 million in the early 1990s, a substantial size by local industry standards.[7] These designer firms, including Calvin Klein, Donna Karan, Ralph Lauren, and Anne Klein, boosted their sales in the 1980s and 1990s by developing "bridge" lines that constitute cheaper derivatives of their "designer" lines and account for 70 to 85 percent of annual sales. More recently, they have increasingly resorted to licensing agreements in order to expand their brand and product coverage in foreign markets, while focusing their core competence on design and marketing activities. Over the years they have acquired strong product-development capabilities by building design teams that support and extend the work of their lead designers. They have become increasingly involved in marketing and retailing by working in close cooperation with retailers to better control product sales. Such strategies rely on advertising campaigns; store-in-store management, where manufacturers are in charge of organizing sales space for their products in department stores; and the creation of their own retail stores, used as marketing and image-enhancing devices. These companies also distinguish themselves by their ability to attract and retain the best talent from the industry's local labor market, on the basis of higher-than-average wages as well as better career development perspectives. While human resources management remains underdeveloped in most local firms, successful large manufacturers resort to formal and informal training in order to enhance the capabilities of their workforce, and they maintain close links with industry-specific training institutions such as the Fashion Institute of Technology and the Parsons School of Design.

These large firms essentially specialize in upper-price products, ranging from "better" for Liz Claiborne to "design" for Calvin Klein or Donna Karan. They simultaneously responded to and stimulated a new market demand for greater variety in product mix and a clothing style known as "sportswear" in the apparel industry (Pashigian 1988). Their success built on major changes in the competitive environment of U.S. apparel firms since the

1970s, marked by the end of regular growth, stable prices, and homogeneous consumption patterns together with a move toward fewer and bigger retailers. To reduce inventories and buy closer to sales, retailers built new partnerships with garment producers in the areas of inventory management, merchandising, and product development (Abernathy et al. 1999). They are rationalizing and streamlining their supplier networks, focusing on those garment firms that are able to meet their requirements in terms of price, quality, and flexibility.

Other New York–based firms, such as Bernard Chauss, Leslie Fay, and the Gitano Group, have reached significant sizes by targeting lower-price segments but have been facing important financial difficulties since the early 1990s, with stagnating or declining sales as well as income losses. While sportswear designers have built strong partnerships with their main retailers, these lower-price manufacturers have been affected by restructuring in the retail sector, losing market share as a result of retail concentration, and bankruptcies. Their market position has also been weakened by the strong growth of private-label products. If retailers cannot compete with prestigious designers in higher-price segments and actually need these products to enhance the image of the stores, they can still advantageously develop their own product lines at the expense of less-known brands in lower-price categories. Specialized private-label chains such as Ann Taylor and the Gap are also penetrating middle-to-upper-price segments, but the bulk of private-label products are positioned in lower-price categories (*Women's Wear Daily* 1995).

In the late 1980s and early 1990s, the development of private-label products fostered the emergence of a new niche for New York manufacturers, in which some firms, such as Cygne Designs, have become important players. Traditional manufacturers typically responded to retailers' private-label demands by proposing derivatives of their own lines, often selling both types of products to a given retailer. By contrast, firms such as Cygne Designs have specialized in private labels, working in close cooperation with retailers to define product lines that meet the needs of their consumer base. Retailers take part in key decisions at each stage of the production process, including product design, market testing, and manufacturing. They can also be linked to private-label manufacturers through equity ownerships. For example, the Limited owns about 7 percent of Cygne Designs' common stock, and until recently, this manufacturer worked for Ann Taylor under a joint-venture arrangement. Through such partnerships, retailers are becoming increasingly involved in design and sourcing activities, mirroring sportswear designers' involvement in retailing. In both cases, the objective is to achieve higher integration within the value chain, in order to support the strength and consistency of a firm's products and brand names.

These new combinations are blurring traditional distinctions between manufacturers and retailers, and in the private-label segment it is still difficult to assess which organizational form will dominate. Indeed, retailers are also developing their own design and sourcing arms, such as Mast Industries and Gryphon Development, owned by the Limited, and Federated Product Development, a division of Federated Department Stores. If retailers give priority to internal private-label development capabilities, manufacturers might not be able to secure a stable position in this market niche. Cygne Designs' persistent difficulties illustrate the dilemma facing private-label manufacturers when retailers favor their own sourcing capacities over outside partners.[8]

The growth strategies of sportswear designers thus appear at this stage to be the most consistent path for achieving sustainable competitive advantage. Smaller firms are successfully emulating these strategies by focusing on particular market niches: for instance, Nicole Miller, which adopted a designer strategy targeted to the bridge segment. Such choices are consistent with Kurt Salmon Associates' (1992) diagnosis identifying three sources of competitive advantage for New York manufacturers: "build a brand," which corresponds to sportswear designers' strategy; "offer superior service," as is done by private-label manufacturers; and be a "niche supplier," as is done by smaller firms in these two categories. Some New York manufacturers apply these generic strategies, but many have been unable to adapt to intensified competitive pressures in an essentially stagnant apparel market. Manufacturers who failed to target and understand a specific consumer base, to invest in product-development capabilities, to offer a broad range of products, and to build close links to retailers find themselves increasingly marginalized within the local industry. Their management style is essentially reactive, and they compete mainly on the basis of costs, which makes them extremely vulnerable to cyclical and seasonal fluctuations in market demand. The growth of large successful firms among New York's women's wear manufacturers has thus translated into growing differentiation between powerful lead firms, niche firms, and peripheral firms in this industry. As I discuss in the next section, these various manufacturers' profiles also present distinct characteristics in terms of sourcing strategy.

The Development of Global Production Networks

Until the 1970s, apparel sourcing was essentially a local or regional activity for New York manufacturers, but the rise of large firms favored an important expansion in the geo-graphical scope of subcontracting networks. Liz Claiborne was among the first New York–based manufacturers to develop what can be called a global production network, involving a complex coordination of complementary activities performed by contractors in a variety of countries. Higher-price designers such as Ralph Lauren and Anne Klein developed similar strategies in the 1980s, arranging for the production of a major part of their bridge lines overseas. Today most of New York's large women's wear manufacturers rely on foreign sourcing for a substantial portion of their products, which can be estimated at 60 to 85 percent of annual sales.[9] The bulk of production is performed in the Far East, where contractors have developed specialized capabilities in the production of fashion-oriented women's wear (Steele 1990), as well as in the Caribbean and Central America, which offer the advantage of greater geographic proximity. Nevertheless, only the most successful large manufacturers have developed global production networks that allow them to maintain a complex balance of production quality, flexibility, and cost control and to achieve sustainable performance in their current market environment. Such sourcing capabilities are built on consistent strategic choices involving both the location of production activities and the nature of relationships developed with contractors.

Location strategies first involve the relative importance of local and foreign sourcing in global production networks. Delivery-time requirements, fabric origin, and production volumes determine such choices. Even though the time involved between production order and delivery has substantially declined for offshore sourcing, from about twelve months in the early 1980s down to eight to twelve weeks in the 1990s, garments sourced in New York City can still be shipped to customers within two to five weeks.[10] In addition, garments made from Asian fabrics, such as silk, will preferably be manufactured there, whereas wool products might be manufactured in the United States. Finally, overseas sourcing is not economical for small-size orders, and Asian producers often require minimum order sizes, so that small lots tend to be produced locally. Although large manufacturers derive most of their sales from a relatively limited number of styles, they still need to source small-volume orders for market tests and reorders, as well as collection lines in high-price segments. Consequently, the consistent management of global production networks aims at maintaining a balance between local and foreign sourcing in which New York retains specific locational advantages for small lot production.

More generally, the choice of location is based on the particular advantages each might offer from the perspective of product quality, operational flexibility, and cost. As highlighted by Gary Gereffi (1994), these advantages are weighed against manufacturers' requirements in various price segments: Those specializing in higher-price garments source predominantly from locations such as Hong Kong and South Korea, where producers offer higher-quality and higher-cost services; and producers in lower-price segments concentrate their orders in lower-cost countries such as China, Malaysia, or Bangladesh in Asia, as well as Central America and the Caribbean.

For New York women's wear manufacturers, selecting a particular location usually means not owning a plant but building a relationship with one or several local garment contractors. It is the nature of these relationships, and the way in which they are combined within a global production network, that allows manufacturers to meet the simultaneous needs for production quality, flexibility, and cost control. From that perspective, the backbone of global production networks is formed by long-term partnerships with a few "core" contractors to whom manufacturers contract out a

substantial part of their production activities and for whom they, in turn, represent important customers. These relationships are based on the development of specific skills, trust, and exchange stability.[11] First, core contractors acquire an idiosyncratic knowledge of manufacturers' products and expectations through a process of learning by doing based on information exchange and joint problem solving with manufacturers.

Second, relationships with core contractors are based on mutual trust. Production managers in charge of supervising manufacturers' subcontracting activities develop friendship ties with core contractors. Trust is not blind, however. As emphasized by one production manager, "It's like a marriage, but constantly reviewed and justified. We have constant discussions and negotiations about lead times, productivity, margins" (interview with the author). Trust brings considerable flexibility in the subcontracting relationship. Manufacturers do not have to exercise direct supervision of contractors' activities, and they intervene in the production process only to help solve problems at the contractor's request. Likewise, prices are not strictly defined *ex ante*, but an agreement acceptable to each party is reached once production is completed. In that perspective, trust allows for the exchange of strategic information on business activities.

Third, exchange stability is both a necessary condition for and an outcome of trust and specific skills. Trust and specific skills require time to develop, and both involve an investment yielding returns over a period of time. A long-term orientation is thus a key component of the relationship, as is the regularity of orders provided by manufacturers to contractors. Investing in the relationship is worthwhile only if it represents or can become a significant part of each firm's activity. This is particularly true for contractors, who are more dependent on manufacturers due to the

derived nature of their activity. As one manufacturer puts it, "Close relationships come
from giving a lot of business, or else it's up for
grabs" (Uzzi 1996, 682). Consequently, manufacturers and their core contractors engage
in joint planning of production activities. Because of the unstable nature of market demand, such planning involves the overall
amount rather than the detailed content of
production activities. Manufacturers reserve
in advance a portion of a contractor's manufacturing capacities, which they might use in
a variety of ways depending on changes in
market demand.

These cooperative arrangements present
many advantages, but they also create some
constraints in manufacturers' sourcing activities. Accordingly, manufacturers do not work
exclusively with core contractors and on a
short-term basis resort to the services of
"peripheral" contractors. As analyzed by Brian
Uzzi (1996, 1997), price and quantity constitute the main parameters of these "market"
relationships. They allow manufacturers to
exert significant pressures on price and to
quickly adjust production volumes to unexpected changes in product demand. In order
not to jeopardize product quality, speed, or
cost competitiveness, manufacturers must find
a balance between these two categories of
contractors. Such complementarities between
core and peripheral contractors are managed
through the selection and training of core
partners. Manufacturers continually search for
new productive resources through their use of
peripheral contractors and select those with
good potential to engage in a training and
development process. Over a period of one to
three years, they increase the amount of business done with selected contractors, accounting for as much as 80 percent of contractors'
production capacities, and they provide technical and managerial support in order to improve quality levels and speed capacities in the

factories. These contractors might eventually
reach a core position in a manufacturer's production network, diversify their clientele, and
raise contract prices. Manufacturers are thus
motivated to continuously seek out and train
new factories in order to lower average costs in
their production networks.

Successful large women's wear manufacturers are thus developing three-tiered production networks involving well-trained contractors, in-training contractors, and peripheral
contractors. Such network segmentation patterns can be found both within locations, as in
New York City, and between locations, with
core contractors being located in higher-cost
countries such as the United States, Hong
Kong, and South Korea, where producers have
long experience in garment making, and
peripheral contractors, which account for the
bulk of production, in lower-cost countries
that have entered more recently into export-
oriented production (Gereffi 1994). The relative importance of core, peripheral, and intermediate contractors in global production
networks varies depending on price segments
and managerial capabilities. In higher-price
segments, manufacturers have more control
over their market position because of brand-
building strategies as well as classic forms of
garment construction that are less amenable
to short-term changes in fashion. Product
quality also has greater weight than cost considerations in sourcing decisions. As a result,
manufacturers are better able to develop stable
relations with core contractors and have less
reason to resort to peripheral contractors. By
contrast, their counterparts in lower-price segments make greater use of peripheral contractors, thereby exerting stronger price pressure on core contractors and providing them
with a less consistent flow of work. Finally,
managerial capabilities play a role in building
and sustaining these tiered contracting networks on a global scale. Relations based on

skills development, trust, and stability are more difficult to manage than market relations based on price and quantity, so that less-skilled managers will lean toward the second option, especially for overseas subcontracting.

For this reason, smaller New York manufacturers adopting a niche strategy prefer to rely on local sourcing. Some have experimented with foreign sourcing but pulled production back to New York, where they can better control quality and flexibility (Friedman 1992, 1993). Indeed, only the largest manufacturers, with annual sales over $100 million, can establish an in-depth presence in a number of countries around the world by setting up overseas production management offices and by building partnerships with a diverse array of local contractors. These sourcing arrangements are an important component of competitive strategies based on brand building, flexible services, or niche specialization. However, many New York–based manufacturers do not carefully weigh quality, timing, and cost parameters in their sourcing decisions.

To conclude, major differences can be found among the sourcing patterns of New York manufacturers depending on their relative position in the industry. Powerful lead firms have mastered the complex tasks of balancing local and foreign sourcing, as well as high-skill and low-skill contractors, in their global production networks. In this group, differences in sourcing patterns depend on market-price segments and managerial capabilities. Niche firms apply similar sourcing strategies but focus on local production, while peripheral firms, both large and small, have underdeveloped sourcing systems that do not allow them to achieve a sustainable competitive advantage.

The analysis shows how the emergence of large lead firms has transformed subcontracting networks in New York's women's wear industry, integrating this industrial district into transnational production chains. As emphasized by Gereffi (1994), New York–based manufacturers such as Donna Karan and Liz Claiborne are "drivers" of global subcontracting networks. These firms still maintain headquarters, product development, and marketing functions in New York City, where they can tap a local pool of talented designers, marketers, and managers. Their strategy is consistent with Saskia Sassen's (1991) thesis that the geographic dispersal of production activities has increased the need for lead firms to concentrate strategic functions in "global cities," which constitute centers of command in the global economy. However, these firms do not resort exclusively to foreign sourcing, and New York contractors retain a niche in their global production networks. Likewise, smaller manufacturers still subcontract production on a local basis. Such strategies are made possible by the persistence of local production capabilities built by new immigrants, which helps explain "why garments are still made in New York" (Waldinger 1986). The next section highlights new patterns of segmentation that emerged among New York contractors under the combined impact of manufacturers' sourcing practices and immigrant firms' development strategies.

New Patterns of Segmentation among New York City Contractors

As shown in Tables 3.1 and 3.2, the new immigrants who have been entering New York's garment industry since the late 1960s are predominantly Asians and Hispanics. While both groups are well represented among production workers, Asians have reached a significantly higher penetration among managers. Waldinger (1986) highlights managerial differences between Chinese immigrants, who represent the largest group of Asian immigrants in New York City, and Dominicans, who predominate

TABLE 3.1.   Ethnic Distribution of Resident Labor Force, New York City Garment Industry, 1980

| | | Percentage Distribution of Ethnic Groups | | | | | | | |
| | | Whites | | Blacks | | Asians | | Hispanics | |
	Total	NB	FB	NB	FB	NB	FB	NB	FB
Managers and Administrators	7,960	66	18	2	0	1	5	5	4
Professionals and Technicians	4,240	59	14	6	6	0	3	6	7
Sales	4,540	79	11	2	1	0	2	3	3
Clerical	16,980	48	8	15	6	0	2	11	9
Craft	14,620	25	25	8	4	0	6	13	19
Operatives	84,560	13	20	6	4	0	17	14	27
Transportation Operatives	2,220	13	8	8	5	0	4	18	43
Laborers	2,740	12	6	12	9	1	20	20	21
Service workers	1,280	20	9	3	5	0	11	20	31
Total Resident Labor Force	139,140	25	18	7	4	0	13	13	20

Source: "5 Percent Public Use Microdata Sample," 1980 Census of Population, in Waldinger (1986, 107).

Note: NB: native-born; FB: foreign-born. Percentages add up horizontally; due to rounding, they may not add up exactly to 100.

among Hispanics: Chinese-owned enterprises tend to be larger and longer-lived, exhibit higher performance levels, and are managed with a longer-term perspective than are their Dominican counterparts. Such differences in business characteristics are related to differences in the profile of owners in terms of education level, prior business experience, and settlement status in the United States, which tend to favor Chinese over Dominican immigrants.

These characteristics have translated into distinct geographic patterns in production activities. On the one hand, during the 1970s an important production pole emerged in the Chinatown area of southern Manhattan. In the 1980s and 1990s, other Chinese factories developed in the Flushing area of Queens and in Sunset Park in Brooklyn, and a growing number settled in Manhattan's traditional Garment District, but Chinatown remained a major hub of Chinese apparel production (Chin 1994; Zhou 1992). On the other hand, Dominican firms did not form a dominant cluster and are dispersed in neighborhoods such as Corona in Queens, Washington Heights in northern

Manhattan, and Sunset Park in Brooklyn, as well as certain buildings of the Garment District (Waldinger 1986). In addition, a third type of immigrant enterprise developed in the central Garment District during the 1980s and 1990s, characterized by Korean ownership and a Hispanic workforce (Chin 1994). According to manufacturers interviewed, this Korean pole is of growing importance in New York's production base. The rest of this section focuses on the development of Chinatown and the recent emergence of the Korean pole of garment production, highlighting firms' organizational characteristics and how they differ from those of traditional contractors belonging to Jewish and Italian ethnic groups.

Growth, Upgrading, and Segmentation in the Production Pole of Chinatown

With the arrival of large numbers of Chinese immigrants in New York City, Chinatown has become a prominent production center in New York's women's wear industry. Whereas the traditional Garment District continued

TABLE 3.2.   Ethnic Distribution of Resident Labor Force, New York City Garment Industry, 1990

| | | Percentage Distribution of Ethnic Groups | | | | | | | |
| | | Whites | | Blacks | | Asians | | Hispanics | |
	Total	NB	FB	NB	FB	NB	FB	NB	FB
Managers and Administrators	9,252	50	18	4	4	0	15	1	8
Professionals and Technicians	4,270	53	19	5	6	0	9	2	8
Sales	5,379	65	10	6	4	0	7	2	6
Clerical	11,008	39	15	15	10	1	9	1	11
Craft	11,205	18	29	9	7	0	17	1	19
Operatives	64,476	7	18	4	4	0	38	1	29
Transportation Operatives	3,238	10	9	22	9	0	10	0	41
Laborers	2,533	5	16	14	8	0	32	0	25
Service workers	829	26	7	7	2	0	17	0	41
Total Resident Labor Force	112,190	19	18	6	5	0	27	1	23

Source: U.S. Census of Population, Public Use Microdata Sample, U.S. Bureau of the Census, Department of Commerce.

Note: NB: native-born; FB: foreign-born. Percentages add up horizontally; due to rounding, they may not add up exactly to 100.

to lose jobs in women's wear, from about forty thousand workers in 1969 to only about twenty-five thousand in 1980, employment nearly doubled in Chinatown over the same period, from about eight thousand to more than sixteen thousand workers. The number of Chinese firms registered in the Chinatown area increased from 8 to 102 between 1960 and 1970 and rose to 430 in 1980 (Abeles et al. 1983). Chinese contractors entered the women's wear industry by specializing in a particular segment: the low-skilled, low-price end of sportswear production. They benefited from an abundant workforce, with a majority of immigrant women from their own ethnic group going to work in apparel production (Zhou 1992). Chinese contractors developed an informal system of employment by which they could respond in a very flexible manner to manufacturers' requirements. Small firm size, family ownership, and kinship ties allowed them to develop trust relationships between managers and workers based on mutual obligation and solidarity, following the pattern of "immigrant enterprise" conceptu-

alized by Waldinger (1986) and Thomas Bailey (1987).

The growth of Chinatown's garment production activities continued in the 1980s and 1990s, but the structure of the local industry evolved considerably during this period. A dominant group of large contractors upgraded their production activities and penetrated higher-price segments, increasingly differentiating themselves from smaller immigrant firms. These new strategic orientations gained attention from the local business press in the early 1990s, as large Chinese contractors were able to produce high-quality garments and compete with technologically advanced producers in the Far East (Brookman 1994; Furman 1993; Struense 1993). These contractors are typically organized in family groups in which various businesses are run by members of the same family under the direction of a central leader. Union officials estimate about a dozen such groups in Chinatown, each including from five to twelve companies. Although some of the companies are small, the main ones are of above-average size, with fifty to one hundred workers and annual sales of $1 million to $2 million.[12] Factories specialize by product, price segment, and activity, which allows the group to offer manufacturers a variety of services, such as pattern making, cutting, warehousing, and sewing, for a broad range of sportswear products. Group leaders have over ten years of experience in the local industry and have acquired in-depth knowledge of contracting activities as well as a favorable reputation among New York manufacturers. They have progressively penetrated higher-price segments by building stable contracting relations with quality-conscious manufacturers, such as Liz Claiborne, Ralph Lauren, and Anne Klein. Such relationships are based on trust and specific skills, as illustrated by this owner's comments: "It's important to understand a designer's mind and its goal concerning a style.... Manufacturers count on the contractor to recognize problems and make judgment calls. A basic trust in quality is also necessary" (interview with the author).

Because of their reputation in the local industry, large Chinese contractors can further limit the impact of seasonality on sales by diversifying their clientele during the slow seasons. As a result, variations in production levels during the year are below 50 percent, while they can reach much higher levels in smaller contracting firms. These achievements are based on continuous improvement of production capabilities through investments in new technologies as well as core workers' skills. Owners emphasize the importance of workers' behavior and motivation in maintaining a competitive advantage. Workers' technical skills are also developed through informal on-the-job training as well as occasional outside formal training. "Multiskilling" is particularly important to allow contractors to adjust quickly to qualitative changes in product demand. These firms are able to attract skilled workers by offering higher-than-average wages,

relative work stability over the year, and good working conditions in terms of health and safety standards. Thus they retain a core of regular employees, among whom turnover is low and who provide the foundation of a competitive strategy based on product quality. To absorb demand fluctuations, contractors resort to a variety of arrangements, including work sharing, temporary work, and subcontracting. Temporary workers and subcontractors are typically less skilled than the core workforce and are assigned less-sophisticated production activities. Thus the workforce of large Chinese contractors tends to be stratified according to skill levels, wage levels, and work stability, along principles similar to those guiding the segmentation of manufacturers' production networks.

Through subcontracting, large contractors are connected to smaller businesses, which remain numerous among Chinatown's firms given the ease of entry into production activities, continuous inflows of immigrants, and high-demand seasonality. This segmentation of Chinatown's garment industry was already observable in the early 1980s (Abeles et al. 1983). Highly unstable work and employment levels characterize these smaller businesses. They typically maintain market-based relations with manufacturers and are submitted to strong price pressures. Such firms can be found in all price segments, although they are numerically more important in low-price, low-quality production. Owners have limited managerial experience and the skill level of production workers is relatively low, most of them mastering only one sewing operation. In addition, the equipment is usually second-hand and obsolete, which prevents these firms from reaping productivity gains as do their larger counterparts. Employment conditions in terms of wages, stability, and health and safety standards can be extremely poor in peripheral factories.

Ethnic Succession in the Garment District

While Chinatown's garment industry grew to become the center of New York's women's wear production, important changes occurred in contracting activities performed in the Garment District, including the decline of traditional ethnic groups as well as the rise of Korean contractors. As their own ethnic groups retreated from production activities and Chinese contractors penetrated higher-price segments, Jewish and Italian contractors found themselves increasingly marginalized in the local industry. Today they typically specialize in shrinking markets such as "evening couture" or occupy marginal positions in the contracting networks of large sportswear designers. These companies have organizational characteristics similar to those found by Waldinger (1986) in the mid-1980s, including small size and aging human resources, with owners and employees whose average age is over fifty. The workforce is specialized in craft production of high-price garments requiring intricate hand sewing, and it receives above-average weekly wages. Employees work intermittently in order to get unemployment benefits during idle times, as opposed to sharing work as is widely done in Chinese firms. Together with the use of formal recruitment channels, these practices indicate a more formal employment system by which contractors may not be able to compete with flexible Asian producers.

While a great variety of ethnic groups can be found working in the Garment District, the most striking development of the 1980s and 1990s has been the fast growth of Korean-owned contracting shops, located predominantly at the west end of the District. This growth is reflected in the membership statistics of the Korean Apparel Contractors Association of Greater New York, which was created in 1980 with a dozen companies and increased its membership to 400 contractors in 1995, of whom 260 are located in the Garment District. The association estimates that it covers about 50 percent of Korean contractors who operate in the Garment District.[13] These contractors have bought factories from their Jewish and Italian predecessors and built on ethnic ties to develop a new cluster of production activities (Chin 1994). Replicating the strategy of Chinese immigrants in the early 1970s, Koreans have entered the industry through the production of low-price sportswear. However, they do not rely on their own ethnic group to mobilize labor, and they chiefly employ Hispanic workers. Korean women are more educated and fewer in number than their Chinese counterparts and have found work in more lucrative segments of the local economy.[14] By contrast, large numbers of Hispanic immigrants, many of whom entered the country illegally, provide a cheap and flexible workforce in this highly competitive segment of the local apparel industry.

The Korean production pole presents segmentation characteristics similar to those identified among Chinatown producers in the early 1980s: A core of large factories organized in family groups maintain regular contracting relations with manufacturers, and they are surrounded by a periphery of smaller firms that absorb cyclical fluctuations in product demand. Interviews in two large Korean factories reveal that they are subject to stronger price pressures and experience more volatile seasonal fluctuations in production than large Chinatown contractors, which translate into lower wages as well as a greater use of temporary workers. The factories are also less sophisticated in terms of technology and worker skills, although they try to retain a stable core of multiskilled workers.

This overview of changes in the contracting segment of New York's women's wear industry reveals a complex pattern of segmentation based on ethnicity, market segment, and size, the last of these being closely linked to the nature of contractors' relations with manufacturers. Small Jewish and Italian contractors operate in the shrinking couture segment, while Chinese and Korean contractors are positioned in the fast-growing sportswear segment. The former occupy a marginal position in the industry, whereas some large contractors have emerged among Asian firms, in both higher- and lower-price segments, by building stable relations with large New York–based manufacturers. Hispanics appear to be involved in production activities mainly as employees, and Hispanic-owned firms seem to play a marginal role in the local industry. This contrasts with the experience of other ethnic groups, which have improved their position by moving either from contracting to manufacturing activities, as did the Jews and Italians, or from low-value to high-value production, as did the Chinese and as Koreans may do soon.

The core-periphery pattern identified among contractors is consistent with Uzzi's (1996) statistical analysis of contracting linkages in the New York "better" dress segment. Studying subcontracting flows between fifty-four manufacturers and 484 contractors, Uzzi found that the failure rate of contractors was lower for those producers that (1) had concentrated exchange ties with manufacturers, meaning that they derived a substantial part of their activities from working with a few manufacturers; and (2) were part of a contracting network including both concentrated and dispersed ties, meaning that other contractors working for the same manufacturers did not develop similarly concentrated exchange ties. One can infer from these results that contractors increase their chance of survival when they occupy a core position in contracting networks that include both core and peripheral contractors.

While the emergence of core contractors is a sign of economic performance and vitality,

the growing range of peripheral contractors also points to high vulnerability and precariousness in New York's garment production activities. From the perspective of employment, the most favorable conditions can be found in core firms operating in higher-price segments, as well as smaller firms belonging to traditional ethnic groups. In the low-skilled segment, labor oversupply resulting from immigration flows is exerting intense competitive pressures, raising concerns over a return of "sweatshops" in New York's garment industry (GAO 1989, 1994).

Conclusion: Assessing the Future of the New York Garment Industry

The transformations reviewed in the preceding sections have deeply affected the social and institutional regulation of competition that characterized the New York garment industry as an industrial district. On the one hand, ethnic fragmentation appears to limit both social solidarity and social mobility within the local industry. Although some forms of cooperation exist between firms belonging to different ethnic groups, for instance, between sportswear designers and their core contractors, manufacturers do not have a sense of moral commitment or responsibility toward the Asian and Hispanic communities in which production activities are performed. Upward mobility also seems to occur predominantly within rather than across ethnic groups, as indicated by the diverse paths the various communities follow. In addition, continuous immigration flows generate an oversupply of labor that eliminates an important condition for local solidarity, namely, the bounded nature of local industrial-district communities (Piore and Sabel 1984). These transformations have resulted from one facet of globalization, the arrival of new Asian and Hispanic immigrants in the local industry, but they are also reinforced by its second facet, the development of global production networks. When considering the foreign ramifications of the local industry, both ethnic diversity and labor oversupply reach impressive dimensions and further limit social cohesion and solidarity within the industry.

On the other hand, changes in market conditions and industrial organization have contributed to intensify competitive pressures among local apparel firms. Stagnant demand and declining real prices for apparel products, greater market uncertainty, and retailers' growing power as a result of larger size and concentration have combined to enhance pressures to cut costs and increase speed and flexibility. New York apparel firms have responded differently to this changing environment, leading to the emergence of distinct competitive profiles based on market specialization, size, and networking strategies, as well as internal skills and capabilities. These new patterns of segmentation among both manufacturers and contractors are further dividing interests within the local industry.

In this context, competitive pressures are disproportionately exercised on production activities, which constitute the most vulnerable segment of the local industry, and on the smallest contracting firms and less-skilled production workers in that segment. Due to the weakening of its social and economic foundations, the local system of industrial relations is no longer able to stabilize contracting and employment relations. Competition is such that neither collective agreements nor labor laws provide a consensual framework for the operation of local garment firms.

Will New York nevertheless remain a key location in the global apparel industry on the basis of its specialization in the fashion-oriented women's wear sector? From an American perspective, Los Angeles appears to be New York's most immediate competitor, and the substan-

tial growth of the former's women's wear industry in the 1980s and 1990s has already offset New York's traditional dominance in terms of employment. Los Angeles has become an important site for the design, marketing, and production of sportswear, capitalizing on the distinctive "California style" of casual and active wear (Institute for the Future 1985; Pitman 1992). Los Angeles also presents the advantages of a nonunion environment (although anti-sweatshop campaigns and government pressures have been particularly strong in recent years in California) as well as greater proximity to producers located in the Far East, Central America, and Mexico. New York, however, retains an edge in arts and fashion that gives the city a distinct advantage in higher-priced, more-sophisticated sportswear. For this reason, sportswear designers such as Calvin Klein and Donna Karan will presumably remained anchored in Manhattan, and the city should retain a strong position in this segment.

The future of New York's private-label segment is more uncertain. The importance of the regional market will probably keep retailers attached to the city, and with them at least some of their design and sourcing activities. Whether these activities will be performed by retailers, by specialized private-label manufacturers, or by both types of firms remains to be seen. Overall, the three competitive strategies of brand building, service flexibility, and niche focus identified by Kurt Salmon Associates (1992) should provide a basis for sustainable competitive advantage to those New York manufacturers that are able to implement them. Traditional manufacturers are increasingly marginalized in this new competitive environment, but the ease of entry into this segment might also continue to attract entrepreneurs, despite the fact that firms' performance might be short-lived.

Local contractors essentially work for New York manufacturers, so their development will derive from the need for local sourcing. The analysis of subcontracting relations in New York City shows that large manufacturers implementing global sourcing strategies do retain a local production base and that niche manufacturers rely entirely on it. Local contractors should thus continue to grow, provided they can meet the quality, flexibility, and cost requirements of these manufacturers. To this end, the efforts toward upgrading and rationalization that large Chinese contractors have implemented need to continue and extend to other ethnic groups involved in production activities. Future trends in immigration also will influence the evolution of the local production base: On the one hand, continuous immigration creates strong competitive pressures that undermine the stabilization and rationalization of the local garment industry; on the other hand, local producers rely on an immigrant workforce and might suffer from a labor shortage if immigration flows were to slow down significantly. Finally, the need among both manufacturers and contractors to develop firms' skills and capabilities highlights the importance of local training institutions, such as the Garment Industry Development Corporation, and the linkages they are building to local firms. These training initiatives are part of a broader range of policies by which new forms of cooperative competition might be fostered in the local industry, in line with the industrial-district argument.

The profile of the New York apparel industry has changed markedly since the 1970s, with the emergence of global manufacturers and their core contractors in new immigrant communities. The industry accommodates much greater diversity in terms of firm size and ethnicity than it did up to the 1960s, and it appears today as a miniaturized version of the very global industry it helped develop. This complex pattern fits well with Sassen's (1991) image of a "global city": Globalization rein- forces the role of key locations, such as New York City, but also produces new forms of segmentation within these urban centers. By doing so, it generates new growth opportuni- ties as well as new tensions in the social and institutional architecture of local industries.

Appendix: Methodology for Collecting and Analyzing Firm-Level Data in New York's Women's Wear Industry

The collection and analysis of firm-level data in New York's women's wear industry aims at developing an understanding of its industrial and social structure by identifying typical pro- files that could summarize the diversity of firms' characteristics in this particular setting. The study was designed to identify possible relationships among: (1) firms' economic char- acteristics in terms of product, market segment, size, age, and performance; (2) social charac- teristics, such as union status and ethnicity; and (3) characteristics of interfirm and intrafirm relations, defined in terms of stability, skill lev- els and development, cooperation versus adver- sarial orientation, and geographic scope.

The method used was what Matthew Miles and A. Michael Huberman (1994) refer to as multiple-case studies, which allows us to form types or families based on similarities and dif- ferences between cases. Firms were selected from the dress (Standard Industrial Classifica- tion, or SIC, 2335) and sportswear (SIC 2339) sectors, which respectively accounted for 33 percent and 46 percent of employment in New York's women's wear industry in 1993, and from within the borough of Manhattan, where 74 percent of the city's employment in wo- men's wear was located during 1993 (New York State Department of Labor, unpublished data). Firms' addresses and the names of chief executive officers (CEOs) were identified

TABLE 3.3. Characteristics of Firms Interviewed in New York City's Women's Wear Industry

	Manufac-turers (n=16)	Con-tractors (n=24)	Total (n=40)
Industry Sectors			
Dresses (SIC 2335)	8	6	14
Sportswear (SIC 2339)	8	18	26
Number of Employees			
≤20	4	5	9
>20 to 40	2	6	8
>40 to 100	5	9	14
>100	5	4	9
Annual Sales (U.S.$ millions)			
≤1	0	11	11
>1 to 10	6	12	18
>10 to 50	4	1	5
>50 to 100	1	0	1
>100	5	0	5
Date of Constitution			
Before 1960	5	0	5
1960–69	4	0	4
1970–79	2	5	7
1980–89	4	9	13
1990–94	1	10	11
Location			
Garment District	16	13	29
Chinatown	0	11	11
Ethnic Group (CEOs)			
Jewish	13	1	14
Italian	1	3	4
Asian	0	19	19
Other	2	1	3
Union Status			
Union	14	20	34
Nonunion	2	4	6

TABLE 3.4. Interview Guidelines

Economic Characteristics
Price segment
Own/private label (manufacturers)
Retail channel (manufacturers)
Sales concentration and seasonality
Average number of styles per year (manufacturers)
Average number of garments per order (contractors)
Product diversification
Perceived importance of design/quality/speed/cost
Range of functions performed/externalized
Year of establishment of the company
Years of CEO's experience in the industry (contractors)
Number and location of companies/establishments
Number of employees
Sales amount and profit levels
Trend in sales and profits (last three years)
Use of new technologies (CAD, EDI, computerized costing)

Social and Institutional Characteristics
Union status of production workers
Union status of trading partners
Ethnicity of production workers
Ethnicity of CEO (contractors)

Contracting Characteristics
Structure of contracting network (location, number, size of manufacturers/contractors, concentration)
Variation in number of contractors/manufacturers over the year
Frequency and nature of interactions
Technical/financial involvement of manufacturers
Contractor selection criteria (manufacturers)
% of relationships older than 3 years
Ease in finding new orders (contractors)

Employment Characteristics
Employment seasonality
Employee turnover
Employment security policy
Compensation level and system for production workers
Hiring network and criteria
Formal and informal training
Work organization
% of multiskilled production workers (contractors)
Human resource development policy
Average age of production workers (contractors)
Benefits provided

through a variety of sources, including a listing of union firms maintained by the ILGWU, the records of public firms, and referrals from other firms. This selection method tends to bias the sample toward large firms as well as unionized firms, as shown in Table 3.3. Field

TABLE 3.5. Typology of Firms' Profiles in New York City's Women's Wear Industry

	Manufacturers			Contractors[a]			
	Core (n=4)	Niche (n=5)	Periphery (n=7)	Core (n=10)	Periphery (n=4)	Intermediate (n=4)	Traditional (n=3)
Economic profile							
Trends in sales and profits	Up/stable	Up/stable	Down	Up/stable	Down	Varied	Down
Sales seasonality	Moderate	Moderate	High	Moderate	High	Varied	High
Product range	Large	Narrow	Narrow	Large	Narrow	Narrow	Narrow
Product category	Sportswear	Varied	Varied	Sportswear	Varied	Varied	Couture
Size	Large[b]	Small	Small	Large[c]	Small	Small	Small
Primary competitive advantage	Quality	Quality	Cost	Quality	Cost	Varied	Quality
Link to buyers	Close/stable	Stable	Unstable	Close/stable	Unstable	Varied	Varied
Product development	Important	Little	Little				
Production-system development				Yes	No	Varied	No
Employment profile							
Employee skills development	Yes	Some	Little	Yes	No	Varied	No
Average wages for production workers	High[d]	Moderate	Moderate	Varied[e]	Low	Low	High
Employee turnover	Low	Moderate	Moderate	Low	High	Varied	Low
Owner experience				High	Low	Varied	High
Employee skills				High	Low	Low	High
Buffering devices[e]				Yes	No	Varied	No
Social and institutional profile							
Ethnicity[f] (CEO)	Euro. imm.	Euro. imm.	Euro. imm.	Asian imm.	Asian imm.	Asian imm.	Euro. imm.
Union status	Varied	Varied	Varied	Varied	Varied	Varied	Yes
Contract with nonunion firms	Yes	Yes	Yes	Yes	Yes	Yes	No
Contracting profile							
Contractors skills development	Yes	Some	No				
Global network	Yes	No (local)	No (imports)				
Contract price pressure	Moderate	Some	High				
Variation in number of contractors	Varied[g]	Moderate	High				
Core-periphery contracting	Yes	Yes	Yes				

[a] Although a total of twenty-four contractors were interviewed, three of them were cutters. Because these activities are not strictly comparable to what the other contractors do, the results are not included in this table.

[b] Annual sales over $50 million.

[c] Annual sales over $1 million.

[d] $300 per week or more, 1994.

[e] Depending on market price segment.

[f] European or Asian immigrants.

[g] Work sharing, temporary workers, subcontracting.

interviews were conducted during the summer and fall of 1994 with forty CEOs, including sixteen manufacturers and twenty-four contractors, as well as five production managers who supervised manufacturers subcontracting activities.

To allow for cross-case comparisons, a similar interview guideline was used in all firms studied and adapted to the specificities of manufacturers and contractors. As summarized in Table 3.4, the main topics covered include firms' economic and social characteristics, contracting relations between manufacturers and contractors, and intrafirm relations. On that basis, firms were grouped according to similarities among their economic, social, employment, and contracting characteristics. The resulting classification distinguishes three main categories of manufacturers and four main categories of contractors. A detailed presentation of the various firms' profiles can be found in Table 3.5 (also see Palpacuer 1996, 1997).

To highlight the dominant patterns of change occurring in the New York women's wear industry since the 1970s, these static, cross-sectional results were combined with secondary data providing a historical perspective on the local industry. In particular, interviews were conducted from 1993 to 1995 with about forty industry experts and representatives of industry institutions such as labor unions, employers' associations, state agencies, training centers, and nonprofit organizations. Of an open-ended nature, these discussions aimed at collecting background information on changes in local industry structure, characteristics of local firms, and their relations to local institutions. They also allowed me to test and validate the typology identified on the basis of firm-level interviews.

Notes

1. U.S. Department of Labor, Bureau of Labor Statistics (BLS), *Current Employment Statistics* (SIC 23), annual survey. Available at <http://www.bls.gov/bls/employment.htm>.

2. Ibid. (SIC 233).

3. Ibid. This source provides the most recent data on employment in New York City, whereas the *Census of Manufactures* provides data for years prior to 1958. Differences in data collection procedures account for variations in reported employment figures, and hence in the relative share of New York City, between the two sources.

4. Although employment subsequently declined under the impact of NAFTA, California remains the primary American site of women's wear production, with ninety-three thousand workers in 2000 (BLS, *Current Employment Statistics*, SIC 233).

5. The price classification of women's wear products corresponds approximately to the following scale of unit retail prices: below $50 (popular), $50 to $100 (moderate), $100 to $200 (better), $200 to $600 (bridge), $600 to $1,200 (design), over $1,200 (couture).

6. Information on business characteristics and financial performance of publicly traded companies is based on 10-K annual reports from the U.S. Securities and Exchange Commission. Information on privately owned companies is based on interviews with CEOs conducted in the summer and fall of 1994 (see Appendix).

7. According to Dun and Bradstreet data for 1992, firms with annual sales over $100 million represent only 7 percent of women's wear manufacturers located in New York City but account for more than 60 percent of local sales.

8. On this topic, see the special issue of *Women's Wear Daily* (1995).

9. This estimate is based on interviews with large New York manufacturers, as well as information provided in 10-K annual reports of public companies.

10. Based on Waldinger (1986, 95) for early 1980s lead time and CEO interviews for early 1990s lead times.

11. This definition is adapted from Uzzi's (1996, 1997) conceptualization of close, or embedded, subcontracting relationships in the New York

City women's wear industry, distinguishing the three main dimensions of trust, fine-grained information exchange, and joint problem solving. While Uzzi (1997) considers exchange concentration an indicator of embeddedness, the relative amount and stability of contract work are here considered as a distinct, conceptually significant parameter in the subcontracting relationship. The two dimensions of information exchange and joint problem solving are also subsumed into the specific-skill development dimension.

12. These estimates are based on interviews with twenty-four contractors, including three large Chinese groups, as well as industry experts (see Appendix).

13. From an interview with the general manager of the Korean Apparel Contractors Association of Greater New York in July 1995.

14. Ibid.

References

Abeles, Schwartz, Haeckel and Silverblatt, Inc. 1983. *The Chinatown Industry Study.* Prepared for Local 23–25, International Ladies' Garment Workers' Union and the New York Skirt and Sportswear Association. New York: Abeles, Schwartz, Haeckel and Silverblatt.

Abernathy, Frederick, John Dunlop, Janice Hammond, and David Weil. 1999. *A Stitch in Time: Lean Retailing and the Transformation of Manufacturing: Lessons from the Apparel and Textile Industries.* New York: Oxford University Press.

Apparel Industry Magazine. 1994. "The Quick Response Handbook." Supplement to the March issue of *Apparel Industry Magazine.* Atlanta: Apparel Industry Magazine.

Bailey, Thomas. 1987. *Immigrant and Native Workers.* Boulder, Colo.: Westview Press.

Blumenberg, Evelyn, and Paul Ong. 1994. "Labor Squeeze and Ethnic/Racial Recomposition in the U.S. Apparel Industry." In *Global Production: The Apparel Industry in the Pacific Rim,* ed. Edna Bonacich, Lucie Cheng, Norma Chinchilla, Nora Hamilton, and Paul Ong, pp. 309–27. Philadelphia: Temple University Press.

Brookman, Faye. 1994. "Chinese Firms Shed Sweatshop Image." *Crain's New York Business* (March 14): 23.

Carpenter, Jesse T. 1972. *Competition and Collective Bargaining in the Needle Trades, 1910–1967.* Ithaca, N.Y.: Cornell University Press.

Chin, Margaret. 1994. "Working in the City: Chinese and Latino Garment Workers." Paper presented at the Eighty-ninth American Sociological Association (ASA) Conference, Los Angeles.

Friedman, Arthur. 1992. "They're Still Making It in New York." *Women's Wear Daily,* August 25, 16.

———. 1993. "New York Manufacturing: Speed's the Thing." *Women's Wear Daily,* August 11, 4.

Furman, Phyllis. 1993. "Leslie Fay Rocking Chinatown Jobbers." *Crain's New York Business* (April 19–25): 3.

General Accounting Office (GAO). 1989. *Sweatshops in New York City: A Local Example of a Nation Wide Problem.* GAO/HDR-89-101BR. Washington, D.C.: U.S. General Accounting Office.

———. 1994. *Garment Industry: Efforts to Address the Prevalence and Conditions of Sweatshops.* GAO/HEHS-95-29. Washington, D.C.: U.S. General Accounting Office.

Gereffi, Gary. 1994. "The Organization of Buyer-Driven Global Commodity Chains: How U.S. Retailers Shape Overseas Production Networks." In *Commodity Chains and Global Capitalism,* ed. Gary Gereffi and Miguel Korzeniewicz, pp. 95–122. Westport, Conn.: Praeger.

Helfgott, Roy B. 1959. "Women's and Children's Apparel." In *Made in New York,* ed. M. Hall, pp. 21–112. Cambridge, Mass.: Harvard University Press.

Institute for the Future. 1985. *The Apparel Industry: The Other California.* Report R-67. Prepared for the California Department of Commerce by Institute for the Future, Menlo Park.

Kurt Salmon Associates. 1992. *Keeping New York in Fashion.* Report prepared for the Garment Industry Development Corporation. New York: Kurt Salmon Associates.

Miles, Matthew B., and A. Michael Huberman. 1994. *Qualitative Data Analysis.* 2d ed. Thousand Oaks, Calif.: Sage Publications.

Palpacuer, Florence. 1996. "Stratégies compétitives, gestion des compétences et organisations en réseaux: Etude du cas de l'industrie New-Yorkaise de l'habillement." Unpublished Ph.D. diss., University of Montpellier, Department of Enterprise Law and Management, Montpellier, France.

———. 1997. "The Development of Core-Periphery Forms of Organizations: Some Lessons from the New York Garment Industry." Discussion Paper, DP/95/1997. Geneva: International Institute for Labour Studies.

Pashigian, Peter. 1988. "Demand Uncertainty and Sales: A Study of Fashion and Markdown Pricing." *American Economic Review* 78, 5: 936–53.

Piore, Michael J. 1990. "United States of America." In *The Re-emergence of Small Enterprises: Industrial Restructuring in Industrialized Countries*, ed. Werner Sengenberger, Gary W. Loveman, and Michael Piore, pp. 261–308. Geneva: International Institute for Labour Studies.

Piore, Michael J., and Charles F. Sabel. 1984. *The Second Industrial Divide.* New York: Basic Books.

Pitman, Beverley A. 1992. *Enforcing Labor Laws in the California Garment Industry.* Report prepared for the International Ladies' Garment Workers' Union. Los Angeles: Graduate School of Architecture and Urban Planning, University of California at Los Angeles.

Sassen, Saskia. 1991. *The Global City: New York, London, Tokyo.* Princeton, N.J.: Princeton University Press.

Schlesinger, Emil. 1951. *The Outside System of Production in the Women's Garment Industry in the New York Market.* New York: International Ladies' Garment Workers' Union.

Schmitz, Hubert. 1995. "Small Shoemakers and Fordist Giants: Tale of a Supercluster." *World Development* 23, 1: 9–28.

Steele, Peter. 1990. *Hong Kong Clothing.* Special report 2028. London: Economist Intelligence Unit.

Struense, Chuck. 1993. "A New Contract for Chinatown: A Cleaner Image." *Women's Wear Daily,* July 8, 1.

Taplin, Ian. 1997. "Struggling to Compete: Post War Changes in the U.S. Clothing Industry." *Textile History* 28, 1: 90–104.

Uzzi, Brian. 1996. "The Sources and Consequences of Embeddedness for the Economic Performance of Organizations: The Network Effect." *American Sociological Review* 61 (August): 674–98.

———. 1997. "Social Structure and Competition in Interfirm Networks: The Paradox of Embeddedness." *Administrative Science Quarterly* 42 (March): 35–67.

Waldinger, Roger D. 1986. *Through the Eye of the Needle: Immigrants and Enterprise in New York's Garment Trades.* New York: New York University Press.

Women's Wear Daily. 1995. "What's in a Name? Is It a Brand, a Private Label or a Store?" Infotrack, a supplement to *Women's Wear Daily,* November.

Zhou, Min. 1992. *Chinatown: The Socio-Economic Potential of an Urban Enclave.* Philadelphia: Temple University Press.

Judi A. Kessler

4 # The Impact of North American Economic Integration on the Los Angeles Apparel Industry

Introduction

Since the 1950s the Southern California apparel industry has defined a look that has evolved into a lexicon of cutting-edge contemporary casual wear, primarily for women and girls. This includes a strong emerging niche of active wear: men's and women's fashions geared to a variety of outdoor and indoor activities from snowboarding to skateboarding. Los Angeles County is the largest apparel production center in the United States. Its garment-manufacturing base has continued to grow, in terms of both employment and company start-ups, while most other U.S. garment production centers have experienced steady, pronounced declines. The distinctive demands of the industry—including rapid turn time[1] and multiple fashion cycles—have created, on the backs of waves of immigrant workers, a strong, geographically concentrated industrial district.

At the turn of the century, the Los Angeles fashion and apparel production industry—the largest in the nation—finds itself in a period of significant transition. This chapter focuses on the evolution of Southern California as a major center of garment production and the changes that occurred there during the 1990s, particularly since 1994. Although a number of contributory factors can be identified, arguably the single most important development affecting the industry at the turn of the century is the decade-long process of North American economic integration, culminating with the passage of the North American Free Trade Agreement (NAFTA) in December 1993.

The results of two surveys of Los Angeles County apparel manufacturers[2] conducted in 1997 and 1998 (Kessler) and 2000 (Kessler and Wong) provide micro-level insights into and statistical data on how North American economic integration and NAFTA have shaped the production strategies, relocation decisions, and hiring practices of Los Angeles manufacturers and, ultimately, the face of the largest apparel production center in the United States. Post-NAFTA production arrangements represent a variety of dynamic cross-border production alliances not possible before 1994 (Kessler 1999a, 1999b). These alliances, in turn, are transforming garment production centers on both sides of the border, transnational networks, and the larger North American apparel commodity chain in which they are embedded.

The Evolution of Southern California's Garment Industry

Garment production in California can be traced back to the 1850s. Before World War I the industry was centered in San Francisco, but Los Angeles replaced the Bay Area as the dominant center of production after the war, when "the burgeoning of the motion picture industry . . . produced a nation-wide interest in Hollywood styles which was quickly and expertly capitalized upon by the state's apparel industry" (Goodman 1948, in Bonacich and Appelbaum 2000, 33). Through the successful promotion of Hollywood-style lines of clothing—the "California look"—and the availability of a large pool of immigrant laborers, Los Angeles became the fourth largest garment center in the country by 1924 (Loucky et al. 1994). Currently, over 80 percent of the California apparel industry is located in Southern California (LAEDC 2000, 1). In terms of employment, Los Angeles County, whose apparel employment in 2000 represented almost 16 percent of total manufacturing jobs in Los Angeles (LAEDC 2000, 1), is ranked the largest garment district in the United States.

In the early years, garment making in Southern California was dominated by the production of men's wear, and most manufacturing was done in-house rather than contracted out. However, the industry ultimately found its niche in casual yet fashionable, moderately priced sportswear, especially for young women (although almost every type of garment is produced in Los Angeles). Most production is now contracted out, either offshore or to local garment contractors, many of whom

are Asian immigrants and who employ mostly Latino and some Asian immigrant workers. Gradually, the Los Angeles fashion district[3] grew to embrace the larger Southern California region, although downtown Los Angeles alone boasts a high concentration of apparel firms, contracting factories, supporting infrastructure, and specialized labor markets, all the hallmarks of a vibrant industrial district.[4]

Although traditionally defined by its huge manufacturing base, the Los Angeles apparel industry thrives in large part because Los Angeles is a major style center, owing to its traditionally close ties to the entertainment industry and its image as a mecca for casual, outdoor, active living. In addition, as a major metropolitan area Los Angeles is home to a wide variety of fashion-related business services and educational institutes. These include financial consultants and legal firms specializing in the apparel sector, cross-border production consultants, apparel design and marketing schools and programs, technical colleges, advertising agencies, compliance and monitoring consultants, and buyer-targeted seasonal apparel shows. Finally, Southern California is home to an enormous population of immigrants, the majority of whom emigrated from Mexico and Central America. Close to 75 percent of apparel production-line operators are of Mexican origin. The plentiful supply of low-cost garment workers has sustained a large sewn-products manufacturing base, while the industry's ongoing labor needs have, in turn, served to attract large numbers of immigrant workers to Los Angeles.

Nevertheless, the clustering effects and centripetal forces of industrial geography are matched by the opposing centrifugal forces of globalization and economic regionalization. Although NAFTA has generated a wave of new Southern California–based services geared to the industry, its effect also has been to pull segments of the apparel commodity chain from Los Angeles to Mexico. This trend will increase as Mexico hones its capabilities and increases its capacity for full-package production.[5] Gary Gereffi suggests that the governing agents in the North American apparel supply chain are likely to be "coordinating hubs of design, marketing, distribution and other services headquartered in several regional nerve centers of the United States (such as Los Angeles)" (1997, 28–29). By all indications, the Los Angeles apparel district is transforming into an industry that will one day be defined by its knowledge-intensive activities rather than by labor-intensive manufacturing. Sewing operators are losing hours, pay, and jobs, and contractors are rapidly downsizing as production leaves the region, while more jobs are being created in the upstream and downstream activities of product development and marketing. One Los Angeles journalist who frequently reports on the industry predicts that "in another decade . . . the Southern California apparel industry will be vastly changed, with greater opportunities for designers, managers and sophisticated production workers but little room for basic sewing machine operators" (Cleeland 1999, A14).

South of the border, Gereffi envisions "the emergence of 'network clusters' composed of fiber, textile, apparel and perhaps even retail companies, each cluster with production bases located in different parts of Mexico" (1997, 28). My findings support Gereffi's predictions: Industrial clusters are rapidly developing in networks that comprise Southern California and garment-specific production regions in Mexico. Because some NAFTA provisions have yet to be phased in, we can expect to see changes in the structure and function of these networks. Players from both sides of the border will seek alliances that best suit their production needs in the context of NAFTA, the capacities of firms, and their positions in the apparel commodity chain.

Embedded in the North American apparel commodity chain, U.S.-Mexican production networks ultimately will assume a variety of spatial and organizational characteristics, depending on the role coordinating agents—U.S.-based textilers, large retailers, brand-name manufacturers, and so on—play and the degree to which they dominate production clusters. This, in turn, has much to do with how NAFTA provisions differentially benefit mills, manufacturers, retailers, and other types of suppliers.

The Transnationalization of Los Angeles–Based Apparel Production

Well before NAFTA's implementation, garment manufacturing in Southern California had become an externalized production activity. Small independent contractors handled the low-value-added activities of cutting, sewing, and trimming (more commonly known as CMT, or "cut, make, and trim"), while the higher-value-added work of pre- and post-production remained in-house. As low-wage production was contracted out, so were the employer risks associated with factory work, including employee turnover, layoffs associated with seasonal production, and workforce unionization. As a result, contract manufacturing became the hallmark of Los Angeles fashion and apparel production. As recently as 1992, however, most Southern California apparel manufacturers continued to resist the lure and problems associated with offshore sourcing and contracted their CMT work close to home, usually within the Los Angeles garment district.

In 1992, Edna Bonacich and Richard Appelbaum conducted interviews with 184 of the largest Los Angeles apparel manufacturers.[6] They found that about 30 percent reported doing some offshore production; of those, 17 percent reported sourcing in Mexico (Bonacich and Appelbaum 2000, 62). Sixty percent of the firms surveyed were still sourcing all production in the Southern California area. When both domestic and offshore producers were asked if they planned to shift production to Mexico should NAFTA be approved, 9 percent had definite plans to do so; 37 percent reported that they had no such plans; and the rest thought they might do so eventually. Between 1992 and 1997, anecdotal evidence, along with a few small surveys,[7] suggested some shift in production from Los Angeles to Mexico since NAFTA.

From July 1997 to March 1998, three and one-half years after NAFTA was enacted, I surveyed a random sample of eighty manufacturers, sixty-seven of which were from the group of 184 firms that participated in Bonacich and Appelbaum's 1992 survey. My sample included about half of the 1992 firms still in operation in 1997 and closely resembles the original data set of 184 firms. In 2000, with Linda Wong (of the Los Angeles–based Community Development and Technologies Center), I conducted another survey of Los Angeles apparel manufacturers from the same yearly revenue category ($10 million or greater) as those of 1992 and 1997, along with a smaller sample of firms with sales of $5 to $9 million per year (Kessler and Wong 2000). (The 1997 survey, which focused primarily on production relocation since NAFTA, was part of a larger research project that examined NAFTA-driven changes in the geography of apparel production and cross-border production alliances.) The 2000 survey reassessed sourcing patterns and also examined post-NAFTA changes in Los Angeles apparel employment across occupational categories. (See the Appendix for details of both surveys' methodologies.) Unless otherwise indicated, the findings discussed below are from the 1997 survey.

Figure 4.1 reveals a significant surge in offshore sourcing by Los Angeles–based apparel firms. In 1997, 65 percent of large manufacturers were sourcing at least some production offshore, up from 25 percent in 1992; the figure increased to 75 percent by 2000.[8] In 2000, 56 percent reported sending production to Mexico, up from 17 percent in 1992. Firms that source production in Asia increased from 3 percent of total respondents in 1992 to 37 percent in 2000.[9] As Figure 4.1 indicates, the proportion of firms sourcing all production locally declined dramatically, from 60 percent in 1992 to 25 percent in 2000. Of the 1997 respondents who indicated whether the move represented relocation or expansion of production (about one-half of the sample), the overwhelming majority viewed the production shift as a relocation. In terms of the labor-intensive segment of the production chain, this suggests a zero-sum outcome: rising employment in Mexico and job loss in Southern California.

In sum, between 1992 and 2000, Southern California's apparel production became more globalized, with Mexico taking the lead as the primary site for offshore production.[10] Sourcing in Asia also increased significantly during the same period. Findings from both 1997 and 2000 suggest that companies which sourced most or all production locally tended to be those in the higher-price-point categories (such as "designer") and those without the resources to establish production alliances with Mexico.[11] However, Mexico has become the major offshore sourcing site for firms that produce the budget to moderately priced clothing that defines the Los Angeles industry. Figure 4.1 summarizes these trends.

According to the California Employment Development Department (EDD) Los Angeles County payroll data, apparel employment increased steadily in the 1990s and peaked in 1997 at 111,900, after which it declined by

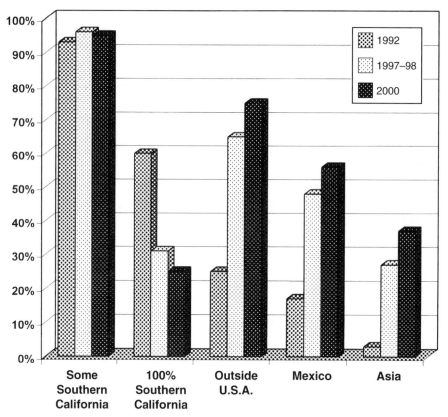

FIGURE 4.1.   Los Angeles County Apparel Firms Sourcing Profile
Source: 1992 data: Bonacich and Appelbaum 1992; 1997–98 data: Kessler 1998; 2000 data: Kessler and Wong 2000.

14,100 between 1997 and 2001 (see Table 4.1). As seen in Figure 4.2, however, employment during Los Angeles' peak apparel production months of February through June began to decline a year earlier, in 1997, three years after NAFTA's inception. This typical seasonal rise in employment all but disappeared by 1999. Information gleaned from the EDD's classified employment ads in local trade publications, as well as from informal interviews with industry experts, points to significant changes in both aggregate unemployment and the types of occupations in which job loss has been concentrated. Although aggregate apparel employment continues its steady decline, most of the

loss has been in the low-value-added occupations of cutters, trimmers, warehouse workers, and, especially, sewing operators. Table 4.2 summarizes a two-year EDD survey of apparel workers, which found that between 1995 and 1997 (the most recent year for which disaggregate employment figures are available) the industry lost more than thirteen thousand sewing-operator jobs.

The decline in low-end jobs may be even more pronounced than these figures suggest. First, the EDD survey was conducted before the industry experienced its most pronounced employment decline, between 1998 and 2000. Second, official figures do not include undocumented sewing operators who lost jobs or hours of work. Third, the EDD also found that in 1996 and 1997 the apparel industry added more than seventeen thousand non-sewing-operator jobs (see Table 4.2), which offsets the aggregate decline in overall employment. As shown in Table 4.2, while sewing operators accounted for 58 percent of total apparel employment in 1995, they represented only 44 percent in 1997.

The Los Angeles garment district faces other problems. Los Angeles lags behind other U.S. apparel centers in terms of technological upgrading, even in basic communications technology such as electronic mail. International exporting of finished goods produced by (but not necessarily in) Southern California firms, while slowly increasing, remains at low levels,

despite recent efforts by industry lobbying groups to promote a global presence of the "Made in California" look. The highly touted government-industry partnership spearheaded by the Los Angeles Mayor's Office and the Southern California Edison Company (Southern California Edison Company 1995) to upgrade the district is yet to be realized. Los Angeles' textile industry is floundering in the face of competition from Asia's textile firms and, more recently, the crippling natural-gas prices generated by California's energy crisis.[12] Finally, sweatshops continue to proliferate while legitimate contractors struggle to keep their heads above water with less-frequent, smaller-volume, rapid-turnaround orders.

The region's largest manufacturers and designers continue to consolidate through

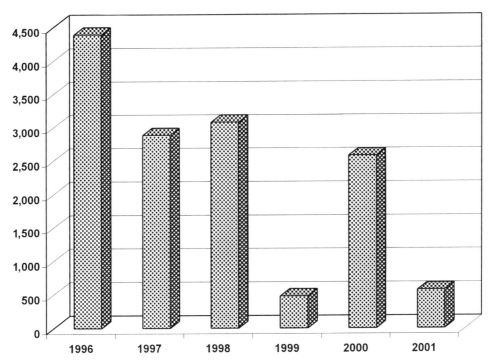

FIGURE 4.2.   Difference in February-to-May Apparel Employment, Los Angeles County, 1996–2001
Source: California Employment Development Department, Labor Marker Information, Apparel (SIC 23) Employment by Month.

TABLE 4.1. Apparel (SIC 23) Employment: Los Angeles County, 1983–2001

	Jan.	Feb.	Mar.	Apr.	May	June	July	Aug.	Sept.	Oct.	Nov.	Dec.	Yearly Average
1983	70,900	73,500	75,100	73,700	72,700	72,700	71,500	70,700	71,900	73,100	74,100	73,700	72,800
1984	73,600	76,600	78,800	77,900	77,400	76,400	74,300	73,300	72,900	74,100	74,200	73,600	75,300
1985	73,400	76,900	78,100	76,900	76,800	75,500	72,900	73,300	74,200	76,500	78,300	77,800	75,800
1986	78,600	81,500	84,200	82,900	83,700	82,500	79,800	80,400	80,700	86,700	88,900	88,300	83,200
1987	88,700	91,500	93,300	92,700	92,900	92,400	89,900	90,000	91,300	91,600	91,800	91,400	91,500
1988	90,000	92,200	92,800	92,000	91,500	90,800	87,300	86,900	88,600	89,300	90,600	90,600	90,200
1989	89,500	93,600	95,200	94,200	94,800	94,800	91,300	91,400	92,700	92,400	93,000	93,000	93,000
1990	92,300	95,200	97,200	97,000	97,000	97,500	94,100	95,000	95,900	96,600	97,000	96,200	95,900
1991	95,000	98,300	99,700	99,000	98,500	97,200	97,700	95,000	95,500	95,800	95,700	95,700	96,700
1992	96,500	99,900	102,500	101,600	100,500	99,600	97,200	96,600	96,700	96,700	96,500	95,100	98,300
1993	94,900	98,900	97,800	94,700	94,900	93,800	90,100	89,600	90,100	89,000	89,200	88,900	92,500
1994	88,500	93,100	98,400	99,900	100,400	100,100	100,000	99,900	101,400	99,100	98,900	99,800	98,300
1995	100,500	105,100	108,700	108,100	108,000	107,300	105,500	105,500	107,000	107,100	107,700	107,800	106,500
1996	105,000	108,600	112,400	112,600	112,900	113,200	111,000	111,900	112,700	110,500	110,800	109,700	110,900
1997	109,500	112,800	115,000	114,800	115,600	114,900	110,900	111,400	111,200	110,100	108,900	107,900	111,900
1998	106,700	108,700	110,700	111,100	111,700	110,700	108,500	109,600	110,100	110,700	110,900	110,400	106,300
1999	98,800	111,000	111,600	111,300	111,400	110,400	107,400	108,000	108,400	107,700	99,000	99,400	101,200
2000	98,500	100,300	103,100	102,300	102,800	102,500	100,000	100,000	100,200	99,400	99,500	99,200	100,700
2001	97,600	99,600	101,500	100,400	100,100	99,000	96,500	96,100	95,900	95,300	95,600	95,500	97,800

Source: California Employment Development Department, Labor Market Division, February 2002; data available at <http://www.calmis.ca.gov/htmlfile/subject/indtable.htm>.

Note: Area in shaded box represents traditional peak production months of February through May.

TABLE 4.2.   Los Angeles County Apparel Industry Employment (SIC 23): Sewing and
Nonsewing, Selected Years

	1995		1997		Change 1995–97	2001 Employees	Change 1997–2001
	Employees	% of Total SIC 23	Employees	% of Total SIC 23			
Total SIC 23	106,500	100	111,000	100	4,500	97,800	(14,100)
Sewing Operators	61,660	58	48,520	44	(13,140)	nd	nd
All Others	44,840	42	62,480	56	17,640	nd	nd

Source: California Employment Development Department, 1995, 1996–97, 2002.

Note: Nd = no data.

buyouts or licensing agreements, widening the gap between the giants and the smaller firms. Of the approximately fifteen hundred non-contractor apparel firms in Los Angeles County in 1977 (LAEDC 2000, 7), probably not more than two hundred generate yearly sales revenues of $20 million or greater. Thus, while small firms dominate the industry numerically, it is estimated that the largest two hundred collectively account for close to two-thirds of the wholesale value generated by all fifteen hundred apparel companies (Bonacich and Appelbaum 2000, 36). Finally, while it once was standard operating procedure for Southern California firms to manufacture "in-house," most apparel production in the region is now sourced out, either to local contractors or offshore. Most notably, the past five years have witnessed a steady, rapidly accelerating production move to Mexico and, to a lesser degree, the Asian region (Kessler 1998). During this period, the average number of Southern California contractors used per firm has declined significantly, from sixteen in 1997 to twelve in 2000 (Kessler and Wong 2000).

Why Mexico?

Not surprisingly, factors related to company profit margins have figured most prominently in decisions to relocate production to Mexico.

Virtually all manufacturers sourcing in Mexico cited competition and rising production costs[13] as major factors precipitating their move. Several companies maintained that while labor costs were a major consideration, other factors were at least as important as the difference in wages between Los Angeles and Mexico. For example, according to one firm's production and sales manager, the needlework required for the company's line of men's knitwear is not done in Southern California; however, Mexico has qualified operators and equipment for this type of production. Similarly, a large manufacturer of swimwear said that while it had become increasingly difficult to find qualified swimwear operators in Southern California, they were in plentiful supply in Mexico, particularly in the region surrounding Mexico City (Kessler and Wong 2000). None of the survey's respondents cited union activity as a factor in relocation.

The companies were asked if Mexico's proximity to Los Angeles enhanced production in terms of turn time. Approximately two-thirds responded affirmatively, while the rest said that Mexico's geographic proximity was not a factor for them. Interestingly, 29 percent of the manufacturers who considered Mexico's location an asset were not sending production there; similarly, about 25 percent of the respondents who reportedly saw no benefit in geographic proximity were producing in Mexico. While

Mexico's closeness to Southern California is important to most manufacturers that are considering offshore production, it is but one of many factors taken into account when strategizing production location. Proximity alone is not reason enough to relocate production. Of utmost importance to most manufacturers is the quality and reliability of their supply chains.

Beyond In-Bond

One manufacturer in the 1997 survey cited the availability of full-package production programs, along with Mexican-manufactured textiles (a production arrangement typically found in the newly industrializing economies of East Asia), as the primary reason for having relocated to Mexico. In fact, this manufacturer planned to shift "as much [Southern California–based] production as possible, as quickly as possible, to Mexico for full-package production." Similarly, in the same survey a large manufacturer of sportswear and swimwear reported plans to move rapidly from a platform of export assembly of precut fabric to full-package production in Mexico:

> I just returned from a meeting with Mexican contractors around Textile City [in Cuernavaca]. We talked about doing full-package work, however it's still in the talking stage. [But] once they are capable, then we will move to full-package arrangements. . . . We have a long way to go with Mexico, but it will happen. . . . Some do well, some don't . . . [however] we have overcome the "time" problem—turnaround is now fine. But the problem is *us*, not *them*. If we provided the assistance they need, they would be fine. . . . Once they have it, they have it.

Most industry experts agree that Mexico is destined to shake off assembly of piece goods and move steadily toward full-package production. Bruce Berton, with Stonefield Jo-

sephson (a leading accounting and consulting firm for Los Angeles apparel manufacturers), envisions true full-package apparel production in Mexico developing over the next three to five years. What many refer to as "almost-full-package"—more than just cutting and sewing but less than complete specification contracting—is becoming more common in Los Angeles–Mexico production alliances (Berton 1997a, 1997b).

Nevertheless, integrated production operations in Mexico face a number of barriers that are distinct to the country's social, political, and economic infrastructure. Unlike East Asia, Mexico lacks the trading companies that broker full-package production (see Appelbaum and Gereffi 1994). For example, in Hong Kong letters of credit are collateralized based on the reputation of the trading company and well-established business networks with banks and manufacturers. Banks will most likely lend up to 80 percent of the cost and charge a monthly interest rate on unpaid balances. By contrast, in Mexico collateral must be advanced either in real estate or dollars deposited as pesos in a private Mexico bank. The bank, in turn, takes about 5 percent off the top for handling, charging an additional 10 percent devaluation fee if the collateral is presented in pesos. The bank then advances about 80 percent of production costs, at interest rates that reportedly exceed 8 percent per month, depending on the size of the firm. The networks of trust that operate between Hong Kong and U.S. apparel firms do not yet exist between Mexico and California's apparel manufacturers. Financing for full-package production will most likely go the route of factoring,[14] which is beginning to expand in Mexico. Also, revisions of Mexico's complicated banking laws should make credit more accessible.

At least some Los Angeles manufacturers are ready to act on their belief that the Mexican apparel industry is ultimately capable of "Asian-style" full-package production.[15] Tarrant Apparel Group, a large, publicly owned Los Angeles–based private-label manufacturer, currently offers full-package services in Mexico through its enormous U.S.-Mexican network of textilers, manufacturers, finishers, and distributors. Tarrant no longer produces garments in the United States. Its Los Angeles headquarters handle product development, design, and marketing, but all production activities, including the acquisition of most raw materials, are carried out in Mexico and Asia.

Compared to the countries of East Asia, Mexico is a relative newcomer in the production of world-class apparel for global companies. Most industry observers expect Mexico to continue to manufacture in the foreseeable future what the maquiladora system was known for before NAFTA: basic apparel, such as T-shirts, undergarments, and other items without much fashion sensitivity. In the case of Los Angeles, it was assumed that firms carrying more fashion-sensitive lines would have them produced in East Asia, if time allowed, or locally.

In 1997, I found a significant correlation between production in Mexico and price point. Manufacturers reporting "budget" and "moderate" price points (less fashion-sensitive clothing) sent more production to Mexico. In 2000, by contrast, there was no significant correlation between price point and Mexican production. This suggests that Mexico is now manufacturing a wider variety of apparel in terms of retail value. The 2000 results should be interpreted with caution, however, since a firm producing at multiple price points may be sending the basics to Mexico and the fashion items elsewhere. The sourcing profiles of firms in both 1997 and 2000 cannot be disaggregated for those companies with multiple price points or sourcing in multiple countries.

Where in Mexico?
The Spatial Distribution of Networks

At the risk of oversimplifying the geographic distribution of production in Mexico, I divide the country into two general apparel production regions: the border and the interior. I further break down the interior of Mexico into four subregions: central (the Federal District, the state of Mexico, and proximate regions), the west coast (which comprises part of the larger Pacific Rim production region), the northern and northeastern states (excluding the regions contiguous to the United States), and the south (including the Yucatán).[16]

There appears to be a significant shift in Southern Californian sourcing, from the western border region to central Mexico. The states of Guanajuato, Puebla, Tlaxcala, and the greater Mexico City area figure prominently as new production sites. Also included is the west coast state of Jalisco, located due west from Mexico City. In general, manufacturers who now source in regions other than the border do so for two reasons: labor costs and quality. I was told that garment workers' wages in the Tijuana and Mexicali industrial districts are almost on par with those of Southern California (although, given the official wage statistics, this may be somewhat of an exaggeration). Nevertheless, labor costs have risen in these areas much faster than in Mexico's interior. It was also reported by the majority of firms with contracts in Mexico that quality of production is superior in the central Mexico factories. The few manufacturers interviewed who were beginning to source a significant proportion of their production in the Yucatán claim they benefit from both low labor costs and high-quality finished products.

While it would seem that garment production will ultimately shift from the border to the interior, a significant minority of firms surveyed prefer arrangements with border contractors. The primary reason they have continued to contract in border districts is production turn time and related problems with ground transportation: Labor costs are higher along the border, but turn time and the risks of ground transport shipment hijackings are significantly decreased.[17] Although the majority of Southern California apparel manufacturers' lines comprise budget and moderately priced clothing, some do require particularly rapid turnaround, depending on the lines and the vendors. Some firms reported that they were better able to monitor quality control by offshore sourcing as close to Los Angeles as possible. Additionally, if runs shipped by border contractors were unacceptable for shipment to retailers, they had some "breathing space" to correct the errors locally. Finally, a few respondents have established extraordinarily successful production networks through interesting mixes of contracting and joint-venture arrangements along the border and the northwestern coast of Mexico.

Garment Services International[18] (GSI) is a case in point. In business as a private-label manufacturer for five years, GSI manufactured better apparel for such notables as Nike, Adidas, and Eddie Bauer and had plans to expand into licensed apparel manufacturing and to develop its own brand labels. GSI distributed its production strategically, sending longer-run full-package programs to Asia (where labor is cheapest) and orders requiring a quicker turn time to its factories in Mexico, while retaining the most rapid turnaround items in its Los Angeles factories. The company owned two "full-service" factories near its Los Angeles headquarters and two CMT factories near the U.S.-Mexico border (Garment Services de México), and it sourced full-package production in Asia. Recently the company was sold and renamed; however, it continues to produce apparel and to source manufacturing globally.

GSI's first foray into Mexico's interior was less than successful. According to its president and co-owner, Jim Reach, "We didn't have the proper procedures in line [and] we failed miserably at the gates" (Reach 1999). After careful planning and consultation with outside professionals who had expertise in U.S.-Mexican production alliances, Reach and his partner moved production south again in early 1998—this time to the border region (where labor costs are substantially higher) and into GSI-owned factories. In August 1999, I visited the Tijuana factory and found that its workers earned well above minimum wage and about double the weekly wages of their counterparts in the interior. Reach was willing to pay more in exchange for the benefits of the border's proximity to his Los Angeles headquarters.

In sum, the advantages to border contracting are quicker production turn time and the ability to better monitor the Mexico contractors. Nevertheless, the majority of manufacturers who source in Mexico have managed to establish adequate production networks (albeit not overnight) that use contractors in the interior, reaping lower labor costs and more consistent quality. Some manufacturers use a mix of border and interior production, spreading their lines and runs across border and interior contractors, depending on their particular production needs. In addition, several manufacturers who are currently contracting along the border region report that they have plans eventually to relocate all Mexican production to the interior, primarily because of increasing labor costs at the border and problems with product quality.

Gereffi (2000) identifies the southern part of Mexico as the "loser" in the restructuring of the North American apparel commodity chains, "in relative, if not absolute, terms." He points out that in 1992 the Yucatán accounted for less than 1 percent of Mexico's maquiladora employees. Between mid-1998 and August

2000, however, the number of maquiladoras in this region grew from 67 (with 16,720 employees) to 131 (with 34,450 employees) (INEGI, in *Twin Plant News* 1999, 2001). Four firms interviewed in 1997 were sourcing in the Yucatán peninsula, primarily in the picturesque colonial city of Mérida. One company, specializing in lines of girls', children's, and infants' outerwear, sends 60 percent of its total volume to contractors in Yucatán, and several Los Angeles apparel consultants speak of a growing full-package production district in Mérida. While southern Mexico's contribution to total apparel exports remains relatively small, industrial districts in the region have been growing rapidly since NAFTA.

The Importance of NAFTA in Shaping Corporate Relocation Decisions

A 1996 report generated by the North American Integration and Development Center (NAID) at the University of California, Los Angeles, asserts among other things that "the lowering of tariffs through NAFTA has not had a significant impact on the rate of growth of imports or exports between Mexico and the United States, or on the composition of trade between sectors recently liberalized by NAFTA and those sectors still awaiting liberalization" (Hinojosa et al. 1996, 10). Moreover, it concludes that the peso crisis of December 1994 "had by far the single largest impact on Mexican trade trends in the last 10 years" (Hinojosa et al. 1996, 34). The report does note that the more labor-intensive sectors (such as apparel) have not yet been fully liberalized vis-à-vis NAFTA. Consequently, many of their adjustments will be felt in the future.

Although the NAID report offers important insights into the impact of NAFTA on local employment patterns across industrial sectors, it is inconclusive on the issue of the relative impacts of the peso devaluation and NAFTA

on apparel-production relocation from Southern California to Mexico. Left unanswered is the degree to which NAFTA and the Mexican peso collapse served as an incentive for Los Angeles apparel manufacturers to relocate production to Mexico. I examined this issue by asking each manufacturer in the 1997 survey to rate the relative importance of six factors in their willingness to relocate to Mexico: (1) economic liberalization in Mexico over the past ten years; (2) the December 1994 peso devaluation and collapse; (3) NAFTA; (4) the stability of Mexico's political system; (5) the cost of labor; and (6) the quality of production. I then posed the question "Which do you consider a greater incentive to relocate production to Mexico—the peso devaluation or NAFTA—and why?" Of the seventy-two respondents to this question, 68 percent considered NAFTA a greater incentive to relocate to Mexico, 7 percent considered the peso devaluation a greater incentive, and 15 percent were not sure. (One respondent thought both were equally important, and six thought that neither mattered.)

Of those manufacturers who cited NAFTA as the greater incentive, close to half elaborated on their response. Although the answers varied, the general sentiment was that, despite its implications, the December 1994 peso devaluation was a one-time occurrence; major production changes should not be based on such phenomena as currency fluctuations; and the long-term benefits of NAFTA far outweigh any short-term benefits to be gained by exploiting the impact of a currency devaluation on labor and other costs. In the words of one large manufacturer of women's, misses', and juniors' sportswear, "A peso devaluation can happen at any time; NAFTA is more permanent." Similarly, a smaller manufacturer, whose company was founded in the early 1990s, said that "NAFTA offers more opportunity [in the long run]. We didn't budge when the peso crashed." Others offered similar comments: "NAFTA makes it all work smoothly.... [It] will result in development [of the apparel industry]"; "NAFTA opened up the market, makes it easier to do production"; "NAFTA makes production more affordable.... [The peso devaluation] has no importance whatsoever." Several manufacturers seemed surprised that the interviewer would pose such a question: "The peso devaluation is 'history'!"

One chief financial officer who had been in the apparel business for forty-five years did not mince words in his response: "The peso crash is a stupid reason to relocate production. [Currency fluctuations] are always a crap game. It could happen any time, and it could recover any time. The exchange rate (peso to dollar) has been very stable at 7.8 for a while. You'd have to be a moron to [relocate production] based on the peso crash!" In fact, this manufacturer, who now sources 70 percent of his production in Mexico, relocated the majority well before the peso collapse. In late 1995 the firm moved toward a more permanent presence in Mexico by building two factories close to the border, while continuing to source from six contractors located in the interior.

Of the five manufacturers who viewed the peso devaluation as the greater incentive to relocate production to Mexico, four cited price and profit as the reason. According to a relatively small manufacturer of misses' and juniors' sportswear and dresses, "If money is what it's all about, [then] the peso devaluation is more important." Another manufacturer said she could make a "bigger profit" as a result of the peso collapse. Ironically, the former had no production in Mexico, and the latter had produced in Mexico at one time but had since pulled back to Southern California. In fact, of the five firms that chose the peso devaluation as the greater incentive to relocate production, only three were sourcing production in Mexico at the time of their interviews. In sum,

while cost and profit are undoubtedly foremost in the sourcing strategies of Los Angeles apparel manufacturers, most perceive NAFTA as more likely than the peso collapse to generate cost savings and profit in the long run. This also modifies the stereotype of the wildly footloose garment maker, jumping from country to country with each currency fluctuation.

Bonacich and Appelbaum join Raúl Hinojosa Ojeda and his coauthors in questioning the magnitude of NAFTA's impact on the Los Angeles industry. They emphasize that U.S. apparel production relocation predates the passage of NAFTA, as represented by a 30 percent annual growth rate of U.S. apparel imports from Mexico between 1989 and 1993. They further argue that although this figure did reach 45 percent per year in the three years after NAFTA's inception, it does not necessarily indicate that production is leaving Los Angeles for Mexico; some of the growth could be attributed to Los Angeles–based companies, already sourcing offshore in Asia or the Caribbean, that decided to move production to Mexico after NAFTA (Bonacich and Appelbaum 2000, 63).

In theory this could be true; but the authors' own data suggest otherwise. Their 1992 survey, conducted two years before NAFTA took effect, found only a few Los Angeles firms (3 percent) sourcing in Asia and even fewer in Central America and the Caribbean (Bonacich and Appelbaum 1992). Since 1992 the number of firms with production in Mexico and the number of firms with production in Asia (and firms with production both in Mexico and in Asia) have increased significantly, suggesting that the distinct characteristics of Mexico and Asia—geographic proximity, capabilities, capacities, and costs—have made both sites increasingly popular for offshore apparel production.

Moreover, the individual needs of the manufacturers determine whether and where to source offshore. For example, production programs that require relatively quick turnaround (two to ten weeks) are more likely to be done in Southern California (if they are highly fashion-sensitive) or Mexico, while longer-turn-time production of any sort (thirteen to eighteen weeks) is more suited for Asia. In fact, most large Los Angeles manufacturers source strategically—that is, they send production to multiple offshore sites, depending on the price point and fashion sensitivity of their line. The Bonacich-Appelbaum survey also found that very little Los Angeles production was sent to Central America or other Caribbean nations in 1992; this continues to be the case in 2000. So it is also unlikely that any significant proportion of NAFTA-era Mexican sourcing is displaced production, either from the Caribbean or from Asia.

In sum, the data that support the direct relocation (or expansion) from Los Angeles to Mexico seem more convincing than the circuitous route posited by Bonacich and Appelbaum (although the authors do acknowledge the growing importance of Mexico as a U.S. garment production site). More recent findings also indicate that Mexican sourcing is predominantly NAFTA driven. Of the thirty-eight respondents in 1997 who reported the year their firm began sourcing in Mexico, 66 percent (twenty-five firms) first relocated production at least one year after NAFTA's inception and 13 percent (five firms) in 1994, for a total of 79 percent relocating after NAFTA. Respondents to the 2000 survey who were sourcing in Mexico were also asked when they had begun sourcing in Mexico and whether NAFTA had been an important factor in their decisions to do so. Of the thirty-five who responded, 81 percent relocated production to Mexico after NAFTA's inception and 69 percent reported that NAFTA was a principal factor in the decision to relocate.

The most compelling and direct evidence of NAFTA's impact on the Los Angeles apparel industry, however, is found in employment trends over the past fifteen years. From 1989 to 1993, the pre-NAFTA time period cited by Bonacich and Appelbaum, during which U.S. apparel imports from Mexico increased by 30 percent, aggregate employment in Los Angeles' apparel industry also increased by at least two thousand workers per year (see Table 4.1).[19] Three and a half years after NAFTA's passage, however, employment leveled off, then began a decline. These trends were concentrated in the area of production activities that Mexico was increasingly assuming: cutting, sewing, finishing, and warehousing.

Why Not Los Angeles? Monitoring, Liability, and the Cost of Compliance

Monitoring for workplace compliance was spearheaded by the U.S. Department of Labor (DOL) in the early 1990s to help manufacturers avoid the shipping of "hot goods."[20] Since 1996 the DOL's Wage and Hours Division has conducted a number of compliance-monitoring workshops and manufacturing training seminars in the Los Angeles area. Overall, the Wage and Hours Division's enforcement strategy—called the "No Sweat Initiative"—is to focus on low-wage industries; its primary targets have been garment manufacturers in New York and Los Angeles. An additional enforcement tool is the Garment Enforcement Report, which provides the industry and consumers with information about contractors that violate the minimum-wage and overtime laws and which manufacturers are doing business with them.

In concert with the DOL's efforts, a joint federal-state Targeted Industries Partnership Program (TIPP) aims to bring the full weight of their combined laws on serious violators through periodic joint "sweeps" of factories. The program has four lead agencies: the

California Division of Labor Standards Enforcement (DLSE), the California Division of Occupational Safety and Health (Cal DOSH), the California EDD, and the DOL's Wage and Hours Division. Since 1996, TIPP has maintained a "garment hot line" for reporting suspected violations. According to a January 1999 report by the Los Angeles Jewish Commission on Sweatshops,[21] about sixty of Los Angeles' largest manufacturers had signed a DOL agreement that required their contractors to sign a compliance-program agreement[22] (Los Angeles Jewish Commission on Sweatshops 1999, 17–18).

Virtually all large manufacturers have monitoring programs,[23] whether they engage in self-monitoring through in-house programs, use independent consultants or auditors, or are members of Compliance Alliance, an organization with its own monitoring protocols. Not surprisingly, a number of manufacturers in my surveys held escalating contractor compliance-enforcement efforts by state and federal officials responsible in part for their production relocation to Mexico. Four manufacturers cited increased enforcement as the primary reason for shifting production. Many more offered unsolicited comments and opinions on what one manufacturer termed "the price of monitoring compliance."[24]

A minority of those surveyed expressed an uncompromising position in the face of government demands for monitoring. One production manager of a sportswear company interviewed in 1997 was very straightforward regarding his take on the issue: "Listen, I can tell you where all of this is leading: if the U.S. [government] puts any pressure on me, I will have absolutely no problem pulling out and moving [everything] to Mexico." His firm is currently sourcing some production in Mexico, but he declined to state how much.

More commonly, manufacturers interviewed in 1997 and 1998 acknowledged that a problem exists (no one who brought up the issue denied the existence of sweatshops in Los Angeles) but felt strongly that they should not be made to shoulder the sole responsibility of monitoring contractors' compliance with laws regarding wages, hours, and workplace safety. The controller of a large manufacturing firm that uses about fifty contractors perceived the dilemma this way:

> We can't meet price point because of the [U.S.] Department of Labor.... They are asking too much of us.... We can't take [on] the responsibility.... If we have to be so selective with contractors, we [won't be able to] find enough in California. [We are faced with] two options: curtail business or go to Mexico and continue to expand. We want to expand.

A controller with another firm voiced similar sentiments:

> We are relocating for price, but you need to understand, it is not just the price of labor; it is the price of monitoring compliance. We just can't afford it, and we just can't keep track of the operations of 20 contractors, 24 hours a day—it's impossible.... We have to monitor the "bad guys" very closely—if we don't, they will end up costing us in fines and confiscated goods.

A chief financial officer at a firm sourcing about 70 percent production in Mexico described in detail the arrangement his company has with an independent auditing firm:

> What we do here is we contract with one of the independent auditors. They work for us. They go in and grade contractors: A, B, or C. "A" is impossible to maintain; "B" is a good, acceptable contractor. Most are "C." We only contract with the "Bs"—we can't find any "As." The bigger, better [contracting] shops get more work, have higher standards, less turnover, and better working conditions. Unfortunately, Los Angeles has small shops compared to other garment districts. The food

chain is fierce in this business. California is now a police state. Monitoring is essential but they [the government] just need to back off a bit, ease off a bit, to keep manufacturing in business.

In August 2000 the DOL's Wage and Hours Division posted the findings of its latest Southern California garment-industry survey. (Federal and state agencies have been conducting compliance surveys every two years since 1994.)[25] The survey, conducted in February and March 2000, found that the overall level of compliance with minimum-wage, overtime, and child-labor requirements was 33 percent, down from approximately 39 percent in 1998. Shops with "thorough monitoring programs" in place fared somewhat better, with 44 percent in compliance; only 10 percent of those without monitoring were in compliance. Nevertheless, the overall quality of Los Angeles' monitoring programs is suspect because over half the shops with supposed comprehensive programs were found to be in violation of U.S. labor law. Of the ninety-three contractors and eight manufacturers inspected, thirty-five were firms previously investigated and found to be in violation. The level of compliance for this group was 37 percent—only slightly higher than the overall compliance level (California DLSE 2000; U.S. Department of Labor 2000).

The issues of manufacturer compliance, retailer-manufacturer joint liability, and labor's right to collective bargaining were brought to the fore in great part by lobbying efforts and campaigns by the Union of Needletrades, Industrial, and Textile Employees (UNITE), other unions, and advocacy groups such as the Los Angeles Jewish Commission on Sweatshops. Activists at California institutions of higher education are part of the larger nationwide Workers Rights Consortium (WRC), a pilot project in which students and faculty from up to one hundred colleges and universities are pressuring their administrations to end the use of sweatshop labor in the production of college apparel. The WRC has won some highly publicized victories, mostly on the East Coast of the United States. However, given the structure of apparel production—its propensity for globalized and decentralized production, a workforce consisting primarily of documented and undocumented immigrant laborers, fierce management resistance to organizing efforts, and tensions between garment workers and major unions—along with the more general decline in unionization and the shrinking welfare state, it is unlikely that Los Angeles garment workers will achieve union representation in the foreseeable future.[26]

A number of factors account for the high level of noncompliance as well as the failure of the "No Sweat" campaign and the TIPP to bring the industry into compliance. First, as of 1998 the U.S. Department of Labor had a little more than nine hundred investigators across the country to cover 120 million workers in 6.5 million workplaces; to say that staff is stretched thin would be an understatement. Similarly, a recent study by the California Works Foundation found that enforcement of laws covering wages, hours, and health and safety at the state level was lower in 2000 than at the turn of each of the previous three decades. Although more than one hundred enforcement positions were added to the DOL's Wage and Hours Division in 1998 and 1999, staff-to-worker ratios are 36 percent lower than they were in 1980 (Cleeland 2001, C1).

Second, although most large manufacturers do have monitoring programs in place (and are extending them to their Mexican contractors), it is difficult to monitor effectively the activities of a shop that is determined to violate labor and safety laws. A manufacturer would need to place monitors in all of its contractors' facilities, twenty-four hours a day, seven days a week, to assure that work was not being sent out as "homework" or subcontracted to noncompliant shops. For a large manufacturer with contractors numbering in the double digits, the cost would be prohibitive. Additionally, most manufacturers argue that if the company has implemented an approved monitoring program, it should not and cannot be responsible for workplace violations that occur in independent contractors' facilities.

Finally, the structure of the apparel industry lends itself to varying degrees of noncompliance, including true sweatshop conditions. The industry remains primarily labor intensive and buyer driven, with profits skewed in the direction of retailers. This translates into pressure on hundreds of manufacturers by a relatively small number of major retailers to fill orders at highly competitive costs. Manufacturers, in turn, farm out the production to those contractors in a pool of thousands who are willing to operate on a slim margin of profit. Often, in order to break even on operating costs, contractors must (or choose to) violate labor laws and pay sewing operators below minimum wage. Sewing operators, who constitute the largest occupational group in the industry, are typically immigrants, poorly paid, and often not proficient in English. Moreover, a significant number of operators are undocumented, working with *papeles chuecos* (false documents). "Rather than view the state inspectors as allies ... workers worr[y] that the [government] raids would cost them precious time at their machines. With piece rates dropping fast, they [have] to work harder and longer to match earnings of just a year ago" (Cleeland 1999, 14). UNITE is the recognized Los Angeles garment workers union, yet it has, by its own admission, fewer than one thousand members in Southern California. Garment workers are unwilling to associate with the union for a variety of reasons, not the least of which is the fear of retaliation or termination by their employers.

The Changing Face of Los Angeles' New Apparel Workforce

Much more attention has been given to NAFTA's impact on socioeconomic development in Mexico than to its effect on regional economies in the United States. To cite declining manufacturing employment or even declining aggregate employment in NAFTA-vulnerable sectors as the universal outcome of North American economic integration ignores the dynamic mix of high- and low-value-added activities embedded in America's new global cities. Unlike the cities of the past, "at the hearts of geographically bounded regions whose economies they center, [global cities] connect remote points of production, consumption, and finance" (Appiah 1998).

As a global city, Los Angeles is fast becoming the center of control and management of an expanding transnational apparel production region, a high-value link in the apparel commodity chain, which, in turn, has fostered the proliferation of a variety of nonmanufacturing apparel-related jobs. At the same time, however, the thousands of immigrant workers employed in garment manufacturing have seen their numbers, employment options, and real wages diminish dramatically.

As noted earlier in the chapter, since NAFTA's inception the Los Angeles apparel industry has witnessed a decline in aggregate apparel-related employment, a loss of thousands of sewing-operator jobs, and a shrinking contractor base. Accompanying these trends, however, has been an increase in apparel-related white-collar employment, suggesting retention and consolidation of high-value production activities that require a growing base of knowledge-intensive workers. Anecdotal evidence gleaned from open-ended interviews and employment ads in trade publications suggests that at least part of the increase in higher-end employment has been generated, directly or indirectly, by NAFTA.

In the first six months of 2000, Linda Wong and I interviewed eighty-one Los Angeles apparel firms. Our principal aim was to explore the effects of NAFTA on production sourcing, employment, and occupational distribution in the Southern California apparel industry. A full account and analysis of our findings is beyond the scope of this chapter. However, the principal findings discussed below suggest that Los Angeles is beginning to shed, in significant numbers, its lowest-value-added production activities, which are now located in Mexico and elsewhere. At the same time, although the industry retains a relatively large apparel-manufacturing base, it is increasingly identified with knowledge-intensive activities on the apparel commodity chain, such as preproduction product development and design and postproduction marketing and merchandising.

As indicated in Table 4.2, Los Angeles County lost at least thirteen thousand sewing-operator jobs during the post-NAFTA period, when sewing activities moved to Mexico and Los Angeles contractor utilization declined. As such, it is reasonable to attribute the loss of sewing-operator jobs to NAFTA-related production shifts. Non-sewing-operator employment, both in absolute numbers and as a proportion of total apparel-related employment, increased (see Table 4.2). We found that half the firms currently sourcing in Mexico have advertised for or hired personnel in Southern California who have NAFTA- and Mexico-related knowledge or expertise. While twenty-eight companies (51 percent) attributed general increases in hires to company growth or increased sales, twenty-two firms (40 percent) reported increased personnel in occupations such as production management, quality control, import-export expedition, and data entry as a result of production relocation to Mexico. By contrast, sixteen firms (29 percent) reported decreased hiring or layoffs as a result of off-shore sourcing in Mexico and elsewhere. Of the sixteen, half reported job reductions in the blue-collar occupational categories of sewing, shipping and receiving, and warehouse work.[27] Tables 4.3 and 4.4 detail these findings.

Findings suggest that NAFTA-driven redistribution of production activities and the concomitant emergence of transnational strategic production alliances have resulted in both the creation of Southern California–based knowledge-intensive jobs in the industry and a significant loss of labor-intensive sewing-operator and other blue-collar jobs. It should be emphasized that the newly created knowledge-intensive jobs are, for the most part, structurally inaccessible to the majority of displaced production workers because of these workers' lack of English proficiency, low levels of education, and insufficient skills and training. Nonunionized and with little political muscle, low-wage apparel manufacturing workers are the least likely to benefit and the most likely to be marginalized by NAFTA-related industry transformations.

Under NAFTA's provisions, U.S. workers may apply for compensation if they are able to prove that they lost their jobs as a result of the trade agreement. The 1996 UCLA NAID report found that neither apparel firms nor garment workers in Los Angeles had filed claims with the government for jobs lost as a result of NAFTA's implementation, despite the fact that apparel firms nationwide are overrepresented in terms of filing such complaints. Thus, on the surface, NAFTA does not yet appear to have had a significant impact on the region. However, the authors of the report convincingly argue that characteristics distinct to the Los Angeles garment district account for the lack of complaints. Los Angeles apparel factories are too small to have the resources to monitor and document NAFTA effects; furthermore, less than 2 percent of Los Angeles apparel workers are unionized and thus without an advocate to voice their need for assistance (Hinojosa et al. 1996, 74–78).[28] Add to this the evidence that employment appears to

TABLE 4.3.   Factors Contributing to Increased Hiring, by Occupation and Number of Firms Reporting (55)

	Company Growth	Increased Sales	Acquisition	Automation/ Technology	Mexico/ NAFTA Production	Offshore Sourcing	Other
All Occupations	15	12	1	3	0	0	0
White-Collar	11	17	0	14	22	1	0
Retail	1	2	0	0	0	0	0
Sales/Mktg./Cust. Srv.	1	6	0	0	2	0	1
Accounts	0	0	0	1	0	0	0
E-Com./Info. Tech./ Mgmt. Info. Sys.	0	0	0	5	0	0	0
Import/Export	0	0	0	0	3	0	0
Office/Data Entry	2	2	0	6	4	0	1
Nonprod. Adm./Mgmt.	1	0	0	0	2	0	0
Non-CMT Prod./ Prod. Asst./Mgmt.	1	2	0	1	6	1	1
Design/Design Asst.	2	3	0	1	0	0	3
Specifications/ Piece Goods	1	0	0	0	0	0	0
Quality Control	2	2	0	0	5	0	1
Skilled Blue-Collar	4	1	0	0	0	0	0
Pattern/Sample Maker	4	1	0	0	0	0	0
Blue-Collar	5	5	0	0	1	0	0
Ship./Rec./Warehse.	2	2	0	0	0	0	0
CMT[a]	3	3	0	0	1	0	0
All Unskilled Labor	0	0	0	0	0	0	0

Source: Kessler and Wong 2000.

[a]Cut, Make (sewing); Trim: Most manufacturers do not employ CMT; CMT work is done by contractors, which were not included in this survey.

be increasing in the higher-value-added occupations, and we may reasonably conclude that Southern California has more displaced garment workers than current complaints and official aggregate employment figures suggest.

Conclusion

Since 1992 the Los Angeles garment industry has experienced significant changes in the sourcing patterns of its manufacturers and a transformation of its workforce. Findings from surveys conducted in 1992, 1997, and 2000 indicate that manufacturers' sourcing patterns have become globalized, with garment-specific industrial clusters in the interior of Mexico emerging as principal sites of offshore production. Large, resource-rich manufacturers represent the lion's share of production relocation. The small number of designers and manufacturers that constitute the fashion-sensitive sector of the industry must, due to rapid turn time and upscale lines, continue to outsource locally. However, greater profit margin per unit offsets Southern California's higher costs of production. The large number of small manufacturers producing lower-price-point lines lack the resources to develop production alliances with Mexico and are, for the most part, captive to Southern California.

While employment in apparel-related sectors decreased steadily on the national level, the Southern California region experienced a net gain in apparel jobs for at least fifteen years. Between 1978 and 1997, every state except California posted a decline in apparel employment. New York, New Jersey, Pennsylvania,

and Massachusetts lost over half their apparel jobs. An exception to this pattern was California, which added about fifty-thousand jobs, most of which were concentrated in Los Angeles. From 1983 to 1997 officially recorded employment grew steadily, from an average of roughly 73,000 workers in 1983 to 111,900 in 1997—a 53 percent increase.[29] Beginning in mid-1997, however, aggregate apparel employment leveled off and began a downward trend.

The Los Angeles apparel industry is emblematic of the uneven distribution of

TABLE 4.4.   Factors Contributing to Decreased Hiring, by Occupation and Number of Firms Reporting (55)

	Company Contraction	Sales Decline/ Fluctuation	Auto-mation/ Technology	Mexico/ NAFTA Production	Offshore Production	Other
All Occupations	4	2	0	1	1	1
White-Collar	11	21	6	1	4	2
Retail	0	1	0	0	0	0
Sales/Mktg./Cust. Srv.	2	5	0	0	0	1
Accounts	0	0	0	0	0	0
E-Com./Info.Tech./ Mgmt. Info. Sys.	0	1	0	0	0	0
Import/Export	0	0	0	0	0	0
Office/Data Entry	2	5	4	0	0	0
Nonprod. Adm./Mgmt.	0	0	2	0	1	0
Product Development	1	0	0	0	1	0
Non-CMT Prod./ Prod. Asst./Mgt.	2	6	0	1	0	1
Design/Design Asst.	3	2	0	0	2	0
Specifications/ Piece Goods	1	1	0	0	0	0
Quality Control	0	0	0	0	0	0
Skilled Blue-Collar	1	1	0	0	0	0
Pattern/Sample Maker	1	1	0	0	0	0
Blue-Collar	6	11	5	5	4	4
Ship./Rec./Warehse.	2	7	4	4	2	3
CMT[a]	4	4	0	0	2	1
All Unskilled Labor	0	0	1	1	0	0

Source: Kessler and Wong 2000.

[a]Cut, Make (sewing); Trim: Most manufacturers do not employ CMT; CMT work is done by contractors, which were not included in this survey.

NAFTA's benefits and the way in which the global economy recreates hierarchy and inequality at the local level. The clear winners are the large, resource-rich manufacturers and retailers that have capitalized on expanded opportunities for international sourcing. The future is less certain for the plethora of small apparel firms without the resources or infrastructure to establish profitable transnational production alliances. While NAFTA bodes well for the industry from a macroeconomic perspective, those least likely to benefit are the hundreds of small manufacturers, thousands of contractors, and many thousands of blue-collar workers who watch without recourse as their orders and their jobs move south. In her case study of the New York garment industry, Florence Palpacuer (Chapter 3 in this book) points out that the smaller garment firms—"second-tier manufacturers"—have neither the resources nor "the sophistication necessary to manage global production networks and focus on local production and its 'quick turn' advantage." The result is a growing number of "peripheral contractors" characterized by low technology, lack of industry experience, and high employee and company turnover. Jamie Peck (1996, 172) refers to this as "in situ restructuring strategy," as opposed to "spatial restructuring strategy," which is built around offshore sourcing.

Several projects are in the works to help apparel contractors upgrade and develop the capacity for private-label manufacturing. Most of these programs have failed, however, principally because they lacked the capital and know-how required to move from garment contracting to manufacturing. Aside from the start-up costs, which are formidable, contractors must develop infrastructures for product development, design, and other pre- and post-production activities. In a similar vein, there has been much talk recently among industry players about upgrading the skills of Los Angeles garment workers. In fact, most training programs currently in operation are geared either to produce more sewing operators in order to maintain a healthy supply of low-wage workers or to offer training in higher-skilled positions, with entry prerequisites far above the skills and education of most sewing operators. Few programs exist, in either the private or the public sector, that adequately address the needs of the thousands of immigrant workers who have been occupationally displaced as a result of NAFTA.

Finally, stepped-up monitoring for compliance and liability has undoubtedly figured in decisions to relocate production offshore. Increased efforts on the part of state and local governments to compel retailer and manufacturer responsibility for wage and safety violations roughly coincided with both the implementation of NAFTA and increases in federal and state minimum wages. Those respondents in my surveys who offered comments on the unionization of apparel workers did not consider union organizing efforts a threat to local production. However, many did cite escalating pressure by the government to hold them responsible for their contractors' work environments as contributing to their decision to relocate production offshore.

As firms increasingly source their production in Mexico, what will be left in Los Angeles? No one can say for certain whether the industry will go into decline or experience resurgence in higher-value, more fashion-sensitive production. Its strength lies in its flexibility, innovativeness, distinct image, and design. Nevertheless, NAFTA is drawing the top end of production (in terms of firm size and resources) to Mexico. Left behind are fashion-sensitive firms that must keep production close at hand (and can afford to do so, based on their price point) and a growing number of small manufacturers that have no recourse but to rely on local, often sweatshop, production.

As the transnational regional apparel economy continues to restructure in the wake of NAFTA, its future on both sides of the border remains unclear. From an industry perspective, the Los Angeles garment center and its hinterlands must let go of what it has already lost and move quickly and strategically to exploit its competitive advantages. It is likely that the Southern California apparel industry will reemerge as a design, information, and high-technology center, efficiently networked to growing apparel production centers in Mexico.

In this scenario, the winners are found at the highest-value-added segments of the apparel commodity chain: retailers, manufacturers, and skilled white-collar workers. The losers occupy the least-remunerated links in the chain: thousands of contractors, sewing operators, and other low-paid blue-collar laborers. As economic integration creates new knowledge-intensive jobs, the fate of thousands of small manufacturers, contractors, and displaced immigrant garment workers challenges the integrity and resources of a region in transition from garment making to fashion creation, and from a site of local garment makers to a coordinating hub of global apparel production.

Appendix: Methodology

The research reported in this chapter was primarily obtained through two surveys, thereby providing the only longitudinal study of leading Los Angeles apparel manufacturers. The first survey was conducted by Edna Bonacich and Richard Appelbaum in 1992 and included 184 Los Angeles County manufacturers with annual sales in excess of roughly $10 million (out of a population of approximately 255 apparel firms), accounting for an estimated two-thirds of the dollar value of wholesale production (for details, see Bonacich and Appel-

baum 2000). The follow-up survey was carried out by Judi Kessler from August 1997 to March 1998. The 1997–98 survey represents the first phase of a larger study that examines Mexico's role in global apparel production as part of the Southern California–Mexico transnational apparel production region.

The 1997–98 sample represents about half of the 184 firms surveyed in 1992 that were still in operation (including eleven companies not surveyed in 1992). Of the 184 firms surveyed in 1992, 7 have since relocated their headquarters outside Los Angeles County; 46 are no longer manufacturing or have closed down; and 4 have changed ownership. Of the 127 remaining firms, 1 was actually headquartered in Northern California at the time of the 1992 survey. Since this firm had a large distribution center in Los Angeles and was surveyed in 1992, it was included in the 1997 population of firms. The 1997–98 sample closely resembles the profile of the firms surveyed in 1992, at least in terms of sales volume. We therefore conclude that it is a fairly representative sample of our original data set. The 66 firms' 1996–97 yearly sales volume ranged from $3.5 million to $132 million. Five percent of the sample had yearly sales under $10 million; 53 percent, between $10 million and $29 million; 20 percent, from $30 to $49 million; 9 percent, from $50 to $69 million. Two percent fell between $70 and $89 million, and 11 percent had yearly sales volumes of $90 million or greater.

Finally, I conducted in-depth interviews with apparel accountants, labor officials, contractors, apparel and textile manufacturers, representatives of government agencies, and leading figures in the industry in both Southern California and Mexico to obtain a more detailed understanding of the changes that had occurred since NAFTA.

In 2000, Linda Wong of the Community Development and Technologies Center and I conducted eighty-one structured and semi-structured interviews with Los Angeles County apparel manufacturers. This sample differed from that of 1997–98 in that it included a group of smaller manufacturers, with $5 million to $9.9 million in yearly revenues. Otherwise it closely resembled the earlier survey. The sample was derived from an updated version of the 1997–98 database of manufacturers, as well as lists provided by the Fashion Institute of Design and Merchandising, which produced a population of approximately three hundred Los Angeles apparel manufacturers with yearly revenues of $5 million or greater. In addition to gathering current data on manufacturers' sourcing patterns, we asked questions about the relationship between offshore production and NAFTA and the firms' hiring patterns, practices, personnel demographics, and trends in the size of blue-collar and white-collar employee cohorts.

Notes

1. "Turn time" refers to the time it takes to turn apparel specifications into a finished product.

2. A manufacturer is defined as the designer, brand-name company, or producer of private-label garments. Manufacturers do little actual manufacturing per se; instead, they coordinate production, as opposed to garment contractors, who are responsible for cutting, sewing, and finishing. Most Southern California manufacturers outsource most or all production; their primary activities include product development, design, coordination of production networks, and marketing and image creation.

3. Recently the city, prodded by industry leaders, changed "garment district" to the more trendy "fashion district" in order to emphasize the industry's higher-value-added activities.

4. For an in-depth analysis of the constituents and politics of the Los Angeles garment industry, see Bonacich and Appelbaum (2000).

5. Full-package production (also called original equipment manufacture, or OEM) represents a step forward from garment assembly. In the latter, the contractor is responsible for the assembly of precut fabric. In the former, the contractor coordinates the "full package," from the acquisition of fabric, trim, and other materials to the production of a finished product.

6. These firms have yearly sales of $10 million or greater. This population accounts for approximately 13 percent of all Southern California manufacturers. The larger manufacturers, however, represent an estimated two-thirds of the dollar value of wholesale apparel production in the region (for details, see Bonacich and Appelbaum 2000).

7. See, for example, Hinojosa Ojeda et al. (1996).

8. These are respondents in the $10 million or greater yearly sales category, which matches the 1992 and 1997 samples.

9. Note that total sourcing percentages often exceed 100. This is because some firms have multiple sourcing sites.

10. Trade enhancements granted to the Caribbean Basin Initiative (CBI) countries under the new Trade and Development Act of 2000 have opened up Southern California to yet another offshore production region. Future research will reveal whether Los Angeles manufacturers continue to shift production further south and how production processes are apportioned among Southern California, Mexico, and Central America.

11. We were surprised to find that firms once considered too small to source offshore now have a significant production presence outside the United States. Of the subset of twenty-four Los Angeles apparel firms interviewed in 2000 with yearly revenues of $5 to $9.9 million, almost half were sourcing at least some production outside the United States.

12. Once home to an estimated ten thousand knitting machines, Southern California has lost an estimated one thousand machines as mills have been unable to survive the recent skyrocketing natural-gas prices (Dickerson 2001).

13. California state legislation mandated a minimum-wage increase to $5.75, effective March 1998 (see DesMarteau 1997, 44).

14. In the textile and apparel industry, factors advance funds to the manufacturer, based on collateral, previous-account credit approval, and a

commission. The factor, in effect, is actually buying a percentage of the receivables from the manufacturer and assuming full responsibility for their collection (as well as the risk of default).

15. See Gereffi (1999) for a detailed account of East Asian production networks.

16. The author's fieldwork from 1997 to 2000 was conducted in the city of Tijuana (border); Mexico City and the states of Mexico, Puebla, Morelos, and Guanajuato (central); and the state of Nayarit (west coast).

17. According to Bruce Berton (1997a) of Stonefield Josephson, reliable freight transport services provide full insurance coverage of transported goods. However, transportation of goods to the United States remains one of the highest costs of doing business in Mexico. Consequently, manufacturers often try to cut corners by contracting with less-than-reliable ground transport services. There are some indications that recent anti-crime measures implemented in Mexico seem to be paying off: Truck robberies dropped from twenty-one a day in 1997 to sixteen in early 1999, and hijackings were down 16 percent in the first four months of 2000 (Malkin 2000, 74).

18. The name is not a pseudonym.

19. The exception was 1993, a time of recession in Los Angeles' garment industry. The next year saw an increase of almost six thousand apparel workers.

20. The Fair Labor Standards Act prohibits the shipment of goods into commerce that have been *(a)* made in violation of minimum-wage or overtime provisions or *(b)* produced in an establishment at which prohibited child labor is used. This law affects both the contractor and the manufacturer (who owns the goods). Hot-goods garments may be confiscated by federal officials.

21. The Los Angeles Jewish Commission on Sweatshops was a coalition of Jewish educators, religious leaders, and activists. The commission's primary goal was to eradicate sweatshops and afford garment workers the freedom to unionize without recriminations. In general, its strategy was to force the larger Los Angeles manufacturers and contractors into compliance by confronting them with the Jewish religious perspective on labor rights. Most of the chief executive officers and owners of large apparel firms self-identify as Jews and are active in a variety of Jewish charity organizations. The commission, created in 1997, is no longer in existence.

22. In an attempt to extend wage violations to retailers, the California legislature passed Assembly Bill (AB) 633, "The Garment Workers Protection Act," in 1999. The law's original intent was to hold both manufacturers and retailers responsible for minimum-wage and overtime violations by California contractors. Proposed regulations for AB 633 were not issued until July 2001. As of the fall of 2001, the regulations had not yet been finalized for adoption, due to challenges by manufacturers and retailers over interpretations of AB 633's allegedly ambiguous wording. Most industry insiders expect the law to be interpreted in favor of retailers, leaving them once again out of the liability loop.

23. While most of the smaller manufacturers monitor for compliance, some respondents to the 2000 survey indicated that they did not regularly monitor their contractors, and two claimed they had never heard of monitoring.

24. See Gereffi, Garcia-Johnson, and Sasser (2001) for a discussion of apparel monitoring initiatives in the United States, Mexico, and Central America.

25. The U.S. Department of Labor's Wage and Hours Division, California's Division of Labor Standards Enforcement (DLSE), and the Division of Occupational Safety and Health (DOSH) of the Department of Industrial Relations participated in this survey. Civil penalties and Notice to Discontinue labor-law violations were issued to violators by the DLSE. A total of eighty-three civil penalties in the amount of $138,100 were issued to 59 employers out of the 101 inspected; failure to pay the minimum wage accounted for twenty-two of the eighty-three penalties (California DLSE 2000, 2).

26. Having seen the writing on the wall, UNITE has increasingly turned its attention from the rapidly declining U.S. textile and apparel workforce to unorganized workers in the service sectors, whose jobs are less vulnerable to the centrifugal forces of globalization (see Friedman 1999, 6).

27. Most firms cited multiple factors responsible for decreased or increased hiring.

28. Despite the fact that over 23 percent of NAFTA-TAA (Trade Adjustment Assistance)

certified workers nationwide are in the apparel industry and 12 percent of U.S. apparel industry employment is located in Los Angeles County, as of May 1996 there had been *no* apparel-sector TAA applications, let alone certifications, in Los Angeles.

29. These figures are for officially recorded workers and employees only. Taking into account the underground economy, total apparel employment at its peak was probably at least 25 percent higher than state data indicate.

References

Appelbaum, Richard P., and Gary Gereffi. 1994. "Power and Profits in the Apparel Commodity Chain." In *Global Production: The Apparel Industry in the Pacific Rim*, ed. Edna Bonacich, Lucie Cheng, Norma Chinchilla, Nora Hamilton, and Paul Ong, pp. 46–62. Philadelphia: Temple University Press.

Appiah, Anthony K. 1998. "Foreword." In *Globalization and Its Discontents*, by Saskia Sassen, pp. xi–xv. New York: New Press.

Berton, Bruce. 1997a. "Mexico Sourcing Opportunities." A Stonefield Josephson, Inc., Workshop, 1620 Twenty-sixth Street, Santa Monica, Calif. October 15.

———. 1997b. Interview with author, Stonefield Josephson, Inc., Santa Monica, California, December 2.

Bonacich, Edna, and Richard P. Appelbaum. 1992. Unpublished data from the "Los Angeles Apparel Manufacturers' Survey," a project of the Pacific Rim Research Program of the University of California, Oakland.

———. 2000. *Behind the Label: Inequality in the Los Angeles Apparel Industry*. Berkeley: University of California Press.

California Division of Labor Standards Enforcement (DLSE). 2000. *Apparel Industry Survey, Southern California, Year 2000*. Report by the Division of Labor Standards Enforcement, Department of Industrial Relations, State of California, August 25.

California Employment Development Department (EDD). 1998. "Occupational Employment Projections, 1995–2001." *Projections—September*

1998, Employment Development Department— Labor Market Information Division. Available at <http://www.calmis.cahwnet.gov>.

———. 1999. "Employment by Occupation and Wage Estimates for SIC 23." Unpublished data from 1996–97 survey of SIC 23 firms in the Los Angeles–Long Beach Primary Metropolitan Statistical Area. Employment Development Department—Labor Market Information Division.

———. 2001. "Los Angeles County Labor Force Data, 1983–2000." Employment Development Department—Labor Market Information Division. Available at <http://www.calmis.cahwnet. gov>.

Cleeland, Nancy. 1999. "Garment Jobs: Hard, Bleak, and Vanishing." *Los Angeles Times*, March 11, A1, A16–17.

———. 2001. "Study Cites Drop in Enforcement of Labor Laws." *Los Angeles Times*, June 30, C1.

DesMarteau, Kathleen. 1997. "Industry Takes a Hit with Higher Minimum Wage . . . and Warily Anticipates Long-Term Effects." *Bobbin* 39, 4 (December): 44–46.

Dickerson, Marla. 2001. "Repossessions Rise as Textile Firms Unravel." *Los Angeles Times*, June 3, C1.

Friedman, Arthur. 1999. "UNITE's New Members: Beyond Its Core." *Women's Wear Daily*, December 28.

Gereffi, Gary. 1997. "Global Shifts, Regional Responses: Can North American Meet the Full Package Challenge?" *Bobbin* 39, 3 (November): 16–31.

———. 1999. "International Trade and Industrial Upgrading in the Apparel Commodity Chain." *Journal of International Economics* 48, 1 (June): 37–70.

———. 2000. "The Mexico-U.S. Apparel Connection: Economic Dualism and Transnational Networks." In *Poverty or Development: Global Restructuring and Regional Transformations in the U.S. South and the Mexican South*, ed. Richard Tardanico and Mark B. Rosenberg, pp. 59–89. New York: Routledge.

Gereffi, Gary, Ronie Garcia-Johnson, and Erika Sasser. 2001. "The NGO-Industrial Complex." *Foreign Policy* 125 (July–August): 56–65.

Goodman, Charles S. 1948. *The Location of Fashion Industries, with Special Reference to the Cali-*

fornia Apparel Market. Ann Arbor: University of Michigan Press.

Hinojosa Ojeda, Raúl, Curt Dowds, Robert McCleery, Sherman Robinson, David Runsten, Craig Wolff, and Goetz Wolff. 1996. *North American Integration Three Years after NAFTA.* Los Angeles: UCLA North American Integration and Development Center.

Kessler, Judi. 1998. "Southern California: Transition Takes Hold." *Bobbin* 40, 2 (October): 30–38.

———. 1999a. "The North American Free Trade Agreement, Emerging Apparel Production Networks and Industrial Upgrading: The Southern California/Mexico Connection." *Review of International Political Economy* 6, 4: 565–608.

———. 1999b. "North American Economic Integration, Transnational Apparel Production Networks, and Industrial Upgrading: The Southern California-Mexico Connection." Ph.D. diss., Department of Sociology, University of California, Santa Barbara, August.

Kessler, Judi A., and Linda Wong. 2000. "Summary Report: NAFTA Apparel Occupations Project." Unpublished survey.

Los Angeles Economic Development Corporation (LAEDC). 2000. *The Los Angeles Area Apparel Industry Profile.* Los Angeles: LAEDC. May.

Los Angeles Jewish Commission on Sweatshops. 1999. *Los Angeles Jewish Commission on Sweatshops.* Self-published report, January.

Loucky, James, Maria Soldatenko, Gregory Scott, and Edna Bonacich. 1994. "Immigrant Enterprise and Labor in the Los Angeles Garment Industry." In *Global Production: The Apparel Industry in the Pacific Rim,* ed. Edna Bonacich, Lucie Cheng, Norma Chinchilla, Nora Hamilton, and Paul Ong, pp. 345–61. Philadelphia: Temple University Press.

Malkin, Elizabeth. 2000. "Sounding the Alarm in Mexico." *Business Week,* June 26.

Peck, Jamie. 1996. *Work-Place: The Social Regulation of Labor Markets.* New York and London: Guilford Press.

Reach, Jim. 1999. Interview with author, Los Angeles, California, August.

Southern California Edison Company. 1995. *Southern California's Apparel Industry: Building a Path to Prosperity.* Self-published report, February.

Twin Plant News. 1999. "Maquila Scoreboard." *Twin Plant News,* February.

———. 2001. "Maquila Scoreboard." *Twin Plant News,* February.

U.S. Department of Labor. 2000. "Only One-third of Southern California Garment Shops in Compliance with Federal Labor Laws." Press release, U.S. Department of Labor Employment Standards Administration, Wage and Hours Division, August 25. Available at <http://www.dol.gov/dol/esa/public/media/press/whd/sfwh112.htm>.

Robert J. S. Ross

5   The New Sweatshops in the
     United States: How New, How Real,
     How Many, and Why?

Introduction

Starting in the late 1970s, investigative journalists noticed what they understood as the reemergence of extreme exploitation of laborers in the domestic United States apparel industry (e.g., Buck 1979). Academic studies of the issue began to appear in the early 1980s (Ross and Trachte 1983). But two challenges confront the idea that sweatshops are reemerging. One challenge contends that, like the poor, whom "always ye have with you" (John 12:8), sweatshops were always with us, never really going away (Proper 1997a; Alman 1997; Ross 1997). At the other extreme, one of the most knowledgeable of all sociologists studying the apparel industry has argued in a highly technical paper that sweatshops do not exist (Waldinger and Lapp 1993). He and his colleague have not been refuted in print. The task of determining whether the new sweatshops are new—indeed, whether they exist at all—is not a trivial exercise.

Assuming for the moment that sweatshops do exist, if they are new, then, logically, they must have disappeared or become quantitatively insignificant at some point. Causal explanation would require isolating the conditions that changed.

The first task of this chapter is to show the extent of sweatshop exploitation in the apparel industry in the current period. This part of the chapter meets Roger Waldinger's challenge: The answer to "How real?" is subsumed in the answer to "How many?" The next challenge is to show that the type of superexploitation of labor termed "sweatshop" became quantitatively insignificant for some period of time before the late 1960s. This constitutes a response to the question "How new?"

I answer the question of why the new sweatshops emerged by discussing changes in industrial structure, world trade, and state regulatory capacity. The theoretical framework in the background is that of *Global Capitalism* (Ross and Trachte 1990). While Robert Ross and Kent Trachte used the concept of "the disaggregation of the production process over space," the term *global commodity chains* (Gereffi and Korzeniewicz 1994) is both more euphonious and in wider usage among sociologists, and I employ it here. I also touch briefly on the concept "informal economy."

Method and Definition

This research adopts a restrictive but objective definition of a sweatshop: *a business that regularly violates both wage or child-labor and safety or health laws* (U.S. GAO 1988). The definition depends on the Fair Labor Standards Act, which establishes a minimum wage and also requires premium pay for hours exceeding forty in one week. In addition, the Fair Labor Standards Act prohibits child labor and industrial homework in large branches of apparel making. Violations of state and federal workplace safety laws—for example, the regulations enforced by the Occupational Safety and Health Administration (OSHA)—are also included in the definition. The Wage and Hours Division of the U.S. Department of Labor is responsible for enforcing the Fair Labor Standards Act. Local authorities (e.g., fire departments) are also responsible for enforcing some safety laws. The U.S. Department of Labor and the apparel workers union (Union of Needletrades, Industrial, and Textile Employees, or UNITE) often summarize the definition as "multiple labor-law violator" or "chronic labor-law violator." By emphasizing persistent violations, the definition includes nontrivial behavior and excludes occasional lapses.

A clear logic led the General Accounting Office (GAO) of the U.S. Congress to invent this definition. Asked by a congressman to investigate the prevalence of sweatshops in the late 1980s, the GAO first had to define the condition for which it was looking. The GAO arrived at a definition that depends on the legal framework of minimum standards that has evolved in the U.S. context over a period of fifty years. This definition has the same virtue for researchers as it has for the GAO: One can objectively define a violator and thus count (or estimate) the number of violators. It is much harder to study the prevalence of a condition if each of its defining characteristics is subjective and totally contextual. The term *sweat-shop* is a vivid metaphor for a "lousy" job (see below); the challenge for research is to turn metaphor into something measurable.

There is a cost to the clarity thus gained. Even if an employer does pay the minimum wage and does pay an overtime premium for longer hours, the ordinary moral sensibility of our culture might still judge the wage too low. For example, the minimum wage will not lift a family of three out of poverty. By removing the word *sweatshop* from the realm of metaphor and subjective moralism to that of a legal test, the GAO definition leaves many low-paying jobs with "lousy" conditions unsullied by the label. Principally for this reason, the GAO definition is not consensual (Rothstein 1996; Ross 1997b; S. Green 1997; Waldinger and Lapp 1993; A. Ross 1997, 296).

The most common criticism of the legalistic definition is that it is arbitrary, and it confers moral dignity to bad pay. Yet, besides the fact that the GAO definition is most useful for research purposes, it may be defended on other grounds. The framework of social protections embodied in labor and public health law defines what Karl Marx would have called the "historical and moral element," which is part of the determination of the value of labor power (Marx 1867). By reserving the term *sweatshop* for those workplaces that do not meet even the low standards of public law, the definition denotes "superexploitation," that is, something even more extreme than "low pay."

In practice, shops in the apparel industry that violate the wage or overtime laws almost always violate both, which are known collectively as the "monetary provisions" of the Fair Labor Standards Act. An even higher proportion violates OSHA safety regulations. Thus, in the ordinary discourse of enforcement—for example, when the U.S. Department of Labor releases quarterly enforcement reports as part of its "No Sweat" program—chronic and nontrivial minimum-wage violations are taken as *indicators* of sweatshop conditions.

Looking for Covert Sweatshops

In an important article, Waldinger and Michael Lapp (1993) use an indirect and, indeed, ingenious method to claim there is little sweatshop labor in the New York region's apparel industry. A discussion of their method and findings illustrates the ambiguity of the idea of "informal economy" and the dangers inherent in its literal use.

Waldinger and Lapp argue that the consensus estimating technique that suggested as many as fifty thousand sweatshop workers in New York in the 1980s is based on erroneous guesses. They point out that over the 1990s a series of scholars (including myself) have generated estimates by citing each other's guesses.

They then proceed to examine whether indirect measures of sweatshops indicate a marked increase in "covert" workers.[1] They argue that a marked decrease in manufacturing wages as a ratio of value added in manufacturing would indicate an increase in covert production workers. The proportion of production workers to all workers should also decrease if a substantial fraction of production workers are working "off the books"— paid in cash by contractors. Waldinger and Lapp demonstrate that wages as a proportion of value added declined by about 10 percent in the 1970s and 1980s in the nation overall, as well as in New York and California. This decline indicates productivity gains but no differences between the nation as a whole and the areas likely to foster sweatshops. Further, they find no reduction in the number of production workers as a proportion of all workers in the garment industry. They conclude that a low-wage immigrant garment industry exists but that estimates of large increases in covert, or sweatshop, employment are overstated.

While there is reason for skepticism about estimates based on anecdote and even on informed opinion, Waldinger and Lapp's approach demonstrates severe methodological problems. The most important problem is embedded in their definition of shops that are "off the books" and thus in the "informal sector." The authors assume that the bulk of sweatshop workers will not show up as workers on tax or other official payrolls. Yet investigators from the Wage and Hours Division of the U.S. Department of Labor and from the New York Labor Department often find that shops that are multiple labor or health-and-safety law violators do show up in official records (U.S. GAO 1994). Evidence that the majority of sweatshops may be "visible" to some official records appears in the GAO study of tax compliance of sweatshops in New York and California (U.S. GAO 1994)—published after Waldinger and Lapp's 1993 article. In that study, composed of the violators *known* to the departments of labor of the two states, the GAO found that in New York City, fifteen of twenty-one sweatshops filed state taxes at least once between 1990 and 1994; in California, thirty-eight of forty-four had done so. Of the ninety-four sites (including restaurants) studied in the two states, only eight had not filed unemployment payroll taxes.[2]

The idea of an informal economy does not require total invisibility. In apparel shops, for example, workers are often asked to start work *before* they punch in on the legally required time clock. Manuel Castells and Alejandro Portes (1989, 12) note "the systematic linkage between formal and informal sectors, *following the requirements of profitability*" (emphasis added). The informal sector, they say, "is unregulated by the institutions of society in a legal and social environment in which similar activities are regulated." Indeed, as we see in the apparel industry, the subcontracting system allows for an elaborate and complex texture in which the formal and informal, the recorded and unrecorded, are woven among closely related though fictively distinct entities. As between manufacturers and contractors, some contractor practices are closely inspected (e.g., quality control), while others "escape" the notice of the commissioning principal; and the contractors and their subcontractors record some activities that are legal, while others that may be illicit are "cash only."[3]

The last point is especially significant for Waldinger and Lapp's method because it subverts the statistical underpinning of their conclusion. Indeed, their conclusion results in large part from their definition of sweatshops as referring only to firms that are totally covert. They write, "While Chinatown's garment contractors may include many firms that cheat on hours and wage laws ... they are clearly not underground" (Waldinger and Lapp 1993, 15). Violations among New York's Chinatown contractors are difficult to find. Yet Min Zhou (1992) surveyed more than four hundred of Chinatown's women workers and found their *average* wage was below the legal minimum. The Department of Labor found that 90 percent of New York City's Chinatown shops were labor-law violators (U.S. DOL 1997). According to Waldinger and Lapp, however, such employers are not sweatshops because they are not "underground."

Waldinger and Lapp used a very technical input-output technique and found no evidence for a completely off-the-books apparel sector. Their conclusion should have been that the concept of an informal sector is relative, not absolute, instead of the conclusion at which they arrived: that there is no significant sweatshop sector in the apparel industry.

The New Sweatshops: Prevalence

The evidence of sweatshop prevalence derives from reports of state and federal departments of labor and GAO surveys, which, unlike Waldinger and Lapp, examine compliance with the Fair Labor Standards Act and OSHA regulations.

Los Angeles and Southern California, 1994–2000

Four times in the 1990s the U.S. Department of Labor, the California State Labor Commissioner's Office, and California's Occupational Safety and Health Administration cooperated in surveys of garment contractors in Southern California and, in particular, in the Los Angeles region. The California Division of Labor Standards Enforcement (DLSE) initiated a Targeted Industries Partnership Program (TIPP) in 1992, and these surveys were a cooperative venture of TIPP (California DLSE 1996). In 1994 and 1996 the firms surveyed were randomly selected from California Employment Development Department (EDD) records of firms in SIC 2300.[4] Since the first survey (1994) showed that 80 percent of the firms were in the five-county area of the Los Angeles Basin, the 1996 survey focused on this region. The data were then reanalyzed to make comparisons between them valid.

In 1994, 78 percent of the firms had either minimum-wage or overtime violations of the law; these are called the monetary provisions of the Fair Labor Standards Act. Ninety-eight percent had some general kind of violation, most frequently record keeping. The average number of violations (out of ten categories) was four and one-half.[5] By 1996, 61 percent of seventy-six firms studied had monetary violations. (The reduction was not statistically significant according to the California DLSE.) That year almost three-quarters of the firms (72 percent) had serious OSHA violations; 43 percent had minimum-wage violations; and 55 percent had overtime violations. The average back pay owed due to minimum-wage violations in 1996 was $1,592 for each worker; the average back pay owed for overtime violations was $1,643. At minimum wage ($4.75 in 1996), the most a fully employed worker would have received annually for standard workweeks was around $9,500. The back pay due was almost

17 percent of base pay; the overtime pay due was just over 17 percent. If a worker were subject to both violations, she would have been short 34 percent of potential base pay. None of these numbers is trivial for the working poor, although they were lower than the numbers for 1994 (U.S. DOL 1996).

A voluntary program of compliance monitoring, in which the "manufacturers" (i.e., jobbers who hire contractors) undertake to monitor the labor-law compliance of their agents, has been the primary enforcement innovation of the Department of Labor. Compliance monitoring does, according to these surveys, reduce violations noticeably. The percentage of firms with wage liabilities was significantly less for monitored firms (48 percent) than for those not monitored (78 percent). A little less than half the firms studied (48 percent) were monitored.[6]

In 1998 the Department of Labor found compliance rates in Los Angeles had not appreciably increased (U.S. DOL 1998). In August 2000 the department and the cooperating California agencies released the results of their latest study to date: Only one-third of garment contractors examined complied with labor law, and only 37 percent of a random sample of previously cited violators complied with the law (U.S. DOL 2000).

In sum, considerably over one-half of a random sample of firms engaged in apparel manufacturing in Southern California had multiple labor-law violations in the mid-1990s, in particular monetary and environmental law offenses. Estimates of the number of apparel workers in the region run between 120,000 and 150,000. These data justify an estimate that 70,000 to 90,000 workers labor in sweatshop conditions in Southern California. The survey was repeated in 1998 and again in 2000. The U.S. Department of Labor has reported that the level of monetary violations, that is, minimum wage or overtime violations, has remained the same as that in 1996—over 60 percent.

San Francisco, 1995–97

In the smaller labor market of the San Francisco Bay Area, in surveys whose details have not been released, the U.S. Department of Labor found Fair Labor Standards Act (wages and hours) violations at lower levels—43 percent in 1995 and only 21 percent in 1997 (Fraser 1998). No improvement was made in that small (ten-thousand-worker) labor market by 1999: Seventy-four percent of "Bay Area garment businesses comply with the minimum wage, overtime pay and other requirements of the Fair Labor Standards Act, not a significant change from a similar 1997 survey, and up . . . from 57 percent in 1995" (U.S. DOL 1999a).

New York 1997, 1999

A 1997 U.S. Department of Labor survey of ninety-four New York City garment shops was intended, as was the 1994 Los Angeles study, to create a baseline for future findings:

> The New York City survey consisted of a random sample of the latest available information regarding known garment contractors in all five boroughs. Among other purposes, this and other investigation-based surveys help establish a statistically valid baseline of compliance in order to track industry compliance over the long term. (U.S. DOL 1997)

In this study the Department of Labor found that 63 percent of the firms violated the minimum-wage and overtime provisions of the Fair Labor Standards Act, and 70 percent violated the record-keeping requirements of the law. In Chinatown, 90 percent of the firms violated the monetary provisions of the law. That year one hundred thousand garment production workers were estimated to be in the New York area, so 63 percent of the total would be about sixty-three thousand workers—well over the fifty-thousand-worker estimate (Ross and Trachte 1983) that Waldinger and Lapp (1993) criticized so harshly.

Throughout the period under discussion (the 1970s to the 1990s) employment in the apparel industry declined drastically, particularly in New York City. Apparel employment in New York City declined from 340,000 jobs in 1950, to 140,000 in 1980, to an estimated 90,000 in the mid-1990s (Ross and Trachte 1983; Proper 1997b). The fifty thousand sweatshop-worker estimate of the early 1980s constituted a much smaller fraction of the total apparel labor force than the fifty to sixty thousand estimate for the late 1990s. The number of sweatshop workers thus increased both relatively and absolutely.[7] In 1999 contractor violations of the Fair Labor Standards Act in New York continued at an unchanged rate (U.S. DOL 1999b).

Underestimation? Estimation!

Whereas Waldinger and Lapp (1993) exaggerated the invisibility of the sweatshop sector of apparel manufacturing, the U.S. Department of Labor and California DLSE data almost certainly underestimate the size of the sector. The official agencies' violations data are based exclusively on firms that have *some* legal visibility to authorities. Contractors who are totally cash based and have no legal existence do not appear in their data; more important, the labor force of contractors who illegally give workers bundles to sew at home is absent from these data. Large segments of the Dallas garment industry are thus excluded, not to mention New York's Chinatown and numerous Mexican workers in Los Angeles.

On the basis of the data from the two leading production centers of the industry, Los Angeles and New York, more than 60 percent of contractor shops in the visible industry are found to harbor sweatshop conditions. In the late 1990s more than eight hundred thousand apparel workers were on record in the United States (Fraser 1998); this number included over 380,000 sewing-machine operators and

another 150,000 employees in job categories likely to be found in contractor shops, for example, dry cleaning. There are, then, about 538,000 recorded workers in apparel jobs who are vulnerable to sweatshop conditions. In addition, it is likely that another 20 percent of the sewing-machine operators are home workers or unrecorded. Adding 61 percent of the recorded base and all the unrecorded sewing operators produces an estimate of more than four hundred thousand workers laboring in sweatshop conditions in the United States in 1998.[8] Strikingly, employment declined in the central apparel production segment of the industry (the above estimate includes a small portion of knitted products) by a full one hundred thousand workers between 1998 and 2000 (U.S. Bureau of Labor Statistics 2001). The number of sweatshop workers may therefore have declined; the rate of abuse has not.

How New Are the New Sweatshops? Evidence for the Decline of Sweatshops

The evidence for sweatshop decline from approximately 1942 to the late 1970s includes the following sources:

- statements from officials and documents of the International Ladies Garment Workers Union (ILGWU);
- studies done by independent scholars;
- examination of the conditions of Puerto Rican workers in New York City's garment industry in the 1950s.

Quantifiable surveys such as those conducted in the 1990s by the Department of Labor and cooperating state agencies are not available to compare the 1950s to the current period. Instead, with one exception, reasonable inferences drawn from the observations of knowledgeable analysts and our own logical retrospect must suffice to approach the question.

The exception, based on a casually observed fact in a journalist's account of Puerto Rican areas of Harlem in Manhattan in the 1950s, allows a sketchy quantitative estimate of sweatshop conditions in New York in that decade.

The Union Perspective

Publications from and statements by the ILGWU support the view that sweatshops declined for roughly a thirty-year period. As early as 1944, a historian closely associated with the apparel unions wrote in the past tense, "In the old sweatshop days the garment worker lived in an environment, industrial and social, which was a major outrage to every rule of public health" (Stolberg 1944, 299).

In a report prepared for the ILGWU in 1951, Emil Schlesinger[9] also spoke of the sweatshop and sweatshop-related conditions in past tense. His emphasis was mostly on the union's success at countering the effects of the "outside system of production," that is, the nonunion subcontracting firms that once were the sweatshops of the apparel industry. Schlesinger remarked on how, "in the past," an employer would pay his overhead expenses and "with what little there was left, he would pay his workers. If nothing was left, his workers were not paid" (Schlesinger 1951, 6). More clearly, Schlesinger states, "The sweatshops have been wiped out; the days of their existence are among the most shameful pages of recorded history" (Schlesinger 1951, 90).

Also in the 1950s, union officials considered the problem behind them. Speaking at the groundbreaking ceremony for a union-sponsored housing project, ILGWU president David Dubinsky said, as reported in the union's newspaper, "Now 50 years later, the garment workers return to their place of origin. We have wiped out the sweatshop. Now we return to wipe out the slum" (Dubinsky 1953, 268). When Dubinsky referred to this cere-

mony again in 1955, he wrote of its Lower East Side site: "Only a few of the old structures remain standing on this site. When their walls come tumbling down the last sign of the slum and the sweatshop will disappear for ever from this corner of Manhattan" (Dubinsky 1955, 267). He described the sweatshops of the past in somber tones: "There were rooms in these houses where the sun never shone. There were rooms in these houses in which children slaved over bundles of garment work, breathing in the foul air that made them tubercular before they were grown up. There were rooms in these houses in which, in a not too distant past, men and women worked to the point where they dropped" (Dubinsky 1955, 267). In conclusion, Dubinsky stated, "We cannot forget the poverty, the sickness, the homework shops, the child laborers of their neighborhood" (Dubinsky 1955, 268). These statements suggest that in the eyes of the union leadership, sweatshop conditions, as early as the 1940s and certainly by the early 1950s, were no longer characteristic of the apparel workers' conditions in New York's industry.

Such claims might be viewed skeptically by those knowledgeable about union politics. Dubinsky had risen to political dominance in his union through a bitter struggle with Communist rivals who had a political following among Jewish garment workers in particular. They had been militant in the 1920s and bitterly critical of him in the 1930s. Some might claim that, now ascendant while the Red Scare harassed his erstwhile enemies, Dubinsky was merely self-congratulatory. Certainly, Herbert Hill, the labor secretary of the National Association for the Advancement of Colored People (NAACP), thought Dubinsky and his union were puffed up and evasive, for he accused them of tolerating and even endorsing sweatshops for Black and Puerto Rican workers (Hill 1974). I address Hill's claims directly below. However skeptical we might be about

Dubinsky's political motives, others more removed from the ambit of his political career have come to similar conclusions about sweatshop decline.

Documentary and Economic Evidence

In her extensive research on apparel workers in Paris and New York, historian Nancy Green surveyed union records exhaustively. Her conclusion was that "the labor history of the industry as constructed through union records contrasts the sweatshops of the 1900s to the subsequent amelioration of conditions, thanks to union efforts and especially the legendary 1909–1910 strikes" (N. Green 1997, 158).

Green found corroborative evidence for the union's view. Among this evidence is the decline of homework. Briefly, industrial homework in the context of the apparel industry entails taking home sewing from a contractor's shop or being assigned sewing by a contractor without ever working in or going to the factory or workshop. The worst abuses of physical environment and low pay apparently occurred in the crowded tenements of immigrant neighborhoods such as the Lower East Side of New York at the beginning of the twentieth century.

While New York State, in the years directly after the Triangle Shirtwaist Factory fire of 1911, attempted to regulate and partially abolish homework, these laws were apparently ineffective in eliminating substandard conditions (N. Green 1997). Under the National Industrial Recovery Act of 1935 homework was prohibited, but that law was nullified by the Supreme Court. The Fair Labor Standards Act of 1938 began a period of effective federal regulation of this form of exploitation. Under the authority of this act, in 1942 Secretary of Labor Francis Perkins prohibited industrial homework from most branches of the apparel industry, except under permits, and these only under special circumstances such as that of

a handicapped worker (Boris 1994). Green reports that "it was estimated between 1935 and 1955 the number of homeworkers in New York State had dropped from 500,000 (in all fields) to less than 5,000" (N. Green 1997, 64). Furthermore, "in 1962, the New York State Department of Labor abolished its special homework unit due to 'apparent success' in policing homework and enforcing sanctions" (N. Green 1997, 152, citing New York State Department of Labor 1982). It is fair to infer that with unregulated home workers disappearing as a low-wage alternative to workshop labor, conditions in the New York apparel industry had improved by the 1950s.

Given our definition of a sweatshop as a place that violates the Fair Labor Standards Act and other laws, we must consider some sources of data to be contaminated: for example, Department of Labor wage surveys taken from employer-submitted records, where we are not likely to find that employers supplied material to show hourly wages below the legal minimum. Typically, law violators simply require employees to punch in their time cards (or equivalent records mandated by law) hours after the workers arrive for work or before they leave. Thus, too, reports of union success in bargaining for contracts with higher wages than the minimum (Laslett and Tyler 1989) and reports of high wages in New York or low but legal wages in places to which contractors fled to escape the union cannot tell us whether extensive illegal conditions were mitigated.

Uncontaminated by employer motives, census income data are collected from individuals. These retain ambiguity about the number of hours workers had to put in to earn the reported wages. Nevertheless, reporting 1970 census data on Puerto Rican women employed as apparel workers in New York City, Carol Smith indicates, "In 1969, median earnings for Puerto Rican operatives were $3,615" (1980, 71). For a standard workweek, this reported median works out to be $1.74 per hour, above the minimum wage ($1.60) for that year. Women who worked longer than forty-hour weeks for these wages may indeed have been working in de facto sweatshop conditions, but we do not have information corroborating this claim. However, we do have both claims of sweatshop exploitation of Puerto Rican women in the 1950s and 1960s and some investigations relevant to those claims.

Puerto Rican Sewing Operators in New York: Sweatshop as Metaphor

The sweatshop is seared into cultural memory. "Sweated labor" was a specific nineteenth-century usage for industries with middlemen who "sweated" direct homework producers. In Greek the usage *tsekouzisma*, "to squeeze the juices out," communicates the brutality of what came to be seen as an older, transcended moment in capitalist development. In the course of mid-twentieth-century American (and, more broadly, Western) capitalist development, the word's implications broadened. Now the word *sweatshop*, as Nancy Green (1997, 160) points out, has become a metaphor for bad conditions and below-standard pay. For example, in the *New York Times* of July 10, 1998, Steven Greenhouse reported on a long-simmering labor dispute in a New Orleans shipyard. Pay there ranged from $8 to over $13 per hour—hardly illegal—but the shipyard had a bad safety record, paid about $2 per hour less than a comparable yard in Mississippi, and had poor benefits. "It's a sweatshop, with such low wages," said Mike Boudreaux, a mechanic (Greenhouse 1998).

The use of the term *sweatshop* as a metaphor for a "lousy" job complicates historical research. The case of Puerto Rican sewing operators in New York City illustrates the problem and also the relevance of a clear definition. The details of Puerto Rican insertion in New York's garment industry also provide some evidence for sweatshop decline by the 1950s.

Between 1940 and 1960, New York's Puerto Rican population grew dramatically, from 61,000 to 612,000. With education below that of resident New Yorkers and often with language barriers to high-paying employment, Puerto Ricans in New York in 1960 had higher poverty rates than other New Yorkers. They were similar in many ways to today's Latino immigrants in New York. Furthermore, as with contemporary Dominicans (Pessar 1987), Puerto Rican women had a strong ethnic concentration in the New York apparel industry of the 1950s and 1960s: Some economists have asserted that their low-wage labor "saved" the industry in a period when it was experiencing rapid geographic losses (Rodriguez 1979).

At the time of maximum migration flow, at least two prominent observers used the term *sweatshop* to describe conditions of Puerto Rican sewing operators in New York. One was Herbert Hill, longtime labor secretary of the NAACP; the other was the distinguished journalist Dan Wakefield.

In testimony before Congress (U.S. Congress 1963), Hill railed against the political exclusion of Puerto Ricans and Blacks from the leadership of the ILGWU. He discussed the "callousness" with which union leaders tolerated low (but, according to our calculations, lawful) wages in those branches of the industry in which minority people were concentrated. At one point in his testimony, Hill referred to the ILGWU acceding to another union's sweetheart contract with a "sweatshop" employer.[10] (Hill's main purpose in his testimony to Congress and in his provocatively titled 1974 article "Guardians of the Sweatshop: The Trade Unions, Racism and the Garment Industry" was to condemn the ILGWU for discrimination and political exclusion of Puerto Ricans and Blacks, a matter we are neither disputing nor discussing.) In a 1974 article, Hill cited low wages in those branches of the New York garment industry where production workers were predominantly Puerto Rican or Black. He also cited a case history of the ILGWU, in the late 1950s, *opposing* a New York City minimum-wage law that was higher than the federal minimum. Yet Hill never indicated that the low wages he cited as examples were illegal. Indeed, by using the term *sweatshop* in quotes, Hill indicated he was employing the term as a metaphor for low wages and "lousy" conditions.

Another source for the claim that Puerto Rican women faced sweatshop conditions in New York's garment industry in the 1950s is journalist Dan Wakefield's 1957 reportage on New York City's Puerto Ricans—published two years later as *Island in the City* (1959). The fifth chapter of Wakefield's book is titled "Sweat without Profit" and tells of the new garment contractors in Spanish Harlem employing Puerto Rican women at low wages. Like Hill, Wakefield questions the motivation of the ILGWU in addressing these problems.

Yet Wakefield did not provide much information about the wages actually earned by the female sewing operators. One example he gave was of a woman who was told she would earn $42 per week (the minimum union scale)—slightly higher than the U.S. minimum wage ($1 per hour) at the time. Her take-home pay was only $29. Her employer is quoted as making a vague reference to taxes, suggesting that he was keeping the money that legally should have been set aside as taxes withheld. Yet the narrative does not demonstrate that the employer was paying subminimum wages.

These two sources, fairly clearly in sweatshop-as-metaphor mode, were used as corroboration for a more recent historical judgment. Professor Altagracia Ortiz (1990, 1996) has tracked the history of Puerto Rican women in New York's garment industry through much of this century. Although her main interest is

in the politics of the women's struggles in the ILGWU, Ortiz cites Hill and Wakefield and also oral history archives as evidence for sweatshops in New York in the 1950s. In the interviews, workers told of hard work for little pay. Yet Ortiz's report does not allow us to judge whether these women were paid below the minimum wage of that era, denied overtime payment, subjected to extensive health or safety hazards, or employed at a place with child-labor infractions. The interview material as cited in published work is too imprecise to allow a positive judgment about the existence of sweatshops as we have defined them.

One fact revealed by Wakefield's interviews offers the possibility of a very rough estimate of sweatshop incidence in New York in the 1950s. He reports an interview with a business agent of the ILGWU in East Harlem. The interviewee and Wakefield assume (in contrast to Hill) that a union shop is *ipso facto* not a sweatshop. Given Wakefield's willingness to criticize the union, there is some reason to accept this judgment. The union agent tells of thirty-five steadily operating shops in East Harlem (where the Puerto Rican population was then concentrated); a total of twenty-five were organized (Wakefield 1959, 201). With these slim facts, we can produce some estimates of sweatshop prevalence in 1950s New York City.

If we assume that 70 percent of the ten unorganized shops were substandard (i.e., sweatshops), there were seven sweatshops in East Harlem in 1957. If, in Spanish Harlem of the late 1950s, there were about seven *known* sweatshops, let us further assume that as many were unknown as known, for a total of fourteen. Let us then assume seventeen employees per shop. (The GAO has estimated that in the 1980s there were three thousand shops and fifty thousand workers. Since this is larger than the anecdotal reports of ten to twelve workers, we err only in overestimation.) This calculation would yield 238 sweatshop workers in Manhattan, according to our definition. We assume for this estimate that the almost wholly unionized Garment District in Manhattan had no sweatshops but that the new immigrant Puerto Ricans employed in peripheral areas may have been vulnerable.

We omit Chinatown from these calculations. Its recent immigrant and total population were lower in the 1950s and 1960s than in the 1970s and thereafter. Zhou (1992) reports hardly any apparel employment in Chinatown before the 1970s. We also exclude Staten Island and Queens because neither borough had a significant Puerto Rican population in the 1950s. If we assume equal numbers in the Bronx, Brooklyn, and Manhattan, the total number of workers in apparel sweatshops in New York City in the late 1950s would then be 714.

The estimated number of sweatshop employees in the 1980s in New York City ranged from thirty-three thousand to about fifty thousand (U.S. GAO 1993), so the estimated number in the late 1950s would be under 1.5 percent of the current number. Even if we more than double the 1950s estimate, to fifteen hundred, and use the low end of the GAO estimate as the denominator (fifteen hundred versus thirty-three thousand), the result is 4.5 percent of today's number. If this estimate is anywhere near correct, the problem was *not* quantitatively significant.

Historical Conclusion:
Sweatshops Were Marginal

The combination of union, documentary, and contextual evidence in New York leads to a confirmation of the conclusion reached in 1997 by Alan Howard, working for UNITE: "At various points over the past century the power of the sweatshop to depress the wages and living conditions of workers throughout the industry has been reduced and even neu-

tralized by the power of workers to defend themselves and of government to regulate the industry" (Howard 1997, 151). Although "the sweatshop was never eradicated," it was "steadily pushed to the margins of the industry. . . . By the mid-1960's, more than half of the 1.2 million workers in the apparel industry were organized and real wages had been rising for decades. The sweatshop had been relegated to a minor nuisance, its very marginality the symbol of an American success story" (Howard 1997, 155).

Having established that sweatshops in the apparel industry are real, new, and encompass about 60 percent of the industry, involving over four hundred thousand workers, we turn our attention to why they reappeared in the course of the 1970s.

The New Sweatshops in America: Why?

The appearance of the new sweatshops can be explained by four simple terms, only one of which is widely understood. *Deregulation, concentration, imports,* and *immigration* jointly determine the appearance of sweatshop exploitation in the apparel industry since the 1980s. Of these, immigration may be the least important cause, despite being the most widely recognized.

Deregulation

Deregulation may be accomplished as an announced policy by formally changing state policies. Alternatively, in similar fashion to permitting inflation to decrease social benefits, deregulation may be accomplished de facto by allowing the state's regulatory capacity to decline relative to the economy. This has occurred in the enforcement of the Fair Labor Standards Act of 1938. The data in Figure 5.1,

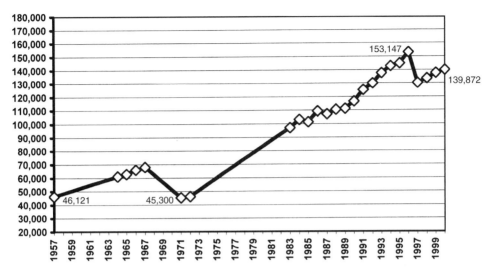

FIGURE 5.1.   De Facto Deregulation: Employees per Wage and Hours Investigator, Selected Years, 1957–2000
Sources: INVESTIGATORS: 1957, 1959, 1964–67, 1971–72: U.S. Department of Labor (DOL) "Budget Estimates," various years, U.S. Department of Labor library, Washington, D.C. 1983–95: Personal communication from Acting Administrator John Fraser, Wage and Hours Division, Employment Standards Administration, DOL, April 21, 1998. 1996–2001: Internal Department of Labor data via interview with Robert DeVore, Wages and Hours Division, U.S. Department of Labor, Budget and Finance Team Leader, May 17, 2001.
EMPLOYMENT: U.S. Bureau of Labor Statistics, Current Employment Statistics data extraction, available at http://stats.bls.gov/webapps/legacy/cesbtab1.htm. Accessed June 8, 2001.

incomplete though they are, show that Wage and Hours Division investigators of the Department of Labor face increased numbers of workplaces ("establishments") with a relatively smaller staff. Each investigator was responsible for fifty-seven hundred workplaces in 1983, eighty-six hundred in 1996, and seventy-five hundred in 1999.

Figure 5.1 also shows a long-range story by using the ratio of investigators to employees outside government.[11] From 1957 to 1995, each investigator's potential responsibility increased from about 46,000 workers to about 153,100 workers, an increase of 350 percent, and then, after a drop, rose again, to 140,000.

As a result of sensational reports of slave labor and celebrity involvement in sweatshops, the number of investigators went up (to 942) in fiscal year 1998, but not enough to deter law breaking–for example, in Los Angeles (see above)—as compared to 1996. One way to summarize the regulatory environment is to say that de facto deregulation has created a haven for scofflaws. Richard Appelbaum and Edna Bonacich (2000) report bitter resentment about law enforcement among Los Angeles manufacturers.

Concentration

The approximately twenty-five thousand contractors in the apparel industry are at the bottom of the industry's food chain. During the 1930s, 1940s, and 1950s, the men's and women's clothing workers' unions gradually developed the ability to control the abuses of the contractor system by compelling the manufacturers (in New York in those days they were called jobbers) to accept "joint liability" for union standards in contractor shops (Schlesinger 1951). This was done through the collective bargaining power of the unions at a time when they represented the majority of the workers in the industry.

Manufacturers' liability for the labor-law violations of their contractors, however, was never part of American labor law. Under the law's "hot goods" provisions, The Fair Labor Standards Act does give the Secretary of Labor the power to prevent the sale of goods produced in violation of the law. Rarely used, the "hot-goods" power has not proved a powerful deterrent. Since the high point of the unions' influence in the industry in the 1950s a new power factor has arisen: the dominant role of retailers.

Both UNITE, the union that represents apparel workers, and a variety of advocacy groups—the National Labor Committee in the United States and the Clean Clothes Campaign(s) in Western Europe, to name but two—have campaigned for legal and ethical change, calling for manufacturers or retailers to take responsibility for the labor conditions under which the goods they sell are made. The "Stop Sweatshops Act," introduced in the U.S. Congress in the 1990s by Representative William Clay and Senator Edward Kennedy, would have made manufacturers liable for labor-law violations committed in the production of the goods they commission. (Action on the bill awaits Democratic congressional majorities.) Campaigns to pressure retailers to "disclose" their contractor chain of supply are another advocacy strategy aimed at piercing the veil of secrecy and impunity that allows jobbers and retailers to pretend to be separate from the labor abuses of their agents (National

Labor Committee 1998a; Clean Clothes Campaign 1997, 1998).

Here is how the Dutch Clean Clothes Campaign articulates their demand:

> We stress that the retailers are responsible and should be made to account for the conditions under which garments are produced at their orders. This holds true for the entire subcontracting chain. They check quality, colour and delivery speed. They can check on wage and working conditions and pay extra for them, if necessary. If we know of a case where workers rights are violated we take this to the retailer they supply to and press them to take action. We ask people to be critical consumers, e.g. to ask for every garment they intend to buy where it has been made and under what conditions. (Clean Clothes Campaign 1998)

There is little immediate prospect for either legal change or behavioral change by retailers. Politically, the "Stop Sweatshops" bill was anathema to the Republican majorities in both houses of the Congress (S. Green 1997). As of mid-2001, the U.S. Senate had a new but narrow Democratic majority, and it is possible that with Senator Kennedy as chair of the Senate Labor Committee the bill might come to the Senate floor. Whatever the likelihood of passage in the U.S. Senate, it is not likely to succeed in the House. The American retailers militantly defend the principle of their separation from and freedom of responsibility for the production of garments they sell.

Despite their insistence of innocence, the big retail chains dominate both clothing sales and clothing production in ways the manufacturers never approached, and the concentration in clothing retail has been growing steadily since the 1980s. Table 5.1 uses the latest publicly available data from the U.S. Census of Manufactures to show that, by 1997, the top twenty department-store chains (including discounters) together with the top twenty specialty-apparel chains controlled 56.9 per-

TABLE 5.1.   Retail Concentration in the "Top 40": Apparel Sales in Top 20 Specialty Apparel Chains plus Top 20 Retail Department Stores,[a] 1972–97

	1972	1977	1982	1987	1992	1997
Retail Value (U.S.$ billions)	15.5	25.1	41.6	66.9	92.3	106.6
Percent of Gross Apparel Sales	37.9	42.4	47.8	52.6	56.9	56.9

Source: Author's calculations from U.S. Bureau of the Census, Economic Census, "Retail Trade," "Merchandise Line Sales," and "Establishment and Firm Size," various years.

[a]Includes discount chains.

cent of all clothing sales—about $92 billion. These publicly available data almost certainly understate the level of concentration and thus the power in the hands of the top few retailers. Using proprietary data from the Kurt Salmon market research firm, Jackie Jones reported that the top five retail organizations held 48 percent of the apparel market, or $168 billion in sales, in 1993 (Jones 1995). The top twelve chains, the same firm estimates, controlled 68 percent of apparel sales in 1996 (*Apparel Industry Magazine*, n.d.). What the U.S. Census data show, rather than the actual level of concentration (which is higher than that shown in the preceding data), is the trend over the last generation.

In addition to their sheer market power as buyers and sellers of goods, the chains act as manufacturers themselves when they contract for the production of private-label goods—and about 30 percent of the clothing sold in the big chains is under their own label. This concentration makes the retail chains the price makers of the industry, the eight-hundred-pound gorillas of the rag trade. Wal-Mart stores alone sell about 20 percent of all apparel at retail in the United States.[12] Concentrated market power is also the source of labor-standards erosion. When retailers order goods and insist on a certain price, they initiate a competitive process, one that may force U.S. contractors to meet a price only obtainable under the labor conditions of poor countries. The demand for such a price is made credible by the fact that

most clothing sold in this country is made in poorer countries; and that is the third determinant of sweatshop exploitation: imports.

Imports

The global commodity chain of the apparel industry consists of fiber production, textile manufacture, design, cutting, sewing, and marketing and retail (see, e.g., Gereffi 1994; Appelbaum and Gereffi 1994). These stages in the production process may be, and in apparel typically are, disaggregated over space (Ross and Trachte 1990). While law enforcement in the United States is weak, the most powerful actors in the global commodity chain of the apparel industry—the retailers—have used their strategic power to capture the largest share of profits (Gereffi 1994; Appelbaum and Gereffi 1994). By sourcing clothing in low-wage areas of the global economy, the name-brand manufacturers and the big private-label retailers are able to appropriate the lion's share of the markups; the direct producers, including their direct supervisors—the contractors—obtain but small shares of the consumer's dollar.

The complex global contracting system produces grimly humorous oddities: A pair of Britannia Relaxed Fit boys' jeans, selling for $17.99 at Kmart and "produced"—that is, contracted for—by the giant VF Corporation, may have been made in Nicaragua or in the United States. The National Labor Committee (NLC) estimates the (U.S. industry standard) labor cost as $2.08 in the United States and $0.14 in Nicaragua. The committee purchased these garments at the same store. Levi Strauss and Company, which sold Britannia to VF, has recently closed eight U.S. plants and three in Europe, laying off seventy-three hundred U.S. workers and seventeen hundred in France and Belgium (National Labor Committee 1998b; Tomkins and Buckley 1998).

One measure of low-wage competition is the level of import penetration. Table 5.2 reports the increase in clothing imports to the United States. Apparel imports, largely from low-wage producers, went from 2 percent of apparent consumption in 1961 to over 52 percent in 1999. These are very conservative estimates. The analysis does not correct, for example, for material cut and then exported to be sewn and reimported ("807/9802" in-bond assembly items under the U.S. tariff code). In addition, the data in Table 5.2 are by value of shipments, not numbers of items. When the U.S. Census analyzes particular clothing lines rather than the whole industry, with all the data aggregated, major product lines show much higher levels of import penetration. For example, 87 percent of men's sweaters (82 percent by dollar value) were imported in 1999, as were 66 percent of suits and 75 percent of sport coats. Ninety-two percent of women's suits, 69 percent of skirts, and 59 percent of dresses were imported in 1999 (U.S. Bureau of the Census 2000). As many others and I have argued (Ross and Trachte 1990; Ross 1997b; Appelbaum and Bonacich 2000), the availability of a global pool of cheap labor has had a powerful effect by weakening workers' bargaining power everywhere and subverting the higher standards of compensation and benefits in the older industrial regions. This has an even more powerful effect in labor-intensive industries like apparel.

The power structure of the industry is heavily influenced by the fact that the major retailers are also major importers. Among the top one hundred importers of apparel, retail chains controlled 48 percent of imports (Jones 1995).

The power of retailers and the market share of imports from countries where workers' material levels of living are considerably lower than working-class standards in the older industrial nations constitute the most important strategic *differences* between the new sweatshops of the late twentieth century and the old ones of its early years. Among the *similarities* of the two eras is the fact that in each case the most exploited workers were immigrants. Popular and journalistic accounts of contemporary sweatshops are well aware of, if not obsessed by, this parallel.[13] To acknowledge the contribution of a particular reserve of labor to overall worker vulnerability is not, however, to accede to the proposition's primacy.

Immigration

The last factor that contributes to the rise of the new sweatshops in the United States is the one most frequently cited by popular accounts and by many academic ones: immigration. The renewal of massive immigration after the 1965 reforms has duplicated, at the bottom of the labor market and in certain regions (e.g., New York and Los Angeles), the industrial reserves of the early twentieth century. In 1980–90, for example, *net* immigration was exactly the same (5.7 million) as it had been in 1900–1910. The inflow continued in the 1990s. By 2000, 11 million U.S. residents had entered the country since 1990, compared to 8 million people who had entered in the 1980s (U.S. Bureau of the Census 2001). Poor people from the Western Hemisphere and middle-class and poor immigrants from Asia now face

TABLE 5.2.   Import Penetration in U.S. Apparel Market, 1961–99

Year	Domestic Production (U.S.$ millions)	Imports (U.S.$ millions)	Exports (U.S.$ millions)	Import Penetration[a] (%)	Import/Domestic Production (%)
1961	13,088	283	159	2.1	2.2
1962	13,948	374	152	2.6	2.7
1963	14,818	400	158	2.7	2.7
1964	15,514	481	196	3.0	3.1
1965	16,426	568	177	3.4	3.5
1966	17,308	637	188	3.6	3.7
1967	18,483	692	207	3.6	3.7
1968	19,628	900	220	4.4	4.6
1969	21,045	1,149	242	5.2	5.5
1970	20,394	1,286	250	6.0	6.3
1971	21,687	1,574	258	6.8	7.3
1972	23,914	1,967	300	7.7	8.2
1973	25,970	2,261	381	8.1	8.7
1974	26,855	2,465	593	8.6	9.2
1975	27,098	2,775	602	9.5	10.2
1976	30,019	3,912	740	11.8	13.0
1977	35,323	4,393	859	11.3	12.4
1978	37,845	5,722	1,035	13.5	15.1
1979	37,350	5,902	1,387	14.1	15.8
1980	40,293	6,543	1,604	14.5	16.2
1981	44,074	7,752	1,628	15.4	17.6
1982	46,681	8,516	1,236	15.8	18.2
1983	49,423	9,976	1,049	17.1	20.2
1984	50,672	14,002	1,026	22.0	27.6
1985	50,784	15,711	991	24.0	30.9
1986	53,323	18,171	1,178	25.8	34.1
1987	62,119	21,503	1,490	26.2	34.6
1988	62,750	22,363	1,988	26.9	35.6
1989	61,447	25,372	2,362	30.0	41.3
1990	61,962	26,602	2,864	31.0	42.9
1991	62,649	27,377	3,746	31.7	43.7
1992	68,844	32,644	4,659	33.7	47.4
1993	70,986	35,475	5,433	35.1	50.0
1994	73,258	38,561	6,009	36.4	52.6
1995	73,780	41,208	6,979	38.2	55.9
1996	73,319	43,075	7,836	39.7	58.8
1997	68,018	50,191	9,279	46.1	73.8
1998	64,932	55,838	9,474	50.2	86.0
1999	62,798	59,156	8,541	52.2	94.2

Source: U.S. Industrial Outlook, various years. 1991–99: *U.S. Statistical Abstract,* 1998, 2000. Production, 1997–99: U.S. Bureau of the Census, *Annual Survey of Manufactures: Statistics for Industry Groups and Industries M99 (AS)-1,* issued March 2001.

[a]Imports/(domestic production plus imports, minus exports).

one another as workers and entrepreneurs in a global apparel industry with branches in the United States.

Immigrants are often blocked in their ability to claim well-paid jobs: by education (or lack of it), by language issues, and by unfamiliarity with their new surroundings. Women, the traditional workforce of the apparel industry, have all these problems and others. The gender-specific issues that make women more vulnerable than men to sweatshop conditions may include ethnic norms that constrain the job search to certain neighborhoods or among relatives; the desire for workplaces that will break rules by allowing little children to be tended on site; and gender norms about appropriate women's work. All these factors constrain the choices women may have and thus heighten their vulnerability to unscrupulous labor practices.

The fact that many contemporary immigrants are illegal is a major aggravation to their handicaps in the labor market. Unwilling to complain to officials for fear of discovery and deportation and afraid to join unions for the same reason, undocumented workers are the most vulnerable. The immigration reform of 1986, which instituted sanctions on employers who hire undocumented workers, has had a major impact on the apparel industry—some of it surprising. Not so surprising is the use of the Immigration and Naturalization Service (*la migra*) as a de facto union buster. Should workers evince union sympathy, "dropping a dime"—that is, telephoning immigration authorities—is a swift and anonymous way of firing them. In fact, employer sanctions appear to be changing the gender division of labor in the apparel business in Los Angeles.

Appelbaum and Bonacich (2000) note, for example, that despite the traditional domination of women as sewing operators in the garment industry in Los Angeles and elsewhere, Hispanic men now represent up to 20 percent

of the sewing labor force. They attribute this to the displacement of these men from industrial jobs in establishments large enough to attract Immigration and Naturalization Service (INS) attention and to the relative invisibility of the myriad small shops in the apparel infrastructure.

Despite the obvious currency of immigration as an explanation for sweatshops, restraint in using this as a master determinant is prudent. In the 1950s, when import pressure was low to nonexistent, when unions were strong, and when state regulation was more robust, poor Puerto Rican migrants to New York were not subject to the kinds of abuses that today's Mexican and Dominicans face in New York and Los Angeles (Ross 1997a). And lest the simple explanation of undocumented status substitute for the broader immigrant explanation, it should be noted that among today's sweatshop workers many are legal immigrants, including Korean workers in Dallas (Um 1996) and Chinese workers in various locations (Fishbein 1996).[14]

Overview and Theoretical Considerations

This chapter has reviewed the new sweatshops in the United States, briefly answering four questions. I showed that sweatshops in the United States were "new" in that there is strong evidence that between World War II and the 1970s regular abuse of low wages, long hours, and dangerous or noxious conditions in the apparel industry became marginal at worst and practically disappeared at best. By adopting the objective definition of "multiple labor-law violations," I have shown, contrary to Waldinger and Lapp (1993), that sweatshops are not invisible to the formal economy, despite their informal and illegal practices. I reviewed the evidence for an esti-

TABLE 5.3.   Typology of Old and New Sweatshops in the United States

Factor	Old Sweatshops (circa 1900–1920)	New Sweatshops (circa 1978–present)
Immigrant Reserve of Labor	Yes (mostly legal)	Yes (many undocumented)
Infrastructure of Labor Protection	No	Yes (weak enforcement)
Global Scope of Commodity Chains in U.S. Production	No	Yes

mate that half the industry and as many as 60 percent of the contractor shops are major labor-law violators. Finally, I reviewed the four causal factors that allowed this form of labor exploitation to return so many years after it was the object of widespread indignation: the declining capacity of the state to enforce labor law; the increasing market power of retailers through concentration of sales; the competitive pressure brought about by massive imports from low-wage export platforms; and the availability of a large pool of vulnerable immigrant labor.

The sweatshops of the era symbolically marked by the 1911 Triangle Shirtwaist Factory fire (McClymer 1998) were made possible by a lack of worker organization, the consequent absence of a legal infrastructure of worker protection, a vast reserve of immigrant labor, and a price-competitive industry where no seller had the concentrated power to extract higher prices in return for labor peace. Imports from societies and economies at very different levels of development were not relevant. Now, worker organization, having briefly been strong, again covers but a minority fraction of the industry. The strong actors in the system have thus been able to maintain high profits and keep the labor share of final price quite small. Imports and the threat of imports discipline the current generation of small entrepreneurs and laborers in much the same way as unbridled price competition did earlier, producing a race to the bottom of the world's industrial standards. Vulnerable immigrants, sometimes grateful for any foothold in the economy and usually desperate for jobs, provide the hands that sew and cut. The similarities and differences between the two eras of sweatshop labor are summarized in Table 5.3.

Nowadays recognition is widespread that globalization is a potent force in everyday life, and a rhetoric that asserts its importance is universal. Global hype is sometimes countered by global debunking ("the importance of trade to the U.S. economy is overstated"), but more often global optimism is challenged by workers' views of the problem of "social dumping" and a "race to the bottom." Rarely, however, is globalization seen as the occasion for theoretical reflection.

Ross and Trachte first connected New York sweatshops to a theory of global capitalism in 1983. They later asserted (1990) that global capitalism was a specific and different form of capitalism from the monopoly capitalism or "Fordism" that preceded it. Yet, despite the universal *empirical* cognizance of global capitalism and the commodity chains of its spatial structure, there has been little theoretical advance. Perhaps the now widespread recognition that an old form of exploitation has reappeared in the new sweatshops will occasion a new willingness to encounter global capitalism as new form of capitalist political economy. In particular, it is one in which workers' strategic resources are challenged by new advantages for their employers. But as in each previous era of capitalism, these are not forces to which it is necessary to acquiesce. Knowledge creates opportunity to act but responsibility as well.

Notes

Acknowledgments: This is a revised version of a paper given at the 1998 annual meeting of the American Sociological Association. Lisa Grandmaison (Clark University, 1999) assisted in the collection and analysis of the data. The work dealt with herein is investigated at greater length and in more depth in *Hearts Starve: The New Sweatshops in Global Context,* by Robert J. S. Ross (Ann Arbor: University of Michigan Press, forthcoming). The quantitative material will be revised and updated in that book.

1. The authors' implicit definition of a sweatshop is one that is "covert" or in the "informal sector."

2. The GAO sample of violators was not representative because it was composed of the violators *known* to the departments of labor in the two states as a result of their investigations.

3. "There is no theoretical reason to exclude from the informal economy the unrecorded practices of large corporations, particularly since they have close linkages with the growth of other informal activities" (Castells and Portes 1989, 13, 15). When seventy-one workers, lured into slavery from Thailand, were discovered in a slave factory in El Monte, California, in 1995, the list of retailers to which the clothing was bound was a who's who of mainstream (and upscale) retailing in California, including Neiman Marcus and the Mays chain (Su 1997).

4. The EDD Tax Branch is one of the largest tax-collection agencies in the nation and handles all the administrative and enforcement functions for audit and collection of unemployment insurance, disability insurance, employment training tax (ETT), and personal income tax (PIT) withholding.

5. The fact that there were so many violations for each violator firm makes it possible to use minimum-wage violations as an indicator variable for "multiple labor-law" violations." This is de facto how the U.S. Labor Department treats the matter in its press releases.

6. Voluntary compliance monitoring is considered a failure by labor rights advocates. Despite apparently boosting compliance rates, almost half of the contractors allegedly monitored are still labor-law violators. Notoriously, among the first firms to claim it monitored its contractors was the infamous Guess? Jeans, which was later found to have repeat violators in its contractor chain (Greenhouse 1997).

7. It should be noted that the restaurant industry, when examined by the U.S. General Accounting Office in 1989, had as high a level of Fair Labor Standards Act violations as did the apparel industry. Generally the violations were of different types. Record-keeping violations were high and child-labor violations much more frequent in the restaurant industry than in the apparel industry. Arguably, large fractions of these violations might be "technical": for example, when a teenager otherwise working legally works past a certain hour in the evening during the school week. In addition, restaurants were sanitary-code violators. Among the more serious violations, sweatshop conditions have been reported when Chinese workers are smuggled into the country and held under conditions of indenture, often working in restaurants (Kwong 1998) There is no other known recent systematic study of industrial concentrations of major Fair Labor Standards Act violations.

8. These calculations are based on the Bureau of Labor Statistics National Industry-Occupation Employment Matrix, using 1996 data. Apparel (SIC 213) is combined with knitting mills (SIC 225). Data extraction is available at <http://STATS.BLS.GOV:80/oep/nioem>. Accessed on December 2, 1998.

9. Schlesinger was an attorney whose history of the apparel industry was written on behalf of the union (ILGWU) of which his father had been an early president.

10. The use of quotation marks is Hill's.

11. The number of investigators working for the Wage and Hours Division of the Employment Standards Administration of the U.S. Department of Labor from 1983 to 1996 was given in congressional testimony by the acting administrator. The number of establishments as defined by the U.S. Census Bureau series *County Business Patterns* is available in that series for all these years. The number of investigators before 1983 can be gleaned from documents in the Department of Labor library in Washington, D.C., but only for the years in Table 5.1. Prior to 1974, the period for which I have located the num-

ber of investigators, *County Business Patterns* reported not "establishments" but "reporting units," which includes only one unit per county per corporation outside of manufacturing. Hence the only consistent time series that matches all the years for which I have the number of investigators is the employment time series of the Bureau of Labor Statistics, *Current Employment Statistics*, available at <http://stats.bls.gov/ces/home.htm> (accessed on March 2, 2002).

12. Here is the basis for that estimate:

a. About 19 percent of Wal-Mart sales are apparel and domestics (source: Wal-Mart Stores Inc., SEC form 10-K, filed on April 10, 2001).

b. Wal-Mart FY 2001 (ending in January 2001) sales were $191.3 billion (form 10-K, exhibit 13).

c. Nineteen percent of those sales are $36.3 billion. Correcting for possible overstatement caused by including domestics (i.e., towels and sheets), use 15 percent, which yields an apparel sales estimate of $28.7 billion.

d. National retail sales of apparel in 2000 were $182.3 billion, indicating that Wal-Mart sold between 15.7 percent and 19.9 percent of all clothing.

e. Retail sales of apparel included $169.3 billion in retail store locations. The Wal-Mart share of $28.7 billion to $36.3 billion of these is between 16.9 and 21.4 percent of in-store sales (see About.com at <http://retailindustry.about.com/industry/retailindustry/library/weekly/01/aa010319a.htm)>.

13. I have found that about 45 percent of news stories about domestic sweatshops in the *New York Times* and *Los Angeles Times* identify the immigrant status or ethnicity of the workers in either the headline or the lead paragraph, and over 50 percent mention these identifiers of the workers somewhere in the article.

14. Among the legal-immigrant sweatshop workers in New York is a sewing operator whose daughter was one of my Harvard students, thus neatly confirming one immigrant stereotype (success of future generations) while subverting another (illegal status as the prerequisite for exploitation).

References

Alman, Ron. 1997. New England director and vice president of UNITE, interview with the author. Boston, October 10.

Apparel Industry Magazine. n.d. "Top Twelve Vertical Retailers in U.S." Clipping found in UNITE library files, Boston, December 1997.

Appelbaum, Richard, and Edna Bonacich. 2000. *Behind the Label: Inequality in the Los Angeles Apparel Industry.* Berkeley: University of California Press.

Appelbaum, Richard, and Gary Gereffi. 1994. "Power and Profits in the Apparel Commodity Chain." In *Global Production: The Apparel Industry in the Pacific Rim,* ed. Edna Bonacich, Lucie Cheng, Norma Chinchilla, Nora Hamilton, and Paul Ong, pp. 42–62. Philadelphia: Temple University Press.

Boris, Eileen. 1994. *Home to Work: Motherhood and the Politics of Industrial Homework in the United States.* New York: Cambridge University Press.

Buck, Rinker. 1979. "The New Sweatshops: A Penny for Your Collar." *New York Magazine* 12, January 29, 40–41.

California Department of Labor Standards Enforcement (DLSE). 1996. *Fourth Annual Report, 1996.* Available online at <http://www.dir.ca.gov/dir/Labor_Law/DLSE/tipp4.htm>. Accessed July 2, 1998.

Castells, Manuel, and Alejandro Portes. 1989. "World Underneath: The Origins, Dynamics, and Effects of the Informal Economy." In *The Informal Economy: Studies in Advanced and Less Developed Countries,* ed. Alejandro Portes, Manuel Castells, and Laura A. Benton, pp. 11–37. Baltimore: Johns Hopkins University Press.

Clean Clothes Campaign. 1997. Group interview with the author. Amsterdam, June 7.

———. 1998. "Consumer Actions and Public Education." Available online at <http://www.cleanclothes.org/1/ccc.htm>. Accessed September 21, 1998.

Dubinsky, David. 1953. "Out of These Slums." *Justice,* December 1. Reprinted in *Out of the Sweatshop: The Struggle for Industrial Democracy,* ed. Leon Stein. New York: Quadrangle/The New York Times Book Company, 1977.

————. 1955. "Remarks of David Dubinsky at the ILGWU Housing Dedication Ceremony." *Justice*, October 22. Reprinted in *Out of the Sweatshop: The Struggle for Industrial Democracy*, ed. Leon Stein. New York: Quadrangle/The New York Times Book Company, 1977.

Fishbein, Jerry. 1996. Organizer, Union of Needletrades, Industrial, and Textile Employees (UNITE), interview with the author. Boston, September 23.

Foo, Lora Jo. 1994. "The Vulnerable and Exploitable Immigrant Workforce and the Need for Strengthening Worker Protective Legislation." *Yale Law Journal* 8: 2179–212.

Fraser, John. 1998. *Hearing on Workplace Competitiveness Issues*. Hearing before the Subcommittee on Oversight and Investigations of the Committee on Education and the Workforce, House of Representatives, 185th Cong., 2d sess. Washington, D.C., March 31. Available online at <http://commdocs.house.gov/committees/edu/hedo&i5-89.000/hedo&i5-89.htm>. Accessed on September 4, 2001.

Gereffi, Gary. 1994. "The Organization of Buyer Driven Global Commodity Chains: How U.S. Retailers Shape Overseas Production." In *Commodity Chains and Global Capitalism*, ed. Gary Gereffi and Miguel Korzeniewicz, pp. 95–122. Westport, Conn.: Praeger.

Gereffi, Gary, and Miguel Korzeniewicz, eds. 1994. *Commodity Chains and Global Capitalism*. Westport, Conn.: Praeger.

Green, Nancy. 1997. *Ready-toWear and Ready-to-Work: A Century of Industry and Immigrants in Paris and New York*. Durham, N.C.: Duke University Press.

Green, Suzanne. 1997. Minority counsel to Senate Committee on Labor, interview with the author. Washington, D.C., April 10.

Greenhouse, Steven. 1997. "Sweatshop Raids Cast Doubt on an Effort by Garment Makers to Police the Factories." *New York Times*, July 18, A10.

————. 1998. "Union Organization Drive Exposes Flaws in Nation's Labor Laws." *New York Times*, July 10, A1, 11.

Hill, Herbert. 1974. "Guardians of the Sweatshops: The Trade Unions, Racism, and the Garment Industry." In *Puerto Rico and Puerto Ricans: Stud-*

ies in History and Society, ed. Adalberto López and James Petras, pp. 384–416. New York: Wiley.

Howard, Alan. 1997. "Labor, History, and Sweatshops in the New Global Economy." In *No Sweat: Fashion, Free Trade and the Rights of Garment Workers*, ed. Andrew Ross, pp. 151–72. New York: Verso.

Iyengar, Shanto. 1991. *Is Anyone Responsible? How Television Frames Political Issues*. Chicago: University of Chicago Press.

Jones, Jackie. 1995. "Forces behind Restructuring in U.S. Apparel Retailing and Its Effect on the U.S. Apparel Industry." *Industry Trade and Technology Review* (March): 23–27.

Kwong, Peter. 1989. *Forbidden Workers: Illegal Chinese Immigrants and American Labor*. New York: New Press.

Laslett, John, and Mary Tyler. 1989. *The ILGWU in Los Angeles: 1907–1988*. Inglewood, Calif.: Ten Star Press.

Marx, Karl. 1867. *Capital*. Vol. 1, part 2, chap. 6. Available online at <http://leftside.uwc.ac.za/Archive>. Accessed September 8, 1998.

McClymer, John F. 1998. *The Triangle Strike and Fire*. Fort Worth, Tex.: Harcourt Brace.

National Labor Committee. 1998a. "The People's Right to Know Campaign." New York: National Labor Committee. Available online at <http://www.nlcnet.org/rtk/rtkl.htm>. Accessed September 21, 1998.

————. 1998b. "Race to the Bottom." Available online at <http://www.nlcnet.org/Press/Newsclip/rtb11_11.htm>. Accessed September 21, 1998.

New York State Department of Labor. 1982. *Report to the Governor and Legislature on the Garment Manufacturing Industry and Industrial Homework*. New York: New York State Department of Labor.

Ortiz, Altagracia. 1990. "Puerto Rican Workers in the Garment Industry of New York City, 1920–1960." In *Labor Divided: Race and Ethnicity in United States Labor Struggles, 1835-1960*, ed. Robert Asher and Charles Stephenson, pp. 105–25. Albany: State University of New York Press.

————. 1996. "Puerto Rican Women in the Garment Industry of New York City, 1920–1980." In *Puerto Rican Women and Work: Bridges in Transnational Labor*, ed. Altagracia Ortiz, pp. 55–81. Philadelphia: Temple University Press.

Pessar, Patricia R. 1987. "The Dominicans: Women in the Household and the Garment Industry." In *New Immigrants in New York*, ed. Nancy Foner, pp. 103–29. New York: Columbia University Press.

Proper, Carl. 1997a. Research staff of UNITE, telephone interview with the author. November.

———. 1997b. In-house calculations from U.S. Bureau of Labor Statistics data. December.

Rodriguez, Clara. 1979. "The Economic Factors Affecting Puerto Ricans in New York." In *Labor Migration under Capitalism: The Puerto Rican Experience*, ed. Centro de Estudios Puertorriqueños, History Task Force, pp. 197–221. New York: Monthly Review Press.

Ross, Andrew. 1997. "After the Year of the Sweatshop." In *No Sweat: Fashion, Free Trade and the Rights of Garment Workers*, ed. Andrew Ross, pp. 291–96. New York: Verso.

Ross, Robert. 1997a. "Kathie Lee Makes a Difference." Paper delivered at Eastern Sociological Society annual meeting, Baltimore, April 11.

———. 1997b. "Restricting Immigration: A Sweatshop Nonsolution." In *An Academic Search for Sweatshop Solutions: Conference Proceedings*, ed. Janice McCoart, pp. 32–45. Arlington, Va.: Marymount University.

Ross, Robert, and Graham Staines. 1972. "The Politics of Analyzing Social Problems." *Social Problems* 20, 1: 18–40.

Ross, Robert, and Kent Trachte. 1983. "Global Cities and Global Classes: The Peripheralization of Labor in New York City." *Review* 7, 3 (Winter): 393–431.

———. 1990. *Global Capitalism: The New Leviathan*. Albany: State University of New York Press.

Rothstein, Richard. 1996. Lecture and interview with the author. Clark University, Worcester, Massachusetts, October 4.

Schlesinger, Emil. 1951. *The Outside System of Production in the Women's Garment Industry in the New York Market*. New York: Hecla Press.

Smith, Carol. 1980. "Women, Work, and Use of Government Benefits: A Case Study of Hispanic Women Workers in New York's Garment Industry." Ph.D. diss., Adelphi University, Garden City, N.Y.

Stolberg, Benjamin. 1944. *Tailor's Progress*. Garden City, N.Y.: Doubleday, Doran and Company.

Su, Julie. 1997. "El Monte Thai Garment Workers: Slave Sweatshops." In *No Sweat: Fashion, Free Trade and the Rights of Garment Workers*, ed. Andrew Ross, pp. 143–49. New York: Verso.

Tomkins, Richard, and Neil Buckley. 1998. "Levi Strauss Shuts Six Plants." *Financial Times* (London), September 30, 29

Um, Shin Ja. 1996. *Korean Immigrant Women in the Dallas-Area Apparel Industry: Looking for Feminist Threads in Patriarchal Cloth*. Lanham, Md.: University Press of America.

U.S. Bureau of Labor Statistics. 2001. Data extracted from National Current Employment Statistics database. Available at <http://stats.bls.gov/webapps/legacy/cesbtab1.htm>. Accessed June 8, 2001.

U.S. Bureau of the Census. 1997. *Country of Origin and Year of Entry into the U.S. of the Foreign Born, by Citizenship Status*. March. Available online at <http://www.bls.census.gov/cps/pub/1997/for_born.htm>. Accessed September 21, 1998.

———. 2000. *Current Industrial Reports*. "Apparel—1999 Summary." MQ315A (99)-5 (MQ23A [99]-5). Released August 2000.

———. 2001. *Current Population Survey: Year of Entry of the Foreign-Born Population by Sex and Citizenship Status*. March 2000. Internet release date: January 23, 2001. Available online at <http://www.census.gov/population/socdemo/foreign/p20-534/tab0106.txt>. Accessed June 11, 2001.

U.S. Congress, House of Representatives. 1963. "Testimony of Herbert Hill, January 31, 1963." 88th Cong., 1st sess. *Congressional Record* 109, Pt. 2: 159–1572. Washington, D.C.: U.S. Government Printing Office.

U.S. Department of Labor (DOL). 1996. "OPA Press Release: Industry Monitoring Credited for Improved Garment Industry Compliance with Minimum Wage and Overtime Laws." May 9. Available online at <http://gatekeeper.dol.gov/dol/opa/public/media/press/opa/opa96181.htm>. Accessed October 29, 1996.

———. 1997. "Office of Public Affairs [OPA] Press Release: U.S. Department of Labor Compliance Survey Finds More than Half of New York City Garment Shops in Violation of Labor Laws." October 16. Available online at <http://www.

dol.gov/dol/opa/public/media/press/opa/opa97369.htm>. Accessed July 2, 1998.

————. 1998. "OPA Press Release: U.S. Department of Labor Announces Latest Los Angeles Garment Survey Results." May 27. Available on-line at <http://www.dol.gov/dol/opa/public/media/press/opa/opa98225.htm>. Accessed June 8, 2001.

————. 1999a. Employment Standards Administration press release: "Most Bay Area Garment Shops Pay Required Wages; Monitored and Established Businesses Do Best." May 18. Available at <http://www.dol.gov/dol/opa/public/media/press/esa/esa99143.htm>. Accessed June 8, 2001.

————. 1999b. OPA press release: "Conditions in New York City's Garment Industry Unchanged, but Tougher Enforcement Leads to Arrests." October 15. Available at <http://www.dol.gov/dol/opa/public/media/press/opa/opa99300.htm>. Accessed June 8, 2001.

————. 2000. "Only One-third of Southern California Garment Shops in Compliance with Federal Labor Laws." USDL-112, August 25. Available at <http://www.dol.gov/dol/esa/public/media/press/whd/sfwh112.htm>. Accessed on March 4, 2002.

U.S. General Accounting Office (GAO). 1988. "Sweatshops in the U.S.: Opinions on the Extent and Possible Enforcement Options." *HRD-88-130BR*. Washington, D.C.: U.S. General Accounting Office. Available at <http://161.203.16.4/d17t6/136973.pdf>. Accessed on March 4, 2002.

————. 1989. "Sweatshops in New York City a Local Example of a Nationwide Problem." Briefing report to the Honorable Charles E. Schumer, House of Representatives. *HRD-89-101BR*. Washington, D.C.: U.S. General Accounting Office. Available at <http://161.203.16.4/d25t7/138958.pdf>. Accessed on March 4, 2002.

————. 1994. "Tax Administration: Data on the Tax Compliance of Sweatshops." *GGD-94-210FS*. Washington, D.C.: U.S. General Accounting Office. Available at <http://161.203.16.4/t2pbat2/152819.pdf>. Accessed on March 4, 2002.

Wakefield, Dan. 1959. *Island in the City: The World of Spanish Harlem*. Boston: Houghton Mifflin.

Waldinger, Roger, and Michael Lapp. 1993. "Back to the Sweatshop or Ahead to the Informal Sector?" *International Journal of Urban and Regional Research* 17, 1: 6–29.

Zhou, Min. 1992. *Chinatown: The Socioeconomic Potential of an Urban Enclave*. Philadelphia: Temple University Press.

Edna Bonacich

---

6   Labor's Response to Global Production

Global and flexible production have had a devastating impact on U.S. garment workers and
on the once-powerful U.S. garment industry
unions. The apparel industry has lost thousands of jobs since its peak in 1973, and every
month brings reports of new job losses. Wages
have stagnated or fallen, and sweatshops have
returned to U.S. cities. For a time, especially
from the New Deal through the 1960s, as a
product of government oversight and strong
unions, sweatshops more or less disappeared
from U.S. garment production. But now they
have returned, as workers slave long hours for
piece rate (i.e., payment by the piece instead of
by the hour) without the basic protections of
minimum wage, overtime, the prevention of
industrial homework or child labor, or benefits
of any kind (Ross 1997; Bonacich and Appelbaum 2000; also see Chapter 5 in this book).

The old apparel unions, the International
Ladies' Garment Workers' Union (ILGWU)
and the Amalgamated Clothing and Textile
Workers Union (ACTWU), have faced huge
losses in membership. They have lost members at an even faster rate than jobs have
declined, as employers have turned increasingly to nonunion shops. Loss of membership
has inevitably been accompanied by a loss of
power, and the unions have had a hard time
protecting those members who remain. In an

effort to recover some lost ground, the
ILGWU and ACTWU decided to merge in
1995 to form UNITE, the Union of Needletrades, Industrial, and Textile Employees.
Faced with what appears to be a dying industry, UNITE has expanded its organizing efforts to include industrial workers who are
linked somewhat or not at all to its old, core
jurisdiction. It seems safe to say that the union
is barely holding on to its garment-worker
membership and is continually losing ground
in this industry, even as it is moving into other
areas.

This chapter addresses the following questions:

1. What are the forces that have weakened
   garment-worker unionizing?
2. How has the union responded to these challenges? What has been tried? What has suc-
   ceeded, what has failed, and why?
3. What can or should be done under these
   circumstances?

These questions and their answers are important not only for the apparel industry but also
for most manufacturing and some service
industries. The garment industry is more
advanced than most in terms of outsourcing
and offshore production, but others are moving along a similar path. Apparel may prove to

be the industry where the most forward-looking experiments in organizing are tried out.

Global and Flexible Production: The Attack on Garment Workers and Unions

Since the late 1960s, severe restructuring has posed a continual challenge to the apparel industry. This trend has taken a number of forms and has been shaped by a number of policies.

Contracting Out

Apparel production has a long history of what now is politely called flexible production. From the earliest stages of mass production of clothing in New York City, work was contracted out from "inside shops" to smaller contracting factories and to home workers. The ILGWU developed from protests against the resulting sweatshop conditions and was able, for a time, to stabilize relations in the industry by binding both manufacturers and their contractors to collective-bargaining agreements.

Since the 1970s, contracting out has risen to new heights. At least in the volatile women's wear industry, contracting out has taken over almost completely, and hardly any inside shops remain. Apparel manufacturers that specialize in design and merchandising have externalized the sewing of garments and other labor-intensive activities.

The industry justifies the contracting system with claims that it is more efficient. Garment contractors specialize in sewing, while the manufacturers are able to focus on their core competencies of design and merchandising. They are better able to deal with the uncertainties of fashion and season by not having to maintain a stable workforce, instead employing contractors on an as-needed basis. Moreover, if one contractor does not live up to required standards of quality, timeliness, or price, the manufacturer can readily switch to another.

All these justifications for increased contracting out may be accurate, but the industry often fails to mention the chief reason behind the practice: Contracting out lowers labor costs and avoids unionization. Labor costs go down for a number of reasons. First, because contractors are employed only on a contingent basis, downtime need not be covered by the manufacturer. The costs of downtime are foisted upon the contractor, who in turn foists them upon the workers. "Piece rate" necessarily indicates contingent workers, because contractors pay their employees only for the work actually done. Regulations mandating minimum-wage and overtime pay are anathema to most garment contractors, who, since they are paid only for the work done, lose money if they have to pay anything extra. In sum, garment contractors are contingent firms employing contingent workers, leading to a double whammy of instability and insecurity for garment workers.

Contracting out also enables apparel manufacturers to avoid responsibility for the regulatory system. They benefit from the production of their garments under illegal, abusive, and cheap labor regimes while being able to turn a blind eye to these conditions. They can claim they are the innocent victims of illegal operators, whose fault it is that labor laws are being broken. This is a convenient fiction, since the manufacturers exercise considerable power over the contractors and set prices such that the work cannot be done legally.

Garment contracting has become a ghetto for immigrant entrepreneurs and immigrant workers in the United States. Widespread racism, combined with the manipulation of immigration law to create an "illegal" workforce, allows for the comfortable acceptance of an especially low-wage, sometimes abused garment-industry workforce. The undocumented immigrants are seen as either willingly accepting these conditions or deserving no better. That they are generally dark-skinned people from Latin America, the Caribbean, and Asia only adds to beliefs about their unworthiness to earn a decent wage and maintain a decent standard of living.

Contracting out is almost synonymous with sweatshop production in this industry. Industry leaders typically refuse to acknowledge the connection. Either they deny that their contractors run sweatshops, claiming that a few "bad apples" are giving the entire industry a bad name, or they blame sweatshops on the contractors. Meanwhile, they happily accept the lower labor costs that improve their profit margins.

Contracting out also serves as a serious inhibitor to union organization (Bonacich 2000). Manufacturers can shift production away from union contractors or from shops that show any signs of "labor trouble." Their ability to move around and select the cheapest contractors severely hurts the capacity of the union to win any improvements for the workers in a particular shop. Organizing drives generally require some steadiness of employment, but in the world of contingent firms employing contingent workers, such steadiness is rare.

On top of this, apparel manufacturers like to keep their contractor lists a secret. They claim that revealing their contractors would hurt their competitive situation, as other manufacturers would try to steal their better contractors. Whether this is true or not, secrecy certainly harms labor organizing. Workers do not know where their fellow workers (working for the same manufacturer) are employed, so joining together becomes immensely difficult.

Mobility and secrecy are a deadly combination for union organizing. Manufacturers maintain a secret and constantly shifting stable of contractors. Today's workers' victory can be canceled out tomorrow by simply moving to another contractor, whose hidden character inhibits the ability of workers and the union to track down where the work has fled. Somewhat similar conditions prevailed in East Coast cities at the beginning of the twentieth century, and they were overcome by mass uprisings of exploited workers who received the support of disgusted community members. Those workers were able to win agreements that protected against the worst violations. But the situation since the 1970s has become worse because mobility has extended offshore, making the relationships even more hidden and the competition much more intense.

Global Production

Garment contracting began to move offshore as early as the late 1950s, but the trend grew slowly at first. By the 1980s it had gained massive momentum, and every year since has shown a large growth in "imports" and a decline in domestic employment. Most of these imports are the product not of free trade by foreign companies but of U.S. apparel manufacturers, especially U.S. apparel retailers, arranging for the production of their goods offshore.

Some U.S. apparel companies have overseas subsidiaries, but by far the most common form of offshore production entails arm's-length relationships. In other words, the manufacturers and retailers set up contracting and licensing arrangements abroad. As with domestic contracting, offshore production relies on employing contingent firms, allowing the U.S. companies to maximize flexibility and to move production to wherever they can get the best deal. The system of mobility and secrecy is thus extended all over the globe, with worldwide effects on labor standards and unionization (Varley 1998; International Labour Office [ILO] 2000).

While there are exceptions, in general U.S. retailers and manufacturers seek out countries where labor laws are weakest and where workers are least able to defend themselves. This has resulted in the employment of many young women from peasant populations that are being dispossessed of their lands and pushed into wage labor. First-generation proletarians are typically less likely to know their rights as workers and may be more desperately dependent on earning a wage. Employers claim they prefer young women because of their hand-eye coordination, but gender subordination is a critical factor in this preference. Employers hope they are getting workers who are shy and soft-spoken, who have never heard the word *union,* and who respect male authority. Needless to say, any worker can learn to stand up and defend herself, and many do. But employers hope to postpone this development as long as possible by selecting the most vulnerable, least protected workers.

If secrecy of production location poses a problem for unions and workers in the United States, the problem is amplified in global production. Tracking down the countries of production, let alone specific factory locations, becomes a formidable task. Furthermore, locations keep changing, so any knowledge that is gained about supply chains is always almost immediately out of date.

U.S. Policies

Global and flexible production are not solely the creation of apparel manufacturers and retailers. The fragmentation of production and its movement offshore have been supported by a number of U.S. policies. On the domestic front, the attack on the welfare state and all its institutions, including labor law, has greatly hurt the garment unions. Sweatshops were substantially reduced during the post–World War II period because of state support for decent labor standards (through the Fair Labor Standards Act of 1938 and its subse-

quent revisions) and for the right of unions to engage in collective bargaining (through the National Labor Relations Act, or NLRA, of 1935 and its revisions). Both types of labor law have been seriously eroded since 1980 (see Compa 2000). The reasons for this attack are complex and not restricted to the United States, but they are beyond the scope of this chapter (see Ross 1997; Bonacich and Appelbaum 2000).

U.S. trade policy has also encouraged the movement of production offshore. Item 807 of the U.S. tariff code (passed in 1930 but used extensively by the apparel industry only since the 1980s) was one of the first regulations to foster offshore garment contracting by cutting tariffs on goods that had been assembled abroad and reimported. The tariff cut encouraged companies to contract out the labor-intensive aspects of garment production, ship unassembled cut goods to countries where labor costs were a fraction of those in the United States, and bring the finished garments back for sale in the U.S. market. Barriers to such arrangements were further eased by the Caribbean Basin Initiative, the North American Free Trade Agreement, policies of the World Trade Organization, and, now looming, the Free Trade Agreement of the Americas. These arrangements, supported by neoliberal ideology, are not simply about "free trade" and "open markets" between equal partners but about the right of U.S. capital to move freely into less-developed countries and to employ, either directly or indirectly, their lower-cost, less-protected labor.

On the U.S. side, immigration policy also plays a critical role in weakening labor's position. The free market in capital is not mirrored with a free market in labor: The border serves as a constraint on workers seeking out the highest-paying, best job available to them. By limiting immigration while not addressing its underlying causes (which include the dislocations created by foreign, often U.S., capital in the countries of origin), a class of rightless immigrant workers is created in the United States. These workers are vulnerable to employer threats of exposure and deportation. Again, any workers can organize, and undocumented workers have been known to wage effective organizing drives. Nevertheless, a lack of the most fundamental rights of citizenship must count as a hindrance to worker organizing. Unions face a special challenge in protecting their undocumented members and potential members.

Complicity of Southern Regimes

Many countries of the global South are trying to industrialize. Frequently, leaders in these countries believe the only route to industrial development is to attract Northern capital and to gain access to Northern markets for their countries' exports. The conditions for both goals are fairly clear: Keep wages low and keep independent, militant unions that push for improvements in wages and working conditions out. "Labor trouble" is to be avoided at all costs, especially in a mobile industry such as apparel, since it will cause the industry to shift its contracting relations to other countries. Thus regimes bent on development, no matter how progressive their intentions, are forced into a posture of repressing labor. Of course, some individuals benefit directly from these arrangements, enriching themselves by skimming off part of the profits.

Repression of Southern garment workers can take myriad forms. It can occur at the level of the national government, regional governments, or even export-processing zone management. Governments and zones can pursue a "no unions" policy, either subtly, through various forms of company or state-backed unions that must be displaced before an independent union can take power, or overtly,

where union leaders are openly fired—and sometimes murdered.

Garment factories in the South vary considerably, ranging from giant, well-lit plants that employ thousands of workers, through subcontracted smaller shops, to industrial homework. Describing the big factories as sweatshops may seem inappropriate; they certainly appear considerably cleaner and in better shape than the garment factories of New York and Los Angeles. But beneath the veneer of industrial order lurk excessively low wages, such that workers cannot possibly support their families. The factory may not look like a sweatshop, but the workers live under conditions that only sweatshops can produce. A disjunction has developed between appearance and reality, in part to satisfy U.S. manufacturers and retailers who (in response to their critics) insist that their contractors maintain clean facilities, even as they pay them too little to enable workers to support themselves in anything like decent conditions.

Government-supported employer efforts to crush independent unions make it difficult for workers to push for needed change. Moreover, over them hangs an implicit threat that if they do manage to improve wages, their employers will pick up and leave the country.

ILGWU and UNITE Responses

Contracting out and the runaway shop are not new to the U.S. apparel industry. Indeed, along with the construction unions and the Teamsters, the garment unions have had to cope with a fragmented and unstable working situation since the nineteenth century. In some ways, it is amazing that these unions were able to build such strength, given their industries' organizational structure.

The ILGWU was able to build itself into a powerful union by using the general strike across entire sectors and by signing "jobbers' agreements" that bound manufacturers who contracted out to use only union contractors. The New Deal and the development of strong, supportive institutions that encouraged the development of unions bolstered these strategies. Even with the passage of the Taft-Hartley Act, which prohibited secondary boycotts (i.e., boycotts against unrelated companies in a effort to pressure them to stop working with a direct union target), the garment unions had the muscle to get a special provision written into the law, the Garment Industry Proviso, which allowed the entire contracting system of an apparel manufacturer to be considered an integrated system of production. Thus much of the U.S. Northeast was able to become unionized (Stein 1977).

The solutions that the ILGWU developed had their own problems. Jobbers' agreements tended to encourage top-down organizing. Contractors would join the union as a means of ensuring that they received work from the manufacturers, creating a strange dynamic between the workers and their direct employers. Too often, union representatives had closer working relations with the contractors than with the workers. Workers still received important benefits from their union contract, including health insurance and a retirement plan. Nevertheless, it was easy for members to remain disconnected from the union and any of the ideals it had originally fought for. This became especially evident in New York's Chinatown, where many immigrant workers came to see the union strictly as a system of health insurance.

The equilibrium established between the companies and the union, supported by the government, managed to diminish the number of sweatshops greatly, although they persisted at the fringes of the industry. The system was always vulnerable to attack, however, especially by movement not simply out of state but out of the country.

Gradually, especially since the late 1970s, government backing for unionization eroded and supportive institutions were weakened. Employers seized the opportunity to take the offensive against the ILGWU and began to use nonunion companies with impunity. Some moved production offshore, aided by a U.S. government that was eagerly pursuing a trade policy encouraging such movement. The union was faced with severe membership loss and declining power in dealing with the manufacturers.

The ILGWU Response before the Merger

In a state of crisis that had been brewing since the 1970s, the ILGWU engaged in a number of campaigns to try to salvage its position. In 1990, Jeff Hermanson, a talented organizer and brilliant strategist, became head of the International's Organizing Department. During the 1990s he made a number of serious attempts to revive the union, including the Leslie Fay strike. Leslie Fay was a large union jobber (manufacturer) that tried to break its contract by shifting production to nonunion contractors, on the grounds that all their competition was doing it. The ILGWU decided to draw a line in the sand and fight the company. A strike was called, and the union won. Shortly thereafter, however, Leslie Fay declared bankruptcy.

Hermanson saw the need for the union to develop an international strategy. It had to help workers in other countries organize themselves so that the industry could not pit workers in different countries against each other. Hermanson helped organize the first unionized factory in an export-processing zone in the Dominican Republic and contributed to a legacy of militant unionism there. He also developed the idea of Garment Worker Justice Centers. These centers would serve as places where workers could come to deal with grievances concerning their jobs and could develop their capacity to fight back. Although these workers were not covered by collective-bargaining agreements and did not become full-fledged union members, the hope was that they would develop union consciousness and contribute to the struggle in their own factories. Over the 1990s justice centers were developed in New York, Texas, and California (Hermanson 1993).

In the early 1990s Guess? Inc., the largest apparel manufacturer in Los Angeles, became the target of a major ILGWU organizing drive. Since World War II a sizable portion of the garment industry had gradually moved to Southern California, which had managed to establish itself as an almost union-free alternative to the East Coast. Employment had grown steadily there, even as it had shrunk in the East. The Guess? campaign was an effort to establish a union foothold in Los Angeles. Hermanson worked closely with David Young, the local director of organizing, in the effort to organize the entire production system of Guess? including its inside shop of cutters and warehouse workers and its contracting network of about forty factories. Because of internal politics within the ILGWU, however, the Guess? campaign faced divided loyalties at the top of the union. Moreover, the merger with ACTWU was in full swing, distracting the union leaders and raising questions about the allocation of resources (Milkman and Wong 2001).

The Impact of the Merger and the Creation of UNITE

The merger between the ILGWU and ACTWU came about because both unions were in deep trouble in the mid-1990s. The ILGWU still had a lot of money in the form of property and investments, even though it was suffering major losses of membership

each year. ACTWU's membership losses were less severe, but it was broke. In general, the ILGWU was viewed as a dinosaur, a fossil unable to move, while ACTWU was praised for its forward-looking organizing model. These judgments were not fair, especially given Hermanson's leadership, but the merger was widely considered to be a joining of ACTWU talent with ILGWU resources. The expectation was that ACTWU's leaders would take over the union, allowing an acceptable period of time for some of the old ILGWU leadership (especially International president Jay Mazur) to retire.

Whatever its faults, the ILGWU had long experience in dealing with fragmented production systems. By contrast ACTWU, itself the product of a merger of the textile union and the men's wear apparel unions, had little experience with the world of sweatshops in the women's wear industry; it was used to organizing in large, reasonably stable factories. The union had taken on the incredibly difficult task of organizing textile factories in the South (and had often failed), but it knew nothing of the tiny, mobile, hidden world of the sweatshop.

Another difference between the two unions was the ethnicity of their members. ACTWU was mainly a white and Black union of native-born workers. The ILGWU was mainly a "yellow" and "brown" union of immigrants from Asia, Latin America, and the Caribbean. The ILGWU in Los Angeles, for example, had become very involved in the organizing of undocumented Latino immigrants, even those outside the apparel industry.

The Guess? campaign in Los Angeles became an important arena for a showdown between the two unions. The campaign had been devised and run by the ILGWU. The basic idea was to work toward an organizing strike that would shut down Guess? and its contractors. The campaign was multifaceted, combining on-the-ground organizing with public exposure of Guess? as a sweatshop producer and with protest actions at their retail outlets, among other tactics. While the possibility that Guess? might move its production offshore was always present, the hope was that moving in the face of a labor struggle would violate the NLRA. Moreover, the union hoped, once a contract was signed, to set limits on offshore production.

The merger of the two unions led to meetings between their organizing leaders. ACTWU particularly was known for its brilliant corporate campaigns. (The ILGWU was not weak in this area either.) It was hoped that the ILGWU's experience on the ground could be combined with ACTWU's corporate know-how to strengthen the Guess? campaign. But this did not happen; the ACTWU leaders opposed the strike strategy, leading eventually to the resignation of Hermanson and Young. ACTWU took over the campaign, which devolved into a legal battle with Guess? Inc. Meanwhile, Guess? used the opportunity to shift most of its production to Mexico and Latin America. The battle was lost, even though it sputtered on for several years and cost UNITE millions of dollars.

The Guess? campaign was a turning point for UNITE's role in the U.S. apparel industry. For one thing, it led to disillusionment with trying to organize the apparel industry in Los Angeles. So much money had been spent, with so few results. The union needed to pull back from that situation and reassess. It still had a large membership base in New York sewing factories that it had to maintain, but the new leadership did not seem interested in opening new fronts in organizing immigrant garment workers.

The union decided to take two approaches. First, it shifted its new organizing efforts to a combination of apparel industry–related tar-gets and other industries that were outside its traditional jurisdiction, such as nursing homes. The apparel-related industries included industrial laundries and distribution centers. In neither case was the industry likely to leave the United States. The women's wear production factories, in contrast, were seen as too fragile to organize. They would simply go out of business or move offshore, leaving impoverished immigrant workers even worse off than they had been.

Occasionally UNITE has taken on apparel-industry organizing. For instance, in 2000 in Los Angeles, under the new leadership of Cristina Vazquez (Milkman and Wong 2000), UNITE organized a strike against Hollander, an old union company that was trying to escape from its contract.

UNITE's second approach to global and flexible production has been to support, join, and develop the growing anti-sweatshop movement, including the important student movement. This movement is concerned primarily with global sweatshops and how they have emerged as a product of the neoliberal world order. Anti-sweatshop organizations have sprung up all over since the mid-1990s, some linked to UNITE and some independent of the union (Shaw 1999). Even when UNITE has played a role in developing an organization, however, the new group has quickly developed its own voice. (This is apparent in the development of United Students Against Sweatshops and its creation, the Worker Rights Consortium.)

Critics of UNITE and of the anti-sweatshop and anti-globalization movements have claimed that these efforts are protectionist. They argue that UNITE is trying to keep apparel jobs in the United States by trying to raise labor standards in countries of the global South, so that those countries can no longer compete on the basis of lower wages, poorer working conditions, and the absence of unions.

But this charge is false. There was a period during the 1970s and early 1980s when the ILGWU ran a "Buy American" campaign in an effort to stop industry flight (Frank 1999), but those times are long over. The ship has left the dock and there is no turning back. UNITE's anti-sweatshop work, along with that of the numerous nongovernmental organizations that have joined it, is a principled form of opposition to declining labor and living standards for workers in other countries. Along with such groups as the AFL-CIO's Solidarity Center, the union is trying to support and encourage organizing in the garment industry around the world with a view to improving conditions for all workers.

New Strategies by Labor

Three major approaches seem to dominate labor's response to global and flexible production at the beginning of the twenty-first century. The first approach involves organizing outside traditional unions; the second, changing the institutional structures of global capitalism; and the third, cross-border organizing.

Working outside the Union: The Los Angeles Garment Workers' Center

In the face of a loss of proactive organizing by UNITE in the Los Angeles garment industry, a group of organizations concerned with the exploitation of immigrant workers came together in 2000 to form the Garment Workers' Center (GWC). Developed under the aegis of the nongovernmental organization Sweatshop Watch, the GWC's formation involved the active participation of the Asian Pacific American Legal Center, the Coalition for Humane Immigrant Rights in Los Angeles (CHIRLA), and the Korean Immigrant Workers Advocates (KIWA), among others. Building on UNITE's

justice center concept and learning from various nonunion immigrant workers' organizations (such as AIWA, the Asian Immigrant Women's Advocates; CHIRLA's organizing of day laborers and domestic workers; and KIWA's organizing of restaurant workers), the GWC serves as a legal aid, research, education, and action center for garment workers. It is headed by Kimi Lee, and in its short life the center has already developed a local presence as a force to be taken seriously. One of its key tenets is that it be multiracial, bringing together Latino and Asian garment workers.

Perhaps this is the best model for organizing workers under the extremely repressive labor regime in the Los Angeles apparel industry. Because shops close down readily, because undocumented workers can be deported, and because garment workers live so close to poverty, traditional union organizing efforts seem doomed to failure. At best they are destined for the long term and are costly, and unions faced with both membership and financial losses feel they cannot afford traditional strategies. The GWC, in contrast, depends largely on foundation money and volunteer labor and takes a less confrontational approach to the workplace. Although it takes on employers and demands that workers be paid what they are owed under the law, it does not push for strikes or collective-bargaining agreements.

Changing the Institutions

A lot of institutional ferment surrounds global production and its obvious negative consequences for workers and their families, both here and offshore. One important development has been the growing movement targeting the World Trade Organization, the World Bank, the International Monetary Fund, and other institutions that are directing corporate-dominated globalization. This movement is able to mobilize massive demonstrations at the meetings of the various bodies, insisting that labor and environmental rights be given a prominent place in all trade agreements. Accusations that the movement—which is a coalition of many forces, including unions, environmentalists, human rights groups, and youth—is against all forms of global integration are a distortion. What the movement wants is greater equality, within and between countries. Its supporters oppose the "race to the bottom" that is developing as a result of countries being forced to compete with each other to offer global capital the lowest possible labor costs, and they want to see basic labor standards put in place.

One might view these efforts as an attempt to create a kind of "global welfare state," with international agencies putting in place and policing rules covering minimum wage, overtime, child labor, women's rights, and rights to organize. An important issue concerns the concept of a "living wage," since a single, global wage standard seems impractical. Instead, activists want to ensure that, no matter what the differences in cost of living are between countries, workers are paid enough to feed and educate their children and to live in decent housing.

An important demand of the movement is for freedom of association by workers, including the right to organize independent unions and the right to bargain collectively with their employers. Serious protections for such rights would go a long way toward alleviating the sweatshop problem. Unfortunately, in too many countries union activity is simply crushed, sometimes with great brutality. One should note that this is not only a Southern problem but is prevalent in the United States as well, despite seemingly protective laws.

Institutional change is also being addressed at the level of companies (manufacturers and retailers). The basic challenge for labor is to bind these higher-level entities to their con-

tractors, so that they are forced to take responsibility for conditions in the contracting shops. The ILGWU fought for joint-liability legislation, with only limited success.

Another approach to the problems that surround global and flexible production is to get companies to develop codes of conduct and to monitor them to ensure that they are being implemented. This concept has extended to municipalities, regarding the uniforms they purchase for city workers (New York City passed related legislation at the end of the 1990s), and to universities (under pressure from University Students Against Sweatshops, or USAS). Cities and universities have set up codes for the companies with which they do business, trying to hold them accountable if their contractors violate the codes. The codes, in other words, act to enforce a kind of joint liability.

U.S. apparel companies have jumped on this bandwagon, establishing their own codes of conduct and their own monitoring systems (see Schoenberger 2000). This can be seen as a preemptive and public relations strategy, as the companies try to ensure the consuming public that they are "sweat-free" and would not think of using any factory that violates basic labor standards. The companies then hire monitoring firms to oversee their contracting empires around the world. The result has been the creation of a new industry of global factory monitors. Various competing organizations have taken up the challenge by recruiting companies to join them, with a view to providing monitoring for their members. The U.S. government–created Fair Labor Association (FLA) is one such organization. UNITE, among other organizations, walked out of the meetings that led to the creation of the FLA, on the grounds that it is an industry-dominated entity. (For the weaknesses of monitoring by companies, see Esbenshade 2000.)

USAS, which has worked closely with UNITE, created its own oversight institution, the Worker Rights Consortium (WRC). One of the cardinal principles of the WRC, unlike the FLA, is to prohibit apparel firms from becoming members of the organization. The WRC is a tripartite entity, bringing together universities, the student movement, and garment-worker advocates from around the world to ensure that companies that license with universities to produce collegiate apparel are living up to the WRC's code of conduct. Rather than relying on self-monitoring of contractors by their employing corporations, the WRC is trying to develop relations with workers via pro-worker nongovernmental organizations, including rights organizations, churches, and unions. Unlike the FLA, which promises companies certification that allows them to claim their goods as sweat-free, the WRC offers no such assurance but instead serves as a watchdog to protect workers and give them a safe place to lodge grievances. Given the great imbalances of power between capital and labor in this industry, students and advocates believe that the companies do not need protection. The WRC can deal with them, but they should not be part of the process of setting WRC standards and policy. In particular, the WRC strongly supports union organizing, which is generally anathema to the industry.

The WRC is a young organization in the process of development, so its model is still being tested. University administrative representatives, especially those from schools with large athletic programs, want to maintain good relations with their licensees, some of whom give those programs generous gifts in exchange for prominently displaying their corporate logos (Klein 1999). Universities are caught between the demands of their students and the demands of their licensees and tend to serve as a conservatizing force on the WRC. Nevertheless, the WRC is a promising model that may provide global garment workers (although in a narrow sector) with some protection for organizing.

Cross-Border Organizing

The obvious answer to the challenges of global capitalism is the development of a global working-class movement. If ever there was a time to apply the slogan "Workers of the World Unite!" it is now. Efforts are going forth in this direction, and various campaigns have been launched (see, e.g., Armbruster 1998 and Armbruster-Sandoval 1999). The AFL-CIO's Solidarity Center is sending organizers to various countries to work with local unionists, and now that it has largely been stripped of its Cold War ideology, the center has more chance of success. Some of the international trade secretariats are also active, including the International Textile, Garment and Leather Workers Federation.

Throughout the 1990s and into the twenty-first century, campaigns have been launched against Nike and the Gap and against various contractors, such as Chentex (in Nicaragua) and Kukdong (in Mexico). There is no need to review each campaign here. The point is that support for workers' organizing efforts has developed around the world, and pressure has been put on the corporations and retailers to stop local contactors from suppressing worker organizing. Since the natural reaction of transnational corporations is simply to withdraw and move their work to another factory or country, additional pressure is put on them not to engage in such an irresponsible action but instead to stay and clean up the mess they created.

The leverage that supporters in Northern countries have is through their role as consumers. Supporters of workers and of unionizing efforts can expose a company's sweatshop and union-busting practices to the public, thereby hurting its image and soiling its brand name (Klein 1999). These kinds of exposés can push a company to get its contractor to conform to worker-supportive demands.

The effectiveness of such strategies remains somewhat murky. Corporations can insist that their contractors change their practices without altering their own pricing policies. The burden of change then falls on the contractor, and the corporation remains only a watchdog. Clearly, more money needs to be extracted at the manufacturer and retailer level in order to get conditions to improve substantially for garment workers around the world.

Toward the Future

In some industries, cross-border organizing means that workers and unions at the branches of a major transnational corporation all work together and coordinate their actions and demands. This was a feature of the United Parcel Service strike (Russo and Banks 1998). In the apparel industry, however, the opportunities for such coordinated strategies are stymied by the looser relations between the transnational corporation and its contractors and the resulting mobility and secrecy that characterize the production network. The lack of a strong union base in the industry in many countries (including the United States) also makes collaborating difficult.

Nevertheless, I believe the major route to social change is empowered workers who are able to demand that change. Developing strong international campaigns that bring together the workers of contractors who operate in more than one country (which sometimes happens among bigger contractors, such as Kukdong) or of multiple contractors who work for the same transnational corporation must be placed high on labor's agenda. These kinds of campaigns require creative thinking

about how to organize far-flung workers. And they require that unions and federations of unions put their best talent and resources to work on the task.

One way to think about international organizing is to consider the entire circulation of capital and where labor has the power to intervene. For example, finance and distribution are critical phases in capital's circulation. In the United States the transportation of imported goods could prove to be a bottleneck that is vulnerable to pressure on behalf of garment workers who are trying to organize themselves in other countries.

Global and flexible production have definitely strengthened the hand of capital and weakened that of labor. This is evident not only in declining union density but also in the severe lowering of labor standards in the industry. Traditional approaches to unionization do not seem to work under these circumstances, yet workers need unity and representation more than ever. New ideas are being tried, both by unions and by various worker-advocating organizations. Hopefully some of them will succeed.

References

Armbruster, Ralph. 1998. "Globalization and Cross-Border Labor Organizing in the Garment and Automobile Industries." Ph.D. diss., Department of Sociology, University of California, Riverside.

Armbruster-Sandoval, Ralph. 1999. "Globalization and Cross-Border Labor Organizing: The Guatemalan Maquiladora Industry and the Phillips Van Heusen Workers Movement." *Latin American Perspectives* 26: 108–28.

Bonacich, Edna. 2000. "Intense Challenges, Tentative Possibilities: Organizing Immigrant Garment Workers in Los Angeles." In *Organizing Immigrants: The Challenge for Unions in Contemporary California*, ed. Ruth Milkman, pp. 130–49. Ithaca, N.Y.: ILR Press.

Bonacich, Edna, and Richard P. Appelbaum. 2000. *Behind the Label: Inequality in the Los Angeles Apparel Industry.* Berkeley: University of California Press.

Compa, Lance. 2000. *Unfair Advantage: Workers' Freedom of Association in the United States under International Human Rights Standards.* Washington, D.C.: Human Rights Watch.

Esbenshade, Jill. 2000. "Globalization and Resistance in the Apparel Industry: The Struggle over Monitoring." Paper presented at the American Sociological Association meetings, Washington, D.C., August.

Frank, Dana. 1999. *Buy American: The Untold Story of Economic Nationalism.* Boston: Beacon Press.

Hermanson, Jeff. 1993. "Organizing for Justice: ILGWU Returns to Social Unionism to Organize Immigrant Workers." *Labor Research Review* 12: 52–61.

International Labour Office (ILO). 2000. *Labour Practices in the Footwear, Leather, Textiles and Clothing Industries.* Geneva: ILO.

Klein, Naomi. 1999. *No Logo: Taking Aim at the Brand Bullies.* New York: Picador.

Milkman, Ruth, and Kent Wong. 2000. "Cristina Vazquez." In *Voices from the Front Lines: Organizing Immigrant Workers in Los Angeles,* pp. 3–10. Los Angeles: University of California, Los Angeles, Center for Labor Research and Education.

———. 2001. "Organizing Immigrant Workers: Case Studies from Southern California." In *Rekindling the Movement: Labor's Quest for Relevance in the Twenty-first Century,* ed. Lowell Turner, Harry C. Katz, and Richard W. Hurd, pp. 99–128. Ithaca, N.Y.: Cornell University Press.

Ross, Andrew, ed. 1997. *No Sweat: Fashion, Free Trade, and the Rights of Garment Workers.* London: Verso.

Russo, John, and Andrew Banks. 1998. "Building Global Trade Union Campaigns and Organizing Structures: Taking the UPS Strike Overseas." Paper presented at UCLEA/AFL-CIO Education Conference, San Jose, California, May 2.

Schoenberger, Karl. 2000. *Levi's Children: Coming to Terms with Human Rights in the Global Marketplace.* New York: Atlantic Monthly Press.

Shaw, Randy. 1999. *Reclaiming America: Nike, Clean Air, and the New National Activism.* Berkeley: University of California Press.

Stein, Leon, ed. 1977. *Out of the Sweatshop: The Struggle for Union Democracy.* New York: Quadrangle/The New York Times Book Company.

Varley, Pamela, ed. 1998. *The Sweatshop Quandary: Corporate Responsibility on the Global Frontier.* Washington, D.C.: Investor Responsibility Research Center.

Part III

The U.S.–Mexico
Border Region

David Spener

7   The Unraveling Seam:
NAFTA and the Decline of the
Apparel Industry in El Paso, Texas

In this chapter I describe the restructuring and job loss in the garment industry of El Paso, Texas, that has accompanied trade liberalization between the United States and Mexico since the late 1980s. As a small city whose "Old West" economy has traditionally revolved around the "four C's—copper, cattle, cotton, and climate" (Mangan 1980, 115), El Paso may seem an unlikely subject for the study of trade regulations and the globalization of the apparel industry. In 1993, on the eve of the passage of the North American Free Trade Agreement, El Paso's civilian labor force numbered 278,500, of whom 24,000 worked in the garment industry.[1] As such, El Paso is just a "bit" player in the international manufacture and distribution of clothing, accounting for only about 2.5 percent of the 973,000 workers who labored in the U.S. garment industry that year (U.S. Bureau of the Census 1993). Appearances can be deceiving, however, and a number of factors combine to make the city an especially interesting and important site for studying change in the garment industry in the aftermath of the North American Free Trade Agreement:

- El Paso has for many years been one of the largest, if not *the* largest, points of production of denim jeans in the United States. Since at least the 1950s, the city has been known as the "Jeans Capital of the World" (van Dooren 1997). Until recently, nearly one-quarter of Levi Strauss and Company's twenty-five thousand U.S. employees worked there, along with several thousand other workers in the employ of Wrangler, Lee Company, and Sun Apparel, among others. On a weekly basis, Levi's plants alone could produce over five hundred thousand pairs of blue jeans in El Paso. In addition, many aspects of blue jeans production in El Paso, involving both large-scale and smaller producers, are linked to the operation of Mexican maquiladoras south of the border.

- In addition to a handful of large-scale blue jeans factories, El Paso has been home to dozens of smaller garment firms engaged in cutting, sewing, laundering, and finishing not only blue jeans but also a variety of women's and misses' outerwear garments. These smaller firms are concentrated in the city center and, taken as a whole, exhibit many of the characteristics typically associated with entrepreneurial industrial districts—a skilled workforce, routine interfirm collaboration based on social network connections among artisan-owners, as well as intrafirm social capital based on shared ethnicity or common participation in immigrant networks by entrepreneurs and their employees (Bull, Pitt, and Szarka 1993; Portes 1995). Unlike successful entrepreneurial garment communities elsewhere, however, the small-scale sector in El Paso finds itself in acute crisis in the face of overseas competition, especially from the maquiladoras. Ironically, some of these smaller garment shops until quite recently collaborated in subcontracting networks with maquiladoras in Mexico on a complementary basis.

- In the 1970s, El Paso was the scene of the massive strike against the Farah Company, one of the last major unionization battles in the garment industry to be won by workers. Winning the strike and union recognition proved to be a Pyrrhic victory for labor, however, as after the strike Farah laid off thousands of workers and moved production offshore (DeMoss 1989; Coyle, Hershatter, and Honig 1984; Honig 1996). The inability of the garment workers to gain recognition of their union *and* prevent the loss of jobs to the maquiladoras in the late 1970s continues to have repercussions throughout the industry today.

- The U.S.-Mexico border region also offers a unique environment in which to observe, in stark relief, the effects that changes in state regulation of the clothing trade have on workers and their communities. In El Paso, the social construction of economic space through state regulation is a striking feature of everyday life. Nowhere is this more evident than in the local garment in-

dustry, many of whose owners and employees maintain an intense interaction with Mexico and Mexicans, a country and people with whom they share a common culture, language, and history. Due to the vagaries of the world apparel market and changing government trade policies, however, the extent to which their economic and social destinies will remain linked is not clear.

- Finally, because the El Paso garment industry is largely peopled by Mexican immigrant women, the brunt of the massive job losses witnessed since the beginning of 1994 are being borne by a particularly vulnerable and poor segment of the local population. Rising immigrant unemployment comes precisely at a time when U.S. immigration and welfare policy has turned especially mean-spirited, leaving newly unemployed garment workers with few appealing alternatives.

The analysis presented in this chapter is based on data from official sources in the United States and Mexico, as well as in-depth interviews and surveys conducted with entrepreneurs and workers in the industry from 1996 to 1998. The chapter is divided into four sections. First, I give an overview of the history and organization of the garment industry and its workforce in El Paso. Second, I describe state regulation of the garment trade between the United States and Mexico under the Multifiber Arrangement (MFA) and the in-bond assembly (maquiladora) program and how this regulation helped structure the garment sector in El Paso. Third, I analyze the reorganization of the El Paso garment industry since the 1989 changes in the Multifiber Arrangement, which has intensified under the North American Free Trade Agreement. This reorganization involves the closing or movement of many sewing operations, both large- and small-scale, to the Mexican side under the auspices of the maquiladora program. By way of conclusion,

TABLE 7.1.   Distribution of the Economically Active Population (EAP) of El Paso, Texas, by Ethnicity and Nativity, 1990 (in percent)

Ethnic/Nativity Group	Total EAP	Garment Industry (manual and nonmanual workers)	Garment Workers (manual only)
U.S.-Born Latinos[a]	40.8	33.9	31.2
Latino Immigrants	24.6	61.1	67.4
Non-Hispanic White Natives	27.7	2.6	0.2
Members of Other Groups	6.9	2.4	1.2
Total	100.0	100.0	100.0

Source: "5 Percent Public Use Microdata Sample," U.S. Census of Population and Housing, 1990.

[a]Over 95 percent of both U.S.-born and immigrant Latinos in El Paso are of Mexican origin.

I offer a few comments on what this reorganization portends for garment-industry enterprises and their workers in El Paso.

The Garment Industry in El Paso

The garment industry has played a major role in the El Paso economy since at least the 1920s, when Lebanese immigrants Mansour and Hannah Farah began to manufacture chambray shirts and denim pants for rail, ranch, and mine workers in the Southwest. The industry expanded after the Great Depression to meet the demand for military uniforms during World War II. After the war garment production continued to grow, fueled by El Paso's cheap, nonunion labor supply. In the immediate postwar period, blue jeans emerged as the dominant garment in the city's apparel sector, a dominance retained through the beginning of the twenty-first century (van Dooren 1997). In El Paso in 1993, "men's and boy's furnishings," which consisted mainly of large-scale blue jeans production, accounted for approximately 60 percent of the city's total apparel employment. In addition, a significant number of establishments and workers have been dedicated to the sewing of ladies' outerwear, including jackets and blouses as well as pants. In the same year, fifty-three of El Paso's

eighty-five registered garment-manufacturing establishments were classified as being dedicated to the production of women's wear (U.S. Bureau of the Census 1993). From these figures we confirm the extent to which smaller-scale establishments that year were concentrated in the production of women's wear.

As has been the case in major U.S. cities on both the East and West Coasts—New York, San Francisco, and Los Angeles, for example—the El Paso garment workforce has consisted largely of women immigrants who have worked for low wages and sometimes in sweatshop conditions. Table 7.1 indicates the extent to which the city's 1990 garment-industry workforce was dominated by Mexican immigrants and Mexican Americans,[2] who, taken together, comprised 65 percent of the city's total workforce (U.S. Bureau of the Census 1990). Less than 3 percent of the entire industry workforce in 1990 consisted of non-Hispanic whites, and virtually all of these were employed in white-collar positions. In 1990 nearly 100 percent of manual garment workers in El Paso were of Mexican origin, and over two-thirds had been born in Mexico.

Table 7.2 provides selected characteristics of the El Paso garment industry's immigrant workforce compared with the all members of the economically active population (EAP) and all Mexican immigrants working in the city in

TABLE 7.2.   Selected Characteristics of the Economically Active Population (EAP) of
El Paso, Texas, 1990

Characteristic	Total EAP	Mexican Immigrants	Mexican Immigrant Garment Workers
Percent who work in the garment industry	5.5	14.0	100.0
Percent female	44.1	44.6	61.5
Percent who have completed high school or its equivalent	73.0	40.0	19.2
Percent who speak English "not well" or "not at all"	12.6	42.6	65.6
Percent who speak Spanish at home	63.3	96.2	96.5
Percent who are U.S. citizens	82.9	36.1	30.4
Percent who immigrated from Mexico, 1985–90	—	11.9	13.7
Percent who immigrated from Mexico, 1980–90	—	29.0	26.4
Median age	36.3	38.4	37.9
Median annual earnings, 1989 (U.S.$)	15,156	9,681	9,062
Percent living below the official poverty line	16.3	33.1	33.7
Median public assistance received, 1989 (U.S.$)	519	855	770

Source: "5 Percent Public Use Microdata Sample," U.S. Census of Population and Housing, 1990.

1990. Immigrant garment workers were much more likely than both the overall EAP and all economically active Mexican immigrants to be women, to have less than a high school education, to speak English poorly or not at all, and not to be U.S. citizens. In addition, Mexican immigrant garment workers had median earnings more than $6,000 lower than local workers taken as a whole and were more than twice as likely to live in poverty—more than a third of immigrant garment workers lived in households whose income fell below the official poverty line, compared to "just" 16 percent in the overall EAP. Like most Mexican immigrants working in El Paso, nearly all immigrant garment workers spoke Spanish at home, and a substantial number—around 40 percent—had immigrated to the United States in the 1980s.

The apparel industry's dominance of the El Paso economy peaked in the early 1970s, when 60 percent of all manufacturing workers and nearly 20 percent of all private-sector workers in the city were employed in the needle trades (Márquez 1995). By the end of the next decade, the apparel industry had declined precipi-

tously, in both relative and absolute terms: Only one-third of manufacturing workers and just 8 percent of all workers were employed in the manufacture of clothing, as around ten thousand jobs in the industry were lost (Honig 1996; Márquez 1995).

There were several reasons for this elimination of jobs in the garment industry in El Paso in the late 1970s and early 1980s. Labor strife was a major precipitating factor. In 1974, one of the largest local employers—the Farah Company, which employed around seven thousand workers in El Paso—finally succumbed to a successful unionization effort after a two-year strike (Coyle, Hershatter, and Honig 1984; DeMoss 1989; Honig 1996). This important union victory proved to be short-lived: Farah and other local manufacturers drastically scaled back their El Paso sewing operations and moved across the border into Mexico to set up as maquiladoras. After the severe devaluations of the Mexican peso in the early 1980s, these firms could avail themselves of labor that was only one-tenth to one-eighth as expensive as minimum-wage labor in El Paso. Some of these companies, such as

Farah, formed Mexican subsidiaries, while others contracted their sewing operations to Mexican national companies.[3]

In addition, the overall stagnation of the U.S. economy in the late 1970s and early 1980s had the effect of depressing clothing sales and prices. Combined with a surge in low-cost Asian imports, this resulted in severe job losses in the garment industry. The decline of the apparel industry in El Paso mirrored the decline in the industry nationwide—1973–91 saw a net loss of over four hundred thousand garment jobs in the United States (U.S. Bureau of Labor Statistics, cited in Blumenberg and Ong 1994, 312). While the Mexican maquiladoras cannot account for many of the U.S. jobs lost in the industry nationwide, the loss of sewing jobs in El Paso after 1974 can be attributed in some measure to maquiladora plants opening in Mexico.[4]

Another important consequence of the successful unionization of Farah was the emergence of a set of small, subcontractor sewing shops, many of which were started by former employees of the larger manufacturers and some of which could accurately be described as sweatshops.[5] Although the informal, underground nature of many of these shops makes it difficult to estimate their number with any degree of accuracy, informants I interviewed in the field suggest that as recently as 1990 several dozen small sewing establishments (with twenty to fifty employees each) were still scattered throughout El Paso's central industrial district.[6]

Employment in this small-scale sector drew lower wages than in the larger plants and was also extremely precarious—when there were orders to fill, workers could labor around the clock; when orders were scarce, employees were laid off. In addition, it was not uncommon for shop owners to fail to pay their workers when they had cash-flow problems, in some cases shutting down their shops entirely and

then reopening in new locations shortly thereafter in order to avoid paying back wages owed (author's field interviews, corroborated in Márquez 1995). Prior to the 1986 Immigration Reform and Control Act, which legalized a large portion of El Paso's Mexican undocumented workers, many of the employees in these small shops did not have a U.S. work permit, which made them extremely vulnerable to exploitation by employers. Even after the legalization program's completion, the depressed state of the garment industry, combined with the continual arrival of new Mexican immigrants to El Paso, kept the supply of cheap labor abundant, limiting the ability of legalized immigrants to better their status and pay.[7]

El Paso under MFA and Item 807

Before the North American Free Trade Agreement on January 1, 1994, much of the structure of the garment industry in El Paso was influenced by regulations contained in the Multifiber Arrangement and those aspects of the U.S. tariff code (Item 807) that governed in-bond assembly of garments overseas. The Multifiber Arrangement (MFA) is a multilateral agreement first negotiated under the auspices of the General Agreement on Tariffs and Trade (GATT) in 1974 and renewed every five years since; in the early 1990s about fifty countries were signatories to the agreement (Bonacich and Waller 1994). Under the GATT Uruguay round, a ten-year phaseout (1995–2004) of the MFA was negotiated, a process that is now in progress (World Trade Organization 2001). The MFA permits signatories to negotiate bilateral agreements regulating the trade in garments. Before the adoption of the North American Free Trade Agreement (NAFTA), the in-bond assembly program for garments that had been developed by the United States and Mexico operated in accordance with MFA rules.

Under Item 807 of the U.S. tariff code, manufacturers may ship U.S.-made components to another country for assembly and then import them back into the United States, paying a duty only on the value added in the other country. This allows U.S. companies to take advantage of lower-cost labor overseas to complete labor-intensive aspects of their production processes. While, in principle, Item 807 may be used anywhere around the world, companies mainly have used it for production in Mexico and the Caribbean countries, whose close geographic proximity to the United States prevents transportation costs from erasing any cost savings to be gained by employing cheaper labor (Bonacich and Waller 1994; Mathews 1995).

Before the adoption of NAFTA, a number of peculiarities in the administration of Item 807 limited the quantity of garments that could be assembled by Mexican maquiladoras for export to the United States (Anderson 1990; Tiano 1994). These served to protect apparel production by both large- and small-scale operations in El Paso. First, only the actual sewing of garments could be carried out "in bond" on the Mexican side, since this was the only part of the garment manufacturing process that was considered to be "assembly." Thus other operations, such as cutting, washing, finishing, and packaging of garments, had to remain in the United States in order for garments to be eligible for 807 treatment. Second, in keeping with the MFA framework, the United States and Mexico negotiated numerical import quotas that limited the annual quantity of garments that could be sewn in Mexico by maquiladoras for subsequent sale in the U.S. market. These annual quotas were made substantially more flexible after bilateral negotiations in 1987–88, with the effect that, beginning in 1989, annual quotas for Item 807

apparel goods were raised by 50 percent or more each year and were automatically adjusted upward any year in which they were filled (Bonacich and Waller 1994; personal communication, U.S. International Trade Commission, November 1996). Thus, for all practical purposes, numerical quotas for apparel maquiladora imports into the United States were eliminated in 1989. Under the bilateral agreement negotiated in 1987–88, the tariff on maquiladora-assembled garments entering the United States averaged around 20 percent on the value added in Mexico, or around 5 percent of the total cost of the garment to the manufacturer (Hufbauer and Schott 1992, 268–72). Because of the rise in the value of the peso relative to the U.S. dollar in the late 1980s and early 1990s, hourly labor costs for sewing operators in Mexico in 1992 were about $0.88, compared to the rate of $4.00–$7.00 per hour that operators in aboveboard establishments could earn performing the same tasks across the border in El Paso.[8]

Given the elimination of quotas and the cost pressures retailers were placing on producers, by 1989 considerable advantages could be gained by expanding production into Mexico. Not surprisingly, Mexico saw a burst of apparel maquiladora employment, particularly in interior cities away from the border. Where in 1988 only about thirty-five thousand workers labored in apparel maquiladoras in Mexico, by 1993 the number had risen to sixty-five thousand (CIEMEX-WEFA 1996; INEGI 1992). During the same period, the value of garments exported through the El Paso and Laredo, Texas, customs ports by U.S. firms to Mexico, a large portion of which were destined for assembly in maquiladoras, rose from $200 million in 1989 to over $625 million in 1993 (U.S. Department of Commerce 1994b). The exports of "men's or boys' trousers of blue denim" (blue jeans) alone rose from just under 4 million pairs in 1989 to over 20 million in 1993 (U.S. Department of Commerce 1994a).[9]

How did the El Paso garment industry organize itself in the face of this binational regulatory arrangement? A number of large-scale producers—among them Action West, Farah, and Sun Apparel—opened or expanded sewing operations in Mexico, whether by means of owned-and-operated facilities or through contractors. At the same time, 807 regulations required that these and other companies' maquiladora-produced garments be cut and finished on the U.S. side. Thus a company such as Farah eventually shut down all its El Paso sewing facilities but maintained a cutting room and finishing and distribution center to complement its Mexican production (Honig 1996; van Dooren 1997). After 1989, as maquiladora production of denim garments expanded in Torreón, Mexico, demand for cutting and finishing services in El Paso was fueled by the need to have cloth cut on the U.S. side in order to qualify for 807 tariff reductions. In some cases, larger firms already established in El Paso opened or expanded their own cutting or finishing facilities there, while others, especially those operating through brokers located elsewhere in the United States, contracted to smaller-scale, independent cutting rooms and finishers around the city.[10] Already before NAFTA, competition from Mexican imports put severe pressures on small-scale sewing operations in El Paso, with many closing their doors.

By the time I arrived in El Paso to conduct interviews in 1996, only a few small-scale sewing operations were still in business (and most of these have since shut down). These hangers-on survived in a number of ways, including by doing special small-batch "rush" jobs for manufacturers or brokers located in El Paso and elsewhere in the United States, by producing specialized garments (such as Harley-Davidson jackets or small-label western wear) for retailers and their brokers, and

by offering smaller U.S.-based companies without overseas experience a relatively inexpensive alternative to organizing production outside the country.

The effects on the El Paso garment economy of this pre-NAFTA boom in Mexican maquiladora apparel production were mixed. On the one hand, it became more advantageous for U.S. manufacturers to contract a greater percentage of their sewing operations to Mexican maquiladoras. This put competitive pressure on El Paso sewing rooms. On the other hand, the boom in maquiladora apparel production in Mexico turned El Paso into a prime location for cutting and finishing operations, since these operations could not be carried out in Mexico if the completed garments were still to qualify for Item 807 tariff treatment. Thus the bilateral trade arrangements in place from 1989 through 1993 probably led to the loss of some sewing jobs and the addition of some cutting and finishing jobs in El Paso, as well as the rapid increase of sewing jobs across the border.

Somewhat paradoxically given these contradictory tendencies in the market, apparel industry employment in El Paso grew substantially in the last pre-NAFTA years. From the 1990 to 1993 average annual employment rose, from 18,400 jobs to 23,600 jobs (see Figure 7.1).[11] Most of this increase in employment did not have to do directly with the binational trade regime, however. In the early 1990s several large blue jeans manufacturers—among them Levi Strauss and Company, Lee Company, Wrangler, and Sun Apparel—expanded their existing operations or opened new plants in El Paso (personal communication, El Paso Office of Economic Development, October 1996; Medaille and Wheat 1997). Lee, Sun Apparel, and Wrangler combined to add more than two thousand employees to the garment workforce between 1992 and 1995 (Crimmins 1995).[12]

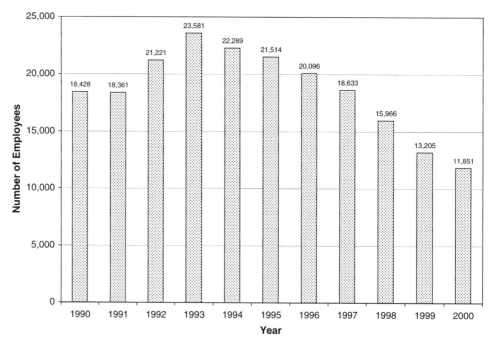

FIGURE 7.1.   Average Annual Apparel Employment in El Paso, Texas, 1990–2000
Source: Compiled from raw data provided by the Texas Workforce Commission.

There were three reasons for this increase in production and employment. First, style changes in the industry in the early 1990s promoted the sale of denim shirts and pants, leading to a 10 percent increase in blue jeans sales between 1991 and 1992, reversing a decade-long slump (Bary 1993). Second, interviews I conducted with employees of Levi Strauss and Company and Wrangler suggest that one of the main reasons for this expansion was the desire to produce garments with a "Made in the U.S.A." label for sale not only in the U.S. market but especially in Europe and Japan, where a pair of standard-cut blue jeans were selling for as much as $100 (corroborated in Crimmins 1995; Medaille and Wheat 1997; van Dooren 1997).[13]

El Paso, with a large, experienced denim-garment workforce, location in a right-to-work state, and some of the cheapest labor in the United States, was an ideal location for expan-

sion. It should also be noted that sewing-machine operators in the Lee, Wrangler, and Levi Strauss plants were paid considerably more (on the order of $7–$9 per hour) than employees in the smaller-scale shops described above, with much greater job security as well as other benefits, such as paid vacations and health insurance. Working conditions were also considerably better than those found in the smaller garment shops, and due to the use of newer and more sophisticated machines designed especially for sewing blue jeans, productivity was much higher as well.

At the dawn of NAFTA, then, El Paso was in the midst of a boom in garment employment, with the local industry dominated by three large employers. Levi Strauss and Company, Lee, and Wrangler had, respectively, forty-six hundred, two thousand, and twenty-six hundred El Paso employees (El Paso Office of Economic Development 1996). The expansion of these companies in El Paso also gave rise to considerable employment in the laundering of jeans, some of which was conducted by their owned-and-operated finishing plants and some of which was contracted to large-scale independently operated finishing plants.[14] In addition to laundering jeans produced locally in El Paso, Levi Strauss and Company's owned-and-operated finishing facilities laundered jeans produced by its plants in other U.S. locations and by its network of contractors in Mexico and elsewhere in Latin America. Laundering operations accounted for as many as 3,000 of the 23,600 garment jobs in El Paso in 1993. A glowing article in the Texas Comptroller's *Fiscal Notes*, published in February 1995, argued that El Paso's plants' use of advanced technologies and flexible production approaches had enabled them to buck the national downward trend in production and employment and would keep the city's garment industry competitive well into the future (Crimmins 1995).

Post-NAFTA Plant Closures and Layoffs

Changes in the Binational Trade Regime and the 1994 Peso Devaluation

Upon its implementation on January 1, 1994, NAFTA superseded previous agreements regulating binational trade between the United States and Mexico, including the Multifiber Arrangement and trade regulations pertaining to in-bond (Item 807 maquiladora) assembly. NAFTA changes in the existing binational trade regime for garments are being phased in over a period of years, however, so some aspects of the regulation of garments have been carried over from the previous regime.

Nevertheless, three of the most important changes were implemented immediately, on January 1, and had significant consequences for the El Paso apparel industry. First, the quotas for Item 807 apparel that had been raised and made more flexible in 1989 were eliminated altogether. Second, the 20 percent duty assessed on value added to garments assembled in Mexico was eliminated, thus effectively lowering Mexican labor costs to the manufacturer by one-fifth. Third, the washing of garments, including the high-value-added stone-washing process used for jeans, was no longer considered to be a "transformation" of the raw material and thus could be carried out on the Mexican side without tariff penalties being assessed. In addition, tariffs assessed by the United States on nonmaquiladora garments whose fabric originated in North America were lowered to around 9 percent, thus substantially reducing the barriers to Mexican national producers who wished to export their product to the United States.

These changes in the binational trade regime combined with two other developments to put increased pressures on the El Paso garment industry to lower its production costs or lose its market share. First, the overall stagnation in apparel sales in the United States by the mid-1990s, due to overproduction early in the decade, sluggish retail sales generally, and changes in women's fashions favoring simpler, more functional designs, put increased pressure on local producers to lower their prices to the buyers. Second, the unexpectedly drastic devaluation of the Mexican peso in December 1994 and its continued free fall during the first months of 1995 dramatically lowered labor costs in Mexico relative to those prevailing in the United States; this change in relative costs came in addition to the 20 percent effective lowering of Mexican labor costs attributable directly to NAFTA.

Changes in the binational trade regime combined with the radical lowering of Mexican labor costs accompanying the peso devaluation had a devastating impact on El Paso's garment sector. Job losses in the industry that have been certified by the U.S. Department of Labor as due to the implementation of NAFTA totaled 5,415 by May 1999,[15] representing about 75 percent of the 7,200 net jobs lost in the industry by the end of the third quarter of 1998. (See Figure 7.1 for the evolution of garment employment in El Paso, 1990–2000.) Nearly two-thirds of these certifications were for Standard Industrial Classification (SIC) 2325, "men's and boys' trousers and slacks" (i.e., blue jeans), and another one-fifth were for SIC 2339, "women's and misses' outerwear," which was also dominated by denim pants and other denim garments. Nearly one-third of these certifications were made on the basis of companies transferring production to Mexico, with the remainder due to increased penetration of Mexican imports after the implementation of NAFTA. The list of forty-nine companies that laid off a significant number of workers includes the names of such large-scale operators as Sun Apparel (803 workers) and its Greater Texas Finishing plant (150 workers),[16] Farah (375 workers), and El Paso Apparel Group (200 workers), as well as smaller, local companies such as CMT Industries (120 workers who manufactured women's blazers), JAM Enterprises (50 workers), a local cutting room,[17] and Final Finish (75 workers), a local jeans laundry. Unlike earlier periods of job loss in the El Paso garment sector, this round occurred during a period of national economic boom, with increasing disposable income among consumers and strong growth in retail sales around the nation.

As jobs were disappearing from El Paso, garment maquiladora employment in Mexico experienced another dramatic surge in growth. In 1993 around 74,000 garment workers labored in 404 maquiladoras throughout Mexico. By 1995 employment had risen to 94,000 employees working in 450 maquiladoras. At the end of 1996, the econometrics firm

CIEMEX-WEFA reported there were 110,000 garment workers laboring in 515 maquiladoras in Mexico. By the year 2000, 270,000 workers were sewing garments in 1,058 maquiladoras (INEGI 1993, 1995, 1996, 2000). The low-cost competition from these maquiladoras, many of which produced high-quality garments for the same manufacturers that had plants in El Paso or for the same retailers that contracted production to El Paso manufacturers, has played a fairly direct role in much of the job loss El Paso's apparel sector has experienced since January 1, 1994.

In contrast, the massive layoff of Levi's employees that followed the company's announcement of El Paso plant closures, first in November 1997, then in September 1998, and again in February 1999, could not be directly attributed to increased maquiladora production or NAFTA. It is to the proximate causes of these plant closures and their longer-term relationship to NAFTA that we now turn our attention.

The Levi Strauss and Company Plant Closures and Layoffs

By the mid-1990s, Levi Strauss and Company was El Paso's largest private employer,[18] operating seven plants in the city and employing around forty-six hundred workers.[19] The company had instituted a flexible work-team approach, automated parts of the jeans-assembly process, and renovated work stations in its local plants. These innovations were credited with significant improvements in productivity (Crimmins 1995). Levi's five sewing plants in El Paso produced more than half a million pairs of "Made in the U.S.A." 501 and 505 jeans per week at peak production. Hourly pay for workers ran as high as $9.00, and the company offered generous fringe benefits, including paid health care, paid vacation, dependent-care benefits, and a retirement plan. The company enjoyed cordial relations with the

Union of Needletrades, Industrial, and Textile Employees (UNITE) in its unionized Cypress plant and offered comparable pay and benefits packages to both union and nonunion employees. Company revenues had been growing throughout the 1990s, and Levi Strauss and Company announced record worldwide sales of $7.1 billion for fiscal year 1996. This represented a 6 percent increase over 1995 and was led by demand for Levi's brand products (not including Slates or Dockers) in both the United States and Europe (Levi Strauss and Company press release, February 26, 1997). El Paso, with a large poor and undereducated population, seemed especially blessed to have such a successful and beneficent employer offering so many jobs to workers with only a high school diploma or less.

Already in early 1997, however, Levi Strauss and Company's management team had decided that the company needed to cut overhead costs for its U.S. business—which were well above the industry average—by at least $80 million per year. A hiring freeze was instituted, and management informed employees that approximately one thousand salaried positions nationwide in the company would be eliminated within a year. Around the same time, the company announced that it would reduce its El Paso workforce by 10 percent by the end of the year, a goal it hoped to reach mainly through attrition (Weddell 1997).[20] A short time later, by mid-1997, Levi's cut operating hours at its El Paso plants by 20 to 25 percent, effectively cutting full-time workers back to a part-time paycheck (but with full-time benefits). Then, on November 3, 1997, the ax fell: The company announced it was shutting down eleven U.S. facilities that employed a total of 6,395 workers, including three sewing plants in El Paso—Airway, Eastside, and Lomaland—that employed sixteen hundred persons (Levi Strauss and Company press release, November 3, 1997). The ax fell

again in September 1998 when the company closed two Texas finishing centers due to declining demand for their services after the shutdown of the eleven manufacturing plants. One finishing plant was located in Amarillo, while the other was El Paso's Pelicano finishing center, resulting in the combined layoff of another 382 workers (Levi Strauss and Company press release, September 28, 1998). On February 23, 1999, Levi Strauss announced that it would close ten plants in North America (nine in the United States and one in Canada), including El Paso's Cypress plant, whose 688 workers lost their jobs later that year (Vaughan and Bizar 1999). In keeping with the company's generally benevolent policies toward workers under the leadership of Robert Haas, laid-off workers were granted generous severance packages consisting of eight months' notice, three weeks of severance pay for each year of service, extended medical coverage, and as much as $6,000 for retraining, relocation, or business start-up expenses (Levi Strauss and Company press releases, November 3, 1997, September 28, 1998, and February 23, 1999; Vaughan and Bizar 1999).[21]

Through the end of 1998, Levi Strauss officials publicly stressed that the closing of plants in El Paso and elsewhere in the United States had not resulted from any decision by the company to transfer production overseas, whether to Mexico, elsewhere in Latin America, or China.[22] Rather, they gave excess capacity, brought about by improved efficiency, and a softening of the denim apparel market as the main reasons for the cutbacks (Levi Strauss and Company press release, November 3, 1997; Colliver 1998). Indeed, Levi Strauss and Company's fiscal-year 1997 worldwide sales dropped 4 percent to $6.9 billion and then, in fiscal year 1998, another 13 percent to $6 billion. These declines were due primarily to the poor market performance of Levi's brand-name products (Levi Strauss and Company press releases, February 9, 1998, and February 16, 1999).

That the denim apparel market had softened was challenged by industry analysts who noted that Levi's rival, the Gap, was posting double-digit increases in annual sales (Colliver 1998). Instead, analysts suggested that Levi Strauss and Company's problems were twofold. First, by focusing excessively on the manufacturing process, Levi's had failed to keep abreast of changing denim fashions, especially in the important teenage market (Colliver 1998; King 1998; Munk 1999). Levi Strauss and Company went from a 48.2 percent share of the market for men's jeans (ages sixteen years and above) in 1990 to just 25 percent in 1998, losing out not only to VF Corporation's Lee and Wrangler brands but especially to lower-cost private labels, which went from just 3.2 percent of the market to over 20 percent during the same time frame (*Tactical Retail Monitor*, cited in Munk 1999, 85). Second, many analysts believe that Levi's touted team-production innovations and company-wide reengineering flopped badly, leading to increased labor and overhead costs, chaotic management, and disgruntled workers (Chanove 1999; King 1998; Munk 1999). The plants closed in El Paso were beset by both sets of problems, for they produced traditional five-pocket Levi's jeans exclusively and suffered through several years of transition from assembly-line piecework to team production and back to modified piecework again (Chanove 1999).[23]

By the time disappointing 1998 sales and new layoffs were announced in February 1999, Levi Strauss and Company had undergone a major internal reorganization to respond to these problems. In its announcement of 1998 sales, the company emphasized that its new focus would be on increasing sales and winning back market share by giving apparel consumers what they wanted in the form of new products and brands and then by intensely marketing its brand names:

During the second half of 1998, LS&CO. moved to an entirely new business model—consumer focused brand management. This new model, with its intense focus on the consumer, is intended to enable the company to build its existing brands as well as a larger portfolio of brands, whether these are sub-brands or new brands. As part of this new strategy, LS&CO. is devoting more resources to innovative marketing and product design in all of its three divisions worldwide. (Levi Strauss and Company press release, February 16, 1999)

In announcing the 1999 layoff of 5,900 employees (30 percent of its remaining 19,900-employee workforce in the United States and Canada), the company acknowledged what it had denied at the time of the 1997 layoffs: that the company was, in fact, shifting most of its production overseas in order to remain competitive in the industry. This cost-saving shift would, in effect, finance the company's new marketing and retail ventures, as stated by John Ermatinger, president of Levi Strauss–The Americas:

Our strategic plan in North America is to focus intensely on brand management, marketing and product design as a means to meet the casual clothing wants and needs of consumers. *Shifting a significant portion of our manufacturing for the U.S. and Canadian markets to contractors throughout the world will give the company greater flexibility to allocate resources and capital to its brands.* These steps are crucial if we are to remain competitive. (Levi Strauss and Company press release, February 22, 1999; emphasis added)

Interviewed by the *San Francisco Examiner,* Levi Strauss and Company CEO Bob Haas was even more direct about the need to cut labor costs:

We can't swim against the tide. We have invested tens of millions of dollars to try (to) find a way to make our owned-and-operated factories enough of an asset [to offset wage differences]. We've invested in automated equipment, in training and incentives, but, frankly, today's announcement is just facing the realities. . . . We can't ignore the fact that certain jobs are not going to be sustainable in North America. They're better done in other countries. (Quoted in Emert 1999)

An internal source I interviewed before the 1997 layoffs, however, suggested that even then the company's senior management was contemplating the shift of company resources away from owned-and-operated manufacturing plants in the United States and into product diversification and retail marketing of its brand names. This would inevitably entail increasing reliance on the company's network of five hundred overseas contractors and owned-and-operated facilities.[24] Not surprisingly, this would include heavier reliance on contractors in nearby Latin America, especially in post-NAFTA Mexico. An interview with the same internal source in July 1998 revealed that from 1994 to 1998, Levi's trained and certified thirty-nine contractors in Latin American countries, including Costa Rica, Honduras, Guatemala, and Mexico. In 1997 and 1998 the company's Miami office began to place special emphasis on Mexico with the approach of the January 1, 1999, lifting of tariffs on the cutting of garments in Mexico. This NAFTA measure would facilitate the company working with "full-package" contractors in Mexico.[25] By then the company's Miami branch was dedicating considerable resources to an aggressive effort to develop and certify contractors in interior Mexican cities such as Aguascalientes, Oaxaca, Puebla, Querétaro, and Torreón.[26]

As this discussion demonstrates, El Paso's largest garment layoffs by its biggest private employer could not be attributed in any immediate sense to changes in the binational trade regime. Rather, their proximate cause had to do with Levi Strauss and Company's inatten-tion to fashion trends and marketing, on the one hand, and its inability to lower high overhead costs sufficiently by raising productivity through organizational innovations and automation, on the other. As a result of declining market share and automation, the company suffered from overcapacity in the U.S. market. At the outset, when the company decided to close plants in El Paso and elsewhere in the United States, it was not in order to shift production to its overseas contractors to fill demand for its products at lower cost. Rather, the company sought to unburden itself of its financial commitments to high-cost plants and workers in the United States in order to shift resources into design, marketing, and sales, so that it could boost sales and regain market share. In this sense the company's strategy was one of classic "flexibilization" designed to improve competitiveness by reducing its fixed investments in a volatile market.

At the same time, the company was able to pursue this strategy only because it already had a network of five hundred contractors in place worldwide, as well as the ability to develop others in a relatively short period of time. Moreover, in the wake of NAFTA and the peso devaluation, it made sense for Levi Strauss and Company to turn increasingly to Mexico as a production site, a country where it already had a considerable presence in the form of owned-and-operated plants and subcontractors. While the Levi's jobs that disappeared from El Paso were not immediately transferred to Mexico, many of them would eventually reappear across the border if the company's reorganization was successful. Thus, while their disappearance from El Paso could not have been caused by NAFTA, their reappearance in Mexico very well might be. With labor costs in El Paso eight to nine times higher than in most Mexican cities, and total production costs four to five times higher,[27] there was little hope that the jobs would be coming back to Texas even if the company regained the ground it had lost in recent years.[28]

Mercifully for El Paso, as of July 2001, VF Corporation's Wrangler and Lee divisions (which together employ around four thousand workers) had not yet resorted to the massive plant closures and layoffs that Levi's had. While VF Corporation has made no announcements that it plans such closures in the foreseeable future, El Paso economic development officials fear that it could happen. By 1996, Wrangler had failed to meet its new-hire requirement to qualify for tax abatements negotiated with the city. City officials I interviewed in May 1997 reported that they had learned that both Lee and Wrangler were increasing their Mexican operations, and this worried them. A Wrangler official I interviewed in June 1996 noted that the company was then beginning to operate maquiladoras in Mexico and was in the process of opening a new plant in Torreón. Still, he said, the company wanted to go up only to 15 percent international production, a level that would not affect El Paso production much. In addition, he believed that a "Made in the U.S.A." label was still valuable for the sale of western wear.[29]

However, an engineer at VF Corporation's Wrangler, whom I interviewed in July 1998, said that the company was then moving into Mexico aggressively, with new owned-and-operated plants already open or in the planning stages in Torreón and Chihuahua City. This informant reported that Wrangler was especially looking to open sewing facilities in small Mexican towns where it could be the largest employer. The El Paso plants were being used to train technical and managerial personnel for the new Mexican facilities. According to this informant, Wrangler planned to double its owned-and-operated plant capacity in Latin America between 1997 and 2002. Given the similarities between VF Corporation's and Levi Strauss and Company's El Paso operations and wider corporate structure and strate-

gies, El Paso city officials are probably right to worry about the possibility of layoffs by VF Corporation as well.

The Unraveling Seam

The plants that have closed and the jobs that have left El Paso are not likely to return. Given the competitive nature of the world apparel market and the reduced barriers to trade and investment that are a consequence of GATT and NAFTA, it seems likely that El Paso's remaining major garment employers will follow in the footsteps of Farah and Levi Strauss and Company, continuing to scale back their operations in the city as they increase production levels in Mexico and other overseas locations. With the remaining barriers to cutting and finishing in Mexico now removed by NAFTA, these cutbacks will not be limited to sewing operations. Cutting and finishing facilities that are contracted to major El Paso employers or that perform such operations for Mexican maquiladoras are likely to fall away as these operations, too, are carried out in Mexico to an increasing extent.

In 2001 the entire Mexican manufacturing sector was extended the same tariff treatment as maquiladoras, and this development should further cement the competitive disadvantage of El Paso as a major production site for denim apparel. This is not to say that the garment industry will cease to play any role in the El Paso economy. One can imagine companies maintaining warehouses and distribution facilities there, and undoubtedly some market segment in "western wear" will remain to be served by "Made in the U.S.A." garments. Nevertheless, the tendency appears to be toward continued contraction of production in El Paso. As shown in Figure 7.1, employment in the industry has fallen to less than half its level pre-NAFTA: Average annual employment in the industry was just 11,900 workers in the year 2000.

The situation of the small and medium-scale firms operating in the industry in El Paso appears particularly dire. Few are likely to survive as presently constituted. Protected to some extent from Mexican competition through the 1980s, the small-scale sector's chief "comparative advantage" relative to other regions in the United States was the ready availability of cheap immigrant labor. In addition, much of this cheap labor was also highly skilled in the needle trades. By the 1980s, however, the availability of cheap immigrant labor with industry experience had increased substantially in other parts of the United States, particularly in Los Angeles, Miami, and New York. Moreover, as several informants in El Paso pointed out to me, the urban geography of El Paso does not lend itself to sweatshop employment on the same scale as do these more heavily and densely populated cities, where it is much easier to hide illegal workshops in warehouse districts and private residences with little fear of detection by the authorities. With the MFA restrictions rescinded under NAFTA, the small-scale garment sector in El Paso has little to offer by way of cost savings, no matter how much it "sweats" its workforce.

With assistance from the City of El Paso in the early to mid-1990s, some small-firm owners participated in the formation of the El Paso Fashion Development Center. The goal of the center was to encourage the formation of a vibrant, fashion-oriented garment district consisting of small firms cooperating in the production of high-end, small-batch garments for sale in boutiques around the United States. The strategy of the center was to encourage experienced producers to get out of the business of mass-produced garments, such as blue jeans, and begin to focus on more complex garments made from other fabrics, such as silk and polyester. A number of the more successful firms in the city's small-scale garment sector had been able to survive into the mid-1990s by following exactly this strat-

egy, and the idea was to get other firms to follow suit.

The Fashion Development Center seems not to have met with much success, however, and its strategy has little potential given the structural obstacles facing the industry in El Paso. At least one of the "fashion" firms contracted out its sewing to home workers, who exploit unpaid family labor to sew these firms' stylish garments. In spite of the fact that they were already making use of the cheapest labor available to them on the U.S. side, the owners of this firm also began to contract sewing across the border in Mexico in search of the labor cost savings that competition requires them to obtain. Fashion garments involving complicated patterns are routinely sewn in low-wage, low-tech shops around the world, and it is improbable that a significant niche in this market remains to be filled by El Paso. Moreover, while local firms have a great deal of production experience, they generally lack the design and marketing experience they would need to compete effectively with major fashion garment centers elsewhere.

Not all the small garment subcontractors in El Paso have gone out of business, however. A handful have either moved operations to the Mexican side or have themselves become brokers who source production to subcontractors in Mexico. The former option seems more viable for Mexican immigrant owners, some of whom have business experience in Mexico and are thus familiar with the commercial and regulatory environment. For example, one immigrant cutting-room owner I interviewed in 1996 planned to make as much money as he could until the NAFTA phaseout of cutting restrictions occurred. After that, he planned to take the capital and machinery he had accumulated to open a cutting room in either Torreón, Coahuila, or in Chihuahua City.[30] Another had already moved his sewing operations across the border and planned to move his cutting and finishing operations across by early 1997. Two long-term Anglo owners of a small garment operation whom I interviewed in 1996 had begun to contract out all their sewing operations to the Mexican side several years earlier. In spite of the fact that these owners did not speak Spanish fluently and had no previous experience doing business in Mexico, through their network of contacts in the industry they were able to locate a suitable set of subcontractors with whom to work in Torreón.[31]

When I was in the field in 1996–97, a few owners of small shops were hanging on in spite of the odds stacked against them. This group of owners had to lay off employees. They admitted that they should probably get out of the business altogether, but they resisted doing so because they have the garment business "in their blood." Most of these had worked their entire adult lives in the industry, having started their careers at one of the larger, "traditional" employers, such as Farah or Billy the Kidd. In their forties or fifties at the time I interviewed them, they had started their own businesses on the basis of their skills and network of contacts in the local industry. These artisan-owners had no experience doing other kinds of work and were "too old" to learn a new trade or move out of the area in search of another job or a place to start another garment business (such as in Mexico).

Although other analysts of small-scale enterprise in the garment industry (Dore 1983; Portes and Guarnizo 1991) have commented on the positive aspects of social capital put to use in this sector, social capital in El Paso's garment district seems not to have done much to ameliorate the devastating effects of international deregulation of the apparel industry. The social capital that owners of small garment factories in El Paso have relied on typically has been accumulated over the course of many years of living and working in a particular local environment where dense networks have formed on the basis of the peculiarities of the trade regime on the U.S.-Mexico border. The social capital

of many garment business owners, particularly those who are El Paso natives as opposed to more "cosmopolitan" latecomers, is not especially exchangeable outside the district, as it was constructed prior to NAFTA. As James Coleman (1988) noted, social capital tends to be quite "sticky," that is, it is not easily transferred from one activity or context to another.

Some garment entrepreneurs have attempted to reconfigure their businesses to survive in the face of the new trade regime. They have typically done so by closing their operations on the U.S. side and setting up as small maquiladoras in Mexico or by getting out of direct production altogether and taking up the role of intermediary between their old customers and the new direct producers on the Mexican side of the border. The social capital of such entrepreneurs has aided in this shift to some extent, but it has not done much, if any, good for their U.S.-side employees, who have almost invariably lost their jobs in the process. While these border-hopping entrepreneurs may in principle be happy to offer jobs to their U.S. employees in their new operation in Mexico, the pay and working conditions offered make this option no alternative at all for most garment workers. Thus the social capital of most garment entrepreneurs and workers in El Paso's small-scale sector has provided little security as the trade protections that gave rise to such capital in the first place have been leveled by NAFTA.

The results of my 1996–97 survey of employees of seven small- to medium-scale garment shops and one Levi's plant in El Paso confirm what was already widely known about the composition of the sector's workforce: It is dominated by Mexican immigrant women with little formal education. Most of the two hundred workers interviewed in eight plants were women who were born in Mexico and who had completed only a primary school education. They spoke Spanish at work and had little formal work experience outside the garment industry. A significant minority had worked previously in the maquiladora sector in Ciudad Juárez. Some continued to live in Juárez and commuted to their jobs in El Paso on a daily basis. Most of the women had dependent children and in many cases did not live with their spouses.

As already noted, Levi's workers enjoy much better pay, benefits, and working conditions than their counterparts in the small-scale sector. Not surprisingly, Levi's workers interviewed for this study were more likely to be men, to have completed high school or its equivalent, and to have been born in the United States. In short, jobs at Levi's are among the better manual jobs to be found in El Paso, and workers there are correspondingly somewhat better qualified than garment workers in the small-scale sector. At the same time, many Levi's workers were immigrants with a social profile that was not markedly distinct from garment workers in smaller establishments.

Mexican immigrant garment workers are poor by U.S. standards but much better off doing the work they are doing in El Paso than they could ever expect to be performing the same work in Mexico. Upon losing their jobs as garment workers, most would find it quite difficult to locate comparably gainful employment in El Paso, given their inability to speak English and low levels of educational achievement. The experiences of displaced garment workers to date support this conjecture. In 1997, El Paso accounted for 60 percent of Texas claims for retraining and job-hunting assistance made by NAFTA-displaced workers, and most of these were garment workers (author's interview with Harry Crawford, Texas Workforce Commission, May 5, 1997).

New jobs are being created in El Paso in a number of growth industries. Some of these derive directly from the city's location on the border with Mexico and serve the in-bond assembly industry. For example, a dozen or so companies that mold plastic inputs for ma-

quiladoras were attracted to El Paso in the late 1990s. These companies, however, typically have hired employees who have completed more years of education and were able to speak, read, and write English better than most immigrant garment workers. In addition, only a few hundred such jobs have been created.

According to the city's Office of Economic Development, a number of other major companies opened facilities in El Paso in the late 1990s. These companies, which included the telecommunications giant MCI and Acer Computers, were moving to El Paso not because of its proximity to Mexico but rather because of its double-digit unemployment rate. Simply put, tight labor markets elsewhere in the U.S. motivated companies in search of cheap domestic labor to consider El Paso. Again, the human capital requirements of these companies prohibited most displaced garment workers from filling the new jobs created: In spite of the fact that most of the new jobs pay little more than $6 to $7 per hour, applicants are required to be high school graduates and to speak English fluently.

While the arrival of new companies has helped somewhat, job growth outside the garment industry in El Paso has tended to be sluggish in recent years. In fact, an analysis conducted in 1995–96 by the El Paso Office of Economic Development showed that overall job growth in the 1990s had failed to keep up with growth in the city's economically active population, suggesting continued high unemployment in the city in the early years of the twenty-first century. Indeed, El Paso has the highest unemployment of any major city in Texas. The city's average annual unemployment rate for 2000 was 8.2 percent, compared to just 4.2 percent for the state of Texas as a whole. Worse still from the immigrant garment worker's point of view, the Personal Responsibility and Work Opportunity Reconciliation Act of 1996 took away from immigrants the most important welfare benefits for which

they once qualified. This is all the more alarming because over one-third of Mexican immigrants in the city lived in poverty even before
post-NAFTA layoffs began. Given these circumstances, the future looks bleak for the
thousands of *mexicanos* who built El Paso's
dominant industry and, in so doing, clothed
millions of people around the United States
for several generations.

Notes

Acknowledgments: Generous support for research
reported in this paper was provided by the Ford
Foundation, Mexico City and New York offices, in
the form of a grant to the Population Research Center of the University of Texas at Austin. The author
also thanks Randy Capps and Kelly Fenton for their
able research assistance.

1. Except where otherwise noted, figures on
employment in El Paso are based on data provided
by the Texas Workforce Commission (TWC), the
state government agency in Austin charged with
overseeing and providing workforce development
services to employers and job seekers of Texas. A
substantial portion of these data may be accessed on
the TWC Web site at <http://www.twc.state.tx.us>.

2. By Mexican American I mean persons who
were born and raised in the United States but who
trace their family's origins to what is now or once
was Mexico.

3. By the end of the 1980s, Farah carried out
more than 60 percent of its production overseas,
principally in Mexico, Ireland, and Hong Kong
(DeMoss 1989, viii). Farah began by establishing
its own factories in Ciudad Juárez and Chihuahua
City but later came to rely almost exclusively on
contractors (van Dooren 1997). In 1996, Farah,
which at the time of the 1972 strike was El Paso's
largest private employer, did not even appear on the
list of the city's top twenty employers (El Paso
Office of Economic Development 1996). By that
time the company's productive operations in the
city were limited to one cutting room and a distribution facility (Honig 1996).

4. Between 1980 and 1991 only about thirty
thousand apparel jobs had been added to the maquiladora sector, bringing the total to just over
forty-six thousand (INEGI 1992).

5. Ironically, some of these shops were started
with assistance from labor organizations that provided support to striking Farah workers. In interviews with the author for an unrelated study conducted in 1994, veteran organizers from La Mujer
Obrera ("The Woman Worker," a nongovernmental organization in El Paso founded by former Farah
Company employees) described how, in little more
than a year, the organization went from helping laid-
off strikers start their own shops to picketing these
same shops on behalf of their exploited workers.

6. That small to medium-size shops used to
account for a considerable portion of total apparel-
industry employment in El Paso is reflected by the
fact that registered garment establishments with
fewer than 100 employees accounted for over 10
percent of all official garment employment in 1989;
establishments with fewer than 250 employees accounted for nearly 40 percent (author's estimate
based on figures in *County Business Patterns*, U.S.
Bureau of the Census 1989). The actual figures may
have been higher, given the informal nature of many
of these small enterprises.

7. In this regard it is important to remember
that it is not only the immigrant workers' legal status that determines their job prospects but also
their human-capital characteristics and the local
labor market supply-and-demand conditions. The
job opportunities available in El Paso even to legal
residents of the United States remain quite limited
if they cannot speak, read, and write English well
and have completed only a few years of formal
education.

8. It should be noted, however, that the $0.88
per hour figure for Mexico is inclusive of fringe
benefits, whereas the figure for El Paso is for hourly
wages only, exclusive of any benefits. Thus the
Mexican wage is somewhat inflated, while the El
Paso wage is somewhat deflated. Mexican wage figures are taken from INEGI 1992. El Paso figures are
from retrospective interviews the author conducted
with several garment-shop owners in 1996–97.

9. The figures for pairs of blue jeans are for
exports through *all* U.S. customs ports, not just

Laredo and El Paso (although these two ports handled around 80 percent of all U.S. surface exports to Mexico).

10. Cutting-room operators I interviewed in El Paso contracted to a variety of larger companies that engaged in maquiladora production in the Mexican interior. These larger companies included Sun Apparel, Denver-based Rocky Mountain, and Kentucky Apparel. Two also cut for Mexican "full-package" companies based in Torreón and Puebla.

11. These figures, derived from the author's calculations using raw data provided by the Texas Workforce Commission, include employment in "laundry, cleaning, and garment services," SIC 721, which includes stonewashing of jeans. In 1992–93 around three thousand persons were classified as working in SIC 721.

12. Not surprisingly, the percentage of area garment workers employed in establishments with fewer than 250 employees declined from around 40 percent of the total in 1989 to just 23 percent in 1993 (author's estimate using data from *County Business Patterns*, U.S. Bureau of the Census 1993). This was due to the growth in employment among this handful of large companies combined with the decline in employment among smaller establishments. Data collected by the Texas Workforce Commission and the U.S. Bureau of the Census (as published in *County Business Patterns*) do not, unfortunately, distinguish among establishments dedicated to specific operations in the production of garments—thus we cannot observe the quantitative changes in cutting versus sewing or finishing employment.

13. Indeed, a Levi Strauss and Company press release dated February 26, 1997, notes that its European sales in 1996 were led by the traditional "Made in the U.S.A." 501.

14. Levi's, for example, contracted to at least two local laundering firms, one of which employed up to one thousand workers.

15. NAFTA-TAA (Transitional Adjustment Assistance) certifications are available electronically on the World Wide Web from Public Citizen's Global Trade Watch site at <http://www.citizen.org/pctrade/NAFTATAA/weball_1.HTML>. The data presented by this anti-NAFTA advocacy organization come from the U.S. Department of Labor and are comparable to those available from the North

American Development Bank's Community Adjustment and Investment Program at <http://naid.sppsr.ucla.edu/nadbank/application.html>. The data reflect the number of workers who have applied for and been certified to receive NAFTA Trade Adjustment Assistance from the U.S. Department of Labor's Employment and Training Administration. While some observers have argued that job losses in other parts of the country are falsely attributed to NAFTA (Richards 1997), in El Paso there is little doubt that NAFTA has contributed to the elimination of the jobs that the U.S. Department of Labor has certified.

16. Sun Apparel's El Paso plants produced garments for Ellemeno, Faded Glory, Arizona, Polo, Sasson, Fila, and Hunt Club (Medaille and Wheat 1997; Greater Texas Workers Committee 1997). El Paso–based Sun Apparel was acquired by the Jones Apparel Group in October 1998, a major women's wear firm based in Bristol, Pennsylvania (Hoover's Online, retrieved from <http://www.hoovers.com/capsules/14954.html> on May 15, 1999). Jones previously contracted to other El Paso companies to produce women's wear, including ladies' jacket maker CMT Industries. Fifty-five percent of Sun Apparel's revenues comes from production of Polo jeans for Ralph Lauren in owned-and-operated facilities in the United States and through a network of Mexican contractors in Mexico (Hoover's Online, retrieved from <http://www.hoovers.com/capsules/57198.html> on May 15, 1999).

17. Cutting rooms enjoyed a temporary market niche since the complete elimination of U.S. tariffs on garments cut in Mexico was not phased in until January 1, 1999. Several of the operators of cutting rooms I interviewed in 1996 indicated that until that time they expected to be busier than they had ever been. Two that were affiliates of larger companies that had owned-and-operated plants in Mexico or already worked through Mexican sewing contractors expected to move their cutting operations into Mexico by 1999. The independent operators were either planning to get out of the business by then or were already exploring the possibility of moving into Mexico themselves.

18. Information presented in this section is based on a combination of visits to Levi's plants in El Paso and San Antonio, formal and informal interviews

with company officials in both cities, interviews with managers at two finishing plants contracted to Levi's, official press releases obtained from the company Web site, and a review of published sources.

19. At the time the company employed around twenty-five thousand workers in thirty-two manufacturing plants and finishing centers in the United States.

20. A source within the company whom I interviewed in June 1996 believed that by that time the company had already begun slowly to decrease its El Paso workforce through natural attrition.

21. This package was in sharp contrast to what was offered to 1,150 Levi Strauss workers who were laid off in San Antonio in early 1990 when the company abruptly closed a Docker's plant and moved production to Costa Rica. In that instance, workers received no advance warning of the plant closure and little more than severance pay commensurate with years of service. Since 1990 a nongovernmental organization known as Fuerza Unida has been pressuring Levi's to make more extensive reparations to workers it claims were not justly compensated by the company or were left with job-related disabilities that prevented them from finding new jobs. Today, Fuerza Unida activists argue that Levi's generous severance packages are, at least in part, the consequence of the group's campaigns against the company for the last nine years (personal interview with Petra Mata, Fuerza Unida coordinator, November 1998; Fuerza Unida 1998; see also Zoll 1998).

22. The company's April 1998 decision to resume production in the People's Republic of China drew fire from human rights activists and U.S. worker representatives who believed the company was transferring high-cost production from the United States to that authoritarian and low-wage country (Landler 1998; Zoll 1998).

23. In addition, a group of El Paso workers successfully sued the company for having discriminated against them after they had filed workers' compensation claims. Plants in El Paso had especially high workers' compensation overhead costs, and the company had designed a special injured-worker "reentry" program to lower these costs. In September 1998 an El Paso jury awarded the work-

ers $10.6 million in damages (see *Wall Street Journal* 1998).

24. At the start of 1996, Levi's began producing its top-of-the line 501 jeans in its owned-and-operated plants in Mexico. This marked the first time that 501 jeans had been sewn in Latin America (personal communication from Jorge Mendoza, based on interviews he conducted with Levi Strauss–Mexico employees, Mexico City, June 1996).

25. The company already operated or contracted to a number of Mexican finishing plants in cities such as Torreón, Querétaro, and Puebla.

26. Interestingly, one of Levi's El Paso finishing contractors whom I interviewed in 1996 told me of his plans to open finishing plants in an industrial park near the U.S. border in Meoqui, Chihuahua (a major competitor, Aquatech, already had opened a plant there), as well as near Ensenada, Baja California. Thus we see that Levi's departure from El Paso could encourage some of its local contractors to move into Mexico as well.

27. Overall costs in Mexico were less than labor savings because of added transportation costs and the greater productivity of workers on the U.S. side due to investments there in automation and other productive technologies.

28. Neither, presumably, would the jobs return that were eliminated by Levi's contractors in town, including Final Finish, Stitches, and International Garment Processors.

29. Wrangler plants in El Paso produced jeans for its own label as well as for Wal-Mart, Kmart, Target, and Maverick.

30. Although I was not able to contact this entrepreneur for an update, his firm now appears on the U.S. Department of Labor's list of NAFTA-TAA certified layoffs, suggesting that the firm either went out of business or did, in fact, move into Mexico.

31. These entrepreneurs' choice of interior Mexican locations as a place to set up operations corroborates the finding of other recent studies of the garment industry in Ciudad Juárez, namely, that there is relatively little integration between the maquiladoras in Juárez and garment producers based in El Paso. The Juárez producers, rather, maintain relationships with either their parent com-

panies or suppliers in the northeastern and south-eastern United States (see Chapters 8 and 9 in this book; van Dooren 1997; Verkoren 1996).

References

Anderson, Joan. 1990. "Maquiladoras in the Apparel Industry." In *The Maquila Industry: Economic Solution or Problem?* ed. Khosrow Fatemi, pp. 103–16. New York Praeger.

Bary, Andrew. 1993. "Bye-Bye Blue-Jean Blues: Denim Is Back in Style: That's Good News for V.F. Corp." *Barron's*, October 4, 15.

Blumenberg, Evelyn, and Paul Ong. 1994. "Labor Squeeze and Ethnic/Racial Recomposition in the U.S. Apparel Industry." In *Global Production: The Apparel Industry in the Pacific Rim*, ed. Edna Bonacich, Lucie Cheng, Norma Chinchilla, Nora Hamilton, and Paul Ong, pp. 309–27. Philadelphia: Temple University Press.

Bonacich, Edna, and David V. Waller. "Mapping a Global Industry: Apparel Production in the Pacific Rim Triangle." In *Global Production: The Apparel Industry in the Pacific Rim*, ed. Edna Bonacich, Lucie Cheng, Norma Chinchilla, Nora Hamilton, and Paul Ong, pp. 21–41. Philadelphia: Temple University Press.

Bull, Anna, Martyn Pitt, and Joseph Szarka. 1993. *Entrepreneurial Textile Communities: A Comparative Study of Small Textile and Clothing Firms.* London: Chapman and Hall.

Chanove, Roland G. 1998. "Between Religion and Science: Implementing Total Quality Management and Other Models of Organizational Change along the US/Mexican Border." Unpublished Ph.D. diss., Department of Sociology, University of Texas–Austin.

CIEMEX-WEFA. 1996. *Maquiladora Industry Outlook.* Philadelphia: CIEMEX-WEFA.

Coleman, James. 1988. "Social Capital in the Creation of Human Capital." *American Journal of Sociology* 94, supplement: s95–s120.

Colliver, Victoria. 1998. "Levi's Will Make Fewer Jeans." *San Francisco Examiner*, November 6. Electronic edition.

Coyle, Laurie, Gail Hershatter, and Emily Honig.

1984. "Women at Farah: An Unfinished Story." In *A Needle, a Bobbin, a Strike: Women Needleworkers in America*, ed. Joan M. Jensen and Sue Davidson, pp. 227–77. Philadelphia: Temple University Press.

Crimmins, Julie. 1995. "Dressed for Success: El Paso Apparel Makers Buck National Employment Trends." Texas Comptroller's *Fiscal Notes*, February, 11–12.

DeMoss, Dorothy. 1989. *The History of Apparel Manufacturing in Texas, 1897–1981.* New York: Garland Publishing, Inc.

Dore, Ronald. 1983. "Goodwill and the Spirit of Market Capitalism." *British Journal of Sociology* 34: 459–82.

El Paso Electric Economic Development Department. 1996. "Employment Trends 1990–1995 by Three-Digit SIC Code." Unpublished memorandum. El Paso, Tex.: El Paso Electric Economic Development Department.

El Paso Office of Economic Development. 1996. "Top 20 El Paso Employers." Mimeograph. El Paso, Tex.: El Paso Office of Economic Development, July.

Emert, Carol. 1999. "Levi's to Slash U.S. Plants: Competitors' Foreign-Made Jeans Blamed." *San Francisco Chronicle*, February 23. Electronic edition.

Fuerza Unida. 1998. "Levi's Lays Off 6400 More Workers." *Hilo de la Justicia / Thread of Justice: Campaign Bulletin of Fuerza Unida* 1, 1: 1, 3.

Greater Texas Workers Committee. 1997. "Ralph Lauren: Injustice against NAFTA Displaced Workers in El Paso." Mimeograph. Retrieved from <http://www.corpwatch.org/trac/corner/alert/ralph.html> on May 15, 1999.

Honig, Emily. 1996. "Women at Farah Revisited: Political Mobilization and Its Aftermath among Chicana Workers in El Paso, Texas, 1972–1992." *Feminist Studies* 22, 2: 425–52.

Hufbauer, Gary Clyde, and Jeffrey J. Schott. 1992. *North American Free Trade: Issues and Recommendations.* Washington, D.C.: Institute for International Economics.

Instituto Nacional de Estadística, Geografía e Informática (INEGI). 1992, 1993, 1995, 1996, 2000. *Estadística de la industria maquiladora de exportación.* Aguascalientes, Mexico: INEGI.

King, Ralph T. 1998. "Infighting Rises, Productivity Falls, Employees Miss Piecework System." *Wall Street Journal,* May 20. Electronic edition.

Landler, Mark. 1998. "Levi Strauss, Citing Rights Gains, to Expand Role in China." *New York Times,* April 9. Electronic edition.

Mangan, Frank. 1980. "A City Matures." In *Four Centuries at the Pass: A New History of El Paso on Its Four Hundredth Birthday,* ed. W. H. Timmons, pp. 106–16. El Paso, Tex.: Centuries 81 Foundation.

Márquez, Benjamin. 1995. "Organizing Mexican-American Women in the Garment Industry: La Mujer Obrera." *Women and Politics* 15, 1: 65–87.

Mathews, Dale T. 1995. "Export Processing Zones in the Dominican Republic: Their Nature and Trajectory." Ph.D. diss., Department of Development Studies, University of Sussex, United Kingdom.

Medaille, Bill, and Andrew Wheat. 1997. "Faded Denim: NAFTA Blues." *Multinational Monitor* 18, 12 (December). Electronic edition.

Meyerson, Allen R. 1997. "Borderline Working Class: In Texas, Labor Is Feeling Trade Accord's Pinch." *New York Times,* late ed., May 8 D1.

Munk, Nina. 1999. "How Levi's Trashed a Great American Brand." *Fortune,* April 12, 83–90.

Portes, Alejandro. 1995. "Economic Sociology and the Sociology of Immigration: A Conceptual Overview." In *Economic Sociology and the Sociology of Immigration,* ed. Alejandro Portes, pp. 1–41. New York: Russell Sage Foundation.

Portes, Alejandro, and Luís Guarnizo. 1991. *Capitalistas del trópico.* Santo Domingo, Dominican Republic: FLACSO.

Richards, Bill. 1997. "Layoffs Not Related to NAFTA Can Trigger Special Help Anyway." *Wall Street Journal,* June 30, A1.

Tiano, Susan. 1994. *Patriarchy on the Line: Labor, Gender, and Ideology in the Mexican Maquila Industry.* Philadelphia: Temple University Press.

Twin Plant News. 1999. "Maquila Scoreboard." *Twin Plant News* 14, 11 (June): 62–63.

U.S. Bureau of the Census. 1989, 1993. *County Business Patterns.* Washington, D.C.: U.S. Bureau of the Census.

———. 1990. "Five Percent Public Use Microdata Sample." Washington, D.C.: U.S. Bureau of the Census.

U.S. Department of Commerce. 1994a. *National Trade Data Base.* CD-ROM. Washington, D.C.: U.S. Department of Commerce.

———. 1994b. *U.S. Exports History, 1989–1993.* CD-ROM. Washington, D.C.: U.S. Department of Commerce.

Van Dooren, Robine. 1997. "The Garment Industry in El Paso and Cd. Juárez: Automate, Emigrate, or Eliminate?" Unpublished master's thesis, Department of International Economics and Economic Geography, Utrecht University, the Netherlands.

Vaughan, Vicki, and Jodi Bizar. 1999. "Levi's Cuts Hit Four Texas Plants: Sweep Spares San Antonio Factories." *San Antonio Express-News,* Tuesday, February 23, 1A.

Verkoren, Otto. 1996. "Trends in Manufacturing on the U.S.-Mexico Border, with Special Reference to El Paso (TX) and Ciudad Juárez (Chih.)." Paper presented at the congress of the Latin American Studies Association, Guadalajara, Jalisco, Mexico, April.

Wall Street Journal. 1998. "Injured Workers Sue Levi's over 'Re-entry Program.'" *Wall Street Journal,* May 20. Interactive edition.

Weddell, Jim. 1997. "Glut of Jeans Forces Company to Pare Down." *El Paso Times,* January 24, 1A, 2A.

World Trade Organization (WTO). 2001. "The Agreement on Textiles and Clothing." Retrieved on August 22, 2001, from <http://www.wto.org/english/tratop_e/texti_e/texintro.htm>.

Zoll, Daniel. 1998. "Sweatshop Blues: San Francisco's Levi Strauss Carefully Cultivates Its Good Citizen Image. But Human Rights Activists Are Catching the Company with Its Pants Down." *San Francisco Bay Guardian,* June 10. Electronic edition.

Robine van Dooren

8 TexMex: Linkages in a Binational Garment District? The Garment Industries in El Paso and Ciudad Juárez

Introduction

This chapter describes the organization of garment production in the border cities of El Paso, Texas, and Ciudad (Cd.) Juárez, Chihuahua, Mexico. As is widely acknowledged, El Paso has occupied a unique position in the U.S. garment industry due to, among other things, the dominance of jeans production in the city's apparel sector (McIntyre 1955; van Dooren and van der Waerden 1997; Chapter 7 in this book). The specialization in standardized garments has, since the mid-1990s, created great difficulties for the "Jeans Capital of the World" because of the vulnerability of these types of products to international price competition. However, the fact that El Paso's neighboring city across the border, Cd. Juárez, houses a considerable number of garment companies producing in a relatively low-wage environment leads one to expect to find a cross-border reconfiguration of the commodity chain and, accordingly, a cross-border division of labor. The obvious cost advantage to dividing production between highly labor-intensive assembly activities in Cd. Juárez and

capital-intensive activities in El Paso should lead to the development of complementary, mutually beneficial cross-border linkages between different types of firms on both sides of the border, thus possibly even giving rise to a transborder industrial district.

This chapter investigates the nature and relative importance of local and transborder interfirm linkages, drawing on insights from new international division-of-labor theory as well as the global commodity chain and industrial-district approaches. The competitive pressures that El Paso is experiencing and the wage differential between El Paso and Cd. Juárez make the El Paso–Cd. Juárez region an exceptionally interesting environment for research into the effects of globalization on the development of regional garment-production networks.

In pursuing the description and explanation of transborder linkages in the garment industry, I have organized this chapter in the following manner. First, I examine the industries in both border cities in terms of their roles in the Mexican and U.S. garment industries and of the government policy affecting these sectors. I provide an overview of the characteristics of

both industries—in terms of product orientation, number of companies, and so forth—and
of the relative importance of the industries to
both cities. Second, I briefly examine a variety
of production linkages between garment producers in both border cities. Contrary to expectations arising from the new international
division-of-labor and industrial-district theo-
ries, local linkages and transborder linkages
between El Paso and Cd. Juárez are relatively
unimportant. I indicate several reasons that lie
behind this surprising finding. The third part
of the chapter then examines the linkages that
do exist, connecting El Paso to production in
the Mexican interior and production in Cd.
Juárez to northern states of the United States.

In discussing the research findings, I use
the term *regional* when referring to the El
Paso–Cd. Juárez border region as a whole and
the term *extraregional* in reference to linkages
between companies in either of the two cities
and companies outside the region. I use the
term *local* when discussing developments in
either of the two cities. The data presented
here are taken from research conducted in El
Paso and Cd. Juárez during the first months
of 1996 and based on a diverse sample of sixty
garment companies in the region.[1] Sample
companies were chosen randomly, based on
their willingness to cooperate and not on statistical sampling requirements. I conducted
personal interviews with managers or owners
according to a standard questionnaire.

The Regional Garment Complex
in a Binational Context

The current phase of internationalization and
globalization of production in the world economy heavily affects the clothing industry. In
the face of increasingly fierce price competition from manufacturers in low-cost production locations, large U.S. garment manufac-

turers are trying to counter their labor-cost
disadvantage (which is especially harmful in
the mass production of basic garment products) by developing production networks that
connect different types of companies in different countries and different industrial sectors (Gereffi 1997b). In shaping these networks, manufacturers increasingly are focusing
attention on Mexico, especially since the implementation of the North American Free
Trade Agreement (NAFTA). Linkages with
Mexican contractors offer not only the advantage of a low-priced labor force but also greater
control over production and shorter lead times,
compared to production in other Latin American and especially in Asian countries. Both
U.S. manufacturers and marketers increasingly
appreciate the advantages of production in
Mexico and are trying to incorporate these advantages into their production strategies by
developing linkages to actors in the Mexican
garment industry. This development is possible because of the relative ease in separating
the apparel-production process into several
distinct steps; the availability of an abundant,
inexpensive labor force; and good transportation and communication in Mexico.

The existence of cross-border linkages in
the apparel industry would thus seem to be in
line with the theory of the new international
division of labor. According to this theory, the
above-mentioned conditions promote a spatial division of labor in which the most labor-
intensive processes (e.g., assembly of garments)
are shifted to low-labor-cost locations (Fröbel,
Heinrichs, and Kreye 1980). Recent changes
have led to a tremendous increase in Mexican
garment exports to the United States. Mexico
is now approaching China in terms of the
dollar value of its total exports to the United
States, and some have noted that Mexico has
even overtaken China in certain production
categories (Khanna 1997; Gereffi and Bair
1998).

TABLE 8.1. Population, Employment, and Wages in El Paso and Cd. Juárez, 1997

El Paso		Cd. Juárez	
Population	682,000	Population	1,011,786
% Unemployment	11.8	% Unemployment	1.8
% Employed in manufacturing	20.6	% Employed in manufacturing	66
Number of garment companies, 1995	82	Number of garment companies, 1994	149
Average hourly wage, U.S. apparel worker, 1995	$7.48	Minimum hourly wage, seamstress, wage zone C, most interior locations in Mexico	$1.34
Average hourly wage, El Paso apparel worker, 1995	$6.00	Minimum hourly wage, seamstress, wage zone B, Mexico	$1.39
		Minimum wage, Cd. Juárez worker, wage zone A	$1.45

Sources: U.S. Department of Labor, 1995a, 1995b; Desarrollo Economico de Cd. Juárez 1995; INEGI 1995; *Twin Plant News* 1997; and Texas Centers 1998.

Note: All information is given in U.S. dollars. Exchange rate is calculated at 8 pesos to the dollar. Hourly wage figures include all taxes and required fringe benefits and bonuses. However, most employers pay between 60 and 90 percent above this wage through productivity bonuses, saving plans, etc. For detailed information coverage of the wage zones, see *Twin Plant News* 1997, 38.

How are the garment industries in El Paso and Cd. Juárez, twin cities located on either side of the U.S.-Mexico border, affected by the development of linkages between U.S. and Mexican companies and the dramatic increases in Mexico's exports to the United States? In considering the socioeconomic indicators provided in Table 8.1, one needs to bear in mind the relative ease of separating the assembly stage from the rest of the production process for apparel, as well as the high quality of communication and transportation facilities in the U.S.-Mexico border region. The combination of these aspects with the indicated wage differential between the twin cities led to the formulation of a hypothesis for the research on the basis of the new international division-of-labor theory. It was expected that companies in El Paso would counter their labor-cost disadvantage by developing linkages with subcontractors in Cd. Juárez or by setting up assembly plants (maquiladoras) there. Moving assembly to Cd. Juárez would minimize labor costs for the most labor-intensive part of the production process, thereby decreasing total production

costs and increasing competitiveness. The fact that El Paso and Cd. Juárez are bordering cities meant that transportation costs could be kept very low and quality control was relatively easy. Companies located in El Paso would be responsible for administering the networks and distributing to the U.S. market the products assembled in Mexico.

In addition, the spatial concentration of garment producers of different sizes in the two cities guided the research to examine local and regional "backward" and "forward" linkages (i.e., linkages to actors in the pre- and postassembly segments of the production chain) as an indication of the industrial-district characteristics of the region and of each of the two cities. Such linkages, against a common cultural background and supported by local institutions, are thought to provide firms in the industrial district with a competitive edge based on external economies (i.e., they derive incidental competitive benefits from geographical proximity to other actors in the industrial district), joint action, minimal transaction costs, and flexible specialization

(Piore and Sabel 1984; Porter 1990; Schmitz and Nadvi 1999; Humphrey and Schmitz 2000).

In addressing the interrelationships of actors within each city and between the two cities, I adopted the global commodity chain approach (Gereffi and Korzeniewicz 1994), making the production process and the organization thereof a focal unit of analysis. Furthermore, this approach enables a clear positioning of the developments in the region within the broader North American garment context.

This study found, contrary to expectations, that cross-border linkages between the industries in both cities and local linkages within the cities were limited in number. Instead, linkages seemed to be skipping the border, connecting El Paso to cities in the interior of Mexico, such as Torreón/Gómez Palacio and Aguascalientes, and Cd. Juárez to large apparel cities in the United States, such as New York and San Francisco. An overview of the surprisingly limited nature of linkages between the industries in both cities and, more important, an explanation of this finding as well as a description of alternative linkages are presented after a short discussion of the main characteristics of the garment industries of El Paso and Cd. Juárez.

El Paso

El Paso is not the biggest or even one of the biggest apparel production centers in the United States. Nevertheless, it is an interesting location for research on the garment industry. First, it is one of the cities in the southern United States whose garment industry has, until recently, expanded, contrary to the national trend. In addition, jeans overwhelmingly dominate garment production in El Paso. As David Spener notes in Chapter 7, El Paso is "one of the largest, if not *the* largest, points of

production of denim jeans in the United States." Large-scale mass-production plants of branded manufacturers such as Levi Strauss and Company and the VF Corporation have dominated the local garment sector for a long time. The statistical data presented in Table 8.2, which examine the most important cities for apparel production in the United States, indicate El Paso's position in the context of the U.S. garment industry.[2] Although it lags behind several big cities, El Paso deserves a place among leading apparel cities.

Considering the number of apparel establishments in the cities listed in Table 8.2, the difference between large metropolitan areas and the border cities examined becomes quite clear. New York is typical of the northeastern U.S. cities, which have witnessed a sharp decline in apparel production and employment. The negative trend in these northeastern cities and in other metropolitan areas, such as Miami, accounts for the steady decline in national production and employment since the late 1960s.

The garment industry outside the traditional apparel zone of the Northeast has been doing much better. The number of companies in Los Angeles doubled over the past four decades, with employment growing significantly as well. However, until the mid-1990s the border cities were the best examples of phenomenal growth in the garment industry. The number of companies in the border cities of El Paso, McAllen, and San Diego grew vigorously between 1967 and 1995. The data in Table 8.2 reflect the tail end of a shift in garment production from the Northeast to the South of the United States that started in the 1930s. In the course of this shift El Paso became one of the most important garment centers in the South. Since 1995, however, a negative trend has set in for the garment industry in El Paso. In 1996 the number of apparel-related companies there dropped from

TABLE 8.2. Numbers of Companies and Employees in the Garment Industry for Selected U.S. Cities

	1967			1977		
	No. Comp.	No. Empl.	Avg. No. Empl./Comp.	No. Comp.	No. Empl.	Avg. No. Empl./Comp.
United States	16,314	1,142,047	70	13,259	1,021,927	77
Major Metropolitan Areas						
New York	6,711	216,226	32	4,635	138,842	30
Los Angeles	1,135	41,233	36	2,099	66,798	32
Miami	226	8,919	39	652	21,773	34
Border Cities						
El Paso[a]	20	11,140	557	55	13,977	254
San Diego[a]	16	2,154	135	45	3,866	86
McAllen	3	365	122	8	1,958	245

	1987			1995		
	No. Comp.	No. Empl.	Avg. No. Empl./Comp.	No. Comp.	No. Empl.	Avg. No. Empl./Comp.
United States	14,635	838,423	57	15,007	652,129	43
Major Metropolitan Areas						
New York	3,290	108,075	33	3,505	62,329	18
Los Angeles	3,048	84,640	28	4,069	94,552	23
Miami	623	16,520	27	531	12,254	23
Border Cities						
El Paso[a]	67	13,213	197	82	13,999	171
San Diego[a]	99	2,358	24	132	3,523	27
McAllen	16	3,352	210	18	4,823	268

Source: U.S. Department of Commerce 1968, 1979, 1989, 1997.

[a]For both El Paso and San Diego, the difference between the increase in the number of establishments and the number of employees is remarkable. For El Paso, the number of companies more than quadrupled, whereas the number of employees grew by only 27 percent. For San Diego, the exact numbers are different but the magnitude of the difference between the two is similar. The explanation for this phenomenon, certainly for El Paso, may well lie in the fact that the development of the industry in the region was triggered by big companies while the later growth occurred through small and medium-sized companies, many of which were set up by the former employees of the big companies. (See Chapter 7.)

eighty-two the previous year to seventy-two, and the number of employees fell from 13,999 to 13,488 employees (U.S. Department of Commerce 1997). Job losses in the industry have continued since then.

Until the mid-1990s employment in the garment industry of the border cities grew considerably as well, but at widely varying rates. The differences in the growth of employment are reflected in the average numbers of employees per plant for the various cities in Table 8.2. The high average number of employees for companies in McAllen and El Paso is especially striking, since it is well above the average for the other cities. For El Paso this can be explained by the presence of the branded manufacturers and other big companies. This may apply to McAllen also, since it possesses the same locational advantages as El Paso in terms of its proximity to the border and an abundance of cheap labor—two factors that are generally known to attract big manufacturers of standardized, basic products such as jeans and T-shirts.

Thus the average number of employees in El Paso factories is directly related to the second unique feature of the garment industry in El Paso: the dominance of jeans and other denim products. In 1996 more than 56 percent of all companies in El Paso produced "men's and boys' furnishings," and more than 41 percent "women's and misses' outerwear" (U.S. Department of Commerce 1997). One of the products in both subsectors is jeans, and the fact that a large number of the companies in these subsectors produce jeans appears to justify El Paso's nickname of "Jeans Capital of the World." By contrast, the three metropolitan areas examined in Table 8.2 specialize in the more fashion-sensitive women's and misses' outerwear products such as dresses and blouses.

Ciudad Juárez

The industry in neighboring Cd. Juárez provides an interesting contrast to the one in El Paso. The appearance of the garment industry there is a relatively recent phenomenon and is related to the maquiladora program. In the 1960s and 1970s the maquiladora program attracted all kinds of industries to the border region, among which the clothing, automotive, and electronics industries were the most important. In 1982, 132 out of a total of 585 maquiladora plants in Mexico were located in Cd. Juárez, only 18 of which were operating within the apparel industry (Gelderloos 1984). By 1996 their number had hardly grown: At that time 16 apparel maquiladora plants were located in Cd. Juárez. Apparel maquiladoras in Cd. Juárez assemble different types of basic, standardized garments and dominate the

local apparel sector in terms of number of employees.

The establishment of a large number of nongarment maquiladoras led to high demand for work clothes and uniforms, especially in the automotive industry (van Dooren and van der Waerden 1997; and Chapter 9 in this book). As a consequence many small and medium-sized uniform producers emerged, which currently form the largest number of companies among garment makers in Cd. Juárez. Besides the uniform producers and maquiladoras, wedding-dress producers for the local and regional market are an important group of companies in the city, more so in terms of numbers of plants than in terms of employees.

Table 8.3 gives an indication of the number of clothing companies and employees in several Mexican cities for 1994.[3] The data illustrate that Cd. Juárez deserves a place among the important clothing centers in Mexico, despite the fact that the garment industry is among the smaller industries in the city. The characteristics of Cd. Juárez as compared to other cities are rather unremarkable. An explanation for high average number of garment-company employees in the interior cities of Torreón/Gómez Palacio and Aguascalientes might be the recent increase in large-scale investments by U.S. companies and the presence of relatively large Mexican manufacturers in these cities, as a number of people in the Mexican clothing industry who were interviewed during the course of the research pointed out.

Under NAFTA the Mexican garment industry and its employment have boomed. Although Cd. Juárez could absorb part of this overall growth in garment production, the growth has concentrated in locations outside the border region (Solunet 1996). At the end of 1991 the number of apparel maquiladoras had grown to 152 along the border and 156 in the interior, and this trend has intensified since

TABLE 8.3. Number of Companies and Employees in the Clothing Industry in Several Mexican Cities, 1994

	No. Comp.	No. Empl.	Avg. No. Empl./ Comp.
Garment Centers, Interior of Mexico			
Torreón/Gómez Palacio	105	2,581	24.6
Aguascalientes	316	8,816	27.9
Puebla	339	3,408	10.1
Border Cities			
Reynosa	66	1,106	16.8
Tijuana	150	2,712	18.1
Cd. Juárez	149	2,964	19.9

Source: INEGI 1995.

(Mexican Investment Board 1997). The difference between Cd. Juárez and other border cities and locations in the interior lies in the higher wage levels in the border region in general and the tight labor market in Cd. Juarez in particular.

Policies Affecting the Mexican and U.S. Clothing Industries

Clothing is the only industrial sector that has its own international trade regulatory system, the Multifiber Arrangement (MFA), which was first negotiated in 1974. Under the MFA the United States and the European Union negotiate bilaterally with individual exporting countries in order to limit the volume of imported clothing that reaches their markets. In accordance with MFA regulations, the United States developed the 807 program, which permitted the import of garments assembled outside theUnited States with duties paid only on the value added in the assembly process abroad. The main condition of the program was that to qualify for the lower tariff rates, only assembly could be done

abroad, while cutting and—in the specific case of jeans—laundering had to be performed in the United States. The 807 regime applied to a large number of low-cost production locations but in practice was used almost exclusively for assembly programs in Mexico and the Caribbean Basin Initiative region. The 807 program gave rise to a very particular distribution of production activities between the United States and these lower-wage countries (van Dooren and Verkoren 1998).

The MFA and 807 restrictions have been largely replaced by NAFTA regulations, meaning that garments produced from fibers made in North America may be exported freely to any of the NAFTA countries without incurring duties. This has already affected the configuration of the apparel commodity chain spanning the United States and Mexico. Mexican manufacturers are increasing in importance and are becoming involved in a greater number of production activities as new links on the commodity chain move to Mexico (Gereffi 2000). Meanwhile, the U.S. competitive position is under great pressure due to relatively high labor costs in the United States.

Structure of the Regional Garment Industry

A typology of the companies included in the El Paso–Cd. Juárez sample has been created in order to group together those sample companies that are expected to be most similar in terms of behavior and position in the industry. It is thus easier to discern trends in behavior and the development of interfirm cross-border linkages. The typology is based on "size" and "type" of company. The number of employees determines the size of a company: A company with fewer than ten employees is considered small, a company employing between ten and one hundred employees is considered medium-sized, and large companies are those that employ more than one hundred employees.

The determination of the type of company is based on the position of companies in the industry. In this research, types of companies are defined as follows.[4] *Branded manufacturers* are engaged in all activities in the areas of design, cutting, assembly, laundry, and marketing and are autonomous in decision making in these areas. They produce under their own brand name, own manufacturing plants, and may contract out some of their production. They are prevalent in the men's and boys' segment of the industry. Examples of branded manufacturers are Levi Strauss and the VF Corporation that produces the Lee and Wrangler jeans brands. *Marketers* are engaged only in design and marketing activities and do not have any production capacity of their own but instead rely on contractors. *Contractors* are companies that produce garments for marketers, retailers, or branded manufacturers. In many cases the contractors are supplied with the design and sometimes all material inputs by the firms that contract with them to do work. Similar to contractors in terms of position and production activities are the *subcontractors*. These are generally smaller-scale producers, often hired by contractors to do a specific production activity, a phenomenon that is referred to as "specification contracting."[5] However, they can also engage in "capacity contracting" when they are hired to produce part of an order that exceeds the production capacity of a contractor. *Finishers* are companies that are specific to the production of jeans, since they specialize in the laundry of jeans, giving them their characteristic color, while often also taking care of other finishing activities, such as pressing, rescreening, and ticketing. The *suppliers* to the garment industry are those companies that supply the industry with the necessary inputs of fabric, thread, needles, and so forth. They are not directly involved in the manufacturing of garments.

Finally, *maquiladoras* are companies located in Mexico, operating in accordance with the 807 program rules, whose production activities are limited to assembly activities only, with fabric supply, design, cutting, finishing, and distribution handled by their U.S. counterparts. Often these maquiladoras are subsidiaries of large U.S. manufacturers.

Of all these types of companies, neither suppliers nor marketers are represented in the sample. Table 8.4 provides a short summary of the characteristics of the various groups of companies included in the sample.

As the table shows, the garment industry in the region consists largely of subcontractors, contractors, branch plants, and a relatively large number of independent producers. The table also shows the importance of the cutting and sewing aspects of the commodity chain in the region.[6] It is interesting to note that finishers, subcontractors, and contractors are limited in the scope of production activities that they perform, regardless of size. The independent producers are the most well rounded companies in the region, since all companies in this group are involved in all production activities.

Some other interesting aspects of the sample are not immediately clear. The size of the sample firms ranges from a sample maker who works on his own to a branch plant of the VF Corporation with twelve hundred employees. All the small firms have specialized, either in the production of a niche product or in one particular stage of the production process. The El Paso part of the sample includes branch plants of branded manufacturers, contractors, subcontractors, and finishers. The majority of the sample companies in El Paso are involved in the production of jeans. Less important products are general sportswear, coats, and T-shirts for women.

The sample companies in Cd. Juárez can be divided into three main groups: the maquiladoras, producers of uniforms, and producers of wedding dresses. None of these three sorts of

TABLE 8.4. Typology of Companies in the El Paso–Cd. Juárez Sample

Group	Type of Company	Total No. Companies	No. in El Paso	No. in Cd. Juárez	Size	Main Production Activities
I	Small subcontractors	6	6	—	1–9	*Cutting, sewing, marking*
II	Small and medium-sized (sub)contractors	15	12	3	10–99	*Cutting, sewing*
III	Large contractors	6	6	—	>100	Design, *cutting, sewing*
IVª	Independent producers	16	8	8	1–99	*Design, cutting, sewing,* embroidery, *finishing*
V	Branch plants and maquiladoras	13	3	10	>100	Design, cutting, *sewing, finishing*
VIᵇ	Finishers	4	4	—	—	Finishing

Source: Research, El Paso–Cd. Juárez, February–May 1996.

Note: Italic indicates activities performed by most companies in the samples.

ªThe fourth group (IV) are the small and medium-sized independent producers. The group consists of sixteen companies and is, at first sight, the most heterogeneous, containing two producers of designer high fashion, two producers of sports clothing, two producers of wedding dresses, five producers of uniforms, one wholesaler, one embroiderer, and three "independent" garment producers (including the only nonmaquiladora producer of regular clothing encountered in Cd. Juárez). Most companies in this group are "niche" firms since they serve relatively small markets.

ᵇThe last formal group (VI) are the finishers, of which there are four in the sample. They form a group on their own, regardless of their respective numbers of employees. (Three finishers employ fewer than 25 employees while one has 825 employees.) The small finishers are all single-plant companies, while the big finisher is part of a multiplant company.

companies fit into the traditional classification of garment companies as manufacturers, marketers, contractors, subcontractors, and finishers since they are all more or less independent of other companies in the industry. The wedding-dress makers and uniform companies are thus considered "independent." The maquiladoras are mostly branch plants of U.S. firms and have accordingly been grouped under branch plants. The maquiladoras produce T-shirts, coats, and sportswear. Only one nonmaquiladora producing "regular clothing" (in this case jeans) was found. Thus one product group dominates production much less in Cd. Juárez than in El Paso, and the composition of the industry is highly varied internally and very different from that of the U.S. city.

Linkages within the Regional Garment Industry

It has become clear that the garment industries of El Paso and Cd. Juárez are quite different.

Not only is the composition of the industry different in terms of types of companies, but the types of products produced by the companies differ substantially between the cities. The bulk of companies in El Paso produce jeans, whereas the industry in Cd. Juárez produces a broader range of products, ranging from women's wear to uniforms, with little emphasis on jeans. This seems to indicate a limited compatibility of the industries on either side of the border.

Notwithstanding these differences, an examination of linkages between companies on both sides of the border is interesting because of the compelling cost-based logic of a division of labor between the apparel sectors in these two cities. Such an examination at the local level is also useful in this context because it is generally accepted that strong and multiple linkages bring about a competitive edge for the companies involved in them (Markusen 1996; Rabellotti 1995; Crewe 1996). The importance of interfirm local or regional linkages is closely related to other concepts: local embeddedness and industrial districts. An embedded firm is a firm that has many backward and forward linkages within its regional industrial environment. Such linkages, especially between small and medium-sized firms, when based on geographical proximity, sectoral specialization, and vertical disintegration (the process in which manufacturers abandon in-house performance of certain production activities in the chain) are also thought to provide the basis of the competitive advantage of industrial districts (Schmitz 1995; Nadvi 1999). These partially overlapping concepts are useful in this context, because, as Louise Crewe (1996, 258) notes, in a globalizing world economy "the bases for competitive advantage are often intensely local, hinging on a unique social, cultural and political milieu." Both concepts can give an indication of the relative importance and quality of this local milieu for the success of the apparel firms located in El Paso and Cd. Juárez. In analyzing these issues, I use the commodity chain as an analytical tool. The subsequent focus on the production process provides a suitable way to interconnect the above-mentioned issues at the local level and to connect the developments at the local level to the dynamic in the North American garment industry and the ongoing reconfiguration of the North American commodity chain as a whole.

In the analysis, the presence and importance of intraindustry linkages at the local and regional level will be examined and interpreted as an indication of the local embeddedness of the firms and the industrial-district characteristics of the region. Different types of linkages within the regional garment industry are examined. Of primary importance in this regard are the subcontracting relationships and supplier-producer linkages in the region; the presence and importance of regional subsidiaries and clients and other aspects of industrial districts are also briefly included in the discussion.

Regional Subcontracting Relationships

Despite the general advantages associated with subcontracting relationships, and especially regional subcontracting relationships,[7] in the El Paso–Cd. Juárez region these relationships are limited in number. Only twenty-six companies in the sample (43 percent) use subcontractors, and only twenty of these companies, or one-third of all sample companies, use regional subcontractors. There does not seem to be a significant difference between the two cities, nor between the different types of firms, regarding the overall use of subcontractors. In Cd. Juárez the wedding-dress makers work with home workers, and the uniform producers work with small subcontracting companies, which are used mostly to enhance production capacity during peak periods. In El Paso one-third of the sample companies have business relationships with subcontractors, and the different types of companies all engage in these relationships to a similar degree.

By far the most notable characteristic of regional subcontracting is the almost complete absence of cross-border subcontracting agreements. Contrary to the hypothesis described at the beginning of this chapter, companies in El Paso do not use relatively cheap contractors or subcontractors in Cd. Juárez as a way of lowering their own costs, thereby possibly gaining a competitive edge relative to companies located further from the border. No companies in El Paso use only subcontractors in Cd. Juárez, while only two companies in the Texas city use subcontractors in both El Paso and Cd. Juárez. This is a rather puzzling discovery, given the short distance and significant wage differential between the two cities. One maquiladora in Cd. Juarez uses a subcontractor in El Paso. This maquiladora produces jeans and contracts out to a laundry in El Paso for finishing, since prior to NAFTA laundry had to be done in the United States in order to comply with the 807 regulation.

Regional Supplier-Producer Linkages

In quantitative terms, regional relationships between suppliers and producers are found to be relatively important; 90 percent of the regional producers buy some of their supplies from suppliers in the region. Cross-border supply relationships are more limited in number: None of the companies in El Paso bought from suppliers in Cd. Juarez. This contrasts sharply with the importance of suppliers in El Paso for companies in Cd. Juárez. For Cd. Juárez, 61 percent of the suppliers were located in El Paso while only 24 percent were local, and the remaining 15 percent were located outside the region. The importance of El Paso as the primary source for Cd. Juárez's inputs can be attributed to the fact that suppliers of certain inputs are much more readily available in El Paso because of the greater relative importance of the garment industry to that city's economy.

In evaluating the apparent importance of regional supplier-producer linkages, one should note the difference between regional sales offices and suppliers.[8] As many as 96 percent of regional suppliers are sales offices of suppliers, and only chemicals used in laundries and labels for jeans are made locally. This reinforces the general conclusion that supplier-producer linkages cannot securely embed companies in the regional industry because of the sales office nature of the suppliers.

Regional Subsidiaries

The main reason for discussing local subsidiaries is that under the 807 program many U.S. companies set up assembly plants in Mexico, the so-called maquiladoras. Since the 1970s the linkages between U.S. manufacturers and their subsidiaries have become one of the most important transborder linkages. Also, a greater number of local subsidiaries could result in a higher degree of local embeddedness among

multiplant companies and possibly a higher propensity to collective action in the district.

Except for the branch plants and maquiladoras, a relatively small number of companies across all groups in the sample have regional subsidiaries. Ten branch plants or maquiladoras have subsidiaries in the El Paso–Cd. Juárez region. However, the embeddedness of these companies in the regional economy is questionable because these big companies have a broad scope in terms of where they choose to locate their subsidiaries. The biggest of these companies, such as Levi Strauss and VF Corporation, see the entire world as their market as well as their potential production site. They are "footloose"[9] and do not seem to have tight links to the garment industry in the region. This is also exemplified by their limited use of local subcontractors, a characteristic for which maquiladoras especially are notorious (Sklair 1993; Gereffi 2000). In the case of the maquiladoras, the subsidiaries in El Paso to which they are linked are almost without exception warehouses and administrative plants (van Dooren and van der Waerden 1997). The maquiladoras are not linked, either through subcontracting or through intrafirm linkages, to "upstream" or "downstream" aspects of the commodity chain in the areas of cutting and finishing. Again, this is surprising, as companies still prefer to perform these activities in the United States in order to avoid duties. (Finishing capacity in the Mexican border region is still limited but has increased since 1996.) Only eighteen companies in the El Paso–Cd. Juárez region, ten of which themselves are branch plants or maquiladoras, have linkages to regional subsidiaries.

Clients

Regional clients do not play a very important role in the garment industry in Cd. Juárez and are even less important to the industry in El Paso. The garment industry of El Paso is geared almost entirely toward the U.S. market because almost all nonregional customers are located in the United States; there is only one producer in El Paso that has a customer in the Mexican interior. The Mexican market is not a target of the garment industry in El Paso.

For Cd. Juárez, regional customers are spread over both cities, although the majority are on the Mexican side of the border. This is largely due to the autonomous nature of many producers in Cd. Juárez and their orientation toward the local market. It is also important to bear in mind that because of the nature of the product that the uniform and wedding-dress manufacturers make, their customers are final consumers (in the case of the wedding dresses) or industrial plants—mostly automotive maquiladoras—for which the uniforms are merely a noncritical input (van Dooren and van der Waerden 1997; Chapter 9 in this book). For the maquiladoras, by contrast, only 6 percent of their customers are located in the region. They produce almost solely for the U.S. market, through clients whose head offices are located in major U.S. cities. Thus, despite the fact that local customers are more important to companies in Cd. Juárez than to companies in El Paso, local customers generally are not very important to the garment industry of the region.

Minimal Linkages, Little Embeddedness

Instead of one regional garment-oriented industrial district bound together by cross-border linkages, it would seem more accurate to speak of two local garment industries in the El Paso–Ciudad Juárez region. Overall, the industries in both cities exhibit a roughly equal and limited degree of local linkages through relationships with subcontractors, suppliers, subsidiaries, and clients. The various groups of companies seem to be similarly limited in their local embeddedness, and neither of the two cities displays clear industrial-district characteristics.

In light of insights from the global commodity chain approach, one of the clearest obstacles to the development of multiple interfirm linkages in the region is the overriding importance of the assembly links of the chain. No significant activities in the areas of design, textile production, marketing, or even distribution are being undertaken in the region, and linkages are limited to some cutting and finishing. Consequently, the scope for true backward and forward linkages in the region is limited and competition between the companies in the region is fierce.

When one considers the characteristics of the region from the perspective of the industrial-district literature, one has to conclude that, despite geographic concentration and sectoral specialization, neither the region nor either of the two cities displays the multitude of interfirm linkages that would indicate an industrial-district type of development. Not only has the dominance of large-scale manufacturers probably been one of the main obstacles to the development of linkages,[10] but institutional support for the industry in the region is limited, and even assumptions of a similar sociocultural background for the actors in the industry are questionable.[11] Thus the concentration of large and relatively footloose companies in El Paso and Cd. Juárez, intense competition in a limited number of products in El Paso, and an overall concentration on the assembly link of the production chain appear to be the most important barriers to an industrial-district type of development in the region.

The evaluation of the absence of cross-border linkages reaffirms the need for a more nuanced view of labor in new international division-of-labor theory (see also Elson 1988;

Scheffer 1992). This study found only limited evidence of the expected cross-border division of labor. Although this finding may appear to challenge the new international division-of-labor theory, it more accurately underscores the importance of the availability of low-cost labor in determining the relocation of labor-intensive production activities and thereby in constantly constructing new international divisions of labor. Not only should the availability of a large reserve of cheap labor be given more importance than is generally done, but labor costs should be related to alternative locations. The limited nature of cross-border linkages can thus be attributed partly to the fact that the local business climate in Cd. Juárez—characterized by high labor turnover, a tight labor market, and relatively high wages—is not ideal for the production of garments for the U.S. market, particularly when compared to other locations in Mexico.

The Linkages That Do Exist

Two types of nonregional linkages are examined in this section: (1) linkages that connect companies in El Paso to production in the Mexican interior and (2) the linkages of maquiladoras in Cd. Juárez with U.S. headquarters located outside El Paso.

The cities of Torreón, Coahuila, and Gómez Palacio, Durango; Aguascalientes; and Tehuacán, Puebla, are significant sites for garment production in Mexico, and especially for linkages with U.S. firms, because the industry is relatively more important in these cities than along the border. This has resulted in the availability of an experienced labor force and production capabilities that extend beyond the assembly activities.[12] Also, wages and labor turnover are generally lower in these cities than in the border region (from personal interviews, conducted in the course of fieldwork in

1996, with Cor Zwezerijnen, technical director of a large manufacturer in El Paso; Jesse Romero, a garment broker in El Paso; and Blanca Santoyo, director of the Garment Development Center in El Paso). It is important, however, to emphasize the slow development of linkages between U.S. companies and firms in the Mexican interior: When this research was conducted in 1996, only 18 percent of companies in the El Paso region had subsidiaries in Mexico at all, and only 7 percent used Mexican contractors outside Cd. Juárez. Subsequent research carried out in 1998 nevertheless indicates that an increasing number of linkages between El Paso and the Mexican interior are developing.

Subsidiaries and Contractors in the Interior

El Paso manufacturers have been somewhat cautious about investing in Mexico, and it is only since 1997 that the rate of investment has picked up speed. In the first months of 1996, eleven companies in the El Paso–Cd. Juárez region had invested in production in the Mexican interior. Branch plants and especially maquiladoras are most extensively linked to production in Mexico, which indicates that the propensity to invest in Mexico increases with experience. Some big contractors and even a small and a medium-sized contractor have also invested directly in the Mexican interior.

The major destination of investments by companies in the El Paso–Cd. Juarez region is the urban area of Torreón/Gómez Palacio. (For a more detailed analysis of this area, see Chapter 10 in this book.) Almost all companies with linkages to the interior have invested there. This phenomenon can be attributed to the location and orientation of the various Mexican garment cities. As Jesse Romero put it: "In Torreón I would venture to say that 80–90% of the factories are set up to do foreign work. . . . In Aguascalientes and Puebla these percentages are lower because the distances to the US market are larger and the cities are more oriented to the Mexican market in Mexico City" (personal communication, May 1997). This conclusion is endorsed by Cor Zwezerij-nen, the technical director of a large manufac-turer, who estimates that as many as 95 percent of the companies in Torreón/Gómez Palacio produce for the U.S. market—the majority as contractors but others as joint-venture part-ners of a U.S. company.

Subcontracting is often seen as an initial step, allowing the firm to acquire a feel for doing business in Mexico while avoiding long-term commitments. But it is also done by com-panies that have gained a lot of experience with contractors over a long supply relationship and now have substantial confidence in the quality of their products. The geographic concentra-tion of contracting relationships is largely the same as that of direct investments and is also centered in the Torreón/Gómez Palacio area in northern Mexico. Only four companies in El Paso have linkages to contractors in the Mexican interior. As an example of such link-ages, Figure 8.1, based on 1996 fieldwork data, depicts one of the companies, which success-fully complemented its domestic production with a mix of direct investment and contract-ing in the border region and an extensive con-tracting network in the Mexican interior. I have called this company Verde.

In 1996, Verde owned four plants in El Paso, two in Cd. Juárez (another opened in 1998, after the research was conducted), and one in Ojinaga, a Mexican border city east of El Paso–Cd. Juárez. The plants in El Paso did design, cutting, and distribution, while all the sewing was done in Mexico. The head of man-ufacturing at Verde said that owning plants in Mexico had a number of advantages: Produc-tion was easier to manage and coordinate be-tween plants, resulting in increased control, flexibility, and reliability. Despite these advan-tages, the company expected to maintain a sta-ble number of Verde plants in Mexico rather than increase them because it wanted to con-centrate on design, marketing, sales, and ser-vices while having reliable contractors who were responsible for production.

Verde's good experiences with contractors were based on the consistent nature of demand for jeans, which has allowed the firm to provide its contractors with steady work all year. The experience it gained over the years led Verde to add linkages with three contractors in Chi-huahua and between eight and ten in Torreón. These contractors produced 75 percent of Verde's total production. Verde has had both long-term (as long as ten years with some) and shorter-term relationships with these contrac-tors. The distribution of orders in the low sea-son depends on the seniority of the contractor and the quality and services it offers.

The company has found the right balance between domestic and Mexican production activities and between owned plants and con-tractors, and it intends to keep this balance unchanged, at least in the near future. The 1996 geographic distribution of Verde's link-ages to other actors in the garment industry and the activities performed by these actors are represented in Figure 8.1.

Despite the potential gains, by 1996 only eleven companies researched had foreign direct investment in the Mexican interior, and four companies in El Paso and no companies in Cd. Juárez had taken advantage of the possibility of contracting in Mexico. In 1998, however, branded manufacturers expanded their pro-duction in Mexico through contracting link-ages, at the expense of production in El Paso. In 1997, Levi's announced the closure of a number of its El Paso plants; Sun Apparel also closed a plant, and a number of other large-

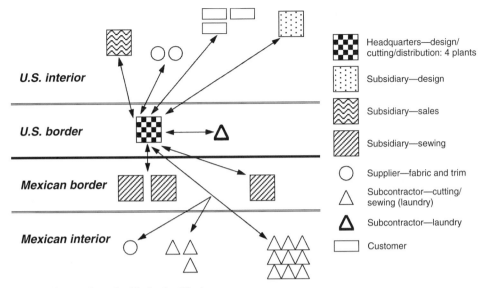

FIGURE 8.1.   Supply Chain for Verde

scale producers have followed suit or indicated their plans to do so (see Chapter 7 in this book). These and other companies are extensively and increasingly involved in subcontracting arrangements with Mexican producers.

Linkages of Companies in Cd. Juárez

Only the maquiladoras in Cd. Juárez have extraregional production linkages, and their local embeddedness and extraregional Mexican linkages generally appear to be quite limited. A number of the maquiladoras in the sample have subsidiaries located elsewhere in Mexico. These subsidiaries seem to produce in isolation from one another, each maintaining its own linkages to its headquarters and other relevant actors in the United States. Two maquiladoras of a large apparel-producing corporation, which I will call Rojo and Azul, provide an example of a typical maquiladora linkage pattern.

Both Rojo and Azul produce ladies' jackets and suits, for which they receive design, fabric, accessories, and decorations from the head office in Philadelphia. The maquiladoras deal directly with a thread supplier in Dallas instead of ordering thread from the sales office of this same supplier in El Paso. All other inputs are shipped directly from Philadelphia to Cd. Juárez. The jackets and suits are finished in Cd. Juárez, after which they are shipped to El Paso, Nashville, or Philadelphia to be distributed. Rojo and Azul do not have any linkages to local suppliers or subcontractors, nor do they have productive linkages with each other. Their local linkages are thus very limited. The geographic distribution of the linkages of the group with other actors in the garment industry and the activities performed by these actors are represented in Figure 8.2.

The pattern of linkages between the maquiladoras and other companies in Mexico and the United States is shaped by the 807 program. The regulations of the 807 regime limit the productive scope of maquiladoras to assembly activities. As a result, all garment maquiladoras, even those belonging to the same company, could serve as functionally

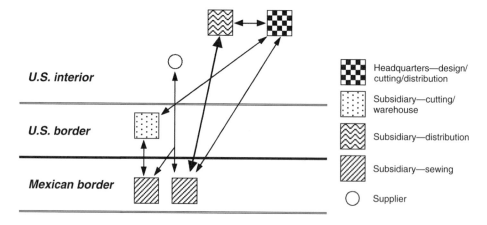

FIGURE 8.2.   Supply Chain for Rojo and Azul

equivalent substitutes for one another. Their noncomplementary character eliminates any reason for linkages between them. The regulations of the 807 program are designed to retain all nonassembly activities in the United States, which is why the linkages that existed in 1996 were all directed north of the border. Although it may seem advantageous to perform other production activities in the U.S. border region, this was hardly the case in 1996. This is currently changing, especially since the elimination of duties on cutting in Mexico were lifted in 1999.

Naturally, under NAFTA the 807 restrictions no longer apply to cross-border relationships between firms in the apparel industry. However, the development of linkages between maquiladoras and other actors in the local or regional industry seems questionable, if not improbable, in an environment such as Cd. Juárez. Prospects for the emergence of such linkages and the development of locally integrated production seem brighter in one of the more traditional centers for garment production, which have local production capabilities in nonassembly activities.

Conclusion

The analysis presented here leads to several conclusions. First, the garment commodity chain in both El Paso and Cd. Juárez is limited to only a few types of production activities. In El Paso production is heavily concentrated in cutting and sewing activities and, to a lesser extent, in laundry and finishing. In Cd. Juárez the maquiladoras, which dominate the sector in terms of both production volume and employment, still perform only sewing activities and a limited degree of finishing. Designing, textile manufacturing, distribution, and marketing activities do not take place in the region. Linkages to other actors in the cities are limited in number. Firms are not deeply embedded in their local business environment and thus are probably not very committed to its survival or to designing a cooperative strategy to increase its competitiveness.

The virtual absence of cross-border linkages between the industries in El Paso and Cd. Juarez—which also indicates the neglect of a potential way to retain a competitive advantage in the region—is due largely to the characteristics of the relatively tight labor market in Cd. Juárez, where garment companies have to compete for employees with electronics and automobile plants that offer higher wages. Although the wage differential between the two border cities is significant, it apparently is not large enough to offset the attraction of even lower wages elsewhere in Mexico.

As a consequence, the linkages necessary to complete the garment production process—namely, linkages to design, textile manufacturing, distribution, and marketing capabilities—"skip" the border in favor of extraregional locations. Overall, the patterns of existing linkages seem to point to the importance of North American networks over regional or local production networks, a trend likely to intensify under NAFTA. Bearing in mind the importance of these production networks for the North American garment industry's competitiveness, as noted by Gary Gereffi (1997b), this case illustrates both some of the losses to be encountered by segments of the North American garment industry in shaping production networks and the still-footloose character of the assembly link in garment production networks. Large manufacturers, as organizing agents of the production networks, despite their overwhelming presence in El Paso have hardly been able or willing to draw small and medium-sized regional producers into their networks. Since, for such companies that do not produce for a local niche market, the ability to tap into these networks has proven to be of vital importance to their survival, the vast majority has gone out of business over the past couple of years. Further, the presence of numerous branded manufacturers' plants in El Paso may no longer guarantee the position of that city as what Gereffi (1997a, 13) calls "a coordinating hub of the North American apparel commodity chain," since recent closures have proven that these manufacturers are willing to leave El Paso. These closures have already left unemployed

an enormous number of workers, who for various reasons will have difficulty finding alternative employment, and this trend is likely to continue.

By contrast, the maquiladoras in Cd. Juárez seem hardly affected by the liberalization under NAFTA in the short and medium term, although they may lose in the long run. With its tight labor market and the competition between production facilities in many industrial sectors, Cd. Juárez is not an ideal hub for a North American garment production network. Better opportunities are offered by interior locations such as Torreón/Gómez Palacio, Aguascalientes, and Tehuacán.

Epilogue

In 2001, five years after the initial research presented here on the U.S.-Mexico border, the trends underway appeared to have completed their course. The garment industry in El Paso has almost entirely collapsed; its current position as support and distribution hub for North American garment production is only a bleak (and possibly temporary) reminder of its former status of "Jeans Capital of the World." On the other side of the border, El Paso's pain has clearly not been Cd. Juárez's gain. As was expected, the industry in the Mexican border city has remained stable and relatively isolated. More surprising may be the fact that although some of the weaknesses of the industry in El Paso have been largely overcome in Mexico's "Jeans Capitals of the World" (such as Torreón), these cities may yet be headed in a similar direction (van Dooren and Smakman 2001; van Dooren 2001).

Notes

1. I use a narrow definition of the garment industry, excluding the nonclothing subgroups of the Standard Industrial Classification (SIC) apparel group. This is especially relevant in Cd. Juárez, where many of the apparel maquiladoras produce nonclothing items such as upholstery for the auto industry, curtains and bedding, belting, and the like.

2. The data presented in Table 8.2 are based on SIC codes 231 to 237, since these are the subgroups that form part of the garment definition used in this research. The subsectors "fur goods," "miscellaneous apparel and accessories," and "miscellaneous fabricated textile products" are thus not included in these tables.

3. The definition of the clothing industry in Mexico used in this research is based on the statistical data provided by INEGI under subsector 3220, "Confección de prendas de vestir."

4. A clear overview of the various garment companies and their positions within the industry is provided by the U.S. International Trade Commission (1995, 3).

5. The distinction between contractors and subcontractors is somewhat theoretical, especially since distinctions between types of companies have become blurred as different types of firms have started to combine sourcing strategies to reduce costs and risks.

6. An aspect not shown by Table 8.4 is that companies in Cd. Juárez, with the exception of the independent producers for the local market, are not involved in cutting. This is due to the 807 regulations mentioned earlier.

7. Generally, contracting is seen as a means to reduce costs, reduce investment risks, enhance production flexibility, and allow for small-batch production. Short delivery times and effective supply response, low transportation costs, convenience in access and control, and cultural similarity are some of the additional advantages of regional subcontracting.

8. Local suppliers produce locally, while local sales offices sell supplies made outside the region. Sales offices of suppliers are relatively footloose and not closely integrated in the regional business environment. They are attracted to a localized concentration of industry but cannot serve to attract companies to or embed them in the local environment.

9. Whereas, formerly, the demand for "Made in the U.S.A." products, public opinion, and the effect on their image of large numbers of layoffs may have deterred these companies from relocating freely, these companies currently seem less able to withstand competition from and the attraction of production in low-cost locations, as exemplified by the recent closures of many plants owned by companies such as Levi Strauss and Sun Apparel in El Paso (see Chapter 7 in this book).

10. Traditionally the industrial-district literature has emphasized the importance of the sectoral specialization and geographic concentration of small and medium-sized companies (Schmitz 1995). With few exceptions (Scott 1992; Schmitz 1995), the role of large-scale producers in districts has received much less attention.

11. During the research it was found that biases and prejudices about doing business in Cd. Juárez are still prevalent in El Paso. This might be an indication that the common cultural and social background of garment actors in both cities, one of the characteristics of industrial districts, is not strong enough to link them together. One basic dissimilarity is that whereas large companies in El Paso were generally run by Anglo-Americans, the shop floors and the smaller-scale companies were dominated by Hispanics.

12. This may also imply that the initial potential for full-package production is greater in these traditional garment centers than in the border cities, where the garment sector is much more dominated by maquiladoras. Integrated production and full-package capabilities may, as noted by Gereffi (1997b), be of decisive importance for the future of garment manufacturing in Mexico.

References

Crewe, Louise. 1996. "Material Culture: Embedded Firms, Organizational Networks and the Local Economic Development of a Fashion Quarter." *Regional Studies* 30, 3: 257–72.

Desarrollo Económico de Ciudad Juarez. 1996. *Sistema de informacion regional* no. 5. Ciudad Juárez, Mexico: Desarrollo Económico de Ciudad Juárez, AC.

Dickerson, Kitty. 1995. *Textiles and Apparel in the Global Economy*. 2nd ed. Englewood Cliffs, N.J.: Prentice-Hall.

Elson, Diane. 1988. "Transnational Corporations and the New International Division of Labour: A Critique of Cheap Labour Hypotheses." *Manchester Papers on Development* 4, 3: 352–76

Fröbel, Folker, Jurgen Heinrichs, and Otto Kreye. 1980. *The New International Division of Labour*. Cambridge: Cambridge University Press.

Gelderloos, Gonneke. 1984. "Het labyrint van der armoede. Een arbeidsmarktonderzoek in de Noord-Mexicaanse grensstad Ciudad Juarez." Unpublished M.A. thesis, Utrecht University, The Netherlands.

Gereffi, Gary. 1997a. "Competing through Networks in the North American Apparel Commodity Chain." Paper presented at the Workshop on Global Production Systems and Labour Markets, International Institute for Labor Studies, Geneva, Switzerland.

———. 1997b. "Global Shifts, Regional Response: Can North America Meet the Full-Package Challenge?" *Bobbin* 39, 3 (November): 16–31.

———. 2000. "The Mexico-U.S. Apparel Connection: Economic Dualism and Transnational Networks." In *Poverty or Development: Global Restructuring and Regional Transformations in the U.S. South and the Mexican South*, ed. Richard Tardanico and Mark B. Rosenberg, pp. 59–89. New York: Routledge.

Gereffi, Gary, and Jennifer Bair. 1998. "Special Report: Mexico. US Companies Eye NAFTA's Prize." *Bobbin* 39, 7 (March): 26–35.

Gereffi, Gary, and Miguel Korzeniewicz, eds. 1994. *Commodity Chains and Global Capitalism*. Westport, Conn.: Praeger.

Humphrey, John, and Hubert Schmitz. 2000. "Governance and Upgrading: Linking Industrial Cluster and Global Value Chain Research." IDS Working Paper no. 120. Brighton, United Kingdom: Institute of Development Studies, University of Sussex.

Instituto Nacional de Estadística, Geografía e Informática (INEGI). 1995. *Censos economicos 1994. XIV censo industrial, XI censo comercial y XI censo de servicios*. Aguascalientes: INEGI.

Khanna, Sri Ram. 1997. "Trends in US Textile and Clothing Imports." *Textile Outlook International* 69 (January): 66–109.

Markusen, Ann. 1996. "Sticky Places in Slippery Space: A Typology of Industrial Districts." *Economic Geography* 72, 1: 55–72.

McIntyre, Mitchell. 1955. "The Clothing Industry of El Paso from 1919 to July 1955." Unpublished Ph.D. diss., University of Texas at El Paso.

Mexican Investment Board. 1997. *Mexico, Your Partner for Growth. The Textile and Apparel Industry in Mexico*. Mexico City: Mexican Investment Board.

Nadvi, Khaled. 1999. "The Cutting Edge: Collective Efficiency and International Competitiveness in Pakistan." *Oxford Development Studies* 27, 1: 81–107.

Piore, Michael, and Charles Sabel. 1984. *The Second Industrial Divide*. New York: Basic Books.

Porter, Michael. 1990. *The Competitive Advantage of Nations*. London: Macmillan.

Rabellotti, Roberta. 1995. "Is There an Industrial District Model? Footwear Districts in Italy and Mexico Compared." *World Development* 23, 1: 29–40.

Scheffer, Michiel. 1992. *Trading Places: Fashion, Retailers and the Changing Geography of Clothing Production*. Utrecht: KNAG.

Schmitz, Hubert. 1995. "Collective Efficiency: Growth Path for Small-Scale Industry." *World Development* 23, 1: 9–28.

Schmitz, Hubert, and Khalid Nadvi. 1999. "Clustering and Industrialization: Introduction." *World Development* 27, 9: 1503–14.

Scott, Allan. 1992. "The Role of Large Producers in Industrial Districts: A Case Study of High Technology Systems Houses in Southern California." *Regional Studies* 26, 3: 265–75.

Sklair, Lesley. 1993. *Assembling for Development: The Maquila Industry in Mexico and the United States*. La Jolla: Center of U.S.-Mexican Studies, University of California, San Diego.

Solunet. 1996. *The Complete Twinplant Guide*. El Paso: Solunet.

Texas Centers. 1998. Internet address: <http://www.utep.edu/txcr/Demgr/Empl.html>.

Twin Plant News. 1997. "Professional Daily Minimum Wages." *Twin Plant News,* January, 17.

U.S. Department of Commerce. 1968, 1979, 1989, 1997. *County Business Patterns.* Washington, D.C.: U.S. Government Printing Office.

U.S. Department of Labor. 1995a. *Mexican Labor Trends, 1992–1993.* Washington, D.C.: National Trade Data Bank.

U.S. Department of Labor. 1995b. *Employment, Hours and Earnings, United States 1990–1995.* Washington, D.C.: U.S. Government Printing Office.

U.S. International Trade Commission. 1995. *Industry and Trade Summary: Apparel.* Publication 2853. Washington, D.C.: U.S. Government Printing Office.

van Dooren, Robine. 2001. "The Garment Boom in La Laguna, Northern Mexico: The Role of and Opportunities for Rural SME's." Paper presented at European Association of Development Institutes (EADI) workshop on "Linking the Local to the Global: Small Enterprises in Global Markets: Technology Transfer, Export Opportunities and Organisational Upgrading," Campobasso, Italy, March.

van Dooren, Robine, and Floor Smakman. 2001. "The Impact of International Buyer Strategies on the Local Apparel Industry in Mexico and Malaysia." Paper presented at the Association of American Geographers (AAG) conference, New York, February.

van Dooren, Robine, and Talitha van der Waerden. 1997. "The Garment Industry in El Paso and Cd. Juárez: Automate, Emigrate or Eliminate?" Unpublished M.A. thesis, Utrecht University, the Netherlands.

van Dooren, Robine, and Otto Verkoren. 1998. "Grondstoffen (IV)." *Geografie* (January): 15.

Jorge Carrillo, Alfredo Hualde,
and Araceli Almaraz

9   Commodity Chains and Industrial
Organization in the Apparel Industry
in Monterrey and Ciudad Juárez

Introduction

Since the mid-1980s, Mexico's economy has
developed in a context that is substantially
different from its former import-substitution
industrialization model.[1] The opening of the
economy to international competition has modified the modes of conduct of both the government and private firms, as well as their mutual
relations. This change has been important not
only for Mexico but also for its nearest and
most important neighbor, the United States,
which upon the ratification of the North American Free Trade Agreement (NAFTA) formal-
ized its status as Mexico's most important trade
partner.

Mexico's unilateral trade opening preceding NAFTA produced macroeconomic imbalances and social tensions among firms. One of
the most frequently expressed fears was that
Mexico's small and medium-scale enterprises
would be left unprotected against an avalanche
of foreign imports. This situation was forecast
especially for industries such as apparel, where
the trade opening took place very rapidly: In

1985, 100 percent of Mexican clothing production was protected by import licenses that
were done away with in 1988, while the average tariff on garments fell from 50 percent in
the second half of 1985 to 20 percent by
December 1987. Other protectionist measures
were reduced or eliminated in textiles as well
(Mendoza and Pozos 1997). The trade opening, according to the pessimists, would sharpen
competition to the point that the survival of
many Mexican small and medium-sized enterprises would be threatened.

Nevertheless, even now, in the early twenty-
first century, it is difficult to assess the outcome
of the trade opening for the Mexican garment
industry in clear-cut terms. At the beginning of
the opening, a significant drop occurred in both
employment and number of firms in the industry. Textile and apparel's joint share of Mexican gross domestic product in manufacturing
fell from 13.8 percent in 1980 to 10.8 percent
by 1990. These industries' share of manufacturing employment also fell significantly, from
18.1 percent in 1980 to 15.9 percent in 1990.
From 1991 to 1994 the real value of textile and

apparel output fell by 20 percent. Since the beginning of 1994, however, macroeconomic data show a substantial increase in both production and exports in the Mexican apparel industry. In 1995 exports grew by 50 percent, and the trade balance for apparel in 1996 showed a surplus of $722 million (Dussel 1997; Bair 1997). Similarly, substantial growth has occurred in garment maquiladora employment, which increased from 64,000 workers in 1993 to 180,800 in 1997 and 285,600 in 2001 (INEGI 1998, 2001). This growth has taken place principally in nonborder areas, where employment grew from 31,430 workers to 134,170 between 1993 and 1997. In contrast, along the border employment in garment maquiladoras increased by only about 15,000 jobs, from 22,065 in 1993 to 37,655 in 1997. Rapid expansion of garment maquiladoras has also meant that the percentage of total maquiladora employment in Mexico accounted for by the apparel industry has increased from 10.6 percent to 19.1 percent in just five years.

These positive trends at the national level were a direct consequence of the peso devaluation that occurred at the end of 1994 and the deregulation of trade in garments and textiles enacted with the implementation of NAFTA. According to some analysts, NAFTA is facilitating a particular division of labor in which the United States textile industry supplies raw materials to garment-producing firms located in Mexican territory that now have unrestrained access to the lucrative U.S. market. This schema varies, however, by both the specific type of garment under consideration and the site of its production in Mexico. In fact, the trade opening has not produced a single, uniform effect on textiles and garments in Mexico. Although thousands of businesses failed, many survived and many new enterprises were created.

An important research task, therefore, is to consider the strategies adopted and the com-petitive advantages possessed by firms that have either remained in the industry or recently entered it. Some firms have transformed themselves into distributors of foreign goods. Others have taken advantage of their ability to import inputs in order to sew garments in small establishments. Certain communities in the Bajío (a region in central Mexico), for example, have become maquiladora garment districts (Vangstrup 1995). Other authors have described a plethora of production situations and highlight the tenuous distinction that exists between formal, informal, and clandestine shops (Suárez and Rivera 1994, 215). One factor that contributes to the opening of new plants in Mexico as well as to the expansion of production in existing plants is the strategy of large retail chains in Mexico (e.g., Comercial Mexicana) to increase the proportion of purchases they make from domestic suppliers in the face of rising prices for goods from Asia and other countries outside the North American market. Similarly, U.S. branded manufacturers such as Levi Strauss and Company have begun to contract a significant proportion of their global production to Mexican maquiladoras (Mendoza and Pozos 1997).

In this chapter we set out to examine this diversity of Mexican garment-production situations through an analysis of a sample of enterprises located in two northern cities: Ciudad Juárez, Chihuahua, and Monterrey, Nuevo León. In conducting our analysis, we adopt a commodity-chain perspective. Since the late 1980s the development literature has demonstrated the need to examine the links between suppliers and clients in specific industrial regions instead of focusing exclusively on individual enterprises or on specific branches of industry (Becattini 1988; Castillo 1988–89; Gereffi 1995, 2000; Gereffi and Hempel 1996). This approach permits us to track the competitive advantages (or disadvantages) accruing to a good at different points along its production-distribution chain. In addition, it allows us to understand how a region or a city is integrated into the productive fabric of its own and other countries.

This chapter is organized into three sections. In the first section we explain the methodology of our study and discuss the characteristics of the garment industry in each city, including the restructuring it has undergone over the last few years. In the second section we analyze how production chains are structured by distinct types of interfirm networks operating in each city. Finally, we reflect on the study's findings and their implications for the further evolution of the garment industry in Mexico.

The Restructuring of the Garment Industry in Monterrey and Ciudad Juárez

Our analysis focuses on two cities in northern Mexico that have followed quite distinct paths to industrialization. Monterrey, capital of the state of Nuevo León, has been a center for industrial growth in Mexico since the beginning of the twentieth century. Its development has been led by several large industrial *grupos* based there, such as ALFA and VITRO.[2] Ciudad Juárez, by contrast, is a border city in the state of Chihuahua whose development has been more recent, occurring in conjunction with the rise of the maquiladora industry since the 1960s.

During the 1980s the large industrial groups in Monterrey, in spite of some difficulties, managed to restructure their enterprises in order to compete successfully on the international stage while preserving their dominance in specific domestic markets (Pozas 1993; Pozos 1996). In the macroeconomic crisis that began in 1982, Monterrey's industrial companies underwent a dramatic restructuring that involved significant plant closures and layoffs brought on by the large dollar-denominated debts they had taken on at the end of the 1970s. One of the most important closures was that of Fundidora Monterrey, long a symbol of the city's industrial strength, which employed eleven thousand direct-production workers in 1986. The ALFA and VITRO groups laid off seventeen thousand and eleven thousand employees respectively (Pozas 1993).

Nevertheless, with the help of a debt-restructuring plan designed by the federal government,[3] Monterrey manufacturers managed to extricate themselves from the most acute phase of the financial crisis in which they were mired. Later, by means of a series of new restructuring moves that included the acquisition of technologies, improvements in management techniques, and the formation of strategic alliances with foreign companies, the Monterrey groups found themselves among the most internationally competitive producers of beer, cement, and glass (Aguilar 1992). Thus VITRO teamed up with Whirlpool and became the majority shareholder in Anchor Glass (Aguilar 1992; Pozas 1993; Pozos 1996). Other industrial groups, such as CEMEX, acquired the leading cement producers in Mexico, as well as four U.S. cement companies. CEMEX became the main producer of cement in Mexico, accounting for 85 percent of the country's exports of this product.

Several factors explain the depth of the restructuring of Monterrey industry in spite of the difficulties that it experienced during the 1980s. First, the corporate structure that the industrial bourgeoisie of Monterrey developed is based on the intertwining of family ties, business interests, and political influence. The enterprises of the *grupos* are vertically integrated to a large extent, meaning that all or most suppliers of components or parts needed to manufacture the product belong to the *grupo*, and this has helped them achieve important economies of scale, although this tight integration can be a source of rigidity in periods of crisis like that of the 1980s. Second, Monterrey's industrial sector maintained strong links with the local and national financial sector. Third, Monterrey industrialists have been innovative and have dedicated considerable resources to research and development (Pozos 1996, 69). Fourth, in spite of recurrent conflicts with the federal government, Monterrey industrialists have repeatedly demonstrated their indispensability to the health of the national economy. In fact, the overall policies of opening and deregulation undertaken by the federal government in response to the 1980s crisis coincided with many of the industrialists' demands. Likewise, strategic institutions such as the Instituto Tecnológico y de Estudios Superiores de Monterrey have participated in and influenced the government's economic planning and programming since the mid-1980s. Finally, in periods of economic opening, Monterrey's industrial groups have readily applied their considerable resources and talents to forging dynamic strategies that permit them to compete effectively in international markets, especially when compared with other regional bourgeoisie in Mexico and Latin America (Pozos 1996).

The economic history of Ciudad Juárez has been quite different. Juárez's industry grew as a result of tendencies in the world economy in which U.S. enterprises—and later those from Asia—searched for new forms of competitiveness by moving production to Mexico's northern border. Proximity to U.S. corporate headquarters, the cheap cost and docility of their labor force, tariff advantages, and improvements in industrial infrastructure converted the Mexican border cities into a major site for direct foreign investment in Mexico. For this reason, in contrast with Monterrey, local entrepreneurs have dedicated themselves principally to the development of the industrial parks in

which maquiladoras may be located. Of greatest interest here is that textile production rather than garment assembly was the subbranch that developed the most in Ciudad Juárez.[4]

The textile-apparel complex also has different relative importance in the two cities. In Monterrey it is one of the six most important manufacturing industries (Aguilar 1992). The textile and garment industry in Monterrey was founded in the early twentieth century with local capital, especially from certain families of Middle Eastern origin (Martínez Sánchez 1997). Some of these garment factories converted themselves into maquiladoras after the trade opening.

With regard to Ciudad Juárez, the government of the state of Chihuahua considers the clothing industry to be one of several "clusters" to be promoted as part of its industrial policy.[5] NAFTA will permit the transfer of certain operations from El Paso, Texas, to central and southern Chihuahua due to its advantages in availability of water and lower labor costs. Thus, Chihuahua could develop inducements to direct investment by garment firms in rural areas with an abundant labor supply. This is reinforced by the importance of elements such as "just-in-time" production, key to the marketing of clothing, which offers opportunities to Chihuahua owing to its location on the border with the United States (DRI/McGraw-Hill and SRI International 1994). Nevertheless, not everyone agrees on the importance of proximity to the border. For example, a recent study notes the scarcity of productive links between textile and garment firms in Ciudad Juárez and El Paso. This study suggests, moreover, a probable decline in the industry along the border in Juárez as more production emerges in the cities further into the Mexican interior (Verkoren 1997). In fact, as the Chihuahua government study itself recognizes, the development opportunities for the textile-garment cluster may be thwarted by a series of competitive threats from the Asian countries, the United States, and other Mexican states that are seeking to attract foreign investment.

Thus the textile-garment sector is important in both cities. In Monterrey it is important as one of the city's traditional industries that grew significantly during the 1990s. In Ciudad Juárez its importance derives from the advantages it has gained since the signing of NAFTA.

Research Questions and Methodological Considerations

We must ask ourselves just how similar the garment industry is in these cities. In both cities, is it oriented toward the same market niches? Are we talking about firms dedicated to the production of fashion or highly standardized garments? What types of interfirm networks have developed as a function of product type? On what basis does competition occur?

These are some of the questions that we set out to answer in our study of twenty-five firms, fourteen in Monterrey and eleven in Ciudad Juárez. Our strategy consisted of identifying major garment industry employers in each city and conducting formal interviews with their plant managers. Our main goal was to interview enterprises that had "backward linkages" in order to gain a greater understanding of the direct impact of such linkages on enterprises in aspects such as working conditions, competitiveness, and firm trajectories based on location, number of employees, and a given firm's position within local networks.

By using this strategy we were able to identify both the direct and indirect suppliers of lead firms with a minimum number of interviews and thus efficiently map the various types of interfirm networks operating in each city's textile-garment complex. In addition, the strategy allowed us to compare results among individual firms in the entire sample as well as among firms in particular network positions. The principal limitation of our sample is that it is not statistically representative for the industry, either in terms of the two cities in question or for the set of suppliers of each firm that was interviewed. A crucial factor impeding the gathering of a random sample of firms was the absence of any list of firms that contained information on the relationships among different establishments.

Profile of Individual Firms in the Sample in Each City

In this section we present the principal socioeconomic characteristics of the firms covered in our study and the types of productive linkages they have established. Of the fourteen enterprises studied in Monterrey, six were dedicated to the production of inputs such as thread, cloth, and poplin, while the other eight manufactured various types of garments. Only one of the firms in Ciudad Juárez produced cloth; the rest manufactured finished goods, mainly uniforms, although one of them produced T-shirts and two manufactured pants.

In our sample, eight of the fourteen Monterrey firms and all but one of those in Ciudad Juárez were "small to medium-scale enterprises"—that is, firms that had from 16 to 249 employees, using the official Mexican government classification system. The remaining plants were large-scale establishments with 250 or more employees. Nevertheless, taking all the plants together, the average number of employees per plant in Monterrey was 256, while in Juárez it was 220 (compared to the average number of 224 employees in garment maquiladoras nationwide) (CIEMEX-WEFA 1998).

Most employees were direct-production workers. While at the national level only 49 percent of employees in manufacturing plants are direct-production workers, in the plants we surveyed nearly 80 percent were engaged in direct production in each city. In spite of the high percentage of direct-production workers, around 9 percent of employees were engineers or technicians, a figure comparable to the national average, while administrative employees accounted for only 15 percent of plant employees in both Monterrey and Ciudad Juárez. In both cities about half of direct-production workers in the plants sampled were women (52 percent in Monterrey and 47 percent in Ciudad Juárez). The proportion of female workers is more or less 20 percent lower than that of garment maquiladoras and lower than that of garment plants producing for the Mexican domestic market as well.[6] Most jobs in the plants we surveyed were permanent. In spite of this, employee turnover rates were high in both cities—especially in the Juárez plants, where average turnover was over 10 percent per month. (In Monterrey it was a more manageable 5 percent.) These figures are nevertheless lower than the 12.9 percent rate found in 1989 for the maquiladora sector as a whole (Carrillo 1993). According to the plant managers we interviewed, this decrease in turnover rate is a reflection of the current economic crisis in Mexico and the corresponding rise in real unemployment.

On average, Monterrey plants began operation twenty-five years before our research, whereas the average Juárez plant had opened fourteen years before. It is interesting to observe that around a third of the plants in our sample had been founded between 1900 and 1969 and nearly half had opened prior to 1990. Here we find important differences between Monterrey and Ciudad Juárez, however. The Monterrey plants were older, on average, than the plants identified in Ciudad Juárez. In Monterrey only four of the fourteen plants studied had been founded since the beginning of the 1980s, and of these only one had opened in the 1990s. Meanwhile, in Ciu-

dad Juárez only two of the eleven plants surveyed had opened prior to 1980.

With regard to plant ownership, three points are important to consider. Around half of the plants we surveyed were owned by a Mexican firm, around a third were privately held, and the rest were subsidiaries of U.S. companies. Here we also see an important difference between the two cities. While in Monterrey more than three-quarters of the plants were subsidiaries of another firm (the remainder were owned by private individuals), in Juárez the majority of plants were owner-operated. Reflecting our purposive oversampling of suppliers, over three-quarters of firms were majority Mexican-owned, and the average proportion of total capital invested in each plant by Mexicans was nearly 90 percent. In Monterrey most firms were 100 percent Mexican-owned, while in Juárez around two-thirds were controlled by Mexican investors with an average of nearly 70 percent of capital investment from Mexican sources.

The average amount of capital invested in each establishment in 1995 was around $160,000. Finally, with regard to gross sales and exports, average 1995 sales were U.S.$13.7 million, while exports reached $5.8 million on average. Sales figures did not vary markedly by city, with average sales of U.S.$12.8 million in Monterrey and $14.3 million in Juárez. The significance of exports did diverge considerably, however, with around 40 percent of Juárez plants' sales deriving from exports, compared to under 15 percent for their Monterrey counterparts. The relatively low proportion of exports by the Monterrey firms places them in a vulnerable situation in the face of fluctuations in the internal market. In Ciudad Juárez, American maquiladoras are the only firms that export, while the Mexican firms are small shops that sell their finished products—industrial uniforms—to the maquiladoras. Finally, although the small size of our sample means we must interpret such figures with caution, we observe that the average value of exports per plant in our sample has grown at an annual rate of over 50 percent between 1993 and 1995.

There is no clear product specialization among the firms in our sample. In the case of Monterrey, seven of the fourteen firms we studied were suppliers to the producers of finished garments: Three firms produced thread, two manufactured poplins, one wove fabric, and another made cardboard boxes. Among the remainder that produced finished garments, three were dedicated to the manufacture of men's shirts, one of the garments that has been traditionally produced by Monterrey's industry. There were also two plants producing uniforms (one specializing in secretarial uniforms and the other in industrial uniforms), one producing men's briefs, and another that produced baptismal gowns. In Ciudad Juárez, industrial uniforms (mainly robes) predominated, although one of the firms we studied also manufactured school and sports uniforms. Other types of garments are also produced: Three firms manufactured pants and shirts, one made T-shirts, one made gloves, another made cloth and flannel, and one even produced ladies' underwear. Research conducted after our study has noted that garment shops in Ciudad Juárez are quite flexible—that is, they are able to switch products in accordance with seasonal fluctuations in demand (Morales 1998).

The principal customers of the plants we studied tended to be located in the same city as the plants, especially in the case of Monterrey. Three-quarters of the plants we studied in that city and half of those in Ciudad Juárez reported that their principal client was located in the same city.

With regard to competitiveness, only a third of the enterprises surveyed indicated that their situation has improved since the beginning of the 1990s. About one-half of the plant managers we interviewed reported their market situation as stable, while the rest stated that their situation has been deteriorating. This perception contrasts with the more optimistic assessment reported in a study of auto-parts and electronics maquiladoras.[7] In Monterrey, 60 percent of plants reported no change in their competitiveness while 40 percent stated that it had improved in the 1990s. This contrasts with the situation facing plants in Ciudad Juárez, where only 22 percent reported a notable improvement in their market situation, a third detected some improvement, and nearly half (44 percent) stated that their competitiveness had worsened during the decade.

The principal competitive advantages reported by Monterrey plants were the "high quality" of their products and "low costs." In Juárez, the principal advantages mentioned were the quick delivery of orders, "low costs," "high-volume production," and "new product development." The pressures that obligated Monterrey firms to change their competitive strategies were mainly limited to "cost reduction"; two plants reported "reduction in delivery time." In Ciudad Juárez the order of these pressures was reversed: More than half the plants surveyed reported pressures to reduce delivery times, and the remainder noted pressures to lower costs.

The main competitors of the firms we visited were for the most part located in Mexico (around 70 percent of the firms in Monterrey and a little more than 50 percent of those in Juárez). Only six plants reported that their principal competition was located in the United States, while two plants placed their main competitors in Central America and the Caribbean and one plant located them in Asian countries outside China and Japan. The location of these competitors reflects the overall trends in the apparel industry internationally, where Asian and Central American countries play an important role. These findings also suggest that an intense competition for market share exists among Mexican enterprises themselves.

The main problems facing Monterrey plants were the lack of credit, low profit margins, and excessive competition. Meanwhile, the main obstacles reported in Juárez were "problems with red tape" at the border, "excessive competition," and "lack of clients," in that order. One of the major problems affecting profitability is difficulty in receiving payment from clients. In the case of the plants producing uniforms in Ciudad Juárez, for example, clients have up to ninety days to pay and remit the amount owed in pesos. The uniform producers, however, must meet short deadlines for delivery and are obliged to use imported cloth (paid upon receipt in U.S. dollars). Employee turnover is another significant problem for the Juárez firms, with many workers moving into other sectors where wages are higher and employment is more stable.

The findings can be synthesized into an "index of global competitiveness" for each plant in our sample.[8] The average global competitiveness index for the sector was negative (-0.40), somewhat worse in Monterrey (-0.45) than in Ciudad Juárez (-0.34). A similar finding occurs with regard to the level of plant modernization, which we measured with an "index of modernization" that also took on negative values in all the plants we visited, whether they exported or not.[9] Nevertheless, in Monterrey the average modernization index score was slightly positive, whereas in Ciudad Juárez it was negative (-0.46). The index of employment quality also showed negative results: -0.39 in Monterrey and -0.28 in Ciudad Juárez.[10] With the exception of the modernization index, these results coincide with external certification of quality-control processes: None of the Monterrey plants had been International Organization for Standardization (ISO) 9000 certified, and just two had been certified by the J. C. Penney Corporation, considered a leader in the apparel industry in setting quality standards. For its part, in Ciudad Juárez one plant was certified as meeting ISO 9000 standards and three were certified by organizations following procedures similar to those of JCPenney.[11]

The situation looks better when we examine the plans of these plants for the future. In our study we found that three-quarters of the Monterrey plants planned to expand their capacity; more than 60 percent expected to increase their exports and add new products to their line; around 15 percent hoped to open new plants; and 20 percent planned to enter into strategic alliances with foreign or domestic partners. Although in general these percentages are greater than those of the plants in Ciudad Juárez, the plans for growth are also substantial in the other city: Over half of the firms we visited expect to expand their capacity; nearly half plan to increase their exports; over half will add new products; nearly one-fifth will open new plants; and up to a third expect to enter into strategic alliances with foreign or domestic partners.

Our sample consists principally, then, of maquiladora and nonmaquiladora plants that face serious economic problems, have difficulties with both competitiveness and modernization, and mainly serve the domestic market. It is interesting, therefore, that even in Northern Mexico's export zone there exists a relatively backward garment sector that, in spite of being linked to direct or indirect exports (by way of the maquiladoras), is not enjoying the benefits of the trade opening and industrial integration with the United States.

Types of Interfirm Networks in Monterrey and Ciudad Juárez

Monterrey: Three Types of Linkages

Within the textiles branch in Monterrey we have identified three types of networks: (1) *traditional networks*, based on vertically integrated

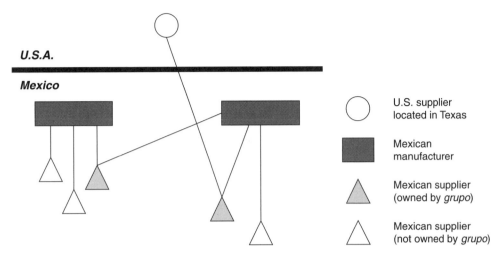

U.S. supplier
located in Texas

Mexican
manufacturer

Mexican supplier
(owned by *grupo*)

Mexican supplier
(not owned by *grupo*)

FIGURE 9.1.   Traditional Interfirm Networks in Monterrey

enterprises selling to the domestic market; (2) *original equipment manufacture (OEM) networks*, revolving around export-oriented lead firms; and (3) *original brand manufacture (OBM) networks*, also based on vertically integrated firms selling to the domestic market. The first of these networks exhibits the greatest degree of vertical integration among participants. The Monterrey plants with predominantly local supplier-client relationships belong to Mexican parent companies and have been active in the city for several decades.

1. The traditional network: A local grupo *serving the domestic market.* The most complete textile-apparel network we discovered in Monterrey was composed of four establishments belonging to the same parent company (see Figure 9.1). The *grupo* began in 1934 with two plants whose main products were poplin, gabardine, and satin fabrics. These plants had two client firms that were also part of the *grupo*. The poplin was used by one of the client firms in the production of men's shirts. The other customer of the two "upstream" firms was involved mainly in the manufacture of uniforms for school and industry. Nevertheless,

the textile-garment network we describe here is not limited to these four supplier-client firms, since the manager of the shirt factory is also the owner of seven other garment firms, six of which are located in Monterrey.

The information obtained from our interviews makes it possible to piece together the principal features of the group and the relationships that exist among its several enterprises. In general we found the group to be highly integrated into the local community with regard to suppliers and clients, and even competitors. Managers of these plants perceive that their principal competition comes from other Monterrey firms. There are, however, some indications that these plants are integrated into markets beyond the Monterrey metropolitan area. Perhaps the most interesting of these is the fact that one of the plants that weaves cloth, founded in 1934, began purchasing cotton from a Texas supplier at the beginning of the 1990s. The other "outside" suppliers that this group used are located in Chihuahua and other regions in Mexico and supply the plant that manufactures uniforms. Nevertheless, although in principle there is an ample local supply of fabrics and accessories

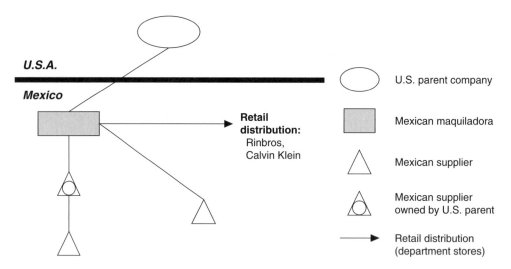

FIGURE 9.2.   Original Equipment Manufacturing Networks in Monterrey

such as thread and buttons, plant managers still spoke to us of problems with obtaining needed inputs in a timely manner from suppliers that could meet their quality and cost requirements.

In general, the enterprises composing this group are of a traditional type, with little use of automated equipment and a workforce that is valued mainly for the quality of its manual skills. Something has changed, however, in recent years. Our findings show that the two measures most frequently implemented to improve competitiveness since the 1980s have been downsizing of personnel and introduction of certain production techniques such as just-in-time production, statistical process control, and total quality management.[12] These organizational techniques have not been accompanied by technological upgrading except in the case of one of the fabric suppliers, 70 percent of whose machinery was automated. Laying off workers has led to changes in the remaining workforce such that workers are now younger and better educated but have less tenure with the firm. Managers complain of a shortage of trained workers and a lack of work ethic in the local labor market. In addition, one

of the managers we interviewed complained of problems with his workers' union.[13] Hence we observe here a local network that has modernized to some extent yet continues to be dependent largely on the Mexican domestic market and particularly on the local Monterrey market. As such, in spite of the relatively important size of the group and its component enterprises, this cluster is still far from competing effectively in a global market for apparel.

2. Original equipment manufacture (OEM) networks. The second type of garment production network we identified in Monterrey involved original equipment manufacturing for a number of brand-name clothing companies, including Rinbros[14] and Calvin Klein. The manufacturer in Monterrey is a maquiladora whose headquarters is located in the United States. This maquiladora is doubly linked to the local market in Monterrey (see Figure 9.2). Its supplier of fabric is another subsidiary of the same U.S. parent firm. In turn, the fabric supplier purchases its textile fibers from an independent local firm. These inputs are consumed by the maquiladora in the production of men's undergarments. All plants in this network have

Mexican suppliers, whether in Monterrey itself or in central Mexico. The lead firm in the network also manufactures undergarments for Mexican department-store clients such as Casa Ley and Eagles.

3. Original brand manufacture (OBM) networks. The last type of garment production network we identified in Monterrey is one in which local manufacturers produce garments under their own brand name and sell to large-scale merchandisers primarily in Mexico (Figure 9.3). The main items manufactured by these firms are: (1) finished ladies' outerwear, such as dresses, blouses, casual shirts, women's suits, and skirts; (2) uniforms; and (3) cloth and fibers such as thread.

The suppliers of the enterprises in this third type of network, unlike those in the other two types, are located in central Mexico as well as in Monterrey itself. Their principal clients were department stores operating in Mexico, such as Soriana, Coppel, Tiendas del Sol Unimax, Prestige, and Wal-Mart (which now has stores in several Mexican states). A second type of client they identified were distributors of brands such as Wilson, and in third place,

two groups of local buyers of secretarial uniforms, such as Grupo Confia and Lamosa.

To summarize, the Monterrey metropolitan area has three types of interfirm networks in the garment industry that have two principal characteristics in common: (1) the purchase of inputs from local suppliers or suppliers located in central Mexico and (2) a high degree of specialization in the type of goods produced that corresponds to the special needs of clients with particular characteristics (brand-name distributors, department stores, or firms that require secretarial uniforms). The process of product specialization among Mexican companies that have traditionally been oriented to the domestic apparel market has allowed the garment industry to continue to develop in Monterrey. The export-oriented OEM-type network has permitted certain OBM plants to survive the current economic crisis in Mexico by using their excess capacity to export under another company's brand name, thus gaining knowledge of overseas markets. Finally, the enterprises linked to the OBM-type network have managed to supply department-store chains that have multiplied since Mexico's trade opening in the late 1980s and early 1990s.

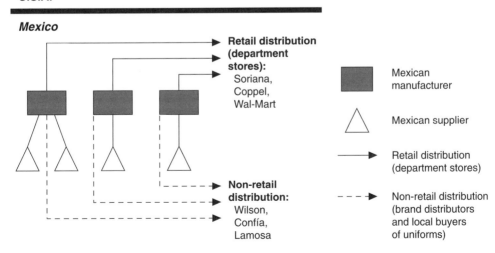

FIGURE 9.3.   Original Brand-Name Networks in Monterrey

Ciudad Juárez: Two Models of Vertical (Dis)integration

1. International subcontracting without local linkages: The traditional maquiladora model. This model is represented by garment maquiladoras operating with foreign capital, such as Converters, Contract Apparel, Boss, and even some joint-venture operations such as Frederick de México. These enterprises are subsidiaries of foreign firms that operate plants in both the United States and Mexico. Their establishment in Juárez to serve the U.S. market dates back to the early 1970s. These are plants that export 100 percent of their production and have no suppliers anywhere in Mexico, not even in Juárez itself. They sell directly to U.S. stores such as JCPenney, Marshall's, and Philadelphia Company. As a consequence they must have either ISO 9000 or JCPenney certification. Their status as subsidiaries ties them to decisions made in U.S. corporate headquarters with regard to technology, investments, and suppliers. In this sense a traditional vertical relationship exists between parent company and subsidiary.

These plants import all their inputs, such as fabric, thread, and accessories (zippers, plastic pieces, reinforcements, etc.), either because there are no Mexican suppliers of these items or because those that do exist are unable to supply the necessary quality in a timely and reliable manner. They are generally medium-sized plants, with sales that range from U.S.$1.4 million to $10.6 million. Plants may have as much as $10 million invested in them. They assemble a variety of products, the most important of which are ladies' clothing (undergarments such as brassieres, girdles, blouses, and tights), pants, robes, gloves, and sheets. They compete with other foreign firms in Mexico and Central America. In fact, excessive competition is their principal problem, aside from coping with the Mexican state bu-

reaucracy, especially with regard to its customs procedures.

In response to competitive pressures, some of these plants are forming strategic alliances, laying off workers, developing new products, and planning to expand operations away from the northern border. In the meantime these plants have already adopted modern management practices to guarantee flexibility, quick turnaround, and high quality. Finally, these are enterprises that employ a sizable number of women (although not in all the plants), paying wages that range from U.S.$5.50 to $10 per day.

In sum, here we are talking about typical export-oriented maquiladora plants, with no local linkages, that produce directly for department stores, which in another publication we have termed "first-generation maquiladoras" (Carrillo and Hualde 1997). Their exclusive role is garment assembly. The value added that they generate is much less than that generated by the product development and marketing that occur in the United States. The interfirm networks in which these plants are enmeshed are binational and do not seem to be changing their pattern of geographic dispersion and lack of vertical integration (Figure 9.4). According to the Asociación de Maquiladoras de Ciudad Juárez, by 1998 there were seventeen garment-producing maquiladoras in the city, employing around forty-four hundred workers (Morales 1998, 76).

2. International subcontracting with local linkages: Indirect suppliers. Unlike the previous model, here we find small-scale, domestic enterprises that supply maquiladoras not with inputs but rather with uniforms and robes for their employees who work on production lines in the electronics and auto-parts sectors. The main objective of these suppliers is to avail themselves of a particular niche in the local market created by the great cluster of maquiladoras in Ciudad Juárez. As such, they are

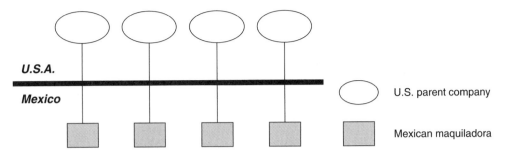

U.S. parent company

Mexican maquiladora

FIGURE 9.4.   Traditional Maquiladora Networks in Juárez

"indirect suppliers" (in contrast with direct providers of inputs or production-specific services). These plants employ mainly women, although some owners prefer to hire men. Worker incomes range from U.S.$7 to $10 per day, comparable to wages paid by large-scale enterprises locally. All the capital invested in these plants, which have been operating since the mid-1980s, is from Mexican sources.

Most of the owners of these plants are Juárez residents who are carrying on their families' tradition in the garment industry. Typically, they worked at another job in the industry before opening their own shop with money from personal savings or received from other family members. These entrepreneurs often own more than one small plant. Annual sales per plant range from U.S.$10,000 to $300,000, and the amount of investment sunk into each plant ranges from U.S.$20,000 to $40,000.

The principal production inputs purchased by these small, locally based plants are fabric, flannel, thread, and buttons. They supply themselves with these items directly from stores either in Juárez or immediately across the border in El Paso, Texas (where they are billed in dollars). Their clients include some of the largest maquiladoras in Juárez, such as Favesa (Lear Seating Co.), Autoelectrónica (Yasaki), RCA (Thompson), Delphi (General Motors), and Delmex (International Telephone and Telegraph).[15] These clients gener-

ally pay in Mexican pesos ninety days after orders are delivered, meaning that the uniform producers, most of whose capital resources are quite limited, are effectively obliged to extend credit to their transnational-corporation clients. This problem is compounded by the fact that no local suppliers can compete in terms of price and speed of delivery, which obliges firms to purchase inputs in dollars across the border in El Paso. Thus these producers are negatively affected by the peso-dollar exchange rate. In addition, the uniform producers are totally dependent on the types of cloth and colors available from local merchandisers (including those in El Paso), who frequently must special-order items they do not have in stock. This can be the source of considerable delays.

Some of the shops we studied were ISO 9000 certified, but this certification was incidental, owing to the fact that their main clients were important parts suppliers of the three largest U.S. automakers. Because they are small and independently owned and operated, all production decisions are made autonomously. Their principal competitors are small local manufacturers like them. Because the maquiladoras insist on ever lower costs and quicker turnaround time, this competition means plants face strong pressures to comply with clients' demands. In the face of this pressure the small plants' strategy has been to

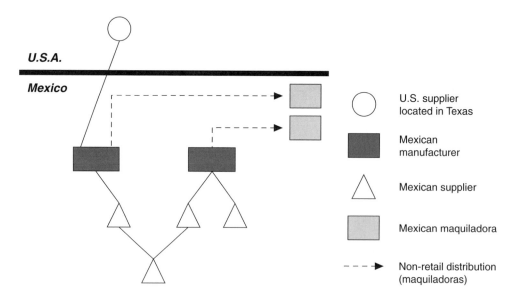

FIGURE 9.5.   Interfirm Networks in Juárez: Vertical Disintegration with Local Linkages

specialize in certain products and make the needed adjustments in machinery and shop-floor layout to make the most efficient use of their resources and to be able to fill clients' orders quickly.

As mentioned earlier, customs procedures, lack of credit, and problems with government officials are among the main difficulties facing these small garment shops in Juárez. Operating in their favor we find their low costs and organizational flexibility, which allow them to meet their customers' needs quickly. Thus we found that these plants have implemented techniques to improve quality and, most important, guarantee a quick turnaround of orders. Although they do not have any grand plans for the future, some managers we interviewed expect to open another plant and enter into alliances with other small firms in the industry.

In sum, we can say that these garment plants are very different from those examined above: They are not maquiladoras, they do not export, and they serve a strictly local market niche. Their operation is tightly linked to and dependent on a dynamic export-oriented industrialization model. Unfortunately, they still face severe limits to their growth, increasing their value added, and achieving higher levels of vertical integration. These limits are imposed by lack of credit, cash-flow problems resulting from customers who are slow to pay, and having to purchase inputs with dollars while receiving payment in pesos. Thus we have a model that, in spite of establishing productive backward linkages, nevertheless faces serious obstacles to increasing profits, investing in human resources, and realizing higher value-added activities (Figure 9.5). Figures from the Cámara Nacional de la Industria de la Transformación indicate there were many more firms in this sector of the local garment industry—around forty—than there were in the maquiladora sector, but average plant size was only around ten employees, meaning that the total workforce of the sector—fewer than four hundred workers—was far smaller than that of the garment maquiladoras (Morales 1998, 58).

Conclusions

The form taken by local interfirm linkages differs between the two cities we have examined. Moreover, within each city we find different types of interfirm networks. In Monterrey we identified three types of networks. The kinds of linkages that prevail are related not only to orientation toward the domestic versus the foreign market but also to the type of client served and where that client is located. In this way the most vertically integrated and most solidly organized firms that rely on domestic suppliers of inputs are, somewhat surprisingly, the most vulnerable to the vagaries of the national market. By contrast, exporting firms, which generally enter the foreign market as a way of using excess capacity, produce under contract for brand-name retailers and receive lower profits but, in exchange, gain access to a market that is more stable and expanding more rapidly than the Mexican market. Finally, we found a few enterprises that have been able to sell their own products with their own brand names on the domestic market, relying on department stores and retail chains for distribution. We still do not know if these types of networks also display significant differences in terms of their competitiveness and short-term business strategies.

In Ciudad Juárez we identified two types of interfirm networks in the textile-apparel complex, one with local linkages and one linked with firms outside the local community. The more locally linked network has auto-parts and electronics maquiladoras as its major clients. This network is based on an intersectoral relationship where the customer (a subsidiary of a foreign auto-parts or electronics firm) hooks up with local Mexican suppliers of uniforms and other products from textile manufacturers. In the second type of interfirm network, plants produce exclusively for export. Here we are mainly talking about foreign-owned maquiladoras with little product specialization that supply department stores and other name-brand apparel markets.

Export maquiladoras in Ciudad Juárez exhibit market behavior that is similar to other sectors, namely, they are internationally competitive; rely on U.S. firms to market their products; and base their competitive strategies on price, quality, and quick, reliable delivery. There also exists another segment that is much more dependent and vulnerable and has little potential to develop greater value added. These small nonmaquiladora firms produce industrial uniforms, robes, and the like for large-scale auto-parts and electronics maquiladoras, but they lack security in the marketplace. Such enterprises are seriously limited given that (1) they purchase imported inputs in stores in Juárez or directly in El Paso, Texas (where they pay in U.S. dollars); (2) they are paid by clients in pesos (in spite of the fact that these clients are, by and large, subsidiaries of U.S. companies); and (3) in effect they are obliged to extend credit to their maquiladora clients insofar as they are paid up to ninety days after delivery of an order. When these problems are added to low profit margins, a large number of competitors, the unavailability of credit, and the constant pressure from clients to lower costs, the combined effect is to make these plants among the most unprotected in the industry along the border. These indirect suppliers are convinced that increased interfirm collaboration is the only way to overcome the limitations associated with their small size. Unfortunately, no plans exist, either on the part of firm owners or on the part of the government, to promote mergers or alliances among firms in this sector that would allow them to achieve economies of scale that could improve their competitiveness.

In this sense, we have two completely different textile-apparel industries in Ciudad Juárez and Monterrey, not only in terms of the market they serve but also in how they connect with their respective markets. The distinct types of interfirm networks that we have found in the garment industry in two Mexican cities allow us to conclude that even among manufacturers of similar products, important differences exist not only in terms of the structure of establishments but also in terms of their potential for upgrading and expansion.

In conclusion, we note how the complexity of industrial processes can confound development theory. The maquiladora model (understood as third-party international subcontracting) is supposedly more vulnerable to economic fluctuations than the model of vertical integration. Our results demonstrate the opposite— namely, that in a situation of economic opening and integration, it is the maquiladoras that are more stable. In the same way, and according to the logic of organizational development, the maquiladora model purportedly generates less value added and does a poorer job of promoting local industrial development than models based on OEM or, especially, OBM. The results from Monterrey suggest that OBM firms have had to abandon their own labels and convert themselves partially or totally into maquiladoras. In other words, instead of having upgraded and converted themselves into OBM firms for the international market, they have "devolved" and become international subcontractors that nevertheless have improved their competitiveness and profitability for having done so. In addition, we find that the niche for locally owned and operated garment shops in Ciudad Juárez is directly dependent on the maquiladora sector of the auto-parts and electronics industry there.

During the 1900s, Mexico tried to develop efficient industrial agglomerations in the form of interfirm networks, production and marketing collaborations *(empresas integradoras)*, and industrial clusters.[16] This was done with the direct support of all levels of government

as well as of local institutions that participate in these types of initiatives, such as educational institutions, trade associations, and consulting firms. The main objectives were to develop suppliers and to increase value added in the sector through industrial upgrading in specific regions of the country. In spite of important advances made in some localities such as Monterrey and Ciudad Juárez, policy makers have heretofore given too little attention to the development of existing production niches occupied by local firms. Such development, unfortunately, is not and has not been a priority for local and sectoral policy makers. Moreover, the competitive pressures introduced by NAFTA and Mexico's world trade policies present new challenges to the survival of many domestic garment producers. It remains to be seen whether new industrial policy initiatives will be able to rescue these firms and the niches they occupy from extinction.

Notes

Acknowledgments. The authors thank David Spener, Gary Gereffi, and Jennifer Bair for their careful reading of earlier drafts of this chapter. Translated from Spanish to English by David Spener.

1. The "import-substitution industrialization model" refers to a set of policies widely adopted in Latin America from the 1930s through the 1970s and 1980s (depending on the country). The main objective of the model was to foster industrialization by producing domestically goods that would otherwise be imported. Imports were discouraged through a variety of tariff and nontariff barriers, and the state played a major role in directing the industrialization process and picking the "winners," that is, the sectors and firms that benefited most from these policies. See Villarreal (1990).

2. A *grupo* is a set of closely related firms that typically belong to several related families. Not only are the related firms integrated into the *grupo*, but the bigger *grupo*s also often own large shares in

banks. ALFA consists of twenty-two enterprises dedicated to diverse production activities, including iron and steel; wood, paper, and cellulose; petrochemicals; and textiles. VITRO is composed of forty-nine enterprises and five joint ventures that produce various types of glass, plastics, and nonmetallic minerals, as well as several service enterprises (Pozas 1993).

3. The plan was known as FICORCA, or Fideicomiso para la Cobertura de Riesgo Cambiario (Exchange Rate Risk Trust Fund).

4. According to the 1994 *Censo Industrial de Chihuahua*, without taking into account maquiladoras, employment in branch 3213, production of textile materials, grew in Ciudad Juárez from 5,300 employees in 1988 to 17,070 in 1993, while in garment assembly employment declined slightly, from 3,105 to 2,965 employees.

5. The government's industrial policy project is known as Chihuahua Siglo XXI (DRI/McGraw-Hill and SRI International 1994).

6. Since our sample was not drawn strictly at random, the relatively high incidence of men working in these plants should not be taken as representative of the gender distribution of garment employment as a whole in either Monterrey or Ciudad Juárez.

7. Carrillo, Mortimore, and Estrada (1999) report that of the seventeen maquiladoras they studied in 1995 (five television maquiladoras in Tijuana and twelve auto-parts maquiladoras in various border cities), managers at 80 percent of the plants indicated that their plant competitiveness had improved from 1990 to 1995.

8. We constructed the global competitiveness index using a factor analysis that included per capita sales, the sales growth rate, capital investment per worker, percent of production exported in 1995, and the export growth rate. Values for the index range from -1 to $+1$, such that -1 is perfectly uncompetitive and $+1$ is perfectly competitive.

9. The modernization index was constructed using percent of equipment that is automated, percent of expenses dedicated to research and development, certification processes, and use of specialized work organization techniques.

10. The employment index was constructed by combining previous indexes, using in this case four variables: wages, union density, training hours, and turnover. Higher wages, higher levels of unionization, more training hours, and lower turnover indicate better employment quality. Values for the index range from -1 to $+1$, such that -1 denotes the worst employment quality and $+1$ the best.

11. If these percentages seem low, we must remember that we are talking about small- to medium-scale enterprises, the great majority of which are domestic (eight of eleven in Juárez and all fourteen in Monterrey). There exists a clear tendency in the electronics and automobile industries, and to a lesser degree in the garment industry, to certify quality-control processes. These certifications represent a great commitment on the part of firms to standardize their quality-control processes and enter into continual upgrading. Certification has an important impact on work since all members of the organization are obligated to participate in this process.

12. "Statistical process control" (SPC) is a method for checking the quality of products through a random sampling process generated by computer. Originally tested in the United States during the 1940s, the technique later was successfully adopted by Japanese firms. "Total quality management" is a philosophy and set of practices developed by Japanese firms to ensure that high levels of quality characterize the final product, the manufacturing process, and the employee's contribution to that process.

13. Some of these enterprises also produce for service-sector businesses. These plants make other garments such as pants, shirts, and overalls, but for another type of client.

14. Rinbros is a well-known brand in Mexico.

15. These maquiladoras produce TV sets and auto parts such as seat covers, wire harnesses, and electronic sensors.

16. By "clusters" we here mean linkages among firms in the same sector in the same geographic region (Humphrey and Schmitz 1995).

References

Aguilar Barajas, Ismael. 1992. *Industria manufacturera de Nuevo León. Un análisis sectorial de sus principales empresas exportadoras.* Monterrey, Nuevo León: CAINTRA/ITESM.

Bair, Jennifer. 1997. "Embedding the Local in the Global: The North American Apparel Industry and the Emergence of a Regional Economy." Paper presented at the Twentieth Congress of the Latin American Studies Association, Guadalajara, Jalisco, Mexico, April 17–19.

Becattini, Giacomo. 1988. "Los distritos industriales italianos." *Sociología del trabajo* 5: 3–17.

Carpi, Juan Tomás, Miguel Torrejón, and Juan Such. 1997. "Producción flexible, redes empresariales y sistemas territoriales de pequeña y mediana empresa: La industria textil valenciana." *Sociología del trabajo* 30: 21–42.

Carrillo, Jorge, ed. 1993. *Condiciones de empleo y capacitación en la industria maquiladora de exportación.* Tijuana: Colegio de la Frontera Norte and Secretaría de Trabajo y Previsión Social.

Carrillo, Jorge, and Alfredo Hualde. 1997. "Maquiladoras de tercera generación. El caso de Delphi–General Motors." *Comercio exterior* 47, 9 (September): 747–58.

Carrillo, Jorge, Michael Mortimore, and Jorge Alonso Estrada. 1999. *Competitividad y mercado de trabajo: Empresas de autopartes y televisores en México.* Mexico City: Plaza y Valdés/UAM/UACJ.

Castillo, Juan José. 1988–89. "La división del trabajo entre empresas." *Sociología del trabajo* 5 (Winter): 19–40.

CIEMEX-WEFA (Center for Econometric Research on Mexico). 1998. *Maquiladora Industry Analysis* 11, 2 (May). Philadelphia: CIEMEX-WEFA.

DRI/McGraw-Hill and SRI International. 1994. *Chihuahua: Mexico's First Twenty-first Century Economy.* Chihuahua: Editorial del Gobierno del Estado de Chihuahua, Desarrollo Económico del Estado de Chihuahua y Desarrollo Económico de Ciudad Juárez, Chihuahua.

Dussel, Enrique. 1997. "La evolución de las exportaciones de la confección mexicana hacia los Estados Unidos." In *Pensar globalmente y actuar regionalmente: Hacia un nuevo paradigma industrial para el siglo XXI,* ed. Enrique Dussel, Michael J. Piore, and Clemente Ruiz Durán, pp. 79–153. Mexico City: Universidad Nacional Autónoma de México and Fundación Friedrich Ebert.

Gereffi, Gary. 1995. "Global Production Systems and Third World Development." In *Global Change, Regional Response: The New International Context*

of Development, ed. Barbara Stallings, pp. 100–142. New York: Cambridge University Press.

———. 2000. "The Regional Dynamics of Global Trade: Asian, American, and European Models of Apparel Sourcing." In *The Dialectics of Globalization—Regional Responses to World Economic Processes: Asia, Europe, and Latin America in Comparative Perspective,* ed. Menno Vellinga, pp. 31–62. Boulder, Colo.: Westview Press.

Gereffi, Gary, and Lynn Hempel. 1996. "Latin America in the Global Economy: Running Faster to Stay in Place." *NACLA Report on the Americas* (January–February): 18–27.

Humphrey, John, and Hubert Schmitz. 1995. "Principles for Promoting Clusters and Networks of SMEs." Discussion Paper no. 1. Geneva: United Nations Industrial Development Organization, Small to Medium Scale Enterprises Program.

Instituto Nacional de Estadística, Geografía e Informática (INEGI). 1998, 2001. *Industria maquiladora de exportación: Estadísticas económicas: Mayo.* Aguascalientes: INEGI.

Martínez Sánchez, María Luisa. 1997. "Estrategias competitivas en la industria de la confección en Nuevo León." Working paper. Monterrey, Nuevo León: Facultad de Filosofía y Letras, Universidad Autónoma de Nuevo León.

Mendoza, Jorge, and Fernando Pozos. 1997. "Mecanismos de distribución de ropa importada, 1988–1995. El caso de México." Paper presented at the Twentieth Congress of the Latin American Studies Association, Guadalajara, Jalisco, Mexico, April 17–19.

Morales, Julio Cesar. 1998. "Instrumentos de política industrial y estrategias empresariales en la industria textil y del vestido en Ciudad Juárez, Chihuahua." Unpublished master's thesis, Colegio de la Frontera Norte, Tijuana, Baja California, Mexico.

Pozas, María de Los Angeles. 1993. *Industrial Restructuring in Mexico: Corporate Adaptation, Technological Innovation and Changing Patterns of Industrial Relations in Monterrey.* San Diego: Center for U.S.-Mexican Studies, University of California at San Diego.

Pozos, Fernando. 1996. *Metrópolis en restructuración: Guadalajara y Monterrey, 1980–1989.* Guadalajara: Editorial de la Universidad de Guadalajara.

Suárez, Estela, and Miguel Angel Rivera. 1994. *Pequeña empresa y modernización: Análisis de dos dimensiones.* Mexico City: Universidad Nacional Autónoma de México.

Vangstrup, Ulrik. 1995. "Moroleón: La pequeña ciudad de la gran industria." *Espiral: Estudios sobre estado y sociedad* 2, 4: 101–34.

Verkoren, Otto. 1997. "Trends of Manufacturing Employment on the US-Mexico Border with Special Reference to El Paso and Ciudad Juárez." Paper presented at the Twentieth Congress of the Latin American Studies Association, Guadalajara, Jalisco, Mexico, April 17–19.

Villarreal, René. 1990. "The Latin American Strategy of Import Substitution: Failure or Paradigm for the Region?" In *Manufacturing Miracles: Paths of Industrialization in Latin America and East Asia,* ed. Gary Gereffi and Donald L. Wyman, pp. 292–320. Princeton, N.J.: Princeton University Press.

Part IV

Interior Mexico

*Gary Gereffi, Martha Martínez,
and Jennifer Bair*

10   Torreón: The New Blue Jeans
      Capital of the World

The Maquiladora Debate
in Mexico

The North American Free Trade Agreement
(NAFTA) has dramatically increased the export dynamism of the Mexican apparel industry. The sheer increase in the country's clothing exports to the United States, from $1.6
billion in 1994 to almost $6.5 billion in 1998, is
impressive evidence of this claim. NAFTA has
also promoted the consolidation of apparel
export-production centers. This chapter concentrates on one of these production centers,
the Torreón region, which has been called the
new blue jeans capital of the world.

Torreón is a dynamic industrial cluster of
five hundred thousand people located in the
northern Mexican state of Coahuila, about four
hours by car from the Texas portion of the U.S.
border. It is located in the heart of La Laguna
region, well known for its cotton and dairy
products. Torreón's apparel industry as discussed in this chapter is actually a cluster of
three cities, as it straddles the nearby municipalities of Gómez Palacio and Lerdo in the
neighboring state of Durango. Following an
economic recession in the early 1990s, Torreón
has been one of the main beneficiaries of Mex-

ico's recent export boom. Although Torreón is
also home to other export-oriented manufacturing sectors, such as auto parts and machinery, the apparel and textile industries have been
the star performers in terms of export growth
and job creation.

Despite these undeniable gains, a verdict on
the consequences of NAFTA for both Torreón
and Mexico has yet to be reached. Much of the
debate about NAFTA in academic and policy-
making circles on both sides of the border has
addressed the question "Is NAFTA good policy, and if so, for whom?" The maquiladora
form of production occupies center stage in
this debate. Maquiladoras are factories that
assemble products for export from imported
components that enter the country duty-free.
Proponents of the maquiladoras assert that the
system is a valuable source of export revenue
and job creation for Mexico. The program's critics, however, see it as the ultimate example of a
"new international division of labor" that traps
developing countries in the dead-end role of providing cheap labor for low-value-added assembly
operations. Because the vast majority of inputs
assembled into final products in the maquiladoras are imported,[1] the maquiladoras do not
stimulate growth in the rest of the economy.

This debate rests implicitly on three assumptions: (1) that the change in Torreón (and in other Mexican production centers) from local production to export manufacturing is a direct consequence of NAFTA; (2) that the unavoidable consequence of the free-trade agreement is the maquilization of Mexico; and (3) that maquiladora production does not promote development. These assumptions conceal and oversimplify the dynamics of export industrialization and regional development in Mexico. The question should not be whether NAFTA promotes Mexican development but rather under what conditions particular regions in Mexico benefit from free trade. Is NAFTA promoting the maquilization of Mexico, and if so, which factors could be expected to lessen this effect? What role does foreign capital play in establishing favorable or unfavorable conditions for local firms? How do local institutions and conditions mediate this process?

Before answering these questions, it is necessary to identify what it is about the maquiladora production system that creates undesirable developmental outcomes. Mexico's maquiladoras are foreign- or domestically owned factories that traditionally have been geared toward assembling products for export from imported components. These inputs are imported to Mexico duty-free, and when the assembled products are exported after assembly, only a minimal duty is assessed on the value added in Mexico, chiefly labor. Maquiladoras exist in a number of manufacturing sectors, although the main products assembled in maquiladoras are autos and auto parts, consumer electronics, and apparel. Although the maquiladora system began with the U.S.-Mexico Border Industrialization Program in 1965, most of the growth in maquiladora production has occurred since the mid-1980s. The program initially applied only to in-bond factories located along Mexico's northern border, but this geographic restriction has since been eliminated and maquiladoras currently are located throughout the country. Because of the labor-intensive, low-value-added nature of maquiladora production, critics argue that this system promotes almost no industrial upgrading or technology transfers, creates minimal linkages to the local economy, and generates very little wealth that can be retained in the country.

In contrast to this traditional view of the maquiladoras, a revisionist perspective about the significance of this export-oriented sector for Mexican development emerged in the late 1980s and early 1990s. Researchers began to call attention to a so-called second generation of maquiladoras. Although local inputs to the production process remained low, the mix of activities being performed by Mexican workers in the maquiladoras became more diverse, expanding beyond low-value-added assembly. The empirical focus of this research included production of auto parts in northern Mexico, televisions and other electronics in Tijuana, and computers in Guadalajara. In each of these industries, scholars argued, the maquiladoras were maturing from assembly sites based on cheap labor to manufacturing and even profit centers whose competitiveness lay in a combination of high productivity, good product quality, and wages well below those prevailing north of the border (Shaiken 1987; Gereffi 1996; Carrillo 1998).

NAFTA presents yet another twist in the ongoing maquiladora debate. Because NAFTA removes most of the restrictions on backward and forward linkages between the maquiladoras and national firms, the enclave nature of the maquiladoras could change as export-oriented plants become more integrated into the rest of the economy. In effect, NAFTA levels the playing field and allows all companies to set up the same kinds of cross-border production networks that traditionally characterized only the maquiladora sector.[2] These developments present two scenarios, which are reflected in the literature on the maquiladora sector in the era of NAFTA. Some see regional integration as an opportunity for a wide array of Mexican firms to attain the productivity and quality levels associated with the country's leading maquiladoras and therefore to increase their competitiveness in foreign (primarily U.S.) markets. Others argue that NAFTA further exacerbates the existing asymmetries in Mexico's industrial landscape, with large U.S. firms standing to obtain all the main benefits that NAFTA provides. Instead of expecting the maquiladora sector to become integrated with the rest of the Mexican economy, this camp predicts the "maquilization of Mexico," whereby the entire country is converted into a site for low-value-added export-oriented production for the U.S. market, to the benefit of foreign capital and the detriment of national firms and Mexican workers (Dussel Peters 2000; Tardenico and Rosenberg 2000).

Our own research suggests that Mexico in general and Torreón in particular appear to be moving away from typical maquiladora manufacturing toward a more integrated form of full-package production. Instead of just doing assembly, firms in Torreón are performing all the other required manufacturing activities, including the purchase and production of raw materials, cutting, laundering, finishing, and, to a lesser extent, distribution. This new full-package system differs from maquiladora production in terms of both external linkages and local linkages. As apparel production in the Torreón region moves from maquiladora to full-package manufacturing, we expect to see a transformation in the relationships between Torreón suppliers and their American clients. Linkages among local firms, which are nonexistent under the maquiladora system, should become more salient. Full-package production forces local firms to develop ties with suppliers and subcontractors (both local and foreign) in order to satisfy the demands of marketers

and retailers, which generally do not engage in any production activities.

Although in an era of globalization both local and external linkages are vital for the survival of firms, there is no integrated framework that analyzes their interplay. The global commodity-chains literature, with its distinction between producer-driven and buyer-driven commodity chains (Gereffi 1994), suggests multiple models of export-oriented industrialization. Development outcomes depend largely on the type of industry and the type of lead firm coordinating the international trade and production networks that are dominant during a particular phase of a country's development strategy (Gereffi and Wyman 1990). In the same way, the movement of a country or a firm from one segment of the commodity chain to another explains changes in profit margins, quality of jobs, and technology transfers, among other factors. While producer-driven chains have received significant scholarly attention in research on large, integrated multinational corporations, the dynamics of buyer-driven chains, such as the ones responsible for Torreón's rapid growth as a jeans-production center, are less well understood despite their growing importance in terms of Mexico's export-oriented strategy.

The importance of local linkages is addressed by the industrial-districts literature. The original industrial-district model was based on the Emilia-Romagna region—the so-called Third Italy—where small and medium-sized enterprises with a craft tradition in products such as footwear and apparel organized into geographically concentrated and sectorally specialized clusters. The advantages provided by participation in the clusters allowed these small-scale manufacturers to compete successfully in global markets on the basis of high quality and flexible specialization. Features of this model include high wages for a local workforce with strong skills, significant horizontal networks between firms within the cluster based on cooperative competition, and supportive government policies and institutional infrastructure. The ability of industrial districts to succeed in global markets despite high labor costs led to the conclusion that these clusters represented a "high road to competitiveness" for firms and workers in developed countries (Piore and Sabel 1984; Pyke and Sengenberger 1992; Humphrey 1995; Markusen 1996).

The global commodity-chains and industrial-district frameworks are complementary. While the former concentrates on the power dynamics created by global production systems and the consequences of having a particular location within these systems, the latter focuses on the local linkages that can be used to create competitive advantages in a global economy. Development outcomes depend not only on the dynamics of the global economy but also on the local resources (social, material, financial, or institutional) that are available or can be created. A change of the maquiladora system would necessarily imply transformations in both internal and external linkages in order to move toward higher-value activities and positions. The rest of this chapter attempts to show how Torreón's blue jeans firms have been transformed from producers for the domestic market to maquiladora exporters, then to full-package exporters and, possibly in the future, to lead firms. Particular attention is placed on comparing the network arrangements, both local and international, related to the Torreón region under the maquiladora system and under the new model of full-package production. Finally, once we have established how much Torreón's production setup differs from typical maquiladoras, we discuss the consequences of such a system on key developmental variables: local linkages, technology transfer, employment, wages, working conditions, and rural-urban disparities.

Methodology

We conducted our fieldwork in Torreón in July 1998 and July 2000.[3] Open-ended strategic interviews with Mexican-owned, U.S.-owned, and joint-venture firms, industry associations, and local government organizations were coupled with plant visits and the use of secondary materials to document recent changes in the industry. Our initial contacts with major export firms in Torreón were made through earlier interviews with U.S.-based textile manufacturers, apparel companies, and retailers. This strategy enabled us to identify and interview the majority of Torreón's leading textile and apparel manufacturers, as well as a number of their second-tier contractors.

Our sample included nine apparel companies and two textile mills. Although around 350 different apparel firms operate in the Torreón area, the nine companies included in our sample directly produce or coordinate around one-third of the total production of the region. Given the disproportionate role played by leading firms in the sector and our interest in understanding the power dynamics that exist in the industry, our oversampling of large and foreign firms is justified. We should note, however, that additional research is needed to complement our findings in terms of wages and working conditions in the factories that occupy the lowest tier of Torreón's hierarchical production and subcontracting networks.

This method is superior to random sampling techniques for two reasons. First, a relatively small number of firms in the United States are driving the restructuring of the North American apparel commodity chain, and our approach allows us to identify these firms and the companies they work with in specific sites such as Torreón—in terms of both their main suppliers or partners in the local cluster and the tiers of smaller subcontractors that are not linked directly to the U.S. market. Second, this approach guarantees us better access to these firms since we do not contact them "cold" but rather are referred to them by a company we have already interviewed higher up on the commodity chain, another local firm in the cluster, or the local chamber of apparel manufacturers.

Interviews were conducted primarily in Spanish on-site with the company's plant manager, director of foreign operations, or owner, depending on the firm, and they lasted an average of two hours. The interviews were followed by a tour of the production facilities. In Torreón these included, in addition to the traditional sewing factory associated with apparel production, textile mills; laundries; finishing plants where the garments are pressed, inspected for quality, and packed; and a distribution center. As well as providing an opportunity to evaluate the working conditions and industrial relations, these tours permitted us to speak with additional informants, such as production trainers and line supervisors, whose perspectives on the operation complement the data collected in the initial interview.

We conducted strategic interviews with lead firms in the United States as well as with our informants in Torreón. The strategic interview is a semistructured interview format and differs from a traditional survey-style interview in that there is no standardized questionnaire. Rather, the interviewers use a protocol that lists key questions as a template to ensure that critical issues are addressed with each respondent. The questions listed in the protocol are open-ended, and the protocol is not intended as an exhaustive list of the topics the interview will address. Instead, these questions are used as probes that help the informant understand the kind of information the interviewer is interested in.

Torreón's Emergence as the New Blue Jeans Capital of the World

At the time of our fieldwork in July 1998, the Torreón area was producing an average of 4 million pairs of jeans a week. In contrast, El Paso, Texas—a major production center for Levi Strauss and Company and Torreón's predecessor as the blue jeans capital of the world—produced only 2 million pairs of jeans a week at its peak in the early 1980s. To keep pace with this dramatic increase in production, employment in Torreón's approximately 350 apparel factories had also grown considerably from twelve thousand jobs in 1993 to sixty-five thousand in 1998.

There are several reasons for Torreón's export success. Although not located along the northern border where the country's in-bond, export-oriented maquiladora sector has historically been strongest, Torreón is still close and well connected to the United States. This gives it a distinct advantage over other production sites in the interior of Mexico, particularly since quick turnaround time and reliable delivery of even basic apparel products such as blue jeans (which are not generally considered to be high-fashion items) are critical for U.S. retailers and manufacturers. The Torreón area has a significant cotton textile tradition, which is allowing the site to emerge as a model of integrated manufacturing, with denim production and apparel assembly occurring in the same Mexican cluster.

This dynamism in the export of jeans is a relatively new phenomenon in the Torreón region. In 1993, Torreón produced only five hundred thousand pairs of jeans a week, most of them under the provisions of the 807/9802 maquiladora program[4] and mostly limited to assembly activities. Apparel export manufacturing became important for the region only in the mid-1980s. Prior to that time, apparel production was almost exclusively dedicated to the domestic market. The blue jeans industry in Torreón since has undergone a series of shifts: from local production to maquiladora exporting to full-package manufacturing. Four historical factors have driven this evolution:

1. the peso devaluations;
2. the implementation of NAFTA and the subsequent elimination of tariffs and trade barriers;
3. the presence of new organizational buyers, especially retailers and brand marketers; and
4. the existence of local capital and expertise applied to apparel production.

The effects of each these factors are explained in the subsequent sections.

The Peso Devaluation Effect

The Torreón region has a strong tradition in the apparel and textile industry. Textile mills have been located in the region since the late nineteenth century. During the 1940s and 1950s companies such as Fábricas El Venado, Fábricas de Ropa Manjai, Metro, and Guadiana were founded to satisfy the need of the national market for work clothes, particularly for rural settings. These companies specialized in the production of jeans and other denim items. During subsequent decades, as jeans evolved from being "work clothes" to an object of fashion and moved from rural communities to the streets of cities, local companies developed their own brands (e.g., Jesús, Medalla Gacela). Under the import-substitution strategy, which prevailed in Mexico from the 1940s through the 1970s, there was little international competition, and Mexican suppliers dominated the domestic market.

The Mexican peso crises in 1982, 1985, and 1988 and the subsequent hyperinflation changed the environment for these companies. Since they were totally dependent on the local market, the reduction in buying power and the related contraction of local demand jeopardized their income. However, inflation affected these companies in a more fundamental way. The jeans industry requires the availability of working capital to acquire the raw materials and labor necessary for production; this working capital is recovered by selling the jeans (plus a profit), and then the production cycle begins again. But jeans manufacturers must wait a period of time (generally a month) to receive payment for their products. Under conditions of hyperinflation, the money received for a pair of jeans produced a month ago may not be enough to make a new pair of jeans now, which left manufacturing unprofitable and impossible to sustain.

The only viable option for the survival of these companies was to redirect their efforts from a stagnant local market to the more solid U.S. market. Export prices are set in dollars and therefore are not affected by the changes in a volatile economy. However, this shift in orientation had its downside for Torreón companies. Although these firms performed all production activities related to the manufacturing of jeans (assembly, cutting, laundering, finishing, marketing, and design), they discovered that their quality was not up to international standards. Torreón firms were unable to offer full-package production with the quality requirements of the American clients. For this reason the few companies that managed to survive had to specialize in assembly and became maquiladora subcontractors for American manufacturers such as Sun Apparel, Levi Strauss and Company, and Farah. This transformation meant, in reality, a de-skilling and a reduction in the value added by Torreón firms.

Although this reorientation toward the international market signified an increased dependency on American manufacturers and brokers, the basis for an export boom in the region was being created. Even though they concentrated on sewing, Torreón firms learned how to man-

TABLE 10.1.   Main Clients for Torreón Apparel Exports

Type of Clients	1993	1998
Manufacturers	Farah (M) Sun Apparel (M)	Sun Apparel–Jones of NY (BM, M) Aalfs (M) Kentucky Apparel (M) Grupo Libra (M) Siete Leguas (M) Tarrant (M) Tropical Sportswear (M) Red Kap (M)
Brand Marketers	Wrangler (BM,M) Levi Strauss and Company (BM,M)	Wrangler (BM,M) Levi Strauss and Company (BM,M) Action West (BM,M) Polo (BM) Calvin Klein (BM) Liz Claiborne (BM) Old Navy (BM) Tommy Hilfiger (BM) Donna Karan (BM) Guess? (BM) Chaps (BM)
Retailers		Gap (BM,R) The Limited (BM, R) Kmart (R) Wal-Mart (R) JCPenney (R) Sears (R) Target (R)

Note: Firms aligned to the right are hybrids.

M, Manufacturers; BM, Brand Marketers; R, Retailers.

ufacture quality products and deliver them in a timely fashion. Lead firms such as Sun Apparel played an active role in "pushing" Mexican suppliers to meet international standards and to increase their production capacities, which helped them to become full-package producers.

The Mexican peso devaluation crisis in December 1994, after three years of relative stability, had mixed effects on the blue jeans industry. The exchange rate jumped from 3.4 pesos per dollar in December 1994 to 6.8 pesos per dollar in January 1995 (IMF 1999). For the apparel industry the immediate consequences of the devaluation were an increase in the number of U.S. clients interested in the Torreón region, an increase in the number of Mexican apparel assembly plants, and an increase in the production capacity of already existing firms. Table 10.1 shows that prior to 1994 only four U.S. manufacturers—Farah, Sun Apparel, Wrangler, and Levi Strauss and Company—had a significant presence in the region. By 1998 the number of clients had grown to more than two dozen. At the same time the number of jeans manufactured in the

TABLE 10.2. Apparel Industry Indicators for La Laguna Area[a]

Variables	1993	1998
Apparel Employment	12,000	65,000
Output of Jeans (pairs per week)	500,000	4 million
Output per Company (pairs per week)	Max. 50,000	Max. 230,000
Mexican Denim in Export Production	1–2%	5%
Assembly Price per Piece	U.S.$0.90–1.10	U.S.$1.20–2.05
U.S. Retail Price	U.S.$10–40	U.S.$10–80
Activities with Mexican Ownership	Assembly	Assembly Laundry Cutting Finishing Textiles Trim and Labels U.S. Sales Offices
Types of Companies	Specialized Apparel Firms	Diversified Corporate Groups and Textile Exporters[b]
Regulation of Work Conditions	Mexican Legislation	Mexican Legislation and Foreign Buyers' Codes of Conduct

[a]Torreón is the center of La Laguna, a highly integrated economic region formed by two additional cities, Gómez Palacio and Lerdo, and several rural communities. Although each city is a distinct political entity, together they form an integrated production zone.

[b]Examples of these new companies are Grupo Lajat, Grupo Soriana, and textile producers such as Parras-Cone and Textiles Lajat.

region jumped eightfold, from 500,000 to 4 million pairs per week (see Table 10.2).

The NAFTA Effect

The maquilization of apparel activities in the Torreón region was primarily due to the Mexican peso devaluations and not to NAFTA. What, then, was the effect of NAFTA on the industry? The most elementary consequence was a change in the rules of the game for producers in Mexico. For the apparel industry, NAFTA meant the progressive elimination of U.S. tariffs and nonmonetary barriers to all apparel production activities, including laundering, cutting, and finishing, as well as the use of Mexican inputs such as textiles (denim), buttons, labels, and so forth. For the global apparel industry, NAFTA meant a transformation, at least potentially, of the cost structure of production. For the first time activities other than assembly could be performed in

Mexico without the restrictions created by the quota system or the 807/9802 program. The cost reductions that NAFTA made possible provided a rare window of opportunity to obtain a competitive advantage. Companies that decided to move their operations to Mexico around or shortly after the implementation of NAFTA would enjoy lower production costs than other companies.

Figure 10.1 shows how these new conditions reoriented production activities in the Torreón region. In 1993 the region was dedicated exclusively to apparel assembly. By 1996 Mexican-made denim, trim, and labels were used for blue jean exports, and laundering and finishing were also carried out in Mexico. By 2000 cutting and distribution were established in the region as well. However, Figure 10.1 indicates that marketing and retail, the most profitable activities in the apparel industry, are still exclusively performed in the United States. This deepening of the apparel com-

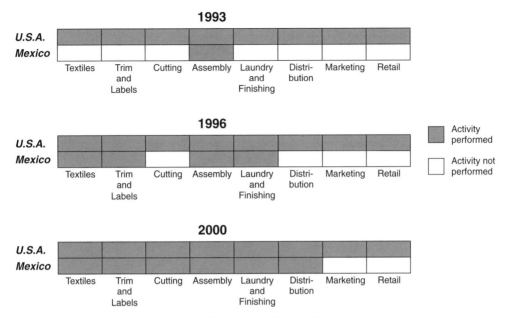

FIGURE 10.1.   Apparel Commodity Chain: Activities and Location

modity chain in Mexico suggests that NAFTA has allowed Mexico to develop full-package production capabilities, where not only assembly but all other required manufacturing activities, including the production and purchase of raw materials, are performed within the country. It is important to note, however, that the capability to carry out all manufacturing activities in the making of a pair of jeans does not by itself constitute full-package production. An additional activity, which is usually difficult to locate in a value-added chain, is the *coordination* of all production activities in order to offer clients a finished product. This raises a new factor that has intensified the coordination functions in the Torreón region: the explosive growth in the volume of orders placed by U.S. retailers and brand marketers.

New Organizational Buyers and the Move to Full-Package Production

The 807/9802 model of export production before NAFTA was linked to large U.S. apparel manufacturers that provided the inputs for Mexican assembly. The possibility of lower-cost full-package production after NAFTA enticed U.S. retailers and marketers to consider Mexico as an alternative to Asia for their sourcing needs (Gereffi 1997). Table 10.1 not only shows an increase in the number of U.S. clients with operations in the region but also highlights the entrance of new kinds of players: brand marketers (who develop distinctive labels, such as Nike, Tommy Hilfiger, and Liz Claiborne) and retailers. Both retailers and marketers require full-package supply because they dedicate themselves to design, distribution, and marketing rather than to production activities.

Besides creating demand for full-package supply, retailers and marketers have transformed Torreón's production patterns in three fundamental ways. First, they introduced high-volume orders to the region. In 1993 the biggest firms could assemble a maximum of 50,000 pairs of jeans per week. In 1998, Sun Apparel and its subcontractors produced

230,000 pairs per week in Torreón alone, just under half of Sun Apparel's total jeans production in Mexico. Despite this tremendous jump in capacity, Torreón firms are still experiencing pressure to keep growing. For example, Original Mexican Jean Company (OMJC) and Siete Leguas are two of the jeans manufacturers in the region, and they both dedicate most of their production (all of it in the case of OMJC) to manufacturing jeans for JCPenney's private-label Arizona brand. With a joint production capacity of 300,000 pairs of jeans per week in 1998, both companies plan to double their production capacity in the near future.

The second transformation is the manufacturing of more-expensive and higher-quality jeans. In 1993 the maximum retail price of a pair of jeans assembled in the region fluctuated around U.S.$40; this price increased to $80 in 1998. Since 1994 the piece rates for local assembly have risen in part because of the increased demand but also because of the production of jeans with higher retail prices.

The third factor is the introduction of branded apparel. One important characteristic of the leading firms is that they base their competitive advantage on the power of their brands and the images they create. Companies such as Liz Claiborne, Calvin Klein, and Donna Karan, and even retailers such as JCPenney, Kmart, and Sears, try to distance themselves from the often exploitative conditions in maquiladora production because they are concerned about tarnishing their image among consumers (see Gereffi, Garcia-Johnson, and Sasser 2001).

As a result of these factors, production in the Torreón region has dramatically changed. Table 10.2 offers several indicators of this transformation in the region. In 1998 the Torreón area produced 4 million pairs of jeans per week, with at least 25 percent being full-package production. Although no accurate estimate can be provided, the rest of production is moving to what is locally known as "half-package"—that is, the assembly, cutting, laundering, and fin-ishing of jeans is performed locally but the inputs, such as denim, trim and other materials, are provided by the U.S. client.

The Role of Local Capital and Knowledge in Torreón's Development

All three factors mentioned above are to a certain degree external to the Torreón region. However, local industrial development, even after the implementation of NAFTA, is also dependent on the resources and characteristics of the Torreón cluster, as well on the strategies and decisions taken by specific local firms. Brand marketers and retailers have "pushed" American manufacturers to move their operations to Mexico, but due to an explosive demand they have also "pulled" Mexican firms to increase their production volumes and their range of activities. The existence of local knowledge and capital has allowed Torreón firms to take advantage of the opportunities created by the demand for full-package production.

Torreón firms after the 1980s crisis went through a process of recovery. Although the legislation that made maquiladoras possible had existed since 1965, firms in Torreón had used this export system only when the local market conditions were unfavorable. In a historical context, the reorientation toward maquiladora production meant a momentary relapse for the regional industry. Mexican firms lost status and control, and they were also forced to reduce their value added. The knowledge acquired in more than thirty years of apparel production stopped being useful to them during this period. However, NAFTA and the related entrance of new organizational buyers made it possible for the few traditional companies that survived the turbulent times to use the expertise developed during their years of making apparel for the local market. Grupo Libra and Siete Leguas are two examples of companies that were established decades before NAFTA, when Mexico was still pursuing an import-substitution strategy. Both managed to survive the turbulent 1980s, emerging as full-package suppliers for U.S. clients.

Grupo Libra has demonstrated great flexibility in adapting to changing environments. By the late 1970s and early 1980s, Libra was beginning to see the potential in the international market. When the crisis of 1982 hit the Mexican economy, 100 percent of Libra's customers were American firms. By 1985, Libra was already offering full-package production in addition to its assembly services. Grupo Libra benefited greatly from the export boom. It has become the second largest manufacturer in the Torreón area, with a local production capacity of two hundred thousand pairs of jeans per week. Since 1996 the firm has dedicated itself exclusively to full-package production and has developed distribution systems to manage and replenish the stock of some of its U.S. clients. Libra is perhaps the only Mexican firm seriously to consider buying or developing its own brands in order to directly enter the American jeans market.

Siete Leguas represents a similar success story. Founded in 1957 as a producer of jeans for agricultural workers, the company did not reorient itself to the export market until 1988. Although it had always been a relatively small company (producing 25,000 to 30,000 jeans per week in 1982–85), by 1988 its production capacity was reduced to 3,000 pairs per week. The company's first American customer was Action West, although this association lasted only for three months. At that time Sun Apparel arrived in the Laguna region and offered a better deal. During its association with Sun Apparel, Siete Leguas not only learned international quality standards but also increased its production from 3,000 to 60,000 pairs of jeans per week. No longer in association with Sun Apparel, the firm has constructed its own facilities for cutting, laundering, and finishing jeans. With a production

capacity of 150,000 pairs of jeans per week, Siete Leguas is widely recognized as the one of the best and most innovative apparel producers in the Torreón region.

Besides local expertise in the apparel industry, an important characteristic that has allowed Mexican firms and communities to take advantage of free trade is the existence of significant sources of local capital. The Torreón region has highly diversified corporate groups that, although limited in number, are attracted to the apparel industry. Diversified Mexican companies are able to bring capital to the partnerships, while the U.S. firms bring experience and knowledge of the American market and its requirements for export success. Although it is too early to assess the extent to which these relationships will result in skill and knowledge transfer to Mexican companies, the major industrial groups involved in the Torreón ventures are wealthy and sophisticated enough to potentially buy out their U.S. partners and assume control of the interfirm networks that link the Torreón cluster to U.S. buyers.

Together these four factors—the peso devaluations, the implementation of NAFTA, the entrance of new lead firms, and the existence of local resources—are reshaping the Torreón apparel cluster. How different is full-package production as developed in the Torreón region from the traditional maquiladora model? A review of network structures in 1993 and 1998 provides a good indicator of how much the production relationships have changed since NAFTA.

Pre-NAFTA Maquiladora Production Networks

Many of the disadvantages of the typical maquiladora model can be explained by the types of relationships it fosters among firms. Figure 10.2 represents the networks typically formed between Torreón suppliers and the U.S. companies that placed their orders in 1993, under

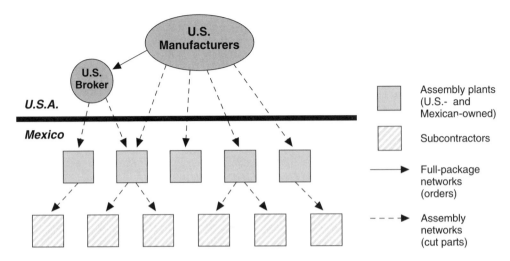

FIGURE 10.2.   Pre-NAFTA Blue Jeans Assembly Networks

the provisions of the 807/9802 program. The simplicity of the model points out exactly what the problem is: A few manufacturers and brokers provide the orders for a large number of Mexican assemblers. The asymmetry in the relationship is reinforced by several factors. First, the most important survival factor for assembly plants is achieving a continuous flow of orders from U.S. clients, which allows them to maintain constant operations during the whole year. For U.S. companies, by contrast, one of the main purposes of subcontracting assembly in Torreón under the maquiladora program was to handle seasonal "peaks" in demand, which would make permanent relationships with firms difficult or undesirable. Second, all subcontractors offered the same service: assembly. Without the possibility of differentiating themselves from their competitors, Torreón subcontractors were easily replaced. U.S. firms could give orders to certain subcontractors in April and move them to other firms or even different regions in Mexico by May. Third, the subcontractors have few or no horizontal ties between them, so no coordination mechanisms are in place to regulate competition or to mitigate the consequences of this

unbalanced power distribution. The lack of horizontal coordination facilitates the mobility of the companies placing the orders, allowing the American firms to "pressure" their subcontractors in order to obtain lower prices.

Another important problem for Torreón subcontractors is only partially addressed by Figure 10.2. The network diagram concentrates on the Mexican firms and their contacts with U.S. clients, particularly manufacturers and brokers. However, the diagram does not show the firms and networks to which Mexican firms do *not* have access. On the U.S. side of the border a complex set of activities, firms, and relationships form the structure of the blue jeans industry, especially its high-priced fashion segment. A major source of power for the U.S. firms placing the orders was that they monopolized access to the most profitable nodes in the American market. A handful of manufacturers and brokers benefited by serving as a point of contact between the otherwise unconnected Mexican subcontractors and their American clients, in particular brand marketers and retailers.

This "structural hole" (Burt 1992) in the jeans supply chain is based on two dimensions.

First, there is an absence of skills. By providing only assembly services, Mexican firms were unable to deal directly with brand marketers and retailers because these companies were looking only for full-package suppliers that had the ability to manage textiles, cutting, laundering, and finishing. Second, the gap is not only technical but also relational. Torreón subcontractors simply lacked the knowledge of the North American apparel supply chain and its main actors required to generate new options. Most Mexican firms, with the exception of Grupo Libra, which was searching for more clients and had opened sales offices in the United States, were dependent on the few U.S. manufacturers or brokers that were actively looking to subcontract their assembly in Mexico.

Post-NAFTA Full-Package Networks

Four years after the implementation of NAFTA, the network configurations created by the maquiladora model and the strategies of U.S. firms regarding their Mexican subcontractors had been profoundly transformed. Figure 10.3 indicates just how much network configurations in the Torreón region were altered in a few years. Changes occurred in the capabilities of the network as well as in the characteristics of the actors and the structure of the relationships between them. Perhaps the most important feature of the post-NAFTA organizational arrangement is that the part of the network located in Mexican territory is offering full-package production. Under the coordination of manufacturers in Mexico, textile production, cutting, laundering, and finishing are carried out in order to deliver finished products to U.S. retailers and manufacturers. Some companies, such as OMJC, distribute the jeans directly to American stores and manage their inventory information.

Although full-package production represents an undeniable improvement in capabilities that go well beyond the maquiladora model, a structural gap still exists between the

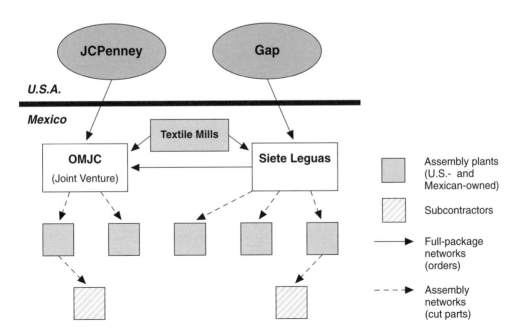

FIGURE 10.3. Post-NAFTA Full-Package Networks in Torreón

networks located in Mexico and those across the border controlled by the U.S. buyers placing the orders. Marketing and design, the two most profitable segments in apparel, remain completely under the control of U.S. companies. Of the largest Mexican-owned apparel firms in the area, only Grupo Libra and Kentucky-Lajat (a U.S.-Mexican joint venture) have sales offices in the United States. No Mexican firm has its own brand in the U.S. market. The next big step for firms located in the Torreón region is thus to create or acquire their own brands so that they can target and contact prospective U.S. clients directly.

Another salient transformation in local networks is in the characteristics of the firms forming the networks. Although the majority of assembly operations comprised small Mexican firms in 1998, a new set of organizational actors has emerged. American manufacturers that did not have any significant operations in Mexico before the implementation of NAFTA have moved to Torreón. At the same time, because of the new activities and higher profit margins of full-package production, diversified Mexican corporate groups are developing an interest in the apparel industry. Both trends have promoted the creation of new joint ventures. For example, one of the firms shown in Figure 10.3, OMJC, the third largest manufacturer in Torreón in terms of output,[5] is a joint venture between Aalfs, a U.S. apparel manufacturer, and a Mexican family (the Martín family) that has interests in retail, restaurants, dairy farming, bakeries, and banks. A more unorthodox joint venture was formed by Grupo Lajat (which owns LP Gas, a major supplier to Mexico City) and Kentucky Apparel in 1995. Kentucky-Lajat was launched as a joint venture with production in both Mexico and United States, in which each partner owned 50 percent of the business in both countries. In July 1999, Grupo Lajat bought out its U.S. partner, and in November

of the same year Kentucky Lajat's U.S. manufacturing operations were shut down.

Grupo Lajat also exemplifies the entrance of a new kind of player into the Torreón region: textile firms oriented to the export market. At the same time that the Kentucky-Lajat joint venture was being established, Grupo Lajat, which has significant investments in cotton production in several regions of Mexico, decided to establish a textile mill. Textiles Lajat made around 3 million yards of denim per month in 1998. Most of this production (around 90 to 95 percent) was destined for products exported to the United States. The mill at the time had a total of six or seven clients; the two other major customers, in addition to Kentucky-Lajat (which bought only 30 percent of its sister company's production), were VF Corporation's Lee and Wrangler.[6] The second major textile manufacturer that produces much of the denim used in jeans marketed under major U.S. brand names is Parras-Cone. This textile mill represents a collaborative effort between North Carolina–based Cone Mills and one of Mexico's oldest and largest textile companies, Compañia Industrial de Parras, S.A. de C.V. Their new denim mill, which produced around 570,000 yards of denim per month in 1998, is located in the town of Parras, about two hours outside Torreón.

Besides attracting new actors to apparel production, the fundamental changes that took place in the late 1990s have forced companies that were established in the region before 1994 to reconfigure their structures and strategies. For some Mexican firms the new conditions have meant moving up the ladder of apparel manufacturing. Those local firms that are able to develop high-quality production and increase their capacity and the variety of activities they perform become "hot commodities" for American clients. But what about the American manufacturers that used to hire assembly firms in the region? For them the growth in demand and in the number of clients has reduced their control over subcontractors and has increased assembly prices. Sun Apparel, Wrangler, and Levi Strauss and Company have responded to these new challenges not by moving their operations out of Torreón but by consolidating them.

Sun Apparel responded to the challenge of reduced control and higher prices by injecting direct investment into the region and constructing its own assembly and laundering plants. Although in 1998 it still had thirty-one subcontractors in its supply network, Sun Apparel directly assembled 180,000 pairs of jeans and laundered 280,000 jeans per week (around 35 percent of its exports to the United States) through its subsidiary, Maquilas Pami. Likewise, Wrangler changed from occasional subcontracting to the construction of a high-technology hub and a series of assembly plants in Torreón's neighboring rural communities.[7] Although Levi Strauss and Company has avoided setting up its own plants in Mexico, it has faced the new competitive environment by dramatically reducing the number of its subcontractors in Mexico from 120 in 1997 to 17 in 1998, even though production capacity was kept at 1 million pairs of jeans per month by increasing the size of orders with the remaining subcontractors. One of Levi's biggest suppliers in the Torreón region, Fábricas de Ropa Manjai, constructed a new, highly automated sewing, cutting, and laundering facility in order to meet the demands of high-volume, high-quality production for Levi Strauss and Company.

The nature of interfirm networks has also been reorganized. First, the emergence of more segments of the apparel commodity chain in the Torreón area allows for greater local linkages, as Mexican producers of denim, trim, labels, dyestuffs, chemicals for laundering, and so forth are supplying the export-oriented industry. Second, higher demand and

a larger number of possible clients have relieved some of the pressures of dependency. Although exclusivity is still important for the survival of Mexican firms, particularly in the case of small assembly contractors, American clients are now competing to get the services of the best assemblers and manufacturers. For the first time Mexican firms can begin to choose their clients.

Consequences for Local Development

The ultimate critique of the maquiladora is and has always been the exploitation of cheap labor. Do the new relationships and opportunities for Mexican firms that we identify above translate into real advantages for Mexican workers? We believe that the full-package system has clear advantages over maquiladora production. Labor-related benefits of the new system can be classified into six different areas: employment; wages and benefits; working conditions; upgrading of personnel; unions; and rural communities.

Employment

Between 1993 and 1998 apparel employment in the Laguna region where Torreón is located increased 300 percent, while employment in commerce and services grew only 3 percent; construction, 80 percent; and the auto industry, 100 percent. The general dynamics of employment in the region can be summarized as follows:

- Total employment in the region has grown significantly (30 percent from 1993 to 1998).
- Most of this growth has been concentrated in manufacturing (68 percent of new employment created from 1993 to 1998 represents manufacturing jobs).

- Apparel and textiles have become the most important source of employment in the region.
- As a consequence of this growth, unemployment in the city of Torreón decreased from 7.6 percent in February 1995 to 3.1 percent in December 1997.

In addition to the expansion of employment opportunities in the Torreón apparel cluster, it is equally important to note that activities associated with the strengthening of the supply chain—such as textile production, laundering, and cutting—are bringing new types of jobs to the region to complement the growing number of sewing jobs. These new jobs include not only basic production activities, such as cutting fabric, but also the supervisory and technical positions needed to maintain highly automated, capital-intensive operations like Torreón's new textile mills. The growth of textile production in Torreón is particularly significant in terms of employment, since textile jobs typically pay more than apparel jobs. For example, 1998 average hourly labor costs in the Mexican textile industry were $2.23 an hour, as compared to $1.51 in apparel (Werner International, Inc. 1998).

Wages and Benefits

Workers in the industry are paid according to a piece-rate system whereby they receive a base wage, which is typically a multiple of the local minimum wage, plus additional earnings "per piece" when they achieve certain productivity levels or fulfill set production quotas. It is widely agreed that Mexico's minimum wage, which varies by geographic region, is not a living wage, and consequently many companies pay a multiple of it, such as 1.5 times the legally allowed minimum. When we completed our fieldwork in Torreón in July 1998, the local minimum wage was 182 pesos per week. Base

wages in the companies we interviewed generally ranged between 220 and 280 pesos a week, but most workers earned more due to the piece-rate system. Maximum average salaries ranged from 500 pesos to 750 pesos a week. The exchange rate in July 1998 was approximately 8.7 pesos to the dollar, meaning that the minimum wage was equivalent to U.S.$21.00 per week and the maximum salaries ranged between U.S.$57.50 and $86.20 a week.

High turnover and a tight labor market in Torreón have been driving wages up in the region's apparel plants, and this trend has not gone unnoticed by the factory's owners. High and persistent turnover was repeatedly cited in our interviews as the most pressing problem Torreón's employers face. In the summer of 1998 the employers initiated discussions among themselves in an effort to find a "solution" to the problem of wages rising as a result of Torreón's increasingly tight labor market. The employers particularly wanted to address the practice of companies pirating away each other's workers with wage increases, but at the time of our fieldwork their efforts in this regard had not been successful.

Working Conditions

The presence in the region of visible clients with high investments in their brand names prompts improved working conditions. Large retailers and marketers do not want their brands associated with the exploitation of workers or with unsafe working conditions. Companies such as the Gap and JCPenney have created and imposed detailed codes of conduct related not only to the final quality of the product but also to the quality of the process. Any plant or company that fails to fulfill these requirements, including compliance with local labor laws, safety practices, and even the conditions of the bathrooms, is in danger of losing its contracts. In addition, since most plants and factories have been constructed since 1994, they were designed to provide a safe working environment, with proper ventilation, lighting, ergonomic equipment, and the like. In general the working conditions of many of these Mexican plants are better than those offered by local competitors and often are better than those in similar factories in the United States.

Upgrading of Personnel

The analysis of this dimension is complicated by the characteristics of the local labor market and of the industry. Highly competitive labor markets have forced many companies to slash educational requirements to a minimum, with some companies not even asking for basic writing and reading skills. In general U.S. companies are more likely to require a minimum educational level (typically completion of elementary school) than are their Mexican counterparts. Given the greater technological complexity of textile production, the area's textile mills are more demanding than the region's sewing factories, requiring a high school education for all their workers. Companies provide limited options for upward mobility and relatively few positions for skilled workers and professionals. However, the low educational requirements can be seen as favoring the most impoverished stratum of Mexican society. Wages are not tied to education but to productivity, offering an opportunity for the most disadvantaged workers in Mexico to earn a decent wage. Furthermore companies frequently provide opportunities for workers to continue (or even begin) their education.

Unions

In tandem with the liberalization of the economy, the Mexican government has reduced the power of unions to a minimum. The role of unions in the apparel industry in the Torreón region has been limited in many cases to helping the firms and their managers deal with the workers. Effective representation and collective bargaining are virtually nonexistent. Instead, workers exercise their power by moving from one company to another fairly often. They use their mobility as a source of bargaining to obtain small wage increases and nonmonetary benefits such as transportation, free lunch, classes, raffles, and prizes. However, this is an advantage contingent on a continued high demand for labor.

Rural Communities

A few manufacturers are evading the turnover problem in Torreón by relocating production to outlying rural areas. Many of the collective farms that were a centerpiece of Mexico's agricultural program for decades and that were privatized under the administration of Mexican president Carlos Salinas de Gortari are located around Torreón in the Laguna region. The privatization of these cooperatives, known as *ejidos*, has created a supply of landless rural workers with few employment opportunities. Consequently, rural communities have become a dependent periphery, with wages 30 percent lower than in urban areas. Furthermore, rural communities often perform only assembly work and have no access to the technological advances mentioned above.

Although concerns may be raised about the proletarianization of this formerly agricultural labor force with the arrival of sewing factories, such objections must be evaluated in light of the limited employment and industrialization opportunities available to these communities.[8] At the time of our fieldwork, the practice of relocating apparel production to these areas was limited. Around 10 percent of apparel jobs are located in rural communities, while the rural labor force represents 30 percent of the total labor force in the greater Torreón region.

Conclusions

The main conclusion that can be drawn from the Torreón case is that the apparel industry in the region is far removed from the standard maquiladora model. Although the number of assembly firms has grown considerably in Torreón since the implementation of NAFTA in 1994, new developments challenge the "maquilization of Mexico" scenario. A comparison between the region today and in 1993, when the maquiladora model was dominant, shows how the network linkages, both external and internal to Torreón, have been profoundly transformed in less than five years. New types of organizational actors have emerged, providing additional resources and a wide variety of organizational strategies and structures. Finally, the combination of full-package networks, the explosive growth of demand for Torreón's exports, and the emergence of new actors has contributed to an amelioration in the conditions for workers. Since these shifts are quite apparent, two questions become pertinent: First, if not maquiladora, then what exactly is the production model in the Torreón region? Second, is this kind of transformation likely to occur in other regions of Mexico?

Answering the first question returns us to the global commodity-chains and industrial-district approaches. Since external as well as internal linkages have been created in the Torreón region, both literatures are relevant for the description and explanation of changes in production relations. In at least one sense, however, the commodity-chains literature better describes the process and the driving forces of the transformation to full-package supply in Torreón. (See Bair and Gereffi 2001 for a more detailed analysis of these issues.) The establishment of direct linkages with a variety of lead firms, particularly retailers and brand manufacturers, has been the engine running the growth and transformation of the Torreón

region. The strategic needs of these lead firms led them to transfer diverse activities to Mexico. The economic forces unleashed in the apparel supply chain have attracted new investments, created pressures for growth, and promoted the transfer of technologies. The transformation process is thus explained by the power and ability of these actors to take advantage of the opportunities that NAFTA has created.

Even if external actors are the main drivers of change, we should not underestimate the importance of local factors. Local expertise, capital, and entrepreneurial vision have contributed significantly to the shape and structure of the apparel industry in the region. However, Torreón is far from being an industrial district. If what characterizes a district is the formation of effective institutions as well as cooperative mechanisms among firms, these elements appear to be in short supply in the Laguna region. If certain firms in Torreón have acquired the role of network coordinators, their relationship with small firms tends to be hierarchical and unequal. Horizontal cooperation between firms is rare. Networks are created to fulfill volume demands, and standardization is the norm. Neither the firms nor their clients frequently seek flexibility and adaptability. Furthermore, any institutional development seems to be two steps behind externally driven changes. For example, it was only after NAFTA that the local industry association was created, and even in 1998 its scope and influence were limited. Although the industry association tries to create a forum to address common issues confronting local firms, the main ones being labor shortages and rising wage rates, few specific measures have been implemented.

This argument is closely related to our second question: Is this kind of development likely to occur in other regions of Mexico? Both the peso devaluations and the implementation of NAFTA are events with national implications. The unsustainability of production for the local market, the attractiveness of export production, and the potential advantages of exporting by way of NAFTA are factors that have affected not only the Torreón region but the rest of Mexico as well. However, we believe that the expanded U.S. market access provided by new lead firms and the available local resources have been key factors in preventing the "maquilization" of Torreón. Furthermore, these factors are subject to regional variations.

Continued growth and expansion of the Torreón apparel cluster are not guaranteed. Follow-up fieldwork conducted in 2001 revealed that a slowdown in the U.S. economy had negatively impacted on the region, and U.S. clients were placing fewer orders with local apparel manufacturers (Bair and Gereffi 2001). Industry experts estimated that jeans production had declined by as much as 20 percent between October 2000 and May 2001, compared with the previous year. During the same period, an estimated eight thousand Torreón apparel workers lost their jobs. This vulnerability to consumer demand north of the border is the unfortunate consequence of increased dependence on the U.S. market.[9]

The risks caused by a high level of concentration on one export market apply to all apparel-exporting clusters in Mexico. The decline in demand from U.S. clients that has hurt the Torreón cluster has undoubtedly affected virtually all apparel-producing regions in Mexico. Compared to these other exporting regions, the overall prospects for Torreón remain bright. The Torreón case makes clear that being able to attract the right kind of lead firms to a particular region is a prerequisite for Mexican communities to move away from maquiladora production toward a more development-oriented, full-package manufacturing model. These new lead firms create

opportunities for Mexican suppliers to go beyond the typical maquiladora role, but they create only "opportunities," not guarantees of success. The presence of local capital, skills, entrepreneurial drive, and other resources are necessary but not sufficient conditions to strengthen the position of Mexican firms in the apparel commodity chain. The demonstration effect that lead firms have created may encourage more U.S. manufacturers to move their operations to Mexico, but this must be coupled by the efforts of savvy Mexican entrepreneurs to upgrade their operations or to start new export firms. Thus, even though external forces drive the changes in Torreón, local factors mediate this process.

Since the conditions that foster full-package production and a more favorable position for Mexican firms are local, the possibility for uneven consequences of NAFTA among different regions of Mexico is high. Due to labor shortages and relatively high wages, some manufacturers (even the new big Torreón manufacturers) are moving their assembly operations to rural communities around Torreón or to the southern part of Mexico (e.g., the Yucatán and Campeche). What these manufacturers are trying to do is partially to replicate the conditions of the maquiladora model. By establishing factories or subcontracting work with small plants in rural communities with few alternative sources of employment and limited access to lead firms, they seek to retain the high degree of control over cheap production that we associate with the maquiladora model. If NAFTA has not resulted in the maquilization of Mexico as a whole, it may still result in the maquilization of rural and southern Mexico (Tardanico and Rosenberg 2000).

The role of regional policy under the new conditions created by NAFTA is clear. Regional and local governments should create incentives to attract U.S. buyers (retailers, brand marketers, and manufacturers) to their locations and provide support for Mexican firms so that they can satisfy the needs of these demanding clients. This experience provides a basis for Mexican firms to move up the apparel commodity chain into higher-value-added activities themselves. Without this process, the maquilization of many communities may be the unavoidable outcome of NAFTA.

Notes

1. Historically only 1 to 3 percent of these inputs have been produced locally within Mexico.

2. For example, the duty-free importation of U.S.-made inputs for assembly in Mexico—the primary advantage of the maquiladora program—is now generally available for all firms with cross-border trade and production networks, not just the maquiladoras. While the full phase-in of NAFTA implied the official end of the maquiladora program in January 2001, "maquiladoras," defined as companies that perform mainly assembly operations for the export sector, will continue to exist.

3. All three authors participated in the July 1998 fieldwork, while Jennifer Bair and Gary Gereffi carried out the July 2000 fieldwork. For a more detailed discussion of the latter research, see Bair and Gereffi (2001).

4. In the United States the maquiladora program is also referred to as the 807 program, for the numbered clause of the U.S. trade law that described this type of cross-border production sharing. The numbering of the relevant clause was later changed to 9802, so it is commonly referred to in the literature as 807/9802 production.

5. OMJC produces about 140,000 pairs of jeans a week for clients such as JCPenney, Levi Strauss and Company, and Tommy Hilfiger.

6. Textiles Lajat was sold to Parras by Grupo Lajat in December 1998.

7. Wrangler is a subsidiary of VF Corporation, a major U.S. apparel manufacturer whose brands include Lee, Vanity Fair, Jansport, and Healthtex. (See Chapter 2 in this book for a discussion of VF.) Wrangler was formerly the largest division of the

Blue Bell Corporation, which was acquired by VF in November 1986, and it remains the largest company within VF Corporation. Wrangler has a high degree of autonomy vis-à-vis its parent company, and decisions about where to locate production facilities such as the one in Torreón are made at the divisional level.

8. The incorporation of these regions into full-package networks may even be creating ownership opportunities for workers. At least one Mexican manufacturer whose subcontracting network includes a number of factories located in the former *ejido* areas was instrumental in establishing these factories as worker-owned companies controlled by the employees living in the community.

9. Heavy reliance on the U.S. export market is a general feature of the Mexican economy. In 2000 the United States received 89 percent of Mexico's total exports, up from 83 percent in 1993 (INEGI 2001).

References

Bair, Jennifer, and Gary Gereffi. 2001. "Local Clusters in Global Chains: The Causes and Consequences of Export Dynamism in Torreon's Blue Jeans Industry." *World Development* 29, 11 (November): 1885–1903.

Burt, Ronald S. 1992. *Structural Holes: The Social Structure of Competition.* Cambridge, Mass.: Harvard University Press.

Carrillo, Jorge. 1998. "Third Generation Maquiladoras? The Delphi-General Motors Case." *Journal of Borderlands Studies* 13, 1 (Spring): 79–97.

Dussel Peters, Enrique. 2000. *Polarizing Mexico: The Impact of Liberalization Strategy.* Boulder, Col.: Lynn Reinner.

Gereffi, Gary. 1994. "The Organization of Buyer-Driven Global Commodity Chains: How U.S. Retailers Shape Overseas Production Networks." In *Commodity Chains and Global Capitalism,* ed. Gary Gereffi and Miguel Korzeniewicz, pp. 95–122. Westport, Conn.: Praeger.

———. 1996. "Mexico's 'Old' and 'New' Maquiladora Industries: Contrasting Approaches to North American Integration." In *Neoliberalism Revisited: Economic Restructuring and Mexico's Polit-*

ical Future, ed. Gerardo Otero, pp. 85–105. Boulder, Colo.: Westview Press.

———. 1997. "Global Shifts, Regional Response: Can North America Meet the Full-Package Challenge?" *Bobbin* 39, 3 (November): 16–31.

Gereffi, Gary, Ronie Garcia-Johnson, and Erika Sasser. 2001. "The NGO-Industrial Complex." *Foreign Policy* 125 (July–August): 56–65.

Gereffi, Gary, and Donald L. Wyman, eds. 1990. *Manufacturing Miracles: Paths of Industrialization in Latin America and East Asia*. Princeton, N.J.: Princeton University Press.

Humphrey, John, ed. 1995. Special issue on "Industrial Organization and Manufacturing Competitiveness in Developing Countries." *World Development* 23, 1 (January).

Instituto Nacional de Estadística, Geografía, e Informática (INEGI), Banco de Información Económica. 2001. Data available at <http://www.inegi.gob.mx>. Site consulted in July.

International Monetary Fund (IMF). 1999. *International Financial Statistics*. Washington, D.C.: IMF.

Markusen, Ann. 1996. "Sticky Places in Slippery Space: A Typology of Industrial Districts." *Economic Geography* 72, 1: 293–313.

Piore, Michael J., and Charles F. Sabel. 1984. *The Second Industrial Divide*. New York: Basic Books.

Pyke, Frank, and Werner Sengenberger, eds. 1992. *Industrial Districts and Local Economic Regeneration*. Geneva: International Institute for Labour Studies.

Shaiken, Harley, with Stephen Herzenberg. 1987. *Automation and Global Production: Automobile Engine Production in Mexico, the United States, and Canada*. Monograph Series 26. La Jolla: Center for U.S.-Mexican Studies, University of California, San Diego.

Tardanico, Richard, and Mark B. Rosenberg, eds. 2000. *Poverty or Development: Global Restructuring and Regional Transformations in the U.S. South and the Mexican South*. New York: Routledge.

Werner International, Inc. 1998. *Hourly Labor Costs in the Apparel Industry*. New York: Werner International, Inc.

Enrique Dussel Peters, Clemente Ruiz Durán, and Michael J. Piore

11   Learning and the Limits of Foreign Partners as Teachers

Recent Economic Trends

The garment industry is being hailed as the outstanding success of the North American Free Trade Agreement (NAFTA), at least from the Mexican point of view. Garment exports to the United States have expanded from less than $500 million in 1991 to $7.4 billion in 2001. Moreover, since 1994, when the agreement actually went into effect, that rate has continued to increase as more and more producers move facilities from other parts of North America and the Caribbean Basin to Mexico. But NAFTA is the culmination of the process of opening the Mexican economy to trade, a process that began in the mid-1980s, and the increase in imports from Mexico associated with that process has also been dramatic. As shown in Table 11.1, in the period leading up to NAFTA (1988–93) the annual increase in real imports averaged 42.9 percent. Tables 11.2–11.4 additionally reflect that maquiladora exports have been the driving force in Mexico's garment industry. Specifically, temporary imports to be reexported (i.e., imports that are transformed temporarily, without payment of tariffs or taxes and without value added, through programs such as the maquiladora

program) remain the core of garment exports (Alvarez Galván and Dussel Peters 2001).

Independent of the recession in Mexican exports since 2001, the import figures reflect in part that the Mexican garment industry is increasingly a subcontracting operation, an extension of the pattern of development initiated under the maquiladora program where access to U.S. markets is mediated by foreign companies that design the product, supply the materials (in garments, often in the form of cut pieces), specify the production process, and then take over the final output for sale abroad. The annual increase in imports for plants operating under this program in 1988–93 averaged 62 percent.

But the import figures also reflect a darker side of the structural changes occurring in the Mexican economy. The opening has had a devastating impact on traditional producers; the country has increasingly lost its domestic market to imported foreign goods. It is hard to identify this loss precisely, because figures for the industry as a whole mask the division between the expanding and contracting sectors, and so many of the losses have been in small firms in the informal sector that the official figures do not capture at all. The magnitude of

TABLE 11.1. General Data on Garment Industry, 1988–99[a]

	1988	1989	1990	1991	1992	1993	1994	1995	1996	1997	1998	1999	Cumulative Change 1988–99	Cumulative Change 1988–93	Cumulative Change 1994–99
GDP (share over total)	0.86	0.75	0.71	0.70	0.69	0.64	0.61	0.60	0.65	0.70	0.69	0.70	0.68	0.70	0.67
GDP growth (1988 = 100)[b]	100.0	103.6	114.5	120.0	124.2	121.4	124.3	116.6	136.2	147.2	153.9	162.9	4.5	4.0	6.1
GDP growth (1988 = 100), total economy[b]	100.0	104.2	109.5	114.1	118.2	120.5	125.9	118.1	124.2	132.6	139.3	144.5	3.4	3.8	3.7
Employment (share over total)	0.91	0.90	0.91	0.92	0.92	0.96	0.96	0.97	1.15	1.34	1.47	1.64	0.95	0.85	1.03
Employment growth (1988 = 100)[b]	100.0	99.9	100.9	101.5	101.2	105.8	106.1	106.9	126.7	147.8	161.9	180.9	5.5	0.5	11.3
Employment growth (1988 = 100), total economy[b]	100.0	102.9	107.8	111.0	112.8	114.1	117.0	113.6	117.5	121.9	127.3	130.5	3.6	0.8	6.2
Productivity growth (1988 = 100)[b]	100.0	103.7	113.5	118.3	122.7	114.7	117.1	109.1	107.5	99.6	95.0	90.1	-0.9	2.8	-5.1
Productivity growth (1988 = 100), total economy[b]	100.0	101.3	101.5	102.8	104.8	105.6	107.6	104.0	105.7	108.8	109.4	110.7	0.9	1.1	0.6
Real wage growth (1988 = 100)[b]	100.0	101.0	99.5	103.0	107.9	108.1	108.5	88.0	80.5	83.6	85.4	90.2	-0.9	1.6	-3.6
Real wage growth (1988 = 100), total economy[b]	100.0	100.7	101.1	107.0	116.3	123.2	127.5	109.1	103.5	109.8	113.0	116.8	1.4	4.3	-1.7
Exports (share over total)	0.40	0.38	0.34	0.40	0.43	0.45	0.51	0.69	0.85	1.12	1.47	1.45	1.05	0.40	1.16
Export growth (1988 = 100)[b]	100.0	117.7	124.5	141.8	130.0	140.4	180.2	339.2	468.1	571.1	754.1	842.3	21.4	7.0	36.1
Export growth (1988 = 100), total economy[b]	100.0	101.5	106.3	114.2	115.6	124.7	142.1	197.5	233.8	252.7	267.2	290.1	10.2	4.5	15.4
Imports (share over total)	0.61	1.11	1.20	1.23	1.51	1.53	1.11	0.72	0.61	0.76	1.01	0.93	0.94	1.31	0.87
Import growth (1988 = 100)[b]	100.0	219.7	301.9	374.2	577.7	595.1	527.0	250.0	268.9	420.3	599.1	589.7	17.5	42.9	2.3
Import growth (1988 = 100), total economy[b]	100.0	121.3	149.2	181.1	225.0	223.0	269.0	195.8	245.4	311.6	359.2	396.8	13.3	17.4	8.1
Trade balance/GDP	-3.35	-13.60	-17.93	-19.07	-28.05	-27.44	-21.26	-0.99	6.17	5.64	2.30	5.12	-9.4	-18.2	-0.5
Trade balance/GDP, total economy	-0.52	-2.02	-2.62	-4.64	-6.91	-5.76	-6.94	0.04	-0.87	-3.27	-5.88	-5.35	-3.7	-3.7	-3.7

Source: Authors' estimates based on data obtained directly from INEGI (Instituto Nacional de Estadística, Geografía e Informática).

[a]Refers to Branch 27 (Garments) in the Mexican National Accounting System; does not include the maquiladora industry.

[b]The periods 1988–99, 1988–93, and 1994–99 refer to the average annual growth rate.

TABLE 11.2. Mexico: Exports, Imports, and Trade Balance, 1990–2001[a]

	1990	1991	1992	1993	1994	1995	1996	1997	1998	1999	2000	2001	Cumulative Change		
													1990–2001	1990–93	1994–2001
U.S.$ Millions															
Garments[b]															
Exports	78	524	822	999	1,500	2,520	3,557	5,417	6,430	7,563	8,427	7,836	45,674	2,424	43,250
Imports	361	667	1,062	1,124	1,474	1,737	2,309	3,208	3,625	3,517	3,472	3,323	25,878	3,213	22,664
Trade Balance	−282	−142	−240	−126	26	783	1,248	2,209	2,805	4,046	4,955	4,513	19,796	−790	20,586
Total Economy															
Exports	26,838	42,687	46,195	51,832	60,833	79,823	96,000	110,380	117,500	136,703	166,424	158,542	1,093,757	167,552	926,205
Imports	32,802	51,724	64,213	67,548	79,374	72,475	89,469	109,798	125,246	142,063	174,473	168,275	1,177,460	216,287	961,173
Trade Balance	−5,964	−9,037	−18,018	−15,716	−18,541	7,348	6,531	582	−7,746	−5,360	−8,049	−9,733	−83,703	−48,735	−34,968
Percentage (Over Respective Total)															
Garments[b]															
Exports	0.29	1.23	1.78	1.93	2.47	3.16	3.71	4.91	5.47	5.53	5.06	4.94	4.18	1.45	4.67
Imports	1.10	1.29	1.65	1.66	1.86	2.40	2.58	2.92	2.89	2.48	1.99	1.97	2.20	1.49	2.36
Growth Rate (Percent)															
Garments[b]															
Exports	—	569.5	56.7	21.5	50.2	68.0	41.1	52.3	18.7	17.6	11.4	−7.0	52.0	66.4	26.6
Imports	—	84.9	59.3	5.9	31.1	17.9	32.9	39.0	13.0	−3.0	−1.3	−4.3	22.4	25.5	12.3
Total Economy															
Exports	—	59.1	8.2	12.2	17.4	31.2	20.3	15.0	6.5	16.3	21.7	−4.7	17.5	14.1	14.7
Imports	—	57.7	24.1	5.2	17.5	−8.7	23.4	22.7	14.1	13.4	22.8	−3.6	16.0	15.5	11.3

Source: Authors' estimates based on Bancomext (2002).

[a]Includes maquiladora activities.

[b]Refers to chapters 61 (articles of apparel and clothing accessories, knitted or crocheted) and 62 (articles of apparel and clothing accessories, not knitted or crocheted) of the Harmonized Tariff Schedule.

TABLE 11.3. Mexico: Export Structure, 1998–2001[a]

	1998	1999	2000	2001
U.S.$ Millions				
Garments[b]				
Total	6,404	7,554	8,427	7,831
Temporary	6,090	7,318	8,196	7,625
Definitive	313	236	232	206
Total				
Total	117,442	136,703	166,424	158,547
Temporary	97,518	114,814	137,251	131,429
Definitive	19,924	21,889	29,173	27,118
Percentage (Garment Total = 100)				
Garments[b]				
Total	100.00	100.00	100.00	100.00
Temporary	95.11	96.87	97.25	97.37
Definitive	4.89	3.13	2.75	2.63
Percentage (Over Respective Total)				
Garments[b]				
Total	5.45	5.53	5.06	4.94
Temporary	6.25	6.37	5.97	5.80
Definitive	1.57	1.08	0.79	0.76

Source: Authors' estimates based on Bancomext (2002).

[a]Includes maquiladora activities.

[b]Refers to chapters 61 (articles of apparel and clothing accessories, knitted or crocheted) and 62 (articles of apparel and clothing accessories, not knitted or crocheted) of the Harmonized Tariff Schedule.

this effect is suggested by one estimate for 1991–93, when official imports in garments, not including maquiladoras, rose 59 percent; when used and contraband clothing are included, the increase was 175 percent (according to information provided by one firm interviewed for this study). In real terms the value of production in garments increased by only 0.6 percent over the period.

These figures changed dramatically after the devaluation of the peso in December 1994. In 1995 imports of garments, excluding maquiladoras, declined by a startling 53 percent. But a good part of that decline reflects the suppression of Mexican domestic demand and cannot

be sustained over the long run. In fact, in 1997 imports of garments began to rise again—by 56 percent—wiping out over 60 percent of the import decline in the previous two years. The losses in the domestic market to imports are particularly surprising given that Mexico's comparative advantage should lie precisely in these low-wage, labor-intensive industries. Considerable adjustment is to be expected in the face of newly emergent foreign competitors. It is not clear, however, why that adjustment should involve a loss of the domestic market. In principle, if Mexico can be competitive on the international front, it should be able to compete on the domestic front at least as well.

This chapter reports the findings of a study designed to explore why comparable competition on the international and domestic fronts has not been the case in Mexico. The findings are based on material gathered in the period from 1994 to 1996 as part of a larger project still continuing on the adjustment of Mexican firms to the opening of the economy to trade. While the focus here is on the clothing industry, the study on which it draws is focused on traditional industries more broadly, and material from shoes, furniture, and ceramics supplements that drawn directly from the clothing industry in developing the argument.

The findings moreover have potential implications extending beyond these industries to the Mexican manufacturing sector as a whole. The dichotomy we observe in the garment industry between the larger, more capital-intensive firms that are prospering under the new trading regime and the smaller, more labor-intensive firms that are not replicates a pattern reflected in the broader aggregates for Mexican manufacturing. Indeed, the most successful Mexican industries in recent years have not been those where one would have expected the country's comparative advantage to lie but rather capital- and skill-intensive industries associated with relatively advanced technologies

TABLE 11.4. Maquiladora Exports of Garments in Mexico, 1990–2001[a]

	1990	1991	1992	1993	1994	1995	1996	1997	1998	1999	2000	2001	Cumulative Change		
													1990–2001	1990–93	1994–2001
Garments															
Firms	290	350	393	399	412	522	650	786	907	1035	1119	958	7,821	1,432	6,389
Employment	42,677	48,759	57,972	65,973	82,513	107,015	147,196	183,241	219,079	262,994	286,584	234,800	1,738,803	215,381	1,523,422
Total															
Firms	1,789	2,013	2,129	2,143	2,064	2,267	2,553	2,867	3,130	3,436	3,703	3,450	31,544	8,074	23,470
Employment	439,474	486,146	510,035	546,588	600,585	681,251	799,347	936,825	1,043,483	1,195,371	1,307,982	1,081,526	9,628,613	1,982,243	7,646,370
Percentage Over Respective Total															
Garments															
Firms	16.21	17.39	18.46	18.62	19.96	23.03	25.46	27.42	28.98	30.12	30.22	27.77	24.79	17.74	27.22
Employment	9.71	10.03	11.37	12.07	13.74	15.71	18.41	19.56	20.99	22.00	21.91	21.71	18.06	10.87	19.92
Growth Rate (Percent)															
Garments															
Firms	—	20.7	12.3	1.5	3.3	26.7	24.5	20.9	15.4	14.1	8.1	−14.4	11.5	11.2	12.8
Employment	—	14.3	18.9	13.8	25.1	29.7	37.5	24.5	19.6	20.0	9.0	−18.1	16.8	15.6	16.1
Total															
Firms	—	12.5	5.8	0.7	−3.7	9.8	12.6	12.3	9.2	9.8	7.8	−6.8	6.2	6.2	7.6
Employment	—	10.6	4.9	7.2	9.9	13.4	17.3	17.2	11.4	14.6	9.4	−17.3	8.5	7.5	8.8

Source: Authors' estimates based on INEGI: <http://www.inegi.gob.mx>.

[a]Includes maquiladora activities.

such as automobiles and electronics. Exports are furthermore concentrated in a relatively few large firms. Illustrative of this pattern, for 1993–99 the principal three hundred exporting firms and maquiladoras were responsible, on average, for 93 percent of Mexican exports.[1]

The pattern creates two fundamental problems, one of macroeconomic management and the other of social cohesion. The problem of macroeconomic management results from the fact that as the country loses its domestic market, the propensity to import increases as a result of growth in the gross domestic product (GDP); expansion produces a growing deficit in the country's balance of trade that must be sustained by an inflow of foreign capital. This makes the country highly vulnerable to the threat of capital flight and periodic foreign-exchange crises of the kind that erupted most recently and dramatically in December 1994. These crises are managed by severe cutbacks in domestic demand and rising unemployment that, in turn, threaten social coherence.

The changing structure of industry also has a direct effect through its impact on opportunities for social mobility. This is particularly true in clothing. The traditional garment industry is a cascade of operations, each of which can be, and in practice is at one time or another, separated off and subcontracted, creating almost a continuum of firms arranged in a hierarchy of skill, power, and profitability. At the bottom of that hierarchy are firms that do simple sewing on the cheapest garments, often as home workers. Toward the top are a range of firms that actually design the garments and cut the material into pieces that are subcontracted for sewing, again arranged in a hierarchy of price and quality. At the peak are firms that wholesale and retail the garments, often in combination with design. In the United States the latter tend to be large companies of the kind that are now entering into maquiladora production in Mexico, but in Mexico, as in France and Italy, many small producers own, or at least owned, a couple of retail outlets. When all the elements of the structure exist in close geographic proximity, it is possible to start at the bottom as an unskilled home worker sewing cheap garments and work one's way up the hierarchy, gradually acquiring more skills and business sense and contacts with progressively higher levels on the chain. In our interviews in Mexico City we encountered several family firms that were the products of this process: The proprietors had begun their working lives helping their mothers with piecework at home.

The new kinds of subcontracting relationships between Mexican producers and foreign buyers typically cut off the chain of subcontracting in Mexico at both ends: The span of control along the subcontracting chain is considered too long for the quality and reliability they are seeking, and they limit production to the Mexican partners' own facilities. At the same time, they absorb the design and marketing links of the chain. The result is to create a sharp divide between workers and contractors that can be bridged only by people with accumulations of capital and industrial expertise that a typical worker could never hope to acquire on the job. As Mexican firms lose design and marketing capability they also become increasingly dependent on foreign partners, and in that sense mobility, even for those with capital and expertise, is limited as well.

Methodology

The study is organized around the concept of a commodity chain (Gereffi 1994), or, as it is called by other authors, a production chain or supply chain (Fine and Whitney 1996). A commodity chain consists of a series of linkages stretching from raw-materials production at one end through manufacture and assembly to wholesale and retail distribution at the other end, and it generally encompasses important segments of a limited number of interdependent industries. The process of industrial transformation can be understood in terms of the relationships along these chains. On any particular chain certain points constitute leadership positions, and organizations that occupy these positions formulate strategy and drive the transformation process. Leadership, however, varies over time and across industries. In automobiles, manufacturing has historically driven transformation. In recent years retailers have driven transformation in the traditional industries that are the focus of this study (Gereffi 1994). In this study we sought to map out the chains and the transformation process through open-ended interviews with key actors.

Because of their strategic importance in the garment industry, we began interviewing retail managers, particularly managers in the discount retail chains that have proliferated in Mexico at the turn of the twentieth century. We focused in these interviews on their experience with local sourcing. The discount chains are linked directly or indirectly to foreign companies that purchase in bulk throughout the world. They thus constitute superhighways for the entrance of foreign merchandise into the Mexican economy, but they could as well serve as export channels for Mexican goods going abroad. We then moved to interview American companies buying from Mexican producers; a range of the Mexican producers, including companies producing for exports as maquiladoras and on their own account as well as companies focused exclusively on the domestic market; government agencies and nongovernmental organizations (NGOs) concerned with the promotion of the Mexican garment industry; and various other individuals and firms offering ancillary services to the industry.

The sample is in no sense random. Respondents were selected because of the strategic importance of the place they occupied along the supply chain. Where possible, we used personal contacts to obtain access. Although, as it turned out, that access was obtained in over half the cases through cold calls, respondents clearly agreed to talk to us in many cases because of our credentials and the belief that we had useful contacts with government officials or with potential customers. The closest our study came to a generally random selection process was in Mexico City, where we selected the tallest building in the garment district, took the elevator to the top floor, and systematically went from shop to shop seeking interviews. The reception there was mixed, ranging from a three-hour interview in one shop to a three-minute exchange in another. We offered all our respondents confidentiality and anonymity; few, however, seemed to put much credence in that offer.

Overall, in the period from 1994 to 1996, we interviewed managers in three discount retail chains that had recently opened in Mexico; three U.S. companies actively engaged in upgrading Mexican partners; nineteen Mexican clothing producers, five of which were operating as maquiladoras and two that designed for and sold directly to the international market; and one international consulting firm engaged in training personnel for "greenfield" sites (i.e., investments in new plants, machinery, and equipment) in Mexico. In addition, we spent two days at a fair in Cancún organized by Bancomext (Banco Nacional de Comercio Exterior) to introduce U.S. buyers to Mexican garment producers. A total of thirty U.S. companies and thirteen Mexican producers attended this event. We talked with most of them informally and, in addition, observed one-on-one meetings between buyers and potential suppliers in which the former evaluated the latter's collections. We also met with groups of local producers in Puebla and Aguascalientes, which were essentially group interviews. We met with leaders of the industry associations and state economic-development officials in both Puebla and Aguascalientes, with federal officials in Mexico City, and with two NGOs working on upgrading small garment producers in different parts of the country. We also conducted, as explained below, a separate study of *empresas integradoras*. Material on garments is supplemented with material collected separately from other traditional industries.

Principal Findings

All the traditional industries, but especially clothing, are sensitive to fashion. This gives Mexico the particular advantage, relative to other low-wage developing countries, of proximity to the U.S. market. The advantage is even greater when producers are using U.S. materials that must be shipped into Mexico before the finished goods can be shipped out. (This advantage should be even greater still in the domestic market.) The magnitude of that advantage is suggested by one brand-name retailer who reported that shipment from Mexico to its Texas warehouse took four days, compared to thirty days from Korea. Another brand-name retailer, a U.S. shoe company, estimated total time to market, from initial order to receipt of the finished goods, at seven to eleven weeks in Mexico compared to fourteen to fifteen weeks in Hungary or Italy, eighteen in Portugal, and twenty-three to twenty-five weeks in Brazil, China, or Indonesia.

Against this advantage, the discount retail chains and American companies purchasing in Mexico all identified a common set of obstacles to sourcing in Mexico. Mexican producers were unable to meet quality standards; they could not produce in sufficient volume; their production cycle (or turnaround time) was too long; and they failed to meet promised delivery schedules. These were all viewed as production problems, the legacy of the sheltered markets in which Mexican producers have traditionally operated. They are distinct from the inexperience of Mexican companies with the commercial practices and procedures involved in selling internationally, which have been a problem for Mexican companies seeking to export for the first time. The American firms we interviewed were all prepared to handle the commercial problems for their Mexican suppliers, and commercialization was obviously not a problem in dealing with discount retail chains in Mexico itself. Therefore the central question to emerge from the interviews is: Why haven't Mexican producers been able to learn how to meet international production standards? Or, since some Mexican producers can meet these standards, how might Mexican producers be induced to learn faster or in larger numbers?

The Nature of the Learning Process

An answer to this question is suggested by the experience of American companies that have tried, with varying degrees of success, to develop Mexican sources. We interviewed several companies about this process. The companies were selected in an opportunistic fashion and not on the basis of a systematic survey. But we believe that companies actively engaged in upgrading their suppliers in Mexico are relatively unusual. Mexican firms do not typically engage in the practice of upgrading their suppliers themselves.

The impact of maquiladoras on the rest of the Mexican economy has been extremely limited.[2] The most extensively studied have been the automobile assembly plants (see, for example, Shaiken and Herzenberg 1987; Robinson 1988). The plants of U.S. companies import virtually all the parts that they use. Japanese companies have encouraged their home suppliers to locate around them in Mexico; these suppliers have not developed a second tier of Mexican contractors. Recently, as the cost of production in Japan has increased, a special effort has been made to increase sourcing in Mexico, but it has consisted almost exclusively of enhanced efforts to identify *qualified* Mexican producers, not to upgrade them. Information on other industries is more limited but is consistent with the automobile findings: Neither foreign firms operating in Mexico nor Mexican firms themselves have been particularly active in upgrading their supplier networks. In this sense the discount retail chains are typical.

The companies we interviewed, which did make efforts to upgrade Mexican contractors, all managed brand names and all sourced worldwide, purchasing in the United States and in a number of different developing countries. They made it clear that in Mexico, as in most countries in the world, few producers can meet their standards initially. They thus made a substantial effort to develop new sources. In Mexico this typically involves, first, comparative shopping in Mexico itself to find producers whose products meet some minimum standards of quality at the outset. The U.S. company then visits the producer and interviews the management to see whether the company has interest in and is capable of upgrading its quality and producing in the volumes and time constraints that American purchasers typically require. This is a two-stage process that begins with an initial half-day visit. It is then followed by a whole-day evaluation that serves as a diagnostic tool as well as the basis for a business decision.

If the parties agree to go forward, the American partner then undertakes to teach the Mexican company how to meet its standards. This involves a series of exchanges in which Mexican personnel are virtually tutored by their American counterparts—sometimes in the Mexican plants, sometimes at the facilities of the American customer in the United States, often in both places. One large shoe company, for example, when it began sourcing in Mexico, opened an office in Mexico City and has two engineers working out of that office permanently assigned to each sourcing plant. A large clothing retailer reported that it takes at least one and often one and a half years from the time it starts working with a potential Mexican partner to the time it receives its first order. To illustrate this, one retailer reviewed a typical case: The process began with several preliminary visits of its personnel to Mexico and of the potential partner to company headquarters in the United States. Once upgrading was begun in earnest, the process involved six trips of a three-person U.S. team to Mexico and eight visits of a similar team of Mexicans to the United States, then heavy involvement of U.S. personnel in the initial production runs in Mexico.

The learning process here involves what is known in the literature variously as practical, implicit, or tacit knowledge. Its essential characteristic is that it is difficult to transmit verbally or in written instructions and instead it is taught by demonstration on the job as production is carried out. The U.S. garment firm, for example, in a process reminiscent of what in England is called "sitting by Nellie," has its own people work side by side with the inspectors and watch what they are doing, picking up the faults that the new inspectors miss and pointing out to them, case by case, what is wrong with the garment.

Historically, managerial theory and advanced management practice have paid little attention to knowledge of this kind. For American manufacturing in particular, a sharp distinction was made between formal and informal engineering, and management looked only to the former for improvement. But since the mid-1980s, under the pressure of heightened competition, particularly from Japan, the priority accorded to formal knowledge has been abandoned. A number of the techniques borrowed from the Japanese or developed in response to the pressures of Japanese competition, such as total quality control and the *kanban* system of on-time delivery,[3] are essentially ways of deliberately managing tacit knowledge, making it explicit, subjecting it to debate and discussion, and forcing progressive improvements in production processes (Nonaka 1995). Part of what Mexican firms are required to do is thus not so much to learn a standard set of practices as to catch up with a managerial revolution that has been occurring in industrialized countries only recently and even there is far from complete.

In other ways this new emphasis on tacit knowledge is a competitive advantage for Mexico. It places an enormous premium on experience in the industry. It values the knowledge that comes out of growing up within an industry. As a result the existing skill within the traditional industries of Mexico constitutes a considerable human capital. That skill is, however, an asset specific to the industries in which it resides; it will be lost if those industries fail to make the transition and the resources are dispersed elsewhere in the economy. Moreover, to make the transition and become competitive in world markets, this existing capital needs to be combined with modern managerial techniques. Finally, the process of introducing those techniques clearly involves a substantial commitment on the part of both the Mexican suppliers and their U.S. customers; it takes resources and its takes time to upgrade Mexican facilities. The latter seems to range from a year to a year and a half.

Because it takes time and resources, the process of upgrading is clearly an investment. But the investment is basically one of skill

transfer of a particular kind. The transfer must be made directly from the foreign client to the Mexican contractor. Once transferred, the skills are embedded in the ongoing practices of the organization; they reside in the contractor, and if the contractor walks away from the relationship, he or she takes the skills along. Unlike plant and equipment expenditures, there is no physical asset that can be used to secure the investment and reprocessed if the contractor reneges on any agreed-upon payments. To the extent that the skills are particular to a given client and of no use in other contracting relationships, there is little reason for the contractor to walk away. But most of the skills are quite general; there is inevitably a specific component, but typically the skills increase the capacity of the contractor to produce quality goods efficiently for any client or, for that matter, for sale directly on the market. Thus the Mexican firm, once upgraded by its foreign client, has every incentive to jump ship and sell its newly acquired skills to the highest bidder.

We encountered two cases in our interviews where the Mexican partner had apparently done this. One blue jeans contractor had been trained by an American company with whom he initially had an exclusive agreement, but when we interviewed him, he had abandoned that relationship to work for a number of different U.S. companies and was about to launch his own brand. In the second case a U.S. shoe company reported that it had acquired one of its Mexican contractors by persuading the firm to leave the company originally responsible for upgrading its facility. In several other plants we visited the company was obviously thinking about taking off on its own. Why, then, would clients ever make investments in upgrading contractors in Mexico?

One possible answer is that the contractor repays the client-tutor by charging prices below the market value for the goods that it provides during the learning period. This is not generally true. In the cases we studied, no merchandise was exchanged until *after* the contractor had learned how to produce to the client's standards. But it is possible that some upgrading arrangements are financed in this way. The transactions here are so complex, however, that it is possible that they are secured in other ways. The upgrading is not necessarily limited to tutelage. The Mexican partner is sometimes required to make complementary investments in plant and equipment. In several cases the American customers required their contractors to set up physically separate facilities for the export portion of the business in order to segregate exports from the overhead associated with commercialization of manufacturing production in Mexico itself. The partnership generally includes access to material supplies at favorable credit terms and often to credit itself, which is a considerable advantage to Mexican producers given the high interest rates and general shortage of capital that have accompanied the opening of the Mexican economy. Indeed, at real interest rates ranging as high as 30 percent, this backdoor access to the U.S. short-term credit market may be the most valuable part of the relationship for the Mexican partner and the biggest deterrent to jumping ship.

If arrangements of these kinds were able to solve the investment problem, one would expect tutelage to be widespread, whereas it appears, as noted above, to be extremely limited. Whatever forms of security can be worked out in these ways, they are evidently not enough to diffuse the tutelage arrangements broadly. What is it about the companies we encountered that enabled them to overcome the problems that seem to deter other firms?

We offer several conjectures on this score.[4] The most plausible is linked to the characteristic that appears to distinguish these companies from others engaged in outsourcing in Mexico. The American companies we interviewed are all brand-name producers with a worldwide sourcing strategy. Brand identification enables them to sell their product at premium prices and thus generates an economic rent. That rent can be shared with contractors in the form of favorable fees, thereby binding the contractors long enough to enable the company that provides training to earn a return on its investment. A global sourcing strategy generates further returns. In these strategies Mexican sourcing serves to diversify risk. In addition, the short turnaround time relative to other foreign locations enables the U.S. company to balance its product line by including a high-fashion component that attracts customers who then purchase other parts of the collection. Without a nearby supplier the turnaround time would be too long to keep up with the market. These returns are also a kind of economic rent that can be shared to bind the contractors to the tutoring company.[5]

The second conjecture rests on the fact that the knowledge about how to upgrade producers in low-wage economies is a relatively recent innovation. The companies we interviewed in Mexico were all pioneers in global sourcing. Their strategy in this regard is new, developed over the last ten to fifteen years to take advantage of the low wages prevailing in developing nations in order to service the markets of advanced industrial countries without becoming hostage to the political and commercial risks of the extended supply chains this entails. Other companies sourcing in Mexico, to say nothing of Mexican companies that buy from local contractors, simply may not have the skills required to upgrade their supply networks, and the skills may not be generally available on the market. This, rather than the difficulties of securing the investment, may explain why particular companies and not others are engaged in upgrading contracting networks.

Still another possible explanation is that what those companies offer to their suppliers is not a single set of techniques but rather continuous access to state-of-the-art manufacturing production as it evolves over time. Again, their global sourcing strategy should put them in a unique position to do this. It enables them systematically to benchmark and compare practices across a wide variety of producers, to orchestrate a competition among them, to select the best practices, and to diffuse these rapidly across their contracting network. Such techniques for the management of supply networks are part of the repertoire of techniques for the management of tacit knowledge that have developed toward the end of the twentieth century and that are now widely applied in advanced industrial countries. But they are not universal even in the United States and Western Europe, let alone in relationships that span borders and countries at very different levels of economic development. Some of the practitioners of these new techniques encourage their contractors to work with several clients, even competitors, thereby stretching the contractors' capacities and generating a wider range of approaches to feed into the fund of alternatives that the mother company is able systematically to compare in order to generate continual improvements over time. Thus the approach does not necessarily require Mexican contractors to work exclusively for the clients who initially upgraded their facilities, and one of those clients whom we interviewed confirmed that it did not seek exclusive relationships.

If this is what is going on in the companies upgrading Mexican facilities, however, the capacity of a Mexican firm to compete internationally once it does jump ship must deteriorate progressively over time unless it manages quickly to hook up with a new foreign partner. The practices observed in the one contractor that had become cut off from his original American partner suggested that this might be the case. This is also suggested by the fact that the American partners whom we interviewed continue to station their own personnel in the Mexican partners' facilities even after the initial training period and regularly send additional personnel for random quality inspections at the production site.

Minimum Order Size

In principle the problem of quality and efficiency within productive establishments can be separated from the issue of minimum order size, which many clients and particularly the large discount retail chains cited as reasons why they did not source locally. To solve the second problem, many of our respondents suggested association arrangements in which a number of producers pooled their resources to take on a large order.

The government has recently created a new institutional structure, *empresa integradora*, designed to house such arrangements and facilitate their development. This seems a promising approach to the problem of minimum order size, but this organizational form has been slow to take off, and few such *integradoras* actually exist in Mexican manufacturing. To find out why, we conducted an in-depth study of twelve *empresas integradoras* in Cuernavaca, Puebla, Jalisco, Mexico City, and Tijuana. Regional cultural factors, the education and training of the entrepreneur, and the availability of financial resources were all found to be critical to *integradora* success. Established cooperative relationships between manufacturers and the decentralized division of labor among manufacturers also appeared to facilitate success. One *integradora* grew out of an association that for years had worked together at trade fairs and bought fabric together. The division of labor among manufacturers involving marketing, inspection, and other tasks serves to decentralize authority and to enhance trust among members of the *integradora*.

Although some small producers have formed *empresas integradoras*, these efforts have faced many obstacles and relatively few such associations exist in Mexico. Among the most important challenges faced by *integradoras* are building a culture of trust, gaining access to credit, and overcoming bureaucratic barriers. Many small producers are reluctant to enter into such associations and generally share little information about their sources of fabric and other production issues. Accountability is also an important issue. A particularly dramatic example of this problem was one large *integradora* outside Puebla. As one home-based manufacturer explained, each producer paid the salary of a coordinator who later ran off with all the money.

Empresas integradoras also encounter difficulty in gaining access to credit and find bureaucratic obstacles when they seek to export. Like other garment manufacturers, *integradoras* face extraordinary interest rates and payment cycles that lag behind loan schedules. The *integradoras* often compound rather than simplify credit problems because of the reluctance of financial institutions to lend to such associations. As one manufacturer explained, "There were complications in lending to five long-standing businesses. Someone would have to put up their house and become the leader, which we didn't want." Finally, *integradoras* have experienced delays in getting export authorization because of the lack of coordination of government programs.

In the garment industry, however, the focus on the limits of the government's *integradora* program may be misplaced. It is after all standard practice, not only in Mexico but throughout the world, for a "jobber" to meet large orders through a network of subcontractors. The jobber is, in other words, already functioning as a kind of *integradora*. Thus the jobber could upgrade its suppliers in the same way that some foreign retailers work with larger suppliers. If it is possible to upgrade these jobbers' networks and maintain standards within them, it may not be necessary to develop new contracting institutions. In this sense any set of policies that manages to diffuse the tutelage arrangements that exist between foreign clients and Mexican contractors would also resolve the problem of minimum order size.

Consultants

This leads to the question of why Mexican garment firms have been so reliant on these foreign partnerships at all. Why can they not hire consultants to help upgrade themselves? Indeed, not all foreign firms rely on their own personnel to develop production facilities or contractors abroad; a number use consulting services. We identified and interviewed one such firm in the garment industry. Among its other services it offered training in both production and management for shops in the developing world seeking to export. The firm will staff and train the personnel of a new production facility from scratch. Its program for doing so has strong parallels to the in-house programs we encountered. It first hires a cadre of managers. In Mexico, interestingly, it draws for this purpose primarily on people who started but, often for financial reasons, were unable to finish a technical education. The consulting firm uses its own personnel to train the managers in production techniques and then hires the production workers for the new facilities. The managerial candidates under the supervision of the consultant's personnel then train the production workers. At the same time the managers in the new facility receive special functional training, including a classroom component. All production training is on-the-job, using a variant of the tutelage we described earlier. Our respondent estimated the total time needed to launch a new factory in Mexico at six months to one year, which is somewhat shorter than the in-house programs discussed above. Although the source of the discrepancy is not clear, the standards of efficiency and quality may not be identical; the type of product may also vary. Most of our respondent's clients seem to be multinational companies in the United States producing relatively standardized products with limited fashion content, but they claimed to offer the same services to Mexican producers for any type of clothing. We did not, however, find Mexican firms using this type of service.

We were more successful in the furniture industry, where we found an association of firms in Ciudad Hidalgo, a relatively remote city in Michoacán that had hired a consultant to help upgrade the quality and efficiency of their operations. We visited the city some time after the consultant, who had provided extensive advice on how to upgrade the quality of the product line and the efficiency of the production facilities, and we interviewed in-shop the proprietors of several of the enterprises about what they had learned. It was clear in these interviews that the people in these shops had changed their practices at the consultant's behest, but they had essentially learned the new practices by rote. They had no idea of the underlying principles from which the consultant was working. This, in turn, reflected the fact that they had never seen the kinds of products with which they were competing in the international marketplace, which the consultant was using as a template to improve their own. Nor had they seen the foreign shops whose practices the consultant was trying to get them to adopt. Thus one shop has redesigned the work flow on the consultant's advice, but aisles were clogged with work in progress that completely undermined the rationale for the streamlined plant layout it had introduced. In another shop, the proprietor showed us how the consultant had suggested

they turn the knots on the wood to the interior of the cabinet to improve the outside finish, but he then indifferently forced the lock and bent the key on his model piece when he opened it up so that we could feel the knots on the inside pieces of wood.

These experiences with the consultant in the furniture industry led us to believe that a key ingredient in upgrading partnerships in the garment industry is the visit of Mexican personnel to the partners' facilities in the United States that *precedes* the visits of the partners' personnel to the Mexican facilities. It seemed that the consultant would have been much more successful if he had first put his clients on a plane and flown them to the United States, or even to Mexico City, to see and discuss the products with which they were competing and to visit production facilities on which his advice was modeled. Indeed, he might then have been able to teach his clients not only how to do what the foreigners were doing but how actually to think through and critique their own practices themselves. This approach might be attractive not simply for the traditional firms that have been left out of the export boom but even for Mexican producers that have found foreign partners. This would be especially true if, as some of our conjectures about the tutelage process suggest, what Mexican producers are getting from their foreign partners is simply the most up-to-date production practices, not the skills of their foreign partners that the economy really needs to survive in international competition on its own—that is, the capacity for continuous improvement in practice over time and to assume the tutelary role vis-à-vis their own subcontractors.

The other factor that is involved in the dependence on foreign partners for learning, as opposed to hired consultants, is credit. The difficulties of securing investment in tacit knowledge that limit the willingness of foreign partners to invest in upgrading Mexican facilities also make it difficult for the Mexicans to obtain capital to invest in themselves. This problem has been greatly aggravated by the general shortage of working capital and the extremely high interest rates that have accompanied the opening to trade, even before the peso crisis in December 1994 and much more so afterward. At the same time the credit crisis increases the advantages of a foreign partner enormously, if you can find one, because one then has access to the partner's suppliers in the United States on favorable credit terms. Indeed, several of our interview respondents suggested that they could obtain working capital through foreign partnerships on relatively favorable terms at times when such capital would not be available on any terms in Mexico. The extreme example of what the capital shortage was doing was one small producer who was reduced to buying just enough material in the morning so that he could produce a day's output, sell it in the evening, and have enough money to buy material for another day's production. Such practices foreclose economies of scale in purchasing and production altogether.

In principle, these credit problems call for an "investment subsidy" or a specialized loan program. But such a program would not be easy to administer, especially in Mexico. Applicants would have to be screened for eligibility and then monitored afterward. The general scarcity of credit promotes a strong incentive to divert funds to other purposes, and without collateral it is difficult to penalize such diversions. The difficulties here are compounded by the nature of small firms in the garment industry and the Mexican banking system. The garment industry is populated by family firms in which the household and business accounts are often intermingled and confused. It requires a strong local banking system with roots in the community to distinguish the viable firms and judge the integrity of the enterprise. But the Mexican banking system has passed through a process of nationalization and reprivatization that has left the industry centralized in Mexico City, without locally oriented branches.

Bootstrapping

Given what an investment subsidy designed to diffuse foreign practices appears to entail, it is worth considering a much more broadly conceived policy to actually develop the requisite capacities within the Mexican economy, without foreign intermediaries, by what one analyst has termed "bootstrapping" (Sabel 1995). Could a developing country such as Mexico actually discover or invent world-class management practices for itself? The reason to think it might be able to do so is that development of the skills at stake here has not historically taken place through tutelage arrangements. Rather, these skills emerged first in the efforts of the Japanese economy to catch up with the West in the aftermath of the Second World War. Japan entered the postwar period with a reputation for cheap, second-rate manufactured goods, not unlike that of Mexico's traditional industries today. It managed in the 1950s to set a course of development that by the 1970s had made it preeminent in the efficient production of high-quality mass-produced goods, rapidly gaining share in the home markets of its erstwhile competitors in the United States and Western Europe. In the 1980s these Western competitors then sought to meet the Japanese challenge by appropriating the techniques the Japanese had invented in order to catch up and use them to recapture their original lead. In both episodes of competitive transformation, foreign practices played an important role, but in neither case was the process essentially one of direct transfer of foreign practice.

The latest round of transformation in the United States and Western Europe has had three key ingredients. First, companies developed a set of standards and benchmarks to identify concretely where their performance was deficient. Second, they sought to identify the precise institutions and practices that differentiated the benchmark procedures and practices from their own. In the attempt to do so, they occasionally went as far as to establish joint ventures with Japanese partners in order to get firsthand exposure to their ways of doing business. But they did not ever slavishly imitate the Japanese. Instead, and this is the third of the key ingredients, they initiated a series of internal debates and discussions about what the critical elements of Japanese practices were, whether these could be adopted whole, and, if not, how they might be altered to fit into their own organizational practices. When it was not possible to identify precise procedures used elsewhere, they nevertheless sought to invent approaches that might produce the desired result. The new practices and procedures that constituted the revolution in Western management in the 1980s were not those actually borrowed from Japan but the practices and procedures invented to facilitate the borrowing, namely, discussion and debate structured by a set of benchmarks and standards on the one hand and a set of alternative institutions and practices on the other. These are what constitute the new techniques for managing tacit knowledge. They are basically the techniques foreign retailers are applying to develop and maintain the global sourcing networks that their Mexican partners are being drawn into.

U.S. manufacturers in the 1980s generally sought to catch up with their Japanese competitors as rapidly as possible, in a single spate of institutional reform. It was only relatively recently, after they had bridged the initial gap, that they began to think in terms of continuous improvement, using the same procedures and benchmarks or, when they are already in the vanguard, standards and targets to stay

ahead of the game. By contrast, the Japanese in the postwar period had recognized that they could not catch up in one sudden transformation and sought instead to raise their performance gradually over time. For these purposes it is important not simply to have not simply a single standard or set of benchmarks but rather to think in terms of a hierarchy of standards that the practice can ascend gradually over time. This hierarchy of standards needs to be matched to a typology that divides the market into segments that the firm can move across as its standards rise. Mexico's position in international competition is closer to Japan's in the 1950s than to that of the United States and Western Europe in the 1970s, and this idea of a hierarchy of standards and markets would seem an important addendum to the North American approach. A number of people with whom we talked were already thinking in these terms: A Japanese government official working to increase the backward linkages of the Japanese automobile assembly plants used a three-tier system to rate potential Mexican suppliers; U.S. companies looking for contractors in Mexico use a similar system. But in such a system, it does not appear that a policy designed to stimulate a bootstrapping process would be much more difficult to initiate than one more narrowly focused on investment subsidies.

International Matchmaking: An Illustration

The limits of government policy are illustrated by one particular program we were invited to examine closely, a program managed by Mexico's Foreign Trade Bank (Bancomext) in partnership with the Ministry of Commerce (Secretaría de Comercio y Fomento Industrial, or SECOFI) to link Mexican producers with outside clients. The program was conceived as a matchmaking operation, in which buyers from major U.S. and European department stores were invited to Mexico to meet with potential suppliers. This program was run for several different industries. In the garment industry, the first meeting was held in 1994. The Mexican producers brought samples of their merchandise, and the buyers set up booths where they met with the producers individually to examine and criticize their products. Enormous effort was put into the organization of the meetings; the then secretary of commerce, who was also the chief Mexican negotiator for NAFTA, actually called the chief executive officers in the United States to urge them to send representatives. But virtually no effort was put into evaluation and follow-up. No one really knows whether Mexican companies managed to obtain any business from this exercise and, if not, why they failed to do so. It is completely unclear whether the meetings were a successful policy initiative and, if not, what precisely could be modified to make them more successful.

The program was nonetheless administered again, in October 1995, in essentially the same way in which it was administered in 1994. This time, however, there was considerably more discussion and evaluation of the results. Several of the conclusions that emerged are worth emphasizing, partly to illustrate what was lost by failing to reflect on the experience the first time around but also because they feed into the specific policy recommendation we are about to put forward. The first conclusion is that the large U.S. chains that were the focus of the first two meetings are the wrong targets. Their standards of quality and minimum order sizes are too far out of reach of the bulk of Mexican producers. The Mexican industry can do better by targeting buyers from other Latin American countries, whose levels of income and taste are closer to its own, and smaller (but somewhat obscure) retail chains in

the U.S. that order in lesser quantities. The second conclusion is that the promotion of Mexican products should focus on areas with a distinct national style, such as Mexican handicraft styles or formal garments for children (baptismal and communion dresses, for example). The third conclusion is that the kind of Mexican producers most likely to benefit from programs of this kind are unable to meet the new orders without access to working capital and hence that, to be effective, these matchmaking operations need to be supplemented by programs providing short-term credit to small enterprises. Bancomext developed a pilot credit program for a group of producers that obtained orders at the 1995 meetings from a Colombian department store.

The Bancomext example suggests that the first step toward an effective policy is a new approach to thinking about policy itself. In a sense, what is required is to introduce into the management of government programs those techniques for managing and systematically upgrading practical knowledge that have emerged in manufacturing production. But a prior task is to create a wider space for a principled approach to industrial policy, to articulate a philosophy of government that, while more active and interventionist than the framework that currently dominates government thinking, cannot be reduced to traditional clientelistic actions.

Toward a New Philosophy of Industrial Policy

Our examination of the problems of the clothing industry suggests that a principled approach to industrial policy might be built around three basic suppositions. The first of these would preserve the basic insight of neoliberal thought by recognizing that the market is a powerful instrument both for motivating economic activity and for coordinating and directing the allocation of scarce resources, and that economic science provides a way for understanding how the market works toward these ends. Second, it must be recognized that, whatever the ideological attractions of a market economy, the scientific case for its effectiveness in no way precludes the interventions of the Mexican state. This is because the unregulated operation of the market leads to a particular distribution of income and power in the society that is not inherently just or necessarily compatible with long-term social and political stability. This important caveat to the neoliberal argument for market-oriented economic policies must be distinguished from the third point: A separate and distinct rationale for state action lies in the considerable difficulty in fully understanding how a market economy operates (in theory, let alone in practice).

What we do understand implies that an effective market economy must be supported by a set of supplementary institutions and that even when those institutions are in place there can be significant instances of market failure, as appears to be the case, for example, in the transfer of practical knowledge that we have been examining. These principles suggest an approach to policy that is guided by the market and instructed by developments in the private sector without being completely dependent on the market to produce desirable results or necessarily acquiescing to market developments. They imply as well that, in public policy no less than in the production and commercialization of goods and services, constant discussion and reevaluation of practice must supplement theoretical economic knowledge.

Toward an Alternative Policy

What might an alternative policy look like? First, it should be conceived as an effort to extend the process of adjustment already taking place in the private sector. Second, it must build on mechanisms for evaluation and learning as well as pressures and processes designed to produce continual improvement over time. Third, it should build on the experience of and borrow mechanisms developed for this purpose since the mid-1980s in the laggard sectors of advanced industrial countries that have been trying to catch up with their competitors in the international marketplace.

These general principles, when applied to a policy designed to bootstrap traditional industries in Mexico, suggest an approach that focuses less on specific sets of government policy initiatives and more on the role of government in catalyzing discussion and debate. The basic goal, in other words, is to develop a heightened public awareness of the need to upgrade the productive apparatus and commercial practices throughout Mexican society. More than any particular policy measure, the idea is to orchestrate a national discourse; to draw as many people as possible from a broad spectrum of the society—from the worker on the plant floor to the politician in the legislature—into the enterprise of making Mexico more competitive at home and in the international marketplace; to generate a critical perspective on productive and commercial practices in the business and political community. The aim should be to focus discussion and debate as much as possible on practice and away from ideology and abstraction. Models of how to do this include the case method used in business and legal education, grand rounds in medical education, and the design studio in art and architecture, in which students are assigned a particular problem and their solutions are then criticized by a jury of faculty. A particular example of how this might be done, one that might serve to initiate the process, is to invite state development agencies to a seminar in which each agency presents for discussion and debate two case studies, one of a major development success and one of a development failure. Industry chambers, particularly in traditional industries, could be encouraged to sponsor similar seminars in which each local chamber is asked to work up and present one case of a rapidly developing enterprise (or contracting network) and one case of a declining enterprise or network.

As part of the effort to focus and direct the debate, the government should encourage the development of standards and benchmarks. These provide both a target for policy and the criteria for judging its success. The federal government might do this by requiring that any project it funds build in a set of standards to serve as a threshold for admission to the project, as well as a second set of standards that serve both as a program target and a set of criteria for evaluating the outcome. The standards might in principle focus on outcomes—for example, delivery time, quality, efficiency, and the like. But standards should also focus on processes, such as inspection, inventory control, quality control, quality circles, and so on.

The process of generating these standards, the debate about what appropriate standards and benchmarks are, is at least as important as the standards and benchmarks themselves. An example of the kind of standard-setting process that needs to be encouraged is Guanajuato 2000, which the footwear chamber in that state created as a threshold that firms had to achieve to gain access to a set of state-run development programs. There is now a debate at the national level as to whether this standard should be extended to the shoe industry as a whole or whether other states should be encouraged to develop their own standards. A third alternative would be to use as a national standard the International Organization for Standardization (ISO) 9000 of the European Economic Community.[6]

The kind of debate that is emerging around Guanajuato 2000 is the key to the policy we are proposing. The debate is actually more important than the particular way in which the issue is resolved. If properly orchestrated, it will force the participants to reflect on practice. Nevertheless, the outcome of the debate may not be irrelevant; there is a lesson here too. We tend to think, as suggested earlier, that it is important to avoid a single set of absolute standards. The relevant standard depends very much on which segment of the market the industry is targeting at any moment. The standard should shift upward over time as the country develops or with technological advances. Standards should thus be a moving target. And a variety of standards at any moment will help to pick out benchmarks and call attention to alternative practices. The fact that Guanajuato has set a standard different from ISO 9000 means that ISO 9000 firms can serve as a source of ideas for where the industry might move next. Were Guadalajara to develop a higher standard than León, practice in Guadalajara could become a benchmark for further upgrading. The León standard, the Guanajuato standard, and the ISO 9000 standard would then constitute a hierarchy across which firms or contracting networks might think of moving over time.

The development of standards needs to be accompanied by a parallel effort to develop a typology of market segments that can then be set alongside the hierarchy of standards to guide industrial strategy. This is the broader lesson embodied in the Bancomext insight that Mexican producers are more likely to find markets at this time in Latin America or among smaller retail chains in the United States than in the prestigious New York department stores at which their development program was originally directed. Divorced from this broader lesson, the Bancomext policy is likely to trap the industry in a low level of development. But linked to a typology of markets and a hierarchy of standards, it becomes a way station in a strategy for the gradual upgrading of the productive system over time. The development of market typologies can be fostered, like the development of standards, by requiring that a market analysis be built into any development project that the federal government funds. Such an analysis should identify the segment of the market to which the targeted enterprises are currently catering and the segment toward which the project is designed to help them move.

Conclusions

It is useful to return in conclusion to the central theme of the paper: There is a growing division within the Mexican economy between, on the one hand, a relatively small group of producers that have managed to adjust to the opening of the economy to trade and are prospering in the newly created North American market and, on the other, a large group of smaller producers that have been unable to meet international standards of quality and reliability and are floundering even in their own national marketplace. The garment industry is thus in many ways symptomatic of the Mexican manufacturing sector: The rapidly expanding subcontracting industry dominates the aggregate statistics and makes the industry the outstanding success, at least from the Mexican point of view, of the NAFTA strategy, but it masks the stagnation and decline of the smaller, traditional producers and the progressive loss of the domestic market to imports. In an economy with significant excess labor reserves, there seems no reason why the second development pattern should follow from the first, especially in a traditional sector such as garments, which is extremely labor-intensive and has a fund of tacit knowl-

edge embodied in a skilled labor force and a cadre of managerial and technical experience. In garments at least Mexico should be able to expand its exports through subcontracting relationships and retain its domestic market. It became apparent early in this study that its inability to do so is associated with problems of quality and reliability within the traditional sector, and we looked for clues among firms that had successfully overcome these problems—largely with the help of an American partner—as to how the lagging firms in the industry might do so.

Ultimately we arrive at two rather different solutions. One is to take the upgrading process in the successful firms as a model and to try to transfer or extend it to the lagging sector. The model seems to have two salient characteristics. One is how the foreign partner works as a tutor to its Mexican contractors. An extension of this model would presumably look for consultants to play this role. The other characteristic is the investment in intangible assets and the difficulties of securing such investments when they are made by parties other than those in which the newly transferred knowledge resides. The importance of the credit implicit in these arrangements has been augmented by the general shortage and high interest cost of working capital in Mexico and by how maquiladora-type arrangements facilitate access to working capital in the United States. A direct attempt to extend this model through, for example, a government development program would thus concentrate on the provision of consulting services as a substitute for the role of the foreign partner and on special loan programs to overcome the capital constraints that small producers appear to face. The difficulties with implementing such a program and the limitations of upgrading through consultants lead us to consider a second strategy of bootstrapping, in which the laggard firms are encouraged to upgrade themselves through a process of self-criticism and self-examination in light of visits to best-practice facilities and benchmarks that measure the gap between best and prevailing practices.

The bootstrapping strategy might actually be better suited to the traditional garment sector than the tutorial approach in maquiladora firms. The traditional sector, as noted, consists of a long chain of subcontracting relationships that stretch from the design and cutting rooms backward to progressively smaller shops and, ultimately, to home workers. Historically there has been considerable mobility along this chain, with pools of people at each stage thinking strategically about how to gather the knowledge and contacts required to move up to the next level. People are, in other words, already involved in a process that looks very much like bootstrapping, and in this sense the strategy we are proposing in many ways simply formalizes, codifies, and, hopefully, improves on a process already in progress.

In any case, it does not appear necessary to choose between the two approaches to upgrading, any more than it seems necessary to choose between exports and the domestic market. The benchmarking and broader debate around which the bootstrapping strategy is built should serve to facilitate the learning arrangements associated with either the foreign partnerships or consultants. And in the case of foreign partnerships, it might allow the maquiladoras to create or maintain the skills in design and marketing downstream and management in a subcontracting chain upstream that they now seem to give up when they enter into a relationship with a foreign partner for upgrading.

Notes

Acknowledgments: This was a joint research undertaking of the Massachusetts Institute of Technology (MIT) and the Universidad Nacional Autónoma de México. It was supported by funds from the World Economy Laboratory at MIT and a grant from the MacArthur Foundation to the Center for International Studies at MIT.

1. Own calculations based on an *Expansión* survey of the 500 largest firms in Mexico. The exact number of firms varies from 1993 to 1999; it goes from 264 firms in 1993 that accounted for 92.3 percent of total Mexican exports, including maquiladoras, to 286 firms in 1999 that accounted for 89.0 percent of total exports (*Expansión* 1993–99).

2. This finding is pervasive in the literature (see, for example, Gonzales-Aréchiga and Ramírez 1990a, 1990b, 1990c; Wilson 1992). On linkages within Mexican industry itself, see Rabellotti (1995). It is not clear, however, whether the apparent weakness of these interindustry linkages is a peculiarly Mexican phenomenon. Only the last of the studies cited in this note compares Mexico to other countries, and this is a comparison with Italy, where the interfirm linkages are believed to be unusually strong.

3. The *kanban* system is a complex administrative and production organization that includes a just-in-time supplier-client system to manage tool changes, product changes, material purchasing, and planning. It thereby reduces stocks and work in progress.

4. Formal models that capture elements of this process have been developed by Caballero and Hammour (1996) and by Hansen (1992; 1995). The problem of inducing investments in upgrading here is a specific instance of what Caballero and Hammour call the "appropriability" problem. These conjectures are thus basically about how the appropriability problem is resolved by particular firms.

5. In the current depressed conditions of the Mexican economy, the investments that the new discount retail chains made initially may also act as a rent and provide an inducement for them to take on the task of upgrading local contractors. The investments are a sunk cost. To earn a return upon them, the companies must try to minimize their losses, hold what customers they can, and survive until domestic demand revives. One strategy for doing this would be to substitute lower-cost Mexican goods for the products they were importing from abroad, but to

do so without losing the reputation that differentiates them from other retail outlets. The contribution of this strategy to survival and the long-term profit that survival will generate is thus a kind of rent that could be used to bind the producers that it trains.

6. ISO 9000 is a set of evolving international standards for businesses or organizations that initially developed in the United Kingdom in the 1970s. These guidelines and requirements apply to such tasks as inquiries and orders, doing the job or work, checking the work, and delivering the product. The intended effect of the systematic evaluation and implementation of these procedures is to improve the quality and productivity of economic units.

References

Alvarez Galván, José Luis, and Enrique Dussel Peters. 2001. "Causas y efectos de los programas de promoción sectorial en la economía mexicana." *Comercio exterior* 51, 5: 446–56.

Bancomext (Banco Nacional de Comercio Exterior). 2002. *Sistema de comercio exterior-México* (SICM). Mexico City: Bancomext.

Caballero, Ricardo, and Mohamad L. Hammour. 1996. "On the Ills of Adjustment." *Journal of Development Economics* 51, 1 (October): 161–92.

Expansión. 1993–99. "Las empresas más importantes de México." *Expansión* (Mexico City).

Fine, Charles, and Daniel Whitney. 1996. "Is the Make-Buy Decision Process a Core Competence?" MIT Working Paper, Massachusetts Institute of Technology, Cambridge, Mass., January.

Gereffi, Gary. 1994. "The Organization of Buyer-Driven Global Commodity Chains: How U.S. Retailers Shape Overseas Production Networks." In *Commodity Chains and Global Capitalism*, ed. Gary Gereffi and Miguel Korzeniewicz, pp. 95–122. Westport, Conn.: Praeger.

Gonzales-Aréchiga, Bernardo, and Jose Carlos Ramírez. 1990a. "Estructura contra estrategia: Abasto de insumos nacionales a empresas exportadoras." In *Subcontratción y empresas transnacionales: Apertura y restructuración en la maquiladora*, ed. Bernardo Gonzales-Aréchiga and Jose Carlos Ramírez, pp. 241–87. Tijuana: El Colegio de la Frontera Norte.

———. 1990b. "Perspectivas estructurales de la industria maquiladora." In *Subcontratción y empresas transnacionales: Apertura y restructuración en la maquiladora*, ed. Bernardo Gonzales-Aréchiga and Jose Carlos Ramírez, pp. 41–44. Tijuana: El Colegio de la Frontera Norte.

———, eds. 1990c. *Subcontratción y empresas transnacionales: Apertura y restructuración en la maquiladora*. Tijuana: El Colegio de la Frontera Norte.

Hansen, Gordon. 1992. "Industry Agglomeration and Trade in Mexico." Unpublished Ph.D. diss., Department of Economics, Massachusetts Institute of Technology, Cambridge, Mass.

———. 1995. "Incomplete Contracts, Risk, and Ownership." *International Economic Review* 36, 2 (May): 341–63

Nonaka, Inkujiro. 1995. *The Knowledge-Creating Company: How Japanese Companies Create the Dynamics of Innovation.* New York: Oxford University Press.

Rabellotti, Roberta. 1995. "External Economies and Cooperation in Industrial Districts: A Comparison of Italy and Mexico." Unpublished Ph.D. diss., University of Sussex, Brighton, U.K.

Robinson, Elizabeth. 1988. "A Comparative Study of the Economic Effects of External and Internal Linkages Achieved through Compensatory-Type Investments: The Mexican Automobile Industry." Unpublished Ph.D. diss., Department of International Business, George Washington University, Washington, D.C.

Sabel, Charles. 1995. "Bootstrapping Reform: Building Firms, the Welfare State, and Unions." *Politics and Society* 23, 1: 5–48.

Shaiken, Harley, and Stephen Herzenberg. 1987. *Automation and Global Production: Automobile Engine Production in Mexico, the United States, and Canada.* La Jolla: Center for U.S.-Mexican Studies, University of California at San Diego.

Wilson, Patricia A. 1992. *Exports and Local Development: Mexico's New Maquiladoras.* Austin: University of Texas Press.

Ulrik Vangstrup

12   # Knitting the Networks between Mexican Producers and the U.S. Market

Introduction

Knitwear producers in small towns in Mexico have recently begun exporting to the United States as well as to Latin American markets. The most significant challenge they face is the complexity of dealing with foreign clients and not a lack of overall competitiveness, as has been suggested on the basis of research carried out in the 1980s (Wilson 1993, 79). In recent years it has become clear that large Mexican manufacturers have significant export potential, but so far success in the export market has eluded small companies (*El financiero* 1996). Furthermore, the large exporting companies appear to have few linkages to the small national firms, which means the latter have limited direct as well as indirect exports (Pozas 1993, 87). This chapter explores the prospects for expanding linkages between one segment of the Mexican textile industry—sweater producers—and foreign customers, taking into account the industrial organization of the sector, its management, and the role of private and public business associations in promoting exports. The main focus is on what is learned through manufacturer-buyer export relationships: changes in attitudes, knowledge, and skills for both the management

and the labor force in companies involved in export operations.

In the central and western Mexican states of Hidalgo, México, Michoacán, Guanajuato, and Jalisco are numerous towns[1] in which manufacturing activities have taken place since the 1960s, while in others continuous manufacturing operations date from the beginning of the twentieth century. In the 1960s the industrialization of the Mexican metropolis and the expanding national markets established a new socioeconomic context, stimulating the decision of local entrepreneurs to produce basic consumer goods, such as garments and footwear. Towns with early experience in manufacturing were already exporting to the United States during World War II (Arias 1992, 1994), but the majority of recently established firms have produced exclusively for the national market. Mexican knitwear manufacturers in the 1990s and into the early twenty-first century, especially those producing sweaters and similar garments, are concentrated in these small urban areas. Typically they have fewer than fifty employees and are family owned and managed. Most Mexican enterprises that fall into this category have difficulty surviving on the national market, let alone successfully entering export markets (Calvo and Méndez 1995).

Contrary to the general tendency among small domestic producers, however, some enterprises in the knitwear sector thrived in the 1980s and 1990s. Investing heavily in advanced knitting, embroidery, and assembly technology, they have been able to produce at the demanding quality levels required for export to the markets of the industrialized countries. In this chapter I first discuss the current organization of the knitwear sector into industrial clusters and how producers can forge linkages to buyer-driven commodity chains. Second, I discuss the economic development of the sector in the 1990s, and third, I analyze cases[2] in which businesses and other economic actors have been engaged in establishing commercial relations with export markets based on full-package supply relations. I discuss three cases that can be regarded as "success stories," and the lessons learned from them are compared to the less-successful cases of exports mediated through producer associations or consortia.

Industrial Clusters as Links in International Commodity Chains

In this section I outline a model for analyzing enterprises in the knitwear sector and their interactions with export markets. For small and medium enterprises (SMEs) in this sector to succeed in exporting, they should seek to develop particular linkages to buyer-driven commodity chains by engaging in full-package supply relations (see Gereffi 1997; Chapters 3 and 11 in this book).

It is difficult for a Mexican producer to establish full-package supply to the U.S. market since it often involves a prolonged period of product development, from making fabrics to cutting and assembling the final product—

all supervised by a client located far away, speaking a foreign language. Being part of a buyer-driven chain, however, has the advantage that once the company is geared up to meet the demands of foreign buyers (e.g., produce to the required quality levels), additional market opportunities are available. Most manufacturers in the Mexican sweater industry are located in industrial clusters and can be perceived as links in a commodity chain.[3]

Enterprises located in industrial clusters may achieve a comparative advantage over nonclustered firms because of gains derived from collective efficiency. It is not the purpose of this chapter to establish which of the two types of organization is the most efficient or desirable from a developmental point of view but rather to assess the export experience of businesses that tend in this particular sector to be located in industrial clusters. It is my hypothesis that the organization of businesses in industrial clusters can facilitate the success of new business strategies, including exports. The analysis of the specific commodity chain for the Mexican knitwear sector is limited to manufacturers, the cooperation and joint action between manufacturers, and their relations to third parties, such as export agencies and overseas buyers.

The concept of collective efficiency was inspired by the flexible-specialization debate of the 1980s, provoked primarily by the influential work by Michael J. Piore and Charles F. Sabel (1984). One of the examples that Piore and Sabel drew on was the Italian case of SME industrialization organized in industrial districts. Hubert Schmitz formulated this new research paradigm at the end of the "lost decade" of Latin American development, in the years after the financial crisis of the early 1980s. Building on his previous research on small business in Brazil (Schmitz 1982, 1985), he suggested that the model of industrialization that Piore and Sabel believed to exist in

Italy could also be found in industrializing countries, although the organization and the gains from clustering would differ in the two contexts (Schmitz 1989, 30).

Schmitz initiated research on what he considered a "model" case of SME agglomerations in the Sinos Valley in Brazil: the success story of Brazilian footwear producers (Schmitz 1995a). He defines collective efficiency as the combined effect of *external economies and joint action* (see also Schmitz 1997). He summarizes the potential of collective efficiency in SME clusters in the following way:

> A group of small producers making the same or similar things in close vicinity to each other constitutes a cluster, but such concentration in itself brings few benefits. It is, however, a major facilitating factor for a number of subsequent developments (which may or may not occur): the division of labor and specialization amongst the small producers; the emergence of suppliers who provide raw materials or components, new and second-hand machinery, and spare parts; the emergence of agents who sell to distant national and international markets; the emergence of specialized producer services in technical, financial and accounting matters; the emergence of a pool of workers with sector-specific skills; joint action of local producers, which can be of two types, individual firms cooperating or groups of firms joining forces in business associations or consortia. (Schmitz 1997, 4)

Schmitz has emphasized the importance of joint action among producers as the trigger of initiatives that can upgrade the competitiveness of entire clusters—for example, participation of groups of entrepreneurs in trade fairs abroad (Schmitz 1995a, 1995b).

Collective efficiency is a promising starting point when analyzing the socioeconomic processes within clusters of enterprises. It is a limitation of the concept, however, that it is difficult to apply in terms of the economic per-

formance of the individual firms or groups of enterprises making up the cluster. While I offer a reconsideration of the concept elsewhere (Vangstrup 1999), the main interest here is the potential for joint action among producers located in industrial clusters with respect to creating export linkages and, in particular, to delivering full-package supply. A number of researchers working within the collective-efficiency framework have assessed joint action as the driving force behind successful establishment of export linkages.

Similarly, Schmitz (1997) has argued that increased export orientation is the main factor transforming embryonic clusters into efficient ones in terms of business performance. Schmitz (1995a, 1995b), Pamela Cawthorne (1995), and Khalid Nadvi (1999) describe cases of clusters[4] that have successfully reached export markets, identifying joint action combined with an efficient business organization as the driving force. It seems, however, that successful integration of small and medium-sized producers into export markets through buyer-driven commodity chains is more the exception than the rule in Latin American, African, and South Asian countries. For example, Evert-Jan Visser (1996) has studied the case of a Peruvian textile cluster that did not accomplish its goal of initiating exports, although Visser provides several examples of joint actions among producers in pursuit of this goal.[5]

The Organization and Economic Performance of the Mexican Knitwear Industry in the 1990s

Foreign-trade statistics are an important element in assessing the development pattern of an industry, especially for an industry as dependent on global processes of consumption and production as the textile industry. The export performance of selected cate-

TABLE 12.1.   Mexico's Textile and Apparel Exports, Selected Categories, Including Maquiladoras (in U.S.$1,000)[a]

	1993	1994	1995	1996
Knitted Fabrics (Chapter 60)[b]				
Nonmaquiladora	7,268	11,779	38,725	52,615
Maquiladora	1,307	683	188	267
Total	8,575	12,462	38,913	52,882
Knitted Garments (Chapter 61)[b]				
Nonmaquiladora	44,581	59,491	183,223	333,123
Maquiladora	168,945	342,138	678,422	941,098
Total	213,526	401,629	861,645	1,274,221
Woven Garments (Chapter 62)[b]				
Nonmaquiladora	73,963	120,055	261,403	448,618
Maquiladora	710,985	978,285	1,340,569	1,834,367
Total	784,948	1,098,340	1,601,972	2,282,985

Source: INEGI (1994, 1995a, 1996, 1997).

[a]Mexican trade statistics are published in both Mexican pesos and U.S. dollars. Since the author did not have access to U.S. dollar figures for 1995 and 1996, Mexican pesos were converted into dollars using the average exchange rate provided by the International Monetary Fund. For the 1993–96 period the average peso–U.S. dollar exchange rates were 3.12 (1993), 3.38 (1994), 6.42 (1995), and 7.60 (1996).

[b]"Chapter" numbers refer to the standardized WTO product categories.

gories, covering an array of products, is presented in Table 12.1.

The increase in exports in all three categories is spectacular. The export of knitted fabrics, which are relatively capital-intensive, virtually excludes in-bond, maquiladora production, while exports in the labor-intensive garment sectors have depended heavily on maquiladoras. In knitted garments, the exports by nonmaquiladora producers have increased 747 percent from 1993 to 1996 and the export by maquiladoras 557 percent, but the latter from a higher level. What is most interesting are the sweaters, blouses, and T-shirts subgroups[6] of this category. The exports by nonmaquiladora producers of these products are presented in Table 12.2.

The export growth is not simply a reflection of the December 1994 peso devaluation but more of a process that was already apparent in the 1994 data. It is important to note the low level from which exports developed: Among the seven subcategories 1993 exports totaled

$11.8 million, whereas in 1996 exports of the same subcategories were $194 million. The U.S. market is the single most important destination for these exports.

In terms of the size and location of Mexican knitwear producers, the economic census of 1993 identified a total of 1,632 knitwear-producing enterprises. The census operates with five categories, which include 232 hosiery producers, 667 sweater producers, fifty-seven underwear producers, ninety-five cloth producers, and 581 producers of outerwear and other products (INEGI 1995b, 17). An interesting characteristic of the group of sweater producers is that they are predominantly located in small towns in central and western Mexico.

Table 12.3 lists eleven sweater-producing localities that vary in their importance as centers of knitwear production, along with the number of producers located in each locality in 1993. To these can be added a few larger urban areas such as Aguascalientes, Puebla,

TABLE 12.2.   Exports of Selected Knitwear Products by Nonmaquiladora
Manufacturers, 1993–96 (in U.S.$1,000)[a]

	1993	1994	1995	1996
61.05.10:[b] Men's and boys' shirts/cotton	1,504	642 (−57%)	4,532 (706%)	14,568 (321%)
61.05.20:[b] Men's and boys' shirts/synthetic	649	760 (117%)	1,295 (170%)	1,847 (143%)
61.06.10:[b] Women's and girls' blouses/cotton	2,929	5,279 (180%)	6,588 (125%)	10,988 (167%)
61.06.20:[b] Women's and girls' blouses/synthetic	139	196 (141%)	3,746 (1,911%)	12,609 (337%)
61.09.10:[b] Underwear T-shirts/cotton	2,640	7,945 (301%)	55,763 (702%)	123,203 (221%)
61.10.20:[b] Sweaters/cotton	1,146	2,941 (257%)	5,631 (191%)	13,433 (239%)
61.10.30:[b] Sweaters/synthetic	2,818	5,574 (198%)	15,103 (271%)	17,401 (115%)

Source: INEGI (1994, 1995a, 1996, 1997).

[a]Percentages indicate increase over the previous year's exports. Mexican trade statistics are published in
both Mexican pesos and U.S. dollars. Since the author did not have access to U.S. dollar figures for 1995
and 1996, Mexican pesos were converted into dollars using the average exchange rate provided by the
International Monetary Fund.

[b]"Chapter" numbers refer to the standardized WTO product categories.

and Tulancingo, but the production in these areas is not comparable to the output of small-town manufacturers. This places the knitwear industry, especially the sweater segment, in a situation that is contrary to most industries owned by Mexican capital, the latter being concentrated in the three largest urban areas: Mexico City, Guadalajara, and Monterrey.

The published census does not distinguish between the five subcategories on the county or *municipio* level, making it difficult to asses the number of sweater producers. But to my knowledge the knitwear producers in the eleven localities are almost entirely sweater producers, although some areas, in particular Moroleón, have a number of fabric manufacturers (i.e., producers who perform only the knitting process, not garment assembly). It is also probable that the 1993 census is underestimating the number of knitwear producers, especially those located in small towns.[7]

Market Integration and Economic Performance of Sweater Producers in the 1990s

Sweater production is located primarily in small towns as a result of economic and social processes that have evolved over decades. In the industrial centers in which knitwear production was first established, Mexico City and Guadalajara, the industry could not grow quickly enough to catch up to the proliferation of enterprises in the smaller towns, and the industry entered a decline from which it has not recovered (Lailson 1980). In the bounded social spaces of the small-town clusters, individuals and whole families were mobilized as textile entrepreneurs, coinciding with a gradual technological upgrading and an integration between businesses and informal markets.

The most important technological element in sweater production is knitting technology. Much secondhand machinery has entered

TABLE 12.3.   Knitwear-Producing Industrial Clusters

Location	Number of knitwear producers according to the 1993 economic census
Moroleón, Guanajuato	178
Uriangato, Guanajuato	66
San José Iturbide, Guanajuato	24
Villa Hidalgo, Jalisco	63
San Miguel el Alto, Jalisco	60
Santiago Tangamandapio, Michoacán	0[a]
Cuautepéc, Hidalgo	16
Santiago Tulantepec, Hidalgo	6
Jilotepec, Estado de Mexico	13
Coscomate, Estado de Mexico	n.d.
Chiconcuac, Estado de Mexico	11
Total	437

Source: INEGI (1995b).

[a]Although the INEGI census data indicate no knitwear producers in this locality, Wilson (1991) discovered fifty knitwear enterprises there in the mid-1980s.

Mexico from the United States, whereas new machinery was imported from Japan or Europe, especially Italy, Spain, and Germany. Knitting technology has developed from rudimentary artisanal manual devices to computer-controlled machines in a few decades. In contrast to many other sectors, the Mexican knitwear manufacturers have managed to acquire state-of-the-art technology, so that the most advanced machines are found in Mexico. Another important technological development that manufacturers have widely implemented in recent years is computerized embroidery machines capable of stitching logos on almost any kind of apparel, including sweaters. The highest concentrations of embroidery machines in Mexico are found in the towns of Moroleón and Uriangato, which together had approximately three hundred embroidery machines in 1998.[8] An important aspect of both knitting and embroidery machines is their low economies of scale, making it possible for small firms to operate in the industry.

Mexican knitwear producers depend on national synthetic-fiber and -yarn manufacturers. Synthetic yarn constitutes close to 100 percent of their yarn input and 85 to 90 percent of variable costs. The cost of yarn increased more than 100 percent after the 1994 devaluation, and for most producers it has not been possible to increase sales prices to the same extent. The knitwear sector was also affected by Mexico's general trade liberalization, with 1992 being the most difficult year. Nevertheless, at least some clustered enterprises experienced high growth in the 1990s, and the industry of Moroleón established itself as the indisputable center of knitwear production in Mexico. The average annual growth in investments in the 1992–96 period reached 19.1 percent, and the average accumulated investment per company in 1996 was $550,000.[9]

The situation faced by home-market producers has improved significantly since 1994 for two reasons: first, the December 1994 peso devaluation, which increased the prices on imported goods; and second, the imposition of a 35 percent import tax on knitwear imports (Chapters 61, 62, and the majority of 63, according to the World Trade Organization, or WTO, product categories) from countries with which Mexico does not have any trade agreements, for instance, a non–World Trade Organization member such as China (SECOFI decree DOF.30.V.95).[10] This change is reflected in the importation of sweaters (Chapter 61.10 in the WTO classification) to Mexico, which has developed as follows in the 1993–96 period:[11] $62 million (1993), $59 million (1994), $20 million (1995), and $22 million (1996) (INEGI 1994, 1995a, 1996, 1997).

Enterprises within industrial clusters have been using seven different marketing strategies: informal markets, mail-order sales, sweater fairs, national department stores, franchise-based retail chains, producer consortia, and exports. While the latter four are discussed in the case studies to follow, I comment here on the significance of the informal markets, the *tianguis*, which have made up the most important marketing strategy for clustered enterprises. Informal markets were established in three of the eleven localities (Moroleón, Uriangato, and Villa Hidalgo), and they flourished in Chiconcuac—an old market town close to Mexico City and not far from Cuautepéc and Santiago Tulantepec—after the 1982 devaluation as consumers began to demand and search for cheaper garments.

At present, local retailers buy apparel not only from the local industry but from all over Mexico. In Villa Hidalgo the customers mainly arrive from the northern parts of the country, while in Moroleón they come from the central and southern parts and in Chiconcuac from Mexico City. During the last four months of every year, which constitute the high season, several hundred buses arrive on market days. Moroleón producers benefit not only from the local commerce but also from the *tianguis* in the conurban area of Uriangato and from a third *tiangui* established in 1996 in the town of Yuriria, a few miles from Moroleón. In 1997, Villa Hidalgo had approximately 595 clothing retailers;[12] I have no precise data for the other areas. The existence of informal retail markets a close distance from the producers in an industrial cluster is an important factor for industrial success from the mid-1980s onward.

The Export Experience of Three Successful Exporting Companies in the Mexican Knitwear Sector in the 1990s

I begin the analysis with a discussion of three enterprises that have initiated exports as a result of direct contacts they developed with foreign economic actors. The companies are growing increasingly independent of the in-dustrial clusters in which they are or previously have been located. In the next section I discuss the export strategies of companies located in enterprise clusters. They have changed their marketing strategies—that is, export sales versus sales to national department stores—as a result of their engagement in business associations and consortia.

The Salvatierra Company

Two companies that were founded in Moroleón have a long export experience. I refer to them as the Salvatierra and Celaya companies. Both began exporting in the 1980s. During the last ten years they have become less dependent on the local industrial cluster to the extent that they relocated from the Moroleón cluster in the 1990s to communities with little textile production, away from what management perceived as a deteriorating business environment caused by labor shortage.

The Salvatierra company was owned by the Soto family since the early 1960s, and it is now managed by the founder's oldest son, who recently took over this responsibility from his father. When asked how they got started as exporters, Soto explains that in 1987 his company was contacted by a Canadian firm that wanted to source from Mexico. The Salvatierra company accepted the business proposal, although it was not very attractive, because it provided the company with production in the low season and it could be an important experience. The Salvatierra company soon shifted its focus to the U.S. market and maintained this orientation in subsequent years. It has recently diversified its client base, which now includes Sears and a New York broker, and it has also begun exporting to other countries in Latin America. Since the early 1980s the Salvatierra company has been selling through Mexican department stores, and at present it works with ten different stores. It sells almost nothing in the *tianguis*, which is rather exceptional for knitwear producers.

In 1994 the owners decided to move the assembly operations to another town, twenty-five miles away. Although this was a difficult decision to make, the move was necessary because a stable labor force was no longer possible in Moroleón during the peak period of production. The expansion of the knitwear industry means so many jobs in the peak period that workers are able to "shop around" in terms of employment opportunities. Soto feels that he now has a much more flexible labor force, for which he is paying only about half the wage rate that is typical for Moroleón. Soto is planning to build a new factory in the town where assembly takes place in order to achieve a more integrated production process. Currently all fabrics are still made at the plant in Moroleón and shipped to the assembly plant.

The Celaya Company

The owner of the Celaya company, Mr. Vázquez, graduated from business school in the United States and returned to Mexico with the idea of using his newly acquired skills, including the ability to speak English, to export to the U.S. market. Vázquez has several relatives who have been involved in the textile industry in Celaya and Apaseo el Alto. He chose to set up his business in Moroleón in 1987 in order to take advantage of the business opportunities there. That year Vázquez came into contact with a major garment distributor located in New York, and they began a long-term cooperative relationship. The U.S. distributor designs and develops the specifications for knitted baby garments that the Celaya company produces. The distributor sells the baby garments to department stores, such as Wal-Mart and JCPenney.

Right from the start Vázquez did things differently than most producers in Moroleón. He quickly got into exports, exporting almost 100 percent of production during the next four years. In 1991 exports were negatively affected by the overvaluation of the peso, and the Celaya company started to sell on the national market through department stores. In 1994, Vázquez decided to move the business to Celaya, and he resumed exports after the 1994 devaluation.

When Vázquez operated in Moroleón, he did not invest in knitting machinery, preferring instead to establish a network of approximately eight subcontractors that manufactured the fabrics. He hired a young woman from the town to help him manage this supply network, which involved working with the fabric manufacturers to overcome their difficulties in producing to the exact specifications required by the New York client. Later this woman became a partner in the firm, and she is now the production manager of the Celaya plant.

Vázquez decided to leave Moroleón because of the deteriorating work environment. The Celaya company had difficulties with both its subcontractors and its own employees. Vázquez characterizes the labor market in Moroleón as "devastating" for a business like his. The workers demand a salary but are disloyal to their employer and show up for work "whenever they feel like it." In Moroleón, Vázquez paid a salary of 600 Mexican pesos[13] per week to the seamstresses, while he claims to pay only 150 in Celaya to the female workers.

In 1996 a number of important changes occurred in the enterprise, which was by then located in Celaya. The company hired two engineers, a male mechanical engineer and a female textile engineer. The mechanical engineer was put in charge of fourteen recently bought knitting machines. The textile engineer oversees production, together with Vázquez's assistant, whose responsibilities also include maintaining contacts with the company's U.S. customers. The most important change in terms of production has been better control of the production processes in order to establish better quality control. The company has plans to construct a new plant outside Celaya.

The changes that have occurred in the Celaya company have grown out of the firm's experiences in Moroleón as well as its relationship with American buyers. The difficulties with producing in Moroleón convinced Vázquez of the need to improve the company's organization by integrating the whole production process in the same plant, and the company's stable relations with its U.S. customers made it possible for the firm to make the long-term investments necessary for this reorganization. Although the Celaya company maintains its long-standing relationship with the New York distributor that helped launch its production in 1987, it has also recently begun working with a second buyer also located in the United States. By late 1996 the Celaya company had orders for the next six months, with guarantees for additional contracts in the future. Furthermore, its long-term customer from New York put Vázquez in contact with a U.S. supplier for secondhand knitting technology from whom his company is now buying, and the U.S. distributor is partly financing the purchase of this machinery.

The San Miguel el Alto Company

In 1968 an industrialist from Guadalajara established a factory in San Miguel el Alto, Jalisco, producing sweaters and sweatshirts. In 1974 the factory had about three hundred employees and had established a formal corporate structure, with professional administration including a sales division—something that was not found prior to the 1990s in the sweater industry, in the industrial clusters mentioned previously. In 1974 the company expanded when it established a mill to produce synthetic yarn. In the 1970s and 1980s new divisions were added, producing elastics, hosiery, and knitted fabrics, and an industrial group took form. Apart from its own growth, the company had an important impact on the subsequent industrial development of San Miguel. In 1974 fifteen local families owned workshops in the textile industry, each employing about ten workers (Martínez Saldaña and Gándara Mendoza 1976, 225–30).

The company is still family owned and partly managed by the founder and his two sons, but professional managers have played an important role in the company's restructuring. Between my first visit to the factory in November 1995 and my second visit in August 1996, the enterprise underwent fundamental changes and focused on exports as the most important element of its business strategy. In 1995 the company had its first experience with exporting to the United States, working with Phillips–Van Heusen as well as department stores. For exports to succeed, it was necessary to implement a whole new organization of production, especially with regard to the assembly of garments. In 1995 the company hired two new managers to implement changes: One was an Argentine engineer, an expert in production systems, and the other was a Mexican sales manager, fluent in English and used to dealing with the expectations of American clients.

Assembly is now organized around a new production scheme—modular production—that resembles a combination of teamwork and just-in-time organization of internal work processes. The sewers, 120 mostly young women, work in groups or modules of six to eight workers, in which all assembly activities are performed. The company has invested in new computer-controlled sewing machines that make quality control easier. Under modular organization, it is possible to determine the number of garments to be made in a given time period because capacity is always known. This organization also increases flexibility since the modules can work with different styles simultaneously, and it increases worker commitment and quality. The actual production of each module is written on a blackboard together with the production goal for the day. Other plants in the town perform the knitting and cutting, but the operations are strictly coordinated.

The goal is not to knit anything before it can be immediately cut and assembled in order to avoid inventory, and the organization has reduced the throughput time from knitting to the finished garment from thirty-five days to five hours. According to the managers, their main problem is the absence of good supervisors, which they explain by the plant's remote location, making it difficult for them to work more than one shift of nine hours per day. The advantage to the company of the location and lack of alternative employment is the low level of operator salaries, which are similar to those paid by the Celaya company. The company used to contract out assembly operations to local firms, but these operations were internalized in order to improve quality. With the exception of labor, the company is therefore becoming increasingly independent of local inputs. The company still buys some fabrics from a few manufacturers located in Moroleón.

The changes in organization were necessary to increase production volume and improve quality at the same time. Both factors have been essential to the company's export success. Whereas in 1995 the San Miguel el Alto company produced approximately five thousand dozens of garments, in 1996 they planned to produce more than eighty thousand dozens.[14] While a substantial part is destined for the national market, more than $1.4 million worth of that production will be exported, primarily to the United States and Canada but also to Venezuela. The company plans to increase production annually by 1 million units until it reaches 5 million units, and it expects to export the majority of this volume to the United

States. The sales manager explained that the company was actually rejecting clients, since it lacked the additional assembly capacity it would need to expand its customer base.

Discussion of the Three Cases

I regard these three enterprises as successful cases of transition from suppliers to the home market to full-package suppliers to the U.S. market. These transitions were made possible by improvement of the companies' organization—for example, they are relying now on an increased number of specialized managers. They are exporting low-priced garments, made with basic fabrics almost exclusively from synthetic fibers. Operating in this highly competitive segment provides these companies with a strong incentive to improve their organization in order to increase efficiency. In all companies, learning processes have occurred over the years that have resulted in an improved organization of production and higher-quality output. The learning processes develop through interactions with foreign clients, combined with the challenges of day-to-day management.

The speed with which changes are implemented as a result of learning processes varies. For example, while the Salvatierra company has slowly improved its organization over the years, the Celaya and San Miguel el Alto companies have done so in a short period of time. The San Miguel el Alto company initiated a search process to identify the best managers and most suitable partners, while the Celaya company did not have the same financial and organizational resources and found new managers in its immediate environment. The company's long-standing contact with the U.S. client was essential for it to initiate the changes. The integration between the production of yarn and fabrics is an enormous advantage for the San Miguel el Alto company, since its access to yarn both increases revenues and facilitates planning. Knowing the right clients is essential, and good clients can be scarce. The Celaya company seems to have benefited the most from its client relations, while the Salvatierra company is dissatisfied with its client relations, primarily because of price. The San Miguel el Alto company has the strongest client position of the three since its organization permits it to choose the clients its wants, but this company has also been through a long process of adaptation in which client relations were a major facilitating factor.

The three enterprises are embedded in a range of different networks. They have access to federal agencies, such as the Banco Nacional de Comercio Exterior (Bancomext) and Nacional Financiera (NAFIN), and in some cases direct linkages to state governments. They have developed their organizations to the extent that they do not need the facilitating aspects of location in industrial clusters—that is, a specialized workforce and technology. They train workers themselves and have implemented technology according to their needs, not because of prevailing norms of technology in industrial clusters. The clustered enterprises are exposed to an economic environment in which there are both constraining and enabling factors that influence their possibilities of engaging in exports. In the next section I analyze the role of business associations and producer consortia in promoting exports.

Business Associations in Export Promotion: Credit Unions and Producer Consortia

This section deals with two types of associations: the credit unions and the producers' consortia, both emergent from legislation passed during the administration of President Carlos Salinas de Gortari (1988–94). The credit unions located in Moroleón and Cuautepéc are discussed together with producer consortia in Cuautepéc and Villa Hidalgo. I first discuss the institutional setup of the producer consortia and credit unions together, arguing that the political motives behind their establishment and the objectives they fulfill are similar.

Between 1991 and 1994, during the Salinas administration, some four hundred credit unions were established as intermediaries for Nacional Financiera, the Mexican development bank (*El financiero* 1997). NAFIN has played an important role in the development of large corporations in Mexico, both private and public. The bank dramatically changed its policies during the Salinas administration: While previously it channeled almost 100 percent of its funds to public corporations, after 1987 the private sector received 94 percent of its total support (Rojas and Rojas 1997, 25). In a policy paper, NAFIN's role is stated the following way: "The institution has shifted from being the development bank of a proprietary government to become the development bank of a solidary government" (NAFIN 1992, 3). From 1989 on, the bank began granting credits only through intermediaries—that is, commercial banks and credit unions.

The stated objective of both credit unions and producer consortia is to improve the competitiveness of Mexican SMEs in the global economy. They were created as local institutions, initially branch-specific, so that they could be "experts" of the local manufacturing and service industry they were serving. Like the producer consortia, credit unions were owned by local entrepreneurs, but the final decision on approval of credits was made solely by NAFIN. It was, however, possible for a credit union to provide credit with its own resources without consulting NAFIN. Credit unions make their revenues by charging a markup on interest rates and through the other services they may provide. The possibility of providing services, for example, in organizing sales, is also the main difference between credit unions and commercial banks.

After three years of fast growth, the Mexican peso crisis and the change in administration put an end to most credit unions. In 1998, NAFIN continued to work with fifty-six of what were originally more than four hundred credit unions, one of which was the credit union of Cuautepéc (NAFIN 1998).

The producer consortium system of *empresas integradoras,* or integrated enterprises, is parallel to the credit union system. The important difference is that the consortium has less access to credit, since NAFIN does not want to finance collective projects, only the individual members. This indicates that NAFIN had little confidence in the accountability and viability of producer consortia. The legislation on which the producer consortia are based was passed by the Salinas administration in 1993. The immediate aim of the organization was to encourage SME producers to cooperate in the production of services, improving the competitiveness of the members working in the same sector. The presidential decree lists the following services that can be provided by the new organization to the member companies: implementation of new technology, commercialization, design, subcontracting, financing, and other types of consulting (*Diario oficial* 1993).

The number of producer consortia increased in the 1990s, reaching 128 in 1997. Interestingly enough, textiles and apparel are the sectors that have generated the most producer consortia in recent years. Between January and October 1997, 6 consortia were established in the textile sector and 10 in the apparel sector (SECOFI 1998). The Mexican producer consortia[15] have received more scholarly attention than has the credit union program.

The Credit Union of Moroleón

The Moroleón credit union was established in 1991 and by late 1994 had 108 members. The credit union has been successful in providing credit to the local industry but was forced to discontinue its activities after the December 1994 peso crisis. According to the staff, the discontinuation was not because of its economic condition, which was good, but because of NAFIN's politically motivated decision to cut off credits. Although it is not supposed to be a key objective of credit unions, the director of the Moroleón credit union took an early interest in promoting exports. Management courses in exports were arranged, but the most important influence was through selecting local partners for interested foreign companies that contacted the credit union director as a result of his high profile in the local business community.

Although few producers were interested in the management courses that the credit union offered or in exporting, some contacts developed. The first entrepreneur to engage in exports was Mr. Martínez, who had been well connected to the credit union and its manager for several years. Martínez took an interest in the possibilities of exporting because of personal financial problems resulting from the 1994 crisis. He received export orders from a New York–based broker but discontinued the relationship because of problems with the payments, and because he felt the broker was too demanding. Martínez later began to subcontract for a Mexican producer[16] located in Celaya who, for a number of years, had been exporting to South America and the United States. Martínez earned less this way but was more satisfied with the relationship. He feels it is better for the workshop to specialize in production, leaving the international marketing to others and exporting only indirectly.

The Producer Consortium of Villa Hidalgo

In 1994 a group of three workshop owners, looking to identify new marketing strategies, decided to contact one of the national department stores. The department store preferred to work with larger producers and suggested that the three companies create a group. In 1993 two of the three producers had been on a trip to Italy together, along with seven other local producers, in an effort to learn how the Italians organized themselves in small garment-producing towns. Another objective of this trip was to investigate the possibility of purchasing new knitting technology. NAFIN initiated and partly financed the trip. Several members of the group told me they were very impressed by what they saw in Italy and thought they should replicate the form of cooperation between producers that they witnessed there. In early 1995, NAFIN invited the same group to visit a successful producer consortium of apparel producers in Atotonilco, Jalisco. After this the producers decided to establish a consortium under the terms of the *empresas integradoras* legislation, and their organization soon numbered twenty-three producers.

Their first project was to design a common line of clothing that they would offer to national department stores. On the day of their first business meeting, for which they had invited a designer from Guadalajara, another person from Guadalajara, Miguel Sedano, visited Jesús González, the president of the local business chamber and also one of the initiators of the consortium. González invited Sedano to participate in the meeting, at which Sedano explained his own ideas for exporting to the United States. Sedano told the owners of the companies assembled for the meeting about his experience as a sales manager working for a large sweater plant in Guadalajara, and he offered to work with them in initiating exports.

The leading members of the consortium agreed to work with Sedano with the goal of exporting sweaters to the United States. Sedano explained that their first action would be to make samples for a U.S. client with whom he already had contacts. The American client, whom Sedano introduced to the consortium, was an important New York–based garment broker. The company had suppliers in more

than fifteen developing economies and was interested in adding Mexico to its list of supplier countries. The broker's interest in Mexico was due primarily to the country's proximity, making it possible to reduce both transportation and financial costs considerably while increasing flexibility. The broker's representative stated that the company would place orders of as much as $10 million in Mexico on a yearly basis if an agreement could be reached. The client required that the Villa Hidalgo producer consortium develop a new spring line in collaboration with one of its designers, finishing the sample making by mid-December in order to start production and shipping in January.

The workshop owners, however, were not prepared for this time-consuming and tedious work, which required fundamental changes in their organization. They were used to making very few models that they repeated year after year, so in the beginning they simply saw it as a waste of time. The person who best understood Sedano's modus operandi and the resulting demands the U.S. broker was placing on the consortium members was the president of the consortium, Antonio Moreno, who was also the owner of the largest sweater plant in Villa Hidalgo, the only one that could rival most of the Moroleón workshops with its German flatbed computerized machines. Moreno was also a member of the group of three producers who had initially contacted the Mexican retail chain. At this point Sedano felt that he could trust Moreno, whom he thought capable of influencing the other owners.

Moreno's company, called Originales Futura, and another, Maroly, also making use of computerized machinery and a computer programmer, made most of the samples while smaller workshops made the simpler ones. All the producers felt that sample making was a problem since it had to take place in the high season, during which an idle machine would mean a loss. An owner using automatic machinery explained that he had to spend three weeks making a single sample. In the workshops that possessed computerized machinery the process went much faster, but it was still a problem.

The American client signed a contract in April 1996 directly with Sedano, who decided that the producer consortium should make thirty-seven sweater styles and the Aguascalientes plant the remaining thirteen, for a total of five thousand dozens. In August 1996 the producer consortium began exporting, and later in 1996, Bancomext, which had contacts to a potential client in Costa Rica, contacted them. This client needed women's garments that were rather simple compared to those the consortium was shipping to the United States, making it possible for a number of owners with less developed technology than that of the two largest members to fill this order. The workshops belonging to Moreno also began exporting to Chile independent of the consortium as a result of contacts with Bancomext.

This export experience brought major organizational changes to the two largest workshops, Originales Futura and Maroly. They became responsible for almost all of the assembly, while the rest operated as subcontractors producing part of the knitted fabrics. The quality requirements of the U.S. broker made it necessary to change many routines in assembly and finishing. The consortium president decided to integrate the assembly and finishing in the two largest plants in order to achieve the necessary quality.

There was little discussion among the partners about the business and the needed investments and changes in structure. Several owners talked to me about investing in knitting technology that would be more appropriate for the American market, but the necessary steps have not been taken. There are two reasons for this: The smaller member companies were content with their sales on the national mar-

ket, and they felt the two largest companies had taken over the consortium.

The future looked promising at first glance, but the consortium never returned to exporting again. The reason was lack of trust among most of the participants and a difficult financial situation. Apparently, some members had no confidence in the new manager, who they felt was too strongly connected to Moreno. This caused the manager to leave the consortium in December 1996. Moreno's company was able to export smaller orders to JCPenney in 1996 and 1997, but in 1998 it had given up exporting for the time being because of good sales in the domestic market. Moreno felt that the export experience had been important, since it was no longer a problem to produce the quality demanded by the department stores.

The Producer Consortium and Credit Union of Cuautepéc

The producer consortium of Cuautepéc (La Corporación Industrial de Tejido de Punto, or COITEP) differs from that of Villa Hidalgo in one important aspect: It merged with the Credit Union of Cuautepéc and therefore enjoys strong financial support. The credit union was established in 1993 and the consortium in 1995 by the same group of producers, and this later facilitated the merger between the two organizations. An additional difference between the Cuautepéc credit union and most other credit unions is that NAFIN did not cut its credit after the 1994 devaluation, due to a better economic situation and possibly better political contacts to NAFIN.

Shortly after the establishment of COITEP, a number of interesting initiatives were taken aimed both at improving the members' situations on the national market and at initiating exports. COITEP bought two advanced computerized knitting machines and established a chain of sales outlets. The members financed one of the knitting machines while the credit union financed the other, with the intention of using it partly to produce "in common" for COITEP's exports. When not being used for this export production it could be "rented" to individual consortium members, who could buy production time according to their needs.

The chain of sales outlets the consortium owned proved to be a success. The first two shops were located in Chiapas, and in 1996 six more opened in central Mexico, all on a franchise basis. Despite this, the consortium ran into economic difficulties, primarily because of the investments in the two knitting machines. An additional reason was the lack of commitment on behalf on the members, since they did not provide the shops with the necessary merchandise in the high season. The credit union took over all assets in 1996; the consortium continued to operate as a sales agent on the national market and as a distribution center for the credit union. The producer consortium was established by a group of credit union members who wanted to engage in new activities, but because of financial problems they had to merge with the credit union, although they were still officially two distinct organizations.

In the period after the 1994 peso devaluation, the main concern of the credit union director and the board was to avoid bankruptcy for the whole union. After the merger of the two organizations a new set of initiatives was taken involving both, but under the supervision of the credit union director and his staff. The director developed three sales strategies: (1) increased sales on the domestic market through department stores, (2) setting up their own retail chain, and (3) the initiation of exports. In 1996 the credit union hired four new staff members to implement the three strategies, and the consortium hired a manager to make contacts with department stores. Administration of the retail chain and exports were now handled solely by the credit union, while the department-store business was dealt with by both organizations.

The results were promising at first, as Mexican department stores (e.g., Aurrera and Wal-Mart/Mexico) were interested in sourcing from national producers since the devaluation had made their prices competitive. Members of the credit union were invited to present their collections to interested buyers; the new credit union staff developed the designs that the stores requested; and members shared the large orders. The credit union purchased the acrylic yarn, lending it to the producers. Orders were made directly with the credit union, which paid the producers sixty days after orders were delivered.

In January 1997 the credit union director was no longer very optimistic: Although the members had experienced a good season in terms of sales, they had difficulties securing the commitments of the department stores. Because of the improved market situation of the *tianguis*—especially Chiconcuac, which is where the Cuautepéc producers sell most of their output—the producers were reluctant to fulfill their orders with the department stores, which offered smaller revenues while being more demanding. The credit union had accepted orders of sixteen thousand dozens from the department stores but could only deliver ten thousand. In addition, the producer consortium made orders of fifteen hundred dozens that it managed to deliver.

By early 1997 the retail chain was a success in terms of sales, and more outlets were to be opened. The planned export program had not begun, but the sales at department stores would be continued. The results of these initiatives were mixed, but the economic situation of the member producers and the credit union as such improved in 1996. The better financial situation is partly due to the new marketing strategies but mainly because of more sales in the *tianguis*.

Discussion of the Producer Organizations

The producer associations and consortia discussed above operated as organizing agents. I argued earlier that such organizing agents may contribute to the diffusion of knowledge about and changes in attitudes and skills related to exporting. The three case studies have shown, however, that it is difficult to establish an efficient working organization.

In Moroleón the credit union did not actually have a clear strategy about how to promote its member companies, but the experience shows that considerable upgrading can take place if a company is connected to the right customer. This case also exemplifies that the manufacturer-buyer relationship is not a one-way process; customers can and should learn through their interactions with manufacturers. During its second attempt to source from Moroleón, the New York–based client invested more time and offered better working conditions, although no long-term relationship was established.

The Villa Hidalgo producer consortium managed to export, but lack of financial control by the partners, combined with mistrust between managers and the partners, made the project fail. The Cuautepéc consortium and credit union did not manage to export, but it became a supplier to the national department stores. The members preferred, as did most members of the Villa Hidalgo consortium, to continue working primarily on the national market.

From an efficiency point of view, the optimal business association is what the producers in Cuautepéc attempted: to establish close connections among a private business association, the consortium, and a semipublic association such as the credit union. I believe this organization is superior to the Villa Hidalgo consortium, because the latter lacked working capital and financial expertise, and better than the Moroleón credit union, because it did not have a staff to undertake the management of the new marketing strategies.

The case studies of these business organizations show that they have potential but also that they are fragile: A mixed or negative experience can ruin interest among and support from the members, and disagreement between partners and managers is common. Managers of business associations develop their skills over time, through interaction with clients and as a result of adjusting their daily routines to the requirements of buyers. It is likely that disagreements between the managers and partners develop because managers do not feel that the individual owners manage their businesses according to the needs of the organization and because the producers are not used to dealing with highly skilled employees.

A logical answer to the problem would be to create institutional setups that can accumulate such knowledge by learning from past experiences, but such attempts have been infrequent in Mexico. For example, the credit union program was dismantled without a proper evaluation of its costs and benefits. The problem is not that the Mexican government is unable to intervene but that government agencies have not been capable of learning from the successes and failures when it comes to promoting exports from SMEs.

Conclusions

In this chapter I have examined the Mexican domestic sweater industry in order to assess the potential of entrepreneurs and enterprises to participate in subcontracting relationships with foreign clients. The case studies of the three successful exporters have shown that for Mexican companies to export through buyer-driven networks, changes in management practices are necessary. These can be fostered both internally and by interaction with foreign clients. The practices associated with exporting are different from those that have prevailed among enterprises operating on the national market, which sell the majority of their production to the *tianguis,* where customers prefer low prices and accept low quality in finishing. This is in contrast to the North American market, where finishing quality has to be high even in the low-priced segment, which all the companies studied are serving.

Management practices and the organization of the firm are becoming more efficient in the 1990s. While this may not be true of all enterprises, it is especially true for enterprises located in the Moroleón industrial cluster. Important reasons for this include the recent technological upgrading of the sector and increased competition in the national market. Management practices in Moroleón in many cases have also been influenced by the entry of second-generation entrepreneurs, often professionals with former work experience.

Despite their potential benefits, in some situations external "dis-economies" develop in industrial clusters. For example, in the Moroleón industrial cluster dynamic growth in the sweater sector created a labor shortage. This led entrepreneurs to leave the community, and often the firms that chose to leave were among the best-organized companies and those most capable of managing the transition to exporting, for example, the Salvatierra and Celaya companies. Many producers in Moroleón believe that low assembly quality, which they attribute to the unstable labor situation, is the most important impediment to companies that want to initiate export programs.[17] There are producers in Moroleón that are improving the physical conditions of their facilities and offering workers better conditions (e.g., year-round employment) in the hopes of lowering turnover.

Larger companies in the apparel sector tend to be relatively successful exporters. It is important, however, to study as well the export potential of clustered companies. First, the vast majority of manufacturers in the sweater sector are located in industrial clusters, and these clusters collectively contain the largest export potential in the knitwear segment of the apparel industry. Second, developing relationships with foreign clients is an important means of improving the sector's overall competitiveness. Increasing competitiveness for the sector will also benefit the companies that serve the home market, which is becoming increasingly open to global competition. The benefits exporting companies receive in terms of improved overall competitiveness are probably the most important reason to export.

Different institutional environments mediating manufacturer-client relations have been analyzed based on the concept of joint action among manufacturers, the second element of the collective-efficiency model. The conclusion is that the learning experience within business associations has been more individual than collective. The important learning effects have been internal to the firms, and this experience has not been diffused equally among the members. At the same time the staff members of these various associations have benefited from the "export learning curve," but this learning process has not been institutionalized. Consequently, business associations and producer consortia are not efficient facilitators of exports.

Mexican knitwear producers are not in the same position as many other Mexican companies, which lack the technology and capacity to engage in exports or even to compete successfully on the domestic market. To the contrary, many knitwear producers have high technological levels and have improved their organization significantly in recent years. From a visit to Moroleón and Villa Hidalgo during the summer of 1998, I learned that few new enterprises had engaged in exports, but the attitude in the producer communities, at least in Moroleón, had changed. Because of stagnation in the domestic market in 1998, several producers that before had been skeptical declared that they would now pursue an export strategy. Whether they will achieve this goal remains unclear. The Mexican domestic garment industry is indeed highly volatile, but indications are that a more efficient and internationally competitive industry is being formed, with the potential of becoming a significant part of international subcontracting networks.

Notes

1. Patricia Arias lists seventy-one localities with fewer than fifty thousand inhabitants in the states of Michoacán, Jalisco, and Guanajuato in which people are involved in manufacturing not related to agriculture (Arias 1992, 261–66). In some of these, particularly in Michoacán, production is more artisanal than industrial.

2. Cases of exporting companies were identified in the enterprise clusters in the towns of Moroleón, Villa Hidalgo, and Cuautepéc. All enterprises with export experience were sought out and interviewed, along with local organizations that promoted exports—namely, credit unions, producer consortia, and an export agency. Enterprises with export experience in the same sector but located outside clusters were identified in four other localities: Celaya, San Miguel el Alto, Aguascalientes, and Guadalajara. In all cases, interviews focusing on economic performance and organization in general and relations to foreign clients in particular were conducted with owners and managers, in most cases on several occasions over the four-year period from 1995 to 1998. All names are pseudonyms, with the exception of those of politicians.

3. I owe this point to Florence Palpacuer's contribution to this book (see Chapter 3). My conception of commodity chains follows the definition of Terence K. Hopkins and Immanuel Wallerstein, cited in Gereffi (1992, 93–94); see also Humphrey (1995, 158) for his account of the theoretical con-

nections between industry clusters and commodity chains.

4. The authors analyze clusters in Brazil, Pakistan, and India in the footwear, surgical instruments, and textile sectors, respectively.

5. Visser made an interesting comparison between clustered and nonclustered enterprises in the Peruvian apparel sector. The benefits of clustering seemed to erode when the national market was opened to international competition. Clustered producers had a tendency to invest in retailing instead of in production when faced with increased competition. Furthermore, they were less capable than nonclustered enterprises of establishing subcontracting linkages that could have improved their performance (Visser 1996, 208–9, 171).

6. The most important subgroups for the knitwear producers in relation to this study are sweaters, blouses, and T-shirts. An important subgroup not dealt with is hosiery.

7. The economic census is based on interviews with owners of permanent establishments (INEGI 1995b, 3–6). A census not based on interviews would exclude nonregistered enterprises and therefore be of little value in Mexico. It is likely, however, that many enterprises are simply not included because the census interviewer did not detect them. For example, according to the census there are no knitwear businesses in Santiago Tangamandapio. However, Fiona Wilson (1991) examined the industry of this city and discovered about fifty knitwear enterprises there in the mid-1980s. Another example is Cuautepéc, which, according to the census, had only sixteen producers in 1993, while the Credit Union of Cuautepéc had forty-seven members in the textile sector in 1995; they had been operating for several years and are only a fraction of the total number of producers (Unión de Crédito de Cuautepéc 1996). There may also have been changes in how the census is carried out and therefore differences in the quality of the data from 1988 and 1993. The simple fact that the number of enterprises in the knitwear sector went up from 908 in 1988 to 1,632 in 1993 suggests that this is the case. Although the sector expanded in some areas in the period, I believe that the census was simply more accurate in 1993 than in 1988.

8. Interview with a supplier of machinery in Moroleón, July 1998.

9. Investments in technology (1992–96) are used as a proxy for economic performance. The data are based on a sample of ten enterprises out of the approximately three hundred companies in the locality employing computer-controlled knitting and embroidery equipment.

10. This was a governmental decree by the Secretaría de Comercio y Fomento Industrial (SECOFI), Mexico's Ministry of Trade and Development, acting on behalf of the president of Mexico. It was published in *Diario oficial de la nación.*

11. Before 1993, Mexican statistics did not distinguish between maquiladora and nonmaquiladora producers.

12. Interview with the town treasurer in Villa Hidalgo Town Hall, July 20, 1998.

13. Approximately U.S.$80 in late 1996.

14. U.S. wholesalers normally trade garments in dozens and not in tens or hundreds.

15. Alba Vega (1997) did a case study of the first producer consortium in Mexico. Enrique Dussel Peters, Clemente Ruiz Durán, and Michael J. Piore (Chapter 11 in this book) discuss the shortcomings of the institutional design of Mexican producer consortia.

16. This company is not the one discussed earlier. There were two exporting companies in Celaya in the sector, and it was not possible to arrange a meeting with this latter company.

17. At a meeting organized by Coordinadora de Fomento al Comercio Exterior (COFOCE) and Grupo Guanajuato Textil on September 10, 1996, a questionnaire was administered with the objective of identifying the problems and priorities of the sector. The majority of the forty entrepreneurs present identified apparel assembly as their most significant problem.

Bibliography

Alba Vega, Carlos. 1997. "Las empresas integradoras en México." *Comercio exterior* 47, 1: 43–49.

Arias, Patricia. 1992. *Nueva rusticidad mexicana.* Mexico City: Consejo Nacional para la Cultura y las Artes.

———. 1994. *Irapuato: El Bajío profundo.* Guanajuato: Talleres Gráficos del Gobierno del Estado de Guanajuato.

Boston Consulting Group and Bufete Industrial. 1988. "Sector textil." Report. Mexico City: Boston Consulting Group and Bufete Industrial.

Calvo, Thomas, and Bernardo Méndez, eds. 1995. *Micro y pequena empresa en Mexico: Frente a los retos de la globalización.* Mexico City: Centro de Estudios Mexicanos y Centroamericanos.

Cawthorne, Pamela. M. 1995. "Of Networks and Markets: The Rise and Rise of a South Indian Town, the Example of Tiruppur's Cotton Knitwear Industry." *World Development* 23, 1 (January): 43–56.

Diario oficial. 1993. "Decreto que promueve la organización de empresas integradoras." *Diario oficial de la nación,* May 7, pp. 37–38.

El financiero. 1996. "Empresas sin cultura exportadora." *El financiero,* November 9, p. 10.

———. 1997. "Uniones de crédito en la mira de CNBV." *El financiero,* January 11, p. 4.

Gereffi, Gary. 1992. "New Realities of Industrial Development in East Asia and Latin America: Global, Regional, and National Trends." In *States and Development in the Asian Pacific Rim,* ed. Richard Appelbaum and Jeffrey Henderson, pp. 85–112. Newbury Park, Calif.: Sage Publications.

———. 1997. "Global Shifts, Regional Response: Can North America Meet the Full-Package Challenge?" *Bobbin* 39, 3 (November): 16–31.

González Ruiz, Edgar. 1995. *Guanajuato: La democracia interina.* Mexico City: Rayuela Editores.

Humphrey, John. 1995. "Industrial Reorganization in Developing Countries: From Models to Trajectories." *World Development* 23, 1 (January): 149–62.

Instituto Nacional de Estadística, Geografía e Informática (INEGI). 1994, 1995a, 1996, 1997. *Anuario estadístico del comercio exterior de los Estados Unidos mexicanos.* Mexico City: INEGI.

———. 1995b. *XIV censo industrial—industrias manufactureras productos y materias primas—resumen general.* Mexico City: INEGI.

———. 1995c. *La industria textil y del vestido en Mexico.* Mexico City: INEGI.

Lailson, Silvia. 1980. "Expansión limitada y proliferación horizontal: La industria de la ropa y el tejido de punto." *Relaciones* (College of Michoacán), no. 3: 48–102.

Martínez Saldaña, Tomás, and Leticia Gándara Mendoza. 1976. *Política y sociedad en México: El caso de los altos de Jalisco.* Mexico City: Secretaría de Educación Pública–Instituto Nacional de Antropología e Historia.

Nacional Financiera (NAFIN). 1992. "Credit Support Programs." Policy paper. Mexico City: NAFIN.

———. 1998. From the NAFIN Web site: <http://www.nafin.gob.mx/>.

Nadvi, Khalid. 1999. "Collective Efficiency and Collective Failure: The Response of the Sialkot Surgical Instrument Cluster to Global Quality Pressures." *World Development* 27, 9 (September): 1605–26.

Organisation for Economic Co-operation and Development (OECD). 1996. *Networks of Enterprises and Local Development: Competing and Co-operation in Local Productive Systems.* Paris: OECD.

Piore, Michael J., and Charles F. Sabel. 1984. *The Second Industrial Divide: Possibilities for Prosperity.* New York: Basic Books.

Pozas, María de Los Angeles. 1993. *Industrial Restructuring in Mexico: Corporate Adaptation, Technological Innovation and Changing Patterns of Industrial Relations in Monterrey.* San Diego: Center for U.S.-Mexican Studies, University of California at San Diego.

Rojas, Mariano, and Luis Alejandro Rojas. 1997. "Transaction Costs in Mexico's Preferential Credit." *Development Policy Review* 15: 23–46.

Secretaría de Comercio y Fomento Industrial (SECOFI). 1998. From the SECOFI Web site: <http://www.secofi.gob.mx/>.

Schmitz, Hubert. 1982. *Manufacturing in the Backyard: Case Studies on Accumulation and Employment in Small-Scale Brazilian Industry.* London: Frances Pinter.

———. 1985. *Technology and Employment Practices in Developing Countries.* London: Croom Helm.

———. 1989. "Flexible Specialisation: A New Paradigm of Small-Scale Industrialisation?" IDS Discussion Paper no. 261. Brighton: Institute of Development Studies, University of Sussex.

———. 1995a. "Small Shoemakers and Fordist Giants: Tale of a Supercluster." *World Development* 23, 1 (January): 9–28.

———. 1995b. "Collective Efficiency: Growth Path for Small-Scale Industry." *Journal of Development Studies* 31, 4 (April): 529–66.

———. 1997. "Collective Efficiency and Increasing Returns." Working Paper no. 50. Brighton: Institute of Development Studies, University of Sussex.

Suarez Aguilar, Estela. 1994. *Pequeña empresa y modernización: Analisis de dos dimensiones.* Cuernavaca: Universidad Autónoma de México, Centro Regional de Investigaciones Multidisciplinarias.

Vangstrup, Ulrik. 1995. "Moroleón—La pequeña ciudad de la gran industria" *Espiral* (University of Guadalajara), no. 4: 101–34.

———. 1999. "Collective Efficiency and Regional Industrial Clusters in Mexico—Assessment of a Theory of Local Industrial Development." Ph.D. diss., Department of Geography and International Development Studies, Roskilde University, Denmark.

Visser, Evert-Jan. 1996. "Local Sources of Competitiveness—Spatial Clustering and Organisational Dynamics in Small-Scale Clothing in Lima, Peru." Ph.D. diss. Amsterdam: Thesis Publishers.

Wilson, Fiona. 1991. *Sweaters: Gender, Class and Workshop-Based Industry in Mexico.* London: Macmillan.

———. 1993. "Workshops as Domestic Domains: Reflections on Small-Scale Industry in Mexico." *World Development* 21, 1: 67–80.

Unión de Crédito de Cuautepéc. 1996. "Informe de la Unión de Crédito de Cuautepéc, 1995." Unpublished document. Cuautepéc, Hidalgo, Mexico: Unión de Crédito de Cuautepéc.

Jorge Mendoza, Fernando Pozos Ponce, and David Spener

---

13   Fragmented Markets, Elaborate Chains:
      The Retail Distribution of Imported
      Clothing in Mexico

Since the beginning of its opening to inter-national trade in 1986, the Mexican economy has undergone a series of transformations. Some of these arose as a consequence of the continuation of the financial crisis that erupted in 1982. Others were the result of Mexico's new relationship to the world economy in general and with the United States and Canada in particular. Mexico's reinsertion into the world economy called into question the patterns of production, distribution, and service provision that prevailed during its import-substitution period. For this reason many entrepreneurs, some with experience in the international market and others who were complete novices, developed new strategies to keep their enterprises competitive during an uncertain period of economic restructuring that continues to this day. Many manufacturers underwent radical restructuring in response to the new productive and marketing challenges, while others simply could not meet the competitive challenge and closed their doors, contributing to soaring unemployment levels during the peak years of the crisis in the mid-1980s (Calva 1996). Other firms abandoned manufacturing but survived by converting

themselves into distributors of the foreign imports that flooded the Mexican market during these years. Moving to the sale of these products offered greater short-term profits to such firms and avoided the problems inherent in upgrading their manufacturing processes. In fact, three of every ten small-to-medium-scale enterprises in Mexico switched from manufacturing to the distribution of imported manufactures, a move that typically involved a reduction in employment in these firms (Pozos 1996a, 130).

The garment industry has been transformed by the globalization of markets and productive restructuring in Mexico. Since 1988 it has gone from being an industry featuring moderate growth and exports to one undergoing dramatic expansion, especially in the export-oriented sector, such that Mexico has replaced the Asian countries as the leading exporter of garments to the United States (Gereffi 1997, Table 1; Ramzy Casab, president of the Cámara Nacional del Vestido, cited in *Ocho columnas* 1996). At the same time clothing consumption in Mexico grew substantially, from around U.S.$9.2 billion in 1988 to U.S.$12.2 billion in 1992. A substantial portion of this increased consumption consisted of apparel imported from the United States and a number of Asian countries, which grew from 3 percent of total consumption in 1988 to nearly 12 percent by 1992, quintupling in dollar value (see Table 13.1).[1] This import boom stimulated employment growth in both formal and informal sale of clothing in Mexico, especially in the major urban centers of Mexico City, Guadalajara, and Monterrey, which also became regional distribution centers for consumer apparel (Gereffi 2000; Guzmán 1993, 22).

In this chapter we focus our analysis on the final segment of the apparel market channel,[2] namely, the sale and distribution of finished garments to private consumers in Mexico. Our objective is to advance understanding of the evolution of distribution channels in the garment industry in Mexico during the period of trade opening that began in the 1980s and continued through the 1990s, upon the signing of the North American Free Trade Agreement (NAFTA). We begin by reviewing the dynamics of the Mexican consumer market for clothing during this period, including changes in the share of apparel sales captured by imported garments as well as the principal countries of origins of such garments. Next we discuss the principal types of enterprises responsible for the retail sale of apparel in Mexico and the market segments they serve. In the third section we undertake a special examination of the important role informal channels play in the distribution of imported garments in Guadalajara. We conclude by raising several questions regarding the continued evolution of apparel-distribution channels in Mexico that may be answered by future research. These questions arise in response to the transformation of commercial practices in the Mexican apparel industry, which has simultaneously featured dramatic growth in large-scale commercial firms and the persistence of a substantial informal sector populated by many thousands of microenterprises.

The Mexican Apparel Market, 1988–2000

The consumer market for clothing in Mexico reflects the differences between Mexico and the United States–Canada in terms of the age structure of the national population. In the latter two countries, residents under twenty years of age account for 32 percent and 31 percent of the total population, respectively, whereas in Mexico they are 50 percent of the population. For this reason the sale of children's clothing is considerably more important in Mexico (28 percent of all clothing sales) than in either the United States (19 percent) or Canada (17 percent) (INEGI 1996a). With regard to the distribution of clothing purchases by gender, in 1995 more women's garments were sold than men's, but the total value of men's clothing exceeded that of women's (INEGI 1996a). Also, in contrast to the markets in the United States and Canada, clothing purchased in Mexico is for the most part produced in Mexico, even though the amount of imported clothing consumed in Mexico rose dramatically after the country's unilateral trade opening in the late 1980s and early 1990s.

We can identify two distinct periods in the Mexican consumer clothing market in recent years: an *expansion stage* in consumption that lasted from 1988 to 1992, followed by a *contraction stage* that ran from 1993 through 1995 (see Table 13.1). During the expansion stage, total consumption of garments in Mexico rose from U.S.$9.2 billion in 1988 to U.S.$12.2 billion in 1992, an average annual growth rate of around 7 percent. Put another way, clothing purchases in Mexico grew by about one-third in just four years. This high rate of growth reflected an increase in per capita clothing consumption.[3] Additionally, the consumption of garments grew more rapidly than the total consumption of goods, suggesting that the participation of garments in average consumption also rose somewhat during this period.[4]

TABLE 13.1.   Mexican Consumption of Domestically Produced and Imported Finished Garments, 1988–2000

Year	Total Private Consumption[a]	% Change[b]	Domestic Garments and Accessories			Imported Garments and Accessories		
			Dollar Value[a]	% of Total	% Change[b]	Dollar Value[a]	% of Total	% Change[b]
1988	9,193,424		8,917,621	97.0		275,803	3.0	
1989	9,857,523	7.2	9,315,360	94.5	4.5	542,164	5.5	96.6
1990	10,933,508	10.9	10,190,030	93.2	9.4	743,479	6.8	37.1
1991	11,294,765	3.3	10,357,300	91.7	1.6	937,466	8.3	26.1
1992	12,170,314	7.8	10,746,387	88.3	3.8	1,423,927	11.7	51.9
1993	11,831,525	−2.8	10,388,079	87.8	−3.3	1,443,446	12.2	1.4
1994	11,472,782	−3.0	10,141,940	88.4	−2.4	1,330,843	11.6	−7.8
1995	9,067,013	−21.0	8,486,724	93.6	−16.3	580,289	6.4	−56.4
1996	9,527,028	5.1	8,898,244	93.4	4.8	628,784	6.6	8.4
1997	10,155,812	6.6	9,191,010	90.5	3.3	964,802	9.5	53.4
1998	10,480,798	3.2	9,139,256	87.2	−0.6	1,341,542	12.8	39.0
1999	10,522,721	0.4	9,186,335	87.3	0.5	1,336,386	12.7	−0.4
2000	11,311,925	7.5	9,875,311	87.3	7.5	1,436,614	12.7	7.5

Source: INEGI, "Sistema de cuentas nacionales de México," available at <http://dgcnesyp.inegi.gob.mx/bdine/m10/m100352.htm>. Retrieved May 28, 2002.

[a]In thousands of 1993 U.S. dollars. Based on authors' calculations using INEGI data expressed in constant pesos.

[b]Relative to the previous year.

The increase in consumer purchases of clothing in the 1988–92 period can be attributed to several factors. First, the Mexican economy experienced moderate growth during these years, and real wages (except for those at the bottom of the range) also grew.[5] Moreover, the price of garments relative to other consumer goods fell significantly in these years.[6] In addition, this period witnessed an important reduction in both tariff and nontariff barriers to the importation of clothing. In response to this relaxation of protectionist measures, the consumption of imported clothing in Mexico rose markedly, from just 3 percent of the total in 1988 to nearly 12 percent in 1992. During this period the main exporters of finished clothing to Mexico were the United States and Hong Kong, with 64.9 percent and 17.5 percent of the 1992 total, respectively (see Table 13.2).[7]

The contraction phase of clothing consumption began in a mild manner between 1992 and 1994, when consumption fell by 6 percent; it then plummeted dramatically by 21 percent in 1995, during the deepest stage of the recent economic crisis in Mexico (see Table 13.1). The reduction in clothing consumption in 1993 is explained by the recession in the Mexican economy that resulted from the contraction in private investment in the face of uncertainty with regard to the U.S. Congress's ratification of NAFTA.[8] In 1994, although the Mexican economy recovered somewhat, clothing consumption continued to fall. During that year private consumption of imported clothing began to fall after several years of sustained growth. This decline is explained in part because the relative price of imported clothing increased as a consequence of exchange-rate adjustments made that year, as well as by the institution of protectionist measures aimed at curbing the import of East Asian garments. The peso devaluation of December 1994 reduced the sale of domestically produced clothing as well, since

TABLE 13.2. Mexican Imports of Garments and Accessories by Country of Origin, 1989–97

Country	1989	1990	1991	1992	1993[a]	1994	1995	1996	1997
Total (in %)[b]	100	100	100	100	100	100	100	100	100
Total (in U.S.$1,000s)[c]	266,775	354,625	441,255	1,016,802	1,200,875	1,688,981	1,774,972	2,314,633	4,752,753
Colombia	0.2	0.3	0.4	0.5	0.5	0.5	0.1	0.2	0.1
North Korea	0.2	0.2	1.8	1.5	0.1	0.1	0.0	0.0	0.0
South Korea	2.1	1.1	0.2	0.0	2.2	1.6	0.5	0.4	0.1
China	3.5	2.9	0.0	0.0	0.0	0.0	0.2	0.1	0.1
Spain	1.3	1.7	1.5	1.3	1.4	2.0	1.3	1.0	0.5
United States	63.3	52.3	51.2	64.9	69.2	74.4	88.5	93.4	96.3
Hong Kong	13.0	21.5	21.1	17.4	9.1	5.2	2.2	0.9	0.9
Italy	2.6	4.5	5.4	2.8	4.0	2.9	1.3	0.8	0.2
Japan	0.1	1.3	0.4	0.1	0.1	0.1	0.0	0.0	0.1
Panama	6.0	7.2	6.3	2.8	0.3	0.1	0.0	0.0	0.0
Thailand	0.5	0.5	0.5	0.7	1.7	1.6	0.3	0.1	0.0
Taiwan	0.0	0.0	2.2	1.4	2.0	1.3	0.5	0.4	0.1
Uruguay	0.4	0.5	0.6	0.3	0.3	0.2	0.0	0.0	0.0
Canal Zone (Panama)	1.1	0.1	0.8	1.0	0.1	0.0	0.0	0.0	0.0
Other countries	4.4	4.7	5.9	4.2	7.3	8.4	4.6	2.5	1.4

Source: INEGI, *La industria textil y del vestido en México* (1996a, 1997).

[a]Beginning in 1993, data include maquiladora-related imports.

[b]Percentage totals for individual countries do not equal 100 exactly, due to rounding to the nearest one-tenth of a percent.

[c]Banco de México, *The Mexican Economy* (1996, 1997b, 1998). Total imports are in current dollars.

it occurred at the beginning of the holiday season, in which a large proportion of annual clothing sales typically is made.

In 1995 the Mexican economy experienced its largest contraction since the 1930s, as real gross domestic product (GDP) fell by 6.9 percent.[9] For its part, total consumption of clothing decreased much more (21 percent), owing to the drop in disposable income and real wages as well as the rise in garment prices relative to other goods.[10] Furthermore, the drop observed in the value of imported garments (56 percent) was much greater than that for domestic garments (16 percent) as a consequence of the devaluation of the national currency. Thus the share captured by imported garments in total clothing sales fell from a peak of 12.2 percent in 1993 to just 6.4 percent in 1995, as consumers substituted cheaper domestically produced garments for more-expensive imports.

It is important to recognize the severity of the contraction in the consumption of garments in Mexico as a consequence of the economic crisis. Total consumption of clothing in 1995 was 5 percent less than that registered in 1988, representing a rollback of more than seven years of gains in absolute levels of consumption. Moreover, per capita consumption of clothing—which is an indicator that allows us to approximate the effects of the crisis on the welfare of the population—suffered a dramatic decline of 16 percent when we compare 1995 with 1988. Given all this, the share of total consumer spending in Mexico that was captured by garments—which in 1993 and 1994 had fallen to 4.2 percent and 3.9 percent, respectively—in 1995 contracted significantly to just 3.4 percent, a level that was also substantially below that of 1988.[11] Modest macroeconomic recovery in Mexico began in 1996, with a 5 percent increase in GDP and a 2.2 percent increase in consumption of private goods and services. Total consumption of clothing increased 5.1 percent over 1995, and

as the peso strengthened against the dollar consumption of imported clothing also rose by 8.4 percent (see Table 13.1).

Although the Mexican public's consumption of both domestically and foreign-produced clothing was considerably less in 1996 than it was in 1992, Mexico's garment imports grew rapidly throughout this period (see Table 13.2). Where, in 1992, Mexico imported just over U.S.$1 billion in "garments and accessories," by 1996 the figure had more than doubled to U.S.$2.3 billion. Even more dramatically, imports from the United States eclipsed those from all other countries, as its share of Mexican imports grew from 65 percent in 1992 to 93 percent in 1996. The continued growth of garment imports to Mexico and the increase in share captured by the United States are a direct consequence of the dramatic expansion of maquiladora production of garments in the wake of NAFTA and the 1994 peso devaluation. The import of synthetic and natural fiber garments for the maquiladora industry grew by 32.5 percent from 1994 to 1996, and the maquiladoras' share of imports of these garments grew from 58 percent to 78 percent of total imports.[12] We now turn our attention to the types of firms that served the increasingly dynamic and volatile Mexican retail market for clothing.

The Types of Enterprises Engaging in the Retail Sale of Clothing in Mexico

A number of different types of enterprises engage in the retail sale of new clothing in urban Mexico. These vary along a continuum of size and degree of formality of establishment and range from large-scale department stores (*tiendas departamentales*) and self-service outlets (*tiendas de autoservicio*) to "markets on wheels" known as *tianguis* and door-to-door sellers

TABLE 13.3.   Principal Types of Retail Clothing Outlets in Mexico

Type	Description
Tiendas departamentales	Department stores
Tiendas de autoservicio	Self-service stores (i.e., items purchased without the assistance of a sales clerk). Includes supermarkets, general-merchandise discount stores, warehouses, and membership clubs. Generally large-scale establishments but also includes some clothing specialty chains with smaller individual establishments.
Tiendas de ropa	Clothing stores. Mainly small-scale and privately held.
Tianguis	"Markets on wheels" that move from place to place in a Mexican city, so that one operates in a particular part of the city on a given day of the week. Similar to "flea markets" in the United States, except that *tianguis* sell new as well as secondhand goods.
Mercados and *bazares*	Market stalls and bazaars.
Aboneros	Door-to-door sellers of clothing and other goods who extend credit to customers, allowing them to pay for goods in installments.
Other outlets	Includes street vendors and non-*abonero* door-to-door sales.

known as *aboneros*. Table 13.3 presents a typology of enterprises selling garments in Mexico and describes the characteristics of each category. As shown in Table 13.4, the Mexican retail clothing market is roughly divided into thirds at both the national level and in the nation's three largest cities (which are also the three largest urban markets for retail clothes). In 1996 formal, large-scale department stores and self-service outlets accounted for a bit more than a third of clothing sales. Another third of total sales were by clothing stores *(tiendas de ropa)*, most of which are small-scale, formal establishments. Finally, about one-third of clothing purchases by Mexican consumers were made through a variety of small-scale, informal enterprises, including *tianguis, aboneros,* and street vendors. In the remainder of this section we discuss the dynamics of the coexistence of these three distinct market segments and their possible future evolution. In particular we discuss the simultaneous expansion of the large-scale, formal sector of the market and the small-scale, informal sector.

Since the 1980s, and increasingly in the 1990s, Mexico has witnessed a rapid growth of retail sales of all types of products, including clothing, through large-scale, multicity chains of department stores and self-service outlets.[13] As in the United States, the rise of department stores and discount chains has taken considerable market share away from small-scale, independently owned stores.[14] These types of outlets have come to play a very important role in the retail sale of clothing, so that by 1997 sales of the biggest eight stores in Mexico City, Guadalajara, and Monterrey accounted for 37 percent, 33.6 percent, and 33.8 percent, respectively, of total retail clothing sales (Trendex North America 1998). The development of self-service outlets has taken two distinct forms. On the one hand, department-store chains have increased the size of their individual stores and the breadth of their product lines. Thus this sector, which had typically been composed of supermarkets, has incorporated hypermarkets and, more recently, megamarkets and "membership clubs" as well.[15] The expansion of large-scale self-service outlets has offered an increased role for foreign investors, who have initiated joint ventures and mergers with domestic firms in order to take

TABLE 13.4.   Percent Share of Mexican Retail Clothing Sales Captured by Enterprises of Different Types[a]

Type of Enterprise	Nation		Mexico City[b]	Guadalajara[c]	Monterrey[d]
	1995	1996			
Formal, large-scale					
Tiendas departamentales	29.2	24.9	27.3	28.2	29.2
Tiendas de autoservicio	12.7	10.7	13.1	8.2	15.6
Subtotal	41.9	35.6	40.4	36.4	44.8
Formal, mainly small-scale					
Tiendas de ropa	31.1	32.0	32.1	35.7	28.4
Informal, small-scale					
Tianguis, mercados, and *bazares*	16.3	18.7	18.3	14.9	13.6
Aboneros	4.2	5.2	3.3	6.6	4.3
Other outlets	6.5	8.5	5.9	6.4	8.9
Subtotal	27.0	32.4	27.5	27.9	26.8
Total	100.0	100.0	100.0	100.0	100.0

Source: Kormos, Harris and Associates and Shaw Direct (1996a, 1997).

[a]Metropolitan figures are for 1995.

[b]Mexico City captured 27.4 percent of national retail clothing sales in 1995.

[c]Guadalajara captured 5.2 percent of national retail clothing sales in 1995.

[d]Monterrey captured 4.4 percent of national retail clothing sales in 1995.

advantage of the latter's existing locations and market experience. For their part, Mexican domestic firms have preferred to associate themselves with foreign firms and thus broaden their scale of operations rather than face the foreign firms as new competitors in their traditional markets.[16]

The market position of small independent retail establishments has also been affected by proliferation of informal microenterprises, which by 1994 numbered around 3 million in Mexico.[17] These enterprises mainly serve a low-income clientele that is attracted by cheaper prices, does not possess credit cards, and may have difficulty accessing large-scale self-service outlets that are not located conveniently near their neighborhoods. In 1992, at the peak of the expansion phase of garment consumption in Mexico, nearly 166,000 microenterprises engaged principally in the sale of clothing in

urban areas.[18] Eighty percent of Mexican microenterprises had no fixed place of business and no employees. These informal businesses included *tianguis,* street vendors, market-stall sellers, and *aboneros.* In 1992 around half of the microenterprises dedicated to clothing sales had opened within the previous three years, that is, they were born in the years immediately after Mexico's trade opening (INEGI-STPS 1996).

Market-research studies conducted by industry consultants in Mexico indicate that the formal and informal sectors of the retail market for apparel serve different consumer segments (Kormos, Harris and Associates and Shaw Direct 1996a). As indicated in Table 13.5, middle- and upper-class consumers make from two-thirds to three-quarters of their clothing purchases in department stores and clothing stores, from 10 to 15 percent in self-

TABLE 13.5.   Mexican Retail Clothing Sales in 1995, by Type of Enterprise and Class of Customer

Type of Enterprise	Class of Customer		
	Upper-class and upper-middle-class	Middle-class	Working-class
Formal, large-scale			
Tiendas departamentales	37.0	31.7	18.5
Tiendas de autoservicio	9.9	13.9	13.9
Subtotal	46.9	45.6	32.4
Formal, mainly small-scale			
Tiendas de ropa	36.5	31.9	28.4
Informal, small-scale			
Tianguis, mercados, and *bazares*	6.7	11.7	27.2
Aboneros	2.9	4.1	4.7
Other outlets	7.0	6.7	7.3
Subtotal	16.6	22.5	39.2
Total	100.0	100.0	100.0

Source: Kormos, Harris and Associates and Shaw Direct (1996a).

service outlets, and one-fifth or less from informal channels. Working-class Mexicans, by contrast, carry out about 40 percent of their clothing purchases through informal outlets, especially *tianguis,* markets, and bazaars, and about 14 percent through self-service outlets. They are especially unlikely to shop for clothes in the expensive department stores, making less than 20 percent of their purchases in such establishments. While working-class Mexicans constitute the majority of all clothing consumers in Mexico, they do not make the majority of clothing purchases. In 1994 upper- and upper-middle-class Mexicans, who made up just 10 percent of consumers, accounted for half of the value of all clothing purchased in the country (Harris 1995).

The contraction of the Mexican clothing market from 1992 through 1995 reduced the sales of all types of retail clothing sellers. The unexpected devaluation of the peso in late 1994, in addition to reducing overall clothing sales drastically, led to the substitution of domestically produced garments for imports. The decline in clothing sales after 1992 had a significant impact on the informal retail clothing sector. The number of microenterprises engaged in the sale of clothing and footwear fell from its peak of 166,000 in 1992 to 151,000 in 1994, with employment falling from 248,000 to 227,000 (INEGI 1994). During the same period, in contrast, the number of microenterprises in all industries at the national level actually grew, from 2.6 to 3.0 million. As the apparel market began its recovery, however, the number of clothing microenterprises expanded to 208,000 in 1996 and employed more than 285,000 Mexicans (INEGI-STPS 1992, 1994, 1996). As shown in Table 13.4, informal outlets increased their share of total clothing sales in Mexico from 27.0 percent of the market in 1995 to 32.4 percent in 1996. In this first year of market recovery, the National Association of Self-Service and Department Stores reported that clothing sales among its members continued to fall, though not as precipitously as they had from 1994 to 1995 (ANTAD 1997b). Accordingly, the share of Mexican clothing sales captured by department stores and self-service outlets fell from about 42 percent in 1995 to 36 percent in 1996 (see Table 13.4). At the same time the share of sales made through clothing stores was essentially unchanged.

Thus in the first years after the establishment of NAFTA we find a Mexican consumer apparel market whose characteristics are changing rapidly in terms of the overall volume of sales, the country of origin of garments, and the principal sales outlets. Recent years have seen a rapid expansion of large-scale clothing retailers in the form of department stores and self-service outlets that now claim a substantial portion of the market. As leaders of buyer-driven commodity chains (Gereffi 1994), these retailers, which now include U.S. giants such as JCPenney, Wal-Mart, Dillards, Price Club, and Sam's, have begun to import large amounts of clothing from abroad, especially Asia, while they also source an increasing amount of their own production in Mexico.

At the same time the informal sector has expanded considerably in recent years. It currently accounts for a substantial portion of the overall apparel market and plays an especially important role in serving the needs of Mexico's working-class consumers (who are the majority of consumers). Although they clearly do not drive garment commodity chains in the way that their large-scale counterparts are able to do, informal apparel sellers contributed substantially to the growth of clothing imports during the first years of the Mexican trade opening leading up to NAFTA. Standing between these two sectors, and having experienced loss of market share to both, we find the clothing stores, a large proportion of which are small-scale locally owned and operated establishments. While it is clear that the expansion of the department stores and self-service outlets has significantly altered the dynamics of the Mexican apparel market in the wake of free trade, we must nevertheless

bear in mind that small-scale establishments, both formal and informal, still make up as much as half of total apparel sales in Mexico.

We now turn our attention to the operation of small-scale and informal distribution channels for imported garments in Guadalajara, Mexico's second largest urban area. Guadalajara, known as "la gran ciudad de la pequeña industria" (the big city for small business) (Arias 1985), is also the country's second largest apparel market and serves as a regional trade hub for western-central Mexico. We undertake this examination of such channels in order (1) to better understand their coexistence with the large-scale firms that lead buyer-driven commodity chains; (2) to illustrate their role in the opening of the Mexican market to imported clothing in the early years of the trade opening; and (3) to speculate as to what type of role they will play as the North American apparel market is consolidated and macroeconomic recovery continues in Mexico.

Guadalajara: Case Study of Informal Distribution Channels for Clothing[19]

In Guadalajara informal distribution channels for clothing play a substantial role in the market: Twenty-one and a half percent of clothing sales in the metropolitan area are accounted for by *tianguis*, markets, bazaars, and *aboneros* (see Table 13.4). If we add to this the 35.7 percent of clothing sales that are made by clothing stores (which in this city are mainly small businesses), we find that in Guadalajara up to 57 percent of all clothing sales are made by small-scale enterprises, many of which operate in the informal sector.[20] Furthermore, there is a close relationship between small-scale formal establishments on the one hand and informal sellers on the other, since many informal sellers purchase their imported merchandise wholesale from small formal establishments.

The Import Clothing Boom, 1988–94

Beginning in the late 1980s a large volume of imported garments entered the Mexican market, mostly from the United States. Most if not all apparel imports from Asia passed through the port of Los Angeles, California, and then entered Mexican territory through inland ports of entry, especially in Tijuana and Nuevo Laredo. Many of these Asian garments were sold to small-scale Mexican firms through brokers in Los Angeles' dynamic garment district. Thus the "true" country of origin of imported apparel in Mexico was frequently murky, since clothing traded in Los Angeles consisted of both U.S.- and Asian-made garments.

In Guadalajara the dramatic growth in imports promoted the creation of a new downtown district for retail clothing sales, in and around the traditional San Juan de Dios Market, a section already dedicated mainly to the sale of imported clothing. Around four hundred small stores in this area are located along each of four streets (Alvaro Obregón, Esteban de la Torre, Medrano, and Sixty-fourth Street) (Pozos 1996b, 130). Fifty percent of these stores are dedicated exclusively to the sale of clothing. Elsewhere in the city we find approximately two hundred *tianguis*, 36 percent of which sell only apparel items (Torres 1988, 330; corroborated in personal communication by Pozos with the staff of the Cámara Nacional de Comercio de Guadalajara, June 1996). Small formal businesses and *tianguis* combined account for around three thousand jobs in the sale of clothing. These jobs are quite diverse both in terms of class of worker (employers, the self-employed, salaried workers, and unpaid family workers) and in terms of income level.[21]

No single firm or group of firms in Guadalajara's retail garment district appears to dominate the distribution channels, whose outlets are small-scale establishments or informal enterprises. Furthermore, there are few barriers to entry for firms wishing to enter these distribution channels. To a great extent this is because any businessperson, whether large- or small-scale, can travel to Los Angeles to acquire merchandise, so that no firm is "controllable" by other firms up- or downstream from it in the distribution channel.[22] Thus in our fieldwork we did not discover that any single importing firm or group of firms supplied most small garment-selling enterprises in the city (as is the case in some Mexico City informal markets for other types of products in Mexico—e.g., Mexico City's Tepito market—which are controlled by powerful syndicates). Nor did we find that small-scale garment sellers had begun to turn to large-scale discount chains as their wholesale suppliers.[23]

The inability of individual firms or groups of firms to monopolize clothing imported into Guadalajara's garment district encourages multiple structures for distribution channels. At one end of the continuum we find channels composed of segments that are vertically integrated to some extent, where an import/export firm sells garments to retail/wholesale establishments and these, in turn, supply *tianguis* vendors, who then serve as suppliers to *aboneros* selling clothing door to door. At the other end are channels whose segments are completely independent of one another, where the retail/wholesale clothing store, the *tianguis* vendor, and the *abonero* purchase garments directly in Los Angeles and sell directly to the final consumer, completely independent of one another. Between these two extremes we find channels with other kinds of characteristics, which for reasons of space we do not describe here. More important, we need to explain the factors that seem to have prevented the concentration of control of imported-garment distribution channels in just a few hands.

One of the factors that promotes vertically fragmented channels with autonomous firms for each transaction is the potential for individual

TABLE 13.6.   Distribution of Value Added among Three Types of Distribution Channels for Imported Clothing in Guadalajara, 1997

Type of Seller	Men's Wear: Printed T-Shirt[a]		Women's Wear: Dresses		Children's Clothing: Dresses or Outfits	
	Typical Seller's Markup (%)[b]	Typical Value Added to Garment (%)[c]	Typical Seller's Markup (%)[b]	Typical Value Added to Garment (%)[c]	Typical Seller's Markup (%)[b]	Typical Value Added to Garment (%)[c]
Importing firm	25.0	25.0	30.0	30.0	36.0	36.0
Clothing store	35.0	43.8	40.0	52.0	25.0	34.0
Tianguis vendor	30.0	50.6	25.0	45.5	20.0	34.0
Abonero			15.0	34.1	16.0	32.6
Typical Total Value Added (%)	—	119.4	—	161.6	—	136.6

Source: Constructed by authors with data obtained through field interviews in Guadalajara and Los Angeles, May–June 1997.

[a]This channel ends with sale to the final consumer by the *tianguis* vendor; hence the empty cells for the *abonero*'s markup and value added.

[b]The typical "seller's markup," SMU, is given by the equation $SMU = 100*(b - a)/a$, where a = the price paid by the seller when she or he purchases the garment from the supplier immediately preceding her or him in the channel, and b = the price she or he charges the next purchaser in the channel. Percentages shown at each transactional level of the chain may *not* be summed to give a total markup for the garment.

[c]The typical "percent value added," PVA, is calculated with respect to the garment's cost at point of purchase in Los Angeles. At any transactional level it is defined by the equation $PVA = 100*(d - c)/p$, where c = the price paid by the seller when she or he purchases the garment from the supplier immediately preceding her or him in the channel; d = the price she or he charges the next purchaser in the channel; and p = the cost of the garment at the point of original purchase in Los Angeles. Percentages shown at each transactional level of the chain may be summed to give a total PVA for garments passing through the channel.

firms to bypass intermediaries in the channel in an attempt to realize greater profits. Thus, for example, the clothing store, the *tianguis* vendor, and the *abonero* who buy their products directly from suppliers in Los Angeles and sell directly to the final consumer realize significantly greater profits relative to those who sell to other segments of the channel.[24] In these cases each segment adds value to the garments in order to realize its specific profit without the price of the garment rising above a competitive level. Here we insist that in a fragmented, undeveloped market such as that represented by working-class residents of Guadalajara, each segment of the channel provides a needed distributive service that ensures diverse buyers receive the clothing they desire at prices commensurate with their ability to pay. Thus the segments' markup is not merely the collection of a middleman's economic "rent" but in fact

adds value to the product through the labor of small-scale entrepreneurs and their associates (see Sayer and Walker 1992).

To better illustrate this phenomenon, in Table 13.6 we present three examples of distribution channels for imported garments that are widely consumed in Guadalajara: men's printed T-shirts, women's dresses, and children's outfits (*vestidos y conjuntos*). In the first column for each type of garment, the table shows the percentage that each buyer-seller marks the price up beyond what was paid to the buyer-seller immediately "upstream" in the channel. The second column represents the size of that markup in percentage terms relative to the value of the garment at its point of purchase in Los Angeles. Figures in the second column are summed to show the total percentage of value added to the garment along its distribution channel after it leaves Los Angeles.[25]

Of the three examples represented in Table 13.6, dresses are the type of garment with the greatest value added along the entire distribution channel, showing an average increase of 162 percent between the point of sale in Los Angeles and the point of final consumer purchase in Guadalajara. Thus, for example, a woman's dress purchased wholesale in Los Angeles for 60 Mexican pesos receives a 30 percent markup from the importer (18 pesos). Next, one of the small retail/wholesale clothing stores near the San Juan de Dios market purchases the dress for 78 pesos, marks it up 40 percent (31 pesos), and sells it to a *tianguis* vendor for 109 pesos, who in turn marks it up another 25 percent (27 pesos). Then the *tianguis* vendor sells it to an *abonero* for 136 pesos, who in turn marks the dress up another 15 percent (21 pesos) and sells it to the final consumer for 157 pesos. As we see, in this way each segment of the channel appropriates for itself a part of the total value added to the dress, which is still sold on the market for a competitive price.

The type of distribution channel represented by this description of the movement of a dress from Los Angeles to Guadalajara was the most common one we found in our field studies. Nevertheless, a large number of independent entrepreneurs and firms bypass intermediaries and purchase goods directly in the Los Angeles garment district. Obviously, these merchants must have sufficient financial resources to travel to Los Angeles, but they are aided by the fact that there are a number of fairly inexpensive direct flights between the two cities. For large-scale sellers, travel costs represent a relatively small investment, while for the small-scale sellers such expenses are considerably more significant. Still, small-scale sellers are often able to minimize their expenses by (1) relying on family members or friends in Los Angeles to purchase and ship to them the garments they need and (2) making less frequent trips and purchasing garments that per-

mit a greater markup, such as women's dresses or prestigious brand-name gentlemen's clothing.

Another factor that facilitates merchants' purchases of garments in Los Angeles is the presence of Mexican immigrant and Mexican-American employees in the stores and warehouses of the garment district. Although most of the owners of establishments in the Los Angeles garment district that we interviewed were Koreans or Iranians who did not speak Spanish,[26] their Mexican employees filled the ethnic and linguistic gap that separates the Guadalajara and Korean entrepreneurs. In this way the Mexican businessperson in Los Angeles finds herself in an environment that is in many respects quite similar to what she would encounter in her own city, including the classic haggling over price and terms, in which the entire transaction is carried out in Spanish. Of course, the employees of these stores and warehouses consult in English with their Korean employers to close certain deals, offer price discounts, or inquire as to the availability of certain seasonal fashions. This ethnolinguistic factor allows an "average" Guadalajara merchant to travel to Los Angeles and obtain garments to sell in her city of origin with a far greater profit margin than the merchant who acquires her product in Guadalajara itself.[27]

The 1994 Peso Crisis: Import Substitution Redux

As noted previously, the devaluation of the peso in December 1994 produced a significant downturn in Mexican imports of clothing from the United States and East Asia.[28] In response to the devaluation, Mexican merchants reverted to the sale and distribution of domestically produced apparel, which suddenly became cheaper than imported garments. This obviously benefited Mexican garment manufacturers, whose export potential also increased dramatically with the devaluation. (See Chapters 1 and 2 in this book.) In states such as Jalisco and Nuevo León, many garment factories that had produced mainly for the domestic market converted themselves into exporting maquiladoras (interview with Jaime Barba de Loza, president of the Cámara del Vestido de Jalisco, reported in *Ocho columnas* 1996; see also Chapter 9 in this book).

During the phase of expansion in garment imports, Mexican consumers became accustomed to certain models, logos, and brand names emanating from the United States and East Asia. For this reason Guadalajara clothing merchants insisted that domestic manufacturers of garments modify their products after the devaluation in order to make them more similar to those that consumers had become used to purchasing. Examples include printed T-shirts that have a strong market, especially among the young. Before the peso devaluation, some of the most popular shirts sold were imports that were adorned with the logos of U.S. sports teams, such as the Dallas Cowboys, the Los Angeles Lakers, and the Chicago Bulls. The same shirts still appear to be on the market in large numbers. Close inspection reveals, however, that the tags on the shirts that give cleaning instructions, type of cloth, and country of origin now read, in English, "Made in the U.S.M." Clearly this tag is intended to give the consumer the idea that the shirt was produced in the United States of America, with "U.S.M." referring to the "United States of Mexico," a translation of the complete name of the Mexican republic. As a result, the great majority of consumers are able to purchase T-shirts that are "identical" to those they purchased before the devaluation, but at a more affordable price.

The overall decline in the consumption of imported clothing in Mexico has had direct effects on distribution channels at both the national and international levels. In response to Mexican merchants switching back to domestic garment producers as suppliers, Los Angeles garment sellers had to offer Mexican clients better prices to stimulate sales. For this reason many of the Los Angeles sellers have resorted to their own version of tag-switching: They put "Made in the U.S.A." labels on cheaper Asian-produced garments, which allows them not only to avoid Mexican tariffs but also to offer a lower-priced alternative to U.S.-made imports. Still, the reduction in the consumption of imported clothing in Mexico has signified important losses. Los Angeles garment sellers we interviewed reported that their sales to Mexican merchants declined by approximately 70 percent from 1994 to 1995.

Conclusions

Since at least the late 1970s, analysts of international economic development have written extensively about the rise of export-oriented manufacturing in developing countries of the periphery and semiperiphery of the world system. A great deal of attention has been focused on the garment industry, which has played a pioneering role in this process. Countries such as Mexico are studied as cost-saving production sites for transnational manufacturing. Much less attention, however, has been paid to the opening in these countries of large consumer markets to foreign products. In the case of Mexico we see that this may be a significant oversight, especially with regard to apparel, which by 1992 constituted a $12 billion market, over $1 billion of which consisted of imports. Because of the unexpected collapse of the peso in NAFTA's first year of operation, the steady growth of sales of imported clothing since 1988 was reversed in the mid 1990s. By the year 2000, total private consumption of clothing had finally returned to its pre-crisis share of total consumption (see Table 13.1).

That the Mexican consumer market was a potentially lucrative one for foreign firms is attested by the rapid expansion of large U.S. retail chains into many Mexican cities in the 1990s. Such firms, whether independently or in concert with Mexican partners, quickly gained major market shares for a variety of consumer goods, including apparel. In the case of apparel, some of the leading firms that established a network of production contractors in Mexico during this period also began to attack the Mexican consumer apparel market aggressively. This was a theoretically significant development as buyer-driven commodity chains came full circle, with developed-country firms bringing their Mexican-made goods to an emerging market that was itself located in the developing world.

At the same time a substantial share of the consumer market for apparel, including that for imported garments, continued to be served by small-scale and informal enterprises. These enterprises were not "driving" the commodity chains for which they were the retail outlets but rather purchased goods either directly from manufacturers or from brokers located in Los Angeles' garment district.[29] Although they "took" the prices offered by suppliers from whom they purchased garments wholesale (whether in Mexico or in the United States), they played a vital role in serving a clientele of low-income consumers in a market characterized by an underdeveloped physical and financial infrastructure. In this context, these small-scale entrepreneurs were not so much price-gouging "middlemen" interposing themselves between suppliers and the public as they were necessary links between producers and a highly fragmented market, with their earnings commensurate to the value they added to the product by ensuring that it reached its intended consumer. Moreover, while it may be true that the fragmented markets served by small-scale and informal clothing-distribution channels are

relatively small in terms of monetary value and potential profits to be made by transnational enterprises, both these markets and the distribution channels that serve them are of substantial social significance. Millions of Mexican consumers and thousands of workers are vitally dependent on them.

We do not yet know the extent to which the expansion of large-scale self-service outlets and corporate chains of clothing stores may erode informal distribution channels in urban Mexico. If the self-service outlets, because of the volume of merchandise they move, can offer discounted prices that overcome the advantages of informal sellers (physical proximity to customers and limited overhead in the form of taxes, rent, employee benefits paid), they may continue to gain market share as the Mexican economy recovers. As lead firms in buyer-driven commodity chains that include production sites in Mexico, the United States, and elsewhere in Latin American and Asia, both the discount chains and the department stores will surely play a major role in determining the extent to which imported clothing becomes more important in the domestic apparel market.

Small-scale and informal sellers of garments are likely to retain distinct competitive advantages for a substantial segment of the Mexican market. Mexico's neoliberal economic model has, in general, fostered the development of separate markets and separate social worlds for the upper and lower classes. This may extend to the world of apparel sales. It is quite conceivable that U.S.-style department stores and discount warehouses will continue to serve a relatively affluent clientele with the automobiles and credit cards that make shopping in these sorts of outlets attractive, while the *tianguis*, markets, and bazaars will serve a more working-class clientele, greater in number but with considerably less purchasing power and more willing to purchase goods of lower quality (including factory seconds and cheap, even fraudulent imitations of name-brand garments).

Indeed, not only does the informal sector serve the lower and working classes in Mexico; its entrepreneurs and employees are themselves typically drawn from these same classes. Though we did not find this to be the case in our fieldwork, an additional possibility is that the two sectors may eventually become linked so that informal and other small-scale sellers make wholesale purchases of some types of garments from large-scale discount outlets. Whether or not they retain independence from lead firms in the formal sector, small-scale and informal sector enterprises are likely to play a significant role in the clothing of Mexicans for the foreseeable future.

Notes

Acknowledgments: Research whose results are reported in this chapter was supported by a grant from the Ford Foundation to the Population Research Center (PRC) of the University of Texas at Austin. The authors worked as part of a PRC team investigating the interrelationships among small-business activity, urban poverty abatement, and international migration in the U.S.-Mexico transborder region.

1. Here we should note that official data do not capture the large amount of clothing that enters Mexico as extralegal contraband.

2. Our use of the term *market channel* in place of *commodity chain* follows that of Dannhaeuser (1991), an economic anthropologist. Dannhaeuser's use of the term, in turn, follows that of Kotler (1980). In the interest of clarity, in this chapter we frequently use the term *distribution channel* to describe those portions of garment commodity chains that distribute imported garments in Mexico. We do this in order to avoid confusion between "chain stores" that are major sellers of such garments and the distribution "chains" in which they are inserted. As argued by Dannhaeuser (1991, 316), the market channel for a commodity is structured around the number of trade levels that exist between producer and consumer and by the number, size, and type of enterprises that occupy each level. Some market channels are complex and vertically fragmented, with many firms located at each transactional level. In these channels no single firm exerts effective control over other firms. Other channels are more tightly coordinated and vertically integrated, so that a single enterprise or group of enterprises dominates and controls the operation of the entire channel (Dannhaeuser 1991). In the case of peripheral or semiperipheral countries, we must consider another aspect of these channels as well: the relative formality or informality of the activities carried out by an enterprise at each of its transactional levels.

3. The growth in per capita consumption is inferred from an annual population growth of less than 2 percent per annum. Figures on growth in garment sales are taken from INEGI (1996b).

4. Thus the share of garments in total consumer expenditures rose from 4.2 percent in 1988 to 4.4 percent in 1992. These figures are calculated in constant 1993 prices (INEGI 1996b).

5. Average annual growth in gross domestic product between 1988 and 1992 was 3.5 percent. Manufacturing salaries and the average salary nationwide grew in real terms each year from 1989 through 1994, although they fell significantly in 1995. In contrast, the minimum wage in Mexico fell in real terms throughout this period (CIEMEX-WEFA 1996).

6. Between 1988 and 1992 the price index for clothing fell by 20 percent relative to the index of prices for all other consumer goods in Mexico (INEGI 1996b).

7. The figures for this period exclude semifinished and unfinished garments imported into Mexico for assembly in maquiladoras.

8. In 1993, Mexican gross domestic product experienced a real growth rate of just 0.6 percent, while real gross investment fell by 3 percent (CIEMEX-WEFA 1996).

9. In 1995 private consumption fell by 12.9 percent and total investment shrank by nearly 40 percent (CIEMEX-WEFA 1996).

10. Real wages in manufacturing fell by 11.4 percent in 1995, while the average wage for all sectors

dropped by 9.7 percent (CIEMEX–WEFA 1996). Furthermore, the price index for garments rose three points higher than that of the general consumer price index (INEGI 1996b).

11. These indicators are calculated using constant 1993 prices. If instead we rely on prices in current pesos, the share of total consumer spending captured by garments was 5.2 percent in 1988, falling to 4.6 percent in 1992 and further, to just 3.4 percent, in 1995. This contrast owes to the lag in garment prices with respect to the consumer price index. In other words, the fall in the relative price of clothing (both domestic and imported) more than compensated for the important increases in the unit volume of sales, such that garments' share of current consumer spending effectively declined.

12. Figures reported are based on calculations made by the authors using the Banco de México's *Indicadores del sector externo* (1995, 1997a).

13. For example, the Asociación Nacional de Tiendas de Autoservicio y Departamentales (ANTAD) reports that between 1988 and 1992 the number of establishments designated as megamarkets, hypermarkets, and department stores grew by 63 percent, 50 percent, and 37 percent, respectively (1997a). According to ANTAD, a "megamarket" is a self-service outlet (*tienda de autoservicio*) with more than ten thousand square meters of floor space that manages all product lines. A "hypermarket" is a self-service outlet with between forty-five hundred and ten thousand square meters of floor space that manages a large number of, but not all, product lines. "Department stores" sell and exhibit products that are classified by department, such as clothing and housewares. These categories are defined in ANTAD's *Directorio 1997* (1997a).

14. In 1993 the retail discount chains and department stores with the greatest sales in the country were (in descending order): Cifra, Gigante, Comercial Mexicana, Liverpool, Chedraui, Soriana, Hermes, Sears Roebuck, Sorimex, Nazas, Salinas y Rocha, El Palacio de Hierro, and Almacenes Coppel (Harris 1995).

15. Membership clubs are stores with floor space greater than forty-five hundred square meters that are focused on wholesale and semiwholesale sales and directed to certain sectors through memberships; these stores sell hardware, perishables, and general merchandise (ANTAD 1997a). There are also some specialty discount-clothing stores that fall in the self-service outlet category that are typically smaller establishments.

16. It should be mentioned that the Cifra group established a joint venture with Wal-Mart, which now operates both supermarkets (Aurrerá and Superama) and department stores (Suburbia). Other examples of joint ventures among discount chains are Comercial Mexicana–Price Club–Kmart and Gigante–Sam's Club.

17. Owners of small-scale formal retail establishments in Mexico frequently complain of *competencia desleal* (unfair competition) on the part of street vendors and other informal enterprises, since the informals do not abide by the same government regulations or have to factor high overhead costs into their prices. Particular ire is reserved for street vendors who "use public space for private gain" (see Mendoza 1994).

18. The number of microenterprises selling new and used clothing also includes footwear. A "microenterprise" is defined as an economic unit employing up to six people, including owner and employees, whether or not they are paid. For manufactures this number rises to sixteen persons (see INEGI-STPS 1994, 1996).

19. Findings reported in this section derive from fieldwork conducted by Pozos among garment sellers in Guadalajara and in the garment district in Los Angeles in May and June 1997. In Guadalajara thirty structured interviews were conducted with sellers of different types of garments. In Los Angeles fifteen such interviews were conducted with Korean and Iranian garment sellers.

20. This needs to be taken as an upper-bound estimate, since clothing stores as a category include some larger retail companies with multiple retail locations in Mexico. In Guadalajara, however, smaller independent retail establishments dominate this category.

21. This information is drawn from fieldwork conducted in the retail garment district in downtown Guadalajara as well as in several of the city's *tianguis*.

22. The Los Angeles garment district is the point of provision for the majority of new clothing imported into Mexico. The public sellers in this

district affirm that Mexicans were among their most important customers until the end of 1994; Mexicans imported clothing for men, women, and children from a variety of countries until the Mexican government placed a quota on Asian clothing. This obliged the Los Angeles businesspeople to switch the "made in" tags on Asian-made clothing to tags showing (falsely) that garments were "Made in the U.S.A." and thus could be legally imported into Mexico (interviews with garment sellers in Los Angeles, California, June 1997).

23. In Guadalajara, for example, there is only one Wal-Mart and one Price Club in the city that could serve as distributors to informal enterprises, and their prices are for the most part higher than those found in the informal sector. The higher prices charged in the "discount" self-service outlets might help explain why they lost market share of clothing sales nationwide to the informal sector.

24. It is important to bear in mind that these fragmented distribution channels are serving fragmented consumer markets. *Tianguis* vendors and *aboneros*, for example, frequently serve consumers who do not have easy access to department stores or self-service outlets due to a poor urban transportation infrastructure and traffic congestion that raise the time and money costs of shopping. In addition, *aboneros* sell goods on credit to consumers who often do not qualify for credit cards accepted by larger-scale clothing outlets in the formal sector. This complexity in terms of consumer access to different market segments also means it is difficult to make across-the-board statements as to whether informal and small-scale sector prices are higher or lower than those charged by large-scale, formal enterprises. As a consequence, the former are largely able to keep for themselves the additional profits gained by purchasing garments directly in Los Angeles. The more important point is that market fragmentation helps protect informal garment sellers from price competition by the department stores and self-service outlets.

25. Data reported in Table 13.6 are based on Pozos's field interviews in Guadalajara and Los Angeles. At least three interviews were conducted with sellers at each transactional level in the channel for each type of garment. (Some firms sold more

than one of three garment types shown in the table.) With regard to men's printed T-shirts and children's outfits, little variance in markup or value added was encountered from one firm to another. Somewhat more variance was found with regard to women's dresses, due to the difficulty of finding identical dresses being sold by several firms at each transactional level. Generally speaking, Pozos found similar prices being charged for similar products throughout the Guadalajara market.

26. Light, Bernard, and Kim (1999) provide figures on the nativity of owners of garment businesses in Los Angeles in 1990. Forty percent were Asian-born, with Koreans constituting 19.3 percent of the total; 6.5 percent were born in the Middle East, with nearly all of these from Iran (3.7 percent) or Iraq (2.1 percent); 13.2 percent were born in Mexico, Central, or South America; and 28.5 percent were U.S-born.

27. This information derives from fieldwork and interviews performed by Pozos in the Los Angeles garment district in 1997. The authors wish to thank Judi Kessler, then at the Department of Sociology of the University of California at Santa Barbara, and Raul Hinojosa of the North American Integration and Development Center of the University of California at Los Angeles for a helpful orientation to the workings of the Los Angeles garment district.

28. Garments produced in Taiwan, Hong Kong, Malaysia, and South Korea entered Mexico through intermediaries located in the Los Angeles garment district.

29. We were unable, in our case study of Guadalajara, to follow the commodity chain beyond the point of purchase of garments by Mexican entrepreneurs in Los Angeles. As a consequence, we cannot comment on the power relations between Los Angeles garment sellers (some of whom were also manufacturers) and their suppliers, whether these were in Los Angeles or in Asia. In particular we are unable to characterize the chain leading "upstream" from that point as "buyer-driven" or "producer-driven." More important for our purposes is the finding that Guadalajara's entrepreneurs were independent of their suppliers in Los Angeles and served the Guadalajara market autonomously.

References

Arias, Patricia, ed. 1985. *La gran ciudad de la pequeña industria*. Zamora, Michoacán: Colegio de Michoacán.

Asociación Nacional de Tiendas de Autoservicio y Departamentales (ANTAD). 1997a. *Directorio 1997*. Mexico City: ANTAD.

———. 1997b. "Indices comparativos de ventas 1995–1996." Mimeograph. Mexico City: ANTAD.

Banco de México. 1995, 1997a. *Indicadores del sector externo*. Mexico City: Banco de México.

———. 1996, 1997b, 1998. *The Mexican Economy*. Mexico City: Banco de México.

Calva, José Luis. 1996. "La reforma económica de México y sus impactos en el desarrollo económico: El empleo y el bienestar." In *Estrategias regionales y nacionales frente a la integración económica mundial*, ed. Javier Orozco and Ricardo Fletes, pp. 148–83. Guadalajara: Universidad de Guadalajara/El Colegio de Jalisco.

CIEMEX-WEFA. 1996. *Perspectivas económicas de México (julio)*. Philadelphia: CIEMEX-WEFA.

Dannhaeuser, Norbert. 1991. "La comercialización en las areas urbanas en desarrollo." In *Antropología económica*, ed. Stuart Plattner, pp. 303–44. Mexico City: Alianza Editorial/Conaculta.

Gereffi, Gary. 1994. "The Organization of Buyer-Driven Global Commodity Chains: How U.S. Retailers Shape Overseas Production Networks." In *Commodity Chains and Global Capitalism*, ed. Gary Gereffi and Miguel Korzeniewicz, pp. 95–122. Westport, Conn.: Praeger.

———. 1997. "Global Shifts, Regional Response: Can North America Meet the Full-Package Challenge?" *Bobbin* 39, 3 (November): 16–31.

———. 2000. "The Mexico-U.S. Apparel Connection: Economic Dualism and Transnational Networks." In *Poverty or Development: Global Restructuring and Regional Transformations in the U.S. South and the Mexican South*, ed. Richard Tardanico and Mark B. Rosenberg, pp. 59–89. New York: Routledge.

Guzmán, Alenka. 1993. "Hilados y tejidos de fibras blandas, base de la cadena productiva." *Estrategia industrial* 10, 116: 19–24.

Harris, R. J. 1995. "Apparel Retailing in Mexico." *Textile Outlook International* (May). Available at <http://www.textilesintelligence.com/tistoi/>.

Instituto Nacional de Estadística, Geografía e Informática (INEGI). 1994. *Manual del entrevistador. Encuesta nacional de micronegocios 1994*. Mexico City: INEGI.

———. 1996a, 1997. *La industria textil y del vestido en México*. Aguascalientes: INEGI.

———. 1996b. *Sistema de cuentas nacionales de México 1988–1995*. Aguascalientes: INEGI.

Instituto Nacional de Estadística, Geografía e Informática and Secretaría de Trabajo y Previsión Social (INEGI-STPS). 1992, 1994, 1996. *Encuesta nacional de micronegocios*. Mexico City: INEGI.

Kormos, Harris and Associates and Shaw Direct. 1996a. *A Status Report on the Mexican Apparel and Footwear Retail Markets*. Mexico City: Kormos, Harris & Associates and Shaw Direct.

———. 1996b. *El mercado mexicano de ropa y calzado. Datos comparativos del 1er. semestre 1995–1996*. Mexico City: Kormos, Harris & Associates and Shaw Direct.

———. 1997. *Mexican Apparel Market, Retail Outlet/Fiber, Quarterly Market Monitor. January–December 1996*. Mexico City: Kormos, Harris & Associates and Shaw Direct.

Kotler, Philip. 1980. *Principles of Marketing*. Englewood Cliffs, N.J.: Prentice-Hall.

Light, Ivan, Richard Bernard, and Rebecca Kim. 1999. "Immigrant Incorporation in the Garment Industry of Los Angeles." *International Migration Review* 33, 1: 5–25.

Mendoza, Jorge. 1994. "The Characteristics and Behavior of Street Vendors: A Case Study in Mexico City." Ph.D. diss., University of Texas–Austin and Instituto Tecnológico y de Estudios Superiores de Monterrey.

Ocho columnas. 1996. "México, el país que más exporta ropa a E.U." *Ocho columnas*, October 31, p. 6F.

Pozos, Fernando. 1996a. *Metrópolis en reestructuración: Guadalajara y Monterrey 1980–1989*. Guadalajara: Universidad de Guadalajara.

———. 1996b. "Economic Restructuring and Change in Urban Specialization in Mexico." In *Globalization, Urbanization and the State:*

Selected Studies on Contemporary Latin America, ed. Satya Pattnayak, pp. 117–44. London: University Press of America.

Puga, Cristina. 1992. "Medianos y pequeños empresarios: La difícil modernización." *El cotidiano* 50: 126–29.

Sayer, Andrew, and Richard Walker. 1992. *The New Social Economy: Reworking the Division of Labor.* Cambridge, Mass.: Blackwell Publishers.

Siglo 21. 1997. "La industria del vestido tiene un comportamiento 'decreciente.'" *Siglo 21,* August 2, p. 26.

Ten Kate, Adrian, A. Mateo, and F. de Mateo. 1989. "Apertura comercial y estructura de la protección en México: Estimaciones cuantitativas de los ochenta." *Comercio exterior* 39, 4 (April): 312–29.

Torres, José. 1988. *El comercio y su transformación 1940–1987.* Guadalajara: Gobierno del Estado de Jalisco/Universidad de Guadalajara.

Trendex North America. 1998. *An Overview of the 1997 Mexican Apparel Market.* Toledo, Ohio: Trendex North America.

Part V

Central America
and the Caribbean

Michael Mortimore

14   # When Does Apparel Become a Peril?
On the Nature of Industrialization
in the Caribbean Basin

A Stylized History of the Economic Growth of Countries

In a world of over two hundred countries, it can be argued that only about 10 or 15 percent of them—basically the members of the Organization of Economic Cooperation and Development (OECD)—can be considered to have "made it" in terms of growth and development. They have done so in the sense that they have enjoyed a sustained economic growth over many decades, if not centuries, that has allowed them to reach a significant level of per capita income; the level may be set at U.S.$20,000 a year (Mortimore 1997). Figure 14.1 captures this notion in terms of the "winners' circle" of prominent examples of such successful countries.

The remarkable rise of some nations in terms of their growth and development began with the Industrial Revolution in England. It can be argued that the original winners (such as the United Kingdom and the United States) advanced at relatively low annual rates of growth (at 2 percent or less) over centuries to reach a level of sustained income per capita

that placed them in the winners' circle. Relative latecomers from the Old World, such as France and Germany, achieved the same goal in less time by growing at a faster rate (about 2.5 percent a year). Japan, the first of the Asian nations to achieve winner status, advanced at about double the rate of the original Anglo-Saxon winners. Other European countries, such as Italy and Spain, boosted the Japanese rate of growth by 50 percent. East Asian newly industrializing countries (such as South Korea, Taiwan, and Hong Kong) were, until recently, outdoing even these speedsters (5.5 percent a year) in approaching the targeted income levels, and China, while far from the goal, is advancing at an even faster rate (7.5 percent a year). Within this small group of prominent countries in or approaching the winners' circle, latecomers have been able to outperform their predecessors by "making it" in less time by increasing their per capita income at a quicker pace.

What explains the success of these winners? Undoubtedly, numerous factors influence this outcome. Three central factors taken into account here are:

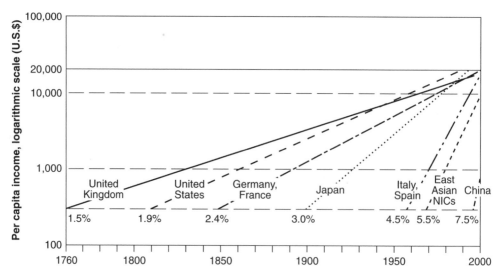

FIGURE 14.1.   The Winners' Circle: A Stylized History of the Economic Growth of Nations. *Source:* Based on J. Ramos, "Industrial Policy and Competitiveness in Open Economies," *CEPAL Review,* no. 34 (September 1996).

- an intense process of industrialization;
- the extension of that process into the international market in the form of exports of manufactures; and
- the creation of firms that might be considered national champions in the sense that they are nurtured in the national economy but develop into world-class global competitors.

A glance at any of the countries in the winners' circle brings to mind some of the principal aspects of their original industrial specialization, the nature of their successes in exporting manufactures, and even the names of some of their national champions that operate in the international market. Examples range from U.S. electrical machinery producers (General Electric and Westinghouse), automobile makers (General Motors and Ford), and computer companies (IBM and Microsoft); to Japanese consumer electronics companies (Matsushita, Sony, and Toshiba) and automobile makers (Toyota, Nissan, and Honda); to newcomers from East Asian newly industrializing

countries (NICs) in the computer (Acer, Hyundai), consumer electronics (Samsung, Lucky Goldstar), and automotive industries (Hyundai, Kia, Daewoo), to name but a few.

Apparel as an Engine of Growth

The apparel industry was an important manufacturing activity and an element of the success in the industrialization processes of the winner countries before those processes shifted the center of value, adding more sophisticated activities such as the manufacture of computers, electronics, and automobiles. Vestiges of that original industry can still be encountered in the export profiles of those countries. The upgrading of OECD countries' industrial activities opened the door to developing countries with the right competitive situations, especially Asian ones, to deepen their industrialization processes with regard to apparel, gaining international market shares at the same time. Over the last quarter century the apparel industry has developed along two axes: (1) the Asian competitors that supply all markets and (2) the specific clusters of regional suppliers created around the principal markets (North America, Europe, and Japan).

Although apparel is an activity of declining importance in the OECD economies as their industrialization processes move into more technologically sophisticated activities, many winner countries are still formidable apparel exporters according to the Competitive Analysis of Nations (CAN) computer program of the United Nations Economic Commission for Latin America and the Caribbean (UN-ECLAC).[1] Italy is the third most important supplier (even though its world import market share dropped from 11.6 to 5.1 percent during 1985–2000); the United States is sixth (actually increasing its share from 0.6 to 2.7 percent); Germany is eighth (a drop from 5.6 to 2.1 percent); France is thirteenth (3.8 to 2.1 percent); and Portugal is sixteenth (falling from 2.6 to 1.6 percent). With the exception of Italy, which has specialized more in high fashion, and Portugal, which is at a less technologically advanced stage of its industrialization process (apparel still accounts for a significant proportion of their exports—4.6 percent and 11.9 percent, respectively, in 2000), apparel represented less than 2 percent of the exports of the other OECD winner countries by 2000. The apparel industry was an engine of growth in the early phases of industrialization, especially when these countries were improving their international competitiveness in that industry, but that is no longer the case for those countries.

Two other important surges in apparel imports during 1985–2000 are noteworthy. With regard to Asian countries there are three aspects to point out. The first is the central role of Chinese exports (rising from 8.5 to 23.8 percent of the market), a feature that firmly ensconced that country as the world's most important exporter of apparel. Second, the more dynamic Asian economies generally saw their apparel exports peak during this period both in terms of market share and the proportion of their total exports represented by apparel. Even though they retained important positions as world exporters of apparel (Hong Kong, second; Indonesia, tenth; South Korea, eleventh; Thailand, thirteenth; Taiwan, sixteenth; the Philippines, twenty-first), the impulse apparel had given their industrialization processes was weakening. Just the opposite was happening to a group of less-dynamic Asian economies, for which apparel constituted a growing part of market share and a higher proportion of total exports. These countries were working their way up the ranking (India, eighth; Bangladesh, ninth; Sri Lanka, twenty-third). This would suggest that, in Asia, apparel as the engine of growth was most apparent in China but was shifting from the more-dynamic East and Southeast Asian economies to the less-dynamic South Asian ones.

The most novel aspect of the evolution of apparel exports to the world market during 1985–2000 was that groupings of new entrants were forming around regional markets. For example, around the European market a number of new supplier countries were winning market shares and increasing the proportion of apparel in their total exports (Turkey, fifth; Tunisia, fourteenth; Romania, eighteenth; Morocco, nineteenth; Poland, twenty-fifth). In the case of the North American market a similar situation was occurring (Mexico, fourth; Honduras, twentieth; the Dominican Republic, twenty-second). In other words, great changes were taking place in the apparel market in which new suppliers were displacing old. However, many of the new supplier countries exported only to regional markets, rather than to all major markets, and it was not clear what effect this had on the use of apparel as an engine for industrialization.

Evidently, the apparel industry has been an important stepping-stone for winner countries (both those in the OECD and several of their Asian challengers) to get their industrialization processes rolling and to generate solid export streams to the international market. During 1985–2000 the importance of apparel (Standard International Trade Classification, or SITC, 842 through 846) in the total imports of the OECD rose from 2.4 to about 3.1 percent, placing it among the dynamic industries in international trade, though that dynamism declined toward the end of the 1990s. Moreover, the import market share of countries other than OECD ones jumped from 61.1 to 77.3 percent of the total. This situation offered concrete opportunities to developing countries that were internationally competitive. That dynamism stemmed in good part from the relocation of existing apparel production, especially to developing countries, rather than from surges in world demand for apparel products (Audet 1996; ILO 1996; van Liemt 1994).

Table 14.1 indicates the twenty-five most important country suppliers of apparel to the North American market (Canada and the United States together) by import market shares during 1985–2000. To a certain extent the North American market reflects the global trends apparent in the OECD market—that is, Italy still retains a strong participation, occupying fourteenth place with an import market share of 2.5 percent in 2000, and the Asian challengers are very present. China was in second place with an import market share of 11.2 percent in 2000, while dynamic Asian economies occupied positions three, six, seven, nine, and ten, but with sharply declining market shares over 1985–2000. The surprise of the North American apparel market is that Mexico is in the first spot, challenging the Asian countries, and several Caribbean Basin countries (Honduras, the Dominican Republic, El Salvador, Guatemala, and Costa Rica) are doing the same thing. Although

the twenty-five principal suppliers still account for over 80 percent of total imports of apparel to the North American market, the composition changed considerably over the period and a regional cluster involving supplier networks in Mexico and the Caribbean Basin was evident.

The Situation of Small Countries

Small countries face an especially difficult task in making it to the winners' circle. In scale-based industries (those that need minimum production volumes to be competitive), for example, they are challenged to reach minimum efficient economic scales of production. They cannot rely on a sufficiently large national market, one that allows them to reach the required levels of productive efficiency, in order to develop the kind of operations that will permit them to venture into the international market with the aim to become significant competitors. They often start off their industrialization processes in simpler, more labor-intensive industries, such as apparel, and look to trade agreements or economic integration initiatives to expand their markets in order to sustain their industrialization processes and to permit national champion companies to arise and evolve into world players.

This is by no means a trivial observation. Small countries are increasingly becoming the norm in today's world. Eighty-seven countries have populations under 5 million; fifty-eight possess populations of fewer than 2.5 million; and thirty-five have fewer than half a million. Measured in another way, half of the countries of the world have a smaller population than the U.S. state of Massachusetts (*The Economist* 1998, 65).

The Caribbean Basin is a case in point. Five of the small countries of the Caribbean Basin are found in the list of the twenty-five main

TABLE 14.1.   The 25 Principal Country Sources of Apparel (SITC 842–846) for the North American Market[a] during 1985–2000

Rank	Country	Market Share in North America[b]			Apparel as % of Country's Total Exports		
		1985	2000	% Change[c]	1985	2000	% Change[c]
1	Mexico	1.6	14.0	754.4	1.3	6.2	371.0
2	China	8.3	11.2	34.3	28.7	6.4	−77.5
3	Hong Kong	22.7	8.2	−63.7	36.7	39.4	7.5
4	Honduras	0.2	4.0	2,201.6	5.7	78.2	1,277.0
5	Dominican Republic	1.4	4.0	183.1	19.9	52.6	164.3
6	South Korea	13.7	3.8	−72.3	18.0	5.6	−68.8
7	Indonesia	1.6	3.4	115.6	5.0	18.2	261.9
8	India	2.4	3.3	37.3	14.1	17.8	25.9
9	Taiwan	15.5	3.3	−78.6	13.4	4.6	−65.5
10	Philippines	2.7	3.2	21.5	17.2	13.3	−22.8
11	Bangladesh	0.8	3.2	303.3	53.7	79.6	48.2
12	Thailand	1.6	3.1	85.7	15.5	10.6	−31.7
13	El Salvador	0.1	2.6	3,811.4	2.3	78.6	3,300.2
14	Italy	4.3	2.5	−42.4	6.4	5.4	−15.1
15	Sri Lanka	1.6	2.4	50.4	70.0	69.6	−0.6
16	Guatemala	0.1	2.4	2,737.0	2.3	52.9	2,181.4
17	Macao	1.4	1.9	41.0	54.2	87.5	61.4
18	Turkey	0.6	1.7	165.9	15.4	31.9	106.8
19	Pakistan	0.5	1.5	190.1	25.1	40.3	60.8
20	Malaysia	1.4	1.4	−1.7	8.3	3.2	−61.1
21	Costa Rica	0.7	1.3	93.3	16.7	19.7	18.5
22	Cambodia	0.0	1.2	—	16.4	97.1	491.2
23	Israel	0.3	0.8	206.7	1.9	3.9	107.3
24	Colombia	0.3	0.7	134.5	2.7	5.6	107.9
25	Egypt	0.0	0.7	—	1.6	47.2	2,886.2
	Total top 25 (percent)	83.8	85.9	2.5	Avg. 13.4	Avg. 10.5	−21.6
	Value world imports (U.S.$ billion)[d]	15.6	58.2				

Source: Calculated from the United Nations Economic Commission for Latin America and the Caribbean (UN-ECLAC) computer program on international competitiveness, TradeCAN (Competitive Analysis of Nations), 2002 edition.

[a]North American market = Canada and United States.

[b]The import value for 1985 is a three-year average (1984–86); for 2000, a two-year average (1999–2000).

[c]Percentages are based on actual values for the years indicated, rather than the rounded figures shown in the table.

[d]Imports of apparel (SITC 842–846) to North American market from all countries.

suppliers of apparel to the North American market. These small countries possessed import market shares of much less than 1 percent each in 1985, and all are making dramatic advances. Honduras rose to fourth position, increasing its share from 0.2 to 4.0 percent during 1985–2000. The Dominican Republic was in fifth position (an increase from 1.4 to 4.0 percent); El Salvador in thirteenth (0.1 to 2.6 percent); Guatemala in sixteenth (0.1 to 2.4 percent); and Costa Rica in twenty-first (0.7 to 1.3 percent). In the case of every one of these countries, apparel accounts for between one-fifth (Costa Rica) and about four-fifths (Honduras and El Salvador) of the country's total exports to the North American market.

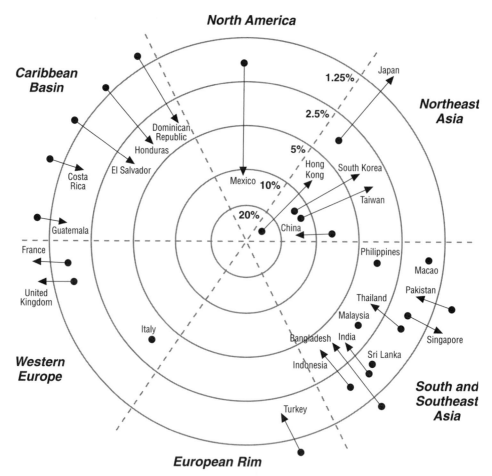

FIGURE 14.2.   Shifts in the Regional Structure of North American (U.S. and Canadian) Apparel Imports (SITC 842–846), 1985–2000.

The rings indicate the share of total North American imports in U.S.$ by partner country: Ring 1 (innermost), 20%+; ring 2, 10–19.9%; ring 3, 5–9.9%; ring 4, 2.5–4.9%; ring 5 (outermost), 1.25–2.4%. The total value of North American apparel imports (SITC 842–846) was U.S.$15.6 billion in 1984–86 and U.S.$58.2 billion in 1999–2000. The 2000 position corresponds to the ring where the country's name is located; the 1984–86 position, if different, is indicated by a circle. The arrows represent the magnitude and direction of change over time.
Source: Calculated using the TradeCAN 2002 edition computer program of UN-ECLAC.

The apparel industry represents their *principal export link* with the international economy, with the exception of Costa Rica. As shall be demonstrated, however, this is a peculiar link in the case of the Caribbean Basin.

Figure 14.2 indicates that in the North American market there are two major apparel-supplying groups of developing countries: Asian ones and Latin American (essentially, Caribbean Basin and Mexican) ones. Mexico is the principal supplier, followed by China, Hong Kong, Honduras, and the Dominican Republic. The next level of suppliers is basically Asian (Korea, Indonesia, India, Taiwan, the Philippines, Bangladesh, and Thailand). In the next group figure El Salvador, Guatemala, and Costa Rica. The Caribbean Basin is a significant and growing apparel supplier base for the North American market.

Other major markets also display regional aspects. In the *Western European* market the principal developing-country suppliers are China, Turkey, and Hong Kong. The next level of suppliers come mainly from the European Rim (Tunisia, Romania, and Morocco) but include Bangladesh and India. The next group of suppliers is a mixture of European Rim and Asian suppliers. The Caribbean Basin suppliers are completely absent. The European Rim represents an important and growing supplier base for the Western European market, similar to the relationship between the North American market and its Caribbean Basin suppliers. The *Japanese* market is supplied basically by one source country: China. South Korea represents the second most important developing-country source of apparel. The next level of developing-country suppliers consists of Hong Kong, Thailand, and Indonesia and, to a lesser extent, Taiwan. The Japanese market is supplied almost exclusively by other Asian countries; major suppliers from both the European Rim and the Caribbean Basin are totally absent.

In other words, there are two predominant realities in the supply of apparel to the distinct constituents of the OECD market. On the one hand are the Asian countries led by China, the dynamic Asian economies, and the newcomers from South Asia, which have impressive import market shares in all major elements of the world market: North America, Western Europe, and Japan. On the other hand, one encounters significant and growing import market shares for Mexico and the Caribbean Basin in the North American market and for the European Rim in the Western European market. The Caribbean Basin plays a significant supplier role solely in the North American market.

The examples of the Dominican Republic and Costa Rica illustrate this point. Tables 14.2 and 14.3 provide the relevant information on the competitive situation of these countries in the North American market. Table 14.2 indicates that the Dominican Republic has significantly increased its overall import market share in that market (from 0.26 to 0.32 percent during 1985–2000).[2] That improvement was concentrated in manufactures not based on national resources (0.16 to 0.39 percent); in both manufactures based on natural resources (0.38 to 0.20 percent) and primary products (0.40 to 0.09 percent) the Dominican Republic saw its import market shares contract. During the 1985–2000 period the structure of Dominican exports to the North American market was transformed from natural resource–based (47.9 percent of total exports in 1985) to manufactures not based on natural resources (86 percent of the total in 2000). Over three-quarters (77.9 percent) of Dominican exports were concentrated in just ten product groups at three digits of the second revision of the SITC (SITC—Rev. 2) in 1996. The Dominican Republic was gaining market share in all of them, and eight of the products corresponded to the group of fifty most dynamic items in the North American market. Four of these ten principal export items pertain to the apparel industry, and their share increased from 17.6 percent of total exports in 1985 to 50.7 percent in 2000. Without doubt, the apparel industry is the principal link between the Dominican and the North American markets and should therefore represent the extension of the national industrialization process into the international market.

Table 14.3 presents similar information for Costa Rica. That country also improved its import market share in the North American market, from 0.15 to 0.29 percent during 1985–2000. This improvement was rooted in manufactures not based on natural resources (0.06 to 0.28 percent). During this period, the export

TABLE 14.2. Dominican Republic: Its Competitiveness in the North American Market, 1985–2000

			1985	1990	1995	2000
I. Market Shares			0.26	0.31	0.38	0.32
1. Primary products[a]			0.40	0.25	0.20	0.09
2. Manufactures based on natural resources[b]			0.38	0.25	0.26	0.20
3. Manufactures *not* based on natural resources[c]			0.16	0.32	0.44	0.39
Low-technology[d]			0.54	1.02	1.46	1.31
Medium-technology[e]			0.04	0.11	0.15	0.15
High-technology[f]			0.03	0.03	0.05	0.05
4. Others[g]			0.77	0.47	0.33	0.20
II. Export Structure			100	100	100	100
1. Primary products[a]			23.6	10.4	5.6	2.9
2. Manufactures based on natural resources[b]			24.3	11.9	8.9	8.0
3. Manufactures *not* based on natural resources[c]			39.3	71.3	81.9	86.0
Low-technology[d]			32.9	56.7	65.9	67.6
Medium-technology[e]			5.1	12.8	13.5	15.2
High-technology[f]			1.2	1.8	2.6	3.2
4. Others[g]			12.9	6.4	3.7	3.2
III. 10 Principal Exports (SITC—Rev. 2)	(x)	(y)	29.7	59.9	70.6	77.9
842 Outer garments, men's and boys' of textile fabrics	*	+	5.4	13.4	16.5	18.5
846 Undergarments, knitted or crocheted	*	+	5.6	8.1	12.6	15.4
843 Outer garments, women's and girls' of textile fabrics	*	+	5.7	10.2	10.6	9.2
872 Medical instruments and appliances, not elsewhere specified	*	+	0.0	4.3	7.0	7.9
845 Outer garments, other articles, knitted or crocheted	*	+	0.9	4.7	5.7	7.6
772 Electrical apparatus for making and breaking electrical circuits	*	+	1.3	3.9	4.2	5.4
122 Tobacco, manufactured		+	1.8	1.3	1.9	4.2
897 Jewelry, goldsmiths' and silversmiths' wares, etc.	*	+	3.7	4.8	3.5	3.7
612 Manufactures of leather, parts of footwear, etc.		+	3.4	6.3	6.1	3.5
931 Special transactions and commodities not classified	*	+	1.8	2.9	2.4	2.5

Source: Calculated initially by way of TradeCAN 2002, then checked using the original COMTRADE database. Product groups defined according to the second revision of the Standard International Trade Classification (SITC—Rev. 2).

[a]45 primary products usually with simple processing; includes concentrates.

[b]65 manufactures: 35 from agro-industrial/forestry, 30 others (mainly metals—excluding steel—petroleum products, cement, glass, etc.).

[c]120 non-resource-based manufactures that represent the sum of the low-technology, medium-technology, and high-technology product groups (groups marked d, e, and f, below).

[d]44 low-technology manufactures: 20 from the textile/apparel cluster and 24 others (paper products, glass products, jewelry, etc.).

[e]58 medium-technology manufactures: 5 from the automobile industry, 22 from processing industries, and 31 from engineering industries.

[f]18 high-technology manufactures: 11 from the electronics/electrical equipment cluster, 7 others from pharmaceutical products, turbines, aircraft, scientific and precision instruments.

[g]9 unclassified product groups, mainly from Chapter 9 of the SITC.

(x) Product groups included (*) in the 50 most dynamic ones that correspond to the indicated market during 1985–2000.

(y) Product groups in which market share was gained (+) or lost (−) by the indicated exporting country during 1985–2000.

TABLE 14.3. Costa Rica: Its Competitiveness in the North American Market, 1985–2000

			1985	1990	1995	2000
I. Market Shares			0.15	0.19	0.23	0.29
1. Primary products[a]			0.65	0.68	0.83	0.71
2. Manufactures based on natural resources[b]			0.07	0.07	0.10	0.11
3. Manufactures *not* based on natural resources[c]			0.06	0.13	0.17	0.28
Low-technology[d]			0.19	0.46	0.57	0.43
Medium-technology[e]			0.02	0.03	0.05	0.08
High-technology[f]			0.02	0.02	0.02	0.44
4. Others[g]			0.03	0.07	0.12	0.16
II. Export Structure			100	100	100	100
1. Primary products[a]			64.5	45.9	38.4	24.3
2. Manufactures based on natural resources[b]			7.9	5.4	5.9	4.8
3. Manufactures *not* based on natural resources[c]			26.7	47.2	53.5	68.1
Low-technology[d]			20.2	40.6	43.3	25.0
Medium-technology[e]			5.3	5.2	7.9	8.6
High-technology[f]			1.2	1.4	2.3	34.5
4. Others[g]			0.9	1.6	2.3	2.8
III. 10 Principal Exports (SITC—Rev. 2)	(x)	(y)	62.2	64.5	62.6	75.9
759 Parts and accessories for computers, etc.	*	+	0.2	0.0	0.2	29.0
057 Fruit and nuts (not oil nuts) fresh or dried		+	33.9	27.2	24.1	15.5
846 Undergarments, knitted or crocheted	*	+	5.0	9.8	12.1	8.1
842 Outer garments, men's and boys' of textile fabrics		+	3.7	9.6	10.9	5.7
776 Thermionic valves and other semiconductors, not elsewhere specified	*	+	0.3	0.1	0.1	3.8
071 Coffee and coffee substitutes		+	12.5	6.0	4.1	3.6
872 Medical instruments and appliances, not elsewhere specified	*	+	0.0	0.5	1.9	3.4
931 Special transactions and commodities not classified	*	+	0.8	1.3	1.7	2.6
845 Outer garments, other articles, knitted or crocheted	*	+	0.5	3.1	4.0	2.3
843 Outer garments, women's and girls' of textile fabrics		−	5.4	6.8	3.5	1.9

Source: Calculated initially by way of TradeCAN 2002, then checked using the original COMTRADE database. Product groups defined according to the second revision of the Standard International Trade Classification (SITC—Rev. 2).

[a] 45 primary products usually with simple processing; includes concentrates.

[b] 65 manufactures: 35 from agro-industrial/forestry, 30 others (mainly metals—excluding steel—petroleum products, cement, glass, etc.).

[c] 120 non-resource-based manufactures that represent the sum of the low-technology, medium-technology, and high-technology product groups (groups marked d, e, and f, below).

[d] 44 low-technology manufactures: 20 from the textile/apparel cluster and 24 others (paper products, glass products, jewelery, etc.).

[e] 58 medium-technology manufactures: 5 from the automobile industry, 22 from processing industries, and 31 from engineering industries.

[f] 18 high-technology manufactures: 11 from the electronics/electrical equipment cluster, 7 others from pharmaceutical products, turbines, aircraft, scientific and precision instruments.

[g] 9 unclassified product groups, mainly from Chapter 9 of the SITC.

(x) Product groups included (*) in the 50 most dynamic ones that correspond to the indicated market during 1985–2000.

(y) Product groups in which market share was gained (+) or lost (−) by the indicated exporting country during 1985–2000.

structure of Costa Rica was transformed from one heavily based on natural resources (72.4 percent of total exports in 1985) to one in which manufactures not based on natural resources came to represent the larger part (68.1 percent in 2000). Seventy-six percent of total exports are accounted in the top ten, and four of those export items are from the apparel industry, representing four of the eight dynamic items. The share of apparel in Costa Rica's total exports to the North American market rose appreciably, from 14.6 percent in 1985 to 18.0 percent in 2000. Costa Rica gained market share in nine of these ten items. In this case, while apparel was a significant link between the Costa Rican and North American markets and represented in part the extension of the Costa Rican industrialization process into the international market, the new investment by Intel to assemble and test microprocessors in Costa Rica caused those items to constitute that country's principal export.

These countries are representative of the general situation in the Caribbean Basin: To different degrees, these small countries had placed their eggs in the apparel basket of the North American market. Their apparel exports go *solely* to that market, suggesting that either they are not plentiful enough to be spread around or they are not competitive enough to enter other markets. We shall see that the manner in which these countries supply the North American market determines to a large extent the impact that the apparel industry has on the growth and development trajectories of the Caribbean Basin countries.

The Caribbean Basin Assembly Model

Gary Gereffi (1994) has demonstrated that the nature of the apparel commodity chain has changed considerably over time. Buyer-driven chains have progressively supplanted producer-driven chains—that is, companies that buy apparel (usually by contracting out fashion articles of their own design) for sale to their upscale clientele are increasingly calling the shots in the U.S. industry, compared to companies that produce standard clothing for distribution to retailers. In the U.S. market large retail stores (Sears, Wal-Mart, JCPenney, Kmart, etc.) and branded marketers (Liz Claiborne, Donna Karan, Polo, Tommy Hilfiger, Nike, etc.) have come to possess greater influence over the whole chain itself.

Gereffi (1997) has also suggested that this evolution allowed "full-package" suppliers from developing countries in East Asia to play a more important role by providing the complete article that the buyers required, cutting the U.S. clothing manufacturers out of the relationship. East Asian national companies capable of organizing the complete production of the article, from inputs to assembly, were fortified in the process. The national companies capable of providing all the organization necessary to convert retailers' or branded marketers' designs into finished products that met the buyers' required volumes on time, as well as fulfilling their quality standards, became significant competitive forces in the apparel industry, particularly in women's wear. Moreover, they also provided a strong boost to the national growth and development trajectory.

East Asian full-package suppliers from Taiwan, Hong Kong, and South Korea achieved this status by establishing their own regional production systems, which organized integrated production from textiles and cloth through the apparel assembly process to final delivery to the retailers or branded marketers. Some even developed into international competitors of their original clients. This gave a significant impulse to their domestic economies. Although these countries appear to be losing import market shares in the OECD market, in fact, for production-cost and quota reasons, their apparel companies often export their products from overseas factories that assemble components from the home country of the Asian manufacturers and traders. Hence, while their market shares in final markets for direct apparel exports decline, their exports of textile and cloth inputs to offshore assembly sites (such as China, Thailand, and Indonesia, and even in the Caribbean Basin) rise. Thus full-package suppliers in Taiwan, South Korea, and Hong Kong have developed their own networks of assembly operations in other parts of Asia and, increasingly, around the world. Full-package suppliers and simple assembly for export operations coexist in Asia, unlike in other regions of developing countries.

The situation is considerably different for apparel production in the Caribbean Basin. The apparel companies operating there tend to be subsidiaries of branded manufacturers (especially for women's underwear) or foreign or national companies that compete for assembly contracts (for men's outerwear mostly) from the overseas buyers of the large U.S. retailers. The latter do not provide full-package services. The overseas buyers or the branded manufacturers themselves handle all the other aspects of the package. Thus, simplifying somewhat, one can distinguish two realities in the apparel industry of developing-country suppliers of the international market: an Asian version, in which local companies of the East Asian NICs act as full-package suppliers of mostly women's wear to large retailers and branded marketers, and a Caribbean Basin model, which isolates the assembly process itself in those countries, mainly by providing women's underwear through subsidiaries of branded manufacturers or men's outerwear through foreign or national subcontractors to overseas buyers. The Asian "full-package" manufacturer-trader version can be starkly contrasted with

what can be called the Caribbean Basin *special access–export processing zone–low-wage version* (hereafter the Caribbean Basin assembly model). These differences are of central importance for defining apparel's local impact in terms of national growth and development.

The North American apparel connection has been responsible for the huge increase in apparel exports from Latin America. Textile and apparel exports from Latin America to the U.S. market grew from $3.4 billion (12 percent of total U.S. imports of such) in 1990 to $14.5 billion (27 percent) in 1997; 14.2 percent of apparel exports originated in the Caribbean Basin and 11 percent came from Mexico during 1997 (USITC 1998). Caribbean Basin countries were gaining ground as apparel suppliers to the U.S. market; however, they did it in a very different manner from the East Asian competitors.

The original Caribbean Basin (but not Mexican)[3] assembly model was considered to have *special access* because it rested heavily on the so-called production-sharing mechanism of the U.S. tariff code. This Harmonized Tariff Schedule (HTS)[4] 9802 provision allows U.S.-sourced apparel inputs to be assembled offshore, with tax paid upon reentry to the U.S. market solely on the value added (essentially wages) outside the country. The share of U.S. textile and clothing imports following this scheme has risen from $1.4 billion (6 percent of all such imports) in 1987 to $8.9 billion (21 percent) in 1997. The Caribbean Basin (56 percent of the apparel imports by way of HTS 9802), together with Mexico (37 percent of such), provided over 90 percent of textile and apparel imports to the United States through this mechanism (USITC 1997a). Quite distinct from Asian countries, a substantial proportion of all Latin American exports to the United States entered by way of the HTS 9802 mechanism in 1996: Dominican Republic (58.7 percent), Costa Rica (35.4 percent),

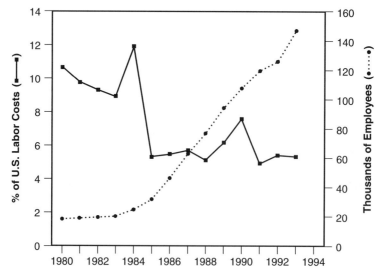

FIGURE 14.3.   Dominican Republic: Relationship between Relative
Labor Costs and EPZ Employment

Honduras (54.6 percent), Guatemala (34.2 percent), El Salvador (62.1 percent), and Jamaica (53.6 percent). It is in this sense that one can speak of a special access for apparel from the Caribbean Basin.

The Caribbean Basin also made increasing use of *export processing zones* to give an incentive to the assembly trade related to the HTS 9802 mechanism. Between 1980 and 1992, for example, the importance of export-processing zone (EPZ) operations to total exports rose from 11 to 68 percent in the case of the Dominican Republic and from virtually nothing to 21 percent in Costa Rica (Willmore 1996). The EPZ provides total tax exemption for the imports of inputs and components and the export of final products, as well as total or temporary exemption from income, profit, and profit-remittance taxes. Complementary aspects concern providing operational facilities in terms of foreign exchange, limited access to the national market, and expedited customs service. The EPZ facilities and tax exemptions represent the national counterpart to the U.S.

HTS 9802 mechanism intended to provide additional incentive to U.S.-based apparel firms to make use of assembly operations in the Caribbean Basin.

The third element of the original Caribbean Basin model of apparel exports to the U.S. market rested on *low labor costs.* Figure 14.3, for example, shows that after the massive devaluation of the national currency in the Dominican Republic in 1985, the relative wage cost there declined from the equivalent of 12 percent of that in the United States to a little over 5 percent. At the same time employment in the EPZs exploded from fewer than 40,000 workers to about 150,000 in 1993. Reduced wage rates (measured in dollars) resulting from the huge Dominican currency devaluation of 1985, itself related to the external debt crisis, explain more than any other single factor why EPZs took off between 1986 and 1993. For example, the number of EPZs in the Dominican Republic grew from eight to thirty; the number of companies installed in them jumped from 168 to 447; the value of gross exports shot from

$246.2 to $1,250 million; and the value of net foreign exchange earnings from EPZs blossomed from $88.4 to $368.5 million (Reyes Castro and Dominguez 1993). This was a significant factor in the recuperation of the economy of the Dominican Republic. Moreover, exports (mostly natural resources) from the non-EPZ part of the economy had entered into a nosedive, falling from about $900 million in 1984 to about $500 million in 1993. Exports from the EPZs rocketed from $200 million to about $1,250 million over the same period (Mortimore, Duthoo, and Guerrero 1996).

Thus the example of the Dominican Republic poignantly captures the relationship of special access to the U.S. market, the use of EPZs, and low wages, which characterize the Caribbean Basin assembly model, to wildly increased exports of apparel to the U.S. market. Unfortunately, the Caribbean model also has its costs.

The Downside of the Caribbean Basin Assembly Model

Each of the three components underlying the Caribbean Basin model of apparel exports to the United States possesses severe deficiencies with respect to its ability to assist these small countries in making it to the winners' circle. First, *special access* represents a direct challenge to the national industrialization process. The HTS 9802 mechanism penalizes practically all value added outside the United States. This limits its use to activities in which low wages are prominent (and compensate for the U.S. duty on value added) and in which local physical inputs are not needed or desired by the manufacturer or buyer. It is extremely difficult for the national government of the assembling country to implement policies that effectively promote further local integration of the industry. This is the case for both higher-level training of the workforce, which would eventually require higher wages for more skilled and complex work performance, and the incorporation of local suppliers of product inputs (thread, buttons, let alone major inputs such as cloth or cutting operations). Thus the HTS 9802 mechanism tends to truncate the industrialization process itself, isolating the assembly operation in the Caribbean Basin to the detriment of any integrated national industrialization process in the assembly country.

Another weak point in the special-access relationship between the Caribbean Basin and the U.S. market has to do with what are known as "calls" in U.S. legislation. A U.S. firm that feels it has been unduly affected by what may be considered an abnormal increase in imports to the United States can request a decision by the U.S. Department of Commerce to determine if import disruption has taken place. The Department of Commerce can issue "calls" (or warnings) to the local textile offices that allocate quotas in exporting countries in order to restrain the growth of such items. This phenomenon took place in March 1995, when calls were issued to Caribbean Basin producers of underwear and pajamas, some of the more important apparel exports of the region. While most assemblers of these items adapted to the U.S. demands, Costa Rica—which was one of the more severely impacted countries—took the case to the World Trade Organization and won, although the damage done to that country's underwear and pajama exports was not compensated. In this sense special access sometimes is less special than it appears for the countries involved.

Another problem associated with special access is that some assembly countries become more special than others. For example, the implementation of the North American Free Trade Agreement (NAFTA) in 1994 effectively gave Mexico advantages that the Caribbean Basin countries did not possess

(USITC 1997b). Mexico enjoyed the equivalent of a six-point tariff-rate advantage in the U.S. market, was no longer subject to import quotas on many apparel items, and, most notably, could count Mexican inputs as part of the requisite NAFTA content. That gave Mexico a huge advantage compared to the Caribbean Basin countries. For that reason, since the inception of NAFTA the apparel assemblers of the Caribbean Basin have been lobbying the U.S. Congress in search of "NAFTA parity" for their apparel exports. The U.S. Congress has turned them down several times. The U.S.–Caribbean Basin Trade Partnership Act of May 2000 did help Caribbean Basin apparel assemblers cut the NAFTA disadvantage with regard to tariffs; however, it didn't affect the NAFTA rules of origin that allow Mexican inputs to count as NAFTA inputs, unlike those involved in assembly in the Caribbean Basin. Thus not all assemblers are special in the same way.

Deficiencies are also encountered with respect to the *export-processing zone* mechanism, which is the local counterpart to the HTS 9802 mechanism. The intense interest in Caribbean Basin countries to develop new exports in the context of the debt crisis of the 1980s and the structural decline of natural-resource exports led them to enter into "incentive wars" to attract foreign direct investment (Mortimore and Peres 1998). That competition was so severe that the level of incentives came to signify that huge assembly operations, accounting for 40 percent or more of all exports of these countries to the United States, provided virtually no fiscal income for the local government. Moreover, competitive pressures produced the effect that incentives intended to be temporary (eight to twelve years) became renewable and, in practice, endless. Thus, in the heat of the battle to attract foreign direct investment to local EPZs, many governments have given away as incentives virtually all the potential fiscal income to be derived from such

activities. These lost resources could have been used to strengthen the local industrialization process, to promote other exports, or to improve the international competitiveness of the national economy through investments in infrastructure (ports, airports, roads) and basic (electricity, water) and other services (telecommunications, financial services, etc.). Rather than representing a starting point for many industries, as was the case for some of the East Asian NICs (UN-ESCAP 1994), EPZs became an end in themselves that eventually came to limit and distort the nascent industrialization process of many of these Caribbean Basin countries.

Finally, the *low-wage* element of the Caribbean Basin assembly model also demonstrates significant deficiencies. More than fifteen years after the massive national currency devaluations of the 1980s, the labor costs (including the social and fringe benefits) in the apparel industry of the Caribbean Basin countries have been rising steadily (measured in dollars). This translates into pricing many of their apparel-assembly operations out of the market, rather than any real manifestation of industrial upgrading or specialization in higher-value output. Table 14.4 presents labor cost data for forty apparel producers during 1990–98, ordered from the highest (Germany, Switzerland, Italy, and Japan had hourly labor costs over $13.50 in 1998) to the lowest (four Asian countries had hourly labor costs of $0.30 or under in the same year). The Caribbean Basin countries are generally found in the middle of the pack (ranging from positions thirteen to twenty-five). All the Caribbean Basin countries had significant increases in their hourly labor costs during 1990–98: Costa Rica, from $1.09 to $2.52; Dominican Republic, from $0.67 to $1.48; El Salvador, from $0.69 to $1.35; and Guatemala, from $0.45 to $1.28. In other words, labor costs in the Caribbean Basin are increasing faster than in most other areas and are substantially higher than the costs of many

TABLE 14.4.   Labor Costs in the Apparel Industry, 1990–98

Rank	Country	Hourly Costs[a] (U.S.$) 1990	1995	1998	1990–98 Annual Growth Rate (%)
1	Germany	7.23	20.35	18.04	18.7
2	Switzerland	14.19	22.42	17.58	3.0
3	Italy	12.50	13.68	13.60	1.1
4	Japan	6.34	20.95	13.55	14.2
5	U.S.A.	6.56	9.62	10.12	6.8
6	Spain	7.08	7.78	6.79	−0.5
7	Greece	4.33	7.19	6.55	6.4
8	Hong Kong	3.05	4.32	5.20	8.8
9	Taiwan	3.41	5.18	4.68	4.7
10	Portugal	2.30	3.85	3.70	7.6
11	Poland	0.50	1.42	2.77	56.8
12	South Korea	2.46	3.29	2.69	1.2
13	Costa Rica	1.09	2.23	2.52	16.4
14	Hungary	0.92	1.68	2.12	16.3
15	Czech Republic	2.79	1.55	1.85	−4.2
16	Turkey	1.35	1.52	1.84	4.5
17	Mexico	0.92	1.61	1.51	8.0
18	Dominican Republic	0.67	1.52	1.48	15.1
19	South Africa	1.07	1.58	1.39	3.7
20	Morocco	0.92	1.22	1.36	6.0
21	El Salvador	0.69	1.43	1.35	12.0
22	Malaysia	0.56	1.59	1.30	16.5
23	Guatemala	0.45	1.30	1.28	23.1
24	Mauritius	—	1.28	1.03	—
25	Honduras	—	—	0.91	—
26	Thailand	0.63	1.11	0.78	3.0
27	Philippines	0.46	0.72	0.76	8.2
28	Nigeria	0.2	0.24	0.69	30.6
29	Egypt	0.34	0.51	0.68	12.5
30	Sri Lanka	0.24	0.41	0.44	10.4
31	China	0.26	0.25	0.43	8.2
32	India	0.33	0.29	0.39	2.3
33	Kenya	0.47	0.34	0.34	−3.5
34	Bangladesh	—	0.20	0.30	—
35	Pakistan	0.24	0.29	0.26	1.0
36	Vietnam	—	0.29	0.22	—
37	Indonesia	0.16	0.33	0.16	0.0

Source: Werner International, Inc., "Hourly Labor Costs in the Apparel Industry" (1998).

[a]Costs include social and fringe benefits.

of the assemblers of standard apparel found in Asia. Even within the Caribbean Basin region there is considerable distance between higher-cost Costa Rica and lower-cost Guatemala. This suggests that as the level of competition in this industry increases in keeping with the demise of the Multifiber Arrangement (replaced by the Textile and Clothing Agreement endorsed by the World Trade Organization), these countries may be tempted to follow a strategy of competitive devaluations of their national currencies in order to artificially prolong the life of their apparel exports. That would only make matters worse.

A more fundamental concern is that the Caribbean Basin assembly model of exporting apparel to the U.S. market simply does not meet the requirements of the stylized view of the growth of countries presented in the first section of this chapter. It is evident that apparel assembly in the Caribbean Basin resulted in an impressive explosion of exports. However, given the characteristics of this particular manner of exporting, this phenomenon did not represent an intensification of the national industrialization process. Instead, it truncates it. The exports are not the extension of the national apparel industry into the international market; they simply represent the localization of the assembly function itself. As a consequence, national-champion companies are not created in the process. There is no transformation of the industry so that the assembler country extends its industrialization into the more organizationally sophisticated, technologically complex, or fashion-centric aspects of the apparel industry.

The Example of Costa Rica

Costa Rica's apparel exports to the U.S. market increased steadily until 1995, when they declined by over 7 percent, falling from $766.3 million in that year to $710.1 million in 1996 (USITC 1998). Costa Rica saw its apparel exports decline in four of the five principal apparel categories (at three digits of the Harmonized Tariff Schedule) that together accounted for over one-half of such exports:

HTS 347—cotton men's trousers (from $156.6 to $148.2 million);
HTS 352—cotton underwear (from $112.2 to $77.1 million);
HTS 649—synthetic fiber brassieres (from $84.7 to $60.4 million); and

HTS 338—synthetic fiber underwear (from $51.5 to $45.3 million).

In this context it could be said that the Costa Rican apparel industry apparently had developed wrinkles.

A detailed analysis of ten of the principal export items of this industry in 1994 (at six digits of the HTS) revealed that by 1996 each item had lost import market shares, on average by 23.6 percent.[5] Costa Rica was losing U.S. import market shares primarily to Mexico and Central American countries such as Honduras, El Salvador and Guatemala, but not to the Dominican Republic. Was Costa Rica being priced out of the market?

An in-depth study of the international competitiveness of the Costa Rican apparel industry was carried out to respond to that preoccupation (Mortimore and Zamora 1998). A formal questionnaire was administered to sixteen firms in the sector. The information from the interviews and the analysis of results of the questionnaire threw light on the specific competitive situations of these enterprises.

The sixteen firms could be classified into three different groups:

• *Group I:* Very large subsidiaries of U.S. transnational corporations that assembled undergarments for export to the U.S. market by way of HTS 9802, which faced "calls" in 1995 but which had improved their international market shares considerably during 1990–95. They accounted for the lion's share of Costa Rica's apparel exports to the United States. An indicator of their success, aside from their domination of Costa Rican clothing exports, is that their employment doubled between 1985 and 1990 and doubled again between 1990 and 1995. Examples are the subsidiaries of large U.S. branded manufacturers such as Hanes (Sara Lee), Warnaco, and Lovable.

- *Group II:* Other, mostly new foreign subsidiaries that mainly assemble clothing facing quotas in the U.S. market, which they access through HTS 9802, and which have had a less successful performance in general during 1990–95. This group accounts for an appreciable portion of remaining Costa Rican clothing exports, and the employment of this group grew by 50 percent between 1985 and 1990 and by about 40 percent between 1990 and 1995. They are smaller employers than Group I companies and also less dynamic. Examples are the subsidiaries of U.S. firms such as Tropical Sportswear, Cluett Peabody, Todd Uniform, and Gilmour Trading.
- *Group III:* Old national firms, mostly small ones, using the export contract regime that accessed the U.S. market through non-HTS mechanisms and that have had some success at improving their international market shares. Their exports are not significant in the context of the Costa Rican clothing industry. While the employment of these companies doubled between 1985 and 1990, it fell by one-third between 1990 and 1995. Their national market shares have been collapsing due to increased import competition. Examples include the Compañia Textil Centroamericana, El Acorozado, and Tejidos El Aguila.

Given their distinct competitive situations, these companies had different corporate strategies. Group I firms, which possessed more sophisticated, specialized operations in which quality is extremely important, had set up integrated regional production systems in the Caribbean Basin some time ago. Typically, they had subsidiaries in four or five different sites, such as the Dominican Republic, Jamaica, Honduras, El Salvador, and Mexico, as well as in Costa Rica. In this fashion they could adapt to changing national competitive situations (labor costs, social benefits, exchange-rate vari-

ations, and other changed circumstances) by adding or dropping lines of production in particular sites. They had no need to be "footloose." Generally they assembled apparel products for their headquarter firm, which sold the output to retailers in the U.S. market. Their success in Costa Rica allowed them to implement "expansive" strategies until the 1995 "calls" were made.

Group II enterprises had less-sophisticated and less-specialized operations. Low wages rather than quality constituted the principal element of their international competitiveness. In this sense they had more of a strict "cost-center" mentality. They tended to have much smaller corporate networks in the Caribbean, based on only one or two main sites. They were more prone to adapt to changing national competitive situations by moving away when the going got rough; they were more "footloose." Rather than producing for their headquarter corporation, these firms generally competed for the assembly portion of buyers' contracts, often delivering the product directly to the contractor. Given their more limited success, their strategies tended to be more neutral than expansive.

Group III companies were the least sophisticated and least specialized of the three groups. These national firms considered foreign technology to be the principal element of their competitiveness both in Costa Rica and in the international market. They possessed no international corporate network to speak of and were effectively stuck with the national competitive situation. Given the collapse of their national market shares with import liberation,[6] these companies were obliged to compete increasingly for the assembly portion of buyers' contracts in the international market in order to survive. Their strategies can be considered defensive.

The exceptionally interesting finding of this empirical study in Costa Rica is that these three different groups of firms, which implemented different corporate strategies, all provided some exceptionally alarming indications of the problems associated with the Caribbean Basin assembly model for exporting apparel to the U.S. market. For example, one of the parent firms—a major U.S. branded manufacturer, owner of two of the five large Group I firms in Costa Rica (and others in Dominican Republic, Mexico, and more recently other Central American countries)—announced that it was to be restructured (selling off its U.S. yarn and textile operations). It would no longer manufacture many of the goods that it sells. What does that forebode for the relatively high-cost plants in Costa Rica? Closure? Sale? It is to be hoped it will not follow the example of its archrival, Fruit of the Loom.[7] Another example of a Group I firm concerns one that closed one of its three plants in Costa Rica only to expand activities in neighboring Panama.

A Group II company in 1996 simply disappeared from Costa Rica, leaving behind huge outstanding payments, especially wages and social security payments. Workers claimed there was no forewarning of this "fly-by-night" exit over the weekend. Will more follow this example as Costa Rica's international competitiveness in this industry wanes?

The final example has to do with a Group III enterprise. In 1996 one of the four national companies, owned by a prominent local businessman (then president of the National Manufacturers Association), that attempted to survive by competing for export assembly contracts simply went broke due to the increasing competitive pressures.

What does all this mean? At a minimum, it would seem to suggest that the problems of apparel exports by means of the Caribbean Basin assembly model appear to be systemic, not temporary. They do not relate to any particular kind of firm with any particular corporate strategy; rather, all apparel firms see their international competitiveness crumble. If one

was to prepare a kind of Costa Rican scorecard on the capacity of the apparel industry to propel the country toward "the winners' circle" mentioned at the beginning of this chapter, some interesting conclusions can be drawn about this experience.

First, in terms of intensifying the national industrialization process, the reliance on the HTS 9802 format actually truncates the national industrialization process with respect to apparel. Only the assembly stage is located in the country, and aside from wages no significant local inputs are incorporated into the final products. Moreover, the tax incentives related to the EPZ so limit the fiscal income of the state from this central export activity that it cannot be said to provide resources for other urgent developmental activities. The latter include stimulating the national industrialization process, promoting new exports, and improving the international competitiveness of the economy as a whole through infrastructure, basic services, or, indeed, the training of human resources for more sophisticated and better-remunerated tasks.

Second, with respect to extending the national industrialization process into the international market by way of exports of manufactures, it is abundantly clear that these apparel exports are *in no integral way* linked to the national economy. These exports were "competitive" only in the U.S. market, and they could not be directed to other markets when problems arose in that one, such as the "calls" on pajamas and underwear in March 1995. In the particular case of Costa Rica, one could go so far as to say that the World Trade Organization dispute proved that the United States can be a lousy trade partner when one tweaks its nose in international forums.

Finally, does the apparel industry in Costa Rica create national-champion companies that evolve into major players in international markets? The opposite took place when the opening up of the economy produced the import competition that destroyed most of the import substitution–based integrated operations of national firms. These firms do not possess a Caribbean network of assembly operations; hence they advance or decline in keeping with the evolution of the international competitiveness of the Costa Rican economy. Even their ability to compete for buyers' contracts is severely limited by the size and characteristics of the local economy, let alone their ability to manufacture (rather than simply assemble) apparel. They have a hard time surviving.

Conclusion

So, when does apparel become a peril?

- When it takes place by way of a mechanism that is designed exclusively to make U.S. apparel firms more competitive in their own market (by taking advantage of low wages in the Caribbean). What is needed is a policy that explicitly and consciously aims at raising the long-term growth of the host economy, especially to reach the goal of sustained per capita income that will place it in the winners' circle.
- When instead of deepening national industrialization it truncates it.
- When instead of producing exports that represent the international extension of the industrialization process it represents the simple assembly of foreign components.
- When instead of giving birth to national-champion companies that evolve into global competitors it threatens their very existence.

Clearly, when an activity that generates a major part of a country's exports does not serve to raise that economy to a higher level, closer to the goal of a significant and sustained per capita income achieved by the winner countries, that is when apparel becomes a peril.

Dire consequences are foreseen for those apparel exporters that do not possess a local industrialization process at the time that the Multifiber Arrangement comes to an end in 2005, under the auspices of the Textile and Clothing Agreement of the Uruguay Round of the General Agreement on Tariffs and Trade. Then the quotas placed on apparel by the United States and other countries are terminated. These Caribbean Basin apparel assemblers will have a difficult task to compete in the United States (or other markets) against the integrated apparel producers of Asia. The latter produce textiles and apparel at scales of production far beyond the reach of the truncated Caribbean Basin operations. Lacking a competitive local or subregional industrialization process to sustain apparel exports, most Caribbean Basin assemblers probably will collapse in the face of the Asian steamroller.

In the few years remaining before that eventuality, the Caribbean Basin apparel industry can attempt to improve its situation. It must receive NAFTA parity in the North American market not just in terms of tariffs but in terms of national or subregional local inputs counting as NAFTA inputs, thereby promoting some degree of industrial integration. It must look for opportunities for associating in some way with the full-package suppliers appearing in Mexico as a consequence of NAFTA. Finally, it must learn from the East Asian experience in terms of becoming full-package suppliers themselves. All of this requires a stitch in time.

Notes

1. The TradeCAN computer program of the UN-ECLAC measures the international competitiveness of countries. It does so in terms of import market shares (at three digits of the Standard International Trade Classification, SITC—Rev. 2) in five principal markets (Western Europe, North America,

Africa, Asia, and Latin America). A Windows-compatible version in CD-ROM can be purchased from UN-ECLAC. Contact <CAN@eclac.cl>.

2. Two decimal points are needed to capture the changes in import market shares of small countries.

3. Since the inception of the North American Free Trade Agreement in 1994, the first indications of full-package suppliers, mostly U.S. companies, have appeared in Mexico. See Gereffi and Bair (1998).

4. The HTS, a newer classification system than SITC, is superior to the latter because it is used for both trade statistics and trade negotiations.

5. Calculated using the Module to Analyze the Growth of International Commerce (MAGIC) computer program, which measures international competitiveness in terms of import market shares in the U.S. market, at up to ten digits of the HTS. Available from the Mexico subregional office of UN-ECLAC. Contact <cepal@un.org.mx>.

6. That is, by lowering national tariffs, more apparel products from outside Costa Rica enter the national market and take local market share away from national apparel firms.

7. Fruit of the Loom has been imploding, laying off 16,355 of its 29,112 U.S. workers since 1994, suffering operating losses of $283 million in 1997, and provoking complaints of poor service from key clients, such as Wal-Mart and Kmart. The solution proposed by its CEO: Move its domicile to the Cayman Islands to make tax savings. See *Business Week* (1998).

References

Audet, Denis. 1996. "Globalisation in the Clothing Industry." In *Globalisation of Industry: Overview and Sector Reports,* by the Organization of Economic Cooperation and Development (OECD). Paris: OECD.

Business Week. 1998. "Strategies: A Killing in the Caymans." *Business Week,* May 11, 50–54.

The Economist. 1998. "Little Countries: Small but Perfectly Formed." *The Economist,* January 3.

Gereffi, Gary. 1994. "The Organization of Buyer-Driven Global Commodity Chains: How U.S. Retailers Shape Overseas Production Networks."
In *Commodity Chains and Global Capitalism,* ed. Gary Gereffi and Miguel Korzeniewicz, pp. 95–122. Westport, Conn.: Praeger.

———. 1997. "Global Shifts, Regional Response: Can North America Meet the Full-Package Challenge?" *Bobbin* 39, 3 (November): 16–31.

Gereffi, Gary, and Jennifer Bair. 1998. "U.S. Companies Eye NAFTA's Prize." *Bobbin* 39, 7 (March): 26–35.

International Labor Organization (ILO). 1996. *Mundialización de las industrias del calzado, los textiles y el vestido.* TMFTC/1996. Geneva: ILO.

Mortimore, Michael. 1997. "La competitividad internacional: Un CANalisis de las experiencias de Asia en desarrollo y América Latina." *Desarrollo productivo,* no. 40. UN-ECLAC, LC/G.1957. Santiago, Chile: ECLAC.

Mortimore, Michael, and Wilson Peres. 1998. "Policy Competition for Foreign Direct Investment in the Caribbean: Costa Rica, Jamaica and Dominican Republic." *Desarrollo productivo,* no. 49. UN-ECLAC, LC/G.1991. Santiago, Chile: ECLAC.

Mortimore, Michael, and Ronney Zamora. 1998. "The International Competitiveness of the Costa Rican Clothing Industry." *Desarrollo productivo,* no. 46, UN-ECLAC, LC/G.1979. Santiago, Chile: ECLAC.

Mortimore, Michael, Henk Duthoo, and J. A. Guerrero. 1996. "Informe sobre la competitividad de las zonas francas en la República Dominicana." *Desarrollo productivo,* no. 22, UN-ECLAC, LC/G.1866. Santiago, Chile: ECLAC.

Reyes Castro, F., and A. Dominguez U. 1993. "Zonas francas industriales en la República Dominicana: Su impacto económico y social." Working Document no. 73. Geneva: International Labor Organization.

United Nations Economic and Social Commission for Asia and the Pacific (UN-ESCAP). 1994. *Transnational Corporations and Technology Transfer in Export Processing Zones and Science Parks.* ST/ESCAP/1410. New York: UN-ESCAP.

U.S. International Trade Commission (USITC). 1997a. "Production Sharing: Use of U.S. Components and Materials in Foreign Assembly Operations, 1992–95." USITC Publication no. 3077. Washington, D.C.: USITC.

————. 1997b. "The Impact of the North American Free Trade Agreement on the U.S. Economy and Industries: A Three-Year Review." USITC Investigation no. 332–381, Washington, D.C.: USITC.

————. 1998. "Annual Statistical Report of U.S. Imports of Textiles and Apparel: 1997." USITC Publication no. 3102. Washington, D.C.: USITC.

van Liemt, Gijsbert, ed. 1994. *La reubicación internacional de la industria: Causas y consecuencias.* Geneva: International Labor Organization.

Werner International, Inc. 1998. "Hourly Labor Cost in the Apparel Industry, 1996–98." Reston, Va.: Werner International, Infotex Division. Available at <http://www.wernertex.com/index.htm>.

Willmore, Larry. 1996. "Export Processing in the Caribbean: Lessons from Four Case Studies." United Nations Economic Commission for Latin America and the Caribbean (UN-ECLAC) Working Paper no. 42. Port of Spain, Trinidad and Tobago: UN-ECLAC.

Dale T. Mathews

15   Can the Dominican Republic's
      Export-Processing Zones
      Survive NAFTA?

Introduction

Global and regional changes brought on by the World Trade Organization, the North American Free Trade Agreement (NAFTA), and more recently the United States–Caribbean Basin Trade Partnership Act (CBTPA) have had mixed repercussions for the export-oriented industries located overwhelmingly in the export-processing zones (EPZs) of the Caribbean and Central America. This chapter focuses on the Dominican Republic, since that country not only has the largest number of EPZs in the region but also is considered a success in terms of the number of plants drawn to its zones and the number of jobs generated therein (particularly in the garment assembly sector). The Dominican Republic's EPZs in 2000 alone employed a total of 195,660 workers and generated U.S.$4.7 billion in exports (free on board), of which U.S.$2.5 billion were attributed to the garment and textile sector alone.[1] In terms of industrial sectors, this chapter focuses on the clothing sector, given that it is the chief export-pro-

cessing industry in the Dominican Republic as well as in the wider Caribbean and Central America (see Gitli and Arce 2000, 1; Willmore 1996, 5).

The prospects for creation of a lasting and sustainable industry on this basis, however, were threatened by the enactment of the NAFTA until the recent passage of the CBTPA by the U.S. government. It was well accepted that trade diversion in favor of Mexico and at the expense of some Caribbean producers, such as the Dominican Republic, had occurred as a consequence of both the inauguration of NAFTA and the 50 percent devaluation of the Mexican peso at the close of 1994. Although it may be too early to tell if the new U.S. legislation will be decisive in reversing the declining employment in this important sector for countries such as the Dominican Republic, the U.S. International Trade Commission reported in early 2002 that U.S. imports from the Caribbean Basin have risen, particularly with regard to textiles and apparel, and that this trend is expected to continue (USITC 2002, 13).

Export-Processing Zones

Export-processing zones may be considered a special category of free-trade zone. The latter can be classified according to function, the type of plant or business located therein. Among these are:

Export-Processing Zones: industrial parks with firms involved in the assembly or processing of goods for export, also known as "maquiladoras."

Financial Services Zones: areas that house banks, accounting and insurance firms, and cargo companies, among others.

Free-Trade Zones or Free Ports: areas that house firms involved in warehousing, distribution, and packaging and container handling.

Enterprise Zones: areas dedicated mainly to urban renewal of depressed inner cities.

The typical case in the developing world remains the export-processing zone.[2]

More precisely, the EPZ regime allows for the temporary duty-free entry of inputs and intermediate components to be processed, assembled, or in some cases lightly transformed and then reexported.[3] On the one hand, firms operating under these conditions are considered privileged in the sense of not being stymied by cumbersome customs procedures, tariffs, or taxes. In short, they are exposed to market forces that theoretically make them more efficient in comparison with similar non-EPZ firms producing for the (usually) highly protected domestic markets. On the other hand, these industrial parks constitute enclaves with few linkages to the local economy. Firms operating therein purchase little more than labor power from a given host country.

This is the type of free-trade zone that is present in the Dominican Republic as in most of the Caribbean and Central American region but also in parts of North and South America. All Central American countries have EPZs or industrial parks that operate like EPZs. A significant part of the insular Caribbean has either EPZs or similar regimes that apply to individual assembly or processing firms that are not concentrated in "parks" as such. The Dominican Republic is a good case study, given the large number of EPZs in that country as well as the fact that it was one of the first countries to establish such parks.

By the close of 2000 some 195,660 workers were reported employed in 481 industrial establishments located in forty-six EPZs of the Dominican Republic. Employment in the country's EPZs since 1985, as presented in Table 15.1, reflects the adverse reaction of the sector to Mexican competition after the 1994 enactment of NAFTA. The value of exports, by contrast, continues its upward trend throughout the period. The employment figures for 2000 show a recovery of around 4 percent from the previous year. This contrasts with a 3.5 percent drop registered in 1999 compared with 1998. On that occasion the National Council of EPZs (Consejo Nacional de Zonas Francas de la República Dominicana) also attributed the decline to the advantage Mexico had obtained over the Dominican Republic with respect to garment exports to the U.S. market.[4]

The information in Table 15.2 profiles the Dominican Republic's EPZs in 2000 by industrial sector and employment. As has been the case historically, the majority sector is that of clothing and textile products. Of the 481 EPZ plants, 57 percent belonged to the textile or garment industry; in terms of employment, 73 percent of the entire EPZ labor force worked in this industry. This sector is followed by the tobacco and electronics sectors, with 6 percent and 5 percent shares of employment, respectively, and 6 percent and 3 percent of

TABLE 15.1.   Dominican Republic EPZ
Employment and Exports, 1985–2000

Year	Employment	Exports (free on board, U.S.$ millions)
1985	30,902	215
1986	51,231	246
1987	66,012	332
1988	83,815	520
1989	122,946	735
1990	130,045	839
1991	135,491	1,053
1992	141,056	1,194
1993	164,296	2,511
1994	176,311	2,716
1995	165,571	2,907
1996	164,639	3,107
1997	182,174	3,596
1998	195,193	4,100
1999	189,458	4,331
2000	195,660	4,655[a]

Source: Consejo Nacional de Zonas Francas de Exportación.

[a]Preliminary data.

total EPZ establishments. Among the other
EPZ industries, not listed separately in Table
15.2, are leather and sporting goods, plastic
products, agro-industrial products, and luggage. Approximately 79 percent of EPZ firms
in the Dominican Republic exported to the
United States in 1998.[5]

This concentration in apparel processing is
prevalent in most of the rest of the Caribbean.
According to U.S. sources, by 1995 the garment sector accounted for 90 percent of the
value of U.S. imports originating from production-sharing operations[6] in countries benefiting from the Caribbean Basin Economic
Recovery Act (CBERA) (USITC 1997b, 2–5).[7]
None of the other product categories account
for more than 5 percent of the total value of
U.S. production-sharing imports from CBERA
nations; these other categories include medical
equipment, jewelry, and electrical components
such as circuit boards (USITC 1997b, 2–5).

The Apparel Industry

Although the situation is undergoing fundamental change, the trade in apparel has historically been regulated through a series of
Multifiber Arrangements (MFAs) negotiated
bilaterally between importing and exporting
countries. These allowed for the establishment
of quotas on certain sensitive categories of
clothing in order to protect domestic producers in the importing countries.

In the case of the United States, a portion
of MFA clothing imports is subject to tariffs
on foreign value added under provision
9802.00.80 of the new Harmonized Tariff
Schedule (HTS). Products that qualify for
entry into the United States under HTS 9802
are those that are subject to processing or
assembly abroad from mostly (but not exclusively) U.S. components. Since nearly all the
clothing assembled in the Dominican Republic's EPZs is exported to the United States,
with a large part entering, until recently, under
provision 9802.00.80, it naturally has been
subject to such tariff payments on foreign
value added. It is also regulated under the
MFA by a series of quantitative quotas, of
which HTS provision 9802.00.8010 was the
most liberal, to the point of being nearly un-
limited. Although this scheme has changed
with respect to the Caribbean as a consequence
of the enactment of the CBTPA, it is still necessary to review it in order to understand the
performance and evolution of the EPZ sector
in the region since the late 1980s.

The liberal 9802 quota was established in
1986 under the former Tariff Schedule of the
United States as Item 807a and covers articles
imported under a "Special Access Program"
applied exclusively to CBERA beneficiary
countries that have bilateral textile agreements
with the United States. Although two years
later a similar program, known as a "Special
Regime," was established for Mexico, the lat-

TABLE 15.2.   Export-Processing Zones: Industrial Sectors Accounting for More than 2,700 Employees, December 2000

Industrial Sector	No. of Employees	% Total Employment	No. of Establishments	% Total Establishments
1 Textiles	141,945	73	275	57
2 Footwear	7,067	4	18	4
3 Tobacco	12,107	6	27	6
4 Electronics	10,439	5	16	3
5 Medical Instruments	7,206	4	13	3
6 Jewelry	3,128	2	14	3
7 Services	5,855	3	59	12
8 Other Industries	7,913	4	59	12
Totals	195,660	100[a]	481	100[a]

[a]Percentages have been rounded to the nearest whole number and therefore may not sum to 100.

ter reportedly was not as advantageous to that country as HTS 9802.00.8010 was initially for the CBERA beneficiaries (USITC 1994, A-3). With the inauguration of CBTPA in October 2000, this scheme was altered again with respect to the Caribbean. The new state of affairs is discussed later in this chapter.

The bilateral agreements under the Special Access Program for the Caribbean included two types of restraints: (1) "Guaranteed Access Levels," or GALs, that applied only to clothing assembled from fabric formed and cut in the United States and (2) regular quota limits for non-U.S.-formed and -cut fabric. According to the United States International Trade Commission:

> In general terms, a GAL is negotiated for each MFA category covered by a SAP (Special Access Program) bilateral agreement, along with a Specific Limit (SL) or a Designated Consultation Level (DCL) for regular quotas. It has been possible to increase GALs upon exporter request unless market disruption occurs, while SLs are subject to agreed allowable annual percentage increases and DCLs are raised only after bilateral consultation. (USITC 1997c, A-5 to A-6)

In this manner the United States protects its own textile industry (thus preserving domestic jobs in the sector) through a sort of marriage of convenience with Caribbean clothing assemblers, thus bolstering the competitiveness of the industry relative to low-cost Far Eastern producers such as China. Although there do exist operations in the EPZs of the Caribbean that assemble garments from cloth made in the Far East for eventual sale in the U.S. market, these are subject to the more restrictive DCLs and SLs (Bailey and Eicher 1991, 8–9).

Despite this favorable disposition of the United States toward 9802 production in Caribbean Basin EPZs, East Asian firms tend to avoid exporting under this regime, preferring to use non-U.S.-formed fabric.[8] This practice has been confirmed by U.S. government sources (USITC 1994, 2–19), which add that such Asian firms generate more value added in the Caribbean by performing cut, make, and trim operations there. This distinguishes them from U.S. production-sharing operations under provision 9802.00.8010 but also makes their exports to the United States ineligible for duty reductions under HTS 9802.00.80. Nevertheless, restrictive quotas in their home countries as well as rising costs are given as the chief reasons for East Asian producers to relocate to the Caribbean and Central America to supply the U.S. market. Foremost among these producers

TABLE 15.3.   Export-Processing Zone
Investments by Country of Origin:
Investments over U.S.$6 million,
December 2000

Country	Investment (U.S.$1,000,000)
United States	747
Dominican Republic	312
South Korea	75
Panama	36
The Netherlands	8
Taiwan	6
Others	38

Source: Consejo Nacional de Zonas Francas de Exportación.

have been the Koreans, with investments totaling close to U.S.$70 million as of June 1992
(USITC 1994, 2–19).

Although South Korea surpasses all foreign
countries except the United States in terms of
number of establishments in EPZs of the Dominican Republic, recent data attest to a strong
presence of Panamanian investment.[9] According to Table 15.3, Panama-registered investments in EPZs in the Dominican Republic total
U.S.$36 million. This figure is surpassed only
by investments of U.S.$747 million originating
from the United States, U.S.$312 million in
local investment, and U.S.$75 million originat-
ing from South Korea. The Netherlands follows in fifth place, with U.S.$8 million in in-
vestments. Table 15.4 presents data on the
sourcing of inputs according to supplier country. Based on the number of EPZ firms that
source inputs from a given country, the chief
suppliers are the United States and South Korea, with 409 and 33 EPZ firms, respectively,
sourcing inputs from these countries. These
are followed by China and Italy, from which 29
and 18 firms, respectively, source inputs. These
do not take into account the 60 establishments
that source inputs domestically.

To get more precise information, efforts
were made to interview managers of Asian
EPZ firms in the Dominican Republic. The

reluctance of managers of Korean enterprises
to participate in the author's 1991 managerial
survey did not allow for a solid confirmation of
the above-mentioned sourcing practice. Nevertheless, one Dominican–Hong Kong joint
venture involved in the production of sweaters
acknowledged using fabric exclusively from
Hong Kong. This firm was also doing its own
cutting in the Dominican Republic, which
qualified it as a manufacturing, as opposed to a
mere assembly, operation. In contrast to this, a
second joint venture involving a minority share
of Korean capital was carrying out mostly
HTS 9802 production of men's and women's
clothing. No non-Asian EPZ operations in the
sample of Dominican firms were sourcing cloth
from Asia at the time (Mathews 1995, 81).

The option of using fabric made in the Far
East is discouraged by the CBTPA, with its
strict rules of origin. The future of these stric-
tures is, however, less certain with the immi-
nent liberalization of commerce under the
Agreement on Textiles and Clothing (ATC) of
the World Trade Organization (WTO), as well
as China's accession to the agreement.

The responses that countries such as the
Dominican Republic can offer to the challenge
of garment trade liberalization depend on a
series of factors that include dollar labor costs

TABLE 15.4.   Country of Origin for Imports
by Number of EPZ Firms: Origin of
Imports Corresponding to Greater than
Twelve Firms, December 2000

Supplier Country	No. of Importing Firms
United States	409
Dominican Republic	60
South Korea	33
China	29
Italy	18
Puerto Rico	17
Taiwan	15
Mexico	14

Source: Consejo Nacional de Zonas Francas de Exportación.

TABLE 15.5. Value of Principal U.S. Imports of Textiles and Clothing Originating from the Dominican Republic: Products Exceeding U.S.$50 Million in Value During at Least One of the Years between 1989 and 1999

Category	Description	U.S.$ Millions				% Total Imports			
		1989	1993	1997	1999	1989	1993	1997	1999
338	Men's cotton woven shirts	27	49	77	129	4	3	3	5
339	Blouses woven of cotton	17	36	77	122	3	2	3	5
347	Men's cotton trousers	137	278	468	463	21	19	21	19
348	Women's cotton pants	40	129	175	222	6	9	8	9
352	Cotton underwear	14	95	220	279	2	7	10	12
435	Women's woolen jackets	15	74	87	42	2	5	4	2
633	Men's MMF[a] sports jackets	17	27	63	42	3	2	3	2
635	Women's MMF[a] jackets	12	62	66	14	2	4	3	1
647	Men's MMF[a] trousers	46	84	149	168	7	6	7	7
648	Women's MMF[a] pants	20	42	59	45	3	3	3	2
649	MMF[a] brassieres	48	108	151	174	7	7	7	7
659	Other MMF[a] clothing	12	46	65	74	2	3	3	3

Source: U.S. Department of Commerce (2001).

[a]Manmade fiber.

and possible product-diversification strategies. It is important to point out that the Dominican Republic has historically specialized in a narrow range of products, as evidenced in Table 15.5. Over the years cotton underwear has become a prominent export of the Dominican Republic, rising from 2 percent of the value of total garment and textile exports to the United States in 1989 to 12 percent in 1999. Most other items have remained relatively stable in percentage terms, with men's cotton trousers registering the highest value of between U.S.$463 million and U.S.$468 million. However, regional treaties have significantly affected what may otherwise appear to be a booming sector.

NAFTA has already caused major changes in the pattern of the United States' garment trade with its southern neighbors. Prior to 1994 the U.S. tariff structure benefited the importation of garments assembled offshore in the Caribbean maquiladora industry. This state of affairs encouraged the growth of the clothing assembly industry, which became an increasingly important nontraditional sector

in several Caribbean Basin countries, particularly the Dominican Republic. Following the enactment of NAFTA and the devaluation of the peso in 1994, Mexico became a relatively more favorable platform for such clothing exports to the United States, to the detriment of some Caribbean exporters. The adverse impact of NAFTA was not uniformly distributed throughout the region. Those most affected were the ones whose dollar wages were relatively higher, such as the Dominican Republic (Gitli and Arce 2000, 1).

The Impact of NAFTA and the Mexican Devaluation

Mexico and the Dominican Republic are among the principal beneficiaries of U.S. production-sharing operations in the clothing sector. This is evident from Table 15.6, which provides U.S. import values of Multifiber Arrangement fibers that enter under HTS 9802 according to the main beneficiary countries of this program in the hemisphere. The import

TABLE 15.6.   Value of U.S. MFA Imports under United States Tariff
Schedule 9802 (807) by Principal Beneficiaries, 1992 and 1995

	1992 ($U.S. millions)			1995 ($U.S. millions)		
	9802 Regular	Special Program	Total	9802 Regular	Special Program	Total
Dominican Republic	513	536	1,049	798	767	1,565
Mexico	364	521	885	219	2,322	2,541
Costa Rica	379	102	481	141	529	670
Jamaica	74	146	220	203	246	449
Guatemala	255	57	312	362	158	520
Honduras	246	0	246	676	0	676
El Salvador	131	0	131	458	19	477
Haiti	62	0	62	—	5	5
Colombia	204	0	204	—	—	—

Sources: 1992 data from U.S. Commerce Department database; 1995 data from USITC (1996, 5-5).

Note: Years following 1995 are excluded due to the declining use of United States Tariff Schedule (USTS) 9802 as a mechanism for entering the U.S. market because of the gradual liberalization of markets under the Agreement on Textiles and Clothing of the WTO.

figures are divided into the categories of "Regular 9802" production sharing and the "Special Program" that applies to clothing assembled from cloth both formed and cut in the United States.[10]

To highlight the impact of NAFTA and the 1994 devaluation of the Mexican currency on regional garment commerce with the United States, data for 1992 (before NAFTA) and 1995 (after NAFTA) are provided. The evidence is quite dramatic in the case of Mexico's Special Regime. Whereas before NAFTA and the devaluation of the Mexican peso the value of the Dominican Republic's Special Access Program garment exports to the United States surpassed those of Mexico by a margin of U.S.$15 million, the year after the enactment of NAFTA the value of Mexican Special Regime garment exports to the United States reached U.S.$2.3 billion while the Dominican Republic exported only a third of that in value.

As highlighted in the introduction to this chapter, trade diversion has occurred to the benefit of Mexico, and at the expense of much of the Caribbean, as a consequence of the com-

bined effect of the 1994 Mexican peso devaluation and the enactment of NAFTA. Regarding the latter, the removal of the U.S. tariff on value added in Mexico for Special Regime imports under NAFTA provided Mexican clothing with an advantage in the U.S. market. Until the recent enactment of CBTPA, this tariff was still applied to imports from Caribbean Basin countries under Special Program HTS 9802.00.8010. According to the U.S. International Trade Commission, in 1995 the average landed cost for slacks from Mexico was 14 percent lower than that for the same product from the Dominican Republic, with half of that difference attributable to the absence of the tariff (USITC 1996, 5–7).

As a consequence of this situation, Caribbean governments adamantly petitioned for some type of NAFTA parity in order to preserve their garment assembly industries. It is difficult at this early juncture to predict if CBTPA will help garment assembly industries recover in countries such as the Dominican Republic, although there are promising signs. The future becomes even more uncertain in the face of the proposed liberalization of clothing and textile markets, scheduled for completion in the year 2005 under auspices of the WTO. Nevertheless, a series of influential factors can be identified.

The Caribbean Basin Trade Partnership Act under the Trade and Development Act of 2000

Responding more to pressures from influential U.S. commercial and manufacturing interests, such as the American Apparel Manufacturers' Association (AAMA) and the American Textile Manufacturers' Institute (ATMI), than to the clamor of Caribbean governments, the U.S. government approved the Trade and Development Act (TDA) in May 2000. The law, which was enacted on October 1, included the relevant section titled the "Caribbean Basin Trade Partnership Act." It will have a duration of eight years, until September 30, 2008, and grants duty- and quota-free access to the U.S. market to:

1. Apparel articles assembled in one or more Caribbean beneficiary countries from fabrics entirely formed and cut in the United States, from yarns of 100 percent U.S. origin. This includes clothing transformed through embroidery or subjected to other incidental processes, such as stonewashing. This also includes clothing formerly entering under HTS 9802.00.8010 and its precursor Item 807a.
2. Articles cut in one or more Caribbean beneficiary countries from fabrics entirely formed in the United States, from yarns of 100 percent U.S. origin, if said articles are assembled in one or more Caribbean countries with thread of 100 percent U.S. origin.
3. Apparel articles (other than socks) knit to shape in a Caribbean beneficiary country

from 100 percent U.S.-origin yarn and knitted or crocheted apparel (excepting T-shirts) cut and entirely assembled in one or more such countries, from cloth formed in one or more such countries from yarns of 100 percent U.S. origin. For the first year of CPTPA/TDA2000 (that is, until September 30, 2001) the allowable aggregate quantity of these imports could not exceed the equivalent of 250 million square meters. Since then the quota has been subject to 16 percent annual growth rate for a three-year period.
4. Similarly, a ceiling of 4.2 million dozens (batches of twelve) was established for the first year of aggregate imports of T-shirts, excluding underwear, made in one or more Caribbean beneficiary countries from fabric made in one or more such countries from 100 percent U.S.-origin yarn. Said quota will be subject to a 16 percent annual growth rate until the year 2004.
5. Brassieres cut and sewn or otherwise assembled in one or more Caribbean beneficiary countries or the United States or both are eligible for preferential treatment only if the combined cost of all fabric components formed in the United States and used in their production constitutes at least 75 percent of the sum total customs-declared value of the fabric contained therein.
6. Apparel articles cut, sewn, or otherwise assembled in one or more Caribbean countries from non-U.S. fabric or yarn, as long as it is officially certified that these are not available in commercial quantities in the United States.
7. Hand-loomed, handmade, or folkloric textile and apparel goods.
8. Textile luggage assembled in a Caribbean beneficiary country from fabric cut in such a country but entirely formed in the United States from yarns of 100 percent U.S. origin.

Although some opposed the CBTPA of the TDA, it will likely benefit interests in the Caribbean as well as U.S. commercial and manufacturing interests. Charles Bremmer of the ATMI estimates that U.S. importers of garments assembled in the Caribbean will save some U.S.$700 million as a consequence of the law (Welling 2000). In the Dominican Republic, Executive Director José Manuel Torres of the Asociación Dominicana de Zonas Francas (ADOZONA) estimates that some thirty thousand new jobs will be created in his country's "free-zone" sector during the first year of the law's application. This would mean a 25 percent increase in employment and between a $600 million and $1 billion increase in overall free-zone exports (Martinez Fornos 2000).

Although data from the Dominican Republic that could indicate the impact on the country of the CBTPA were not forthcoming at the time of this writing, recent U.S. trade statistics compiled by the USITC for the year 2001 show a marked increase of imports under the program for the Caribbean Basin. Comparing the CBTPA program with the overall CBERA, the USITC notes that the value of U.S. imports under the former "with its added textile preferences were more than twice the magnitude of their CBERA counterparts during 2001" (USITC 2002, 15). In the case of imports from the Dominican Republic, these were just under twice the value, with total CBTPA imports totaling $1.5 billion compared with $810 million worth of CBERA imports (USITC 2002, Table 1).

Despite the benefits the Caribbean expects to derive from the TDA 2000, the CBTPA stops short of granting the clamored-for "parity" with NAFTA. Furthermore, the CBTPA rests on a precarious base since it is a unilateral noncontractual law with a limited duration of eight years. Hence the United States is free to modify it as it sees fit or to disqualify any beneficiary without having to justify its actions

to a dispute-settlement body or mechanism, as would be the case under NAFTA. Other limitations of the CBTPA include its inherent restrictions on value added in the Caribbean, thereby reducing the possibilities for vertical integration of the garment export industry beyond the stage of mere assembly.

As expected, CBTPA favors U.S. inputs and raw materials in the Caribbean garment assembly industry. It stipulates that at least 93 percent of yarns incorporated in articles of clothing produced in the region must be of U.S. origin (Manchester Trade 2000). In effect, no regional textile product qualifies for duty-free entry into the U.S. market if not through its incorporation into an article of clothing. However, products made from cloth knitted in Caribbean beneficiary countries enjoy privileged access to the U.S. market, but only in limited quantities. These quotas were distributed among Caribbean beneficiary countries according to the quantities identified in Table 15.7 (for 250-million-square-meter equivalents of knitted apparel) and Table 15.8 (for 4.2 million dozens of T-shirts).

In the case of the 250-million-square-meter equivalents of knitted apparel, the first-year allocation for Honduras is 25.20 percent, followed by El Salvador with 21.4 percent, Guatemala with 19.4 percent, and the Dominican Republic with 18.13 percent. The allocation of dozens of T-shirts also has Honduras leading with 42.0 percent of the quota in the first year, followed by El Salvador with 20.78 percent and the Dominican Republic with 14.5 percent. In the years after 2004, the U.S. Congress will determine the individual beneficiary quota growth rates. Congressional sentiment in this regard is that these quota growth rates should depend (as the chief criterion) on U.S. export performance to the country in question during the first four years of the CBTPA. In other words, if the increase in the quota of a beneficiary country is accompanied by a corre-

TABLE 15.7.   Quotas for the Caribbean Basin Trade Partnership Act, 2000: Fabric

Country	Year 1	Year 2	Year 3	Year 4
Dominican Republic				
% Share	18.13	16.88	15.61	15.54
Quota[a]	45,334,750	489,607,000	52,518,768	60,652,516
% Growth[b]		8.0	7.3	15.5
CARICOM–Haiti[c]				
% Share	4.93	8.87	14.78	15.27
Quota[a]	12,312,500	25,708,500	49,703,100	59,583,303
% Growth[b]		108.8	93.3	19.9
Costa Rica				
% Share	7.48	6.94	6.43	6.39
Quota[a]	18,690,250	20,138,470	21,637,248	24,947,020
% Growth[b]		7.7	7.4	15.3
Nicaragua				
% Share	1.97	4.43	4.93	4.93
Quota[a]	4,925,000	12,854,250	16,567,700	19,218,532
% Growth[b]		161.0	28.9	16.0
El Salvador				
% Share	21.40	19.90	18.40	18.28
Quota[a]	53,496,000	57,711,450	61,911,056	71,323,192
% Growth[b]		7.9	7.3	15.2
Guatemala				
% Share	19.40	18.04	16.68	16.57
Quota[a]	48,496,250	52,317,740	56,124,976	64,657,775
% Growth[b]		7.9	7.3	15.2
Honduras				
% Share	25.20	23.43	21.67	21.52
Quota[a]	62,995,250	67,959,180	72,904,608	83,988,302
% Growth[b]		7.9	7.3	15.2
Panama				
% Share	1.50	1.50	1.50	1.50
Quota[a]	3,750,000	4,350,000	5,046,000	5,853,360
% Growth[b]		16.0	16.0	16.0
Totals				
% Share	100.00	100.00	100.00	100.00
Quota[a]	250,000,000	290,000,290	336,413,456	390,224,000
% Growth[b]		16.0	16.0	16.0

Source: U.S. Department of Commerce (2001).

[a]250-million-square-meter equivalents.

[b]Relative to the previous year.

[c]Caribbean Community and Haiti.

TABLE 15.8. Quotas for the Caribbean Basin Trade Partnership Act, 2000: T-Shirts

Country	Year 1	Year 2	Year 3	Year 4
Dominican Republic				
% Share	14.50	13.35	12.00	11.00
Quota[a]	609,000	650,412	678,182	721,134
% Growth[b]		6.8	4.3	6.3
CARICOM–Haiti[c]				
% Share	5.00	10.00	16.00	17.50
Quota[a]	210,000	487,200	904,243	1,147,259
% Growth[b]		132.0	85.6	26.9
Costa Rica				
% Share	1.50	1.50	1.50	1.50
Quota[a]	63,000	73,080	84,773	98,336
% Growth[b]		16.0	16.0	16.0
Nicaragua				
% Share	4.00	6.00	7.00	7.00
Quota[a]	168,000	292,320	395,606	458,903
% Growth[b]		74.0	35.3	16.0
El Salvador				
% Share	20.78	19.14	17.69	16.52
Quota[a]	872,655	932,257	999,697	1,083,012
% Growth[b]		6.8	7.2	8.3
Guatemala				
% Share	11.22	10.34	9.55	8.30
Quota[a]	471,345	503,536	539,963	544,128
% Growth[b]		6.8	7.2	0.8
Honduras				
% Share	42.00	38.68	35.76	37.18
Quota[a]	1,764,000	1,884,475	2,020,803	2,437,433
% Growth[b]		6.8	7.2	20.6
Panama				
% Share	1.00	1.00	1.00	1.00
Quota[a]	42,000.00	48,720	56,515	65,558
% Growth[b]		16.0	16.0	16.0
Totals				
% Share	100.00	100.00	100.00	100.00
Quota[a]	4,200,000	4,872,000	5,679,783	6,555,763
% Growth[b]		16.0	16.6	15.4

Source: U.S. Department of Commerce (2001).

[a] 4.2 million dozens T-shirts.

[b] Relative to the previous year.

[c] Caribbean Community and Haiti.

sponding increase in U.S. exports to that country, the country in question will have a greater likelihood of obtaining an increase in its quota growth rate after September 30, 2004.

In judging the CBTPA, it is important to keep in mind the U.S. preelection atmosphere out of which it arose, wherein protectionism was an issue among the U.S. electorate. Furthermore, the Caribbean could not expect to make significant gains in access to the U.S. market when the CBTPA is seen in the context of the wider process of globalization. In this respect unilateral advantages such as CBTPA are slowly being phased out in favor of reciprocal liberalization of markets among trading partners. Until the Caribbean agrees to such reciprocal liberalization of its own market, only limited gains can be made at the negotiating table.

Of perhaps greater importance is the question of whether globalization, as spearheaded by the World Trade Organization, prevails in the future over regional agreements such as NAFTA. While some aspects of the latter currently provide certain bloc-member industries with a margin of advantage over those of non-bloc partners, this advantage may be short-lived. The ultimate outcome will hinge on the interaction of the NAFTA with the Uruguay Round agreements. This will be particularly decisive for the future of the Caribbean garment assembly industry; hence it is necessary to examine briefly the possible implications of the General Agreement on Tariffs and Trade (GATT) for the textile and garment trade.

The Uruguay Round and the World Trade Organization

One of the most noteworthy achievements of the Uruguay Round[11] for developing countries in general was the decision to liberalize the garment and textile trade through the progressive elimination of the quota system, existent for many years under the MFA. Accordingly, the Agreement on Textiles and Clothing establishes a timetable for the gradual elimination of quotas in countries that are members of the WTO. If all members adhere to the agreement, restrictions on the garment and textile trade should be eliminated by the year 2005.

However, the conclusion of the Uruguay Round did not establish that free trade would eventually prevail with regard to clothing commerce, as a degree of tariff protection will remain in place even after the ATC takes full effect. As part of the WTO-ATC, the United States pledged to reduce tariffs applied to textiles in general by an average of 9 percent (USITC 1995, 15–16). In more specific terms, the average U.S. tariff on cotton clothing would be reduced to 15 percent from a pre–Uruguay Round level of 16.6 percent, while that applied to manmade fiber clothing would drop to 23.7 percent from a pre–Uruguay Round average of 25.5 percent (USITC 1995, 14). These two categories are important components of developing-country industries.

Although the elimination of the MFA also means the end of the U.S. quota system under HTS provision 9802, it does not mean that Caribbean clothing exports to the United States under the currently restricted categories of SLs and DCLs will have a chance to expand. It is precisely the U.S. quota system applied to clothing imports from the Far East that has restrained those countries from dominating the U.S. clothing market, at the same time motivating Asian firms to transfer assembly operations to the Caribbean in order to take advantage of unfulfilled Caribbean quotas. The elimination of quotas will likely remove the incentive for Asian clothing firms to relocate to the Caribbean, given that they could export directly from the Far East.

What countries would ultimately benefit from these changes toward liberalization? If the timetable for the elimination of quotas under the ATC is abided by, one possibility is that China and other Far Eastern countries will benefit, at least as far as the U.S. market is concerned. One scenario has the resulting increase in U.S. imports from low-wage Asian countries outcompeting the North American textile industry as well as its complementary assembly segments in the Caribbean, Central America, and Mexico (USITC 1995, 23). This would particularly be the case when China manages to take full advantage of its membership in the World Trade Organization.

A clear picture of the future configuration of the hemispheric garment industry is difficult to discern, owing to the numerous factors that must be considered. Although the issue is complex, it may be helpful to draw a distinction between global agreements administered by the World Trade Organization and relevant regional bloc agreements, such as NAFTA. Although they may not be sufficient to make the U.S. textile commodity chain competitive with Asian imports once the WTO–ATC takes effect, NAFTA's rules of origin clearly favor textile inputs originating from within the bloc.

NAFTA or the WTO: Will the Regional or Global Level Be Decisive?

With the advent of NAFTA at the beginning of 1994, the United States eliminated the quotas on around 90 percent of clothing imports from Mexico; the remaining quotas are scheduled to be eliminated over a period of ten years (USITC 1995, 13). While tariffs on around 30 percent of garment imports from Mexico were eliminated immediately, by the year 2000 tariffs on virtually all U.S. imports of clothing from Mexico that comply with NAFTA rules of origin were supposed to have been elimi-

nated (USITC 1995, 14). It should be recalled that the WTO–ATC establishes the elimination of quotas but not tariffs on the world's textile trade.

NAFTA, like other regional agreements, maintains elements of protectionism despite being considered a trade-liberalizing agreement, due to its restrictive rules of origin in some industrial sectors. In the case of the clothing and textile industry, NAFTA rules of origin require the almost exclusive use of yarn originating within the countries that make up the bloc. In other words, to qualify for full NAFTA benefits (including exemption from tariff payments, which will still be in existence after the WTO–ATC takes effect), clothing and textiles must be made of yarn produced within the bloc (the "yarn-forward" rule).

This rule has been the target of criticism by free-trade advocates, given the protection it affords to North American industries. Gary Hufbauer and Jeffrey Schott (1993, 44) point out that trade diversion would occur in favor of producers within the NAFTA bloc that are not the most efficient in the world. In the scenario that NAFTA prevailed over the ATC–WTO, the ultimate beneficiaries would likely be the North American textile mills and their Mexican assembly complement, through the displacement of cheaper Far Eastern clothing in the U.S. market (USITC 1995, 23). Trade diversion would be reduced to the extent that the letter and spirit of the relevant agreements of the Uruguay Round and the WTO are respected, specifically the ATC (Lustig, Bosworth, and Lawrence 1992, 239).

Conclusions

The enclave nature of EPZs and of the garment assembly industry in particular in the Dominican Republic and the wider Caribbean prevents the industry from becoming a sustainable industrial base that could contribute to economic development in the long run. Garment assembly in the Caribbean is just one small link in the commodity chain and hence contributes very little value added from an industry-wide perspective. Furthermore, this link rests on a precarious foundation of cheap labor. The industry in any one country can prosper or decline depending on regional currency fluctuations relative to the dollar. The light-manufacturing nature of assembly accentuates the footloose and highly mobile nature of operations, enabling firms to easily relocate to the country where labor is cheapest at a moment's notice.

Nevertheless, the lack of viable alternatives for employment creation and the generation of badly needed foreign exchange in the short and medium term make the preservation of this sector a high priority of regional governments, and particularly that of the Dominican Republic. The World Bank reflects this sentiment in its 1997 overview of the Dominican Republic:

> The Dominican Republic stands at an economic crossroads. The performance of the economy during the past 15 years clearly demonstrates both its ability to compete effectively in the international market and the inability of tourism and the free trade zones (EPZs) alone to revive sustainable growth. . . . During the transition to a more open and private-sector driven economy, however, the country's medium term growth prospects will continue to depend heavily on the dynamism of tourism and the free trade zones. (World Bank 1997)

The integration of the region into NAFTA may be necessary in the short or medium term if it contributes to vertical integration of the Caribbean clothing industry, as some authors have suggested will occur with Mexico in the context of NAFTA. For the time being, the passage of the CBTPA means that EPZ firms in the Dominican Republic have the opportunity (albeit limited) to integrate other stages of garment production beyond mere assembly. The integration of the Dominican Republic into NAFTA, although restricting clothing industry inputs to bloc members, theoretically enables the incorporation of yarns produced in any member country. Although the Dominican Republic does not possess a comparative advantage in all the stages of garment production, it does have widely recognized design capabilities that could be incorporated. The question of vertical integration would render greater fruits, however, if approached from a regional or even hemispheric perspective.

Regardless of the final configuration of the hemispheric garment commodity chain under regional agreements, the reality of the situation is that it will be pitted against Asian producers that can offer full-package production at very competitive prices once the MFA is completely eliminated by the year 2005. Hence the hemisphere must pool its resources and allow the different links in the hemispheric clothing commodity chain to deploy themselves geographically according to the relative strengths and resources of countries in order to become competitive enough to confront this "Asian challenge." NAFTA is a step in this direction, although the best option would be to extend the agreement to the entire hemisphere.

For the Caribbean Basin's export industrialization program in general, the priority should be the diversification of the industrial base. The current EPZ strategy is too dependent on the garment assembly industry and should be replaced by a strategy that both widens the industrial base and deepens value added in the existing export sector. Vertically integrated domestic firms are content in many cases to serve the national markets from behind high tariff barriers. This is rapidly becoming less of an option as globalization and regionalism advance. Governments should therefore create the conditions for integrating these domestic industries to the EPZs or for them to begin exporting on their own.

Notes

1. Preliminary figures provided by the Consejo Nacional de Zonas Francas de Exportación.

2. Although reference is made to "assembly" processes, this is understood to include light manufacturing as well.

3. In some cases a limited number of these goods are allowed to penetrate the domestic market.

4. Consejo Nacional de Zonas Francas de Exportación, *Informe estadístico 1998, sector de zonas francas* (Santo Domingo: Departamento de Información y Estadísticas, 1999), 47.

5. 1998 data from the Consejo Nacional de Zonas Francas de Exportación.

6. Production sharing, also referred to as complementary production, is production occurring in more than one country. The majority of such goods enter the U.S. market registered under section 9802 of the new Harmonized Tariff Schedule (formerly section 807).

7. A U.S. preferential market-access program.

8. This was an observation commonly voiced by Dominican EPZ managers and others interviewed by the author in 1991.

9. Data for the year 2000, supplied by the Consejo Nacional de Zonas Francas de la República Dominicana, place at twenty-seven the number of establishments operating with South Korean capital, while those with Taiwanese capital total seven.

10. The Special Program includes both the "Special Access Program" applied to the CBERA countries and the "Special Regime" established by the United States for Mexico.

11. The Uruguay agreements were negotiated under the General Agreement on Tariffs and Trade and came into effect at the beginning of 1995.

References

Bailey, Thomas, and Theo Eicher. 1991. "The Effect of a North American Free Trade Agreement on Apparel Employment in the US." Paper prepared for the Bureau of International Labor Affairs, U.S. Department of Labor, Washington, D.C. October.

Consejo Nacional de Zonas Francas de Exportación. 1998–2001. *Informe estadístico, sector de zonas francas.* Santo Domingo: Departamento de Información y Estadísticas.

Gitli, Eduardo, and Randall Arce. 2000. "Qué significa la ampliación de beneficios para los países de la Cuenca del Caribe?" Report. Heredia, Costa Rica: Centro Internacional de Politica Economica para el Desarrollo Sostenible (CINPE). May.

Hufbauer, Gary Clyde, and Jeffrey J. Schott. 1993. *NAFTA: An Assessment.* Washington, D.C.: Institute for International Economics. February.

Lustig, Nora, Barry P. Bosworth, and Robert Z. Lawrence, eds. 1992. *North American Free Trade: Assessing the Impact.* Washington, D.C.: The Brookings Institution.

Manchester Trade. 2000. "MT's Summary Review of CBTPA Benefits." Report. Washington, D.C. June.

Martinez Fornos, Eva. 2000. "The Dominican Triumph." *Apparel Industry International,* July 31. Accessed at <http://www.aiimag.com/aiieng/jul00stor2.html>.

Mathews, Dale T. 1995. "Export Processing Zones in the Dominican Republic: Their Nature and Trajectory." Ph.D. diss., University of Sussex, Brighton.

United States Department of Commerce. 2001. Fax from Brian Fennessey of the Office of Textiles and Apparel of the International Trade Administration, U.S. Department of Commerce. July 5.

United States Department of Labor–Bureau of International Labor Affairs. 1992. *Trade and Employment Effects of the Caribbean Basin Economic Recovery Act.* Economic Discussion Paper 41. Washington, D.C.: U.S. Department of Labor. October.

United States Government. 2000. *Trade and Development Act of 2000.* Washington, D.C.: Government Printing Office. May.

United States International Trade Commission (USITC). 1984. *Tariff Schedules of the United States Annotated: 1984.* Washington, D.C.: USITC.

———. 1994. *Production Sharing: U.S. Imports under Harmonized Tariff Schedule Provisions 9802.00.60 and 9802.00.80, 1989–1992.* USITC Publication 2729. Washington, D.C.: USITC. February.

———. 1995. *Trade and Industry Summary: Apparel.* USITC Publication 2853. Washington, D.C.: USITC. January.

———. 1996. *Production Sharing: Use of U.S. Components and Materials in Foreign Assembly Operations, 1991–1994.* USITC Publication 2966. Washington, D.C.: USITC. May.

———. 1997a. *Caribbean Basin Economic Recovery Act: Twelfth Report, 1996.* USITC Publication 3058. Washington, D.C.: USITC. September.

———. 1997b. *Production Sharing: Use of U.S. Components and Materials in Foreign Assembly Operations, 1992–1995.* USITC Publication 3032. Washington, D.C.: USITC. April.

———. 1997c. *Production Sharing: Use of U.S. Components and Materials in Foreign Assembly Operations, 1993–1996.* USITC Publication 3077. Washington, D.C.: USITC. December.

———. 2002. *International Economic Review.* USITC Publication 3489. Washington, D.C.: USITC. January–February.

Welling, Holly. 2000. "Caribbean Boon: Lurching after NAFTA." *Apparel Industry Magazine,* August 31. Accessed at <http://www.aimagazine.com/archives/200008/c20000731044226i6855a.cfm>.

Willmore, Larry. 1996. "Export Processing in the Caribbean: Lessons from Four Case Studies." United Nations Economic Commission for Latin America and the Caribbean (UN-ECLAC) Working Paper no. 42. Port of Spain, Trinidad and Tobago: UN-ECLAC. September.

World Bank. 1997. "Dominican Republic: Country Overview." In *Trends in Developing Economies, 1996.* Washington, D.C.: World Bank.

Part VI

Conclusion

Jennifer Bair, David Spener,
and Gary Gereffi

---

16   NAFTA and Uneven Development in
the North American Apparel Industry

The various contributions to this book have documented how NAFTA-inspired firm strategies are changing the geography of apparel production in North America. The authors show in myriad ways how companies at different positions along the apparel commodity chain are responding to the new institutional and regulatory environment that NAFTA creates. By making it easier for U.S. companies to take advantage of Mexico as a nearby low-cost site for export-oriented apparel production, NAFTA is deepening the regional division of labor within North America, and this process has consequences for firms and workers in each of the signatory countries. In the introduction to this book we alluded to the obvious implications of shifting investment and trade patterns in the North American apparel industry for employment in the different countries. In this concluding chapter we focus on Mexico in the NAFTA era, specifically the extent to which Mexico's role in the North American economy facilitates or inhibits its economic development.

We begin with a discussion of the contemporary debate about Mexico's development, which turns on the question of how to assess the implications of Mexico's rapid and profound process of economic reform. Second, we focus on the textile and apparel industries as sectors that have been significantly affected by changes in regulatory environments at both the global and regional levels. Third, we examine the evidence regarding Mexico's NAFTA-era export dynamism, and in particular we emphasize the importance of interfirm networks, both for making sense of Mexico's meteoric rise among apparel exporters and for evaluating the implications of this dynamism for development. Fourth, we turn to a consideration of the national political-economic environment that shapes developmental outcomes for all Mexicans. Although regional disparities within Mexico are profound, aspects of government policy, such as management of the national currency, and characteristics of the institutional environment, such as industrial relations, have nationwide effects, and critics of NAFTA charge that these factors are contributing to a process of economic and social polarization that is ever more evident (Morales 1999; Dussel Peters 2000). Finally, we suggest that the mixed consequences of Mexico's NAFTA-era growth can be taken as emblematic of the contradictions that the process of globalization poses for economic and social development.

The anti-sweatshop campaign in North America is one example of transnational or cross-border movements that are emerging to address the negative consequences of this process. In bringing attention to the problem of sweatshop production in North America, activists are developing strategies that rely on a network logic that is not dissimilar to the approaches reflected in the various chapters of this book.

Mexico's Developmental Debate

In many ways Mexico entered the new millennium with an economic and political profile far removed from the desperate and dark days of the 1980s debt crisis, during what would come to be called Latin America's "lost decade." Having abandoned the import-substitution industrialization model that served as the foundation for five decades of development policy, Mexico appeared to be enjoying the fruits of its strict adherence to neoliberal economic orthodoxy. Across a wide variety of sectors, Mexico's exports to the United States have been booming since the implementation of the North American Free Trade Agreement (NAFTA) in 1994, increasing from $39.9 billion in 1993 to $131.4 billion in 2001 (U.S. Bureau of the Census 2002). Aside from impressive export growth, Mexico has also managed to achieve many of the other objectives associated with Latin America's new economic model: a stable currency, modest inflation, and plentiful direct foreign investment (Reinhardt and Peres 2000; Dussel Peters 2000). On the political front, the historic victory of opposition candidate Vicente Fox suggested that Mexico's decades-long transition from one-party rule had been consolidated.

Despite the seeming abundance of good news, there is a growing sense that all is not well in Mexico. While the liberalization strategy that Mexico enthusiastically embraced in the second half of the 1980s and 1990s has been successful in its own terms, critics have pointed out that Mexico's shift from an import-substituting industrialization strategy to an export-led growth model has been associated with a more unequal income distribution and falling real wages for the majority of the country's workers (de la Garza 1994; Robinson 1998–99; Dussel Peters 2000; Mariña Flores 2001). The most dynamic sector of the Mexican economy in terms of exports and job creation is the maquiladora industry of in-bond plants, while small and medium-sized enterprises have been hard hit by the country's rapid liberalization. NAFTA skeptics claim that the trade agreement and the export-led growth model it represents are leading to the "maquilization of Mexico," with the entire country becoming converted into an export-processing zone for low-value-added activities benefiting large corporations on both sides of the border.

NAFTA is fundamental to the debate about the country's developmental trajectory in both an economic and a political sense. The year of NAFTA's implementation, 1994, was a momentous one in Mexico. President Carlos Salinas de Gortari (1988–94) waged an energetic battle to convince Mexicans that NAFTA would prove a powerful, modernizing force for the country's development, and he made the passage of NAFTA the central goal of his administration. Despite ubiquitous references to the modernization of Mexico throughout the six years of the Salinas administration, the Zapatista uprising on January 1, 1994 proved a poignant reminder that many of the nation's citizens continue to grapple with problems of crippling poverty, social marginalization, and ethnic discrimination. In his Internet press releases the movement's leader, Subcomandante Marcos, made explicit the link between the Zapatista struggle and the implementation of NAFTA. Since that time NAFTA has arguably come to be seen as the apotheosis of

Mexico's economic liberalization and restructuring program, which began with a series of reforms implemented under President Miguel de la Madrid (1982–88).

The rhetorical power of NAFTA as a symbol for Mexico's recent political-economic trajectory may make a measured appraisal of its actual consequences more difficult, though surely even more necessary. Opinion was divided over NAFTA before the agreement was signed, with some arguing that its effects would be primarily positive (Weintraub 1991; Lustig 1994) and others warning that it would exacerbate Mexico's already severe patterns of social and economic polarization (Castañeda 1993; Conchello 1992). U.S. scholars argued that the real economic impact of NAFTA would be slight, despite the heated political rhetoric that it provoked (Krugman 1993; Bosworth 1993). Within Mexico much of the debate about NAFTA turned on the question of its potential implications for the country's political system. While some argued that NAFTA and the process of economic restructuring that it represented would not foster democratization (Poitras and Robinson 1994), others maintained that pressure for political reforms would be the most important unintended consequence of NAFTA (Heredia 1994).

The election of Vicente Fox to the Mexican presidency in July 2000 seems to provide support for this last prediction, although the exact nature of NAFTA's causal role, if any, is unclear. Mexico's far-reaching economic reforms, and in particular its role in the process of North American integration, brought it under more intense international scrutiny, possibly inhibiting the ability of the ruling party (the Partido Revolucionario Institucional, or PRI) to reproduce itself through its customary recourse to illegality and corruption. Much of the tone of the 2000 campaign suggested that the election was a referendum on the direction that the country's economic reforms had been taking over the past decade. Each of the three major candidates—from the PRI as well as from the Partido de la Revolución Democrática (the left-of-center party) and the Partido de Acción Nacional (the right-of-center party)—attempted to distance himself from what were perceived to be the failed "neoliberal" policies of the Salinas and Ernesto Zedillo (1994–2000) administrations. Vicente Fox, whose proposed economic platform was not radically dissimilar from the status quo under the three PRI administrations that preceded him, nevertheless embraced a more populist rhetoric at moments during his campaign (Preston 2000).

Mexicans were undoubtedly voting *against* the PRI rather than *for* Fox in large numbers, and democracy, not economic policy, was the electorate's central concern (Hellman 2000). Although Fox's election signaled a decisive end to the PRI's grip on the levers of state power, the debate about the country's development trajectory remains fierce. Fox claimed throughout the campaign that sustained economic growth on the order of 7 percent a year would be necessary to help pull 27 million poor Mexicans above the poverty line, but Mexico fell far short of that goal for 2001, when the economy registered 0 percent growth. The slowdown in the U.S. economy in 2001 further fueled the debate about Mexico's developmental prospects, with some critics arguing that the economy is too dependent on the U.S. import market and is unable to generate endogenous growth (Dussel Peters 2000).

The chapters in this book examine one limited but important aspect of this debate: how NAFTA is leading to the restructuring of the North American apparel industry. In the remainder of the conclusion, we reference the various contributions here and discuss how an analytical approach focusing on interfirm production and trade networks helps explain the changing geography of apparel and textile production in post-NAFTA North America. In so doing we hope to highlight the value of this methodology in assessing the implications of shifting trade and production patterns for firms and workers in the NAFTA countries.

The Post-NAFTA Apparel Industry in North America

As important starter industries for countries attempting to industrialize, and a significant source of manufacturing employment in many countries (see Chapter 14 in this book), the apparel and textile industries have long been politically sensitive sectors. Although apparel workers in developed countries have received some protection from the Multifiber Arrangement (MFA), Chapter 2 by Jennifer Bair and Gary Gereffi documents the shifting patterns of global trade and production in this industry. Domestic apparel manufacturing in the United States declined steadily from the mid-1970s as imports from an ever-evolving array of Asian exporters penetrated the U.S. market.

However, the apparel industry is not only global in its scope; it is also increasingly regional in its organization. NAFTA was conceived, at least partly, as a means to promote intra–North American trade vis-à-vis other areas of the world. As domestic apparel manufacturers struggled to compete with cost-competitive exporters, many U.S. textile companies and some apparel firms argued that the industry could benefit by using low-wage Mexican workers for the labor-intensive processes of garment production. In this way the North American apparel and textile complex could be strengthened vis-à-vis Asian competitors through a regional division of labor between the NAFTA countries.

Perhaps in no other sector have the implications of NAFTA been as striking as in the apparel and textile industries. Although Mexico was only the seventh largest exporter of apparel to the United States in 1990, by decade's close it had overtaken China to secure the number-one spot. The explosive growth in apparel employment in Mexico aptly reflects this export dynamism. The number of garment workers increased from 231,000 in 1994 to 762,000 in 1998. The Mexican apparel industry today is nearly 90 percent the size of the U.S. industry in terms of employment (compared to approximately 25 percent in 1994), and it is far more significant in relative importance as a source of manufacturing employment in the national economy. In January 1999 employment in the garment industry accounted for 4.5 percent of total manufacturing employment in the United States (Commission for Labor Cooperation 2000). In contrast, the Mexican apparel industry accounted for a full 18 percent of total manufacturing employment in 1998 (INEGI 2001).

Several of the chapters in this book note that the reorganization of the North American apparel industry has had important implications for employment. However, besides the well-known trend of declining U.S. employment in garment production, these authors also underscore the sociological aspects of changing employment patterns. Chapter 4, by Judi Kessler, documents the significance of immigrant labor to the renewed vitality of the Los Angeles garment district, while Robert Ross's examination of the sweatshop issue in the U.S. industry (Chapter 5) emphasizes the vulnerability of this workforce.

Chapter 7, by David Spener, calls attention to a perverse paradox created by the shifting regulatory environment for apparel production in North America: that many Mexican and Mexican American women workers in El Paso, Texas, who came to the United States in search of better economic opportunities, have lost their jobs to compatriots south of the border due to the decline of the apparel industry in southern Texas. Spener's chapter captures many of the issues that are most relevant in interpreting the post-NAFTA reorganization of the North American apparel industry, including the importance of changes in the regulatory environment, the impact of those changes on firm strategy and cross-border production networks, and the devastating consequences that can result for garment workers and their communities.

Networks Matter: NAFTA, Firm Strategy, and Development

This book represents an effort to analyze the importance of interfirm networks in the restructuring of the North American apparel industry and the implications of this restructuring for enterprises and workers. A network approach allows us to examine how NAFTA shapes the strategies and investments of the companies that drive the North American apparel and textile commodity chain, and it also enables us to examine the impact of changing interfirm relations on particular communities that are linked into this chain. This focus on networks provides some leverage over the developmental debate in Mexico, insofar as we can show the difference between pre-NAFTA maquiladora assembly and more integrated production networks that have emerged in the post-NAFTA era. Chapter 10, by Gary Gereffi, Martha Martínez, and Jennifer Bair, shows that firms on both sides of the border are responding to NAFTA by establishing new types of supply chains, while the authors also document the implications of this shift in network structure for local development in the Torreón region.

The role of networks in promoting positive development outcomes, and their limits, is also emphasized by Enrique Dussel Peters, Clemente Ruiz Durán, and Michael J. Piore (Chap-

ter 11). Ulrik Vangstrup's discussion of knitters in central Mexico (Chapter 12) examines how networks between local and foreign firms can promote the development and competitiveness of apparel-producing clusters. Each of these chapters points to the importance of networks that specifically link local companies to foreign buyers. Much attention has been paid in the development literature, most notably in the work on industrial districts, to the importance of horizontal relationships between enterprises in a cluster. The chapters presented here suggest that links external to the cluster are also critical (and perhaps even more so) for the success of export-oriented firms (see also Bair and Gereffi 2001). Chapter 9, by Jorge Carrillo, Alfredo Hualde, and Araceli Almaraz, points to the potential tensions between local and external linkages with the authors' finding that firms in Monterrey and Ciudad Juárez without local linkages are more flexible and competitive in the free-trade environment than are companies with such linkages.

In Part 5, on the Caribbean and Central America, Michael Mortimore (Chapter 14) and Dale Mathews (Chapter 15) explore the potentially negative implications of the assembly networks that dominate export-oriented production in the Caribbean Basin region. Again, the relationship between the regulatory environment and firm strategy is emphasized in the authors' descriptions of the apparel industries in Costa Rica and the Dominican Republic, which are dominated by low-value-added assembly processes carried out in export-processing zones. The passage of the Trade and Development Act of 2000 should help this region compete with Mexico, but in terms of development outcomes the networks that connect apparel manufacturers in the Caribbean Basin to U.S. firms are less promising than the full-package networks that are already emerging in Mexico, as Chapter 10 on Torreón explains.

The Limits of Networks: The Political and Economic Context of NAFTA-Era Restructuring

While all the chapters in this book address the relevance of networks to analyzing the NAFTA-era apparel industry in North America, the authors are also aware that such an approach has its limits. NAFTA is not the only factor affecting the decisions of companies regarding their investment and operation decisions, and the types of interfirm networks that structure the industry are not the only determinant of how workers and their communities fare. The significance of the broader institutional environment in shaping the developmental implications of Mexico's economic restructuring is profound. The management of the currency and the minimum wage in Mexico are two factors that affect many Mexicans, including those who work in the apparel industry. Real wage gains owing to productivity can prove ephemeral in the wake of currency devaluation, particularly in a consumer economy that is now highly dependent on imports.

It is difficult to measure the contribution of NAFTA to the fact that real wages in Mexico remain well below their 1994 predevaluation levels. There are almost 10 million more Mexicans living in poverty today than in 1994, the year that NAFTA went into effect, which undoubtedly reflects the devastating toll of the 1994–95 peso crisis on Mexicans' purchasing power. The precarious economic position of many families attests to the importance of the institutional context within which Mexicans work and live. Critics of Mexico's developmental trajectory argue that the political-economic environment in Mexico leads to an unequal distribution of NAFTA's rewards that disadvantages the majority of Mexicans, who have seen little if any improvement in their daily standard of living (Soria 2001; Mariña Flores 2001).

In their contributions to this book, several authors note the difficulties confronting small and medium-sized enterprises, many of which have been devastated by the transition to a liberalized economic environment for which they were ill prepared. In the apparel industry a large number of these companies have become maquiladoras, assembling apparel for foreign firms. While the discussion of Torreón in Chapter 10 reminds us that the transition to maquiladora production can be an initial step in a process of industrial upgrading to higher-value-added activities, the same chapter reveals that the manufacturers who have benefited disproportionately from the region's full-package export boom are members of a wealthy and interconnected local elite. Thus the optimistic interpretation of the Torreón experience must be balanced by the recognition that full-package orders are filled through hierarchical networks, whose bottom tiers are populated by small subcontractors where lower wages and poorer working conditions prevail.

Assessing the consequences of NAFTA for Mexico is made more difficult by the uneven levels of development that characterize different parts of the country. Theoretically, NAFTA applies equally to all of Mexico, but in reality the dynamics of post-NAFTA dynamism have exacerbated already-profound disparities among the different regions of Mexico (Ruiz Durán and Dussel Peters 1999). Although the maquiladora industry is becoming more widely dispersed through Mexico, and indeed there has been a Southern expansion of the industrialized North from the border to more interior locations, there are still areas of the country that remain marginal to the process of North American integration. The significant costs of Mexico's economic restructuring have been particularly burdensome for the rural poor in southern states such as Guerrero, Oaxaca, and Chiapas, and these regions have not benefited from the post-NAFTA export dynamism that has spurred employment creation not only throughout northern Mexico but also in some interior regions, such as Guanajuato and Puebla.

The regional inequalities that pervade Mexico's geographic and socioeconomic landscape raise fundamental concerns about the impact of economic restructuring on social cohesion and solidarity. Denise Dresser argues that this process of restructuring "cuts to the core of Mexico's redistributive coalitions and system of inclusionary corporatism. The shift from a protected to an open market, and from a state-centered to a private-led economy, affected Mexicans from all walks of life" (Dresser 1994, 127). The toll that the economic reforms have exacted on these traditional redistributive coalitions is particularly apparent in the case of Mexico's industrial workers.

As early as the late 1980s it was obvious that Mexico's peculiar form of postrevolutionary authoritarian corporatism, which linked to the state the two largest official union confederations (the Confederación de Trabajadores Mexicanos, or CTM, and the Confederación Revolucionario de Obreros y Campesinos, or CROC), was no longer viable. The collapse of this model has meant real losses for Mexican workers. Labor's share of manufacturing value added declined from 44 percent in 1970 to 20 percent by 1989. Unions throughout this period appeared powerless to halt the decline in organized labor's political influence. While the corporatist unions remained officially pro-government during the Salinas and Zedillo administrations, their participation in the process of economic reform was minimal. The public debate about NAFTA that occurred in the United States between labor unions and business associations did not have a Mexican counterpart, as the negotiation and adoption of the agreement was skillfully managed by the Salinas administration to produce consensus and ensure conformity with the government's agenda (del Castillo 1995; Thacker 1999).

The Mexican system of industrial relations is one dimension of the institutional environment that affects the distribution of rewards created by Mexico's NAFTA-era economic growth. Interpreting NAFTA's independent impact on the Mexican labor movement is difficult, however, because NAFTA is associated with the wider agenda of economic reform and restructuring that the country has pursued since the mid-1980s (de la Garza 1997). To the extent that NAFTA has helped fuel Mexico's export dynamism and create new jobs, particularly in the maquiladora sector of the economy, it can be considered a positive development for Mexican workers. Indeed, recent studies emphasize that the country is increasingly dependent for job creation on exporting industries in general and the maquiladora sector in particular, as these activities have become the primary (some say, only) engine of growth in the Mexican economy (Álvarez Galván and Dussel Peters 2001; Mariña Flores 2001). In terms of its implications for industrial democracy, optimistic analyses of post-NAFTA developments suggest that the nadir of organized labor in Mexico has passed and that NAFTA presents new possibilities for reforming a labor movement that has been profoundly challenged by the decline of Mexico's corporatist system and the defeat of the PRI.

Although unions in the United States campaigned hard against NAFTA, its implementation has generated renewed interest in cross-border organizing (Moody 1995). One scholar of the Mexican labor movement argues that the "labor side agreement" that was added to NAFTA in order to secure its passage has turned out to be "a viable tool for cross-border solidarity among key actors in the trade union, human rights, and allied movements. The NAALC's (North American Agreement on Labor Cooperation) principles and complaint mechanisms create new spaces for advocates to build coalitions and take concrete action to articulate challenges to the status quo and advance workers' interests" (Compa 2001, 451). In the past the Mexican government and the leadership of the official unions often ignored systematic violations of workers rights because it was understood that genuine freedom of association and industrial democracy would have weakened the corporatist structure through which the organized labor movement was linked to the ruling party. Under NAFTA, however, organized labor on both sides of the border, in conjunction with nongovernmental organizations (NGOs), can use the side agreement as a tool in their struggles to redress violations of Mexican labor law.

As Edna Bonacich's chapter on organized labor in the North American apparel industry (Chapter 6) makes clear, unions in the United States have been struggling to develop new strategies that can effectively counter the geographic mobility and organizational flexibility of contemporary garment production. While the process of developing new approaches has been a contentious one at times, a substantial portion of the U.S. labor movement has recognized the need to match the networking strategies of companies. Not only has NAFTA spurred cross-border activity on the part of capital, but it has also been a visible and powerful symbol to workers in North America that labor, too, must organize and operate across borders.

It is not only NAFTA, however, that has prompted labor unions in the United States to reconsider their relationship to Mexico and Mexican workers. At present, around 10 percent of Mexico's population resides outside the country, and nearly all of these more than 7 million persons live and work in the United States (Mexican Ministry of Foreign Affairs and U.S. Commission on Immigration Reform 1997). Of particular consequence to labor, Mexican immigrant workers are especially concentrated in those domestic manufacturing industries most negatively affected by NAFTA-induced competition, on the one hand, and in those manual service-sector occupations to which U.S. unions are devoting most of their organizing efforts, on the other (Spener and Capps 2001). We see this especially clearly in Los Angeles, where Mexicans form the majority of workers in the nation's largest garment district and have also been the object of successful union organizing drives in the hotel industry.

While unions have not had much success in organizing immigrant garment workers in Los Angeles (Bonacich and Appelbaum 2000), they clearly have become aware of the significance to their own future of organizing Mexican workers. The potential benefits to unions of successfully organizing Mexicans (and other immigrants) can be seen in the increased clout Mexicans have gained in Los Angeles' political arena, as Antonio Villaraigosa was nearly swept into the mayor's office in 2001 with massive union and Latino voter support. And of course, increased cross-border collaboration between U.S. and Mexican unions could well strengthen the hand of labor vis-à-vis capital on both sides of the border.

Labor unions' renewed interest in organizing immigrant workers in the United States comes at an especially interesting moment for U.S.-Mexican relations with regard to immigration policy. At the time of this writing, cabinet-level negotiations were taking place between the executive branches of the two nations that sought to address the issue of illegal Mexican labor migration to the United States, and several legislative proposals were under consideration by the U.S. Congress as well. In a dramatic reversal of its previous position, the U.S. labor movement now strongly supports legalizing the status of undocumented immigrants residing in the country and has renounced its support of sanctions against employers who knowingly employ undocumented workers. Today the American labor movement recognizes that "millions of hard-working people who make enormous contributions to their communities and workplace are denied basic human rights because of their undocumented status" (AFL-CIO 2000). At the same time the union federation strongly opposes the revival of a Bracero-style guest-worker program for Mexicans,[1] which it fears would undermine the wages and working conditions of union members. Meanwhile, experts on Mexican migration to the United States note that both guest-worker programs and amnesty for the undocumented in the past have actually promoted further unauthorized moves by Mexicans across the United States' southern border (see Massey 1998).

With regard to U.S.-Mexican relations, the issues of trade, development, and migration have been tightly bound together historically and will continue to be so well into the future. Mexican maquiladoras were born when the Border Industrialization Program was inaugurated following the cancellation of the Bracero program in 1965, with the intention of providing factory employment to thousands of Mexican men who had been employed as guest workers in U.S. agriculture and who found themselves returned to Mexico with few employment prospects. Some have argued that the successful expansion of the maquiladora export sector was later taken as a model for NAFTA, which, it must be remembered, was promoted at least in part as a job-creation solution to the "problem" of undocumented Mexican migration (Orme 1996). Several developments might lead us to expect that this problem would be less acute today:

- Several hundred thousand manufacturing jobs have been created for working-class Mexicans as a consequence of the expanding maquiladora sector and the further opening of the U.S. market to Mexican imports;

- U.S. employers are more aware of the fact that they face sanctions if they knowingly hire illegal immigrant workers; and
- since the late 1980s the U.S. government has dramatically increased the resources it directs toward curtailing unauthorized crossings of the country's southern border (see Andreas 2000; Dunn 1996).

Despite all these measures, however, undocumented Mexican labor migration to the United States has actually grown exponentially since the early 1970s, and it has shown few signs of abating in the post-NAFTA era (Mexican Ministry of Foreign Affairs and U.S. Commission on Immigration Reform 1997).

Although space considerations do not permit us to examine in any depth the reasons for the failure of industrial-development programs in Mexico to curtail emigration north, three factors are especially relevant to this concluding chapter. First, few of the new manufacturing jobs offer wages, benefits, working conditions, and employment security that are sufficiently attractive to retain workers over the course of their careers and thus prevent them from seeking better opportunities north of the border. Second, overall job creation in Mexico has been decidedly lackluster in recent years, despite the dynamism of the maquiladora sector. Mediocre job growth will prove an inadequate break on emigration in an economy that needs to absorb, on average, a million new entrants into the economically active population each year. Third, the buildup of transborder migrant social networks connecting sending communities in Mexico with many towns and cities throughout the United States has greatly eased the undocumented passage of the latest generation of labor migrants (Massey and García España 1987; Singer and Massey 1998). In this sense we find that working-class Mexicans, in much the same way that the apparel firms examined in this book have done, rely on their own organized networks to help them establish productive, income-generating units in the most profitable locations they can find north or south of the border, as structural conditions change in the "new" North America.

The story of Gerardo Gutiérrez (a pseudonym), a native of Torreón, Coahuila, who was interviewed by Spener in San Antonio, Texas, in June 2001, is a case in point. Now twenty-six years old, Mr. Gutiérrez started working as an operator in a maquiladora sewing Tommy Hilfiger jeans in Torreón when he dropped out of school at age fourteen. On the eve of NAFTA five years later, he was still sewing jeans in the factory for just U.S.$30 per week. Seeing no better future for himself in the maquiladoras, he crossed the border illegally in 1994 with the help of an uncle who was a construction foreman for a large commercial developer based in Dallas. Later he settled in San Antonio, where he has worked in a variety of construction-related jobs. When construction work is slack he helps another uncle living on the border with his business of sneaking fellow undocumented Mexicans across the border to find better-paying jobs in the United States. Regardless of whether new amnesty or guest-worker programs are implemented, many thousands of Mexicans are likely to follow Mr. Gutiérrez in using their own network-based migratory labor strategies to cope with the long-term macrostructural inequalities between their country and the United States. One of the questions to be addressed by future research is whether the U.S. apparel industry will continue to offer Mexican migrants meaningful first-job opportunities once they have entered the United States. Another is whether rapid apparel industry expansion into migrant-sending areas such as Puebla will offer Mexican workers an attractive alternative to employment north of the border.

Gerardo Gutiérrez's story is a poignant reminder that even the regions of Mexico that have benefited from NAFTA-era growth, such as Torreón, can be home to workers who consider their jobs in export-oriented manufacturing industries dead-end employment, offering few possibilities for better wages and working conditions. In areas such as Torreón and Aguascalientes, the local labor market for maquiladora employment is saturated, but employers report that the availability of jobs is not sufficient to deter workers from attempts to *cruzar al otro lado* (cross to the other side). Fieldwork conducted by Bair in Aguascalientes, a booming apparel production center, revealed that managers are losing more and more workers to attempted border crossings, although many are back at their old jobs in a matter of weeks (see Bair 2001). In fact, a causal relationship may exist between maquiladora employment and increased emigration flows, since an increasing percentage of maquiladora workers (even in the sewing factories) are young men who are employed for relatively brief periods and who may use the modest wages such factory work pays to finance their migration attempts.

NAFTA's Mixed Legacy: Globalization, Regionalism, and Transnational Social Movements

In the final section of this chapter, we discuss the recent transnational social activism that has developed as an anti-globalization movement. Since the 1999 "Battle in Seattle," transnational and cross-border movements have emerged around a variety of issues, including the environment and labor rights. This book documents the positive and negative implications of NAFTA on the North American apparel industry in general, as well as the specific effects of the post-NAFTA export boom for development outcomes in Mexico. NGOs, labor unions, and student organizations in recent years have argued that the version of globalization promoted by international financial institutions and the World Trade Organization is an undemocratic one that must be replaced by a more transparent and inclusive approach to issues of global governance. Activists involved in these transnational social movements suggest that free-trade agreements should include clauses guaranteeing minimal labor standards for all workers and that corporations should be held more accountable to consumers in terms of revealing information about their international operations.

It is particularly relevant to note the emergence of transnational activism here, because much of it has focused on the apparel industry. The anti-sweatshop campaign has been among the most visible and successful of the efforts to forge a cross-border movement based on solidarity between First World consumers and workers in developing countries. Chapters of the student organization United Students Against Sweatshops (USAS) exist at more than two hundred universities in Canada and the United States, with members pushing to ensure that the T-shirts, sweatshirts, and baseball caps that bear their school's logo are produced by workers in a sweat-free environment.

In conjunction with other NGOs, such as the Canadian-based Maquila Solidarity Network and the U.S.-based Coalition for Justice in the Maquiladoras, the USAS has been publicizing violations of Mexican labor law in factories that produce for major U.S. brands. Their efforts have been instrumental in attracting media attention to the plight of Mexican workers in a Korean-owned factory, Kukdong, which produces Nike apparel (see Gereffi, Garcia-Johnson, and Sasser 2001, 62–64). The situation at the plant, which is also mentioned in Chapter 6 by Edna Bonacich, has been monitored closely by foreign NGOs after the company dismissed workers who complained about rancid food and low wages in January 2001. Workers wanted to hold elections to vote on the possibility of establishing a new union, claiming that the existing union at the plant failed to represent their interests. The existing union was affiliated with the CROC, a corporatist union with long-standing ties to the PRI (which still controls the government of the Mexican state of Puebla, where the Kukdong factory is located).

One may have expected the power of the old-style corporatist unions to be weakened by the defeat of the PRI's presidential candidate and the victory of Vicente Fox, who ran on the platform of cleaning up Mexico's corrupt political system. However, Fox's administration has been notably silent about violations of Mexican labor law such as those that appear to have occurred at Kukdong, where workers were denied the right to exercise freedom of association. In marked contrast to the tepid response of the Mexican government, NGOs, in collaboration with organized labor in the United States, have campaigned vigorously on behalf of the Kukdong workers. However, the main target of their protests is not Mexican president Vicente Fox, nor the Korean owners of the plant, but rather Nike—the global retailer of athletic footwear and apparel that is one of the company's clients.

Workers' rights activists believe that the real potential for change lies with the most visible and powerful corporations doing business in Mexico. Companies such as Nike or the Gap are sensitive to the negative publicity created by reports of abuses or labor-law violations in plants that produce their products (Gereffi, Garcia-Johnson, and Sasser 2001). This strategy of identifying and targeting the high-visibility brand-name companies, which is at the heart of the anti-sweatshop movement, is based on a network methodology: Although the Kukdong plant is not owned by Nike, it is identified as a link in Nike's production chain for which, activists maintain, the corporation is ultimately responsible. So far the network strategy seems to be effective in creating accountability in the North American apparel industry. Under pressure from NGOs, and particularly the demands of students active in USAS, Nike urged management at Kukdong to take back workers who were fired after they went on strike. The months-long struggle at Kukdong (which was renamed Mex Mode) ended in September 2001 when the company's management agreed to recognize an independent union supported by the workers, and a new collective agreement was signed with the union, SITEMEX (originally SITEKIM). The successful resolution of the conflict was hailed as a precedent-setting victory for maquiladora workers in their efforts to secure industrial democracy.

The transnational and cross-border movements that are emerging in response to the dissatisfaction of wide segments of society with the perceived consequences of globalization are a development worthy of more attention than we can give it here. Our hope is that this book has helped illuminate some of the contradictory dynamics posed by the process of regional integration in the North American apparel industry, especially as they relate to issues of equity and the distribution of NAFTA's costs and benefits. NAFTA has produced winners and losers, and more empirical work is needed to better understand the extent to which the gains accruing from this process of regional integration might promote an agenda of employment creation, poverty reduction, and social development in Mexico. We believe that approaches focusing on cross-border networks are likely to contribute much to our understanding of NAFTA's implications and can help illuminate the complex connections between North America's firms, workers, and consumers.

Note

1. The Bracero program was a U.S. policy that allowed Mexicans to live and work in the United States as agricultural laborers on a seasonal basis. Its abrupt cancellation in 1964 created severe unemployment on the Mexican side of the U.S.-Mexico border, and it was ostensibly to address this problem that the maquiladoras were established.

References

Álvarez Galván, José Luis, and Enrique Dussel Peters. 2001. "Causas y efectos de los programas de promoción sectorial en la economía mexicana." *Comercio exterior* 51, 5: 446–57.

American Federation of Labor and Congress of Industrial Organizations (AFL-CIO). 2000. "Executive Council Actions: Immigration." Press release, February 16. Retrieved February 24 from <http://www.aflcio.org/publ/estatements/feb2000/immigr.htm>.

Andreas, Peter. 2000. *Border Games: Policing the U.S.-Mexico Divide*. Ithaca, N.Y.: Cornell University Press.

Bair, Jennifer. 2001. "Casos exitosos de pequeñas y medianas empresas en México." In *Claroscuros: Integración exitosa de las pequeñas y medionas empresas en México*, ed. Enrique Dussel Peters, pp. 63–105. Santiago, Chile: United Nations Economic Commission for Latin America and the Caribbean.

Bair, Jennifer, and Gary Gereffi. 2001. "Local Clusters in Global Chains: The Causes and Consequences of Export Dynamism in Torreón's Blue Jeans Industry." *World Development* 29, 11: 1885–1903.

Bonacich, Edna, and Richard P. Appelbaum. 2000. *Behind the Label: Inequality in the Los Angeles Apparel Industry*. Berkeley: University of California Press.

Bosworth, Barry. 1993. "The Debate over NAFTA." *Brookings Review* 11, 4: 48.

Cataneda, Jorge. 1993. "Can NAFTA Change Mexico?" *Foreign Affairs* 72, 4 (September–October): 66–80.

Commission for Labor Cooperation. 2000. *Standard and Advanced Practices in the North American Garment Industry.* Washington, D.C.: Secretariat of the Commission for Labor Cooperation.

Compa, Lance. 2001. "NAFTA's Labour Side Agreement and International Labour Solidarity." *Antipode: A Radical Journal of Geography* 33, 3: 451–67.

Conchello, José Angel. 1992. *El TLC: Un callejón sin salida,* 2d ed. Mexico City: Grijalbo.

de la Garza, Enrique. 1994. "The Restructuring of State-Labor Relations in Mexico." In *The Politics of Economic Restructuring: State-Society Relations and Regime Change in Mexico,* ed. Maria Lorena Cook, Kevin J. Middlebrook, and Juan Molinar Horcasitas, pp. 195–219. La Jolla: Center for U.S.-Mexican Studies, University of California at San Diego.

————. 1997. "La flexibilidad del trabajo en América Latina." *Revista latinoamericana de estudios del trabajo* 3, 5: 129–57.

del Castillo V., Gustavo. 1995. "Private Sector Trade Advisory Groups in North America: A Comparative Perspective." In *The Politics of Free Trade in North America,* ed. Gustavo del Castillo V. and Gustavo Vega Cánovas. Ottawa, Canada: Center for Trade Policy and Law.

Dresser, Denise. 1994. "Embellishment, Empowerment, or Euthanasia of the PRI?" In *The Politics of Economic Restructuring: State-society Relations and Regime Change in Mexico,* ed. Maria Lorena Cook, Kevin J. Middlebrook, and Juan Molinar Horcasitas, pp. 125–49. La Jolla: Center for U.S.-Mexican Studies, University of California at San Diego.

Dunn, Timothy J. 1996. *The Militarization of the U.S.-Mexico Border 1978–1992: Low-Intensity Conflict Doctrine Comes Home.* Austin: Center for Mexican American Studies, University of Texas.

Dussel Peters, Enrique. 2000. *Polarizing Mexico: The Impact of Liberalization Strategy.* Boulder, Colo.: Lynn Reinner.

Gereffi, Gary, Ronie Garcia-Johnson, and Erika Sasser. 2001. "The NGO-Industrial Complex." *Foreign Policy,* 125 (July–August): 56–65.

Hellman, Judith Adler. 2000. "Opting for Fox." *NACLA Report on the Americas* 34, 2 (September–October): 6–10.

Heredia, Carlos. 1994. "NAFTA and Democratization in Mexico." *Journal of International Affairs* 48, 1: 13–38.

Instituto Nacional de Estadística, Geografía e Informática (INEGI). 2001. Banco de Información Económica. Data available at <http://www.inegi.gob.mx>. Web site consulted in July.

Krugman, Paul. 1993. "The Uncomfortable Truth about NAFTA." *Foreign Affairs* 72, 5 (November–December): 13–19.

Lustig, Nora. 1994. "NAFTA: Doing Well by Doing Good." *Brookings Review* 12, 1: 47.

Mariña Flores, Abelardo. 2001. "Factores determinantes del empleo en México." *Comercio exterior* 51, 5: 410–24.

Massey, Douglas S. 1998. "March of Folly: U.S. Immigration Policy after NAFTA." *American Prospect* 37 (March–April): 22–33.

Massey, Douglas S., and Felipe García España. 1987. "The Social Process of International Migration." *Science,* August 14, 733.

Mexican Ministry of Foreign Affairs and United States Commission on Immigration Reform. 1997. *Migration between Mexico and the United States.* Mexico City and Washington, D.C.: Mexican Ministry of Foreign Affairs and United States Commission on Immigration Reform.

Moody, Kim. 1995. "NAFTA and the Corporate Redesign of North America." *Latin American Perspectives* 22, 1: 95–116.

Morales, Isidro. 1999. "The Institutionalism of Economic Openness and the Configuration of Mexican Geographic-Economic Spaces." *Third World Quarterly* 20, 5: 971–93.

Orme, William. 1996. *Understanding NAFTA: Mexico, Free Trade, and the New North America.* Austin: University of Texas Press.

Poitras, Guy, and Raymond Robinson. 1994. "The Politics of NAFTA in Mexico." *Journal of Interamerican Studies and World Affairs* 36, 1: 1–35.

Preston, Julia. 2000. "Leading Candidates in Mexico as Close on Issues as in Polls." *New York Times,* July 10, A1.

Reinhardt, Nola, and Wilson Peres. 2000. "Latin America's New Economic Model: Micro Responses and Economic Restructuring." *World Development* 28, 9: 1543–66.

Robinson, William I. 1998–99. "Latin America and Global Capitalism." *Race and Class* 40, 2–3: 111–31.

Ruiz Durán, Clemente, and Enrique Dussel Peters, eds. 1999. *Dinámica regional y competitividad industrial.* Mexico City: Editoral.

Secretariat of the Commission for Labor Cooperation in North America. 2000. *"Standard" and "Advanced" Practices in the North American Garment Industry.* Washington, D.C., Secretariat of the Commission for Labor Cooperation.

Singer, Audrey, and Douglas S. Massey. 1998. "The Social Process of Undocumented Border Crossing among Mexican Migrants." *International Migration Review* 32, 3: 561–92.

Soria, Víctor M. 2001. "El mercado de trabajo en Brasil y México a la luz de la integración regional y la crisis financiera." *Comercio exterior* 51, 5: 425–37.

Spener, David, and Randy Capps. 2001. "North American Free Trade and Changes in the Nativity of the Garment Industry Workforce in the United States." *International Journal of Urban and Regional Research* 25, 2: 301–26.

Thacker, Strom. 1999. "NAFTA Coalitions and the Political Viability of Neoliberalism in Mexico." *Journal of Interamerican Studies and World Affairs* 41, 2: 57–89.

U.S. Bureau of the Census. 2002. "Trade Balance with Mexico." Retrieved on April 16 from <http://www.census.gov/foreign-trade/balance/c2010.html>.

Weintraub, Sidney. 1991. "The Rise of Norte Americanos: A U.S.-Mexican Union." *Responsive Community* 1, 3: 64–74.

About the Contributors

ARACELI ALMARAZ is a research associate at El Colegio de la Frontera Norte in Tijuana, Mexico. She has worked extensively on social and economic conditions in Mexico's maquiladora industry.

JENNIFER BAIR is assistant professor of sociology at Yale University, where she also teaches in the women's and gender studies program. Her current research focuses on the developmental implications of the North American Free Trade Agreement for Mexico and on the political economy of neoliberal reform in Latin America.

EDNA BONACICH is a professor of sociology and ethnic studies at the University of California, Riverside, where she has taught since 1970. Her publications include a coedited book, *Global Production: The Apparel Industry in the Pacific Rim* (Temple University Press, 1994) and a coauthored volume, *Behind the Label: Inequality in the Los Angeles Apparel Industry*.

JORGE CARRILLO is director of the Social Studies Department at El Colegio de la Frontera Norte in Tijuana, Mexico. He has a Ph.D. in sociology from El Colegio de México and is a specialist in the sociology of work. Dr. Carrillo is the author of several books and more than sixty articles in national and international scientific journals.

ENRIQUE DUSSEL PETERS is professor at the Graduate School of Economics, Universidad Nacional Autónoma de México (UNAM), in Mexico City. He earned his Ph.D. at the University of Notre Dame. His publications include *Polarizing Mexico: The Impact of Liberalization Strategy* and an edited volume, *Claroscuros: Integración exitosa de las pequeñas y medianas empresas en México*.

GARY GEREFFI is professor of sociology at Duke University. He received his Ph.D. degree from Yale University and he has published extensively on development strategies and industrial upgrading in diverse regions of the world. His books include *Manufacturing Miracles: Paths of Industrialization in Latin America and East Asia*, coedited with Donald L. Wyman, and *Commodity Chains and Global Capitalism*, coedited with Miguel Korzeniewicz.

ALFREDO HUALDE is a researcher and professor in the Social Studies Department at El Colegio de la Frontera Norte in Tijuana, Mexico. His work "Aprendizaje industrial en la frontera norte de Mexico: La articulación entre el sistema educativo y el sistema productivo maquiladora" received the National Award of Mexico's Ministry of Labor and Social Security in 1998 for research on labor issues.

JUDI KESSLER is an assistant professor of sociology at Monmouth College. She has published several articles on the apparel industry and did her doctoral dissertation on the apparel industry in Southern California and Mexico.

MARTHA ARGELIA MARTÍNEZ is a graduate student in the Sociology Department at Duke University. She is currently research coordinator for the Community Learning Center Project at Monterrey Institute of Technology, Mexico.

DALE MATHEWS obtained his Ph.D. in 1995 from the Institute of Development Studies at the University of Sussex in England. He has taught at several universities in the Caribbean region and works as a researcher at the Institute of Caribbean Studies in Puerto Rico.

JORGE MENDOZA is an economist with a Ph.D. in business administration from Monterrey Institute of Technology (Mexico) and the University of Texas at Austin. He is currently working on a research project on industrial policy in Ireland.

MICHAEL MORTIMORE is chief of the development issues section of the Division on Investment, Technology and Enterprise Development of the UN Conference on Trade and Development (UNCTAD) in Geneva, Switzerland. He received his Ph.D. in Political Economy from the University of Toronto (Canada), and he has written extensively on international trade and investment issues.

FLORENCE PALPACUER is professor of business management at the University of Bretagne-Sud, France. She is conducting research on firms' competitive and organizational strategies in global industries, focusing on apparel and food processing.

MICHAEL PIORE is David W. Skinner Professor of Political Economy at Massachusetts Institute of Technology. His books include *Beyond Individualism* and *The Second Industrial Divide* (with Charles Sabel).

FERNANDO POZOS is professor of sociourban studies at the University of Guadalajara. Currently he is conducting research on the impact that various types of employment arrangements have on workers' quality of life.

ROBERT J. S. ROSS is professor of sociology and director of the international studies stream at Clark University. He is the coauthor (with Kent C. Trachte) of *Global Capitalism: The New Leviathan.*

CLEMENTE RUÍZ DURAN is professor of economics at the Universidad Nacional Autónoma de México (UNAM) in Mexico City.

DAVID SPENER teaches sociology and anthropology at Trinity University in San Antonio, Texas. In addition to writing on development issues, Spener has published a number of works on U.S.-Mexico border relations and Mexican migration to the United States.

ROBINE VAN DOOREN is a Ph.D. candidate at the Institute of Development Studies at Utrecht University. She is currently writing her dissertation on the local impact of globalization in the garment industry.

ULRIK VANGSTRUP received his Ph.D. in 1999 in international development studies from Roskilde University, Denmark. Currently he is coordinator of a small-business support program of the Instituto Tecnológico Superior del Sur de Guanajuato in Guanajuato, Mexico, and board member of the Guanajuato Regional Development Council.

Index

Page numbers followed by letters *f, n,* and *t* indicate figures, notes, and tables, respectively.

Aalfs, 43; joint venture with Martín family, 216; Torreón operations of, 20*t*
AAMA. *See* American Apparel Manufacturers' Association
AB 633 (California), 97*n* 22
aboneros (door-to-door sellers), 270–71, 271*t*, 272, 274; class status of customers of, 273*t;* percent share of Mexican retail clothing sales, 272*t;* profits of, 276
Acer Computers, 155
Action West, operations in Mexico, 145, 209*t*, 213
ACTWU. *See* Amalgamated Clothing and Textile Workers Union
ADOZONA. *See* Asociación Dominicana de Zonas Francas
AFL-CIO, Solidarity Center of, 133
Africa: apparel exports of, 27*t. See also specific countries*
Agreement on Textiles and Clothing (ATC), 21*n* 9, 312, 319–20; beneficiaries of, 320
Aguascalientes (Mexico): Burlington manufacturing plant in, 39; knitwear production in, 250; linkages with U.S. firms, 173; worker migration from, 336
AIWA. *See* Asian Immigrant Women's Advocates
Alabama (U.S.), textile employment in, 45
Alba Vega, Carlos, 264*n* 15
ALFA, 183, 196*n* 2
Almacenes Coppel, 281*n* 14
Alpek, 40
Altamira complex (Mexico), 40
Amalgamated Clothing and Textile Workers Union (ACTWU): losses in membership, 123; merger with ILGWU, 129–30
American Apparel Manufacturers' Association (AAMA), 315
American Textile Manufacturers' Institute (ATMI), 315
Anne Klein: and Chinatown contractors, 64; global production network of, 58; growth strategy of, 56
Ann Taylor, 57
anti-globalization movement, 131–32, 336, 338
anti-sweatshop movement, 130, 132, 337–38. *See also* "No Sweat Initiative"
apparel commodity chain: actors in, 9; changes over

time, 296; components of, 113; lead firms in, 34–36; lengthening of, in Mexico, 210–11, 211*f;* Los Angeles in, 90, 91
apparel industry: actors influencing, 8–9; and economic growth, 3, 288–90; elements of, 229; globalization of, 3–4; post-NAFTA, 330–31; regionalization in, 4–7, 24–28, 26*t*–27*t;* use of term, 20*n* 1. *See also under specific countries and regions*
Appelbaum, Richard, 76, 86, 87, 94, 111
Arias, Patricia, 263*n* 1
Arizona jeans wear, 43, 212
Asia: apparel as engine of growth in, 289; apparel exports of, 24, 26*t;* apparel exports to Mexico, 267, 275; apparel exports to North America, 290, 291*t*, 292, 292*f;* as Caribbean basin competitor, 305; triangle manufacturing in, 25. *See also* East Asia; South Asia; Southeast Asia; *specific countries*
Asian immigrants, in New York City apparel industry, 61, 62*t*, 63*t*
Asian Immigrant Women's Advocates (AIWA), 131
Asian Pacific American Legal Center, 131
Asociación Dominicana de Zonas Francas (ADOZONA), 316
Asociación Nacional de Tiendas de Autoservicio y Departamentales (ANTAD), 281*n* 13
assembly, 28; in Caribbean basin, 296–302, 321; Item 807 and, 144; in maquiladora industry, 33–34; transition to full-package manufacturing from, 28, 29, 37; vs. full-package manufacturing, 28–29, 96*n* 5
Assembly Bill (AB) 633 (California), 97*n* 22
association arrangements, 235–36, 256–61
ATC. *See* Agreement on Textiles and Clothing
ATMI. *See* American Textile Manufacturers' Institute
Avante Textil, 42
Aztex Trading Company, 43–44

backward linkages, 20*n* 5; 807A and prevention of, 36; full-package manufacturing in Mexico and, 10; NAFTA and facilitation of, 37; obstacles to development of, 172
Bair, Jennifer, 196
Bali, 41

ethnicity: of El Paso apparel workers, 141*t*, 141–42, 142*t;* of Los Angeles apparel workers, 7, 12, 20*n* 7, 75, 90; of Los Angeles business owners, 282*n* 26; of New York City apparel workers, 54, 61–66, 62*t*, 63*t;* of New York City business owners, 62, 65. *See also specific ethnic groups*
Europe: outward process trade (OPT) in, 25. *See also* Eastern Europe; Western Europe; *specific countries*
European Economic Community, ISO standards of, 188, 242
export-oriented industrialization, multiple models of, 205
export-processing zones (EPZs), 309; in Caribbean basin, 298–99; in Dominican Republic, 298*f,* 298–99, 308–22, 310*t,* 311*t;* limitations of, 300, 304
exports, apparel: credit unions and, 257; growth in, 4; Harmonized Tariff Schedule (HTS) and, 297–98; incentives for, 262; leaders in, 24, 26*t*–27*t;* by maquiladoras, 228*t;* NAFTA and, 85; to North America, 290–93, 291*t*, 292*f;* OECD countries and, 289. *See also* imports, apparel; *specific countries*

Fábricas de Ropa Manjai, 208, 217
Fábricas El Venado, 208
Fair Labor Association (FLA), 132; Workers Rights Consortium (WRC) compared with, 133
Fair Labor Standards Act (1938): and definition of sweatshop, 101; enforcement of, 110–11; "hot goods" provisions of, 97*n* 20, 112; post–World War II conditions and, 126; regulation of homework by, 107
Farah, Mansour and Hannah, 141
Farah Company, 141; layoffs by, post-NAFTA, 148; operations in Mexico, 145, 209*t;* overseas production of, 156*n* 3; relocation of, 142; strike against, 140
Far East: subcontracting networks in, 58. *See also specific countries*
fashion: and El Paso's apparel industry, 153; and Mexico's apparel industry, 6, 231; and women's wear industry, 54
Fashion Institute of Technology, lead firms and, 56
Federated Department Stores, 57
Federated Product Development, 57
Fenton, Kelly, 156
fiber-forward rule, 48*n* 9
fiber industry: NAFTA and corporate strategies of, 37, 38; research and development in, 34
Fideicomiso para la Cobertura de Riesgo Cambiario (FICORCA), 197*n* 3
Final Finish, post-NAFTA layoffs by, 148
financial services zones, 309
financing: in Mexico vs. Hong Kong, 82. *See also* credit
finishers, 168. *See also* laundering operations
firm(s): embedded, 170; large, NAFTA and, 94; lead (*see* lead firms); niche, 55, 61; small (*see* small firms)
firm-centered approach, 8, 11
FLA. *See* Fair Labor Association
flexible production, 124; impact on labor unions, 123, 134; impact on U.S. garment workers, 123; labor unions' response to, 130–34; U.S. government policies and, 126–27. *See also* subcontracting system
forward linkages, obstacles to development of, 172
Fox, Vicente, 328; election of, 329; silence about labor-law violations, 337

France: apparel exports of, 289; apparel imports and, 25; economic growth of, 287, 288*f*
Frederick de México, 192
Free Trade Agreement of the Americas, and global/flexible production, 126
free-trade zones, 309
Fruit of the Loom, 304, 306*n* 7; and assembly orders, 29
Fuerza Unida, 158*n* 21
full-package manufacturing: advantages of, 10, 29; in East Asia, 296–97; labor-related benefits of, 217–19; in Mexico, 10, 34, 37, 48*n* 12, 82–83, 178*n* 12, 205; post-NAFTA, 23, 46, 211; textile firms and, 36; in Torreón, Mexico, 205, 215*f,* 215–17; transition from assembly to, 28, 29, 37, 211–12; vs. assembly, 28–29, 96*n* 5. *See also* original equipment manufacture
Fundidora Monterrey, closure of, 183
furniture industry, in Ciudad Hidalgo (Mexico), 237

GALs. *See* Guaranteed Access Levels
GAO. *See* General Accounting Office
the Gap: codes of conduct of, 218; and full-package production, 29; in middle-to-upper price segments, 57; operations in Mexico, 209*t*
Garment Enforcement Report, 87
garment industry. *See* apparel industry
Garment Industry Development Corporation, 68
Garment Industry Proviso (U.S.), 128
Garment Services International (GSI), sourcing patterns of, 84
Garment Workers' Center (GWC), 131
Garment Workers Justice Centers, 128–29
Garment Workers Protection Act (AB 633, California), 97*n* 22
GATT. *See* General Agreement on Tariffs and Trade
gender: of apparel industry workers, 116, 155; distribution of clothing purchases by, in Mexico, 267; in offshore production, 126. *See also* men; women
General Accounting Office (GAO): definition of sweatshops, 101; study of tax compliance of sweatshops, 102
General Agreement on Tariffs and Trade (GATT): implications for textile and garment trade, 319–20; Mexico's accession to, 45; Multifiber Arrangement of (*see* Multifiber Arrangement [MFA]); Textile and Clothing Agreement of, 301, 305; Uruguay round of, 143, 319, 322*n* 11
Georgia (U.S.), textile employment in, 45
Gereffi, Gary, 59, 61, 76, 84, 177, 196, 296
Germany: apparel exports of, 289; apparel imports and, 25; economic growth of, 287, 288*f;* labor costs in, 301*t*
Gigante, 281*n* 14
Gilmour Trading, Costa Rican subsidiaries of, 303
Gitano Group, 41; weakened position of, 57
global capitalism, 117; cross-border organizing in response to, 133–34; restructuring of, as labor unions' goal, 131–33
global commodity chain: and industrial districts, 206; use of term, 100. *See also* apparel commodity chain
global commodity chain perspective, 182–83; on export-oriented industrialization, 205; on obstacles to inter-firm linkages, 172; on Torreón region, 220
global competitiveness index, 197*n* 8
global economy, and inequality, 94

Partido de la Revolución Democrática (Mexico), 329

Partido Revolucionario Institucional (PRI, Mexico), 11, 329, 337

Peck, Jamie, 94

peripheral contractors, 60, 94; in New York City apparel industry, 64, 66

peso devaluation, 182; and Dominican Republic, 314; and El Paso garment industry, 147–48; and imports to Mexico, 273; and knitwear manufacturers, 251; and Mexico's garment production, 5; and Mexico's garment retail, 277–78; and relocation of production to Mexico, 85, 86; and sale of domestically produced clothing, 268–70; and Torreón garment industry, 208–10

Philippines: apparel exports of, 26t, 289; apparel exports to North America, 291t, 292f, 293; apparel exports to U.S., 30t; labor costs in, 301t

Phillips–Van Heusen, 254

piece rate, 124

Piore, Michael, 55, 247

Playtex, 41

Poland: apparel exports of, 26t, 289; labor costs in, 301t

Polo, operations in Mexico, 209t

Population Research Center (PRC), University of Texas at Austin, 280

Portes, Alejandro, 102

Portugal: apparel exports of, 289; labor costs in, 301t

poverty, in Mexico, 332

PRC. See Population Research Center

Prestige, 191

PRI. See Partido Revolucionario Institucional

Price Club, in Mexico, 274

price point: production in Mexico and, 83; and relocation decisions, 88

private-label apparel, 48n 8; New York's, future of, 67; in retailers' post-NAFTA strategies, 35, 57

producer consortia, in Mexico, 256–57; knitwear producers and, 257–60; as organizing agents, 261

production sharing (807/9802 production), 28, 29, 322n 6; in Caribbean basin EPZs, 310–11; criticism of, 36; in Dominican Republic, 313

productivity, of U.S. apparel workers, 45

protectionism, U.S., 36, 311, 319

Puebla (Mexico): knitwear production in, 250; Southern California sourcing in, 83

Puerto Rican sewing operators, in New York City, 107–9; wages of, 107–8

Puerto Rico, Sara Lee plants in, 42

quality, in border vs. interior regions of Mexico, 83, 84

quotas, U.S., 319; Caribbean Basin Trade Partnership Act and, 316, 317t, 318t; progressive lifting of, 5

racism, against immigrant workers, 124–25

Ralph Lauren: and Chinatown contractors, 64; global production network of, 58; growth strategy of, 56; strategies in response to globalization, 35

Reach, Jim, 84

reciprocal liberalization, 319

Red Kap, Torreón operations of, 209t

regionalization: in apparel industry, 4–7, 24–28, 26t–27t; vs. globalization, 319, 320. See also specific regions

relocation of production: compliance monitoring and, 94; factors in, 81–87; impact of NAFTA on, 85–87;

labor costs and, 173; to rural communities, 219, 222n 8

restaurant industry, labor-law violations in, 118n 7

retail: capital intensity in, 34; concentration in, 112–13, 113t; in Mexico, 270–74, 271t, 272t, 273t; in Mexico, distribution of value added, 276t, 276–77; in Mexico, employment in, 275

retailers, 35; dominant role of, 112; as importers, 114; and manufacturers, blurring of distinction between, 57; pressure on manufacturers, 90; and private-label products, 35, 57; responsibility for labor-law violations, 112; share of profits, 113; strategies in response to globalization, 34, 35; strategies in response to NAFTA, 37, 43; and Torreón's production patterns, 211; U.S. chains, expansion into Mexican cities, 279. See also specific companies

Rinbros company, 41, 197n 14; and Monterrey, Mexico, 190

Rocky Mountain company, 157n 10

Romania, apparel exports of, 26t, 289

Romero, Jesse, 173–74

Ross, Robert, 100

rules of origin: Caribbean Basin Trade Partnership Act and, 312; North American Free Trade Agreement and, 320

rural communities, relocation of apparel production to, 219, 222n 8

Sabel, Charles, 55, 247

sales offices, of suppliers, 178n 8

Salinas de Gortari, Carlos, 11; and credit unions/producer consortia, 256, 257; economic policy under, 45; and NAFTA, 328; privatization of cooperatives under, 219

Salinas y Rocha, 281n 14

Salvatierra company, 252–53

Sam's Club, in Mexico, 274

San Diego (U.S.), apparel industry in, 164, 165t

San Francisco (U.S.): garment production in, 74–96; labor-law violations in, 104

San José Iturbide (Mexico), knitwear producers in, 251t

San Miguel el Alto (Mexico), knitwear producers in, 251t

San Miguel el Alto company, 254–55

Santiago Tangamandapio (Mexico), knitwear producers in, 251t, 263n 7

Santiago Tulantepec (Mexico), knitwear producers in, 251t

Santoyo, Blanca, 173

Sara Lee Corporation, 41–42; Costa Rican subsidiaries of, 302

Sassen, Saskia, 61, 68

Schlesinger, Emil, 106, 118n 9

Schmitz, Hubert, 247–48

Schott, Jeffrey, 320

Sears: Mexican knitwear producers and, 252; in Mexico, 209t, 281n 14

SECOFI. See Secretaría de Comercio y Fomento Industria

secrecy: apparel manufacturers and, 125; in global production, 126

Secretaría de Comercio y Fomento Industria (SECOFI), 239–40

self-service outlets. See tiendas de autoservicio